THE AGE OF
IMPROVEMENT
1783–1867

A HISTORY OF ENGLAND
IN ELEVEN VOLUMES

General Editor: W. N. Medlicott

THE PREHISTORIC AGE IN BRITAIN
By STANLEY THOMAS

ROMAN BRITAIN
By C. E. STEVENS

THE ANGLO-SAXON AGE
By D. J. V. FISHER

THE FEUDAL KINGDOM OF ENGLAND*
By FRANK BARLOW

THE LATER MIDDLE AGES IN ENGLAND*
By B. WILKINSON

THE TUDOR AGE*
By JAMES A. WILLIAMSON

THE STUART AGE
By IVAN ROOTS

EIGHTEENTH CENTURY ENGLAND*
By DOROTHY MARSHALL

THE AGE OF IMPROVEMENT*
By ASA BRIGGS

LATE NINETEENTH CENTURY ENGLAND
By MAURICE SHOCK

CONTEMPORARY ENGLAND*
By W. N. MEDLICOTT

* Already published
Some of the titles listed above are provisional

THE AGE OF
IMPROVEMENT
1783–1867

by

ASA BRIGGS

LONGMAN

LONGMAN GROUP LIMITED
London

Associated companies, branches and representatives
throughout the world

© *Asa Briggs* 1959

First published 1959
Thirteenth impression 1977

ISBN 0 582 48204 6

Printed in Great Britain by
Richard Clay (The Chaucer Press) Ltd, Bungay, Suffolk

INTRODUCTORY NOTE

ONE of the effects of two world wars and of 'fifty years of ever-accelerating industrial and social revolution has been the growing interest of the citizen in the story of his land. From this story he seeks to learn the secret of his country's greatness and a way to better living in the future.

There seems, therefore, to be room for a rewriting of the history of England which will hold the interest of the general reader while it appeals at the same time to the student. This new presentation will take account of the recent discoveries of the archæologist and the historian, and will not lose sight of the claims of history to take its place among the mental recreations of intelligent people for whom it has no professional concern.

The history will be completed in a series of ten volumes. The volumes will be of medium length, and it is hoped that they will provide a readable narrative of the whole course of the history of England and give proper weight to the different strands which form the pattern of the story. No attempt has been made to secure general uniformity of style or treatment. Each period has its special problems, each author his individual technique and mental approach; each volume will be able to stand by itself not only as an expression of the author's methods, tastes, and experience, but as a coherent picture of a phase in the history of the country.

There is, nevertheless, a unity of purpose in the series; the authors have been asked, while avoiding excessive detail, to give particular attention to the interaction of the various aspects of national life and achievement, so that each volume may present a convincing integration of those developments—political, constitutional, economic, social, religious, military, foreign, or cultural—which happen to be dominant at each period. Although considerations of space will prevent minute investigation it should still be possible in a series of this length to deal fully with the essential themes.

A short bibliographical note is attached to each volume. This is not intended to supersede existing lists, but rather to call attention to recent works and to the standard bibliographies.

W. N. MEDLICOTT

CONTENTS

Contents

Contents

NOTE ON FOOTNOTES AND ABBREVIATIONS

The following abbreviations are used in the footnotes:

B.M.	British Museum.
B.R.L.	Birmingham Reference Library.
E.H.R.	*English Historical Review.*
Ec. Hist. Rev.	*Economic History Review.*
Hist. MSS. Comm.	Historical Manuscripts Commission.
H.O.	Home Office.
J. Ec. H.	*Journal of Economic History.*
J.M.H.	*Journal of Modern History.*
J.R.S.S.	*Journal of the Royal Statistical Society.*
N.R.L.	Newcastle-upon-Tyne Reference Library.
P.A.	*Public Administration.*
P.H.	*Parliamentary History.*
P.P.	*Parliamentary Papers*
P.R.O.	Public Record Office.
S.C.R.	*Select Committee Report.*
T.N.A.P.S.S.	*Transactions of the National Association for the Promotion of Social Science.*
T.R.H.S.	*Transactions of the Royal Historical Society.*

Footnote references have been kept to a minimum, and only in exceptional cases, where there might be doubt about the source, are references made to *Hansard*.

PREFACE

IN the preparation of this book I have received generous help from many friends and colleagues. I am grateful to Professor W. N. Medlicott for reading the manuscript and making many helpful suggestions; to Mr. M. Brock and Mr. A. F. Thompson for extremely useful advice and comments; to Mr. C. Collyer and Mr. D. Read for reading parts of the manuscript; to Mr. P. M. Williams for reading the proofs; to Miss G. Coulson for invaluable and unstinted secretarial assistance; and to my wife for much practical help throughout the whole undertaking. I am also grateful to many librarians for unfailing courtesy and attention, to the writers of those theses whose work I have cited in my footnotes, and to a large number of former research pupils, both in Oxford and Leeds, with whom I have talked over key problems in nineteenth-century history. Any errors and shortcomings in this book are entirely my own responsibility.

ASA BRIGGS

The University of Leeds,
January 1958.

INTRODUCTION

PERIOD AND PROBLEMS

THE division of history into distinct periods is of necessity arbitrary and unconvincing. Artificial unity is given to the reigns of monarchs, and centuries are endowed with collective personalities. Above all, historical curiosity is contained complacently within rickety frontiers.

I have chosen to write in this series about an 'unconventional' period, because I believe that my choice opens up questions for the historian rather than suggests that all the big issues are settled and the tidying-up operations can now begin. My unit of study, the years 1783 to 1867, cuts into what are usually thought of as two contrasting centuries—the age of balance and the age of progress—and ends in the middle of the long reign of Queen Victoria, which is often considered a natural unit in itself.

The reasons for my choice are simple and straightforward. The period from 1783 to 1867 was one of formative changes in the structure of the English economy, the shape of English society and the framework of government. In the background was the new economic power unleashed by the development of a coal and iron technology: in the foreground, the problems posed by its use. From Pitt to Peel, from Peel to Gladstone, we can trace continuities of preoccupation and outlook which were not concealed from the men of the times; and although there were features of the past which recalled or perpetuated older systems of social and political organization, it was the 'march' of events which fascinated contemporaries and sometimes horrified them. They were divided about the merits of 'improvement', but they were at one in admitting that it existed.

No single interpretation of these formative years may be regarded as definitive, but in the scope of 'improvement' and the reactions to it we have a clear-cut theme. The word 'improvement' was not an invention of the 1780s: it had a long and respectable ancestry, and was part of the working vocabulary of Dr. Johnson and Defoe. To the men of the 1780s, however, the 'discoveries and improvements' of their own generation seemed to 'diffuse a glory over this country unattainable by conquest or dominion'. Agricultural and mechanical improvements had produced changes 'unparalleled in the chronicles of the world'. Forty years later even the traditionalist Sir Walter Scott was writing of the 'improvement of national taste and delicacy', and twenty years after that, the statistician G. R. Porter in his *Progress of the Nation* remarked that 'all the elements of improvement are working with incessant and increasing energy'. In his own life-time, he went on, he had seen 'the greatest advances in civilization that can be found recorded in the annals of mankind'. Although a powerful minority of sceptics and prophets scorned the 'visibility of progress', the Great Exhibition of 1851 proclaimed it triumphantly, and even in the 1860s when elements of doubt were penetrating many favourite orthodoxies, the sense of achievement remained. The most important and influential English history book of the nineteenth century, Macaulay's *History of England* (1848, 1855, 1861) began with the claim that the author's 'chequered narrative' would excite 'hope in the breasts of all patriots' for, he went on, taking a broader sweep across time than will be attempted in these pages, 'the history of our country during the last hundred and sixty years is eminently the history of physical, of moral, and of intellectual improvement'.

By the middle years of the nineteenth century, indeed, the economic, social, and political history of England seemed to be falling into shape. The increase in material wealth, the challenge to aristocratic monopoly in government and administration, the rise of British power in the world and the creation of an 'intellectual empire' as well as a 'workshop of all the nations' seemed to be related to each other, each feature a part of the same complex of progress. And, perhaps most important of all, the means seemed as significant as the ends. The great changes which had been accomplished in politics as much as in economics had been produced, as H. T. Buckle, another leading Victorian historian put it, 'not by any great external event nor by any sudden insurrection of the people, but by the unaided action of moral force'.

The 'facts' of improvement were so striking that they made men dream dreams: the word 'improvement' itself which now sounds sober, respectable and emotionally threadbare was capable then of stimulating daring flights of imagination. The rate of progress in the previous decades of English history had led the optimists 'with every right' to conceive that the human race in the future would be transported 'to a state of happiness and virtue, which a fond imagination loves to ascribe to [the] primitive condition of man'. 'Innocence and simplicity', associated with 'the traditions of the theologian and the dreams of the poet', would be recovered in a new age of bliss.[1]

It is obvious from statements of this kind that 'fond imagination' was not the prerogative of the theologian and the poet, and it follows as a necessary corollary that any modern interpretation of what many outstanding Victorians considered to be an 'age of improvement' should be coolly critical and not simply derivative. Fortunately for the twentieth-century historian there were many Victorians who enjoyed puncturing rhetoric and challenging easy optimistic assumptions. By 1867, indeed, there were many signs that far-sighted contemporaries, while still sure of the past, were increasingly uncertain about the future. They could go back to the England of Pitt and Fox—or with more assurance to the England of Castlereagh and Eldon—and measure the extent of improvement. They could anticipate continued speed of change in years to come. But they were less sure about direction. 'From the England of Fielding and Richardson to the England of Miss Austen—from the England of Miss Austen to the England of Railways and Free-trade', wrote J. A. Froude in 1864, 'how vast the change; yet perhaps Sir Charles Grandison would not seem so strange to us now, as one of ourselves will seem to our great-grandchildren. The world moves faster and faster; and the difference will probably be considerably greater. The temper of each new generation is a continual surprise.'

Three years later, in the middle of the excitement of the debates on the Second Reform Bill, it was far from certain that the surprise would be a pleasant one. The previous seventy years of English history had been dominated by the rise of the middle classes. The middle classes had been the carriers not only of Free Trade but of the very idea of improvement itself. Now, with the granting of the vote to the workers of the towns, there was little sure knowledge but much real trepidation about the pattern of future politics. To those who still looked eagerly towards the future, Buckle's 'state of happiness and virtue' began to appear like wishful thinking, im-

[1] See *The Miscellaneous and Posthumous Works of Henry Thomas Buckle* (ed. Grant Allen vol. I, 1885, p. 309).

perfectly grounded in the mood of either intellectual or materialist England. The contradictions of progress were undermining the certainties, and in G. M. Young's phrase, it was already late afternoon and there was 'a chill in the air'.[1]

My book ends, therefore, with a question mark about the shape of the future, a far more realistic ending than a full stop to a study of any historical period. Of course, the historian's question mark will not be the same as that contemporaries employed—along with their other flourishes of punctuation. Not only can we see round the corner which was hidden from the view of Porter, Macaulay and Buckle, but we have made a different assessment of what to them was their immediate past. In general, we are more attentive than they were to the elements of opposition and resistance in specific historical 'situations', more chary of drawing thick connecting lines between historical characters and episodes of different generations, more sensitive to the propaganda element in both economic and political slogans, more eager to probe into the structure both of politics and society. In other words, we have ceased to be 'Whigs'. Equally important, though we may not all have ceased to be 'Radicals', we can see clearly that the victory of the middle classes or even of 'liberal government', about which the mid-Victorians talked so eloquently, was less complete and assured than they assumed.

Nonetheless the commanding themes which stand out for us are the same themes as those the mid-Victorians seized upon—the new relationship between man and nature, expressed in the exploitation of physical power and the use of machinery; the rise of a new class structure, conceived of in 'class' terms, and dependent on a massive working-class base; the transformation of politics and administration, so that the control of oligarchies was diminished and the influence of 'opinion' was given greater play; the improvement of manners and morals among both 'high' and 'low'; and the determination of new attitudes and policies in international relations from Pitt to Canning and from Canning to Palmerston.

Not one of these big themes is concerned with a closed circle of facts and incidents which can be traced simply and conclusively. Each of them, as Dr. Trevelyan has said of the industrial revolution, is a process and not an event.[2] Exact dating, possible only for the chronicler, is far from easy in discussing such basic developments

[1] See *Victorian England, Portrait of an Age* (1936) pp. 110 ff.
[2] *Illustrated History of England* (1956) p. 615.

as the rise of the political party or the social and economic impact of the railways. Even familiar chronological landmarks, like 1815, 1832, and 1867, sometimes seem less conspicuous in the light of modern research. In many ways, for example, the political world after 1832 resembled that which preceded it, while the whole story of 'the leap in the dark' in 1867 makes sense only when it is related to the controversies which preceded and followed the passing of the measure.

When all these complications have been taken into account, there is still, of course, a tale to tell about these years of change as well as an analysis to expound. This book is not a straight narrative history, but it does set out to give the outlines of a story. The story must find a place for Waterloo and Peterloo, Kennington Common and Sebastopol, Nelson and Wordsworth, Watt and Darwin: because little-known incidents and connections must be put in, there is no need to leave familiar ones out. Even when historical researchers have struggled with their monographs and shifted their general interpretations, the outlines of a story still remain. 'We carry our own history about with us', and no period of national history has left a richer legacy in the popular imagination and a more substantial record in the England we see around us than that described in this book.

In one important sense this history is incomplete. It is a history not of Britain but of England, and although for reasons of length and emphasis the exclusion of detailed references to Wales, Scotland, Ireland and the British Empire may well be justified, there is artificiality about the process of separation. Scottish and Welsh society had distinct features and pose problems of their own, although there was a persistent cross influence and overlapping of Scottish, Welsh, and English political and economic history and common means of integration were brought to bear on them all. Ireland was a different case. The difficulties of governing it success- fully were frequently a more serious preoccupation of cabinets in London than the difficulties of governing England itself. This can be measured simply by the volume of official paper devoted to Ireland. At the same time, the difficulties were increased not only by the inability of English politicians to understand the problems of a differently constituted society but by the very nature of the theory of 'improvement' which shaped changes in England. As one English politician-civil servant stated at the height of the Irish crisis of the

1840s when he was opposing a policy of positive state action in Ireland—'for the government to undertake by its own direct agency the detailed drainage and improvement of the whole country, is a task for which the nature and functions of government are totally unsuited'. The *Economist* underlined the same lesson; 'a government may remove all impediments which interfere to prevent the people from providing for themselves, but beyond that they can do little'.[1] It was the strength of such attitudes as much as the inherent temper of the Irish themselves, their religion or their 'national character,' which ensured that Ireland was still a major item on the English political agenda in 1867 and that Irish events would continue to produce sharp crises in English politics. One of the first consequences of the Reform Bill of 1867 and the Liberal victory of 1868 was a new bout of interest in Ireland.

There were signs too in 1867 of a growing interest in wider problems of Empire, in sharp contrast to the melancholy of 1783 when an Empire had been lost and it was difficult to avoid a sense of national disgrace. Between 1783 and 1867, however, the expansionist process continued unabated, and distant frontiers of adventure and exploitation drew English men and English money from the restricting confines of what is after all a small island separated from the main land-mass of Europe and dependent upon the ocean as a gateway to opportunity. Not all the expansion was directed towards the 'formal' Empire painted red on the mid-Victorian maps, and the process of movement and growth must always be considered as a whole and not as a series of official *pronunciamentos* about imperial interests, burdens, and responsibilities. A full history of England in the period from the end of the American War to the Canada Act of 1867 must be related not only to the history of the English-speaking peoples but to the contact of English and foreign 'cultures' in the tropics and the antipodes. India, in particular, posed problems as absorbing as those of Ireland, and different 'schools' of Englishmen as well as great individuals tested their theories and tried out their ideas on Indian soil. Whigs, Utilitarians, Evangelicals, even men of the Manchester School were drawn or driven to concern themselves with Indian as well as with English questions, with the balance sheet of commitment and responsibility, with the serious issues of freedom, authority, plan and force, above all with questions

---

[1] Both remarks are quoted by K. B. Nowlan in *The Great Famine, Studies in Irish History* (1957) ch. III.

of 'scale' which did not always arise in the development of 'improvement' in England itself. 'We are all of us', exclaimed one Member of Parliament later in the century 'members for India.'

The detailed consideration of English history in relation to the other parts of Britain and the Empire is not attempted in this book, which should be considered as an English contribution to a bigger story. The geographical perspectives in which English history is viewed have changed strikingly in the mid-twentieth century when London is no longer the centre of the world and even the most indomitable Englishmen are compelled to take account of English history in relation to the history of other countries. It is necessary in introducing this account of English history to state, however briefly, that the period it spans begins with France on the eve of revolution, with Germany and Italy still 'geographical expressions', with the United States still wrestling with the problems of the Constitution. Frederick the Great, Catherine of Russia, Joseph II, Louis XV, Necker, Washington, Jefferson, and Hamilton should be placed alongside George III, Pitt, Fox, Boulton, and Watt. It ends with France precariously ruled by Napoleon III, Germany and Italy on the eve of final unification and the United States safely through the testing ordeal of the Civil War. In other words much else was 'made' between 1783 and 1867 besides English 'liberalism' or the English 'industrial revolution', and the question marks of 1867 were even more challenging across the Channel and the Atlantic than they were in England itself.

I

ECONOMY AND SOCIETY IN THE 1780s

1. SOCIAL ORDER AND ECONOMIC CHANGE

'BY visiting other countries', wrote an English traveller in 1780, 'a subject of Great Britain will acquire a greater esteem than ever for the constitution of his own. Freed from vulgar prejudices, he will perceive that the blessings and advantages which his countrymen enjoy do not flow from their superiority in wisdom, courage or virtue over the other nations of the world, but in some degree from the peculiarity of their situation in an island; and, above all, from those just and equitable laws which secure property, that mild free government which abhors tyranny, protects the meanest subjects and leaves the mind of man to its own exertion, unrestrained by those arbitrary, capricious, impolitic shackles, which confine and weaken its noblest endeavours in almost every other country of the world.'[1]

Both the style and the content of this equable panegyric were representative of the age. To the natural advantages of geography—location, landscape, climate, and resources—Englishmen had added (or so they and many foreigners thought) the acquired advantages of industry, wealth, liberty, and moderation. Taken together, natural and acquired advantages made up a harmonious whole:

> Thy Seasons moderate as thy Laws appear,
> Thy Constitution wholesome as the Year:
> Well pois'd, and pregnant in thy annual Round
> With Wisdom, where no fierce Extreme is found . . .
> Where Strength and Freedom in their Prime prevail,
> And Wealth comes wafted on each freighted Gale.[2]

---

[1] J. Moore, *A View of Society and Manners in France, Switzerland and Germany* (1780). Cf. J. Andrews, *A Comparative View of the English and French Nations in their Manners, Politics and Literature* (1785).
[2] *The Isle of Wight*, A Poem in Three Cantos (1782).

Not even disputes about the balance of the Constitution or the most effective means of encouraging trade and industry seriously disturbed either the equability or the sense of continuity, which were reflected in loyalties and embodied both in institutions and routines of everyday life. Even radical reformers, for the most part, spoke of restoring old rights rather than creating new ones: 'If ever God Almighty did concern Himself about forming a government for mankind to live happily under, it was that which was established in England by our Saxon forefathers', wrote an anonymous essayist of 1771.[1] When a group of footballers at Kingston-on-Thames were charged in 1790 with riotous conduct while playing in the streets, they pleaded in justification that they were merely celebrating the anniversary of an ancient Saxon victory over the Danes.[2]

The dominance of family ties made for both order and continuity. In the countryside, land belonged to families rather than to individuals and was held 'in trust' from generation to generation; decisions relating to its ownership were usually made in terms of family 'interest', with complex legal instruments of family control. In the City of London and the towns, business organization also was often associated with family partnerships—there was no limited liability and no national capital market—and industrial initiative frequently depended on loans from brothers and cousins. The road to individual advancement usually led not through the workshop as in the nineteenth century or through the school as in the twentieth, but past the altar; for a man to marry his master's daugher, or better still his widow, was a recognized avenue to success. Even the unsuccessful at a humbler level were dependent on family both for livelihood and security, and most often on heredity for occupation. Kinship ties—conceived of as an intricate network of responsibilities within extended families—upheld both 'domestic industry' and small-scale farming, while in the political arena, family 'connexion' counted for more than party.

Society, however, was something more than a vast cluster of families, some born to property, others to poverty. It had its *ranks* and *orders* and its necessary degrees of subordination and authority. They were rarely called in question. Good order was deemed the foundation of all good things, of 'politeness' as well as peace, and social relationships, when they were talked about, were conceived

---

[1] *Historical Essay on the English Constitution* (1771), p. 165. See below, pp. 88–9.
[2] M. Marples, *A History of Football* (1954), p. 84.

of in moral as well as in social terms. It was the Architect of the
Universe who had 'distributed men into different ranks, and at the
same time united them into one society, in such sort as men are
united'. By Divine decree rather than by human contrivance, the
poor, the greater part of society, were placed under 'the superin-
tendence and patronage of the Rich'. In turn, the rich were charged
by 'natural Providence, as much as by revealed appointment, with
the care of the Poor'.[1]

Some thinkers in the eighteenth century, particularly philosophers,
defended a modified version of this view of society in terms not of
Divine decree but of enlightened human self interest. Even when
active benevolence was not displayed in works of charity, natural
economic functions might be equally effective in maintaining social
harmonies. The poet Pope had claimed in his *Essay on Man* (1733)

> That REASON, PASSION, answer one great aim
> That true SELF-LOVE and SOCIAL are the same.

Adam Smith was more specific. 'Society', he wrote, 'may subsist
among different men, as among different merchants, from a sense of
its utility without any mutual love or affection, if only they refrain
from doing injury to each other.' The pursuit of the general interest
of all was encouraged, not hampered, by the division between rich
and poor. 'A prosperous merchant, in augmenting his own private
fortune, will enjoy the agreeable reflection that he is likewise
increasing the riches and power of his country and giving bread to
thousands of his industrious countrymen.'[2]

There were various ways of classifying and sub-dividing the
different ranks and orders which together made up the community.[3]
Many of them were complicated, for the English social system
emphasized minute social distinctions and nuances of status rather
than broad composite groupings. It needed a novelist like Jane
Austen to trace the delicate pattern. There was, however, a bold and
massive social pyramid, which can be described more bluntly. At
the peak of it were the 'great', those who, in Daniel Defoe's phrase,
lived 'profusely'. To belong to the ranks of the great it was still
necessary to be a great proprietor. Those great proprietors who
were entitled to use armorial bearings—the nearest approach to a

---

[1] *The Works of Joseph Butler* (ed. W. E. Gladstone), vol. II (1896), p. 305.
[2] J. Moore, *op. cit.*, vol. I, pp. 327–8.
[3] See P. Mathias, 'The Social Structure in the Eighteenth Century: Calculation by
J. Massie' in *Ec. Hist. Rev.* (1957) for some useful comparisons.

nobility in England—were not separated from other non-titled proprietors by any thick walls of caste: they were not a *noblesse*, as in France. A small group of them, however, were renowned for the extent of their ownership and commitments, and the pull of their 'influence'. Frequent intermarriage, it has been said, gave them the semblance more of tribes than of families. Many of their landed estates were kingdoms in miniature and their London houses were as magnificent as their rural mansions. During the course of the eighteenth century they had extended and consolidated their position. Below them came substantial proprietors, often with great local influence and preoccupations, and the gentry, that characteristic but imprecise English social group, whose ownership of land provided them with their main title to power and prestige. The gentry maintained estates in a style appropriate to their social position, and were at the same time proud of their independence and conscious of their corporate existence as the backbone of the 'landed interest'. In addition there were independent yeoman families, although in many parts of the country they had been a declining group for generations. The yeomen, unlike the great proprietors and many of the gentry, farmed their own land. For the most part the land held by substantial landowners was farmed by tenants, some of them substantial men themselves.

It was a distinctive feature of this eighteenth-century English society that it gave an honoured place not only to the landowner but to the merchant, that it permitted wealth to increase 'on each freighted gale'. In the world of trade and commerce itself there were natural gradations and degrees of authority. A group of substantial merchant magnates, princes of wealth, drawing their riches from all parts of the world, was easily distinguishable from the 'middling sort' of folk, local factors and agents, engaged in domestic trade, men who 'though highly useful in their stations, are by no means entitled to the honours of higher rank'.[1] According to Defoe, the middling sort lived 'very well', while Adam Smith remarked that they were usually regarded as a superior rank to the yeomanry.[2] They continued to improve their fortunes—and some of them their prestige—as the century went by. If land conferred secured possession and perpetuated continuous influence from generation to generation, it could be claimed also that 'to COMMERCE AND

---

[1] *Political Register*, January 1763.
[2] *The Wealth of Nations* (1776), Book III, ch. II.

MANUFACTURE we may justly attribute the stability of empire and
the opulence of individuals; since they encourage a universal spirit
of industry, remove local prejudices, and elevate the mind to
magnanimity and wisdom.'[1]

Below the merchant princes and the 'middle sort' came the artisans,
'who labour hard but feel no want', skilled men with subtle degrees
of 'superiority' and 'inferiority'[2]; 'the country people', a loose
term, including many folk who had always been poor, many who
were socially displaced in the course of the century, and many whose
standard of living fluctuated sharply in 'good' and 'lean' years; 'the
Poor, that fare hard', particularly when they were out of work; and
'the Miserable, that really pinch and suffer want'. It is important
not to consider all these groups below the 'middling sort' as one
homogeneous mass. Francis Place, the London tailor—with his
eighteenth-century style of thinking about social divisions—rightly
complained in the early nineteenth century of the indiscriminate
jumbling together in the term 'lower orders' of 'the most skilled and
the most prudent workmen with the most ignorant and imprudent
labourers and paupers'. 'The difference is great indeed', he went on,
'and in many cases will scarce admit of comparison.'[3]

Properly speaking, it was the last two groups described above
who made up Adam Smith's 'common people', the base of a social
pyramid which few contemporaries believed could or should be
converted into a cube. Adam Smith was not exceptional when he
wrote that the rich, even when they were concerned only with 'the
gratification of their own vain and insatiable desires', divided with
the poor the produce of their improvements. 'They are thus led by
an invisible hand', he remarked in a metaphor which was soon to
be used in many other contexts, 'to make nearly the same distribution
of the necessaries of life, which would have been made, had the earth
been divided into equal portions among all its inhabitants.'[4] Rich
and poor were always 'with us', and no government, however
enlightened, could tamper effectively with inequality by supplying
to the poor 'those necessaries which it had pleased the Divine
Providence for a while to withhold from them'.[5]

---

[1] *The Universal British Directory of Trade and Commerce* (1790).
[2] The Spitalfields silk weavers, for example, were considered as 'inferior artificers',
superior to common labourers but inferior to London artisans, such as watchmakers.
[3] Francis Place Papers, B.M., Add. MSS. 27,834, f. 45.
[4] *The Theory of Moral Sentiments* (1759), Part IV, ch. I.
[5] E. Burke, *Thoughts on Scarcity* (1795).

Within this social framework, a comforting if not always a comfortable system, each man had his station and each station its peculiar responsibilities. The responsibilities were, of course, not always met—for every charitable action there were many callous and brutal ones—but the concept of social order itself often blossomed out in works of corporate as well as private philanthropy. The eighteenth century was rightly proud of its 'improvement' in manners and its ripening sense of social duty. For the care of the sick, the aged, prisoners, foundlings and poor children, new institutions were created during the course of the century, particularly after 1750. 'We live in an age when humanity is in fashion', wrote the London magistrate Sir John Hawkins in 1787, and its influence could be traced in many places inside and outside London both in individual lives and in the growth of voluntary social organizations: on scores of tombstones and memorial plaques in parish churches we read of men like William Whyte, a surgeon of Castor, who died in 1788 and was 'equally distinguished for professional Abilities, the strictest integrity and an active Discharge of the Duties of Humanity'.

If the principal duty of the fortunate—those with property and ability—was to meet their social obligations to others, the principal duty of the poor was to be content with their lot. William Paley in his celebrated *Reasons for Contentment* (1781) explained to them why they had to be. While property provided power and implied responsibility, poverty inculcated virtue. 'How thankful, then, the poor should be that the very circumstances in which they are placed have such a powerful tendency to cherish the divine spirit of dependence and subordination.'[1] Even highly critical and searching writers, like Adam Smith's distinguished Scots contemporary and colleague John Millar (Scotland was the home of modern British sociology as well as of British economics) did not dispute the wisdom of the natural division into ranks and orders. Millar held firmly that any necessary reforms should always be carried out within the framework of 'those established distinctions of Rank, which it is often unjust and always hazardous to abolish'.[2]

Although the view of social order generally accepted was essentially static, there were nonetheless significant features which were modifying the picture even before the disruptive invention of the steam engine transformed the processes of material production.

---

[1] J. Stephens, *The Mutual Relations of the Rich and Poor* (1819).
[2] J. Millar, *Origin of the Distinction of Ranks in Society* (1771).

People were already divided into 'optimists' and 'pessimists', those who welcomed movement and dreamed of its limitless possibilities and those who tried to resist or to challenge it.

Three features were of special importance. First, English society not only permitted but encouraged a considerable degree of individual mobility. Successful merchants, for example, could acquire land in the (limited) land market and convert their wealth into social status, and before long it often became difficult to account for the origins of the fixed property of an established family. 'Trade', wrote Defoe, 'is so far from being inconsistent with a gentleman that, in short, trade in England makes "gentlemen".' Of course, there were many complaints about the 'inundation of new men' both from discontented supporters of the 'old order' like William Cobbett and disturbed 'peers and country gentlemen' who 'looked down on the men raised by merit and industry from obscurity to eminence'.[1] But the frequency of such complaints shows that England before the industrial revolution provided a place for what Adam Smith —and Thomas Malthus after him—called 'the natural effort of every individual to better his own condition',[2] a desire, 'which though generally calm and dispassionate, comes with us from the womb and never leaves us until we go into the grave'. Millar even went on to claim that 'every man who is industrious may entertain the hope of gaining a fortune'.[3] In politics, too, many men without the advantages of birth opened the doors of power, although they often had to pay lavish homage, as Edmund Burke did, to the claims of blood and aristocracy.

Second, within the whole social order there had been for many years a general infusion of increased wealth. An interesting letter to the *Public Advertiser* of 1760, after referring to 'our known division of the people of this nation into the nobility, the gentry and the commonalty', spoke eloquently of the enormous recent changes in the 'customs, manners and habits' of the third group. Trade, the writer went on, 'hath given a new face to the whole nation' and within the 'commonalty' there were many signs of new wealth and new pride.[4] 'To conceive that so great a change as this in the people', he concluded, 'should produce no change in the Constitution'

---

[1] T. Gisborne, *Enquiry into the Duties of Men in the Higher and Middle Classes of Society in Great Britain* (1794).
[2] *The Wealth of Nations*, Book IV, ch. IX and *passim*.
[3] *Op. cit.*, p. 120.
[4] Quoted H. Jephson, *The Platform, Its Rise and Progress* (1892), vol. I, pp. 8–9.

would be to show the same ignorance as a physician who asserted that 'the whole state of the blood may be entirely altered from poor to rich, from cool to inflamed, without producing any alteration in the condition of man.' While the author of the letter was vague about the likely nature of the consequences, his forthright contemporary Dr. Johnson was bold and dogmatic. 'Gold and silver destroy feudal subordination', he remarked tersely.[1] No man, he exclaimed, had the same authority as his father had—except a gaoler —and although Johnson hoped for a reaction against 'this extreme relaxation', instead even the absolute authority of the gaoler was to crumble in face of the resolute assault of prison reformers. Outside the prison walls, smoke was to accelerate the effects of silver and gold: the new 'brass' of the rugged industrialists of the North was to prove far more destructive of deference than the 'freighted gales' of the port of London.

Before the smoke poured out from the mill chimneys, however, there was a third feature transforming the picture. The traditional view of society was troubled during the course of mounting eighteenth-century debates on three basic social questions—the size of the population, the state of the poor, and the provision of education.

Although there were many writers who still believed, as William Cobbett did at the end of the century, that the population of England was decreasing, there were others, more careful in their choice of evidence, who realized not only that the population was increasing but that population change was one of the most important determinants of the structure and prosperity of any society. In 1752 David Hume had written his essay *Of the Populousness of Ancient Nations*, which expounded a thesis some elements of which were very similar to those later made famous by Thomas Malthus. A few years later Robert Wallace further shattered some of the dreams of optimistic eighteenth-century philosophers by suggesting that social improvement would be cancelled out by a large population pressing on food supplies, and that a perfect government would be 'inconsistent with the present frame of nature, and with a limited extent of earth . . . the earth would be overstocked at last.'[2] Thus when writers like William Godwin re-stated the eighteenth-century dream of a continually progressing society in the 1790s, there already

[1] J. Boswell, *Life of Johnson* (1791), 10 April 1778.
[2] R. Wallace, *Various Prospects of Mankind, Nature, and Providence* (1761), pp. 114-6.

existed the rudiments of a theory of population which would check large hopes of continued development. In 1798 Malthus was to present the rudiments in a connected and brilliantly written essay and to capture the mind of a generation.

The second controversy, that about the state of the poor, was intimately bound up with arguments about population. In the last twenty-five years of the eighteenth century there was an increasing preoccupation with the condition of the poor and the foundation of a number of philanthropic organizations designed to assist them. In 1796, for example, the Society for Bettering the Condition of the Poor was set up, with the intention of making 'the inquiry into all that concerns the poor and promotion of their happiness a science'.[1] A year later Sir Frederick Morton Eden produced his famous three-volume survey of the state of the poor. Many writers, however, sharply criticized 'over-indulgence' on the part of philanthropists and public authorities. Joseph Townsend, for example, stated categorically in 1783 that 'no human efforts' could improve the state of the poor and that only hunger could induce 'sobriety, diligence and fidelity'. By far the larger part of the poor, he maintained, would continue to fulfil 'the most servile, the most sordid, and the most ignoble offices in the community'.[2] What Townsend wrote was sufficiently chilling, particularly when underlined by the Christian clergyman Malthus, to question the more benevolent aspects of eighteenth-century poor law administration and, more seriously, to throw doubts on ideas of improvement as a whole.

The third controversy also was concerned with the poor. Should they be educated? During the course of the eighteenth century various attempts had been made, particularly in the charity schools, to teach them reading and writing, or sometimes reading by itself. Such efforts were concerned not with refashioning the way of life of the poor but with keeping them in their due place in society by instruction in the scriptures and the catechism. Despite this limitation of purpose, the charity schools were often attacked on the grounds that 'education' threatened 'the great law of subordination': in the last decades of the century, similar arguments were used against the Sunday schools which had been inspired by Robert Raikes of Gloucester. While defenders of the Sunday School Union, founded in 1785, urged that education produced 'orderly and decent com-

[1] *First Report of the Society for Bettering the Condition of the Poor* (1797).
[2] *A Dissertation on the Poor Laws* (1786).

portment' and deterred children from crime, their critics complained that they 'refined and innervated, and consequently disqualified for the duties of a humble station'. A few years later when the good eighteenth-century philanthropist, Hannah More, opened a school for poor children in the Mendips, she was accused by local farmers of inciting village children to mutiny and disaffection. 'The poor',. declared the wife of the leading local farmer, 'were intended to be servants and slaves: it was pre-ordained that they should be ignorant.' Her husband added the appropriate conclusion. 'If a school were to be set up, it would be all over with property, and if property is not to rule what is to become of us?'[1]

Hannah More found no adequate reply to such a conclusion in the terms of her traditionalist eighteenth-century philosophy, based on individual responsibilities and social order. She was at pains to stress that her object had not been 'to teach dogmas and opinions, but to form the lower class to habits of industry and virtue', but such a modest assessment of her work was a little unrealistic. Her own theory of society—and it was a theory which she derived from the views of her immediate predecessors and her philanthropic contemporaries—broke down precisely at the point where she tried to put it into practice, and in the nineteenth century the great educational pioneer, Sir James Kay-Shuttleworth, was rightly to observe that the establishment of Sunday Schools prepared public opinion for a general advance in elementary education.[2]

While eighteenth-century moral and social theories were breaking down or at least getting caught up in a web of complications, the social order as a whole was subject to far sharper strains and stresses as a result of the industrial advances of the 1780s and 1790s. It was then that England experienced the first phases of its 'industrial revolution'; and, although the concept of an industrial revolution has been queried by certain recent economic historians, during these years the beginnings of a total change in English society can be traced, to which the label 'revolution' still deserves to be attached.

There was, of course, no sudden break with the economic past, no over-night upheaval, no universal transformation. England still remained a predominantly agricultural and trading community; many of the new industrial enterprises grew out of the mercantile

[1] Quoted M. G. Jones, *Hannah More* (1952), ch. VII.
[2] Committee of Council on Education, *On the School in Relation to the Church, the State and the Community* (1847), p. 6.

network which existed before the exploitation of steam power; most of the new industrial units were small and highly localized; Jane Austen could ignore all these hard facts just as she ignored the wars against Napoleon. Yet hard facts, quantitatively measurable, they were, and for those with eyes to see they were 'great and extraordinary' facts, 'almost miraculous', 'unparalleled in the annals of the world'. After 1782, almost every available statistical series of industrial output reveals a sharp upward turn. According to Professor T. S. Ashton's calculations, more than half the growth in the shipments of coal and the mining of copper, more than three-quarters of the increase of broadcloths, four-fifths of that of printed cloth, and nine-tenths of the exports of cotton goods were concentrated in the last eighteen years of the eighteenth century.[1] The disasters of the American War were forgotten in a wave of national prosperity: before long Britain was selling more goods to an independent America than she had ever sold to colonial America. 'Move your eye which side you will', wrote Arthur Young, 'you behold nothing but great riches and yet greater resources.'

The central feature of the industrial revolution was not mechanization but the successful attempt to master natural forces which hitherto had mastered man. In the year 1776, when the Americans drafted their Declaration of Independence and Adam Smith published his *Wealth of Nations*, an enthusiastic versifier hailed the potential inventions, which unlocked Nature's secrets, in proud and prophetic language:

> The time may come when nothing will succeed
> But what a previous Patent hath decreed;
> And we must open on some future day
> The door of Nature with a patent key.

Just over a decade later Erasmus Darwin, grandfather of Charles, wrote his remarkable poem *The Botanic Garden* (1789, 1791) which turned nymphs and salamanders into symbols of the human conquest of power and space; while the young Wordsworth in lines written in 1794 and intended to be added to his *Evening Walk* (1787-9) praised 'those favoured souls

> . . . to whom the harmonious doors
> Of Science have unbarred celestial stores,
> To whom a burning energy has given
> That other eye which darts thro' earth and heaven.'

T. S. Ashton, *The 18th Century* (1955), p. 125.

Opening the door of Nature in workshop, factory, mine, and forge was the great technical achievement of the eighteenth century, although developments in scientific thought and economic activity during the seventeenth century had made the achievement possible and prophets like Francis Bacon had foreseen it. Behind the increase in production which technical advance made possible, was a pride in human capacity. It was this pride which permitted a union of art and industry in the first stages of the industrial revolution, and appealed to the imagination of poets as well as to the reason of economists. In time—before very long, indeed—the union was strained and the appeal was converted into a revolt. The contradictions of economic growth and the social problems it created shocked rather than pleased some of the most sensitive Englishmen. By then, however, it was possible for the majority to consider the technical changes not as exciting new ventures but, less grandiloquently, as extensions of that same spirit of 'improvement' which Defoe had seized upon early in the eighteenth century,[1] and to defend them not because they 'unbarred celestial stores' but because they served to make the population 'moral and happy'. Nonetheless, Victorian trust in improvement—which was always challenged by a minority of Victorians themselves—had a revolutionary foundation, although Englishmen could forget it more easily than Frenchmen across the Channel could forget their political revolution of 1789.

The consequences of industrial expansion continued to proliferate unceasingly. Once opened, the door of Nature could not be closed again. The work of the first generation of pioneers was followed up by imitators and new inventors: discoveries led relentlessly to new discoveries. In a sense, the history of the years from 1784 to 1867 is the history of a continuing industrial revolution, which every new generation saw in different terms until the men of the 1860s began to feel for the first time that they could see the whole process in perspective. Even then the 'revolution' was still unfinished, and the interpretations of it have subsequently been revised time and time again, for the simple reason that we are still caught up in the moving picture which we are trying to describe.

But technical innovations, however important they were in multiplying industrial output, did not make up the whole of the

---

[1] 'Every new view of Great Britain would require a new description. . . . New discoveries in metals, mines, minerals, new undertakings in trade; inventions, engines, manufactures, in a nation producing and improving as we are: These things open new scenes every day.' *Tour of Great Britain.* Preface to vol. III, (1726).

industrial revolution. The changes of the late eighteenth century were social and intellectual as well as technical and economic. They were associated with a great increase in population, a further expansion of trade, the emergence of new social groups—both 'captains of industry' and factory labour—the creation of new political pressures and new social institutions, new modes of thought and action, and, above all, the foundation of a new view of society. The whole view of the social order, which had been transmitted from the past and re-formulated in terms of eighteenth-century philosophy, was transformed under the influence of coal and iron, cotton and steam, growth and 'progress'. But in an English setting it was not transformed all at once or completely: the chain of continuity was tampered with, but it did not snap.

Before the nature and extent of the transformation can be understood, it is necessary to examine in more detail the technical changes themselves, and the social and economic *milieu* in which they were devised.

2. Men, Machines, and Materials

The geographical position of England fitted it to be not only the emporium of a world-wide commerce, as it already was by the middle of the eighteenth century, but a centre of manufacturing industry, for a time 'the workshop of the world'. 'Every facility seems at hand', one writer put it, 'for starting us on a manufacturing career. . . . Those metals which are of greatest utility in the useful arts, and the coal which is requisite in working them, are distributed conveniently, and in inexhaustible abundance, throughout the land. . . . With our insulated position we have a greater line of sea coast, and a greater number of capacious harbours, as compared with the extent of land surface, than any other nation in the world.'[1]

Such an inventory of natural resources was no guarantee of economic growth in the eighteenth century. That England was rich in coal and iron—relatively accessible coal and iron—and in a favourable position to import raw materials like timber and cotton from overseas was a pre-condition of large-scale industrial development, not a cause of it. The value of resources depends upon their usefulness, and their usefulness in turn depends upon changes in knowledge, in techniques and in taste. During the course of the

[1] H. Dunckley, *The Charter of the Nations* (1854), p. 6.

eighteenth century new resources were tapped because of changes of this kind; and by the 1780s they had gone far enough to produce visible results in the form of striking increases in output.

Three major technical advances were of the utmost importance— the mechanization of the textile industry, the emergence of a new technology of coal and iron, and the introduction of steam power. Behind these advances there was a long history of experiment and innovation; before them, in the 1780s, there was a bold vista of possible future expansion. The main course of technical advance could be foreseen for years to come.

Mechanization in the textiles industry affected all basic processes from the preparation of raw materials to the making of finished articles for sale. In the story of technical improvement, it was the relatively new branch of the industry, cotton, unfettered by traditional organization, which led the way, not the old British staple, wool, or the luxury fibre, silk. From the 1730s onwards, inventions in both spinning and weaving (interacting and mutually stimulating) had attracted capital, concentrated labour, increased output and swollen imports and exports. The decade from 1780 saw not only a very sharp increase in output but a number of important new developments in the technical and economic structure of the industry. The great manufacturer, Richard Arkwright, who had set up a chain of successful factories in many parts of the country, had his patents cancelled in 1781 and 1785, and from then onwards the field of enterprise which he had pioneered was open to all. In 1785 also, the steam engine was first applied to spinning by rollers, and the way was prepared for a further concentration of factory industry, no longer of necessity situated by the fast moving country streams but free to settle in the heart of industrial towns. A year later, 1786, the Rev. Edmund Cartwright completed the first working power loom which could be operated by horses, water wheels, or steam engines. Although the application of the power loom made relatively slow progress during the following twenty years, there no longer seemed any doubt that given time both the spinning and weaving processes in the cotton industry could become fully mechanized. Advance was far less rapid in the woollen industry, but the barriers to change were more social and economic than technical: by the time that they had been broken down, the cotton interest had established itself as the most powerful and prosperous industrial interest in the kingdom.

Looking back from a nineteenth-century vantage point, its propagandists could claim that England's 'treasures of iron and coal, its crystal mountain streams, and convenient outlets to the ocean', would never have been exploited in a spectacular manner 'if Providence had never planted the cotton shrub'. Without it, not only would the poor have been robbed of the benefits of cheap calicoes —there was no more 'moral' industry than cotton—but national exports and imports would have grown far less rapidly; 'those majestic masses of men which stretch, like a living zone, through our central districts, would have felt no existence; and the magic impulse which has been felt . . . in every department of national energy . . . our literature, our laws, our social condition, our political institutions, making us almost a new people, would never have been communicated.'[1]

These were large claims, although large claims were doubtless justified in the light of the political victories of King Cotton in the 1840s. Against the background of the 1780s they need to be placed alongside the claims of other examples of technical invention and business initiative.

Unlike the cotton industry, the coal and iron industries, which provided basic resources for a new general technology in place of the old technology of wood, wind, and water, did not depend on large-scale imports of a raw material produced overseas nor did their progress lie in the substitution of machines for human labour. Once Abraham Darby (1709) and his successors at Coalbrookdale had substituted coke for charcoal in the blast furnace, the fortunes of the coal and iron industries, which had been separate from the beginnings of history, began to be linked together in what looked likely to be a permanent union. The dispersion of the iron industry amid the forests and beside the hills gave way to its massing along the coalfields. Darby's achievement, which followed many seventeenth-century failures to solve the same technical problem, anticipated the improvements in the textile industry by many years, but it was not until the latter half of the century that ironmasters outside Darby's Shropshire (and Denbighshire) fully exploited the new discovery. The crucial new invention was that of Henry Cort (and Peter Onions, working independently), who patented a combined puddling and rolling process in 1784 which made possible the large-scale production of wrought iron by means of coal fuel. Fortunately for

[1] *Ibid.*, pp. 7–8.

the growth of the industry, Cort's patent rights were quickly annulled in 1785, and during the next ten years, iron became the master material of the industrial revolution, being used not only by specialist metal industries, like armaments or hardware, but in the form of machinery by almost every industry in the country. At Coalbrookdale itself, even the window sills, and tombstones in the village churchyard, were made of iron. John Wilkinson was the most strenuous sponsor of his favourite metal. Perhaps more than any other individual he made his contemporaries conscious of the technical and aesthetic claims of iron as a peace-time commodity, constructing iron bridges, building iron boats which sceptics declared were bound to sink, manufacturing forty miles of cast iron pipes for the water supply of the city of Paris in 1788 (and also for New York), and insisting that when he died his body should be buried in an iron coffin.[1]

During the late eighteenth and early nineteenth centuries considerable sections of the British iron industry were modernized and expanded. In 1788, over 60,000 tons of pig iron were made in England and Wales, as against 25,000 sixty years before. The figure had risen to 125,000 tons eight years later and the number of blast furnaces had increased from 85 to 125. Steel, which was not used to any significant general extent until the middle of the nineteenth century, was being produced in sealed crucibles at Sheffield by Benjamin Huntsman in the 1740s: by 1787 there were twenty crucible steel works in England, and the secret of production was still not known on the Continent. Before the cheapening of steel and its production in great quantities in late Victorian England—and in even greater quantities overseas—the triumph of iron seemed complete. The Crystal Palace of 1851, with its combination of iron and glass, was the crowning achievement of the new iron age—the wrought-iron gates of Hyde Park came from Coalbrookdale—and even in the World of Utopias, J. S. Buckingham's ideal city of 1849 was designed to be constructed almost entirely of iron.

The abundance and cheapness of iron made many of the immediate consequences of its production far from Utopian: unearthed in large quantities and exploited not by science but by rule of thumb methods, it encouraged waste. The same was true of its sister material, coal. England was singularly fortunate that beneath its surface were the largest coal reserves in Western Europe outside the Ruhr, but their

[1] See W. H. Chaloner, 'John Wilkinson, Ironmaster' in *History Today* 1951).

exploitation depended upon ransacking the rich natural environment rather than taming it. The concentration of coal and iron production created broad acres of 'black country', with the prospect of more efficient fuel and cheaper power as over-riding economic incentives. Already in the early years of the eighteenth century, the coal-producing regions of the far North had been opened up, depending on close ties with the busy London market, and Sir Henry Liddell had asked in 1729, 'what signifies all your Balls, Ridottos, etc., unless Navigation and the Coal Trade flourish?'[1] In the course of the eighteenth century almost every local economic change increased the demand for coal for heating long before it was needed for power. The subsequent expansion of the industry depended not only upon the increase of demand but on finding solutions to technical difficulties in the mines. Efficient pumping devices were necessary before deep and prolonged pit working could be ensured: similarly, to extend the area of the mines, it was essential to improve wagon ways and tracks. Many of these technical difficulties were solved in the course of the century, and the total British annual coal output rose from three million tons in 1700 to 10 million tons a hundred years later. This great increase was merely a prelude to the more than twenty-fold increase during the next century.

The victory of coal and iron would not have been complete without the third great technical advance, which carried coal and iron into all parts of the country—the introduction of steam power. The invention and progressive improvement of the steam engine were regarded with pride by many of those who had seen it brought to perfection, 'the exclusive offspring of British genius fostered and supported by British capital'. 'To enumerate the effects of this invention', one of them wrote,[2] 'would be to count every comfort and luxury of life. It has increased the sum of human happiness, not only by calling new pleasures into existence, but by so cheapening former enjoyments as to render them attainable by those who before never would have hoped to share them. Nor are its effects confined to England alone; they extend over the whole civilized world; and the savage tribes of America, Asia and Africa, must ere long feel the benefits, remote or intermediate, of this all-powerful agent.'

Steam power was legitimately regarded as the 'all-powerful agent' in the mastery of Nature, affording two indispensable advantages to

[1] Quoted by E. Hughes, *North Country Life in the Eighteenth Century* (1952), p. 151.
[2] D. Lardner, *The Steam Engine Familiarly Explained and Illustrated with an Historical Sketch of its Invention and progressive Improvement* (1827).

the pioneers of industry. First, it provided adequate power to manufacture the enormously increased volume of materials in almost every branch of production: water power was intermittent and insufficient. Second, it freed industry from dependence on fixed location: water power was available only at the falls of a river or near fast-moving brooks.

From 1775 onwards James Watt and Matthew Boulton, in a classic partnership of technical inventor and businessman, were producing new-type steam engines which saved the serious loss of energy in the earlier Newcomen machines. In 1782 Watt went on to patent a 'sun and planet motion' steam engine transforming the up-and-down motion of the piston into a rotary motion. From this time onwards it was possible to use steam engines as the means of motive power in factories. Necessity was certainly the mother of this invention. A year earlier Boulton had written to Watt, 'the people in London, Manchester and Birmingham are *steam mill mad*. I don't mean to hurry you but . . . I think we should determine to take out a patent for certain methods of producing rotative motion': the patent of 1782 was the answer. Followed up by other patents (1784, parallel motion: 1788, the 'governor', which facilitated regular and smooth working of the engine and which has recently been heralded as an early pointer towards automation) the 1782 model was of crucial importance in economizing power and in stimulating output in many different parts of the economy. By continuing to hold the key patents until 1800, Boulton and Watt were at the centre of the new industrial scene, selling, in Boulton's picturesque phrase, 'what all the world wants—Power'. A catalogue of their customers is a catalogue of England's most active enterprise. In 1783 John Wilkinson and the Coalbrookdale Company each ordered one of the new engines; a year later Josiah Wedgwood, who had built up a remarkably successful pottery business at Etruria in North Staffordshire, bought a second engine to add to the one he had purchased two years earlier; a year after that, Arkwright bought his first steam engine for use in one of his great spinning factories. Other engines were used in important eighteenth-century enterprises like flour mills, malt mills, breweries,[1] and mills for crushing sugar cane. In

[1] In 1787 George III and the Queen visited Whitbread's brewery in London and saw a new steam engine which had just been installed. 'His Majesty, with becoming science, explained to the Queen and the Princess the leading movements in the machinery'. *London Chronicle*, May 1787. Brewers were among the first industrial establishments to require considerable capital equipment, and historians have recently been paying special attention to their history.

1800 there were 11 in use in Birmingham, 20 in Leeds, and 32 in Manchester. Altogether between 1775 and 1800 Boulton and Watt turned out 496 engines, and their new foundry, opened in 1795, was the largest and best-managed engineering works in the world.

> Soho—where GENIUS and the ARTS preside,
> EUROPA's wonder and BRITANNIA's pride.[1]

The successful partnership of Boulton and Watt illuminates the business background of the three great technical advances made during the course of the century. Indeed, both inventiveness and organizing ability must be given prominence in any study of the industrial revolution.

Inventiveness, which is singularly lacking in some societies and in others is associated with arts and crafts rather than with 'industries', was widespread in eighteenth-century England and depended, as it must always do, on knowledge, skill, and challenge. Some of the knowledge was 'practical' and the skill manipulative, the proud possession of 'ingenious but unlettered mechanics': some was systematic and contemplative, derived from the scientific explorations of the previous hundred years. The quality of inventiveness itself was admired and fostered nationally by such bodies as the Society for the Encouragement of Arts, Manufactures and Commerce, founded in 1754, and in the provinces by organizations like the Manchester Committee for the Protection and Encouragement of Trade (1774). But prodding and propaganda, though valuable, were not decisive. Business opportunity tempted the inventor immediately and directly, despite the risks of craft or mob hostility and the perils of litigation.

Not all inventors had the necessary qualities to exploit their own discoveries, and economic growth depended on the existence of a group of businessmen prepared to show enterprise, as well as on a supply of inventors brimful of new ideas. The businessmen came from all ranks of society, although 'middling folk' predominated. England was not an under-developed country at the beginning of the industrial revolution, but an old and active commercial society in which—within the landed framework—merchants had long been prepared to take risks, to invest in productive outlays, to specialize, and to look to the opportunities of the market. Many of the merchants, particularly in the Provinces, were religious dissenters, as their Christian names show. They were perhaps the best and certainly

---

[1] J. Bisset, *A Poetic Survey round Birmingham* (1802).

the most 'usefully' educated section of the 'middle ranks of society'. Their training and ideals of character led them to seek an outlet in trade and commerce; indeed their civil disabilities forced them to do so if they wished to become 'successful'. Their religious solidarity, symbolized in Quaker meeting house or nonconformist chapel, facilitated not only consciousness of Grace but confident mutual borrowing and lending. Reliance on the Good Book and on keeping good books went together.

The existence of this network of business ability in England made for a smooth 'take-off' from trade to industry. Sometimes there was a direct transfer of capital: even when there was not, the introduction of machinery and the application of steam power, for all their revolutionary long-term consequences, dovetailed into those sectors of the economy where there was already an elaborate division of labour[1] and a 'social system which gives equal respectability to trade and equal security to the capital invested in it'.[2]

What the exploitation of the new technical processes implied was the building up of fixed capital as distinct from working stocks; the speeding-up of production and distribution; the direct management of men and machines instead of their indirect control through the market; the creation of new links between manufacturers and users; and the substitution of factory production for dispersed outwork ('the domestic system'). It is important not to exaggerate either the complete novelty or the immediate impact of this logic of industrial transformation. Merchants continued to play a big part in British industry for decades after the industrialists had established themselves: the accumulation of fixed capital often increased rather than diminished the need for working capital: outwork and middlemen persisted in many trades far into the nineteenth century and on into the twentieth: the number of factory workers remained small in relation to the rest of the population; and, above all, the size of plants usually remained small by modern standards. In this last respect, 'cotton was a lonely hare in a world of tortoises',[3] and to see events in proper perspective it is necessary to remember that as

---

[1] Adam Smith first saw clearly the relationship between the size of the market and specialization. In his view, it was specialization which led 'to the invention of a great number of machines'. *The Wealth of Nations*, as has frequently been pointed out, was written before the emergence of the characteristic technology of the industrial revolution.

[2] H. Becke, *Observations on the Produce of Income Tax* (1799).

[3] H. Heaton, 'The Industrial Revolution', reprinted in A. Ausubel (ed.) *The Making of Modern Europe* (1951), p. 623.

late as 1830 only one person in eighty in England worked in a cotton
factory.

Eighteenth-century industrialists had to be both versatile and
tough. Unlike most of their predecessors, they had to control as well
as to profit from production, to concern themselves with the way
in which things were produced as well as their handling and sale:
unlike most of their successors, they had to carry out very varied
duties which have now passed into specialist hands. The most
important quality they required, however, was an 'eye' for an
opening, a feel of the market. The number of market opportunities
was mounting as a result of the growth of incomes, the increase of
population (which we must consider later), the shift of tastes, particularly the tastes of the 'middle ranks' and the expansion of overseas trade. In the case of textiles, for example, the upsurge of demand
for fine and light fabrics prompted both business skill and technical
invention. In the case of pottery, Josiah Wedgwood soon realized
that there was a profitable market not only for elegant hand-painted
china, like that which he sent to Catherine the Great in Russia, but
also for serviceable and reasonably priced standard ware which
would replace wooden trenchers and pewter platters on dining room
tables.

The eye for an opening was necessarily associated, as it still is,
with sales promotion and advertising. Wedgwood adopted
'branding' of his products: he called his most popular line 'Queen's
Ware'. Matthew Boulton received so many visitors at Soho—
George III himself recommended Catherine the Great to go there
in 1776—that his house resembled an inn rather than a residence.
Wilkinson was a born publicity expert. In his lifetime a ballad was
written about him by his workmen, and after he died, the legend
spread that he would rise from his iron coffin and visit the blast
furnaces seven years after his death. Indeed a large crowd gathered
on the appointed day to welcome his resurrection. But other
business qualities of a less dramatic order were needed by eighteenth-
century industrialists—ability to secure, maintain, and increase
capital; skill in choosing a site; care in forecasting and planning;
success in selecting and managing workers and in keeping books;
and willingness to compete. This last quality was important even
though eighteenth-century industry was riddled with combination,
and holding on to a patent was the surest way of securing large
monopoly profits.

Of these additional qualities, two in particular demand further consideration. Success in selecting and managing workers was to some extent a new art, for the outwork system of production emphasized the nominal independence of the individual worker, even though he might be exploited by both merchant and middleman. Having secured a site and a plant, the new factory owner or manager of a large workshop had to 'discipline and tame a labour force', some of whom might have had little experience of industrial employment. Patience was a more useful quality than toughness, although there was no one recipe for good industrial relations, and in many places relations were bad from the start. The resistance on the part of workers to factory production was often as great as the economic inducement of manufacturers to introduce it. There was usually little reason, however, for the new industrial workers to envy the standards of consumption (as distinct from the wealth) of most of the first generation of their new masters. Ability to secure, maintain, and increase capital involved perseverance and abstinence. Although some of the new industrialists, like Boulton and Wedgwood, were men of outstanding taste and discrimination as well as diligence, others made Industry the sovereign good. Samuel Walker of Rotherham, for instance, and his family acquired a thriving iron business only by ploughing back profits and paying themselves 'wages' which they were prepared to reduce when times were bad. Characteristically their small boat was called *The Industry*. As important in the eighteenth century as the impulse to contrive and invent was the willingness to forego present advantages for the sake of the future. Raised to a virtue by the claims of religion, reduced to a stark necessity by the lack of an effective national industrial credit system, and turned into an 'abstinence theory of capital' by the first rationalizers of the new economic order, this willingness was the mainspring of progress. Not all early businessmen fit neatly into Samuel Smiles's hall of fame—Wilkinson's private life kept him out of it—but all of them to go on being successful needed Smiles's four main virtues—thrift, character, self-help and duty.

There were, however, two general changes in the economy without which economic progress would not have been possible—first the improvement of transport and second the spread of banking. To both these essential economic services in the industrial community the word 'system' is often appended: we talk of a 'transport system' and a 'credit system'. In neither case, however, was there an eighteenth-century blueprint of a system or a national plan for making one. The interests of businessmen themselves—and of other groups—were the levers of change. That 'systems' would eventually emerge and that the State would have to concern itself with the regulation of them was scarcely foreseen in the eighteenth century when the State was managed by an oligarchy, lacked an independent civil service, was abandoning older means of regulation and 'welfare' objectives inherited from Tudor and Stuart England,[1] and was never impelled by the 'strategic' considerations or the authoritarian drive which were often found on the Continent. Decisions about both transport and credit in England were taken by scores of people in scores of places: the Invisible Hand did the rest.

By 1780 important changes in the organization of transport facilities had already taken place. Many of the rivers, which were more useful than the roads as communication arteries, had been widened and improved; the roads themselves had been increased in numbers as a result of the setting up of turnpike trusts which levied tolls on road-users; and, though the coastal trade was still vitally important, the canal era had begun. The peak of the canal age was reached in the years 1790–3 when cheap capital encouraged a 'canal mania' and fifty-three canal and navigation bills, involving a capital outlay of over £5 million, were authorized by Parliament. The canals cut the cost of transport of bulky articles such as coal and stone, often drastically, reduced dependence on river and road, and opened up new areas. In addition, the offer of transferable canal shares, with dazzling prospects of quick gains, provided a tempting alternative to investment in the public funds. Fantastic dividends were sometimes paid—the Oxford Canal, for instance, paid 30 per cent for more than thirty years—although the average dividend was well under 8 per cent. Small investors followed in the trail of keen businessmen like Wedgwood who needed canals for their own traffic. Although the disadvantages of the new means of transport soon became apparent—locks; freezing-up in winter; a jumble of widths, depths, and transport charges; and a tendency to charge monopolistic rates—contemporaries were right to describe canals as among the most spectacular 'improvements' of their generation and to boast with Arthur Young that 'by such noble undertakings is the present age peculiarly distinguished'.

[1] See E. Lipson, *Economic History of England* (1934), vol. III, pp. 267 ff, for mid-eighteenth-century battles against wage-assessment and regulation.

Improvements in banking facilities were as urgently necessary in the late eighteenth century as improvements in transport. Businessmen might obtain fixed capital by borrowing from relatives or merchants or by ploughing back profits, but they needed circulating capital to buy raw materials, to pay wages and to keep their factories and workshops in running order. They needed both small cash, which was in short supply particularly in the industrial districts, and short-term credit. To meet their needs, however imperfectly and unsystematically, country bankers began operating in various parts of the country. They were recruited from three main sources—traders and industrialists, whose main concern was to provide a local means of payment; financial intermediaries, like country attorneys who received money on trust and were familiar with investment opportunities; and remitters of funds between London and the provinces, particularly collectors of government revenue. By 1784 there were more than a hundred country banks in England alone; during the next ten years their number trebled. Whatever their weaknesses—and like the canals, they were far from perfect instruments—they represented 'a specialization and development of financial services that were indispensable to economic progress'[1]; they were custodians of deposits, suppliers of cash (often through local paper notes)[2] and short-term moneylenders. Together they made up a hidden national credit network operating with London as a centre, for they facilitated transfers of money from the saving districts of the country, particularly the agricultural areas of East Anglia and the West Country where there were seasonal surpluses, to the investing areas of the Midlands and the North. London was the pivot of these regional transfers, for country funds made their way to London and London bankers acted as bill brokers and intermediaries. Through them there was a link with the Bank of England also, for the London bankers discounted their bills with the Bank and depended upon it in the last resort for gold. There was thus a contrast between the embryonic long-term capital market, which still tended to be local—the only national capital market was in the public funds—and the short-term credit market, which already depended upon London. The contrast was to lead to many incidents and 'crises' during later stages of industrial growth.

[1] L. S. Pressnell, *Country Banking in the Industrial Revolution*, (1956), p. 1.
[2] Until 1793 the Bank of England never issued a smaller note than £10. In Lancashire, there was little local note issuing; the main medium of transactions was the bill of exchange.

Neither transport nor credit, for all their importance, should be allowed to dominate the changing economic scene in the late eighteenth century. Nor should machines and materials. In the centre of the stage was a growing population: transport, credit, machines, and materials were in the service of men.

It is difficult to dissociate the technical and social changes described above from the growth of population.[1] To many contemporaries, indeed, both phenomena were directly related to the same cause—the general expansion of English economic activity. Just as rising consumer demand encouraged technical improvement so it entailed increasing requirements of labour. 'Is it not evident', asked Arthur Young in 1774, 'that demand for hands, that is employment, must regulate the number of people?'[2] According to him, and to writers who thought like him, the rise in population was easy to explain. Where there was work there would be hands. The economic and social mechanism linking increased demand for labour with population was the higher earnings of the wage worker which permitted him to marry earlier than he would have done and to produce more children. In addition, the demand for child labour encouraged bigger families, for there was only a short interval between babies being mouths to feed and hands to earn.

Few writers since have considered the mechanisms to be so simple; and a prolonged controversy about eighteenth-century population growth has not yet reached the stage when final conclusions may be stated. There are three difficulties in the way. First, the mere counting of heads is not easy. No official census was taken until 1801, although the idea of one was mooted in 1753. The incomplete sources available suggest that the population of England and Wales, which was about 9 million in 1801, had increased by some $3\frac{1}{2}$ million during the preceding fifty years, and that most of the increase had been packed into the last two decades. Second, given the dimensions, the causes of the increase can only be conjectured, not proven. Arthur Young's explanation is impossible to accept. There was no considerable increase in birth rates during the 1780s, and during the 1790s they were falling gently. Most modern research has focused attention on declining death rates—declining

---

[1] The population was still small by modern standards. As Professor W. H. B. Court has put it, 'to understand how human life looked and felt . . . we have to begin by removing six out of seven persons in its present population.' *A Concise Economic History of Britain from 1750 to present times* (1954), p. 5.

[2] *Political Arithmetic* (1774), p. 86.

markedly from the 1780s to the 1810s—as a prime cause of late eighteenth-century population growth.[1] Third, given the crucial importance of the death rate, the reasons for its sharp fall, particularly in the period after 1780, are not easy to assess. Some writers have made much of the eighteenth-century improvement in medical services—the expansion of hospital, dispensary, and midwifery facilities, developments in medical science and in medical education, and the introduction of protective therapy (inoculation against smallpox). In fact, hospitals were places of danger rather than of protection and it was safer to stay outside; changes in obstetric practice were limited to improvements in hygiene; there were no significant discoveries in medical science, and inoculation against smallpox (vaccination was not employed until the 1790s even for the well-to-do) appears to have had little efficacy. The reasons for the fall in death rates must be sought not in therapy or in medical institutions but in general improvements in environment. In so far as the biggest threat to the lives of children and mothers was infection, even relatively small environmental changes could lower death rates which men of earlier ages accepted as 'normal'.

Among such changes were physical improvements in the layout of houses, towns, and villages, the replacement of timber by brick, the construction of sewers, the substitution of washable cotton for heavy cloth, and the greater use of earthenware pottery. Increased use of soap and (in some cases purer) water made personal hygiene easier and more attractive, while the reformation in manners made it more virtuous. 'Cleanliness is indeed next to godliness', proclaimed Wesley. At the same time (strictly limited) technical improvements in agriculture, still to be discussed in detail, accompanied by better transport, storage and marketing facilities, diminished the risk of famine. Finally, although there were few revolutionary medical discoveries, there were many doctors who were trying to advertise simple measures against disease and infection. They did not understand the causes of disease, but they advocated ventilation, disinfection, and control of nuisances. Their noses guided them as much as their intellects and they were sometimes eloquent enough to persuade others to use their noses too. One good example of their activities can be seen in provincial Manchester where a series of fever epidemics in the 1790s led to the

[1] For an important recent analysis, see T. McKeown and R. G. Brown, 'Medical Evidence relating to English Population Changes', in *Population Studies* (1955).

setting up in 1796 of a Board of Health consisting of physicians, 'gentlemen', and businessmen. The Board attacked unwholesome food, lack of cleanliness, overcrowded habitations, the smoke nuisance, and the concentration of infected persons in factories. Unfortunately it won only one of its major battles—that concerned with the setting up of a fever hospital—but its ideas were talked about in other places and indicated that men were becoming aware of problems of social control. If the student of population change in the sixteenth, seventeenth and early eighteenth centuries must necessarily turn to the state of the harvest and the history of the weather for his vital information, the student of population change after 1780 may turn increasingly to the social environment, to the actions of men rather than the commands of Fate. Whatever the exact relationship between the rate of population growth and the first phases of the industrial revolution, both phenomena had this in common, that Nature was being tamed and men were becoming conscious that they were taming it.

There was, of course, a complication which contemporaries could not escape. While the death rate, like the technique of production, was proving amenable to control, the natural growth of the total population seemed to set limits to public well-being. By the turn of the century, many people came to share Malthus's view that population increased geometrically while the supply of food increased only arithmetically. According to this theory, the ultimate price of economic prosperity would be a food crisis which by natural devices would reduce population once more to a level compatible with subsistence. Having dismissed or at least having confronted Fate collectively for the first time, men were thus confronted with a terrible and inexorable law which seemed to be holding the world in an iron grip. Not until the second half of the nineteenth century did most thinking Englishmen abandon Malthus or begin to consider his arguments irrelevant. By then, the population of England and Wales had reached over twenty-two millions (1871) and English industry had expanded to such an extent and had captured such a share of increased world trade that England was ceasing to depend on home-grown food. The opening up of new lands overseas, the greater yield of food per acre and the enormous improvement in the international transport and distributive system had falsified the gloomiest of Malthus's expectations.

The story of this economic achievement during the course of the

nineteenth century, leads naturally back again from men to resources
—to materials and machines. There was, however, one specific link
between these themes which must not be forgotten. So far, the
population of England has been considered quantitatively: it was
in such terms that Arthur Young advanced his simple thesis, and
it is in such terms that modern demographers have usually concerned
themselves with national birth and death rates. Yet to explore the
processes of economic growth, qualitative estimates of the character
of the population are equally necessary. Size of population counts
for less than adaptability in determining the course of industrial
expansion. The fact that during the 1780s and '90s the English
population was relatively well equipped for the more efficient
exploitation of resources and the invention of machines counted
for as much as or perhaps more than the increase of population
itself. 'You cannot extemporize labour', the economic historian
Thorold Rogers wrote a hundred years later, 'that is you cannot call
effective industry into existence by mere demand.'

There were three features of the occupational structure and quality
of the English population which encouraged growth. First, everywhere in England, unlike many parts of the Continent, workers
were free to choose their occupations, although the pull of heredity
was strong in most old trades. Second, in addition to an un-
differentiated mass of general labour there were highly-skilled and
specialized labour groups, particularly in industrial areas such as the
West Midlands where there had been uninterrupted industrial activity
for many generations. As early as 1697 a writer observed that
English 'artisans were allowed the best upon Earth for improvements'.[1] Third, and not least, 'the middle ranks of English society'
not only provided businessmen, but created customers, customers
who demanded not luxuries but those good medium quality goods
which could be turned out in ever greater quantities once new techniques were employed.[2]

It is not surprising that Frenchmen, brought up in a different
kind of social system both before and after the French Revolution
of 1789, were the first to use the word 'revolution' to describe the
immense changes across the Channel. Before the 1780s the rate of
industrial change had been as rapid in France, with its far greater

---

[1] Quoted J. U. Nef, 'The Industrial Revolution Reconsidered', in *J. Ec. H.* (1943).
[2] Robert Bakewell (see below, p. 42) is said to have remarked 'I do not breed mutton
for gentlemen but for the public.' Quoted by R. Wallace, *Farm Livestock in Great
Britain* (1907), p. 75.

population, as in England: after the 1780s the gap between England and the Continent widened every year until after the middle of the nineteenth century. If France had a political revolution in 1789, England had an industrial revolution already in progress.[1] The social implications of both types of revolution were far-reaching and neither could stop short of national boundaries: French ideas and English techniques helped to transform the nineteenth-century world. Yet the cataclysmic character of both is easily exaggerated. To put the changes in industry into their proper perspective, it is necessary to look in more detail at the one industry left out of the picture, the greatest industry, agriculture, and to examine the relationship between town and country in the crucial years of change.

3. TOWN AND COUNTRYSIDE

Despite the advances in industrial techniques and production, England was still essentially an agricultural community in the 1780s. By far the largest number of people were employed on the land, and the village—in all its rich diversity—was a more familiar social unit than the town or the city. A considerable amount of industry was still scattered about the countryside, as it had been in the time of Defoe, and in the rapidly growing new industrial communities themselves a very large proportion of the inhabitants were villagers by origin. Even some of the pioneers of economic change, like Thomas Telford, the road builder, who was first President of the Institution of Civil Engineers (founded in 1818), believed that improved communications were more valuable to agriculture than to industry and that they would help to restore the balance between the industrial and agricultural population. Above all, the state of the harvest determined perhaps more than any other single factor the level of economic activity and the mood of society. Good harvests stimulated credit, gave an impetus to industry, and kept the urban population contented. Bad harvests led to increased imports of food, a restriction of credit, and industrial unrest.

Town and country may each be considered from two angles— first in their social setting, in terms of the rural way of life and its urban counterpart; second, in their economic context, with emphasis

---

[1] This contrast between the two 'revolutions' was noted by (perhaps) the first writer to use the phrase 'industrial revolution,' Adolph Blanqui, *Historie de L'Economie Politique* (1827) vol. II, ch. 28.

on the relationship between men and resources. In both cases, there was a contrast between town and country which on occasion sharpened into a conflict of attitudes and interests. 'Our landed gentlemen', wrote James Watt to a French correspondent in 1787, 'consider us poor mechanics no better than the slaves who cultivate their vineyards.'[1] In parliamentary debates on the corn laws in 1791 there were signs of that economic and social antagonism which was to dominate the history of the 1840s. Petitions poured in from the manufacturing towns protesting against increased protection for corn, and to one writer at least 'the alacrity of the manufacturer' seemed to have triumphed over 'the supineness of the landed interest'.[2] Such open conflict was still exceptional, however, and there were close ties between the land and industry. Some industries, like brewing and milling, depended upon agricultural products, and most agricultural areas welcomed the increase of industrial wealth and of urban demand for farm products. As Adam Smith remarked, the gains of both town and country from these relationships were reciprocal, 'and the division of labour is in this, as in all other cases, advantageous to all the different persons employed'.[3]

A first glance at the countryside would have revealed the presence not of farms but of 'estates', large and small, 'family seats' each with its hall or its manor house, its garden, its parkland, its 'acres'. Such estates were symbols of prestige rather than productive units in the modern sense of the word. Agriculture was a way of life as well as a means of livelihood, for landed proprietors and villagers alike. To recapture that way of life we must go back not only to the social round of the country houses but to country revels, Plough Monday, Harvest Home, and village cricket.[4] We must understand also the strains and conflicts within the village community, the increasingly sharp social divisions, the enormous power of the squire-J.P.

The proprietors were of varying resources, background and lineage. The greatest of them belonged to the aristocratic nobility. They often prided themselves, rightly, on the splendour of their

[1] Quoted by W. Bowden, *Industrial Society in England towards the End of the Eighteenth Century* (1925), p. 155.
[2] Lord Sheffield, *Observations on the Corn Bill* (1791).
[3] *The Wealth of Nations*, Book III, ch. I.
[4] See the *Annual Register* (1798) for an account of the rural sports at Maiden Castle near Dorchester. A cricket match was played for a round of beef, and in addition there were cheese-rolling, cudgelling, sack racing, wrestling, pig-catching, pony racing, and a grinning match with a pound of tobacco as the prize.

homes—many of them newly built in the eighteenth century—and
the beauty of their gardens, often newly planned. The site of the
houses was usually chosen on aesthetic grounds, 'to command the
prospect' and to mingle delights of landscape with the refinements
of taste. Much eighteenth-century investment went not into canals
or factories but into 'display' of this kind, lesser landed proprietors
vying with their more affluent neighbours and building Georgian
houses amid well-wooded parkland. The term 'improvement' itself
was employed on occasion to cover such expenditure.

The conspicuous consumption of proprietors, often dependent
upon mortgages, contrasted sharply with the frugality of manufacturers. 'An Estate's a pond', Defoe had written, 'but trade's a
spring.'[1] Both ways of life, however, were part of the pattern of the
age and some businessmen at least, like Arkwright, could not resist
the spell of feudalism.[2] In estimating the eighteenth-century legacy
it is unfair to set Adam fireplaces against cheap calicoes or Chippendale chairs against iron hardware, for many businessmen were
immaculate in their tastes and many noblemen and squires were
more interested in horse racing and the card table than 'culture'.
Nonetheless, there was something distinctive in the landed contribution to the quality of eighteenth-century living. Palladian mansions,
well-stocked libraries, elegant portrait galleries, landscape gardens
and Gothic follies provide permanent evidence of creative leisure,
of the leisure of a minority who, when they wished to exercise power,
could do so both locally and nationally. The length of their rent roll
was one measure of their 'influence', the size of their household
another. Some of them were prepared to destroy old villages and
rehouse their inhabitants in model houses in order to beautify their
estates. At Milton Abbas, for instance, the first Earl of Dorchester
built a great mansion where the ruins of an abbey stood, restored
the old town, and in 1786–7 built a new model village on a site
nearly a mile away.

Adam Smith maintained that great proprietors were seldom 'great
improvers' and that those merchants who became country gentlemen

---

[1] *The Complete English Tradesman* (1726), pp. 321–2.
[2] See the *Manchester Mercury*, 27 March 1787. 'On Sunday last, Sir Richard Arkwright
. . . arrived at Derby, accompanied by a number of gentlemen, etc., on horseback, his
javelin men thirty in number, exclusive of bailiffs, dressed in the richest liveries ever
seen there on such an occasion. They all rode on black horses. The trumpeters were
mounted on grey horses, and elegantly dressed in scarlet and gold.' Matthew Boulton II
bought the estate and country house of Great Tew in Oxfordshire and travelled to
Birmingham by coach.

were generally 'the best of all improvers'. 'A merchant', he argued, 'is accustomed to employ his money chiefly in profitable projects, whereas a mere country gentleman is accustomed to employ it chiefly in expense': in consequence, the commerce and manufactures of cities 'have been the cause of the improvement and cultivation of the country'. Between 1776 and 1800, however, it became increasingly fashionable for landed proprietors with no trading interests at all to display interest in agriculture as well as in hunting or painting: indeed, there grew up an 'agricultural school' of painting, and great landowners and statesmen, including Thomas Coke of Norfolk, first Earl of Leicester, the Duke of Bedford, and Lord Althorp, were happy to be portrayed in the centre of farmyard scenes. It is misleading to linger too long in the eighteenth-century landscape gardens fashioned by men like Capability Brown, who died in 1783, and to overlook what was happening in the fields, not to speak of the factories and the furnaces. Unlike the French nobility, the English aristocracy and squirearchy never lost touch with the land, and after 1780 some of them began to attach prestige to schemes of agricultural 'improvement'. 'This GREAT IMPROVER', exclaimed Arthur Young when referring to one Irish landlord, '(is) a title more deserving of distinction than that of a great general or a great Minister.'

George III himself led the fashion (as did his political opponent Thomas Coke), organizing model farms on 'Norfolk' and 'Flemish' lines, interesting himself in both stockbreeding and corn-growing, and looking forward rhetorically to the dawn of an age 'that shall pay more homage to the memory of a Prince that gave a ram to a farmer than for wielding a sceptre obeyed alike on the Ganges and the Thames.' For Young, such language came naturally. He was indefatigable in his agricultural propaganda, visiting all parts of the country to see what was being done and writing almost incessantly about his experiences. If many of his facts were inaccurate, his theories unsound, and his projects too rosy—and it is now accepted that the writings of William Marshall provide a more realistic picture—Young nonetheless stood out above all his contemporaries. When, in 1793, he became Secretary to the newly-founded semi-official Board of Agriculture, financed by an annual exchequer grant, he sponsored the preparation and publication of a series of county farming surveys, describing the state of agriculture and the progress of improvement and enclosure. In their revised form, these Reports are invaluable to the historian: they were supplemented by much other useful activity on the part of the Board, including exhibitions and practical advice to farmers.

By the time that the Board was set up, not only fashion but the hope of economic gain was impelling landlords to interest themselves in agricultural improvement. Rising national population meant an increase in the demand for both wheat and meat, while improved transport substantially reduced costs and widened internal markets. England ceased in the 1780s to be a corn-exporting country and became a net importer of wheat, and business-like domestic farming became a reasonable economic proposition. The interruption of trade after the outbreak of war with France made the proposition lucrative. The sun shone for the landlord during this time far more brightly than it had done for many years, and he hastened usually not to make hay but to grow corn.

Leaving aside the 'improving' landlords with their model farms —they were still a minority—and the propagandists with their ceaseless publicity, the day-to-day work of English farming was managed for the most part by tenant farmers, the most substantial of whom were both prosperous and powerful. Unlike France, England had few independent 'peasants', forced by grievance and frustration to demand revolution. Their nearest English equivalent, the yeoman class, 'the nation's pride', had dwindled in numbers before the eighteenth-century challenge to agriculture became clear.[1] Although there was an increase in the number of small independent farmers during the Napoleonic Wars and in some places even before, in most areas they had not been able to escape the effects of 'a long period of attrition by consolidation and purchase and direct eviction'.[2] Wordsworth might muse about 'a republic of peasants and shepherds' in Cumberland, but the concept was more appropriate to poetry than to real life.[3] The trend of the times was favourable to the large tenant farmer with a holding big enough to facilitate 'improved management'. Smaller tenant farmers with limited capital and precarious legal tenure, were often in even greater

---

[1] There were large numbers of small 'cottagers'. See V. M. Labrovsky, 'Parliamentary Enclosures in the County of Suffolk' in *Ec. Hist. Rev.* (1937). For the detailed history of one Leicestershire village, see W. G. Hoskins, *The Midland Peasant* (1957).

[2] See J. D. Chambers, 'Enclosure and Labour Supply in the Industrial Revolution' in *Ec. Hist. Rev.* (1953).

[3] *The Early Letters of William and Dorothy Wordsworth* (ed. E. de Selincourt, 1938) are full of references to Cumberland conditions, where there still existed large numbers of people 'kind-hearted, frank and manly, prompt to serve without servility'. (p. 236).

difficulties than independent men. 'Sensibly dividing the country among opulent men', as one of the advocates of the large farm put it, seemed far from sensible to those who lacked capital to fence their farms, to maintain and increase their livestock, or to pay tithes and poor rates. In the course of agricultural change they became more and not less dependent on the landlord.

The course of agricultural change had followed four main lines from before the beginning of the century—the extension of the amount of cultivated land as a result of enclosure of open fields and the opening up of waste; an improvement in farming practices; the introduction of new crops; and the invention and application of new types of agricultural machinery. These advances have sometimes been described as an 'agrarian revolution', running parallel to the industrial revolution, and following a similar pattern of invention and enterprise. In fact, the word 'revolution' seems inappropriate when applied to a series of gradual changes some of which can be traced back to the seventeenth century and many of which had only influenced farming in a very limited way before 1800. If the 1780s and 1790s were critical years in the story of English farming, it was not because of events and tendencies in the agricultural sector of the economy taken by itself—there were many signs of 'backwardness' there as well as 'improvement'—but because the whole place of agriculture in the economy was beginning to change as a result of the impact of industrialization. Even then, the impact was not an immediate one, sharp and swift, but gradual and cumulative, and it still needs detailed study. As late as 1851 agriculture still employed one out of every four Englishmen over the age of 20, and its total working force far exceeded that of cotton, domestic service, or general labouring.

The four main changes need to be considered in more detail against this imperfectly studied background. Between 1761 and 1780 during the first phase of enclosure by Act of Parliament, 4,039 Acts were passed: there were a further 900 between 1781 and 1800. Open field farming, while not such a rigid or inefficient system as has sometimes been suggested, was incompatible in most places with the long-term tendency to increase the size of farms or with the desire of individuals to specialize in the immediately profitable use of land. The Enclosure Commissioners, appointed to survey and allot land after the passing of an Enclosure Act, seem to have carried out their arduous and often prolonged work of apportionment very conscientiously. The main, but not the only sufferers from their efforts were villagers with few resources or without clear-cut legal rights, those cottagers, for instance, who had enjoyed by custom free access to the limited resources of the waste. The national claims of businesslike agriculture or an efficient supply of food meant nothing to such downtrodden and dissatisfied people, and it was scant comfort to them that they had the sympathy of many philanthropists and even of some landlords. England made the 'take-off' into an industrial society with a divided and discontented village community in many parts of the country. The paradox was that it was not the discontented who were the revolutionaries, but those 'improving' farmers who were prepared to break relentlessly with the past without providing social safeguards and those 'political economists' who believed that philanthropy was more of a curse than a blessing in the progress of industrialization.

The other three lines of development have received less detailed attention from historians. The improvement in farming practices, associated with the work of livestock improvers such as Robert Bakewell[1] and experimenters with crops and rotations, of whom Coke[2] is the best known, made possible greater yields of beef and mutton and the employment of horses of greater power on the farm. The more general introduction of clover and turnips, crops which had made their way from the Continent in the seventeenth century, and the increasing production of potatoes in the eighteenth century, 'improved' stock-feeding. (To William Cobbett's disgust, the potatoes were also used to feed human beings). The invention of new implements and machines was another feature of the century. Most of the improvements in farm practices, however, were strictly localized, and in the case of machinery there was a long lag between invention and application. Even the drill introduced by Jethro Tull in the early eighteenth century was not generally adopted until the nineteenth.

What seems clear in the national story of agriculture is that relatively small local improvements produced immediate results long before the new technical devices of ploughing, sowing, reaping and threshing were generally adopted. The slow movement of new ideas, the lack of basic techniques and the often unsatisfactory

---

[1] Alongside his judgement on himself (see above, p. 35) must be set Arthur Young's comment that 'his beasts were too dear to buy and too fat to eat'.

[2] For Coke, see N. Riches, *Agrarian Revolution in Norfolk.* (1937): R. A. C. Parker, 'Coke of Norfolk and the Agrarian Revolution' in *Ec. Hist. Rev.* (1955).

systems of leases and tenures held back 'revolutionary advances'. Potatoes were produced in large quantities only near the new towns; turnips were not grown in Devonshire; inferior livestock were still being bred in many distant parts of the country; and it was not until improved methods of drainage were evolved after the 1830s that the 'Norfolk system' of farming with its elimination of wasteful fodder and its 'scientific' rotation could be fully adopted on the heavy intractable clay soils of the Midland counties.

Nonetheless, cumulative agricultural changes permitted a rapidly growing and increasingly urbanized population to be fed.[1] It is sometimes argued in addition that they forced men to leave the land and to seek their livelihood in the growing industrial towns. In fact, the growth of towns—one of the most important features of the period—seems to have been stimulated more by the attraction of higher industrial wages and the more varied economic opportunities towns afforded than by the movement off the land of a dispossessed surplus agricultural population. The cottage-owning population of the countryside grew alongside the urban population in many parts of the country during the late eighteenth century. There were three reasons for this. First, the new 'improved agriculture' stopped short in most places at the point where mechanization began, and it continued to demand large numbers of agricultural workers. Second, a stimulus was given in the countryside to rural trades, like those of blacksmiths, wheelwrights, and mechanics, not only by agricultural improvement but also by developments in inland transport. Third, despite the improvements in transport, there were still powerful barriers to long-distance movement. The towns grew as a result of local movements from the surrounding countryside, not of great treks from the countryside to the factories and furnaces. It was at the level of local, not of national, life that the Lancashire reporter to the Board of Agriculture complained that 'the advance of wages and the preference given to manufacturing employment, by the labourers in general, have induced many to forsake the spade for the shuttle.'[2] Nationally, as

---

[1] How well they were fed, particularly after 1790, is a matter of argument. See for two contrasting points of view T. S. Ashton, 'The Standard of Life of Workers in England', in *J. Ec. H. Supplement* (1949) and E. J. Hobsbawm, 'The British Standard of Living, 1790–1850' in *Ec. Hist. Rev.* (1957). There is conflicting evidence relating to diets, but adulteration of food became a serious nineteenth-century problem. The first important treatise was F. Accum's *Treatise on Adulteration of Food* (1820).

[2] J. Holt, *Lancaster* (1794), p. 25.

late as the 1840s, it was noted that no form of economic or social pressure could make the Dorsetshire labourers move.[1]

The growing towns of the late eighteenth and early nineteenth centuries included some old centres of population quickened into new life by the improvement of transport, but there were many new ones. Most towns still remained the heart of rural districts, where local trade was closely related to 'local landed interests': others, however, manufactured and distributed goods not for the local market but for distant places and already belonged more directly to 'the great circulating system of the nation than to the local system to which they (were) superadded'.[2] With a new pattern of economic activity, there were often local shifts in the relative size and importance of communities. In Derbyshire, for instance, Belper, the town of Jedediah Strutt's cotton factories, outgrew older towns in the county, eventually reaching second place after Derby itself: in the Midlands, unincorporated Birmingham doubled its population during the last forty years of the eighteenth century, and there was no exaggeration in the claim that 'a traveller who visits [this city] once in six months supposes himself well acquainted with her, but he may chance to find a street of houses in the autumn, where he last saw his horse at grass in the spring.' Although at the first census of 1801 there was no town outside London with a population of more than 100,000 and only fourteen other towns with a population of between 20,000 and 100,000, it was already clear that 'town life was becoming a kind of index of industrial activity, as it was later to be throughout Europe and North America'.[3]

There is no agreed classification of towns, but it is convenient to separate out four sorts of provincial towns in England in the 1780s—industrial towns, market towns, ports, and specialized centres, such as the old university towns and the new spas and watering places. If the industrial town pointed towards the future, the market town looked towards the past. Most of the towns were still in this latter category. They had owed their rise to their rôle as centres of distribution, but had depended for their influence not only on their markets but on the more advanced occupational specialization which went inevitably with numbers of inhabitants. Some of

---

[1] 'In Dorset we very much vegetate where we are born,' a witness told a committee in 1847, 'and live very close indeed.' Quoted by A. Redford, *Labour Migration in England* (1926), p. 83.

[2] This useful distinction was made by George Eliot in *Felix Holt* (1866), ch. III.

[3] W. H. B. Court, *op. cit.*, p. 42.

them were industrial as well as market centres, Wolverhampton, for example, specializing in locks, Dudley in nails, and Frome in textiles. When William Cobbett travelled through England on his 'rural rides', it was usually the small agricultural market towns which won his praises. He gave high marks, for instance, to Lewes, 'a model of solidarity and neatness', and to Huntingdon, 'a very clean and nice place'. An old manufacturing town, like Frome, he dismissed as 'a sort of little Manchester'. Not all the old towns, however, could by any stretch of the imagination be described as clean, nice, and good. They might possess historic monuments and terraces of new Georgian houses, but lack of attention to civic services, indifference to health and housing conditions, and the absence of spurs to 'improvement' often made old towns dingy and overcrowded. Carlisle, for example, 'a city of considerable extent surrounded by a wall thirty feet high, which is rapidly going to decay', was described in 1785 as 'neither so airy nor clean as might be wished'.[1] The famous 'Carlisle tables' of births and deaths based on local census material, revealed a high annual mortality rate in the years 1779–87.

The new industrial towns in this first stage of their development were often less dismal and unhealthy than has been suggested by social historians. Even embryonic cities, like Manchester and Birmingham, had many solid buildings—the early mills, like the chapels, were designed to last for all time—and, more important, 'new men' struggling against old oligarchies and enthusiastic in the cause of local 'improvement'. It was not because the industrial towns were already 'too large', but because they were growing so fast that they posed problems of health and order which had never been forced on the attention of older and more stable communities; and, although they were eventually almost overwhelmed by congestion, smoke, and squalor,[2] they had an early period of energetic cultural initiative. Among the most interesting local institutions of the 1780s were provincial societies like the Manchester Literary and Philosophical Society, founded by Dr. Percival in 1781, and the older Lunar Society in Birmingham, which included among its members Erasmus Darwin, Boulton, Watt and Dr. Joseph Priestley. Bodies of this kind which stimulated intellectual, artistic, and scientific discussion, are evidence that the new industrial town in its

[1] T. Newte, *Tour in England and Scotland* (1785).
[2] Urban mortality rates rose sharply again from the 1810s to the 1840s.

origins was not the 'insensate' ant heap which Lewis Mumford has depicted in his well-known but misleading *Culture of Cities*. Rather it served many of the traditional civic functions associated with older large communities, encouraging thought and diffusing 'civilization'. The tragedy of growth in the new towns was that the pace of change, the multitude of private economic preoccupations, and the distrust of corporate bodies hindered collective action. Lack of efficient administrative machinery, particularly in the unincorporated communities which possessed only the governmental apparatus of villages, the inadequate development of civil engineering, the strains of a war economy in the struggle against Napoleon, the dominant individualist outlook of busy manufacturing groups, and the social division of the towns between the well-off and the 'masses', darkened the future of communities which often began their history with bright promise. There was no urban Capability Brown, few towns where a single owner could control the development of a site, and no common long-term plan for future generations. By the 1840s, when urban problems acquired a note of strident urgency, the towns were centres of discontent and danger: in the twentieth century, for all their improvements and attractions, they remain often as dark blots on the English landscape.

There was one movement, however, which made some genuine contribution to the well-being of both old market towns and new industrial towns in the late eighteenth and early nineteenth centuries. Between 1785 and 1800 211 local Improvement Acts were passed, and local Improvement Commissioners, following the example set in London, turned their attention to street lighting, paving, clearing nuisances and obstructions, providing watchmen, and improving markets and water supply. Usually their financial powers were strictly limited and schemes for large-scale change were frustrated by private interests: even when they were most successful they concentrated on the centre and the better residential districts of the town. In a later age of open discussion of policy, expert control of operations and improvement of the worst quarters of the town, many of them became vested interests, but in their heyday they carried out tasks which otherwise would never have been carried out at all.

The spirit of improvement could be seen perhaps even more clearly in the third class of towns, the ports, which boomed in a golden age of English trade. The wealthy 'unreformed' corporation of Liverpool, one of the most rapidly growing commercial cities, constructed docks, improved the navigation of the Rivers Mersey and Weaver, and had a share in canal building. In 1786, when the town had a population of about 50,000, a local Improvement Act was passed which opened new streets and paved and widened old ones. Further south, in Bristol, which was ceasing to grow in numbers, the Corporation employed a full-time inspector of nuisances, and there could be no doubt that, whatever was happening to its trade, the city had grown in beauty during the course of the century. In both Liverpool and Bristol there was an elegant provincial society, dependent on a rich merchant class, and a far more variegated local economy than shipping and ship-building. In the old north, Newcastle-on-Tyne had an active and energetic life of its own: its Literary and Philosophical Society (founded in 1793) was as lively as that in any provincial city and its new Assembly Rooms, a symbol of civic pride, were finer than those in any town except Bath. Portsmouth, a more populous town than Newcastle, was drained and paved during the century, while of Southampton, 'the residence of many genteel and respectable families and for a brief time a watering place', one traveller remarked, 'its buildings are elegant and numerous, and its situation, in point of natural beauty and artificial embellishment, can scarcely be excelled in this kingdom'.[1]

The fourth class of towns, the specialized centres, included not only the ancient university towns which had many new buildings and in Oxford 'one of the finest, the largest and most beautiful streets . . . in all Europe',[2] but the spas and watering places, which were an invention of the eighteenth century. Bath, built between 1760 and 1810, set the fashion. Thirty thousand inhabitants lived there in splendour or administered to the splendour of others, and a season in Bath was as much a part of the gentleman's year as a season in London. 'The baths, the rooms, the public edifices, the private habitations', wrote Shaw, 'are all alike entitled to applause, and render this the finest city in the world.'

There were two new English attractions which in time helped to diminish the dazzling monopolistic attractions of Bath—the mountains and the sea. The discovery of the mountains of the Lake District was an important event in English social history, part of the

---

[1] S. Shaw, *Tour to the West of England* (1788).
[2] C. P. Moritz, *Travels through Various Parts of England in 1782* (1782).

turn towards the picturesque, and by 1788, according to Wilberforce, 'the banks of the Thames are scarcely more public than those
of Windermere'. The discovery of the sea as a place of pleasure
owed much to the medical profession and something to royalty.
While in the industrial towns doctors were in the vanguard of the
movement for reform, by the seaside their colleagues were
encouraging patients first to drink sea-water and then to bathe in it.
They had conspicuous success when in 1783 the Prince of Wales,
following in the footsteps of the Duke of Cumberland, visited
Brighton for the first time and four years later took up residence in
the Marine Pavilion, designed by Henry Holland and later completely refashioned between 1815 and 1820 by John Nash. George
III preferred Weymouth, which he first visited in 1789, but Brighton
was the favoured town which enjoyed 'mushroom' growth. The
number of houses more than doubled in the last twenty-five years
of the eighteenth century and almost trebled itself again in the first
twenty years of the nineteenth century. Jane Austen, who knew all
the claims of Bath, made Lydia Bennett imagine that 'a visit to
Brighton comprised every possibility of earthly happiness'.[1]

No account of urban life in late eighteenth-century England would
be complete without a description of the greatest urban centre of all,
the metropolis. Although the provincial life of England was rich
and vigorous, to sturdy provincials London already seemed disproportionately large both in numbers and influence. Its population
was one-tenth that of the whole country. There were many complaints
that for long London had sucked the vitals of trade to herself and
attempted to set the tone of the whole of English society, and yet
she was continuing to grow. As Dean Tucker put it, 'London, the
Metropolis of Great Britain, has been complained of for past ages
as a kind of monster, with a head enormously large, and out of all
proportion to its body. If, therefore, the increase of buildings, begun
at such an early period, was looked upon to be no better than a wen
or excrescence upon the body politic, what must we think of those
numberless streets and squares which have been added since?'[2]

Within the area of greater London, still a collection of small
communities imperfectly bound together, all the contrasts of the
country and the century were fully revealed—elegance and squalor,

---

[1] For Brighton, see E. W. Gilbert, *Brighton, Old Ocean's Bauble* (1954). See also A. B.
Granville, *The Spas of England and Principal Sea-Bathing Places* (1841).
[2] *Four Letters to the Earl of Shelburne* (2nd edn., 1783) p. 44.

polish and crudity, property and poverty, plan and chaos. It was a city which was already big enough to suggest all things to all men. For members of Parliament London was the seat of government: for the aristocracy and the landed interest it was the centre of gravity of social life—of clubs, balls, gambling, fashion and pleasure. Their town houses, frequently situated in the elegant squares of the West End, were graced by the decorations of the Adam Brothers, the furniture of Thomas Chippendale and the portraits painted by Joshua Reynolds, the first president of the Royal Academy (founded in 1768), his rival George Romney, Thomas Gainsborough, who for fourteen years lived at Bath, and John Zoffany. For the merchant classes, London was 'the City', the centre of trade and the 'monied interest', with its institutional centre in the Bank of England, its nerves in the insurance offices, and its limbs in the docks and warehouses. For the artisans and shopkeepers London was a centre of economic opportunity, a home of all trades. For the poor, London was still the setting of a real life *Beggar's Opera*: if the West End belonged to Reynolds and Romney, the East End still belonged to Hogarth. Its courts and alleyways contrasted with the newly laid out squares of fashionable London. 'The East End', wrote an observer describing conditions in the early 1780s, 'especially along the shores of the Thames, consists of old houses, the streets there are narrow, dark and ill-paved. . . . The contrast between this and the West End is astonishing: the houses here are new and elegant; the squares superb, the streets straight and open. . . . If all London were as well built, there would be nothing in the world to compare with it.'[1] Between East End and West End were squalid fringe regions, some of them inhabited by the 'darkest and most dangerous enemies to society': outside both, on the outskirts of London, were new suburbs, still scarcely integrated in the whole. To a more marked extent than in the big provincial cities, the relatively well-off were increasingly moving to the suburbs at the same time that a 'floating population' was pouring into the centre.

It was natural that men in London should welcome that same march of improvement which was already transforming provincial cities and countryside. Westminster, indeed, by its Paving Act of 1762 had set the pace: in 1787 its commissioners were renowned for 'an undertaking which has introduced a degree of elegance and symmetry into the streets of the metropolis, that is the admiration

[1] J. W. von Archenholtz, *A Picture of England* (1797), p. 119.

of all Europe and far exceeds anything of the kind in the modern world.'[1]   Like the provincial cities, London was to continue to create problems—it has never stopped having growing pains—but in the late eighteenth and early nineteenth centuries in its richer districts it was putting on a new and attractive face for future generations.[2]

4. NORTH AND SOUTH

The changing pattern of town and countryside was associated with a general shift in the distribution of the national population and a new weighting in economic importance of different regions of the country.

At the beginning of the eighteenth century the southern counties were the main centres of population. Middlesex, Surrey, Kent, Gloucestershire, Somerset, Wiltshire and Devonshire together accounted for one-third of the population of England. The biggest towns in the country after London were Norwich and Bristol. There were already areas with a relatively high density of population in the North-East around the Newcastle coalfields, in Lancashire and the West Riding of Yorkshire, but in general the South was more important than the North in both agriculture and industry.

As the century went by, the North gained enormously in importance, largely as a result of water power, the growth of the coal and iron industries, and improvements in the transport system. There were no coal-mines within fifty miles of London, Canterbury, Southampton, Oxford or Cambridge, and already England was being divided into two nations, one industrial and the other rural. G. M. Trevelyan has put the change into full historical perspective: 'For the first time since Anglo-Saxon days, the North-western half of England, the ancient Northumbria and Mercia, became of importance in rivalry to the corn-bearing lands of South and East, and to London and its satellite counties.'[3] This tilt in the geographic balance of power was to have important social and political as well as economic consequences. The men of the North were often to despise the values of the traditional South and, looked at through southern eyes, to introduce a crude and candid vigour into English

---

[1] Quoted by M. D. George, *London Life in the Eighteenth Century* (1925), p. 100. For a contemporary picture of early improvement, see J. Gwynn, *London and Westminster Improved* (1766).

[2] See John Summerson's fascinating study, *Georgian London* (1945).

[3] G. M. Trevelyan, *op. cit.*, p. 606.

life which at times seemed to verge on 'barbarism'. A nineteenth-
century conflict between North and South was as much a leading
theme of English as of American history.

The detailed story of the emergence of the industrial North has
yet to be written. Already, however, the broad outlines are clear.
It is impossible to divorce it from geographical and geological
factors. The Pennine Upland, sometimes called the backbone of
England, dominated the new northern industrial area. Stubborn and
unrewarding ground for cultivation, it had become a medieval
wool-producing and textile area on account not of its assets but of
its natural disadvantages. From the 'Aire gap' in the North, linking
Lancashire and Yorkshire, down over the bleak millstone grit
moorlands to the limestone hills of the Derbyshire Peak District,
there were plentiful supplies of soft water but of little else. On the
fringes of the region were coalfields, known for centuries but not
fully exploited. One of them, the Yorkshire, Nottinghamshire, and
Derbyshire field, was to become the biggest in England. A second,
in south-east Lancashire, was to play a key part in the early stages of
the industrial revolution. Finally, iron ore was to be found particularly in south Yorkshire, and first Sheffield, a centre of the cutlery
trade for centuries, and later Rotherham and Doncaster were to add
variety to the northern industrial structure.

In his panegyric of Yorkshire progress, Edward Baines, a Leeds
journalist and newspaper proprietor,[1] paid little attention to Yorkshire's monastic history and concentrated on the long-term assets
Providence had placed at its disposal. 'The causes which raised this
extensive range of mountains—with its heath-covered moors, its
mountain limestone pastures, its fertile clay soils, its numerous
streams, and its rich beds of minerals—from the depths of the
ocean, thousands of years ago, in a great measure decided the
method in which society, industry and population should develop
themselves in the western districts of Yorkshire in modern times.'[2]
It is not surprising that he sang the praises not only of Providence
but of geology. To him this science, which later in the nineteenth
century was to challenge traditional Christian cosmogony, was the
most useful of all sciences, the key to prosperity.[3] 'All these
resources have indeed existed from the earliest ages, but it is only

[1] See below, p. 247.
[2] T. Baines and E. Baines, *Yorkshire Past and Present* (1871-7), vol. I, p. 4. See also
the *History of Cotton Manufacture in Great Britain* (1835).
[3] See below, pp. 479 ff.

in comparatively modern times that the increase of intelligence has enabled those who had them under their control, to render them available for the uses to which they are now applied.' Man had tamed Nature in the North not in a quiet, gradual, co-operative manner, but fiercely, dramatically, and in face of persistent resistance. 'Manufactures have transformed heaths, deserts, quagmires, bogs and scenes of desolation into lands of fertility and abundance.'

The early textile industry sprang up on the hillsides and in the valley bottoms, where swift streams could be dammed to drive water wheels.[1] In the last few decades of the eighteenth century, clusters of cottages around the water mills grew into populous industrial villages and towns, gradually attracting hand-workers from the hillsides. The most favourable sites were those where streams met and there was a mill and a bridge. The introduction of steam power led to a further concentration, and those places were favoured where there were plentiful local supplies of coal. Where none was available in the immediate vicinity, there was a powerful pressure to improve transport facilities so that coal could be imported cheaply and in large quantities.

In Lancashire, changes took place sooner than in the West Riding. A local map of 1780 concentrated on country houses and left out canals: a map of six years later included toll gates, canal locks, coal mines, and factories. Already by 1795, Ann Radcliffe could describe an 'almost continuous street of villages' from Stockport to Manchester and contrast the 'wide desolation' of the sands of Morecambe Bay with the busy smoke and turmoil of the cotton area.[2] The congested cotton area was dotted about with industrial settlements, few of which were old corporate towns. As Thomas Walker, one of Manchester's leading manufacturers in the 1780s put it, 'commerce requires universal encouragement instead of exclusive privileges'.[3] Near to unincorporated Manchester, which was already more of a regional capital than an 'independent' city, there were thriving industrial towns like Bolton, Oldham and Bury. Oldham was a characteristic product of the new age. A map of 1756 shows a handful of scattered hamlets set in unimproved moorland. By 1800

[1] Many advertisements for mill sites appeared in the northern papers e.g. the *Manchester Mercury*, 21 October 1784, 'A stream of water runs through the Pennines, with sufficient fall to run a number of Carding Engines or other Machines used in manufacturing Cotton, Woollens, etc.'
[2] *A Tour of the Lakes* (1795).
[3] T. Walker, *Review of Some of the Political Events which have occurred in Manchester during the last Five Years* (1794).

'one of the most populous towns in the Kingdom' had grown up with two and three storey mills, rows of workers' cottages, and millowners' brick-built houses. Even Preston, an old and dignified eighteenth-century town, 'the resort of well-born but ill-portioned and ill-endowed old maids and widows', was transformed into a smoky workshop. Horrocks built five factories there between 1796 and 1802. Not all the new industrial communities were large. It was a feature of the cotton trade that it created both small industrial hamlets (sometimes with names like Charlestown and Botany Bay) and thriving 'company towns' like Ramsbottom.

The rapidly growing cotton centres of Lancashire were soon linked together by canal, and, more ambitiously, with the less industrialized West Riding of Yorkshire. The first English canal, four years older than Bridgewater and Brindley's canal from Worsley to Manchester, was the Sankey cut, an extension of a river improvement. The Bridgewater Canal reduced the price of coal in Manchester, thereby making possible the enormous expansion of factory production: the Sankey cut, sponsored by the Liverpool Common Council, cut the price of coal in Lancashire's growing port. In 1770 work was begun on the Leeds and Liverpool Canal, 'a navigable communication between the east and west seas'. Leeds was a natural terminal point, for it was already linked with Hull and the Humber and had established its position as the chief commercial city on the eastern margin of the Pennines near to the plain of York. Its place as a market centre of the woollen textiles industry, which was still in the very first stages of transformation, was well established and as early as 1758 a waggon way had been constructed from the coal-mines at Middleton to supply it with coal. Between 1782 and 1793 its town centre was laid out on new lines with streets, squares and 'places', and in 1801 it had over 30,000 inhabitants, four times as many as any other town in the clothing district.

Building the 127 miles of canal between Leeds and Liverpool was an arduous task which was not completed until 1816, but as various parts of the canal were opened, there were impressive local ceremonies—flags, brass bands, and fêtes—and, more important, almost immediate economic gains. The small town of Bradford, for example, which had good local coal supplies and was now linked to the main canal by a short waterway, could salute the Leeds and Liverpool as 'one of the noblest works of the kind that perhaps are to be found in the Universe'. As a result of the opening of the whole canal to traffic, transport costs between Yorkshire and Lancashire were cut by four-fifths, and there was an enormous increase in the volume of trade.

Other links in cross-country navigation, the Aire and Calder, the Calder and Hebble, the Rochdale and the Huddersfield Canals, often involved the conquest of what in any other age would have seemed intractable natural obstacles. To complete the transport picture, it is necessary to include turnpike road improvements and the building of such canals as the Lancaster Canal, promoted in 1792, linking up Wigan with the North, the Barnsley and Dearne and Dove Canals linking up south Yorkshire with the textile district and the creation of the Derbyshire canal system which made possible the still far too little studied early industrial revolution in Derbyshire, a revolution as important in national history as the better known 'revolution' in Lancashire and the West Riding. The first true factory built in England had been Lombe's silk mill (1718–1722) at Derby; Arkwright's mill at Cromford (1771) was the first of his many ventures and was later the scene of the famous Cromford and High Peak Railway; the Strutts had created a 'company town' at Belper and transformed a poor village inhabited by nailers into the second largest town in Derbyshire; one of the first painters of new industrial scenes was Joseph Wright of Derby who in 1789 completed a romantic canvas of Arkwright's Cromford factory.

Although Wright and many other poets and artists of the first phases of the industrial revolution could see romance in the smoke, it is difficult to acquit the makers of new wealth from ruining much of the Lancashire landscape. It is true that towns often sprang up in what had previously been waste ground, that before the rise of the mills there were great tracts of undeveloped land which 'hardly ever saw a plough' and where 'a stack of corn was a great rarity', but many of the new towns lacked the 'taste' of older places and many streams, like the Irwell at Manchester, were turned by the rise of industry into thick black currents of slime. Over the whole region, 'continuous and compact . . . the smoke of unremitting fires hangs permanent', wrote Wordsworth.[1] For the most part, the new men of the North gloried in the smoke and took it as an index of wealth. They were proud of their achievement, and rightly felt that much still had to be accomplished before the economic development of the North was complete.

[1] *The Excursion* (1814).

The growing divergence between North and South should not be allowed to obscure the important industrial development of the Midlands in the eighteenth century. Long before Matthew Boulton transformed Soho, the West Midlands had become an industrialized countryside with Birmingham extending its influence as a regional capital. At the time of the first census of 1801, Warwickshire, Worcestershire, and Staffordshire, although less thickly populated than Lancashire, had far more people to the square mile than agricultural counties like Norfolk and Lincoln, and Birmingham was a bigger town than Norwich or its older local corporate rival, Coventry.

The economic unity of the West Midlands, like the unity of the north of England, depended on geological conditions and the central importance of the River Severn in its system of communications. There were two main coalfields in the area—the old Shropshire field, where coal and iron were produced side by side in what, as we have seen, was a pivotal area in the early industrial revolution, and the South Staffordshire field, where a busy population of miners and metal workers were creating a network of villages and small towns. Coal seemed to hold the secret of growth in the Midlands as much as in the North. St. Fond, visiting Birmingham in 1784, told his fellow countrymen 'with pleasure, and it cannot be too often said to Frenchmen, that it is the abundance of coal which had performed this miracle and has created in the midst of a human desert, a town with forty thousand inhabitants who live in comfort and enjoy all the conveniences of life.'[1] Along with coal and iron, however, and ultimately outliving them as a cause of economic prosperity, were the skill and enterprise of the local inhabitants. When the coal and iron were used up, Birmingham continued to expand as a centre of metallurgical trades of every kind.

Supplementing the communications system of the free River Severn, which had hitherto served as the main trading artery of the region, were the canals. The West Midlands region is further removed from the coast than any other industrial district in England —Birmingham is about eighty-five miles away from both Liverpool and Bristol—and for the area to develop its resources and play a leading part in the national and international economy, improved transport facilities were indispensable. In 1772 the Staffordshire and Worcestershire Canal was completed, joining up with the

[1] St. Fond, *A Journey through England and Scotland to the Hebrides in 1784.*

Severn at Stourport. Five years later the Trent-Mersey Canal had
been completed, and by 1790 it was connected with the Thames
through the Fazeley and Coventry Canal.

Birmingham became increasingly dependent on the canal system.
Its first canal (1769), joining up with the Staffordshire and Worcestershire, was designed with the express object of uniting 'the numerous
hearths and furnaces of industrial Birmingham with the prolific
coalworks of the contiguous mining district of South Staffordshire':
when it was completed, the price of coal in Birmingham fell
immediately by a half. By the end of the eighteenth century, the
canals had already transformed the Birmingham neighbourhood, and
factories and workshops clustered along their banks. The appearance
of this area contrasted sharply with that of industrial Lancashire,
particularly with the stone-built towns and villages overshadowed
by the Pennine moors, but both landscapes were specifically
industrial. Just as the men of Manchester and Birmingham were
beginning to be associated in common economic and political
causes, so in both cities—and in Sheffield and Wolverhampton too—
there was a common break with the traditional scene:

> Grim Wolverhampton lights her smouldering fires,
> And Sheffield, smoke involv'd; dim where she stands
> Circled by lofty mountains, which condense
> Her dark and spiral wreaths to drizzling rains
> Frequent and sullied . . .[1]

The men of the countryside were dependent on the weather for their
livelihood: in the new industrial areas, even the weather itself
seemed to have changed, in this case indubitably not for the better.

The growth of the new industrial regions, of which the North and
West Midlands were most prominent, had important repercussions
on the older industrial areas of the country. Cornwall, with its
important tin and copper mines and its generous supplies of clay
became a raw materials centre rather than a manufacturing district
because it lacked local supplies of fuel. In Sussex iron smelting was
dying out, and only one furnace remained in blast in 1796. The
worsted industry around Norwich, which still seemed prosperous
in the early 1780s, already showed some signs of decay and was
eventually—although not for many years—to disappear altogether.

---

[1] These lines of Anna Seward are quoted by W. G. Hoskins, *The Making of the
English Landscape* (1955), p. 170.

In the East Midlands, at Nottingham and Leicester, the hosiery trade flourished, although factories were virtually unknown. In the South-West, the spinning jenny was introduced only in the 1790s after the competition of the North had become alarmingly threatening. Decline was not to lead to immediate collapse—the reputation of Gloucestershire for fine cloth was maintained, and there was no local shortage either of new machinery or new ideas—but a northern manufacturer was pronouncing a sentence of ultimate doom when he wrote in 1804 that 'the woollen cannot too closely follow in the steps of the cotton trade: that nation which brings forth its goods the best and the *cheapest* will always have a preference, and it is only by means of the adoption of every possible improvement that pre-eminence can be secured.'[1]

5. RICH AND POOR

The social and economic changes of the last decades of the eighteenth century helped to create not only a new North and a new South but a new rich and a new poor, and, more important still, to change the relationships between them. As industry grew, it brought into existence new men of wealth unaccustomed to a position of command in society, and a new industrial labour force, larger in numbers, more regular in its working habits and more directly disciplined than either agricultural workers or skilled artisans ever had been before. It is always difficult to generalize about working conditions or standards of living, but there were certain generalizing tendencies in the new industrial society which contrasted sharply with the agricultural and mercantile society which had preceded it. The contrast was not one between a golden age and an age of slavery, as many people at the time and some people since have suggested, but it nonetheless entailed much social disorganization as well as economic progress.

In a traditionalist rural society the existence of the poor was taken for granted. They possessed little property and were dependent on their 'betters' for the right to work and the right to eat. Their 'betters' were not necessarily very rich; the authority of the moderately well-off squire or the often far from well-off country parson carried natural weight in the local community. There was automatic deference even when there was discontent. There was

[1] Observations on the Cotton Weavers' Act (1804), quoted P. Mantoux, *The Industrial Revolution of the Eighteenth Century* (1928), p. 276. The italics are mine.

also by nature of the smallness of the village some common aware-
ness of the life of the whole community. When conditions were
favourable, there was a plentiful flow of charity: when conditions
were unfavourable, large numbers of people within the parish found
themselves at the mercy not of their neighbours but of the poor law.
The shadow of the poor law, as George Crabbe pointed out, hung
over many eighteenth-century villages. Parish Overseers of the
Poor, appointed by the Justices of the Peace, were entitled by the
Poor Act of 1601 to levy a poor-rate, which might be used to relieve
the sick and aged and to find work for the able-bodied unemployed.
Although there was a common administrative framework for the
management of the poor law, the actual policies adopted by the
overseers varied considerably from place to place, as did wages and
standards of living. At Cowden, for example, when Robert Still and
his family contracted smallpox, the parish supplied a nurse for five
weeks, faggots for the fire, and a lavish assortment of food, including
beef, cheese, mutton, butter, milk, and beer.[1] In other places, dismal
workhouses, let out to contractors, made the welfare of the poor as
perfunctory and as degrading as possible. Some parishes made a
genuine attempt to provide for the pauper children and orphans in
their care; others bound them as apprentices to distant masters.
Some parishes found work for the able-bodied unemployed; most
neglected this duty altogether.

The agricultural changes associated with the growth of the large
farm and the spread of enclosure forced many villagers to a greater
dependence on the poor law. However much they might be exhorted
by the parson or the squire to practise frugality or to work with
greater tenacity, they knew that such qualities of character would
bring few material rewards. 'You offer no motives', Arthur Young
made one of the dispossessed poor exclaim, 'you have nothing but a
parish officer and a workhouse. Bring me another pot.' When at the
beginning of the French wars, prices rose sharply and the rural poor
were faced with increased privations, it is not surprising that in some
villages resort to the poor law became habitual and systematic. This
was the procedure associated with the well-known decision of the
local Speenhamland magistrates in Berkshire in 1795. It had long
been the practice of overseers to help men 'overburdened with
children' by making them some allowance from the parish. The
Speenhamland magistrates were not anticipating persistent 'pau-

---

[1] Quoted D. Marshall, *English People in the Eighteenth Century* (1956), p. 190.

perism' when they decided, in face of a sharp price rise, and growing local hardships, not to try to fix local wages, which in law they were still empowered to do, but to supplement agricultural wages with poor-law allowances which would vary with the price of bread and the size of the labourer's family. Too much can be made of the novelty and immediate significance of the Berkshire magistrates' decision, but in time 'Speenhamland' became a shorthand expression for rural pauperization. The allowances system, sharply criticized by Malthus on the ground that it encouraged large families, could also be attacked by liberal political economists because it impeded mobility of labour. In its beginnings, however, it was a genuine attempt to help the poor, not to ruin them. The criticism of it and its ultimate failure showed how much more complicated the problem of alleviating poverty had become in a society with a growing population and an industrialized sector of the economy.

There were four main immediate difficulties in handling the poor. First, the parish was too small and ineffective an administrative unit. Many parishes could not afford a workhouse and few with workhouses could manage them effectively. In 1782 an Act of Parliament, sponsored by Thomas Gilbert, made an attempt to meet this difficulty by permitting parishes to form unions to build work-houses, and in Berkshire itself there was a vigorous but unsuccessful effort at Faringdon to build a workhouse serving nearly twenty parishes. Second, the settlement laws of 1662 (modified in 1685 and 1693) made birth or residence a necessary qualification for parish relief; these laws, which were not applied rigorously in the case of able-bodied single men looking for work, nonetheless entailed interference and at times degradation. The growth of an industrial economy depended on freedom to move without social risk. Third, parishes in large towns, particularly London, were at a far graver disadvantage in dealing with the flooding mass of the poor than were rural villages. In populous places the poor were often hidden away from public view, driven to begging and tempted to crime. No amount of philanthropy or social compunction could solve their problems. Urban society encouraged anonymity and facilitated social segregation. Building bridges between rich and poor had to be a conscious undertaking not, as in the traditional village, a by-product of existing social relationships. Finally, in the traditional village itself, social strains made the problem of poverty more likely to create conflict than ever before. Foreign visitors commented that 'the English labourer is better clothed, better fed, and better lodged than the French',[1] but English observers close to the scene, like the Rev. David Davies, the Rector of Barkham in Berkshire, saw that what was happening in people's minds was as important as what was happening to their bodies. 'Hope is a cordial', he remarked, 'of which the poor man has especially much need, to cheer his heart in the toilsome journey through life. And the fatal consequence of that policy, which deprives labouring people of the expectation of possessing any property in the soil, must be the extinction of every generous principle in their minds.'[2] To Davies, the plight of the poor was not the consequence of defects of character,[3] but defects of character the consequence of poverty. Most of his suggestions for alleviating that poverty, however, were relentlessly disposed of by Malthus, for whom official action was more likely to increase poverty than to make it more tolerable.

It was on the industrial towns and the factories, where new wealth was being created, that the long-term hopes of saving a growing population from poverty were centred, but there the hope was soon dimmed by the smoke, and the evidence of social disorganization seemed to many critics even more alarming than that in the countryside. In the eighteenth century, three points only were clear. First, the wages of the industrial worker were higher than those of the agricultural labourer. They varied even in the same trade from one part of the country to another and from year to year, but they were always higher than those of the farm labourer. Second, the wages of farm labourers and unskilled workers were lowest in those areas where industry did not afford a substantial alternative employment to farming. In rural parishes near the towns 'the flourishing state of manufactures has considerably advanced the price of agricultural labour, and rendered it more adequate to the necessities of the labourer.'[4] Miss E. W. Gilboy has collected statistics from Lancashire which show that unskilled wage rates, which were substantially below those of Oxford in 1700, had left them far behind by the end of the eighteenth century, and had reached the London figure.[5] Third, strictly limited industrial wage gains were secured only in

[1] J. H. Meister, *Letters Written during a Residence in England* (1799).
[2] D. Davies, *The Case of Labourers in Husbandry* (1795).
[3] Contrast Eden's belief: 'If the poor do not prudently serve themselves none can effectively befriend them . . . it is far more useful to teach them to spend less, or to save a little, than to give them much more.' (*State of the Poor*, vol. I, p. 587.)
[4] J. Howlett, *Annals of Agriculture*, vol. XVIII, pp. 574–81.
[5] E. W. Gilboy, *Wages in Eighteenth-Century England* (1934), Appendix II.

return for novel modifications in the worker's way of life. The industrial town and the factory were new social institutions, which demanded new forms of behaviour and created new attitudes. Industrial workers had, above all else, to discover a new attitude to work itself. Seasonal, irregular work to which they were accustomed had to give way to far more regular and disciplined work at least within the factory walls. Time, which had acquired a new significance for the employer, had to acquire a new significance for the employee too, and long hours, the call of the factory hooter, the constant oversight of the overlooker or foreman, the imposition of fines as penalties for breaches of working rules, and the relentless demands of the machines imposed a new and less natural industrial routine. 'Whilst the engine runs, the people must work—men, women and children are yoked together with iron and steam. The animal machine . . . is chained fast to the iron machine, which knows no suffering and no weariness.'[1]

Women and children were the first to feel the strains of the mechanization of the cotton industry. They were adept with their fingers, more docile than men in their response to discipline, and cheaper to employ; and manufacturers were quick to see their advantages. Robert Peel I, for example, had over a thousand children in his workshops; in most mills women were the standard labour force, along with children making up two-thirds of the whole. Some of the first children to be employed in the factories were pauper apprentices transported from distant parishes to the new workshops. The conditions were often deplorable, one model mill in Manchester working its children seventy-four hours a week. Even where conditions were relatively good, there was a severance of all family ties. After Samuel Oldknow had made a bargain with the London parish of Clerkenwell for a supply of seventy children in 1796, some of the children's parents, learning of the destination, came crying to beg to have their children out again 'rather than part with them so far off'.

The employment of women and children was not a new departure in industry. Both had been compelled to work hard in the countryside and in domestic industry. Children's labour in particular had been regarded as morally useful as well as economically necessary, and even the benevolent Rev. David Davies recommended that no

[1] J. P. Kay, *Moral and Physical Condition of the Operatives employed in the Cotton Manufacture in Manchester* (1832), p. 4.

persons should be allowed parish relief on account of any child 'above six years of age who shall not be able to knit'. What the factories did was to spotlight the problem in an age when the number of children in the population was increasing rapidly. It has recently become fashionable to dismiss as 'romantic' the language applied by shocked contemporaries to factory conditions, but alongside the well-managed factories there were many which deserved the name of one notorious factory in Lancashire called 'Hell's Gate'. 'It can only be considered as so much pure unmixed evil, moral, medical, religious and political', one writer said of labour conditions in 1802. 'In great manufactories, human corruption accumulated in large masses seems to undergo a kind of fermentation which sublimes it to a degree of malignity not to be exceeded out of hell.'[1]

Opposition to machinery and to the introduction of the factory system was real and sustained, despite the material advantages offered to the individual in the form of higher wages and to the nation in the form of greater output.[2] The opposition was not simply irrational, based on a preference for the past or an inherent inability to accept discipline. The greatest single objection was perfectly rational, that the factory worker was under the 'absolute and uncontrolled power of the capitalist'.[3] Whether the factory owner was paternalistic, like the Strutts of Derbyshire, who made a genuine attempt to advance the welfare of their workers, or overbearing, falling back on the defence 'I know of no law to restrain me . . . I never heard of any',[4] the ultimate power was in his hands, and it was natural that it should at times be resented. Already in the so-called 'domestic system', many merchants or gentlemen clothiers exercised overriding power, many workers were in effect wage workers, and there was plenty of scope for antagonism between them, the outworkers and the middlemen: in a more advanced industrial system, however, capital was concentrated and visible, and antagonism was now more direct and open. Before long social theorists were to

[1] *Gent eman's Magazine*, vol. LXXII, No. 57 (1802).
[2] For a West-of-England complaint, see D. M. Hunter, *The West of England Woollen Industry under Protection and Free Trade* (1910), p. 22. In 1802 a group of shearmen wrote to an employer: 'Wee Hear in Formed that you got Shear in mee sheens and if you Dont Pull them Down in a Forght Nights Time Wee will pull them Down for you. Wee will you Damd infernold Dog.' For more polite language, see the important evidence in the 1806 report on the Woollen Industry, *P.P.* (1806), vol. III.
[3] Mantoux, *op. cit.*, p. 427.
[4] Quoted *ibid.*, p. 428.

build up general systems of social philosophy around the antagonism between capital and labour and politicians were to make it the starting point of their campaigns.

If the new industrial workers, whether they were employed in factories or not, had to develop a new attitude towards work, they also had to develop a new attitude towards leisure and home life. Many of them continued to try to secure as much leisure as they could, on what was known as St. Monday, for instance, a day of large-scale absenteeism, but they had to fall back restlessly on the very restricted and usually escapist outlets for leisure in new urban communities. New towns like Oldham were deficient in means of 'common enjoyment' for artisans and operatives, however much they catered for the needs of the more sophisticated or intelligent sections of the population. No regular urban calendar took the place of the rural calendar of the past, until organized sport, festivals and outings, gala days, and holidays began to fill out the year later in the nineteenth century, although there was temporary excitement in cockfighting, crude theatricals, drinking and brawling. In any case, long factory hours were a strain on the worker, and the only recognized free day of the week, the Sabbath Day, was increasingly kept holy whether the worker went to church, chapel, or neither. The home might be cleaner and more comfortable than the agricultural worker's cottage and the kitchen less bare, but the surroundings were often more squalid and the outlook less agreeable. There was much 'homesickness' and sense of uprooting. There might be more things to buy—'Beds, Presses, Clocks, Chairs, etc.', as a visitor noticed at Arkwright's town of Cromford—but there was also more pressing need to acquire them. Above all, there was still no social security. Necessity was often as relentless as Nature had been, and the hazards of life were increased rather than diminished. If the spell of magic and superstition was sometimes broken, belief in luck increased, particularly in the isolated mining villages.

By the end of the eighteenth century it was still too soon to establish the lessons of recent experience, but there was already in existence, contrasting with traditionalist rural England, a new urban industrial society where the poor were taken for granted in a different way from their country cousins. They possessed little property, but they were dependent not on their 'betters' but on the newly rich, their economic masters. There was less deference and more opportunity for individual restlessness and organized discontent. The size of the town encouraged social segregation, a division of the urban area between different sections of the population. In some towns, like Birmingham, the rich might still live alongside the poor, but in others like Manchester, as Aikin noted in 1795,[1] the flight to the suburbs by the wealthy had already begun. The local newspaper was taking the place of or at any rate augmenting local gossip. The 'natural' order of the village was giving way first to the disorder and then to the 'artificial' order of the town.

It took time for these changes to establish themselves, and with them a basic change in the relations between rich and poor. The pieces of the pattern, however, were already there. In Birmingham in 1783, for instance, the historian and printer William Hutton, himself the son of a Derby weaver, estimated that out of 209 leading citizens, 3 possessed more than £100,000, 7 more than £50,000, 8 more than £30,000, 17 more than £20,000 and 80 more than £10,000; at that time, the total population of the city was about 50,000[2] and the 'masses' of the population included a large number of highly skilled artisans, many of whom hoped—not too ambitiously—that one day they would join the ranks of the newly rich. In the cotton areas, where men were still proud to say that they had 'risen' from nothing, there was a wider gulf between rich and poor than in the metal-finishing areas. New manufacturing families, like the Peels, were staking large claims which contrasted sharply with the rigid necessities of their operatives. About 1780 a handful of members of the Peel family were employing most of the working population of Bury in Lancashire; in 1788, Robert Peel I bought land in the Midlands at Tamworth and began to accumulate a massive fortune, which was to give his famous son, Robert II, a good start, not in business but in nineteenth-century politics.

Whether the social gulf was wide or narrow, the pattern was the same. The masters took their profits—often, as we have seen, ploughing them back and accumulating more fixed capital in their own hands: the workers were given their wages. Most well-to-do people in the industrial areas were beginning to regard this pattern as self-sufficient and self-justifying. Masters and men, they held, were best left to fend for themselves. It was not that all masters were simply acquisitive 'economic men', but rather that the process of

---

[1] J. Aikin, *Description of the Country from Thirty to Forty Miles Round Manchester* (1795).
[2] There were over 200 publicans. See *History of Birmingham* (1781).

acquisition set the terms on which other social processes were allowed to operate. Room was left for individual mobility—it was considered a virtue in a way which would have seemed impertinent in a village society—but not everyone could move. There still had to be poor, but it was increasingly easy to say that they were poor not because God chose them to be so, but because they lacked the requisite gifts of character and perseverance. It was still possible to feel well-disposed towards them and to offer them charity in hard times, but it was easy, too, to say that they were best left to look after their own future and to go on to dismiss charity as an obsolete and sentimental indulgence.

Such a pattern of relationships did more to break down the traditional view of the social order than the writings of any single theorist or the precepts of any reformer. The newly rich began, in time, to consider their social position not in terms of order and degree, but in terms of *class*, a new concept in English social thinking[1]; the new workers, or at least the most militant amongst them, began to think of themselves not as permanently established 'lower orders', the necessary broad base for the tapering social pyramid, but as 'labouring or working classes',[2] a group far from homogeneous but with realizable ambitions as a group and not as a mere collection of individuals. Concerted action was not new, but the group-consciousness upon which it depended was deepened and extended. In the new towns there were large numbers of working men's friendly clubs and trade societies[3] and employers' associations and combinations, the former looking to 'unions' for strength, the latter banding themselves together to protect their interests both against the farmer and the artisan. The economic framework was in course of construction: the political framework was to take several generations to erect.

[1] The word 'class' was used earlier, e.g. by Defoe, as a category in classification, but not in its late eighteenth-century and nineteenth-century sense.

[2] The phrase 'lower classes' was used by Eden in 1795, *op. cit.* vol. I, p. 404. *Common People* or *lower orders* were the generally used phrases before the rise of class terminology. *Middle Class* was used in 1794 by T. Gisborne. C. Hall in his *The Effects of Civilization on the People of European States* (1805) stated tersely: 'the people in a civilized state may be divided into many different orders; but for the purpose of investigating the manner in which they enjoy or are deprived of the requisites to support the health of their bodies and minds, they need only be divided into two classes, viz. the rich and the poor.' For the later history of class terminology, see below, p. 170 & p. 297.

[3] Machine spinners' unions were founded, for instance, at Stockport in 1792, Manchester in 1795, and Oldham in 1796.

6. WICKED AND GOOD

Another key *motif* in nineteenth-century English history was to
be provided by Vital Religion. Faith in economic progress, which
not even the social complications of steam power could undermine,
was accompanied by—at times controlled and tempered by—
'Evangelical' religion, in its origins a religion not only of outward
observance but of personal salvation. If, as the nineteenth century
went by, the outward observance often hardened into a formal code
which was imposed alike on rich and poor, wicked and good, none
the less, when the roots pushed deepest, outward observance was
simply a natural testimony that an individual had been converted by
Divine Grace. Bible reading, regular prayer, observance of the
Sabbath Day, abstention from gambling and objection to frivolity
were signs of Grace, not self-sufficient virtues: 'by their fruits, ye
shall know them'.

Vital religion was the discovery of a few men, who were prepared
to make enormous personal sacrifices in the eighteenth century to
spread the word; the 1780s were crucial years in their strategy.
Already by 1780, under the influence of John Wesley and his fellow-
Methodists, the Calvinist, George Whitefield, and a group of enthusiastic 'Evangelical' clergymen and laymen within the Church of
England, formal eighteenth-century religion had been challenged
both at its weakest points and in its strongholds.

Formal religion was not necessarily sterile or stagnant religion,
but rather than set itself against the social order and the prevailing
mood and manners of English society it conformed to them. It
emphasized the rational character of Christianity: God was the
Clockmaker of the Universe, Christ the central figure in His Plan,
Christians were expected to be sober, moderate and dutiful. There
was little scope for personal tension in religion, for the probing of
the soul, for a sense of sacrifice, for unrestrained enthusiasm. Dr.
Johnson characteristically defined enthusiasm in his *Dictionary* as 'a
vain confidence of divine favour or communication', and even the
old Dissenting congregations—Presbyterians, Congregationalists,
Baptists, and Unitarians—although they could not escape their legacy
of revolt or forget the principle of freedom of conscience, were as
suspicious of enthusiasm as members of the Church of England.
Quiet, tolerant, cultivated and patient, at least in their leadership,
they drew a sharp distinction between 'candour', which they prized,

and 'cant' which they condemned. For the most part they rested content within the confines of their existing congregations, seeking amity and fellowship rather than trying to increase their numbers or to extend their influence.

Into this world, by 1780, the new 'vital religion' had burst its way, appealing to men and women who were dissatisfied with the 'rational Christianity' of both church and chapel or to those who had previously known little of the claims of religion, rational or otherwise. John Wesley had been particularly successful in appealing to people in districts where the Established Church, through indifference or faulty organization, had failed to meet spiritual needs. The parish was sometimes as ineffective a unit of church organization as it was of poor law administration. Some parishes, like Halifax, were of enormous size; others maintained churches a considerable distance away from the main concentration of population. In many of the rapidly growing industrial areas (Oldham, in Lancashire, for instance) there were no new parishes associated with the new urban centres. Indifference to local spiritual needs, rendered inevitable by pluralism and non-residence, was as real a problem as inadequate parochial organization. There were good and bad priests in the eighteenth century as there must always be, but the close association of the clergy with the social hierarchy and the unconcealed fact that the Establishment, from the bishops downwards, served as a system of patronage and preferment for younger sons and the well-connected, did not favour the spiritual cultivation of the soil. Wesley reacted positively against torpor and abuses: he was indefatigable in pursuing his mission 'to spread Scriptural Holiness throughout the land'. Although he considered himself a loyal member of the Church of England, he refused to be bound by the limits of its outlook or its organization. He respected authority and tradition, but he did not let them interfere with his work or divert him from preaching 'the simple truth for simple folk'. It has been reckoned that he travelled 250,000 miles during his evangelistic tours—it is not surprising that he was as great and as voluble a critic of the English roads as Arthur Young—and that he preached no less than 52,400 times between 1738 and 1791. 'Redeeming the time', to use Wesley's phrase, was a major virtue; time, indeed, meant more to him than it did even to the new manufacturers.

Wesley's vital religion 'warmed the hearts' of large numbers of people, including many who did not become full members of his

United Societies. When he died in 1791, there were about 136,000 'people called Methodists' and nearly seven times as many 'adherents'. Individually he had 'changed' lives, including the lives of hundreds of working folk,[1] the broad base of the social pyramid; collectively, he had done much to make his followers believe that before God the social pyramid melted into thin air. Although he was a believer in both the 'natural' social order and the historic English Constitution, he founded a religious society 'which requires nothing of men in order to their admission into it, but a desire to save souls'. The society was not a democratic one—Wesley himself exercised an authoritarian influence in it and the annual conference was composed of travelling preachers whose only right to attend was an invitation from Wesley himself—but its teachings emphasized first that *all* men and women needed to be 'saved' and second that before God all souls were of equal value. The contrast between equality 'before God' and inequality 'before men' was eventually to turn some of the people called Methodists into effective critics of the social and political order,[2] but for most Methodists the contrast limited interest in the social and political order by making it seem relatively unimportant. By stressing redemption and subsequent good conduct, Methodism turned many of the turbulent and fractious industrial workers into God-fearing and sober people:

> Where weavers expound, as they sit at the loom,
> Where mechanics, inspired, the Gospel explain,
> And weave at a text as well as a chain.

It divided 'wicked' and 'good', but did not follow Calvinist logic and claim that the separation was one between 'elect' and 'damned'. It offered hope of salvation to all who were willing to listen. The hope did much to mitigate worldly dissatisfaction. Old-fashioned traditionalists like Lord Carlisle might plead for 'cheerful rational amusements' which would divert the working men of Lancashire from 'dark, odious and ridiculous enthusiasm' and 'Methodistical

---

[1] 'I was like a wandering bird, cast out of the nest,' the stonemason John Nelson witnessed, 'till Mr. John Wesley came to preach his first sermon in Moorfields. Oh, that was a blessed morning to my soul . . . When he had done, I said, "This man can tell the secrets of my heart: he hath not left me there; for he hath showed the remedy, even the blood of Jesus".'

[2] Wesley encouraged Methodists to read: 'reading Christians will be knowing Christians,' he argued. Quoted by T. W. Herbert, *John Wesley as Editor and Author* (1940), p. 4.

melancholy', but employers on the spot knew better. 'I have left most of my works in Lancashire under the management of Methodists', wrote Robert Peel I in 1787, 'and they serve me exceedingly well.' Generalizing from experience, the Unitarian minister, Dr. Priestley, who disliked Methodist enthusiasm, admitted that to the Methodists were due 'the civilization, the industry, and sobriety of great numbers of the labouring part of the community'. But not all the Methodists remained spiritually blessed and materially poor. Some of them waxed well not as labourers but as masters. We have seen how old forms of Nonconformity, like Quakerism, nurtured business virtues; Wesleyanism, too, by encouraging frugality and industry, helped to make Wesleyans 'successful'. Wesley himself, who had made a special appeal to the unevangelized poor and to social outcasts, saw the spiritual dangers of new wealth among his followers but, apart from emphasizing qualities of individual trusteeship, there was little he could do about it.

When Wesley died in 1791, it was still not clear what would be the relationship between the Methodist societies and the Church of England, yet two steps taken by Wesley himself in the 1780s, the ordination of American 'superintendents' (who styled themselves 'bishops') in 1784, and the drafting in the same year of a Chancery Deed vesting authority after his death in a 'Legal Hundred' of travelling preachers, made separation inevitable. Although as late as 1788 Wesley said that he was anxious to 'live and die a member of the Church of England', he had in fact created, whether he admitted it or not, a new sect, closer to the Church of England than any of the old nonconformist sects, but separated from it by social and organizational barriers.

The Church of England—by law established—remained something more than a sect. It claimed to be a national communion, big enough to contain all shades of thought and feeling, with its rules and ordinances part of 'our happy Constitution and State'. By 1780 it too had felt the full impact of vital religion, not only through the action of the Methodists but through the pressure of clergymen and laymen in its own ranks. Wesley's successes would have been impossible had he not enjoyed the friendship and support of an energetic group of unequivocally loyal priests of the Church of England. They continued to preach 'evangelical' doctrines of personal salvation within the regular ecclesiastical framework, reconciling 'Christian godliness' and 'Christian order'. John Newton, ex-master of a slaving ship and friend of the poet of the group, William Cowper, was one of the two Evangelical clergymen in charge of London parishes in 1780. Far away, Henry Venn used his position as Vicar of Huddersfield to spread similar doctrines in the increasingly urbanized West Riding to such effect that Evangelicalism soon had a firm grip on the industrial North. Later he moved to a Cambridgeshire village from which he could make his influence felt in the university and through the university on the rising generation. There were other men in Cambridge too like Isaac Milner, mathematician and President of Queens' College, and Charles Simeon, Fellow of King's College and incumbent of Holy Trinity, who were influential in organizing 'the best and most fruitful nursery of Evangelicals in the country'. They were often unpopular with 'idle' undergraduates, but they succeeded in firmly anchoring Evangelical doctrines to the Established Church. 'If you knew', said the Whig writer and historian, Macaulay, who was up at Cambridge in Simeon's time, 'what his authority and influence were, and how they extended from Cambridge to the most remote corners of England, you would allow that his real sway over the Church was far greater than that of any primate.'[1]

Macaulay's father, Zachary, a London merchant and for fifteen years manager of the Evangelical journal, the *Christian Observer*, founded in 1801, was a member of the most important concentration of Evangelicals outside Cambridge, the so-called 'Clapham Sect' in South London. It was the Claphamites who forced Evangelicalism into the forefront of public life and carried its doctrines to the rich as well as to the poor. The Rector of Clapham from 1792 was John Venn, the son of Henry Venn of Huddersfield, but the central figure was William Wilberforce, who had been converted to Evangelical Christianity after a visit to the Continent with Isaac Milner in 1785, when he was already Member of Parliament for Yorkshire. For a moment Wilberforce thought of abandoning politics altogether, but he soon came to the conclusion that there was scope for much useful Christian action in public life. Along with other members of the 'Clapham Sect', including Henry Thornton, the wealthy banker and M.P. for Surrey, James Stephen, the lawyer, and John Shore, Governor-General of India from 1793–8 and later first Baron Teignmouth, he pushed 'good causes' to the utmost of his power. Uninfluenced by 'radical' or Whig ideologies, the

[1] Sir G. O. Trevelyan, *Life and Letters of Lord Macaulay* (1876), vol. I, p. 67.

Claphamites sought not political regeneration but the opportunity to save souls through the medium of political action—to free slaves, to abolish duelling, to prohibit cruelty to children and animals, to have the Sabbath 'kept holy', to spread knowledge of the Bible, to reform 'manners'. They did not wish to abolish the distinction between rich and poor or to shatter the traditionalist theory of orders, ranks and degrees, but rather to justify both by introducing into the world a new leaven of righteousness.

Before assessing the full significance of the early Evangelical movement, it is necessary to present another character on the stage— Hannah More. We have already caught a glimpse of her as a philanthropist and educator caught in the dilemmas of reconciling good works and social conservatism in the rural West Country. She had been drawn into practical philanthropy in the 1780s not by a sudden conversion, like that of Wilberforce, but by a gradual process of increasing Evangelical involvement. The campaign against the slave trade drew her into the middle of a circle of active Christians whose faith was 'robust' as well as 'vital'. From 1785 onwards she made a vow to dedicate herself to God 'with a more entire surrender than I have ever made': as a result of her dedication, she became associated with Wilberforce in 1787 and like him turned to the task of reforming the manners and customs not of the poor but of influential people in society. Her slim volume *Thoughts on the Importance of the Manners of the Great to General Society* (1788) was addressed neither to persons of 'eminent virtue, nor to men of flagitious wickedness' but to the 'higher orders' in general. Not without courage, she accused them of teaching bad habits to the poor and warned them against sins of the spirit as well as of the flesh. Above all, she underlined their responsibility for setting the moral tone of society. Her book was a great success, seven large editions being sold within a few months. Her second book *An Estimate of the Religion of the Fashionable World* (1790) was more forthright but equally successful. In it she boldly directed her guns against 'conventional' Christianity, asserting that religion was not 'an act or a performance or a sentiment' but 'a turning of the whole mind to God; a concentration of all the powers and affections of the soul into one steady point, a uniform desire to please him'. Benevolence, urbanity and good taste were not a substitute for Christianity, nor were 'prudence and discretion'. It was this book which gave Hannah More the nickname of 'Bishop' or 'Bishop in Petticoats' as

William Cobbett later called her, and it is indicative of the changed rôle of the Church of England in her age that her acquired authority was as great as the 'natural' authority of any bishop. What Wesley had done for the poor, she was doing for the rich. Although she never flirted with Methodism before or after her 'conversion' in the 1780s, Wesley himself recognized the importance of her evangelical work in a *milieu* he could not reach. 'Tell her to live in the world', was his advice to her, 'there is the sphere of her usefulness; they will not let us come nigh to them.'[1]

Hannah More and the Clapham Sect with whom she was closely associated in the 1790s were responsible for strengthening and revivifying personal standards of morality among 'the great and the gay' in an age of industrial and, after 1789, political revolution. They did much to advertise the merits of 'vital religion' as a substitute for a code of honour among the aristocracy and for prudential and rational Christianity among the middle classes. In 1787 they set up the Proclamation Society to advocate the reformed morality which Wilberforce had succeeded in persuading George III to sponsor in a Royal Proclamation of that year. The society, similar in purpose to the older and lapsed Society for the Reformation of Manners (founded 1692) but far more influential, prepared the way for a whole series of Evangelical organizations of various kinds, during the course of the next fifty years. They were important, as we shall see, in underpinning moral resistance to the 'subversive ideas' of the French Revolution, and, to take a longer view, in ushering in 'Victorianism before Victoria'.[2] Already by 1809 they had accomplished enough to persuade an English woman 'exile' in India to write, 'from what we heard, we supposed that since we had left England, the cool green island had become a land of saints'.

The policy of pursuing the aims of the Proclamation by invoking the law had its dangers from the start: it was just as likely in the long run to produce hypocrites as saints. Hannah More seems to have preferred strictures to legal bans and restrictions, but Wilberforce, a man of charm and vivacity as well as integrity and firmness, was prepared to justify action by the authorities to maintain 'high ideals'. 'I know', he wrote, 'that by regulating external conduct we do not change the hearts of men, but even they are ultimately wrought upon by these means, and we should at least so far remove

---

[1] Quoted by M. G. Jones, *Hannah More* (1952), p. 103.
[2] See below pp. 172–4, pp. 452–3.

the unobtrusiveness of temptation that it may not provoke the appetite which otherwise might be dormant and inactive.'[1] Many restrictions on Englishmen's freedom of activity were to be imposed during the next century in the name not so much of 'liberty' against 'licence' as of 'removing the obtrusiveness of temptation'. The mould of the restrictions gave a particular shape to many habits and institutions in English social life—the English sabbath, for instance—and turned the adjective 'Continental' into an epithet of moral disapprobation.

It is impossible to understand the tide of the new morality without relating its movements to the social contours of the changing age. The future victories of Evangelicalism could scarcely have been anticipated in the mundane, aristocratic, fashionable society of London, Bath and Brighton, yet before the nineteenth century had progressed long, London was invaded far beyond the spearhead of Clapham, and Bath and Brighton, like other popular watering places, became great Evangelical centres. So too did the North of England where there was a natural demand for a revived Puritanism of manners and a religion of personal hope and redemption. The emergence of a new industrial middle class favoured the spread of the new morality which was taught in the Sunday schools. Wesley had preached with spectacular success to the poor; Hannah More had preached with unexpected success to the rich. The long-term success of the 'good' in English society was made possible by neither, but by the increase in influence of the middle ranks of society composed of men and women who found it easier to be 'serious' than to be 'flippant', and often more advantageous to be 'good' than to be 'wicked'. Some of them were impelled by genuine 'vital religion' and needed neither strictures nor prohibitions to guide them: others followed the fashion. As a writer in the *Monthly Review* put it in 1807, when Evangelicalism had begun to touch Dissent as well as the Church of England, 'mediocrity of station' was favourable to 'domestic virtue'. So close was the link that in time respectability became as much a mark of the middle classes as wealth or superior income, and Evangelical arguments originally grounded not in the creed of progress but in that of the Cross were used to justify individual wealth and power as well as national morality. In domestic life social disapproval proved a far more powerful sanction than either the law or the pulpit.

[1] Quoted by M. Jaeger, *Before Victoria* (1956), p. 16.

In the first years of their springtime the Evangelicals with their irrepressible moral energy and skill in the techniques of organization accomplished much which was good, including much which could never have been accomplished by smaller and older religious groups like the Quakers. Even in the long run, when the energy moved through narrower channels, they opened up a moral debate which permitted more sensitive individual moralities to stake their claims. But they also did much that was irrelevant and even harmful. They helped to divide faith and intellect, seeking human knowledge not because they valued it but 'because of the present distress'. In time, as Lecky put it in a trenchant, hostile judgement, 'the popular preacher became the intellectual ideal, and the weakest form of religious literature almost the sole reading of large classes'. Equally important, the Evangelicals succeeded in dividing religion and taste. 'Philosophy, Literature, Art and Science were conceived apart from religion. The world and the Church were not only antagonistic in the biblical sense . . . but severed portions of life divided by outward signs and badges; and those who joined the one or the other were clearly marked off.'[1] Both these negative achievements made impossible the already difficult task of uniting art with industry and taste with progress in an expanding industrial community.

The numbers of Evangelicals should not be exaggerated. In hundreds of parishes there were no great changes in the late eighteenth century. Antipathy towards Roman Catholicism—the religion of a minority in England[2] but of the great majority in Ireland—was as powerful a force within the Church of England as 'enthusiasm', and apathy was probably more powerful than either. There were to be sharp bursts of anti-Catholic feeling long after 1780, and the question of 'Church Reform' was not taken up seriously until after there had been a reform of parliament.[3] By that time Evangelicalism had been challenged by new spiritual forces.

[1] Quoted by J. Tulloch, *Movements of Religious Thought in Britain during the Nineteenth Century* (1901), p. 13.
[2] See B. Ward, *The Dawn of the Catholic Revival in England, 1781–1803*, (1909)
[3] See below, pp. 282 ff.

2

POLITICS AND GOVERNMENT ON THE EVE OF THE FRENCH REVOLUTION

1. George III, Pitt, and Fox

ONE of the closest friends of Wilberforce was William Pitt, the son of Chatham, 'the great Commoner'. They had met at Cambridge University where they were undergraduates together, both of them beginning their university studies in 1773 at the tender age of fourteen. When Wilberforce was converted to Evangelical Christianity a dozen years later, Pitt had already been prime minister for more than three years. It was scarcely surprising that more experienced politicians talked of the kingdom being entrusted to a schoolboy's care. In fact, Pitt had exceptional gifts of pertinacity and character, and, once chosen as prime minister, he behaved as if he had been born to fill the position. Stiff and reserved in public, he never doubted his capacity to lead his country where other men had failed. If Wilberforce was dedicated to the service of humanity, Pitt was prepared to devote every ounce of his energies to the tasks of national revival. Both men were lucky that theirs was an age when young men could make their mark quickly.[1] Boswell listened to Wilberforce speaking in York on the day Parliament was dissolved in 1784 and reported that although Wilberforce seemed like 'a shrimp' when he mounted the table, 'as I listened, he grew and grew until the shrimp became a whale'. That was what happened to Pitt too after 1783. His first ministry lasted for seventeen years and laid the foundations of nineteenth-century England.

When Pitt became prime minister in 1783, however, he did so not as a popular figure well known in the country but at the behest of

[1] Lord Holland is said to have brought up Charles James Fox, Pitt's great rival, to believe that 'the young are always right; the old are always wrong.' Cf. Gibbon's verdict in 1786. 'The country seems to be governed by a set of most respectable boys.' (*Letters*, ed. R. E. Prothero (1897), vol. II, p. 143.)

the King, George III. The political background of his accession to power was the gravest of eighteenth-century constitutional crises, that caused by the American War of Independence, which had begun in 1776 and virtually ended with Cornwallis's surrender to Washington at Yorktown in October 1781. The news of Yorktown was a bitter blow to Lord North's twelve-year-old government which had been bitterly attacked both inside and outside the House of Commons for the last few years. A comparatively small swing of opinion among members who had hitherto supported the ministry was associated in February 1782 with a revolt of 'independent' members of the House of Commons, who joined with relentless critics of the war, of whom Pitt was one.[1] Together they repudiated the war and forced the King to come to terms with men whom he had long regarded as his opponents, and to form a new ministry under Lord Rockingham in March 1782. Before he did so, the King made it clear how critical he felt the situation was. 'His Majesty is convinced', he wrote in the draft of a message to Parliament which he never sent, 'that the sudden change of Sentiments of one branch of the legislature has totally incapacitated him from either conducting the War with effect, or from obtaining any Peace but on conditions which would prove destructive to the Commerce as well as to the essential Rights of the British Nation. His Majesty therefore with much sorrow finds he can be of no further Utility to His Native Country which drives Him to the painful step of quitting it for ever.'[2] In being forced to send for Rockingham George was accepting as his chief minister a man who not only stood for the reversal of the American policy which the King had advocated so fervently, but was anxious also to impose constitutional conditions on the King and to introduce legislation to curb royal patronage. The new ministry was divided, however, and although its favourite objective—an Economical Reform Bill—was achieved, it became even more divided after Rockingham's death in July 1782 and his replacement by Lord Shelburne. In the Shelburne administration, Pitt took office for the first time as chancellor of the exchequer.

'The strangest, though not unexpected revolution that has

---

[1] 'The War,' Pitt declaimed in 1781, 'was conceived in injustice; it was matured and brought forth in folly; its footsteps were marked with blood, slaughter, persecution, and devastation; in truth everything which went to constitute moral depravity and human turpitude were found in it.'

[2] Sir J. Fortescue, *Correspondence of King George III* (1927–8), vol. V, No. 3601, p. 425.

happened in this country for many years', as one contemporary described it,[1] was still not complete. In February 1783 Shelburne in turn was defeated on a motion of censure relating to the terms of peace. For all his intellectual ability he had been an unpopular prime minister, and he had been opposed in Parliament not only by Lord North and his supporters but by Charles James Fox, previously one of the bitterest of North's opponents, a brilliant debater and a close friend of the Prince of Wales. Shelburne resigned at once, and after more than a month of arduous searching for a new ministry which would not prove completely intolerable to him, George III had to give way and accept a government led by the Duke of Portland, a worthy nonentity, and including both Fox, the most relentless of his old opponents, and Lord North, who had once been the most loyal of his friends. It was a measure of George's desperation in the crisis of 1783, that before he yielded to Portland, Fox, and North he twice offered the prime ministership to the young Pitt. He even thought of abdicating, as he had done the year before, or of retiring to Hanover. It was the greatest possible humiliation to him to have to accept a ministry based on the 'infamous coalition' of Fox and his followers, who had bitterly attacked the American war and had threatened to impeach North for mismanaging it, and North, who had 'deserted' him in 1782.[2] It was an equal humiliation to have to accept the terms on which they formed their ministry. Portland demanded a *carte blanche* in the appointment of ministers, refused to show the King the names of any of his ministers except those in the cabinet, and insisted on the right to follow a line of policy determined by the cabinet alone. The sweeping nature of these demands was signal evidence of the drastic domestic consequences of the American upheavals of the previous years. The whole view of government held by the King was being challenged by opponents who wished to substitute a quite different view of government, of which he could in no way approve.

The only course of action open to him was to accept Portland, Fox and North under duress, to refuse to create any peerages at their request, to lull them into a false sense of security and, above

[1] Quoted L. S. Sutherland, *The East India Company in Eighteenth-Century Politics* (1952), p. 365.

[2] As late as 1782, Fox had said of relations with North and his government, 'from the moment when I shall make any terms with one of them, I will rest satisfied to be called the most infamous of mankind. I would not for an instant think of a coalition with men who in every public and private transaction as ministers have shown themselves devoid of every principle of honour and honesty.'

all, to make it known in the right places that he would welcome any initiative to destroy them. At the same time he had to take steps to ensure that when they had been destroyed a new prime minister would be available who could command parliamentary support, and that when in due course a new general election was held that support would be confirmed and augmented.

Pitt was the obvious candidate for prime minister: John Robinson, North's old patronage manager at the Treasury before 1782, was the obvious election manipulator; and Fox and North themselves conveniently supplied the issue which led to the fall of their ministry. In November 1783 they brought forward an East India Bill which in Fox's own phrase was 'vigorous and hazardous'. Not only did its Indian provisions provoke the violent opposition of the East India Company, but its administrative proposals were of such a kind that only the most resolute supporters of the ministry could approve of them. It was suggested that a body of seven Commissioners for India should be set up and that they should be appointed in the first instance not by the Crown but by Parliament. They were to hold office for four years and the Crown could not dismiss them. While this proposal stemmed naturally from Rockinghamite reasoning about the dangers of royal patronage, there were no good constitutional precedents for it, and it was easy to brand Fox and North as ambitious and unprincipled men, seeking dictatorially to concentrate Indian patronage in their own hands and to turn the King into a cypher. Although the House of Commons, where Fox and North between them had a clear majority, carried the India Bill with a majority of 102 votes, the House of Lords was effectively 'influenced' by the King and his servants to throw out the measure. Six days before the Commons passed the bill, Atkinson, an East India Company director and leader of the Company's opposition, wrote to Jenkinson, 'everything stands prepared for the blow if a certain person has the courage to strike it'. George III was never lacking in courage, and two days later he saw Lord Temple, one of his supporters in the House of Lords, and gave him authority to state that any peer who voted in favour of the bill would be considered his 'enemy'. The bill was duly and decisively lost on 17 December 1783, and within twelve hours of its defeat the King dismissed Portland, Fox, and North, and offered Pitt the seals of office. Pitt needed no persuading, for as a result of Robinson's researches he was assured of being able to make a reasonable showing in the

House of Commons until a new general election would provide him with a working majority.

The extremity of the King's anxieties in late 1783 and early 1784 is well brought out in a letter he wrote the day after Christmas. 'The times are of the most serious nature', he exclaimed, 'the political struggle is not as formerly between two factions for power; but it is no less than whether a desperate faction shall not reduce the Sovereign to a mere tool in its hands: though I have too much principle ever to infringe the rights of others, yet that must ever equally prevent my submitting to the Executive power being in any other hands, than where the Constitution has placed it. I therefore must call on the assistance of every honest man . . . to support Government on the present most critical occasion.'[1] Fox's view was diametrically opposed to this. He challenged the manner in which the King had approached the House of Lords through Temple, argued that the confidence of the House of Commons was sufficient in itself to keep a ministry in power regardless of the attitude of the House of Lords or the King's personal wishes, and attacked Pitt as an ambitious renegade who had abandoned his opinions for the sake of office. He had tried as late as November 1783 to draw Pitt into his coalition, and he never forgave Pitt for his acceptance of the King's request to form a government a month later. From that time onwards until Pitt's death in 1806 the two men were implacable political enemies, and their opposition and rivalry gave a special tone to English history. To the constitutional theme of the age as George III saw it, there was added the political theme of Pitt versus Fox, and whenever George III was out of action it was the second theme which predominated.

There were no two men more different in temperament and outlook than Pitt and Fox. The volatile, amiable, and pre-eminently sociable Fox was loved by a wide circle of friends and idolized by his supporters. Even men who disagreed with him admitted his magnetism and charm. The lofty, unbending, and self-sufficient Pitt, loved by few and at best treated with profound respect rather than with spontaneous affection, was never really liked except in the world of high politics. 'I know the coldness of the climate you go into', wrote Shelburne to a man who was about to have an interview with Pitt, 'and that it requires all your animation to produce a

[1] Quoted by Sir Lewis Namier, 'King George III, A Study in Personality,' in *Personalities and Powers* (1955), p. 42.

momentary thaw.'[1] They were both men of great gifts, but while Pitt was to have the opportunity of exercising his talents in office, Fox for most of his life had to employ them in opposition. Their gifts were as different as their temperaments. Fox was fascinated not only by great constitutional questions but by major issues of foreign policy: 'his abhorrence of wrong and his sympathy with human suffering were co-extensive with the habitable globe.'[2] Pitt was especially concerned with financial, economic, and administrative questions, looking to Adam Smith and the study of political economy as a guide, but he necessarily had to concern himself increasingly with an outside world about which he knew almost nothing at first hand.[3] If Pitt's gifts were more relevant to the economic and social needs of his day—the recovery of the national finances after the American war and the encouragement of further economic growth[4] —Fox's wit and warmth were allied with an imaginative power which might have made him an outstanding leader in times of emergency. As it was, it was Pitt who became a symbol of national unity while Fox, bitterly disliked by the King and seldom as assured of as much wholehearted popular support as he believed, was relegated to the rôle of a foil or at best of a partisan.

Between December 1783 and the inevitable general election of the spring of 1784 Fox employed all his gifts of oratory to try to unseat the 'unconstitutional' prime minister, but Pitt gradually strengthened his position both in the House of Commons and in the country. To begin with, his ministry was a very weak one, nicknamed 'the mince-pie administration' because it was not expected to last beyond Christmas. Two of his father's old followers refused to support him, his cousin Temple resigned before the Cabinet had been constituted, and he had to recruit most of his ministers from the House of Lords. He himself was almost the only figure of prominence on the front bench in the House of Commons, with the exception of Henry Dundas who had served continuously under North, Rockingham, and Shelburne. Yet Pitt showed courage while Robinson was completing his efforts behind the scenes, and, by standing firm, gradually cut down the substantial majorities against

---

[1] Lord E. Fitzmaurice, *Life of William, Earl of Shelburne* (1875) vol. III, p. 422.
[2] W. F. Rae, *Wilkes, Sheridan, Fox* (1874) p. 458.
[3] He crossed the Channel only once—for six weeks in the autumn of 1783.
[4] J. Rae in his *Life of Adam Smith* (1895) p. 289, describes a conversation in which Fox admitted he had not read *The Wealth of Nations*. 'There is something,' Fox said, 'in all these subjects which passes my comprehension; something so wide, that I could never embrace them myself or find any one who did.'

him in the Commons, until in March 1784 they fell to one. He not only introduced an India Bill of his own, but took pains to declare his continued support for parliamentary reform, which he had first advocated in 1781 and which he had taken up with determination and energy during the Fox-North ministry when the two sections of the government were pulling in different directions.

His support of reform won him the approval of some of the extra-parliamentary associations which had risen to national prominence during the critical years of the American war. Henry Duncombe, for example, in presenting a reform petition from one of the most important of these bodies, the Yorkshire Association, in January 1784 attacked 'the ambition of daring and desperate men' (Fox and North) totally indifferent to the 'sufferings of the great body of the people' and the 'dignity of the throne'. There were signs in other places in the provinces too that however much Fox might thunder against 'an Administration holding their places in defiance of the House of Commons', there was far less extra-parliamentary concern about strict Foxite 'constitutional principles' than about 'un-principled faction'. A stream of loyal addresses began to flood Parliament attacking Fox and North and praising Pitt's youth, virtue, capacity, resolution, and above all 'purity'. One of them came from John Wilkes, the old leader of Middlesex radicalism: 'to restore this kingdom to any degree of prosperity and greatness', Wilkes exclaimed, 'demands the utmost exertions of virtue and ability, with every support both of the Crown and people at large. I hope you will meet with both.'[1] So noisy, indeed, was the support of this kind that Pitt received and so obvious was it that he would have no difficulty in employing every kind of official influence to win the next election that Fox and his friends were driven into a violent attack on the dissolution of Parliament. They were so convinced that the existing House of Commons was the only brake that could check the 'ambition' of the King and his young minister that they attacked the dissolution as a challenge to the principles of responsible government, a 'settled plan to destroy not the form, but the essence of the House of Commons'.[2]

There was one interesting set of abortive negotiations before the King dissolved Parliament in March. The independent country

---

[1] Quoted S. Maccoby, *English Radicalism, 1762–1785* (1955), p. 409.
[2] For later attacks on 'unconstitutional' dissolutions—what the *Edinburgh Review* described in 1810 as an 'occasional' but 'natural' alliance between 'the mob and arbitrary power'—see B. Kemp, *King and Commons, 1660–1832* (1957), pp 80 ff.

gentlemen in the House of Commons—the group that had played such a big part in the dark years of the war first in carrying a motion in 1780 that 'the influence of the Crown has increased, is increasing and ought to be diminished' and second in overthrowing North in 1782—were anxious to try to reconcile Pitt and Fox and to bring into existence a strong national government based on a 'union of parties'. A series of meetings were held at St. Albans Tavern at which as many as seventy members of the House of Commons discussed the best way of achieving this end. They were unsuccessful, for the conflicts were already too bitter and there was no room for compromise. Fox made Pitt's resignation an indispensable prior condition and pointed to the anti-government votes in the House of Commons as a sign of the unconstitutional basis of Pitt's power: Pitt refused to resign, and both he and his friends directed attention to the growing volume of loyal addresses as a sign of public support. As the parliamentary majorities against him dwindled and the election approached Pitt became more and more self-confident, dismissing the independents as 'ineffectual' and caring little about their reactions. He was, indeed, winning some of them over to his side.

At the general election of March 1784 the King's choice of Pitt was necessarily ratified as Robinson had promised. More than a hundred of Fox's 'Martyrs' lost their seats, and although, as in all eighteenth-century and most early nineteenth-century elections, there was a relatively small number of contested constituencies, the excitement was considerable, particularly in some of the most important counties and in the small number of 'open constituencies'. There was an enormous volume of squib, cartoon, and pamphlet propaganda, the climax of the campaign of loyal petitions and addresses.

It is misleading to ignore the mood of 1784, although less misleading than to overlook, as nineteenth-century historians did, the absence of modern party ties and the crucial influence of patronage in assuring the election result. The Fox-North coalition had been an unpopular one and it was easy to charge it with being an instrument of oligarchy. 'At present', Spencer Stanhope exclaimed at a great meeting in York, 'I fear more the tyranny of Venice than of France.'[1] Pitt stood out by contrast as a 'pure' young leader independent of the great aristocratic factions, and he could depend on the support

---

[1] C. Wyvill, *Political Papers*, (6 vols. 1794–1802) vol. III, pp. 340–1.

of many local leaders who during the worst years of the American war had mobilized 'opinion' against the North government. Dr. Jebb, one of the leading Middlesex reformers and a prominent dissenter, wrote to Christopher Wyvill, one of the leaders of the Yorkshire Association: 'I most cordially wish entire rout to the party of Fox, Burke, and North. England if expiring, could not be benefited by such men'.[1] The Yorkshire Association itself split in 1784, but it was the Foxites who were the break-away minority. So widespread was the dislike of Fox and North and the opposition to an 'aristocratical Republic' that it was possible to argue plausibly at the time, as did the Whig Bishop of Llandaff, that 'it was not so much the prerogative of the Crown that kept Mr. Pitt in his place and set the House of Commons at defiance, as it was the sense of the nation which on this occasion was in direct contradiction to the sense of the House of Commons.'[2] Fox himself believed that he had been 'deserted by the people', although to the end of his life he was always inclined to believe that 'opinion' was manufactured from above rather than generated from below. He certainly did his best to manufacture opinion in Westminster, where with the help not of 'principles' but of the Duchess of Devonshire he won a personal victory as 'tribune of the people'. Pitt did his best (and worst) in the new House of Commons to challenge Fox's return for Westminster, for he was anxious himself to engross as much 'popularity' as possible. In fact, Pitt was remarkably successful in many of the key constituencies, particularly in Yorkshire. Robinson had not anticipated two Pittite victories for that county, but Wilberforce, who drew financial support from many places and was able to mobilize the local Yorkshire forces of discontent, forced his opponents to withdraw from the poll after being shown to be in a hopeless minority on nomination day. The Yorkshire result had a tonic effect on the subsequent elections in other counties. It was Fox himself who had argued in the past that 'Yorkshire and Middlesex between them make up all England',[3] and in Middlesex as well as Yorkshire there was a Pittite victory in 1784.

---

[1] *Ibid*, p. 362.
[2] Quoted M. D. George, 'Fox's Martyrs' in *T.R.H.S.* (1939). For the place of patronage in the election, see W. T. Laprade, 'Public Opinion and the General Election of 1784' in the *E.H.R.* (1916) and the volume he edited, *Parliamentary Papers of John Robinson 1778–1784* (1922).
[3] *The Life of Wilberforce* by his Sons (1838) vol. II, p. 133. The phrase was taken up by Cobden in 1846. See J. Morley, *Life of Cobden* (1881) vol. I, p. 263.

For all Pitt's successes, the real victor in March 1784 was neither the 'people' nor the young prime minister, but George III who had chosen Pitt as the agent of his plans to break what he regarded as a concerted attempt to undermine the Constitution. With the elections concluded, he now had a minister in charge of the administration who could work through Parliament—there were 147 new faces there—and a minister, moreover, who would in no way try to challenge the view of the Constitution which the King held. It is important to note that Pitt never attempted during or after 1784 to fashion for himself a popularity in any way independent of that of the King, and that although he went on to give to the office of prime minister a significance that it had never hitherto possessed, he never tried to assert his claims as prime minister against the King.[1] Nor did he go on pressing for long in the new Parliament for the parliamentary reforms which he had advocated so eloquently in 1782 and 1783 but which he knew the King did not like. The turning point on this crucial issue came in April 1785 when proposals Pitt made to give seventy-two additional members of Parliament to London and the counties by arranging a voluntary and compensated surrender of the franchise in thirty-six decayed boroughs, were defeated in the House of Commons by 248 votes to 174. Pitt made considerable personal efforts to carry this reform—he even summoned Wilberforce back from the South of France to vote for it— but the King was hostile and Lord North took the King's side by quoting the 'horrid sound of silence' in the country as an argument against change. This defeat not only prevented Parliament from gradually and peacefully reforming itself—Pitt had proposed that the same procedure he suggested in the case of the condemned boroughs should subsequently be applied in the case of other decayed constituencies—but confirmed Pitt's inability to lead the country either on his own terms or on the terms of some of his most vigorous supporters in the provinces in 1784. He did not himself complain, nor did he complain in 1801 when the King objected to his proposals for Catholic emancipation and decided with no qualms that he could do without the services of his distinguished and by then experienced prime minister. Pitt was always willing to serve, just as Fox was always willing to oppose, and this, rather than any desire to be popular, was the key to his political career. Freedom for him lay in the recognition of what he regarded

[1] For his view of the prime ministership, see below pp. 123-4.

as necessity, the supremacy of the royal will.[1] It was fortunate for George III and for England that in many spheres of administration Pitt could serve efficiently as well as loyally, that if he was unwilling to assert his will against the King, he was ready enough to direct it forcefully to the realization of purposes which they both shared, that his personal integrity was more generally appreciated outside Parliament than the qualities of any of his predecessors. Above all, he was anxious to apply both his will and his ability to the urgent tasks of recovery and reconstruction which he himself believed were far more important than prolonged discussion of general principles.

There was an enormous temperamental gulf between Pitt and Fox on all these points, and the contemporary description of Pitt and Fox as Hogarth's hard-working and idle apprentices was not without justification. Fox never wanted to devote the whole of his being to political service—his private life was at least as active as his public one—nor was he prepared to subordinate his will to that of his sovereign. On Pitt's death in 1806 he refused to support a motion proposed by Pitt's friends which declared that Pitt had been an 'excellent Minister' whose loss was 'irreparable'. The reason Fox gave was the same reason he would have given in the 1780s—that Pitt 'had countenanced and supported a system of government which had unfortunately prevailed through the whole of the present reign—that of invisible influence more powerful than the public servants of the Crown.' Fox would have been prepared to express his approval of a resolution paying tribute to Pitt's 'transcendent talents and virtues and the disinterested integrity displayed through a long course of arduous services',[2] but he goes down to history protesting incessantly against the terms on which Pitt rendered his 'arduous services' to the community.

It is easy to point to Fox's inconsistencies—almost all his actions need to be studied at different levels of motivation in an intricate pattern of detail—but his protests were all of a piece. There were few men in his generation who believed more fervently that 'liberty is the essence of the British Constitution'. Many men who were willing to employ such language rhetorically were either

[1] 'Where is now the boasted equipoise of the British Constitution?' he asked, 'where is the independence—nay, where is even the safety of any one prerogative of the Crown . . . if its prerogative of naming ministers is to be usurped by this House?' Quoted Earl Stanhope, *Life of William Pitt* (1879 edn.), vol. I, p. 150.

[2] *Diary and Correspondence of Lord Colchester*, (1861) vol. II, p. 31

anxious to take office or content to turn 'liberty' into a convenient partisan slogan. Pitt was able after 1784 to draw on the services of men like these as well as his own followers. One of the most effective diplomatic agents, Sir James Harris, whom he appointed ambassador at the Hague in March 1784, had been a supporter of Fox and Portland: his chief lieutenant in long and complicated commercial negotiations with France was William Eden, first Lord Auckland, who had hitherto been one of his most determined opponents. The view of men like these was well expressed by Harris in a letter written two years before he accepted Pitt's offer. 'In all matters of publick concern', he declared, 'my education, habits and I may add . . . my principles, lead me more to measures than men.'[1] When the crisis of the French Revolution split Englishmen into two camps and forced to the forefront two conceptions of 'liberty', Pitt could further augment his strength and draw in the Duke of Portland himself.

Before the French Revolution led to a consolidation of the forces of 'order' under Pitt's direction and pushed Fox further into the political wilderness, there was one final and illuminating crisis in the relations between George III and the two parliamentary leaders. The King went mad, and from November 1788 to February 1789 was a violent maniac. Pitt and his ministry, recognizing their dependence on the King's support, framed a Regency Bill very closely limiting the powers of the Regent. They knew that the Regent was a personal friend and companion of Fox, that he had welcomed Fox at Carlton House in 1784 after the 'tribune of the people' had been drawn in triumph through the streets of Westminster in his 'chariot of liberty', and that it was more than likely that if he acquired full powers as sovereign he would use royal influence to bring Fox and his friends to power. They also knew that he was a spendthrift libertine whose conduct had helped to force on his father's madness. In 1788 Fox, for all his talk of 'liberty' and constitutional principles, demanded an unrestricted Regency and accused Pitt of believing in the doctrine that 'when the King of England is in good health, the monarchy is hereditary; but when he is ill, and incapable of exercising the sovereign authority, it is elective.'[2] The King, he argued was legally dead and consequently the Prince had of right acquired full sovereignty; all that Parliament

---

1 Quoted A. Cobban, *Ambassador and Secret Agents* (1954), pp. 123–4.
2 *Speeches* (1815), vol. III, p. 423.

could do was to fix the date of the formal transfer of powers. The difference of approach between Pitt and Fox in 1788 shows how dangerous it is in examining late eighteenth-century politics to take professions of 'constitutionalism' at their face value. Every statement about the Constitution made by the King or by the politicians must be viewed in its political context. At a critical moment in English history, Fox put his trust neither in the parliamentary opposition—the concept of opposition was still loose and ill-formed —nor in the 'people', but in the heir to the Throne. Pitt and most of his colleagues stood for 'limitations' which would have made the Prince Regent the sort of ruler Fox had said that he wanted George III to be.

In 1788 as in 1784, however, Pitt was 'popular' outside Westminster because the King was popular, and the Prince of Wales was so strongly disliked that he was hissed and hooted in the streets of the capital. Although a number of the government's supporters in Parliament deserted Pitt and some of the members of his cabinet flirted with an opposition which now seemed to have a good chance of coming into power, the popular fortunes of Fox were far lower in 1788 than when he had attacked 'secret influence' in 1780 and tried to ally himself with movements of discontent in different parts of the country. But 'popularity' no more settled the thorny problems of English politics in 1789 than in 1784. The King was still the centre of the stage, active or insane, and when he got well in February 1789 and began to see his ministers again and to deal with formal business, the 'crisis' came to an end. At the general election of 1790 Pitt further strengthened his position.

Before considering the achievements of Pitt's administration between 1784 and 1790 it is necessary to go behind the bare narrative of events described so far and to examine the Constitution which he and Fox were disputing, and the structure and dynamics of late eighteenth-century politics. For generations historians read their own lessons into the narrative, lessons strongly slanted by the constitutional theories and political exigencies of their own times. It is only in recent years that the conditions and determinants of eighteenth-century politics have been carefully analysed, and while much research is still needed on the 1780s and 1790s, an important transitional period, most of the basic 'rules' and axioms of 'high politics' have been stated in what may well be their final form. There are three features of the political system which it is indispensable to understand—the attitude of contemporaries to the Constitution, the place of patronage in the political process, and the relationship between 'high politics' at Westminster and 'low politics' in the constituencies. All three features were inter-related and, to complicate matters, were in the course of change. Before the French Revolution generated new ideas and the industrial revolution created new problems, there were many signs that the political system of the past was no longer properly adapted to the needs of the present. The French Revolution was to challenge many old views of social and political authority and to influence the context of conservative as well as radical thinking. The industrial revolution was to create a new social structure and a new political vocabulary. In the 1780s, however, the influence of foreign ideas and of industrial changes was comparatively small. Most of the forces making both for movement and stability in local and national politics were the same as in the past.

2. THE CONSTITUTION

Just as it was necessary in examining late eighteenth-century society to begin with that model of social order which continued to grip contemporaries even when its pre-suppositions were being undermined, so in examining constitutional and political processes, it is necessary to begin with an investigation of the 'historic Constitution'.

Most Englishmen—and many foreigners—venerated the Constitution, which they claimed was the bulwark of 'liberty'. They conceived of it in terms of balance, comparing it to a piece of elegant political clockwork, in George III's phrase, 'the most beautiful combination ever framed'.[1] The similes and metaphors used to describe it owed much both to philosophers and to lawyers, but public veneration depended more on pride than on reason. As Pitt said in his speech introducing the parliamentary reform proposals of 1785, Englishmen had been accustomed from their cradles to view the Constitution as a 'pattern of perfection'. The Whig critics of George III appealed to the Constitution as much as Pitt or the King did, not objecting to the conception of balance, but claiming merely that the balance had been tilted in an unconstitutional manner. Even the discontented spokesmen of 'opinion' outside Parliament grumbled because the 'faulty working' of the

[1] *Correspondence of George III*, No. 2991.

Constitution was denying British subjects the benefits which history and constitutional precedent conferred. The old Constitution had to be restored: it was not necessary to manufacture a new one. There was no need even for 'new speculation'.[1] If you went back far enough—to the reign of Alfred the Great, for example—you would discover 'magnanimous government',[2] and all would be well in the present if the Constitution were administered 'as it ought to be'.

This was a radical conception of history, but for the more orthodox too, the concept of constitutional balance seemed to rest on something more than convenience. Out of the constitutional conflicts of the seventeenth century there had emerged a 'mixed monarchy', combining the benefits of absolute monarchy, aristocracy, and democracy without the 'inconvenience of any one'.[3] After years of controversy and conflict, the Glorious Revolution of 1688 had finally succeeded in reconciling individual liberty and the rule of law and in exalting the claims of Parliament. For the men of the eighteenth century the peculiar merit of the post-1688 settlement was that it identified the 'rule of law' with the general laws of nature. The clockwork of the English Constitution was a domestic version of the clockwork of the Universe itself. 'It was at this era (1688)', wrote the well-known foreign constitutional commentator de Lolme, 'that the true principles of civil society were fully established.'[4] The Constitution enshrined them, and to understand their historical origins it was possible to go back long before 1688 itself to the constitutional ideas and practices of previous generations, to what David Hume called a happy series of accidents or what a later English commentator on the Constitution, Walter Bagehot, was to describe as 'a curious accumulation of medieval materials'.[5]

For the men of the 1780s the classical expositions of the contemporary English Constitution were to be found in Sir William Blackstone's *Commentaries on the Laws of England* (1765–9) and de Lolme's *Constitution of England* (1777). Both stressed the importance of checks and balances as guarantees of liberty.

[1] See J. Burgh, *Political Disquisitions* (1774–5). Cf. J. Cartwright, *Take Your Choice* (1776). 'Making our Parliaments *annual* and our representation *equal* can neither of them in any sense . . . be styled innovations. Both of them were the antient practice of the Constitution.'
[2] *The Trial of Henry Yorke for a Conspiracy* (1795).
[3] *XIX Propositions Made by Both Houses of Parliament* (1642).
[4] J. de Lolme, *The Constitution of England* (1784 edition), ch. III.
[5] W. Bagehot, *The English Constitution* (1867), ch. I.

Herein indeed consists the true excellence of the English government, [Blackstone wrote], that all the parts of it form a mutual check upon each other. In the legislature, the people are a check upon the nobility and the nobility a check upon the people . . . while the King is a check upon both, which preserves the executive power from encroachments. And this very executive power is again checked and kept within due bounds by the two Houses. Thus, every branch of our civil polity supports and is supported, regulates and is regulated, by the rest: for the two Houses naturally drawing in two directions of opposite interest, and the prerogative in another still different from them both, they mutually keep each other from exceeding their proper limits. . . . Like three distinct powers in mechanics, they jointly impel the machine of government in a direction different from what either, acting by itself would have done . . . a direction which constitutes the true line of the liberty and happiness of the country.[1]

Blackstone's praise of this system of limited and balanced power was shared by most continental jurists from Montesquieu to de Lolme. Many of them claimed that just because they were foreigners they could see even more clearly than Englishmen the constitutional reasons for the existence of that 'liberty' which Englishmen might easily take for granted. 'A stranger beholding at once the various parts of a Constitution displayed before him, which at the same time that it carries liberty to its height, has guarded against inconveniences seemingly inevitable . . . is struck with a kind of admiration', de Lolme wrote, 'and it is necessary to be thus strongly affected by objects to be enabled to reach the general principle which governs them.'[2] Perhaps he exaggerated the special capacity of foreigners to feel such strong affection: after all, it was Blackstone himself who maintained that 'the thorough and attentive contemplation of it [the Constitution] will furnish its best panegyric'.

The sophisticated as distinct from the public veneration of the Constitution clearly owed much to the dominance of law as the synthesizing element in the study of society. The publication of Blackstone's *Commentaries* preceded Adam Smith's *Wealth of Nations* (1776) by ten years, and had as great an influence on contemporaries. 'This legal classic', wrote one bright young man who had read the *Commentaries* four times before reaching the age of 27, 'is the poetry of law, just as Pope is logic in poetry.'[3] On the other side of the

---

[1] *Commentaries on the Laws of England* (1787 edn.), pp. 154-5.
[2] J de Lolme, *op. cit.*, Introduction.
[3] Quoted C. R. Fay, *Adam Smith and the Scotland of His Day* (1956), p. 96.

Atlantic too, as many copies of Blackstone had been sold in America as in England.[1] We are so used to thinking of economics as the synthesizing element in the study of society, and to underlining the importance of economic factors in both the maintenance of stability and the determination of change, that it now requires a great mental leap (in England at least) to return to the Age of Law and the dominance of lawyers inside and outside Parliament, in the service of the country house and in the ambit of government. It is impossible, however, to understand either the appeal of the English Constitution to educated men of the eighteenth century or the issues involved in the American Revolution without making that mental leap. To Blackstone it was 'the laws of England' which above all else were peculiarly adapted to the preservation of political and civil liberty, just as to the first Americans who murmured words of discontent, legalistic argument was more natural than general talk of political obligation or economic grievance. Jefferson was not exceptional when he justified the American position by direct appeal to Saxon precedent.[2]

Neither the neat picture of checks and balances nor the colourful picture of Saxon freedom and Norman (and eighteenth-century) yoke corresponded very closely to the facts. They were both myths, the one extolling order, the other directing discontent. But like most myths, they were not totally untrue and they both possessed great practical utility. The Constitution of England did serve, as flattering foreigners saw, to prevent England from becoming an absolute monarchy on the French or 'Turkish' model; there was a genuine relationship between law and freedom, which 1688 had helped to 'preserve'; there was no powerful bureaucracy; there was no English *droit administratif*, no *raison d'état* to override the common law or to intimidate judges and jurymen; there was no torture; above all, there was a permanent and stalwart parliamentary buffer against despotism, and a House of Commons which was never at any time empty of elements of opposition. When economic and political factors were weighed together in the same balance, it seemed apparent to sympathetic foreigners that progress and order both followed not from despotism but from freedom, that liberty not restraint cemented national union, and that individual enterprise,

[1] Long afterwards Carl Sandburg depicted Lincoln sitting barefoot on a woodpile in Illinois reading Blackstone.

[2] *A Summary of the Rights of British America* (1774). See also *The Commonplace Book of Thomas Jefferson* (ed. G. Chinard) (1926), pp. 64–5.

not government regulation nor bureaucratic favour, was the road to wealth.

Similarly, though some of the medieval materials employed in the justification of the cause of reform were very curious indeed, they were at least rich raw materials, rich enough to provide the basis for a gradual transformation of radical argument both in England and in the United States from the vindication of historic rights to the demand for natural rights, from talk of restoration of the ancient Constitution to insistence on a genuinely renovated Constitution. By the time that the radical debate shifted, largely as a result of the disturbing influence of industrial growth, the constitutional debate also was being contested in different terms. Eighteenth-century veneration of the law was giving way to pungent criticism of it, and writers like Jeremy Bentham were storming what Blackstone himself once called—with reference not to constitutional but remedial law—'the moated ramparts, the embattled towers and the trophied halls' of an old Gothic castle, erected in the days of chivalry but unsuited to modern inhabitants.[1] By that time also, political economists were coming into their own and approaching the central problems of society in a very different way from eighteenth-century lawyers. All these important transformations in thought and argument were taking place in the forty years from 1780 to 1820. They built a bridge between the eighteenth and nineteenth centuries.

In the 1780s themselves veneration of the historic Constitution —however it was interpreted—was still almost universal and the conception of balance was still the dominant orthodoxy. How far did image diverge from reality? Just how accurate was the mechanical analogy of checks and balances? There was certainly a mixed monarchy, whether the mixture was thought of in terms of monarchy, aristocracy, legislative and federative powers (Locke); of legislative, executive, and judiciary (Montesquieu); or in more concrete English terms of King, Lords, and Commons. According to the last of these analyses, power in England was distributed between King, Lords, and Commons, who together made up a 'supreme, irresistible, absolute, uncontrolled authority', but no single member of the trinity held power in isolation. Mixture, not

---

[1] *Op cit.*, book III, ch. XVII. In the index to Bentham's *Works*, the entries under 'lawyer' include 'the only persons in whom ignorance of the Law is not punished,' 'least of all men exposed to the operations of humanity', 'their interest in technical jargon'. See C. R. Fay, *Life and Labour in the Nineteenth Century* (1920), p. 39.

separation, was the essential characteristic of the functions of government, and 'the impulsion, the soul, the *spiritus rectus* of the British government'—as the *Annual Register* put it in 1807—'depends on the harmonious understanding and co-operating of its members.'[1] This harmonious understanding was dependent on practice rather than upon precept. Not only were the two known extremes of royal autocracy and single-chamber government abhorrent to eighteenth-century thinking about authority, but parliamentary government also could not exist in a developed working form (as the Victorians understood it, for instance) when there were neither organized political parties nor an independent civil service. The King still had to choose his own ministers: he lost his effective powers of choice only when party leaders, backed by parliamentary majorities, almost automatically became 'prime ministers' and when an independent civil service, deliberately kept outside the party fight, was in a position to maintain departmental continuity. In the late eighteenth century, whatever occasional flights of political rhetoric might suggest, the King really was in the middle of the political picture and not above it.

He was, however, compelled to choose his ministers from inside Parliament, and although they were not party leaders in any modern sense, dependent in the last resort on the pressure of opinion outside Westminster or on the efficiency of organized 'party machines', they could not afford to ignore parliamentary support. They were neither royal puppets nor parliamentary dictators. To control parliamentary support—they were never able to monopolize it—they had at their disposal a considerable though limited amount of public patronage—rewards, places, honours, and pensions—and they knew furthermore that the electorate, which lay in the background and was only intermittently and partially mobilized, was narrow and itself amenable to pressure. Thus, as agents of the executive, ministers always had to pay careful attention to the legislature. Had not the two elements in the mixed Constitution been glued together by patronage, the King's government could not have been carried on. Montesquieu's warning that 'England will perish when the legislative shall be more corrupt than the executive' was a misleading theoretical gloss, for executive influence in the Commons was a necessary feature of eighteenth-century government.

There was a further curb on ministers which, although it some-

---

[1] See B. Kemp, *op. cit.*, pp. 84–8.

times made for weak government, always led to open discussion. Ministers knew that whatever their tactical skill in enlisting parliamentary support, they would have to face an opposition in Parliament which depended not only on opinion but on its own private influence and patronage. 'The opportunity which Parliament affords to the young, the bustling, and the ambitious', one writer put it in 1784—with Pitt's blessing—'of canvassing public measures, is one of those salutary counterpoises which our Constitution affords against the weight of the Executive Power. The Opposition in Britain is a sort of public body, which, in the practice at least of our government, is perfectly known and established.'[1] It was not usually a compact opposition—the elements opposed to government were often only loosely and temporarily associated with each other —but it enjoyed great freedom to manœuvre without usually having to worry, as oppositions had to do in the late nineteenth and twentieth centuries, that if its case prevailed, it would have to provide an automatic alternative government. 'The province of this ex-official body', it was held, 'when it acts in a manner salutary to the state, is to watch with jealousy over the conduct of administration, to correct the abuses, and to resist the corruptions of its power.' There was an element of inhibition, of course, in such a definition of its duties, and Fox, who was vetoed by the King in and after 1784, would no doubt have preferred the occasional worry of office to the freedom to criticize on a very wide front.

Out of the battles between government, backed by loyalty and influence, and opposition, also backed by influence but sustained by indignation and reaching after new constitutional principles, the debate about the respective powers of King, Lords, and Commons took shape. It was one of the inevitable consequences of mixed government, as it operated in the eighteenth century, that there could be no precise *constitutional* formulae or even conventions to determine the exact quantum of power possessed by each element in the constitutional trinity. Instead there were persistent *political* conflicts, ebbing and waning with the emergence and interplay of personalities and with the pressure of events.

The American War had not only created a political atmosphere highly-charged with emotion but had entailed a succession of cir-

[1] J. Mackenzie, *History of the Proceedings of the Parliament of 1784* (1785). G. Rose, Pitt's patronage secretary, quoted this observation with approval in his important pamphlet, *Observations respecting the Public Expenditure and Influence of the Crown* (1810). For the limitation to the idea of opposition, see below pp. 112–13.

cumstances favourable to open discussion of constitutional powers and duties. Alongside trans-Atlantic disputes about common law and imperial relations, there were bitter domestic disputes about royal influence in Parliament. As individuals outside Parliament probed the working of the Constitution in an effort to discover the causes of lavish government expenditure, the high burden of taxation, and military defeats, dissatisfied members of Parliament and outsiders alike directed attention to 'the injurious, corrupt, and baneful influence of the Crown'. One group of the discontented pressed for a reduction of royal patronage through 'economical reform', another (overlapping) group for an infusion of independent electors to purify Parliament through parliamentary reform. Both groups, arguing in the name of a balanced Constitution, objected to a system whereby, in the Duke of Richmond's phrase, 'the King's will was the rule and measure of government'.[1] They talked of a betrayal of the Constitution of 1688 and were driven at times to stretch their interpretation of the Constitution to fit their immediate political purposes. Indeed a whole new interpretation of recent English history was advanced.

> The mild and seducing dominion of influence stole upon us [after King George III's accession in 1760] bestowing a greater and a more fatal authority than ever existed in the most arbitrary periods of the government. The gradual creation of a mighty revenue, rising up amidst the glory and prosperity of the Empire, undermined in a few years that nicely-poised Constitution, which unjust power, though exerted for centuries, had only served to strengthen and confirm. The Crown instead of being balanced and curbed in this House, had, during the greatest part of this century, erected its standard within these walls, and thrown the privileges of the people into the scale of the prerogative to govern the nation at pleasure without any control at all.[2]

Many nineteenth-century and some twentieth-century historians of the eighteenth-century Constitution took such interpretations and arguments as 'authoritative' and 'conclusive', particularly when they came from the lips or the pen of Fox. In fact, eloquent and emotive though they were, they were inflated and often inaccurate. At most, they demonstrated how vast were the regions of uncertainty and conflict in the mixed Constitution. On close scrutiny, the much-vaunted mechanical perfection of the eighteenth-century system of

[1] *P.H.* (1781) vol. XXI, p. 666.   [2] *Ibid*, (1797) vol. XXXIII, p. 654.

checks and balances looks instead like an uneasy flesh-and-blood struggle between often ill-equipped and frequently inconsistent antagonists. In a sense, however, liberty, if not the by-product of a balance, was still the by-product of the struggle, since the antagonists spent a considerable amount of time uncovering what they called the 'unconstitutional' intentions of their opponents and neither 'side' was in a position to press its own case to its logical limits.

In examining the older but persistent alternative terminology of balance—that based on monarchy, aristocracy, and democracy—there is the same divergence between ideal and reality. Lords and Commons were constitutionally divided, but socially compact. In both Houses the aristocratic element predominated. If the heads of families sat in the Lords, their younger brothers, sons, nephews and protégés sat in the Commons. Chatham had described the House of Commons as 'a parcel of younger brothers', and the remark was still relevant in the 1780s. The links between the two Houses went much further, however, than ties of kinship at Westminster: far away in the provinces, many of the lords as leading representatives of propertied influence controlled 'elections' to the Commons. In a list of borough patrons, drawn up in 1783, out of eleven men who controlled more than three seats, only four were commoners, and two out of the four were soon afterwards ennobled. This process of ennoblement of newcomers was itself of considerable significance in the late eighteenth century, for a seat in the House of Lords was a powerful attraction to many others besides borough-mongers.[1] It continued to remain so, even though the House of Commons became clearly the more important *political* forum with the greater constitutional weight, and even though from 1776 onwards there was a mounting radical assault on 'aristocratical tyranny' as well as Treasury influence. A petition from the reforming society, the Friends of the People, in 1793 claimed indeed that private patronage (150 M.P.s were elected through the influence of peers) was preventing the House of Commons from acting as a check on 'dangerous oligarchy' as well as on 'despotic monarchy'.

Looked at in the terms which it preferred, however, the House of Commons, with its initial advantages in relation to financial policy, could make much of its increasing political importance. Although an adverse vote—or even a series of adverse votes—in the House of

---

[1] Only in two years of Pitt's first administration—1795 and 1800—were no new peers created.

Commons might not necessarily lead to the fall of a ministry and an adverse vote in the Lords might do so, as in 1783—the Commons was growing stronger in the late eighteenth century because it was less subservient to the government of the day and had to be cultivated instead of commanded. In the formation of ministries, peers might make up the façade, but ministers able to win the goodwill of the Commons were most in demand. In other words, although the House of Commons might be socially 'a second-rate aristocracy', constitutionally it was either the key to smooth government or to constitutional conflict.

'Independence' rather than representation was the basis of its constitutional strength. The sovereign claims of the House of Commons were made in the 1780s against pressure from outside Parliament as much as against royal absolutism, and were sometimes stated with surprising frankness: in consequence, many of those who sought reform did so by emphasizing that their main objective was to make the House of Commons more 'virtuous', more independent of the Crown, not to make it more representative, more dependent on outside opinion. The 1780s were years of transition when there were a wealth of new arguments in favour of reform and considerable differences among the reformers themselves as to the proper relationship between the House of Commons and 'the People'. The internal divisions and conflicts on such issues are well illustrated from the history of the Yorkshire Association which posed the whole social and tactical problem of effective co-operation between 'a popular Party' in the country and the men of 'Virtue and just Political Principles' inside Parliament and within the ranks of 'the great body of Nobility'.[1] They can be illustrated too from a study of the evolution of Fox's ideas on the subject of parliamentary authority from 1780 to 1784. In 1780 the Westminster Committee had condemned 'as unconstitutional and of dangerous import to the country' a declaration of Lord North 'that the people of England could only be heard by their representatives in Parliament'. After he had opposed Pitt's dissolution of parliament in 1784 Fox was challenged by one of his opponents for no longer accepting the view of the Westminster Committee and setting up against 'the people' as a whole that same House of Commons which had been elected to support North in 1780. He was driven in reply to the argument that 'there were circumstances in which the people might

[1] C. Wyvill, *op. cit.*, vol. III, pp. 194–6.

err, and under such circumstances it became an act of duty to resist them'.

This was a congenial argument for most members of the House of Commons, who continued throughout the 1780s to exalt the claims of the House over the electorate, to express jealousy when constituents attempted to put pressure on them by instruction or agitation, and to view with alarm the growth of organizations outside Parliament which claimed to speak in the name of 'the people'. Although there were some defenders of an ideal House of Commons who still thought of it as a popular counterweight to aristocracy, most members agreed with a statement of Lord North in 1784 that

> Those gentlemen who hold that the instructions of the constituents ought on all occasions to be complied with do not know the Constitution of their country. To surrender their own judgements, to abandon their own opinions, and to act as their constituents thought proper to instruct them, right or wrong, is to act unconstitutionally. . . . They were not sent there, like the States General, to represent a particular province or district, and to take care of the particular interest of that province; they were sent there as trustees, to act for the benefit and advantage of the whole kingdom.[1]

There was no difference between this view and that of Edmund Burke, expressed in classic form in his speech to the Bristol electors in 1774. To him, as to North ten years later, Parliament was not a 'congress of ambassadors from different and hostile interests', but a 'deliberative assembly of one nation'. Local communities and the various 'ranks and orders' of the country were represented there, and not individuals, and there was no reason why Parliament could not virtually represent communities and 'ranks and orders' which lacked direct representation. The same point of view was argued confidently as late as the reform bill debates of 1830–2. 'Parliament', wrote Sir John Walsh in 1831, 'is the guardian of the interests, not the echo of the will of the people. It is composed of representatives, not of delegates.'[2]

Such a conception of the rôle of the House of Commons was far from democratic.'If government were a matter of will upon any side', Burke told his constituents in 1774, 'yours without question ought to be superior. But government and legislation are matters of reason and judgement and not of inclination.' Behind such a view there

---

[1] *P.H.* (1784), vol. XXIV, p. 988.
[2] *Popular Opinions on Parliamentary Reform Considered* (1831), p. 38.

sometimes lurked the shadow of a fundamental law anterior to the Constitution, a law which Blackstone, who had described King and Parliament as 'supreme, irresistible, absolute and uncontrolled', nonetheless believed set the framework for all parliamentary initiative. Sometimes the view was stated instead, as Burke stated it, in terms of historic and concrete rights, backed by the claims of reason and judgement. In neither case was there any leaning towards democracy. The nineteenth century was to create a Constitution designed to facilitate the expression of the popular will; the eighteenth-century Constitution was admired and defended because it succeeded in protecting men in the enjoyment of what was already their own. In relation to this basic purpose, the distribution of the franchise was considered primarily as a means; Robert Banks Jenkinson, later second Earl of Liverpool and prime minister from 1812 to 1827, put this point in unequivocal language—'we ought not to begin first by considering who ought to be the electors, and then who ought to be elected; but we ought to begin by considering who ought to be elected, and then constitute such persons electors as would be likely to produce the best elected.'[1]

It was not difficult to go on to argue from this point—the order of argument could equally well be, and was more frequently, taken in reverse—that only property-owners had a 'stake' in the Constitution, even to lay down with Lord Braxfield in 1793 that 'the landed interest alone has a right to be represented', and to conclude contemptuously, 'as for the rabble, who have nothing but personal property, what hold has the nation on them?'[2] King, Lords and Commons were all agreed about the dominance of property, however much they might disagree about their own relationships. Conscious of their stake in the Constitution, property holders were unwilling to convert their constitutional conflicts with the Crown into fundamental debates about natural rights and popular sovereignty. If the King was irritated by the pretensions of an aristocratic opposition, he was not tempted to prefer 'the multitude' to those with rank or landed property. If his opponents were prepared to turn towards the crowds when the occasion seemed propitious, to extol the claims of an 'aristocracy with popular feelings' they usually feared the mob and suspected 'the people'. Eighteenth-century politics moved in circumscribed circles, although

---

[1] *P.H.* (1793), vol. XXX, p. 810.
[2] *State Trials*, vol. XXIII, p. 231.

as we shall see, the circles had a dangerous habit of rippling further and further away from their centre.

3. POLITICAL PROCESSES

To understand political processes in the 1780s, therefore, it is necessary to relate the veneration of the Constitution to the organization of the social structure; governmental power was never used to challenge the natural social order, in which family, property, rank and intelligence were the attributes which counted. Outside Westminster this natural social order with its inherited hierarchy was the basis of local administration. It was the local Justices of the Peace rather than the Cabinet who symbolized 'authority' to most Englishmen, and in this view of the matter most Englishmen were right. England was 'governed' in the 1790s not by 'politicians' or by a civil service, but by a miscellaneous collection of unpaid local authorities, all of which, efficient or inefficient, gave a paramount place to rank and property. Indeed it was rank and property which conferred authority and not the other way round. The ideal of government was often expressed in terms that eliminated the need for a strong executive altogether; obedience and tranquillity were most effective when they depended not on means of compulsion or on the existence of administrative apparatus but on the natural social sanctions of a local community. When the social sanctions were inadequate the Justices combined judicial and administrative functions which gave them far greater local power than that wielded by ministers at the centre.

It is not surprising that against such a local background, most members of parliament at Westminster were not very active in taking up deliberate national political stances. There was a lively and at times dazzling minority of 'politicians' in Parliament, interested in tactics and anxious for office, and a serious and often industrious minority of 'administrators' interested in office and anxious to be left undisturbed in it, but there was a passive majority proud of the title of M.P. but only stirred into action in moments of emergency.

The tasks of the House of Commons as a whole were strictly limited. Although there was a large volume of private and local legislation in which particular M.P.s were directly interested[1]—

---

[1] The main work of preparing and presenting enclosure bills, for instance, fell on the county members, who were often chairmen of the relevant committees. Lord Edward Cavendish Bentinck, second son of the Duke of Portland, for example, presented or reported at least forty-four enclosure bills while M.P. for Nottinghamshire from 1775 to

Horace Walpole once complained that the House of Commons was becoming 'a mere quarter sessions, where nothing is transacted but turnpikes and poor rates'—general legislation was infrequent and certainly was not considered the most important business of the House. If the main duties of the government were to maintain law and order, to wage war and to conduct foreign affairs, the main duties of the Commons were to provide means for these necessary activities and to scrutinize them. In consequence there were regular debates in the 1780s about individual and civil rights, the handling of military, naval, and diplomatic issues, and the incidence of taxation. National politics centred on these themes, although the rhythms of economic expansion and contraction, the state of the harvests, and the vigour of platform agitation in London and the country prevented members of Parliament from being in sole control of their own timetable.

There were 558 members of Parliament altogether, including 45 from Scotland. They were all men of property—unless they were Scottish burgh members or English members who could evade the provisions of an Act of 1710. To be a county member it was necessary to have an assured annual income of £600 a year from land; to be a borough member, an income of £300. The members had been elected to Parliament, however, not on the basis of one uniform national system but on a variety of franchises. In the counties, represented by 122 members, by a law of 1430—a law much discussed in eighteenth-century constitutional controversy—the right to vote was possessed by everyone with freehold property (or certain other titles to possession) worth 40 shillings a year. In the boroughs, represented by 432 members, there was very great diversity of franchise, the right to vote usually depending not on statute but on historic practice and custom.[1]

At one extreme of the electoral scale there were boroughs like Aylesbury, where the right to vote was held by every 'pot-walloper' who was a master of his own fireplace and the pot on his hearth or who held the key of his own door: at the other extreme of the scale were the burgage boroughs, some of them extremely small 'pocket'

1796. See W. E. Tate, 'Parliamentary Land Enclosures in the County of Nottingham,' in the *Thoroton Society Record Series* (1935); 'Members of Parliament and the Proceedings upon Enclosure' in *Ec. Hist Rev.* (1942). For private bills in general, see F. Clifford, *A History of Private Bill Legislation* (1885).

[1] Oxford and Cambridge Universities each returned two members, bringing the total to 558.

or 'rotten' boroughs, where the franchise was restricted to owners or occupiers of certain houses, plots of land or property rights. The most notorious of these places was Old Sarum, a mound of earth without a house, where a solicitor handed the seven voters title deeds to local property just before they voted and immediately took them back again after the votes had been recorded. An American visitor noted in the early 1780s that an enterprising local family supplied the 'curious who visit there with punch, wine and tea'[1]; at election times it was necessary to erect a tent to shelter the returning officer and other officials. In addition to pot-walloper and burgage franchises, there were scot-and-lot electorates, as at Northampton, where all male householders who were not in receipt of poor relief were entitled to vote; freemen electorates, as at East Retford, where the franchise was limited to the freemen of the borough, whatever their title to that distinction (inheritance, marriage, nomination, apprenticeship, or plain purchase); and corporation electorates, as at Bodmin, where the members of the local corporation, itself a closed oligarchy, were the only voters.

The diversity of the borough franchise was less important in determining political behaviour than the size of the electorate and the almost universal dependence on patronage to make the political system work. In almost every place, 'influence' of one kind or another—the pull of government patronage, the claims of a local family, or the lure of money—governed the choice of members. The larger the electorate, the more difficult or at any rate the more expensive it was to control, whatever the formal terms of the franchise. The twenty boroughs with more than a thousand voters— Westminster with its electorate of 11,000 was outstanding—were the scenes of the most active late eighteenth-century election fights and the most open discussion of competing political claims. Sometimes, indeed, the electorates of these places tried to put pressure on their members, who were never in a position to take their constituents' support for granted. But not all relatively big constituencies were of this type. Preston, for example, which until 1786 lacked any sort of residential qualification, was in the firm grip of the local family, the Stanleys, although it was remarked that there was nothing to hinder a regiment of soldiers from marching into the town one night and voting at an election the next morning. Basically, the demand for bribes and favours was as substantial in relatively large consti-

[1] S. Curwen, *Letters and Journals* (1783), p. 67.

tuencies as in small ones, the only difference being that in the former the demand was more difficult to satisfy. In the twenty-six English boroughs with 500 to 1,000 voters, control was more manageable, although considerable amounts of money had to change hands to appease electors who knew that their support might be critical. This range of constituencies included some safe government seats, such as the 'naval boroughs', where the government had substantial patronage at its disposal, and many seats where private patrons could exercise a dominant influence.[1] It was in the smallest boroughs, however, the vast majority of the constituencies, that the pull of ownership and influence was most marked. In the tiniest of them, particularly those where ploughed fields, disused salt pans or heaps of stone were more conspicuous than flesh-and-blood voters, both vote and seat tended to be treated rather like an advowson, as a valuable piece of real property. This same conception of seats and votes as property can be traced in newspaper advertisements offering whole 'boroughs' for sale at election times. Selling seats continued until 1807, the last general election before an Act of 1809 made the practice illegal; selling the property controlling the return of members continued after that date. Such sales were, however, the exception not the rule, and in most constituencies voters required some manipulation. There were towns, like Bath, where there was a notorious thirst for independence; others where 'party spirit' was traditionally strong. Well-known 'politicians' tended to gravitate towards those constituencies which had a reputation for openness and conflict, just as would-be ministerial administrators gravitated towards the safer seats. The former wanted the acclaim of their constituencies, the latter any safe borough where there was little electoral concern for the candidate's 'popularity'. It was characteristic of Fox that in 1780 he gave up Midhurst, a burgage borough, which his father and uncle had hired from a well-known boroughmonger in 1768, and turned to the turbulent and 'popular' electors of Westminster. Ministers too were often prepared to spend considerable sums of money to try to win open constituencies and to prove that the public was on their side. In 1780, for example, over £8,000 of government money was spent in vain at Westminster, £4,000 in Surrey, and more than £4,000 in the City of London.

[1] At the other extreme was Sudbury, 'as open as the day and night too, and it is hard to say who may come in'. Quoted W. T. Laprade (ed), *The Parliamentary Papers of John Robinson, 1774–1784* (Camden Society, 1922).

It has sometimes been argued, as Pitt did in introducing his reform proposals in the 1780s, that the counties were more 'pure' than the boroughs, and that it was there that the real centres of independence —alike of Crown and of aristocracy—could be found. In fact, the aristocracy was strong in most counties,[1] although it was often split into two opposing 'sides'. Some counties like Norfolk and Suffolk were regarded as pre-eminently independent; others like Yorkshire and Middlesex included large urban elements. There was no basic difference in political behaviour between the counties and the boroughs, although there were complications caused by distance and the size of the electorate. Because many county seats were risky and expensive to hold, 'politicians' were wise to shun them, unless like Wilberforce in 1784 they were making a bold bid to advertise their strength. In 1786, for example, Lord Buckingham wrote to his brother that a county seat was such a nuisance to 'a political man' that it would be better to abandon it and to buy something cheaper in a borough. Certainly office-holders, who had to vacate their seats on election to new offices, were bound to find most county seats far less congenial than such boroughs as William Pitt's Appleby, one of Sir James Lowther's group of Cumberland 'ninepins', where there was never any need to make an appearance in the constituency.

The disturbance and expense of elections—Lord Penrhyn spent £30,000 in 1790 in an unsuccessful attempt to control Liverpool, where there were 1,967 freemen with the right to vote—always encouraged electoral compacts, compromises, and local understandings. The number of contested elections was never more than a small fraction of the total. In the counties it was usually only when the great local families disagreed that there was a contest and 'party feeling' was roused, and in most cases in both boroughs and counties what struggle there was took place over nomination, not election. In many of the boroughs, elections were prized as unparalleled opportunities for excitement and profit, rather than as occasions for carefully-weighed political choice. As William Cobbett wrote of Honiton in 1806: 'After . . . I addressed . . . the people of the place, telling them how wicked and detestable it was to take bribes, most

---

[1] 'The idea I gave Lord Rockingham of this county' (Nottinghamshire), wrote a correspondent of Lord Rockingham in 1769, 'was, four Dukes, two Lords, and three rabbit warrens, which I believe, in fact, take in half the county in point of space.' Albemarle, *Memoirs of the Marquis of Rockingham and his Contemporaries* (1852), vol. II, p. 138.

of the corrupt villains laughed in my face; but some of the women actually cried out against me as I went along the streets, as a man that had come to rob them of their *blessing*. The whole of the inhabitants of this borough, the whole of the persons who return two members to Parliament, are bound together in an indissoluble chain of venality.'[1] The electors of Honiton were lucky to be able to count their blessings; in many smaller boroughs, elections were completely dispensed with, and the flow of influence moved unchecked, certain and direct.   Few members found it necessary to anticipate the methods of their successors and indulge, as did Robert Maxwell in 1784, in 'a good deal of smoking, some drinking, and kissing some hundreds of women' in order to win their seats, although the Duchess of Devonshire had more than her fair share of electioneering at Westminster in 1784.

It is not surprising that since the electoral system operated in such a rough and turbulent manner, members of Parliament laid more emphasis on the deliberative than on the representational aspect of their assembly. The memory of the venality of the electorates could be drenched in eloquence or idleness with only the fear of a dissolution of Parliament to revive it. In most cases, members were only loosely attached to their constituents and to the House itself. It was a common occurrence, for instance, for members in the Army and Navy to go on service abroad, or for civilians to accept overseas appointments and still retain their seats; there was even 'an instance or two of individuals who, having been elected, have never appeared at the table even to take the oaths'.[2] Some members never saw their handful of electors even at election times, and some borough-owners, afraid of the creation of a rival 'interest', even went so far as to stipulate that their nominees should not go near their constituencies. As elections drew near, of course, there was some quickening of interest, while in the very big or distinctive constituencies, with a network of local interests to protect and often a considerable volume of local legislation to sponsor, representatives were called upon to give their regular time and service. In most cases, however, members of Parliament devoted as much energy to the work of Parliament as they themselves and not their constituents deemed expedient.

Relations between borough-owners or patrons and members of

---

[1] *Cobbett's Weekly Political Register*, October 1806.
[2] *Hansard*, 3rd series, III, 106, 107.

Parliament were sometimes as casual as relations between constituents and members. There were some patrons like Lord Sackville in 1784, who left his nominee free to vote as he wished; sometimes they enabled bright young men to enter the House of Commons early. Usually, however, they insisted on their nominees following the broad outlines of their own inclinations. Fox was exaggerating when he laid it down as a general rule in 1795 that if a nominated member 'dares to disagree with the duke or lord or baronet whose representative he is, then he must be considered as unfit for the society of men of honour',[1] but there were many nominees to whom the rule did apply with the rigidity of a code. When members of Parliament gathered at Westminster, many of them were no more free in the expression of their opinions than the limited electorates which nominally had elected them. Certainly at least a half of the Commons were 'tied' in various ways. In 1783 John Robinson estimated that there were only 178 'hopefuls' and 'doubtfuls' out of the 558 who could not be placed in any definite category: he expected that there would be 182 of them after the forthcoming election.[2]

Among the 'hopefuls' and 'doubtfuls' were a group of genuine independents, men who demanded favours neither from the government nor from their patrons. Most of them could be included in the group of 'country gentlemen', the most independent of them claiming, like Richard Wilbraham Bootle, M.P. for Chester from 1761 to 1790, that 'he attaches himself to no party, but is governed in the vote he gives, by the unbiased suggestions of his judgement, and the fair operation of that influence only which originates in the several arguments he hears.'[3] In normal times, such men were jurymen rather than politicians, 'watching over the conduct of those who exercise the functions of executive Government' rather than being employed or wishing to be employed 'in exercising those functions themselves'.[4] In times of abnormal strain and uncertainty, they might be compelled to act in concert and to take political decisions of their own; this was the case in the Parliament of 1780–84, when they helped first to get rid of Lord North in 1782 and later in 1784 tried to bring Pitt and Fox into the same broad-based government.[5] They felt more clearly than any other group

---

[1] P.H., 1793, vol. XXXII, pp. 728–9.
[2] W. T. Laprade, *op. cit.*, pp. 66–105.
[3] Quoted by Sir Lewis Namier, *Personalities and Powers*, pp. 60–61.
[4] The language is that of R. B. Jenkinson, second Earl of Liverpool. Quoted *ibid.*
[5] See above, p. 82.

the disadvantage of 'faction', and for all their concern about Crown influence were at one with George III in believing that factious grouping was one of the most serious abuses of the Constitution.

It is difficult to discuss the parliamentary political process in the 1780s without using the emotive term 'faction'.[1] In fact the relations between different parliamentary groups were complicated and deserve to be approached from more than one angle. Members of the House of Commons could be sub-divided (with the virtuous independents left on one side) into a cluster of 'confederacies by which knots of men struggle in a body for places'. But alongside the confederacies or 'connexions', there were 'interests', groups of members concerned not so much with securing office as with safeguarding the interests of social or economic groups with which they were associated. The 'connexions' were not parties, although they were sometimes more than 'factions'; particularly in the case of the Rockingham Whigs who were in power immediately after the fall of Lord North, they were feeling their way towards party arguments which would justify their cohesion, their public spirit and their national loyalty. Edmund Burke, their main spokesman, went out of his way to defend 'party', claiming that in civilized societies it was a natural development, grounded in instinct and affection and elevating in its effects on the individuals who composed it. His definition of party was, however, not so much a description of the practice of his day as a statement of an ideal type: 'a body of men united, for promoting by their joint endeavours, the national interest upon some particular principle in which they are all agreed'.[2] In practice, there were no parties which lived up to this ideal, and Burke himself did not scruple to support the Fox-North coalition of 1783 and 1784 or to appeal to higher claims than party in 1790. As 'party' shaped the nineteenth-century Constitution it took on a different form from Burke's image; in the late eighteenth century the main appeal of 'party' was in the constituencies, where the familiar party labels and colours of 'Whig' and 'Tory' were used to divided the electorate at contested elections. Once assembled, members, whatever their local colours, were bound together not by party discipline but by kinship, friendship, patronage, shared tactics

[1] 'Tho' a little faction now and then gives spirit to the nation,' wrote Adam Smith, 'the continuation of it distracts all public business and puts it out of the power of the best Minister to do much good.' Quoted by W. R. Scott, *Adam Smith as Student and Professor* (1900), p. 241.
[2] *Thoughts on the Present Discontents* (1770).

(and if there was time, strategy), hopes of office, usually in coalition with other groups, and response to genuine leadership.

The 'interests' often cut across the blurred boundaries of 'connexion', or alternatively were used by particular 'connexions' to add to their strength inside and outside Westminster. Among those 'interests' which always had to be taken into account in eighteenth-century politics were the East India interest, the West India interest, the Dissenting interest and the City interest; among the interests without capital letters were those of government contractors, anxious to share the tangible spoils of administration, groups concerned with canals, turnpikes and local improvements, and in the 1780s industrialists, such as cotton manufacturers and iron founders, concerned in a period of economic change to influence government policy. The 'interests' were no more parties than were the 'connexions', indeed, in most respects they were less so, but in their choice of tactics and their capacity to organize they sometimes pointed forward to the politics of the future. The independent country gentlemen, who for all their independence, rightly considered themselves to be the pillars of the oldest and most 'natural' interest of all, 'the landed interest', were just as averse to the pressure-group tactics of bodies like the General Chamber of Manufacturers, set up in 1785,[1] as they were to embryonic party tactics on the part of the most ambitious 'connexions'.

Against this background of parliamentary groupings, the tasks confronting the King in recruiting ministers and securing parliamentary support can be more easily understood. He could rely on the regular service of a number of 'placemen', some of them public servants, but he had to depend also on support from members of the active political 'connexions' and from the 'independents'. From his point of view, such a situation was usually fraught with difficulties. Co-operation between members of different 'connexions', which was usually necessary in order to secure a parliamentary majority, could only be achieved after negotiation. Before a new ministry could be formed, the King—usually acting through intermediaries like the Lord Chancellor—and the political groups had to confer; there was often intricate discussion of personalities and sometimes of policies. Particularly during the last years of the American War and in the critical period between 1782–4, some of the policies being discussed by the politicians were the reverse of the policies desired

[1] See below, pp. 116–17.

by the King. In such circumstances, although the ministers of the King might still properly be regarded as his 'servants', they were claiming some of the rights of members of a modern cabinet, free to determine their own programme of action in a way that they had never been before. In consequence the King, who disliked 'politicians' and did not think in political terms, contended that it was they and not he who were tampering with the Constitution. Lord Shelburne backed him up on this point as Pitt did later. If the King were not to be allowed to choose his own ministers, Shelburne maintained, he would 'resemble the King of the Mahrattas who had nothing of sovereignty but the name'. Charles James Fox, as we have seen, advanced exactly the opposite thesis. If he had had his way, the King's powers would have been exercised, as in the twentieth century, only through ministers, and the 'mixed Constitution' would have been converted into ministerial government.

The parallel with the twentieth century, however, is extremely misleading. To have introduced 'parliamentary government' on a modern model in the 1790s, four absent conditions would have been necessary—a more effective party mechanism than existed in 1784, both inside and outside Parliament; a more effective contact between 'ministry' and 'opinion' which would have permitted alternating party rule; a civil service outside politics which would have ensured administrative continuity; and, above all, a pliant monarch who was prepared to surrender in a few months to a few men rights which were to take years of constitutional change to corrode and to destroy. Merely to state the four conditions is to reveal the enormous gulf between the eighteenth and twentieth centuries. Fox had no clear idea of party; he did not see the benefits of alternating governments, and held that a permanent administration would be 'an amazing advantage' to the country in the 'opinion of Europe' [1]; he had no civil service at his disposal and all the embryonic civil servants were on the 'other side'; and he was confronted by a King who had only accepted him as a minister under duress with the burning desire to get rid of him as soon as possible. The most that Fox could have achieved had his constitutional ideas been pushed to the point of realization would have been a revolution; the least would have been a perpetuation of aristocratic oligarchy, tempered by benign gestures in the direction of the people.

As it was, the political and constitutional conflicts of the 1780s led

[1] *Correspondence*, vol. II, p. 208.

eventually neither to the victory of Fox nor, as seemed more likely in 1784, to the victory of the King. It took decades of gradual change to produce what Sir Winston Churchill has called 'the most deeply founded and dearly cherished' of all national institutions, constitutional monarchy. There was such a complicated interpenetration of ideas and movements in the history of constitutional monarchy that it is quite impossible to isolate one single cause or to point to one specific moment of decision; all that can be said, somewhat tritely, is that the ultimate 'settlement' (if it is a settlement) lay not in logic but in the course of events. To nineteenth-century writers the main difference between the constitutional history of England and the United States was that 'England and her institutions have gone through the purifying furnace of time'.[1] Furthermore, though many people deemed it 'impious and sacrilegious' to tamper with the Constitution, neither Pitt nor Fox during the 1780s accepted the 'finality' of the Constitution. Pitt was willing to investigate 'remedies', and Fox still maintained as he had done in one of his first speeches that 'the greatest innovation that could be introduced into the Constitution of England was to come to a vote that there shall be no innovation in it'.[2]

In the last two decades of the eighteenth century and the first twenty years of the nineteenth century, the relevant factors making for change were the increasing incapacity of the monarchy, the growing importance of differences of opinion about public policy, the greater differentiation of social and political interests, and the improved organization of 'public opinion'. Together with the gradual reduction of patronage which began modestly with Burke's limited attack on sinecures in 1782 (in the name of the 'independence' of Parliament) and was followed up far more successfully though more indirectly in Pitt's chain of economic and administrative reforms (in the name of more effective government), they reduced the influence of the Crown without destroying it. The number of government beneficiaries was drastically reduced both inside and outside Parliament, and although there was an increase in the number of 'working placemen' (including junior ministers) in the House of Commons, the 'spirit of internal reform' led to the gradual abandonment of many of the earlier eighteenth-century anti-placemen cries. The money influence of the Crown which played a

---

[1] A. Crump, *A Short Enquiry into the Formation of Public Opinion* (1888).
[2] *Speeches*, vol. IV, p. 410.

part in maintaining ministerial majorities in 1780 and 1784 had been largely destroyed by 1815. The power of exerting influence through government contracts, which was so important in the middle years of the century, was checked by Pitt's introduction of the system of open bidding, and in 1793, when war broke out, he transferred the buying of army provisions to the victualling commissioners who had previously been concerned only with naval provisions, and set up a separate Transport Board. The political manipulation of government loans was abandoned so boldly that Pitt's obvious willingness not to pull strings but to 'excite competition among monied men' to bid for stock won even the rare approval of Fox. The number of sinecures was reduced (765 revenue offices were abolished in 1789 and another 196 in 1798),[1] and though Pitt created ninety-two new peers and made generous use of political honours, this 'disproportionate' allotment of titles was, as Burke saw, partly the result of other reforms 'having deprived the Crown and the minister of so many other services of recompense or reward'.[2] Not all patronage was destroyed. There were still many means of influence open, but patronage in itself was ceasing to be the only cement which held the English political system together, and before long politicians and political commentators alike were talking of the problems created by its reduction rather than of the greater measure of 'independence' which had been secured.

The King too, for different reasons, was being taken out of a considerable section of the political arena. George III's madness in 1788–9 was merely the prelude to a series of illnesses which reached a climax in 1811 when his son took over the full powers of the sovereign. It was inevitable long before 1811 that the King should neglect business of state and live on his prejudices rather than on his intelligence. He was able to get rid of Pitt in 1801 and to force his ministers to follow his wishes on the single issue of Catholic emancipation partly at least because they knew that if they mentioned the subject another brainstorm might follow.

The withdrawal of the King need not, however, be explained simply in such terms. Although Pitt was the King's servant in the

---

[1] For the history of patronage, which still needs more detailed study, see the very useful article by A. S. Foord,' The Waning of the Influence of the Crown' in *E.H.R.* (1947) and G. Rose, *op. cit.* For the difficulties of giving (or interpreting) exact statistics see B. Kemp, *op. cit.*, pp. 107–8.

[2] Rose claimed that Burke's act of 1782 suppressed 134 offices and Shelburne's reform of 1782–3 another 144, but that 62 new offices had to be created, making a net suppression of 216.

1780s, he was necessarily bound to concern himself with many topics of government which the King had neither the inclination nor the ability to handle. They included some of the most important business of state. By 1784 there was a regular place in the Constitution for an 'efficient Cabinet' consisting of leading ministers, to debate such business, and for a 'chief minister' who, in a phrase of Lord North, 'should plan the whole of the operations of government'.[1] Because of the necessity for managing the House of Commons and maintaining control over diminishing patronage, it was increasingly necessary for this 'chief minister' to be First Lord of the Treasury. Relations between King and cabinet had still not crystallized, however, in any generally accepted set of constitutional principles. The King had the right to demand the cabinet's advice, but the cabinet in turn could consider matters without reference to him, even though the King sometimes queried the practice, and there was legitimate doubt as to how far he was expected on all occasions to take cabinet advice.[2] The task of King and cabinet together was to ensure that the 'King's Government' went on. Not only was this task held to be more important than the drafting of new legislation, but agreement about legislation was not considered to be the test of cabinet solidarity. While ministers might be permitted to disagree about legislative proposals—as Pitt was to do with many of his colleagues in the case of issues as important as parliamentary reform and the abolition of the slave trade—they had to stand together as closely as they could in the day-to-day tasks of administration. It was because his Lord Chancellor, Lord Thurlow, did not do this—nor could he be trusted on big issues, like the Regency Bill—that Pitt was able finally to force him out of the cabinet in 1792.

Not the least important reason for cabinet solidarity was the presence in the House of Commons of elements of opposition to the government. Although, as we have seen, the idea of an opposition—with limited duties—was beginning to establish itself, particularly among the independent men in the House of Commons, there was a feeling that certain kinds of opposition—withholding supplies, for example, or protracted resistance to government—were

---

[1] For an objection to the use of the term *'prime* minister' in 1783—by the Duke of Grafton—see W. R. Anson, (ed.) *Autobiography and Political Correspondence of Augustus Henry, Third Duke of Grafton* (1898), pp. 359-61.

[2] See A. Aspinall, 'The Cabinet Council, 1783-1835, in *Proceedings of the British Academy*, (1952).

not respectable. It was only when 'ministers' seemed to be behaving 'unconstitutionally' that constitutional opposition was fully justified: on other occasions, it could be condemned in the words of Charles Abbot, as 'teasing, barking, cavilling and unprincipled'. Abbot, who did not enter the Commons until 1795, declared that he would always support the minister of the day, 'be he Pitt or Fox; for to me they are as indifferent as Pompey or Caesar'.[1] Even among the dissatisfied political groups themselves, who had a vested interest in 'differences', there was a tendency in moments of difficulty either to withdraw from politics altogether and retire to social or local pursuits or to pin hopes of power not on Parliament but on the Prince of Wales. This second avenue of opposition was not open to the political opponents of George III until 1783, for until then the young Prince George was a minor without a 'court' and with no power; perhaps, in consequence, some of the most daring new theories of 'opposition' were advanced during this period. But from 1783 onwards the 'King to Come' cast his shadow over opposition tactics. Such alignments, which often seemed to justify the identification of 'party' with 'faction', were inevitable when there was no formal machinery of alternating party rule, and connexion and interest counted for more than issues and organizations. There was little chance of the identification ceasing to be accepted until ·the political problems of society became real and not rhetorical, and outside 'opinion' expressed itself clearly at Westminster.

There were signs of both of these last two developments during the period of Pitt's administration. There was a difference of tone between the Parliaments of the 1780s and those which had gone before—new voices were heard and new arguments were being advanced, particularly about economic matters. The 'general public' outside Parliament—Burke estimated that it totalled more than 400,000 people[2]—became better informed about the activities of 'politicians' at Westminster by reports in the press, the organization of propaganda outside the House, and ultimately by the publication of the proceedings of parliamentary committees of enquiry.[3] When Pitt became prime minister, the annual sale of newspaper stamps was double what it had been thirty years before,

---

[1] Abbot became Speaker of the House of Commons in 1802, and retired as Lord Colchester in 1816.
[2] *Works* (1854), vol. II, p. 289.
[3] See A. Aspinall, 'The Reporting and Publishing of the House of Commons Debates' in *Essays Presented to Sir Lewis Namier* (1956).

and by 1793 it had risen again by almost a third.[1] Journalists, who were admitted freely to the House after 1778, were allowed to take notes from 1783 onwards, and by that time the first collections of *Debates* were being published. There was a rise in the volume of reading matter about politics at the same time that there was a burst of platform agitation. For the first time it began to be plausible to make a distinction between 'popular clamour' and 'public opinion'[2] and to organize opinion not only through recognized constitutional bodies but through specially created societies and associations.

During the critical years of the American War expressions of disapproval of official policy were voiced by two main agencies—established municipal corporations (and institutions associated with them) and county meetings. The City of London in particular had played an important part in eighteenth-century politics, and between 1720 and 1782 its Common Council, dominated by small merchants, tradesmen and master craftsmen, was associated almost continuously with opposition to the governments of the day. The parliamentary opposition recognized the importance of attracting the support of City organizations. As Burke remarked, 'we know that all opposition is absolutely crippled if it can obtain no kind of support without doors'.[3] County meetings summoned by the sheriff also had a status and sanction of their own. The only people normally entitled to speak and vote at these assemblies were the freeholders of the county,[4] but in the darkest years of the American War attempts were made by Christopher Wyvill and the Yorkshire Association (there were 16,000 freeholders in Yorkshire) to organize county meetings throughout the whole of the country, to appoint standing committees, and to maintain a central committee to direct the movement for reform. Wyvill's scheme collapsed but the meetings continued, and addresses both from county and from municipal bodies were the main props of Pitt's ministry before the general election of 1784.

There were three other main channels of 'opinion' in the 1780s—reform societies, voluntary organizations devoted to 'causes', and specially created bodies designed to protect 'interests'.

The Society for Constitutional Information was a good example

[1] R. D. Altick, *The English Common Reader* (1957), p. 48.
[2] W. A. Mackinnon, *On the Rise, Progress and Present State of Public Opinion* (1828 edn.), pp. 17 ff.
[3] See the detailed study 'The City of London in Eighteenth Century Politics,' by L. S. Sutherland in *Essays Presented to Sir Lewis Namier*.
[4] B. Keith Lucas, 'County Meetings,' in the *Law Quarterly Review* (1954). Far more detailed work on the history of the meetings still remains to be done.

of the first. Founded in 1780, with one of its main aims the free distribution of reform tracts, it included many men of 'rank and consequence'. At its annual dinner in 1782 toasts were drunk to Magna Carta, 'the majesty of the People' and 'America in arms, Despotism at our feet'. Dr. Jebb, one of its extremely able leaders, believed not only that 'equal representation, annual parliaments and the universal right of suffrage' were 'alone worthy of an Englishman's regard' but that vigorous and carefully planned public agitation was indispensable to the achievement of these objectives. It was the business of reformers, he argued, 'not to prevail with the deputies but to animate the people'.[1] Although the activities of the Society were suspended during most of the subsequent decade, it prepared the way for many similar bodies to come. The 'Revolution Societies' founded in 1788 to celebrate the centenary of the Glorious Revolution owed much to its example.

Among voluntary organizations devoted to a cause, the anti-slavery movement was outstanding. Its religious background has already been touched upon[2]: equally important was its form of organization and the methods it adopted. In 1787 a committee of twelve was appointed, including six Quakers who had set up a committee of their own four years previously. Its task was to procure and publish 'such information as may tend to the abolition of the slave trade'. Behind the committee was a Quaker organizational system which went back deep into the seventeenth century[3]; ahead of it was a sustained agitation which was to be proclaimed by Richard Cobden as a model. Fox and Pitt both agreed with its objectives, but since some of the most powerful economic interests of the day opposed them, it had to concern itself from the start with direct political action. There was an extraordinary criss-crossing of motives and aspirations, 'connexions' and 'interests' in the early history of the anti-slavery question. Alderman Sawbridge, for example, one of the most zealous of London reformers, who moved annual motions in the Commons in favour of shorter Parliaments and was a prominent member of the Westminster Committee, asserted in 1788 that London would be ruined if there were any

[1] J. Disney (ed.), *The Works and Memoirs of Dr. John Jebb* (1787), vol. 1, p. 161.
[2] See above, p. 71.
[3] The Meeting for Sufferings was founded in 1675, and it was this Meeting along with the Committee of six, which published *The Case of our Fellow-Creatures, the Oppressed Africans* in 1784. In the early years of the eighteenth century, it was the Quakers who pointed to all future organizational activities by developing a 'general correspondence together'.

tampering with the slave trade.[1] The failure of Pitt to carry a measure
of abolition shows as clearly as his failure to carry a measure of
parliamentary reform the complexity of political processes in the
1780s. In both cases, the reasons for his lack of success lay in the
fact that Parliament was essentially a chamber not of 'parties' but of
'interests'. In the one case, the strength of the slavery interest was
strong enough to hold back the victory of ideals. In the other case,
the view that Parliament safeguarded the general defence of interests
as a whole was an obstacle to reform, for it could still be pleaded by
all the anti-reformers that the House represented 'virtually' every
interest outside it and had no need of organic reform. It took time
and careful organization for a 'moral movement' of the kind
associated with Clarkson and Wilberforce to achieve its objectives,
just as it took many years for representatives of the new 'industrial
interests' not directly represented in the House of Commons to
come to the conclusion that they could best serve their purposes by
pressing for parliamentary reform.

An attempt was made in the mid-1780s to associate manufacturers
in various parts of the country to defend their industrial interests.
As early as April 1784 Manchester and Birmingham manufacturers
were pressing for a united front and Wedgwood proposed that
'Committees of Commerce, already established in several parts of
the kingdom' should unite together to persuade other towns and
cities to set up similar organizations. A 'general correspondence'
should be established and 'a delegate or delegates from each of them
should meet annually, or at stated times, as often as may be found
necessary, at some central place'.[2] It was not until 1785, however,
that as a result of Pitt's commercial policy the manufacturers united
to form a General Chamber of Manufacturers. 'Common danger',
they said, had induced them to forge a 'general band of union'
whereby the influence and experience of the whole being collected
at a common centre, they will be the better enabled to effect any

[1] R. Coupland, *The British Anti-Slavery Movement* (1933), p. 38. See also F. E. Hyde,
B. B. Parkinson and S. Marriner, 'The Nature and Profitability of the Liverpool Slave
Trade' in *Ec. Hist. Rev.* (1953).
[2] Wedgwood MSS, 18,959. The reason given for common action on this occasion
was to 'prevent the emigration of workmen into the service of foreign manufacturers'.
Already Manchester had taken the lead in opposing Pitt's cotton and linen taxes, and
the General Commercial Committee set up in Birmingham in 1783 was seeking to
correspond with 'commercial chambers in other places'. In November 1784 the Staffordshire potters got together to form 'a standing Body invested with powers to act as
occasion required in the Conduct and Protection of its Public Interests and Concerns'.
Minutes, 1784–90. MSS. 28,404–39.)

useful purposes for their common benefit.'[1] Although the Chamber secured the support of powerful manufacturers in many parts of the country—Boulton, for example, in Birmingham and Thomas Walker in Manchester—the price of its nation-wide organization was an inner conflict of interests which ultimately led to its demise in 1787. To understand that inner conflict it is necessary to turn back to the policy of Pitt as prime minister between 1784 and 1793. Before doing so, however, two points about the Chamber must be noted as portents of the future. First, it was proud. Second, it was misunderstood by 'politicians', including Pitt himself. 'The manufacturers of Great Britain constitute a very large, if not a principal part of the community', their sketch plan began, 'and their industry, ingenuity and wealth have contributed no small share towards raising this kingdom to the distinguished and envied rank which she bears among the European nations.' Pitt, who believed that the interests of the manufacturers 'merited every respectful attention', nonetheless dismissed their organization 'as a few manufacturers collected in a certain Chamber of Commerce', and accused them of wandering into the 'paths of legislation and government'.

Thwarted pride in an 'interest' could relatively easily be converted into consciousness of 'class', and the wandering into the 'paths of legislation and government' was not a desultory and agreeable amble, but the start of a journey which was to take the manufacturers far away from their factories in the nineteenth century. During the debates of 1830–32, while Wellington was still proclaiming the Constitution as the most excellent possible, more acute observers of the social scene were noting how the constitutional structure was losing its traditional hold with 'every increase of our decennial census . . . every mile added to our roads and canals . . . every new sail that entered our docks . . . (and) every additional chimney that waved its sable pennon over the roofs of Birmingham and Manchester.' There was a gulf between 1784 and 1832, but the first bridges were already being constructed while Pitt and Fox were still wrangling about 'secret influence' and the royal prerogative.

4. PITT AND THE NATIONAL REVIVAL

The main achievements of Pitt's administration between 1784 and 1793, the outbreak of the war with revolutionary France, were

[1] *Sketch of a Plan of the General Chamber of Manufacturers of Great Britain*, 4 June 1785 (MSS. 31,314–27).

fourfold—the restoration of the national finances, the carrying out of important administrative reforms, the reorganization of British imperial commitments, and the rehabilitation of Britain in Europe. All four tasks were of the utmost urgency and any government which hoped to survive had to do something about them. Pitt, despite many weaknesses and some inadequacies, was able to do a great deal, and his record fully justifies the title of J. Holland Rose's well-known book, *Pitt and the National Revival* (1911). The prime minister was not directly responsible, of course, for the accumulation of capital, the rise of exports, and the general business prosperity which quickly wiped out the economic losses of the American War, but at least he did nothing serious to impede these signs of renewed economic vitality. He professed himself a disciple of Adam Smith and warned against the effect of 'some public calamity' or 'some mistaken policy' on the well-being of the country.[1] He set an example of absolute integrity and of unremitting industry and preached as strict an economy in the public service as Gladstone was to do in the middle of the nineteenth century. Indeed the Victorians of 1853 felt that they could pay no higher compliment to Gladstone than to say that he was 'the phoenix Chancellor—Mr. Pitt risen from his ashes'.[2] They were wont to trace a line of descent from Pitt through Huskisson and Peel to Gladstone which to them at least would have justified treating the period covered in this book as a completed unity.

Pitt's most remarkable pre-war budget speech was that delivered in 1792, when he surveyed the whole of his work down to that date and related economic achievements to their constitutional background. Comparing the position in 1791 with that in 1783, he showed that the annual governmental revenue had increased by little less than £4 million (about a quarter of the 1791 figure) between the two dates. Of the total increase, about one-quarter was the product of new taxes, about a quarter was gain from the prevention of smuggling and fraud, and the remaining half was the consequence of increasing national income.

It was not difficult to claim considerable credit for all four improvements. Pitt was one of the most ingenious tax-gatherers ever to govern England, beginning in 1784 with taxes on such varied items as horses, hackney coaches, windows, bricks, hats,

---

[1] *P.H.*, vol. XIX, p. 134.
[2] Quoted J. Morley, *Life of Gladstone* (1908 edn.) vol. I, p. 350.

ribbons, and candles, and in 1785 trying to levy a tax on shops. In the budget of 1784 he estimated that he would raise an additional £930,000 by new taxation alone: in 1785 the figure was £400,000. Naturally he was at times unpopular for his taxation policy.

> One would think there's not room one new impost to put
> From the crown of the head to the sole of the foot.
> Like Job, thus John Bull his condition deplores,
> Very patient, indeed, and all covered with sores.

Pitt's window tax was condemned in York as 'impolitic, compulsory, oppressive and unjust', and a projected tax on coal was withdrawn—as was the shops tax—because opposition was too great. Taken as a whole, the taxation policy was sensible, but Pitt not only became unpopular but made mistakes. The window tax not only acted as a penalty on light and air, but held back the progress of the glass industry. The tax on linen and cotton in 1784 was a serious economic mistake and, although Pitt had the sense to withdraw it later, the fact that he levied it at all showed that his understanding of the needs of the new industrial sector of the economy was strictly limited.

The prevention of smuggling and fraud was pure gain except to the smugglers. In order to curb extensive smuggling, Pitt introduced restrictive legislation, the most important example of which was the 'Hovering Act' authorizing the confiscation of certain kinds of vessels built for smuggling purposes and other vessels carrying contraband articles found at anchor or 'hovering' within four miles of the coast. More important, he made the occupation of a smuggler unprofitable by reducing import duties—that on tea, for example, from 119 per cent to 12½ per cent—and extended the excise system, as Walpole had intended to do in 1733, to articles like wine and tobacco.

As far as the increase in public revenue created by new national income was concerned, Pitt could claim somewhat ambitiously that his enlightened commercial policy was a necessary pre-condition of the growth of industry and trade. The value of imports which in the last year of the American War amounted to less than £10 million had doubled by 1790. The value of exports had risen from about £12½ million in 1782 to over £20 million in 1790. Despite this expansion of trade Pitt was unsuccessful in one of his two major ventures in international commercial policy and had only a brief and temporary success in the second. A free trade treaty with Ireland which he proposed in 1785 created such a storm in England that he had to modify his original proposals. In their modified form they were rejected by the Irish Parliament in August 1785. A commercial treaty with France, which was concluded in 1786, had useful results (it led to considerable imports of French wines, which hitherto had been taxed more heavily than Portuguese) but it was rendered ineffective by the outbreak of the French Revolution. On the occasion of both sets of treaty negotiations the industrialists and manufacturers expressed their interest in Pitt's proposals—indeed, it was because of the Irish proposals that the General Chamber of Manufacturers was formed—but whereas they opposed the Irish treaty almost unanimously, they were divided about the treaty with France. Old-established manufacturers still wanted protection: new industrialists were prepared to put their trust in a common market. While the silk manufacturers, the paper makers, and the leather producers were attacking the treaty, Manchester businessmen were drinking to 'the prosperity of free trade, wise government and constitutional revenue'[1] and in Birmingham metal finishers were singing

> And whilst mutual friendship and harmony reign,
> Our buttons we'll barter for pipes of Champaigne.[2]

Pitt's policy in relation to both Ireland and France was opposed on opportunist and political grounds by Fox and his supporters. During the debates on the French treaty, indeed, the Foxites showed themselves to be violently anti-French. Fox himself did not share the mercantilist view that only one country (France) could gain an advantage in a reciprocal treaty of that kind, but preferred instead to criticize in general terms French 'overweening pride and national aggrandisement'. He even went so far as to say that 'France is the natural political enemy of Great Britain'.[3] When after the Revolution had broken out he began to exhibit pro-French sympathies he claimed that his attitude was completely consistent and that before 1789 he had been attacking not the French but the Bourbons. All that is certain is that on both occasions he was attacking Pitt, and that in 1786 he had no reasonable alternative policy to put forward.

[1] *Manchester Mercury*, 15 May 1787.
[2] J. Langford, *A Century of Birmingham Life* (1870 edn.) vol. I, p. 229.
[3] Pitt replied that 'to suppose that any nation can be unalterably the enemy of another is weak and childish'.

Whatever the merits and disadvantages of the Irish and French commercial treaties, Pitt was right when he claimed in his speech of 1792 that 'the security and prosperity of England, the solidarity of credit, the rapid increase of capital, and the rapid expansion of industry' were all 'necessarily connected with the duration of peace'. He declared that the perpetuation of peace 'on a secure and permanent footing must ever be the first object of the foreign policy of this country' and expressed his conviction that 'the season of our severe trial is at an end'. It was an unfortunate prophecy, for the French War was just around the corner and the trial was just beginning. By then, however, Britain's recovery was complete despite financial and economic strains in 1792 itself. 'This island', wrote a pamphleteer in 1792, 'separated from the great continent of Europe possesses more wealth and power and enjoys more tranquillity and freedom than any of those immense nations that people this most important part of the globe.'[1] The contrast between British financial successes and French financial disasters was an important clue to the difference in political features of the two countries. There is an element of truth in the dictum that 'it was arithmetic that saved Great Britain from revolution: it was arithmetic that condemned her neighbour'.[2]

Just as important to Pitt as the expansion of trade and the growth of wealth and power was the reduction of the national debt. At the end of the American War, the debt stood at what seemed to be the prodigious sum of £238 million. Between 1786 and 1793 Pitt managed to cut it by over £10 million. In 1786 he started a sinking fund for the specific purpose of reducing the debt, hoping thereby to offer relief from the 'endless accumulation of taxes'. An independent body of commissioners was to employ £1 million annually for the purchase of government stock, and the accumulation of compound interest on their holding was to be used for the extinction of the national debt. The outbreak of the French wars changed the situation. Not only was the government accumulating a giant new war debt —it took Pitt several years to re-adapt the tax structure to military and naval needs—but because of war expenditure there was an annual budget deficit instead of the surplus of pre-war years. Rather than suspend the sinking fund Pitt preferred to borrow money at a high rate of interest to reduce a debt which paid a low rate of interest. It

---

[1] W. Playfair, *Inevitable Consequences of a Reform in Parliament* (1792).
[2] P. W. Wilson, *William Pitt* (1930), p. 168.

was an unwise policy which had an element both of high moral resolve and of economic absurdity about it. Public credit was maintained, but there were unnecessary and expensive complications. During the years 1793–1815 a total amount of £578 million was raised by the creation of funded debt; of this, £81 million was handed over to Pitt's Commissioners for the Reduction of the National Debt for the purpose of buying up some of the stock which had just been created.[1]

Almost all the financial reforms which Pitt introduced—wise or ill-conceived—owed much to the inspiration of other people. In this respect there is an interesting parallel between Pitt's achievements and those of Peel in the 1840s. Neither statesman was an innovator. Pitt's very first act—the raising of a loan to meet the immediate deficit of £6 million by turning not to privileged subscribers but to public tender—was anticipated by similar procedures in the victualling office of the army and in the ordnance office. His attack on fraud and evasion followed the recommendations of the Revenue Frauds Committee. His ideas on the sinking fund were influenced not only by Dr. Richard Price, the author of well-known tracts on the subject,[2] but by the eleventh report of the Commissioners for Examining the Public Accounts of the kingdom, a most important investigating body appointed in 1780, which in all presented fifteen reports during six and a half years of extremely thorough investigation. 'To them', F. W. Chisholm, the author of the classic Victorian parliamentary paper on *Public Revenue and Expenditure* (1869) remarked, 'the public are mainly indebted for the many reforms which have taken place since that period'.[3]

The reform of financial and fiscal arrangements—in the name of the 'Principle of Economy'—necessarily entailed the reorganization of the cumbrous and ill-adapted system of administration. Pitt, following the advice of the Commissioners and to some extent lines of action already suggested by his predecessors, made important contributions to the settlement of outstanding problems. He abolished numerous sinecures and abstained from making new appointments when vacancies arose. He devised the conception of

---

[1] See for contemporary criticisms, R. Hamilton, *An Enquiry concerning the Rise, Progress, Redemption, Present State and Management of the National Debt* (1813).

[2] *An Appeal to the Nation on the Subject of the National Debt* (1772): *The State of the Public Debts and Finances* (1783).

[3] For an understanding of the work of this body I am much indebted to Dr. J. E. D. Binney, whose unpublished Oxford thesis *The Public Revenue and Expenditure of Great Britain and its Administration, 1774–1792* is an indispensable and detailed source.

a modern budget by creating a consolidated fund into which revenue received from taxes was paid and out of which government payments were made. He established the Audit Office, consisting of a board of five salaried commissioners who took over the work, staff, and books of the older auditors of the imprest. He gave additional work to the under-employed Board of Stamps and went on considerably to rationalize its functions. He set up a Stationery Department to supply other public departments with articles which had previously been bought at a high cost from several different agencies. If there were signs in the last years of his administration that he was slackening in his zest for reform—and signs even in the earlier years that he effected little without the spur of publicity to push him on—he was coping with tasks that demanded exceptional vigour as well as full knowledge.

In relation both to the administrative system and to the organization of his cabinet, Pitt was the man who counted. His views on the proper rôle of the prime minister, though, as we have seen, they left no place for claims against the King,[1] certainly magnified the conception of the office and had more in common with the views of Peel than with those of his predecessors: it was absolutely necessary, Pitt believed,

> that in the conduct of the affairs of this country . . . there should be an avowed and real minister possessing the chief weight in council and the principal place in the confidence of the King. In that respect there can be no rivalry or division of power. That power must rest with the person generally called the First Minister; and that minister ought . . . to be the person at the head of the finances. . . . Notwithstanding the abstract truth of that general proposition, it is no ways incompatible with the most cordial concert and mutual exchange of advice and intercourse amongst the different branches of the executive departments; but still, if it should come unfortunately to such a radical difference of opinion that no spirit of conciliation or concession can reconcile, the sentiments of the Minister must be allowed and understood to prevail, leaving the other members of administration to act under such circumstances.[2]

Such a view, implying departmental co-ordination and the ultimate subordination of his colleagues, reflects Pitt's sense of administrative priorities. He was never a party leader in the modern sense of the

---

[1] See above, p. 84.
[2] G. Pellew, *Life and Correspondence of Lord Sidmouth* (1847), vol. II, p. 116.

word. Although eventually he inspired a strong sense of party among some of his young protégés like Canning and Huskisson, at the end of his first seventeen years of office he had no more than fifty or sixty personal followers. What he had done, however, was to accustom his generation to a high standard of administrative and financial competence. 'Everything that drops from him', Huskisson noted, 'is . . . marked by superior virtue and superior sense.'[1] That Huskisson shared Pitt's view of governmental priorities is borne out in a draft note of 1811 when he expressed a 'firm conviction' that the office of chancellor of the exchequer would not be adequately maintained unless 'this office, united to that of First Lord of the Treasury, is held by the person who leads the House'.[2]

Huskisson was drawn into Pitt's service in 1793 not as a potential future chancellor of the exchequer, but as a clerk 'to read and digest French documents and to see . . . French emigrants'. He thus got to know Pitt only at the turning point of his career—the switch from peace to war. By that time Pitt, for all his hopes of peace, had put Britain in a far stronger position to wage a long war than would have been thought conceivable ten years earlier. In a speech as chancellor of the exchequer in February 1783 Pitt himself had painted in dismal colours the state of Britain and the Empire. The fabric of naval supremacy, he declared, was 'visionary and baseless'; as far as the army was concerned, '3,000 men were the utmost force that could have been safely sent from this country on any offensive duty'; the 'memorable era of England's glory' was in the past and 'she is (now) under the awful and mortifying necessity of employing a language which corresponds with her true condition; the visions of her power and pre-eminence are passed away.'[3] Scarcely had the peace with America been signed, however, than Britain began to count again both in the Empire and overseas. Before long, great economic prosperity, based in part on the continued development of trade with the former American colonies, made many of the doubts and anxieties of the early 1780s wither away. It was a sign of the continued interest in the distant world that Oxford set as the subject of its Latin poem in 1786 'Captain Cook', and that a geographical writer in 1787 could claim that 'the latest Discoveries appear to engross conversation from the politest circles and throughout every

---

[1] Quoted C. R. Fay, *Huskisson and His Age* (1951), p. 71.
[2] A. Aspinall, *Letters of George IV* (1938), vol. I, p. 107.
[3] For this speech and the reaction to it, see C. Whibley, *William Pitt* (1906), pp. 48 ff.

class in the Kingdom'.[1] Not only was Britain's economic power mounting each year, but her future naval power was strengthened by such vital improvements as underwater protection which was made possible by the copper sheathing of ships' bottoms and, just in time, the use of English oak once more instead of the Prussian timber which had been employed as a last resort between the Seven Years War and the War of American Independence. Although for some years Pitt did little to build up the navy, and on the declaration of war with France the effects of 'economy' were still revealing themselves, between 1790 and 1793 there was great activity in the dockyards and by the end of 1792 more than sixty of the eighty-seven ships-of-the-line were in good condition.[2] Sir Charles Middleton, who was comptroller of the navy from 1778 to 1790, had introduced many useful reforms, and struggled hard to free naval tactics from the archaic and rigid 'fighting Instructions' of the late seventeenth century. His work bore fruit during the course of the French wars.

Pitt's interest in some of the important residual tasks of empire is well brought out in two pieces of legislation. The secretaryship of state for the colonies had been abolished in 1782[3], but the empire was not abolished with it. While one empire was being lost in the West, Warren Hastings was saving British power in the East, and Cornwallis was still to have a distinguished imperial career ahead of him before he died in 1815. The trial of Warren Hastings (1788–95), which revealed the worst side of many of the British parliamentarians of the day, was less important in the history of India than the carrying of a new India Bill in 1784 by Pitt, this time in agreement with the East India Company. While leaving the Company's control of patronage and appointments intact, it followed Fox's bill in creating a Board of Control in London, two of the members of which had to be cabinet ministers. It was the duty of the board to approve all political despatches and to issue orders through a secret committee of the directors. In India itself the power of the Governor General was strengthened both by the act of 1784 and by subsequent legislation, and although there were many strains, the new system of Indian government remained in operation until 1858. Cornwallis and Wellesley, Pitt's first nominees, launched it with efficiency and vigour.

[1] T. Bankes, *Universal Geography* (1787), p. 9.
[2] See W. James, *The Naval History of Great Britain* (1860), vol. I, p. 53.
[3] See M. A. Thompson, *A Constitutional History of England, 1642–1801* (1938), p. 439.

Pitt went on in 1791 to give a new foundation to government in Canada. The Canada Act placed all the responsibility for Canadian government on the ministry and Parliament in London, but at the same time it set up representative assemblies elected by a restricted franchise in two newly created Canadian provinces—Upper Canada, with its predominantly British stock, and Lower Canada with its French settlement. The system which divorced power from responsibility was to create growing difficulties in the early nineteenth century, but it lasted until the 1840s.

Both in India and in Canada Pitt was anxious to uphold what he regarded as the best principles of the British Constitution. 'Though the constitution of our Eastern possessions is arbitrary and despotic', he declared during the debates on Warren Hastings (which ended in 1795 with Hastings's acquittal) 'still it is the duty of every administration in that country to conduct itself by the rules of justice and liberty, as far as it is possible to reconcile them to the establishment.' In the case of Canada, he said that it was his wish to make the Canadian government as 'near as the nature and situation of it would admit to the British constitution'.[1]

In Europe, too, Pitt had done much by 1793 to rehabilitate the reputation of his country in the eyes of the world. In 1783 Britain was isolated, and while there were differences of outlook and interest between the allies who had leagued against her during the American War, they were agreed in wishing to prolong that isolation as long as possible.

Pitt's biggest single diplomatic triumph after 1784 was the recovery of the Dutch alliance which had been lost four years earlier when the United Provinces joined the United States and France. The Dutch alliance was important to him not only for European reasons, because of Britain's traditional strategic interest in the Low Countries, but because he feared that the French were anxious to control the Dutch in order to be able to tap the riches of the Dutch East Indies. As a result of the clever tactics of the British ambassador at the Hague, Sir James Harris, the ambitions of the pro-French 'Patriots' in Holland to overthrow the hereditary Stadholderate of the House of Orange were checked. Harris built up a pro-British party in Holland, and when in 1787 the Patriots arrested the Stad-

[1] For an interesting comment, see G. S. Graham, *Canada* (1950), p. 93. 'The parallel between the British and Canadian constitutions resembled Shakespeare's celebrated comparison of King Henry V with Alexander the Great: "There is a river in Macedon. and there is also moreover a river in Monmouth . . . and there is salmons in both".'

holder's wife, the sister of the new King of Prussia, the Prussians co-operated with the British. The resistance of the Patriots crumbled at once and the position of the Stadholder was reaffirmed. The successful outcome of the intervention in the United Provinces was the signing in August 1788 of a defensive Triple Alliance between Britain, Prussia and Holland. Both Fox and Burke welcomed the renewal of Continental connexions and the restoration of the international balance which had been shattered by the American War. 'The councils of England', wrote a pamphleteer, 'conducted on principles, not of a crooked duplicity but of rectitude and magnanimity, excited respect and approbation in the surrounding states, while they diffused prosperity and felicity over every part of the island.'[1] The French, however, were left with a feeling of bitterness which undermined the goodwill Eden had been able to secure during the course of his negotiations about the Anglo-French commercial treaty. There is good reason for regarding the eventual signing of the Triple Alliance as 'an introduction to the greater conflicts of the French Revolution'; it not only added to pressing French problems but provided 'good soil for the growth of revolutionary hatred of England'.[2]

There was a further diplomatic victory for Britain after the French Revolution had broken out. In 1790 the Spaniards took possession of a small natural harbour, Nootka Sound, off Vancouver Island in the Pacific, where an English trading settlement had been established two years before. The British government repudiated the claim of the Spaniards to control all territory washed by the Pacific as far north as 60° latitude, and appealed to its new allies for support. Unable to secure the backing of the French revolutionary government in Paris the Spaniards were isolated and had to back down. It was a small incident, but it demonstrated that Britain was once more in a position through the force of its arms and the support of its allies to resist hostile claims.

The re-forging of continental connexions had its dangers as well as its advantages, and between 1788 and 1791 the international situation was increasingly complicated not only by the French Revolution but by moves further east. The alliance with Prussia brought with it the possibility of Britain being drawn into the complicated and interdependent diplomatic entanglements of Russia,

[1] *A Sketch of the Reign of George the Third From 1780 to the Close of the Year 1790* (1791), pp. 83–4.   [2] A. Cobban, *op. cit.*, p. 213.

Austria, Sweden, Poland, and Turkey, and in particular of incurring the enmity of Russia. It had been possible in 1787 for Britain and Prussia to assert themselves successfully in Holland because the Russians and Austrians had just begun a war against the Turks, and France, unwilling to join them, was completely isolated not only in Holland but in Europe. Britain was not alone in welcoming the freedom of action open to her in that year. Sweden too saw the opportunity of recovering South Finland from the Russians, thereby threatening a Baltic war which would have upset Pitt's desires for the perpetuation of European peace. By the end of 1791 the position had changed. Britain's freedom of action and the unity of the Triple Alliance had both been destroyed. Suvorov, the Russian general, had gained decisive military victories over the Turks, and driven Pitt to fear an enormous increase of Russian power in Europe. Pitt's efforts to check the Russian successes failed ignomiously however, and when he tried to prevent Catherine the Great from annexing the key Turkish fortress of Oczakoff, he faced the resolute opposition not only of Russia but of the 'party' of Burke and Fox at home. There was a moment of danger to his government and a hint of the battles to come about the Near Eastern question in the nineteenth century.[1] Pitt's enforced retreat led inevitably to another shift in the policy of the Prussians who realized the limitations of the alliance with England and prepared themselves to concede Russian claims in Turkey in order to gain territorial concessions from a weak and withered Poland. From the end of 1791 onwards the way was being prepared for the last partitions of Poland between Russia, Prussia, and Austria in 1793 and 1795, the final act of eighteenth-century diplomacy before the map of Europe as a whole was changed by the wars of the French Revolution.

[1] Burke, speaking on the same side as Fox in a foreign affairs debate almost for the last time, asked what other rôle the Turks could play in Europe but to 'spread war, destruction and pestilence' among the great powers. Whitbread held that Russian rule in Constantinople would conduce to 'the prosperity and happiness of the world'. Pitt strongly supported Turkish power and authority.

3

THE IMPACT OF WAR

1. ENGLAND AND THE FRENCH REVOLUTION

FEW societies have been more secure in the belief that they can control their own destinies than the English, particularly the self-confident society of the late eighteenth century. Although the American Revolution had divided and embittered English politicians and created domestic situations of acute tension, and the industrial revolution was posing problems which were to generate new bitterness, the course of events between 1783 and 1789 suggested that the years of crisis were being forgotten. 'The varied and accumulated misfortunes which for a long series of years oppressed, and had almost overwhelmed the commonwealth, were already erased from the recollection. A mild and happy calm had smoothed these troubled waves.'[1] There was bitterness in the rivalry between Pitt and Fox and signs of dispute and conflict in politics outside Westminster, but it seemed as if the consequences of these internal differences would be settled by Englishmen in their own way. Instead, events outside England, the French Revolution and its Napoleonic aftermath, dictated much of what happened inside England in the long period from 1789 to 1815. The way into the nineteenth century led across the battlefield as well as through the cotton mill and the iron foundry. As the Whig lawyer, Cockburn, remarked, 'everything was connected with the Revolution in France, which for twenty years, was, or was made, all in all, everything; not this thing or that thing, but literally everything was soaked in this one event.'[2]

The immediate reaction of most well-informed Englishmen to the fall of the Bastille in 1789, the abolition of French feudal

---

[1] *A Sketch of the Reign* (1791), p. 84.
[2] *Memorials of his Time* (1856), p. 80.

privileges, and the establishment of a new constitutional monarchy
was not unfriendly. George III recognized the hand of justice in the
enforced limitation of Bourbon power: had not the French king
allied himself with republican rebels during the American War?
Pitt, preoccupied with the problems of peace and anxious to find
time to solve them, looked forward to the establishment in France
of a stable regime which would provide Frenchmen with the same
beneficial fruits of freedom as Englishmen: 'the present convulsions
in France must sooner or later culminate in general harmony and
regular order . . . and thus circumstanced, France will stand forth as
one of the most brilliant powers of Europe. She will enjoy just that
kind of liberty which I venerate.'[1] Most of Pitt's political opponents
were genuinely enthusiastic about the prospects, identifying or at
least mixing up in their minds the events of 1789 with the familiar
English themes of the centenary of the Glorious Revolution of
1688. Fox, indeed, considered the fall of the Bastille as 'much the
greatest event that ever happened in the history of the world' and
the draft of the new French Constitution as 'the most stupendous
and glorious edifice of liberty which has been created on the
foundations of human integrity in any time or country'.[2] Only
Edmund Burke from the start thundered against the 'abominable
sedition' and 'distemper' on the other side of the Channel and stated
unequivocally that if the French 'should perfectly succeed in what
they propose, as they are likely enough to do, and establish a democracy, or a mob of democracies . . . they will establish a very bad
government—a very bad species of tyranny.'[3]

Outside parliamentary circles, particularly among radicals who
longed for change and nonconformists who were sharply conscious
of civil disabilities, the private and public language of welcome was
unrestrained. In the Potteries Josiah Wedgwood saluted 'the
wonderful revolution' which threw 'the political world off its
hinges' and inaugurated a new age of enlightenment and wisdom;
in Manchester Thomas Walker, appointed a boroughreeve in 1789,
echoed Fox and exclaimed that the French had 'displayed to the
world the glorious example of renouncing all schemes of ambition
and arousing a system of universal benevolence'.[4] In London, the
veteran dissenting minister, Richard Price, who had been prominent

---

[1] Quoted by Lord Rosebery, *Pitt* (1891), p. 120.
[2] *Speeches*, vol. IV, p. 200.
[3] *Substances of the Speech on the Army Estimates* (1790).
[4] *Review of Some Political Events in Manchester* (1794).

in the attack on the conduct of the American War, thanked God publicly that the people of France were 'starting from sleep, breaking their fetters, and claiming justice from their oppressors'.[1]

The joy of dissenters and radicals, violently condemned by Burke, was shared by poets and intellectuals—a significant partnership, since in the nineteenth century poetry and nonconformity were to point in opposite directions. Blake wore the red cap of liberty in the London streets; Burns, an excise officer, sent guns to the Convention in Paris; Coleridge, a schoolboy at Christ's Hospital, wrote eager verses on the fall of the Bastille; Wordsworth, aged 19, went over to France and revelled in

> . . . a time when Europe was rejoiced,
> France standing on the top of golden hours
> And human nature seeming born again . . .

Southey who, like Wordsworth and Coleridge, was to pass from delight in revolution to resistance against all revolutionary theories and practices, recalled in 1824 how on the outbreak of the Revolution 'old things seemed passing away, and nothing was dreamt of but the regeneration of the human race'.

Such optimistic enthusiasm expressed itself not only in poems and in sermons, but in the revival of old clubs, and the growth of new clubs and associations. The Revolution Society, which met in 1788 to celebrate 1688, sent a congratulatory address to the French in 1789 and urged that 'the two first kingdoms in the world' should together promote the common cause of freedom. In April 1792 a group of advanced young Whigs, including Charles Grey, a confident young aristocrat, formed the Society of the Friends of the People; Fox was not a member, but he did not wish to discourage the enthusiasts who were pressing for 'more equal representation of the people in Parliament'. A less exclusive body, the Society for Constitutional Information, inspired by Horne Tooke and meeting in the Crown and Anchor Tavern, sprang into life again in 1791 and looked to the French example.[2] By stressing the need for buttressing 'the fellowship of the People', it soon broke with the more oligarchic organization to which Grey belonged. In the provinces, in places as far apart as Stockport and Norwich, Coventry and Sheffield, reform and sometimes republican societies were set up. When the

---

[1] *A Discourse on the Love of our Country* (1789), pp. 50–51. Price, an economist (see above, p. 122), could not resist the temptation to mix statistics and rhetoric.
[2] For its earlier history, see above pp. 114–15.

sequence of events in France[1] began to alarm more orthodox Englishmen of a very different mould from Burke, the members of these active groups often turned further and further towards French ideas and institutions. In January 1793, for example, long after the French had overrun Belgium and the September massacres had shaken Paris, the London Society for Constitutional Information elected St. André an honorary member, and followed this up with the election on 1 February of Roland and Barrère. The news was proudly proclaimed to the world for all to know. Members of the provincial societies often called each other 'citizen', and one of the societies even planted a tree of liberty. When radical sympathizers were not looking direct to Paris they looked enthusiastically towards Tom Paine, the honorary French citizen, and author in 1791 of the most famous of the thirty-eight critical replies to Burke's *Reflections on the Revolution in France* (itself a reply to Price). Paine's stress not only on the rights of man but on the conflict between social needs and governmental tyranny shocked many old English parliamentary reformers like Christopher Wyvill, who feared 'wild work' and the rise of a 'lawless and furious rabble',[2] but it excited the new reform groups in the cities. The sale of his *Rights of Man* was estimated at 200,000 copies in 1793. 'We declare', the Sheffield Society for Constitutional Information declared characteristically, 'that we have derived more knowledge from the Works of Mr. Thomas Paine than from any other author or subject.'[3]

The most interesting and significant of the reform societies was the London Corresponding Society, formally founded by Thomas Hardy, a shoemaker, in January 1792. It appealed to working people and consisted largely of them. Unlike other bodies, it charged its members only 1d. a week, with 1s. entrance fee (the annual subscription for the Society of the Friends of the People was a guinea and a half). It was organized into divisions or branches, meeting weekly, each division sending two delegates to its General Committee which also met weekly. It corresponded with similar societies in places outside London—Sheffield, Manchester and Leeds, for example,

---

[1] June 1791, Louis XVI's unsuccessful flight to Varennes; August 1792, his imprisonment; September 1792, the Paris massacres; January 1793, the execution of the King; July 1793, the Terror.
[2] Quoted G. S. Veitch, *The Genesis of Parliamentary Reform* (1913), p. 206.
[3] *Second Report of the Committee of Secrecy appointed by the House of Commons* (1794), Appendix C. After Paines' prosecution for seditious libel his sales increased further. One Scots bookseller sold 750 copies in a week. See P. A. Brown, *The French Revolution in English History* (1918), p. 84.

among the new industrial towns, and Rochester, Bath and Tewkes-
bury in the older England of the south and west. For its zeal in
mobilizing opinion Burke described it as 'the Mother of all Mischief'.
Certainly its ideas were diametrically opposed to those of Burke.
Hardy and his friends emphasized the conflicting interests of
aristocracy and democracy, and proclaimed the solidarity of English
reformers with the French revolutionaries. They concerned themselves not only with political questions of taxation and representation
but, through their outside contacts, with social questions—the
restoration of common land in the village and the reduction of long
working hours in the industrial towns. In their *Address to the People*
in August 1792 they promised 'taxes diminished, the necessaries of
life more within the reach of the poor, youth better educated,
prisons less crowded, [and] old age better provided for.'[1]

They thus pointed the way forward to the development of working
men's politics in the nineteenth century, particularly to Chartism,
although their main strength lay in small independent craftsmen—
weavers, watchmakers, cordwainers, and cabinet makers—and
radical shopkeepers and booksellers.

So strong was the energy and emotional drive behind the radical
ferment of 1792 and early 1793 that it seemed as if the whole pace
of English political argument and agitation would be speeded up.
In fact, however, it was soon to be slowed down. The main effect
of the French Revolution was not to revitalize English politics at
the base of society but to encourage repression from above. By
January 1793 an English Jacobin was remarking that he found it
'prudent to say as little as possible upon political subjects, in order
to keep myself out of Newgate'.[2]

The change can be accounted for in three ways. First, the radical
societies, however enthusiastic, were very much minority societies,
and the feelings of the majority were still easily stirred up by talk
of the 'machinations' of dissenters, the sedition of intellectuals, and
the evils of the French. A significant portent of the balance of
popular feeling was the rioting in Birmingham in 1791. Joseph
Priestley, the Unitarian minister and scientist, who had moved from
Leeds to Birmingham in 1789, had already alienated much local
opinion by his *Familiar Letters to the Inhabitants of Birmingham* in
1789. In July 1791 when Birmingham sympathizers with 'the ideas

[1] *State Trials*, vol. XXV, pp. 590–2.
[2] *Letters of Joseph Ritson* (1833), vol. II, p. 7.

of 1789' set about celebrating the anniversary of the fall of the Bastille,[1] the Birmingham mob went into action and in two days rioting demolished or damaged as many houses of the 'damned Presbyterians' as they could find. The cry of Church and King proved a good rallying point to flay the friends of the Revolution, and George III wrote to Dundas that he could not but feel pleased that Priestley was the sufferer for the doctrines 'he and his party have instilled'. The Birmingham reaction was not an isolated one. In many parts of the country, the same violent expressions of feeling were demonstrated. There were, as Wilberforce remarked later, 'Twenty King's Men to one Jacobin'.

The second reason for the change in approach was the successful imitation of methods of radical organization by the friends of the established order. In November 1792 John Reeves, a lawyer just back from Canada, founded the Association for Preserving Liberty and Property against Republicans and Levellers. It had a room in the Crown and Anchor just above the room where the Constitutional Society met. The new Society was organized to secure the suppression of seditious publications, to convince the public that radical measures being canvassed by 'perverted men' were against the interests of the country, and to set up similar bodies in the provinces. It was successful in all its aims within the next year. A large number of 'groups' were organized in the provinces and dozens of anti-reform tracts were published, including Hannah More's *Cheap Repository Tracts* which have been properly described as 'Burke for Beginners'. The government supported such zeal and initiative besides initiating propaganda of its own. In May 1792 it issued a proclamation against seditious writings. More positively, two new ministerial newspapers were founded and free copies were provided to co-operative provincial weeklies. The intelligence service was strengthened and loyal agents were appointed to ferret out examples of sedition.

Undoubtedly the third reason which made majority opinion swing away from reform ideas and made the government turn towards repression was the course of events in France, which Burke and his friends considered to be 'inevitable', part of a cycle of revolution, terror, dictatorship, and aggression. The September massacres and the trial and death of Louis XVI made many young reformers think again. As the Whig Samuel Romilly put it, 'One might as

---

[1] Priestley himself, fearing local disturbances, did not attend the reformers' dinner; indeed, he tried to persuade them not to hold it.

well think of establishing a republic of tigers in some forest of Africa as of maintaining a free government among such monsters.'[1] Jacobinism in France and an active French foreign policy in Europe 'worked a great change in the public mind in this country'. In April 1792 France declared war on Austria. In November, the French government openly proclaimed a broader international policy in a famous decree inviting all the peoples of Europe to revolt and offering them French assistance; in the same month General Dumouriez occupied the Austrian Netherlands and announced the opening of the River Scheldt. It was not surprising that the pacifist Pitt, who in his budget speech earlier in the year had looked forward to 'fifteen years of peace', should begin to see in French 'annexationism' a threat to British interests and to European order. When in February 1793 France declared war on England and Holland, opinion had already begun to swing round not so much in consequence of Burke's oratory as of the evolution of French policy.

The swing of opinion can be traced quite clearly in the House of Commons itself, and in the change of attitude of the Whig groups which had previously looked to Fox as a leader. In 1791 Burke and Fox broke for ever and Burke took his place on the Treasury bench in 1792. In the last days of 1792 the Duke of Portland, who still feared an open break with Fox, allowed his friends to support Pitt's ministry in order to 'maintain the Constitution and save the country'. In July 1794 the most influential of the Whigs—with the exception of Fox himself and Sheridan—joined Pitt's government, Portland becoming home secretary and William Windham, who asked for 'open steady war against the whole Jacobin faction', secretary-at-war. The French Revolution had reshaped the pattern of English parliamentary politics and consigned Foxite Whigs to the wilderness. Some writers have argued that Pitt deliberately exaggerated the extent of 'sedition' in the country in order to split the Whigs at the centre, yet there is little doubt that the changes at Westminster were representative of significant changes in mood outside Parliament.

From 1792 onwards the government had begun a policy of repression which for a time was far from completely successful. In 1792 a Royal Proclamation condemned 'divers wicked and seditious writings', and Pitt started isolated persecutions of reformers. In August 1793 a series of trials in Scotland gave an

[1] *Memoirs* (1840), vol. II, p. 5.

opportunity for a vindictive judge, Lord Braxfield,[1] to go further even than the government in attacking agitators who set out to unsettle 'ignorant people and the lower classes of the people'. Braxfield argued with studied vehemence that 'a Government should be just like a Corporation; and in this country it is made up of the landed interest, which alone has the right to be represented; as for the rabble, who have nothing but personal property, what hold has the nation of them?' Such statements and the sentences which followed from them were just as provocative to reformers as were the revolutionary excesses of the Scottish radical 'Convention' of 1793 to the friends of order. The result of a series of English trials in 1794 gave some consolation to men who still believed in the freedom of ideas. In May 1794, Hardy, Thelwall, Horne Tooke, and ten other members of the two leading London reform societies were arrested and tried for treason, but with the Whig lawyer, Erskine, prominent in their defence, they were all acquitted. This was the last great victory of English civil liberties for many years. *Habeas Corpus* was suspended in May 1794, and with the support of the Portland Whigs in Parliament and the pressure of local opinion to sustain him, Pitt was able in 1795 to pass two Acts by which it now became possible to speak or to write as well as to act treason and by which all large public meetings were forbidden without special permit. A year later the government raised stamp duties on newspapers and introduced a system of registration of printing presses. Corresponding societies (some of them named in the act) were banned as 'unlawful Combinations and Confederacies', and two further Acts of 1799 and 1800 banned workers' combinations, the embryonic trade unions. Their legal position had been precarious before 1799, and Pitt in this case was not so much enunciating a new principle, as changing the procedure of prosecution and making control of workers' trade associations 'more speedy and exemplary'. He was afraid that trade clubs would provide a cover for political agitation.[2]

The regulations and restrictions, however, were in harmony with opinion. 'There was not a city, no, not a town', Coleridge

---

[1] See above, p. 99.
[2] The vicar of Bolton wrote to the home secretary (11 April 1799) describing a local association nominally concerned with 'the regulation of the wages of weavers' but actually interested in petitioning parliament and playing politics. (*H.O.* 42/17). Pitt was more concerned with politics than with economics in introducing the two Combination Acts.

wrote, 'in which a man suspected of holding democratic principles could move abroad without receiving some unpleasant proof of the hatred in which his supposed opinions were held by the great majority of the people.'[1] By 1796 Coleridge himself was snapping his 'squeaking trumpet of sedition' and hanging up the fragments in 'the Chamber of Penitences', and Wordsworth, shocked at French foreign policy, was reading in events 'the doom of France . . . with anger vexed, with disappointment sore'. Even the radical reformer Thelwall, who had been arrested and acquitted in 1794, argued a year later that although he had 'adored' the principles on which the Revolution was founded, the 'real object' of the revolutionaries had been lost in six years of 'cutting each others throats'.

2. Pitt and the Politics of Intervention

British intervention against France was grounded in the government's appraisal of British interests, particularly British security, and in the support of an impressive but not completely unanimous volume of national opinion. The French declaration of war was merely one incident in a story of growing suspicion and antagonism: it served to prove that earlier fears had been justified. Fox, however, with great courage, warm-heartedness, and persistence, continued even after the outbreak of war to direct attention to French rather than to British grievances and to plead for pacification, while the radical societies, until they were forcibly suppressed, bitterly attacked a war which entailed bloodshed, expense and a threat 'to our trade, our commerce and manufactures'. Unless it is remembered that the war with France was a controversial war in its origins, the subsequent history both of Whiggery and radicalism cannot be understood.

Pitt's decision to wage war against France was not taken for reasons which appealed to Burke and the 'crusaders'. Between 1789 and 1794 the prime minister was unswayed by 'general' considerations—fear for the future of European aristocracies, for example, or even for European monarchies. It was French policy in the Netherlands which made it impossible for him to maintain the rôle of a detached spectator. The French defeat of the Austrians, the fall of Antwerp in November 1792 and the consequent opening of the River Scheldt to traffic disturbed the balance of eighteenth-century

[1] *The Friend* (1809), Essay IV.

diplomacy. The navigation of the Scheldt had been assured to the
Dutch since 1648; it had been guaranteed by France as recently as
1785 and by Britain as recently as 1788. It was French defiance of
treaties, particularly of treaties affecting what were held to be
Britain's vital maritime and commercial interests, which seemed to
strike at 'the security and peace of all independent nations' and to
threaten 'every principle of moderation, good faith, humanity and
justice'. As the foreign secretary, Pitt's cousin, Lord Grenville, put
it in a note to the French ambassador before the outbreak of war in
December 1792, 'England will never consent that France shall
arrogate the power of annulling at her pleasure, and under the
pretence of a pretended natural right, of which she makes herself
the only judge, the political system, established by solemn treaties,
and guaranteed by the consent of all the powers.' The annexation
of the Austrian Netherlands a month later, the execution of Louis
XVI, and the eventual French declaration of war made up the
French reply.

In 1793 Pitt saw no alternative to war except meekly to accept
France's claims. Cautious though he was and anxious to the last to
maintain peace, he soon learned the language if not the practical
grasp of warfare. He spoke in Parliament of opposing those
'principles of ambition and aggrandisement which have for their
object the destruction of England, of Europe and of the world'. A
few weeks after war had been declared, he expanded the list of
'motives' which had guided British actions, as all war ministers are
wont to do. French contempt of British neutrality, 'their pre-
sumptuous attempts to interfere in the government of this country',
their attacks on George III, were all adduced as relevant motives
which helped to transform a war of prudence into a war of honour.
Although Pitt believed that France could not stand a long war on
economic grounds and that the contest would necessarily be brief,
his complex list of 'motives' was itself an indication that the fifth
war with France within the century would not easily be brought to a
conclusion.

If Pitt saw the weaknesses of his opponent, a modern historian
cannot fail to see the weaknesses of Britain. British armed forces,
scattered about the world or tied to the comfortable ways of local
provincial society at home, were pitifully small when compared with
France's half million men in arms or in training. What forces there
were lacked leadership and organization. It was only with difficulty

that the government was able to send 5,000 men to assist the Dutch, and the 5,000 hardly acquitted themselves well. By April 1795 they had been driven back to the mouth of the Ems and had to be evacuated. An attempt with the assistance of French royalists to retain the French naval stronghold of Toulon, which Admiral Hood blockaded and captured in August 1793 ('I am much mistaken', wrote Grenville, 'if the business at Toulon is not decisive of the war') soon failed, weakening British prestige in Europe and giving a young Corsican lieutenant, Napoleon Bonaparte, then aged 24, his first chance to show his paces. In a more distant and familiar theatre of war, the West Indies, on which Pitt concentrated his efforts, there were early victories but subsequent heavy losses, brought about by yellow fever as much as by enemy action. From a strategic point of view nothing had been gained, and by 1797 the opposition of Spain, which was easy to provoke, had been roused. The British navy, which was to prove the decisive factor in long-drawn out wars which raged far away from Europe, had been built up far more efficiently than the army between 1793 and 1797, but the task it faced was far from simple. There were only 16,000 sailors in 1793 as against 110,000 when the American War had ended, and recruiting a new force and discovering new leadership took time. Although Admiral Howe, a hero of the Seven Years War, won the 'glorious first of June' in 1794 and in 1797 the Spanish fleet was beaten off Cape St. Vincent by Jervis and Nelson, there were serious naval mutinies at the Nore and at Spithead in 1797, which seemed to expose the nation to danger at home. It needed the victory over the Dutch at Camperdown in October 1797 to relieve anxieties about the morale of the sailors.

In the long run, British sea power and British economic power were to guarantee triumphs in war as well as in peace, but political disorganization and inefficiency in London and the even more serious disorganization in Vienna, Berlin and the other European capitals held back success. Pitt had no qualifications or experience for running a war; Henry Dundas, secretary for war and the colonies after the formation of the coalition government of 1794, on whom Pitt depended, had grave weaknesses too.

The main task, as Pitt saw it, was to concentrate British efforts in the colonies and provide 'gold', guaranteed loans and direct gifts to maintain Britain's allies on the Continent. Prussia and Austria— and later Russia—needed British financial aid to keep their armies in the field.[1] The weakness of this policy, which during twenty years contributed to the rallying of four 'coalitions' against France, was that it did not buy victories for the allied armies. Even before the final French occupation of Holland, for example, the Prussians had made peace with the French at Basel (April 1795). A few months later Spain withdrew from the rickety coalition and in 1796 made a defensive and offensive alliance with France. While Britain 'filched sugar islands', all Europe's armies were no match for the French, particularly for the young Napoleon, who conquered northern Italy in the brilliant campaigns of 1796 to 1797, and repeatedly defeated the Austrians. Finally, in 1797 Austria signed the Treaty of Campo Formio, which confirmed what the British most disliked, French power in the Low Countries, the French 'natural frontier' on the Rhine, and Napoleon's gains in Italy. It was a sign of French strength and the weaknesses of Pitt's policy that British attempts in 1797 to reach a peace settlement with France were treated with contempt. The Directory, which governed France after the end of the Terror (1795) and employed Napoleon as an instrument who was soon to prove far more powerful than his masters, set impossible terms and prepared to mobilize the combined French, Spanish and Dutch fleets against Britain. Within a week of the signing of the Peace of Campo Formio, Citizen General Napoleon, who had returned to France in triumph after his victories in Italy, was appointed 'Commander-in-Chief of the Army of England'. There were even rumours concerning the membership of an English 'Directory' and the creation of separate republics in Scotland and Ireland. The logic of the French revolution seemed to be inescapable; from the rights of man, the French were passing more than willingly to acceptance of the right of the ambitious Napoleon to mould French destinies.

Although the years 1797 and 1798 were low points in Britain's fortunes and made the whole policy of intervention look untidy and ineffective, they were years when the die was cast and the country as well as the government became committed to a 'cause'. 'The spirit of this country', wrote Pitt, 'has risen so as to be fairly equal to this crisis'. Despite financial troubles and mutiny, domestic unrest both in London and the provinces, and Irish discontent leading to eventual rebellion, the forces of order proved far stronger, psycho-

---

[1] For details of the £16 million of loans and subsidies between 1791 and 1805, see Lord Rosebery, *op. cit.*, Appendices A and B.

logically as well as physically, than the forces of despair.[1] A friendly foreign observer, Mallet du Pan, who like Burke was a theorist of anti-revolution, could detect a mood of 'unbounded confidence almost amounting to presumption'.[2] This was indeed, the tone of the *Anti-Jacobin*, which first appeared in November 1797; and in its Preface, written by the young and brilliant George Canning, friend of Pitt and under-secretary for foreign affairs (1796–9), there was stated, more wittily than by Burke, and for a new generation, the case for unrepentant patriotism, 'It may be thought a narrow and illiberal distinction—but we avow ourselves to be *partial* to the COUNTRY *in which we live*, notwithstanidng the daily panegyricks, which we read and hear on the superior virtues and endowments of its rival and hostile neighbour.'

Patriotism in itself was enough in 1797 and 1798, for the seaborne invasion from the Continent did not in fact take place. Napoleon saw clearly that 'with all our efforts, we shall not for many years obtain command of the sea', and turned away from the Channel towards the Mediterranean. In 1798, with a view to acquiring treasure as well as influence, the French invaded Rome and extinguished the freedom of Switzerland. More ambitiously still, Napoleon went on to seize Malta in June 1798 and to sail from there to Egypt, where he quickly destroyed the armies of the unprepared Mameluke rulers. Dreams of Oriental as well as European mastery seemed for a moment within the effective orbit of his achievement; even the conquest of India as well as Britain, or of Britain through India, seemed not impossible. But such dreams were disturbed if not shattered when Nelson, using British seapower very efficiently, blockaded Egypt and annihilated the French fleet at the Battle of the Nile on 1 August 1798. Once again British national confidence was restored and the uneasy international situation reshaped.[3] Pitt, proud of a great victory, did not hesitate to call his fellow countrymen 'saviours of mankind', even though the salvation was still very provisional. At least Napoleon's army was no longer poised for further movement, but immobilized in a remote desert country, completely dependent for its survival on energetic leadership. Fox,

---

[1] See below, p. 176.
[2] This was the mood of the volunteers, who were mustered in many parts of the country. The newspapers were full of military tailors' advertisements.
[3] The victory was not announced in London until 2 October. It inspired *The Mouth of the Nile, a new Serio-Comic Intermezzo of Pantomime, Song, Dance and Dialogue* at Covent Garden, a command performance of which was ordered by the King.

who persisted in directing attention to British 'tyranny and cruelty' in Ireland, and had lost his place on the Privy Council earlier in the year for referring to 'the yoke of our English tyrants', was quite out of touch with the new English mood.

As a result of the changed international situation, a second European coalition against France was formed in 1799, again with the help of 'Pitt's gold'. Austria, usually willing to return to coalitions whenever possible, and Russia, alienated by Napoleon's drive in the Middle East, associated themselves with Britain. Again, however, it proved far easier to form a coalition than to direct it, and mutual jealousies and suspicions soon came to the surface. After initial victories in Italy the Russians were handicapped in their southern campaigns by lack of co-operation from Austria; in the north, a combined Anglo-Russian force failed to recapture Holland in the summer and autumn of 1799. While it was floundering there, Napoleon, who had successfully slipped away from Egypt, landed in France again in October to receive a saviour's welcome, and by the end of the year had established himself as Consul. To buy time, he made a peace offer not to Pitt but to George III, who abruptly rejected it. Behind the scenes, Napoleon was saying, 'once conclude peace, and then—a fresh war with England!'

Pitt and Grenville's chilly rejection of peace overtures in December 1799—they talked firmly about the restoration of the Bourbons —was based not on doubt concerning Napoleon's long-term intentions but on the forlorn hope that Napoleon's new political power, acquired by a *coup d'état*, could not last. Pitt had been willing to negotiate in 1797, 'to use every effort to stop so bloody and wasting a war', and he was willing to negotiate again in August 1800, but he missed the best opportunity of coming to terms—even then, they would have been truce terms and not peace terms— immediately on Napoleon's appointment as First Consul. By the time that the Treaty of Amiens between Britain and France was signed in March 1802, the second coalition had broken up like its predecessor. Austria, battered by defeats at Marengo and Hohenlinden, signed the Treaty of Lunéville in February 1801: Russia, or at least its mad Tsar Paul, irritated by the British acquisition of Malta in September 1800—a blow to Russian Mediterranean ambitions—had changed sides even earlier, and revived the League of Armed Neutrality, which Catherine the Great had first organized in 1780. In collaboration with the Swedish, Danish, and Prussian governments, the Russians sought to protect all neutral vessels against the arbitrary rights of search claimed by British cruisers. Before Paul had time to complete his anti-British policy with a full French alliance (and possibly, fantastic though it sounded, a Cossack march on India) he was assassinated in March 1801, but although Russian policy was reversed again, it proved impossible to secure an effective new alliance with Britain. The Continent was clearly Napoleon's, although his influence was still limited at the periphery of his empire.

When the peace was signed, Pitt was no longer in power. On 5 February 1801, during the same week that Austria signed the Peace of Lunéville, Pitt resigned the post of prime minister, which he had held since 1783. The issue was not foreign policy, but Catholic emancipation.[1] The King's conscience had proved more stubborn than any foreign enemy, and a reconstructed 'Protestant' cabinet had been formed with the speaker of the House of Commons, Henry Addington (later Lord Sidmouth), a mediocre and uninspiring placeman, as prime minister, Robert Jenkinson, son of Charles Jenkinson (and later Lord Hawkesbury and Earl of Liverpool) at the Foreign Office, and Spencer Perceval, a capable lawyer, as leader of the House of Commons. Pitt agreed to stay in office long enough to carry through the budget and to give Addington his invaluable support during critical weeks of political uncertainty.[2] In the meantime, a series of British naval successes bolstered national confidence. Nelson won a great victory over the Danes at Copenhagen and destroyed the menace of the League of Armed Neutrality. Far away in Egypt, British forces under the command of Abercromby took Cairo and Alexandria and compelled the French to withdraw. Napoleon was master of the European continent, but Britain had kept the sea lanes open and was still strong enough to continue to resist. While the French navy had been reduced by more than a half between 1793 and 1801, the British navy had grown from 15,000 to 133,000 men and from 135 ships of the line and 133 frigates to 202 ships of the line and 277 frigates. These were impressive and ultimately decisive figures, whatever might happen to the land power of European coalitions, and Pitt at the moment of change

---

[1] For details of the crisis see below, pp. 195 ff.
[2] His activity, wrote one pamphleteer, in praising and advising the administration on its assumption of power, induced the public to regard the change as 'a mere juggle'. See A. Hamilton, *Thoughts on the Formation of the Later and Present Administrations* (1804) p. 3.

could rightly claim that 'we have kept our resources entire, our honour unimpaired, our integrity inviolate. We have not lost a single foot of territory, and we have given the rest of the world many chances of salvation.'

Integrity was kept inviolate during the peace negotiations between Addington's far from unpopular government and the French, but there were few signs of intelligence. The undoubted public demand for peace in Britain encouraged Addington to become more and more irresolute the longer the negotiations continued, and to yield on points where firmness was indispensable. Fox praised the 'moderation' of the new ministers and Pitt magnanimously defended the final Treaty of Amiens as 'very advantageous and, on the whole satisfactory', but the Whig Sheridan was nearer the truth when he declared that 'this is a peace which all men are glad of, but no man can be proud of'. Grenville and his friends thundered against it, and so did young and unmuzzled Pittites like Canning. They were right. Of British colonial conquests made during the eight years of war, only Ceylon and Trinidad were retained, the former from Holland, the latter from Spain. The Cape was to be restored to Holland, Egypt to Turkey, and the main bone of contention, Malta, to the Order of Knights of St. John. Within Europe, Bonaparte's empire was to be left almost intact, the only French concessions being withdrawal of French troops from the Kingdom of Naples and the Papal states, and recognition of the Republic of the Ionian Islands. Neither British gains nor French 'losses' were calculated to worry Napoleon or the French, but British failure to secure a favourable treaty of commerce with France and to assist in any effective way either the House of Orange or the House of Savoy was bound to lead to a revulsion of opinion against the Treaty in England. Although Fox and a host of sympathetic British Whigs rushed to Paris, where there was much mutual flattery, London interests which had pressed for peace and had made Addington hasten to negotiate were soon to press for war again. 'Peace in a week, war in a month', was the comment of the old diplomatist Harris (now Lord Malmesbury). The most that could be said for the Treaty from a British angle was that it temporarily appeased a growing current of pacifist opinion and that it did not reduce the long-term determinants of British power, particularly the navy.

Within fourteen months war had broken out again. Technically

Napoleon was right in arguing that it was Britain which had broken the peace, for Addington's government, despite all its 'moderation', refused for strategic reasons to surrender Malta,[1] and when Whitworth was appointed ambassador to France in September 1802 he was instructed to answer no enquiries about its evacuation. In fact, however, it was Napoleon's refusal to rest satisfied with his earlier territorial gains, his continued interest in the east, and his assault on the liberties of the small republics he had himself created in Holland, Switzerland, and Italy that made peace impossible. It was not surprising that faction-ridden Britain, where political groups at Westminster squabbled and intrigued, responded increasingly to the pressure of Grenville and his supporters—'the new Opposition'—and objected unequivocally to the French claim to keep Britain out of all discussion of European issues while France had a free hand to discuss every issue under the sun. In October 1802 Jenkinson sounded Russia about an alliance against France, and at the opening of Parliament supplies were voted for strengthening the army and navy which had been seriously depleted during the previous few months. In March 1803 Whitworth expressed Britain's readiness to recognize the remodelled Italian states only on condition that the French left Holland and Switzerland, acknowledged the integrity of Turkey, and consented to Britain staying in Malta. Such a settlement would have challenged Napoleon's whole conception of French hegemony on the Continent, and simply by suggesting it, the British were inevitably pointing the way to a resumption of hostilities. Even Fox declared that 'if our national rights were involved, if attempts have been made to lower that rank which we had been accustomed to hold among the states of Europe', then a war undertaken in such circumstances would be just. After weeks of tension, Britain sent what was in fact an ultimatum to Bonaparte in April 1803, and on 12 May Whitworth left Paris and war was resumed. It was Napoleon's unlimited ambitions—Pitt had called him 'this last adventurer in the history of revolutions'—rather than British intransigence which lay at the heart of the struggles of the next twelve years.

For the first phase of the prolonged struggles, Pitt came back into power, or rather into office. In April 1804, after months of political

---

[1] The Addington ministry had been persuaded to surrender Malta before news reached London of the defeat of the French Army in Egypt and the French evacuation from Alexandria.

wrangling and manœuvring, Addington at last resigned, and Pitt set about forming a new cabinet. It was a very weak one, for the King vetoed Fox, and without Fox neither the Whigs nor the followers of Grenville, who had formed the most militant group in opposition to Addington, would co-operate. Grenville strongly objected to forming a new administration 'on a principle of exclusion' and demanded the setting up of a government which would unite 'as large a proportion as possible of the weight, talents and character' of the country. Pitt could thus include in his makeshift ministry only his own loyal followers, including Melville (formerly Dundas) and Canning, and some of Addington's ministry, including Hawkesbury (formerly Jenkinson), Eldon, Portland, and Castlereagh. Fox and Grenville were united in opposition, Fox less openly Francophil than before but still standing resolutely against 'the overstrained use of the royal prerogative' and attacking Pitt's policy of relying upon European coalitions. A few months later Pitt irritated his most vigorous supporters, like Canning, by restoring Addington, raised to the peerage as Lord Sidmouth, to the cabinet. This move exacerbated rather than soothed partisan feelings and led directly to a series of scandals and divisions, including the impeachment in April 1805 of Pitt's closest friend, Melville, for speculation with the public funds, and the ultimate resignation of the Addingtonians, who hated Melville. Troubled by such anxieties, seeking in vain to strengthen his ministry by including Fox, and suffering from weak health, Pitt was in no position to intervene effectively in Europe, even had he been more clear which was the right line of action to pursue. Time had not made him a great war minister; administrative inefficiency as well as difficulties of communication made it impossible for him to maintain central strategic control of naval, military or diplomatic forces,[1] and his strongest point was his ability to find eloquent words for the right occasion. He was an ineffective analyst of the continental political situation and he lacked the boldness of imagination to frame a comprehensive military strategy.

Nonetheless, eloquent words counted for much in 1805, and Pitt in a period of great challenge to Britain did far more than Addington could have done to 'weather the storm'. After the resumption of hostilities between Britain and France, Napoleon concentrated most

---

[1] For a fascinating study of the problems and achievements in one area of operations, see P. Mackesy, *The War in the Mediterranean, 1803-1810* (1957). There is no similar detailed study of the West Indies. For interesting but controversial verdicts, see Sir J. Fortescue, *British Statesmen of the Great War* (1911).

of his energies on the conquest of Britain. He turned Boulogne into a great naval base where massed flat-bottomed boats—2,000 of them in all—and light craft prepared to invade Britain with 100,000 men. 'Let us be masters of the Straits for six hours' he said, 'and we will be masters of the world'. To meet the danger, the English constructed martello towers, military canals and beacons on this side of the Channel, and all available forces were alerted. Local poets issued 'Patriotic Clarions' or 'Calls to Glory' and talked of the French tyrant trembling before the British lion.[1] The really decisive check to Napoleon's scheme, however, came with the Battle of Trafalgar.

The French Admiral Villeneuve had succeeded in slipping out of the blockaded naval base at Toulon during the last days of March 1805. The French plan was to collect the various elements of their fleet in the West Indies, to join the Spaniards (who had come back into the war on the French side in December 1804), to disperse the British fleet, and to move triumphantly into the English Channel. By August 1805 it was clear that this plan could not be followed, and Villeneuve had been compelled to take refuge in Cadiz harbour. When on a windless day, 21 October, he tried to get away to sail into the Mediterranean, Nelson was waiting for him. Out of thirty-three French and Spanish ships of the line, nineteen were taken or destroyed. Nelson, Britain's greatest war hero, was killed in the battle in circumstances which have always been preserved in popular tradition, and from 1849 his monument has dominated London's central square. Commenting on Trafalgar immediately after the news of the victory, *The Times* of 7 November—framed copies of which can still be found in twentieth-century households—remarked: 'If ever there was a man who deserved to be "praised, wept and honoured", it is LORD NELSON. His three great naval achievements have eclipsed the brilliancy of the most dazzling victories in the annals of English daring.' Certainly the three victories not only smashed the French Mediterranean fleet, but played a bigger part in ensuring Britain's survival in face of Napoleon than any large schemes of national strategy.

The day before Trafalgar, which shone out for Britain as one dazzlingly bright victory in a year of gloom, Napoleon had struck in the east and virtually settled the fate of the Third Coalition

---

[1] In Birmingham, for example, one merchant offered to place 10 boats of 200 tonnage at the disposal of the government at his Birmingham wharf, and 15 boats of 300 tonnage at Stourport. An innkeeper 'most patriotically' offered all his chaises and horses 'to carry his Majesty's troops, free of expense'.

(Britain, Russia, Austria, and Sweden) which had gathered its forces late in 1804. At Ulm, on 20 October, 30,000 Austrians surrendered to him. Less than a month later he entered Vienna, and on 2 December he overwhelmed a combined Russian-Austrian army at Austerlitz. On 6 December France and Austria signed an armistice, followed soon afterwards by the Peace of Pressburg. Prussia, which remained neutral in this struggle, was heavily defeated in 1806 when she foolishly tried to tackle France single-handed. Two weeks after the crucial battle of Jena, on 14 October, the French were in Berlin sharpening their swords on the statue of Frederick the Great. Finally in June 1807, after a defeat at Friedland, Tsar Alexander of Russia, who had pictured himself as protector of the weak and oppressed and guardian of justice among the nations, met Napoleon privately on a raft moored in the River Niemen and by the Peace of Tilsit came to terms with him about the shape of a new Napoleonic world. All Napoleon's acquisitions were recognized, and once again Britain stood alone.

By the time of Tilsit, Britain was alone without Pitt, who died on 23 January 1806. Tired and exhausted, although only 46 years old, he was as much a victim of the war as the 47-year-old Nelson was its hero. If Nelson's character and personality still provoke controversy, so does the assessment of Pitt's achievements. His solitary nature, his lack of colour, his insensitivity to the appeal of art or of science, his confident sense of superiority over most of his contemporaries, have not endeared him to posterity. Even his friendliest critics have divided his life into two parts—the first down to 1793, when he had plentiful opportunities for constructive achievement, not all of which he took, and the second from 1793 to 1806, when he had to abandon all his early hopes and when he was swept along by tides which he could never control. The difficulties of presiding over the management of a country at war for a prolonged period of time would have been great for any leader; Pitt, like other European statesmen, was carried with the Revolution rather than placed in a position to control it. France set the pace: he had to follow, to meet situations as they occurred, to react rather than to act. In reacting he stood well above most of his European contemporaries; for long he was destined, in Lord Minto's phrase, to be 'the Atlas of our reeling globe'. His chief qualification was the record for integrity and industry which he had established before 1793. He could speak not in the name of a threatened aristocracy but of a threatened country, in terms not only of the past but of the future, not as a figure of an *ancien régime* but as a maker of new policies. In the last resort Britannia not Pitt was the Atlas, but Pitt, for all his inadequacies as a war minister, was usually able to draw on the national reserves of strength. Two tributes to him direct attention to what contemporaries regarded as his outstanding virtues and recall the praises showered upon him as 'the virtuous young minister' in 1784. His friend Wilberforce, one of the few real friends he ever had, observed that 'for personal purity, disinterested-ness and love of his country, I have never known his equal'.[1] The text on his Guildhall memorial is equally pertinent and in its very language catches the mood of the years after 1789. 'In an age when the contagion of ideas threatened to dissolve the forms of civil society', it reads, 'he rallied the loyal, the sober-minded and the good around the venerable structure of the English monarchy.'

3. The Road to Victory

The immediate consequence of Pitt's death was political upheaval. A new administration led by Grenville, who had pleaded for a stronger military policy in opposition to Addington, and joined by Fox, who had believed since 1793 in the possibility of a genuine understanding first with revolutionary and then with Napoleonic France, was no more successful than that of Pitt had been. The road to victory was still long and difficult, there was now no single presiding war minister—effective or ineffective—to give a lead, and it was not until another six years had passed that the skies really began to clear.

Grenville's government was an 1806 version of the 'ministry of all the talents' which he had demanded the previous year, but the 'talents' did not include the Pittites. The main element in the new cabinet consisted of the Foxite Whigs, restored to place after their long years of exclusion. Erskine, the great defending counsel of the 1790s, became Lord Chancellor; Grey, of the Friends of the People, became First Lord of the Admiralty; Lord Moira, political leader of the circle which surrounded the Prince of Wales, who had for long been the main hope of the Whigs, became Master General of the Ordnance; and Fox himself, urgently anxious to negotiate with

[1] See Lord Ashbourne, *Pitt, Some Chapters of His Life and Times* (1898) chs. X and XI.

Napoleon, became foreign secretary. Sidmouth came in again, bringing with him his colleague Lord Ellenborough, while Grenville included two influential members of his own faction—Windham and Spencer.

The new government sought not only to end the war but to lift Roman Catholic disabilities. In neither objective was it successful. On 13 September 1806, Fox followed Pitt to the grave; with him many hopes were buried, but he himself had already buried his own hope of peace with France. Warm-hearted and generous to the last, he did not bequeath the legacy of a united 'party'. Rifts soon appeared in the ministry, and opposition crystallized. The newly re-emerging radicals, including Cobbett, who was passing from 'anti-Jacobinism' to militant radicalism, argued that there was nothing to choose between the Pittites and the Foxites; the advanced Whigs, known as 'the Mountain', disliked the cold and superior Grenville; the disgruntled 'Tories', led by Hawkesbury, Eldon and Spencer Perceval, longed for an attack on 'innovation'; the Pittites, of whom Canning and Huskisson were the most important, dreamed of rebuilding Pitt's fallen ministry according to the same principles.

The Ministry of all the Talents proved just as ineffective in diplomacy and war as Pitt had been.[1] Widely dispersed military and naval actions —including raids on Buenos Aires and Montevideo, an expedition towards Constantinople through the Dardanelles in support of Russian coercion of Turkey, and a disastrous attempt to seize Alexandria—lacked any general strategic purpose and failed to secure any permanently successful results. Sicily was retained and reinforced, but the one theatre of war where activity would have been useful—the Baltic—was left neglected. By 1807 the Russian alliance, on which hopes of decisive victory depended, was crumbling quickly and the withdrawal of subsidies hastened the crumbling. The ministry had only two real successes to its credit—first, Windham's act to abolish enlistment for life, the first step in army reform, and second, the abolition of the slave trade which was carried on a motion of Wilberforce. This latter measure shone out brightly in a dark decade; the abolitionist cause had suffered with many other good causes as a result of the French Revolution, and despite Pitt's sympathy with Wilberforce, and the belief of men like

---

[1] For the hopes it inspired when it took office, see Lord Holland, *An Inquiry into the State of the Nation* (1806).

Grenville, Fox, and Canning in total abolition, there had been little hope of success before 1800. The parliamentary orientations of 1806 and 1807, so unfavourable to effective prosecution of the war, made possible this great reform.

The cause of Catholic emancipation was not to be dealt with so easily. George III, angered by the somewhat underhand attempts of Grey and the Whigs to introduce Roman Catholic officers into the army and to win over the Irish, and knowing that Sidmouth would be on his side in resisting moves towards emancipation as he had been in 1801, asked Grenville for a written pledge that such attempts would stop. Grenville refused; the government resigned, and was replaced in March 1807 by a new and weak administration led by the aged Duke of Portland, the former colleague of Fox, but by this time one of the stoutest supporters of the king. Sidmouth was kept out, but Eldon became Lord Chancellor and Hawkesbury home secretary. Of the younger men, Canning went to the Foreign Office and Castlereagh became minister of war. The government won a clear majority at the general election of June 1807.

Canning signalled his arrival at the Foreign Office by seeking to bring to an end British intervention in Turkey and Egypt and by taking bold and spectacular action elsewhere. Learning from British intelligence services of the 'secret' clauses of the Treaty of Tilsit, which once again left Britain isolated, and anticipating French pressure on Denmark, British ships bombarded Copenhagen and seized the Danish fleet. Later, Danish Heligoland and the Dutch West Indies were occupied. Although the opposition Whigs severely criticized the Copenhagen 'outrage' as a piece of unjustifiable violence, moralists were divided. There were angry debates in the House of Commons, but the government held that British actions were justified by the exigencies of the power situation. Certainly it had shown forethought and initiative, qualities which were also displayed in a different area when Canning managed to rescue the Portuguese royal family just before the French invasion of Portugal, and to escort them safely to Brazil. More important still, he managed to acquire the Portuguese fleet.

Napoleon's assault on the Iberian peninsula, which during the next few years was to expose him to constant troubles and difficulties, was the turning point of the whole Napoleonic War. His motives were, as usual, mixed. The Treaty of Tilsit, by enabling him to concentrate on Britain, forced him to devote greater attention to

economic warfare than he had done before. If he could not invade
Britain, he had to blockade British trade. Before Tilsit, the Berlin
decrees of November 1806 proclaimed the veto of France and its
dependencies on all commerce with Britain and trade in British
merchandise; Tilsit raised this veto to the dignity of the 'continental
system'. The invasion of Portugal in 1807 and the violation of Spain
in 1808 were logical if disastrous steps to take in trying to seal off
Europe from Britain.[1] But his attack on Portugal was inspired also
by annoyance at Portugal's continued friendship with Britain, and
his assault on Spain a year later was influenced by the high opinion
he had of Spanish resources, the low opinion he had (rightly) of the
Bourbon monarchy in Madrid, and his estimate of the ease of overthrowing it.

For once, Napoleon's calculations were disastrously wrong. To
seize the Bourbons and force them to abdicate was easy, but to overcome the Spanish people, who felt no enthusiasm for the Revolution
which Napoleon still carried about with him in his pocket, was very
difficult. The conquest of Madrid by French troops, another
triumphal entry into a foreign capital, was followed a few months
later by the defeat of two French divisions at Baylen (July 1808)
by 30,000 Spanish regular troops assisted by guerilla fighters. No
similar disaster had befallen French troops since the early days of the
Revolution. In order to restore his threatened prestige, Napoleon
had to embark on a large-scale Iberian campaign at a moment when
his commitments in other parts of Europe were far too large.
Although he was able to invade Spain with 200,000 French troops
in November 1808, he achieved nothing but minor successes, and
withdrew again prematurely in January 1809 to leave the issue still
open.

Portuguese and Spanish nationalism provided Canning with a new
moral force in Europe, which greatly strengthened the psychological
ramparts of Britain's continued war against Napoleon. It is true
that Spanish priests and peasantry, the spearhead of national resistance, had no English counterparts, and that their opposite numbers
in Ireland were far from popular in England, but Englishmen of all
parties and groups, including radicals like Cobbett and Cartwright,
warmed to the struggle of a popular movement against a 'foreign
tyrant'. The more the giant Napoleon tried to repress a 'brave, little
people', the more optimistic Englishmen became about the quality

---

[1] For Britain's economic retaliation, see below, pp. 164 ff.

of Spanish resistance, and the more they demanded energetic counter-action. It was the Whig Sheridan who asked in June 1808 before the Battle of Baylen for 'a bold stroke for the rescue of the world'; even Whigs of 'the Mountain', like Whitbread, who had continued to plead for a peace policy in 1807 and went on pleading for one after 1808, temporarily joined in the national clamour. When Spanish 'patriot' representatives reached London in August, they were cheered by the crowds and given public honours at an enormous reception, at which Canning sat beside Sheridan and Erskine next to Hawkesbury.

It would have been unnatural for such political amity to last for long—the Whigs soon became divided about the Spanish struggle as about everything else—but the Peninsular War had more than a psychological importance. It enabled Britain to take the offensive, although not immediately, in a manner which for various reasons had proved impossible in the Mediterranean. It permitted an alternative strategy to that of dispersal of effort, the maintenance of maritime security and the winning of colonial territories. British troops in Spain and Portugal were eventually able, for the first time during the long struggle, to evolve a new discipline and a new organization and to find in Arthur Wellesley, first Duke of Wellington, a general worthy of the challenge. Without British intervention Spanish guerilla resistance might well have collapsed; with it, Napoleon was forced to continue to pour men into Spain, as many as 370,000 in 1810, the largest force he had mustered against a single country. As Wellington said, British troops acted as a magnet, drawing Napoleon on, and Spain was a bridgehead well designed to meet British strategic requirements.

At first, in 1808 and 1809, British intervention was not particularly successful. By the Convention of Cintra (August 1808) an inept British general allowed the French to transfer back to France their defeated troops in Portugal. There was great public outcry in Britain, and poets like Wordsworth joined with enraged politicians in protesting against an 'ignoble and shameful transaction'. This was the worst moment of the Peninsular War, right at the beginning. In January 1809, Sir John Moore, protégé of the Whigs, died a hero's death after the harrowing retreat of British troops to Corunna, but for all the heroism there was still little sign of the turn in events which was soon to come. British troops retained their foothold in Portugal, but the remnants of Moore's army were driven out of Spain. Opponents of the government were predicting at this time that 'the next French battle will be fought in Ireland or perhaps in Kent'.[1]

Before the turn in the Peninsular War, two familiar and recurring events were to take place outside the Iberian Peninsula—the defeat of yet another Austrian campaign against France and a further change of government in London. The two events were connected. In April 1809, the Austrian Emperor, backed by the administration, the army, and the crowds in a way that he had never been before— popular resistance to Napoleon was as contagious as the ideas of the Revolution had been—declared war on France. Once again the Austrians were overwhelmed at the battle of Wagram in July, and by the Peace of Schönbrunn (October 1809) the Austrian army was reduced in size, an indemnity was demanded and Napoleon 'won the hand' of the Emperor's daughter, Marie Louise. The peace was as exasperating as the defeat, and Britain shared in the exasperation. The Austrians had pressed for British action in northern Germany and southern Italy, but there was misunderstanding and lack of co-operation in both theatres and action came too late. South Italian plans were abandoned after the news of Wagram. In the north it was not until three weeks after Wagram that the British government landed 40,000 men in the island of Walcheren at the mouth of the Scheldt. The expedition, ill-prepared, moving without secrecy, badly led and handicapped by unfavourable weather, was a fiasco, and in December the troops had to be withdrawn. The opportunity of rallying a new German coalition had been lost.

Walcheren brought down the divided Portland government which had already been torn apart by bitter hostility between Canning and Castlereagh, a hostility which was to colour the events not only of 1809 and 1810 but of years to come. The nervous, restless, brilliant, and ambitious Canning objected strongly to Castlereagh as war minister, holding him responsible for the Convention of Cintra, Moore's retreat, and the Walcheren expedition. He became convinced, as news of disasters poured in, that 'a *Minister*—and that a Minister in the *House of Commons*—is indispensable to the well-carrying on of the king's government in these times'.[2] His candidate for Castlereagh's position was the elder brother of Wellington, Lord Wellesley, Governor-General of India from 1797 to 1805 and

---

[1] Quoted Mackesy, *op. cit.*, p. 307.
[2] Hist. MSS. Comm., *Bathurst Papers*, p. 362.

ambassador to Spain in 1809. As early as March 1809 Canning offered his resignation to Portland unless Castlereagh were removed from the War Office. The sick and aged prime minister temporized —his inability to inspire or to lead is shown by the fact that *Hansard* does not record any single speech he made during his two and a half years of office—promising in principle to accede to Canning's request, but offering various pretexts for delay. Castlereagh was not informed either of the threat or the promise, and when in September Portland once again postponed Castlereagh's removal from office, Canning resigned. Portland's own resignation followed, as did Castlereagh's when he heard at last what had been intended for him. Before the old ministry was dissolved, Castlereagh challenged Canning to a duel; it ended at the second discharge with Canning receiving a bullet in his thigh.

Canning hoped in 1809 to become a leading minister, if not prime minister, of a vigorous ministry prosecuting the war with renewed energy and according to plan. Instead, the prime ministership passed to Spencer Perceval, Portland's chancellor of the exchequer, the ablest commoner in the cabinet rump. He succeeded in taking office only because of continued Whig divisions. Grenville and Grey, the leaders of the two wings of the formal opposition, failed to agree and with Castlereagh and Canning left on one side and Sidmouth on the other, Perceval ('Little P') was the residual figure rather than the natural choice. His ministry was very weak. Many politicians refused to compromise their political future by taking office, for not only was the ministry precarious in itself but the King's madness (1810) made it likely that the Prince of Wales would soon be in a position to form a new Regency government, consisting of his old friends and supporters, the Whigs. The only important change in the new ministry (apparently paradoxically) was Wellesley for Canning at the Foreign Office. Hawkesbury, who soon afterwards succeeded his father as Earl of Liverpool, was given the War Department.

Round the corner, there were more paradoxes than Wellesley's appointment, some of them real ones. The new ministry was less unpopular in the country than it was in informed political circles. Indeed it provided the nucleus of the administration which won the war and, long before that, won over the Prince Regent and blasted the hopes of the Whigs. 'He is not a ship-of-the-line', Grattan said of Perceval, 'but he carries many guns, is tight built, and is out in all weathers'. He needed all these qualities in 1811, when trade crisis —exports fell by a third[1]—Irish troubles, bad harvests, high taxation and popular discontent added to factional difficulties at Westminster. Before—strangest twist of all—he was assassinated by a madman in May 1812, the only British prime minister to meet that fate, the Whigs had in effect been robbed of all hopes of power, the tide had turned in the Peninsular War, and Napoleon was beginning to plot his calamitous expedition to Moscow.

The blasting of Whig hopes brought to an end a long period of confusion in parliamentary politics and paved the way for a stronger administration, led by Lord Liverpool, which was to last until 1827. The blasting, however, was not achieved in a single explosion: the hopes were undermined before they were destroyed. The Prince Regent, despite all the efforts made by the Whigs in 1810 and early in 1811—as in 1788—to secure for him full regency powers in face of Perceval's opposition, did not choose to replace Perceval immediately after he acquired full power (for one year only) in February 1811. He flinched from large-scale dismissals, took account of sharp Whig divisions, hated Grey, and, more important still, was beginning openly to take the same line as his mad father on the question of Catholic emancipation. When he acquired permanent Regency powers a year later, he made a somewhat cool indirect offer to Grey and Grenville to join a 'coalition' government, but after the offer (which would have meant that the Whigs would have to compromise on the Catholic question) not surprisingly was rejected, Perceval was confirmed in power. Anticipating this 'settlement', the one powerful malcontent in the cabinet, Wellesley, who was anxious to be prime minister himself, resigned. Since joining Perceval's administration, he had formed a lower and lower opinion of his nominal leader and believed that under such 'leadership' there was no chance of winning the war quickly.[2] Perceval's government did not reel, however, under Wellesley's blow. Instead, by bringing in Castlereagh to the Foreign Office and Sidmouth to the Lord Presidency of the Council, Perceval strengthened it. The forces which were to unite under his successor, Liverpool, were concen-

[1] See below, pp. 165–6.
[2] Cf. the view of the poet Southey (*Life and Correspondence* (1849–50), vol. III, pp. 302–3: 'of three points I have now convinced myself, that the great desideratum in our Govt. is a Premier instead of a Cabinet, that a regular opposition is an absurdity which could not exist anywhere but in an island . . . and that parliamentary reform is the shortest road to anarchy'.

trating, while the forces of his opponents remained dispersed. Both Whiggery and Wellesley, backed as ever by Canning, who like the Whigs was in favour of Catholic emancipation, lost their last chance when Perceval was assassinated—in no sense for political motives—on 11 May.[1] Liverpool, who took his place, was defeated in the House of Commons, but it proved impossible to find an alternative combination. Neither the Whigs nor Liverpool and his friends would serve under Wellesley, who was asked to form a government by the Prince Regent, nor could Lord Moira, intermediary between the Prince and the Whigs, secure the support of Grey and Grenville in forming a Whig ministry which they both felt would be too tied to the Court from the start. In consequence, Liverpool was invited to return to office with his old colleagues, and the general feeling that both the Whigs and Wellesley had burnt their political boats, led to an immediate increase of government strength in the House of Commons. Canning unwisely refused offers to join the new administration, which, as a result of the 1812 general election, was placed firmly in the saddle.

Liverpool's success and the Whig failure were perhaps explicable in more general terms than this account of tortuous parliamentary squabbles suggests. From the failure of the Ministry of all the Talents down to 1812, the Whigs were not only divided but bankrupt of constructive ideas. On four occasions they had the opportunity of turning out their rivals; on each occasion they failed. United only in their belief in Catholic emancipation, which was a most unpopular cause and always lost votes at elections, they were equivocal and petty in their approach to the far bigger issue of the war. 'Their criticisms were purely destructive: their objections frequently cancelled out each other; and they could not agree in championing any intelligent strategical plan. Their conduct in Parliament made them very unpopular with the nation.'[2] They even failed to make effective use of the new popular interest in parliamentary reform, which was reviving again after its eclipse in the 1790s and producing new forces of movement. By contrast, Liverpool, a conscientious and capable if uninspiring man, was able to

---

[1] There was a background of violence, however, which gave the incident a political tinge (see F. O. Darvall, *Public Order and Popular Disturbances in Regency England* (1934)). People cried 'God bless him' as Bellingham, Perceval's murderer, went to the scaffold. 'This is but the beginning', Coleridge heard people say (*Letters of S. T. Coleridge* (1895), vol. II, p. 598).

[2] See M. Roberts, *The Whig Party, 1807-1812* (1939), p. 3. This book gives a useful account of Whig groupings and divisions.

co-ordinate the forces of order and to marshal them for the victory against Napoleon.

Limited by lack of financial resources but avoiding the dispersion of effort which Pitt and his successors had perpetuated, Liverpool maintained 'a steady and continued exertion on a moderate scale'. If he shared none of Wellesley's grand strategic schemes, he persisted in the Peninsular venture and gave Wellington sufficient though never lavish support. Already in 1810 and 1811 Wellington had preserved his defences at Torres Vedras in face of the attacks of Napoleon's general Masséna: from the famous lines of Torres Vedras, the British armies marched to the frontiers of Spain and by capturing the key fortresses of Ciudad Rodrigo and Badajoz in April 1812 were able to pass to the offensive. The victories of Salamanca (July 1812) and Vitoria (June 1813) followed. After Vitoria the French had to evacuate all Spain south of the river Ebro and were soon pushed back to the Pyrenees. Wellington chased them back into France, entering Toulouse in March 1814.

These efforts, the result of generalship of the highest order, were not in the forefront of European news in the years 1812–1815. As usual it was Napoleon who stole the stage, but for the first time he was no longer starring in the rôle of conquering hero. At the end of 1811, he had made up his mind to attack Russia, the 'greatest and the most difficult enterprise that I have so far attempted'. With satellite troops gathered from all over occupied or 'allied' Europe in an enormous army of nearly half a million men, he crossed the Niemen in June 1812 *en route* for Moscow. By September the remnants of his cold and hungry army arrived there, only to find the city in flames. By October he was in retreat again amid the icy gloom of a Russian winter. By December, when he had been forced to leave his 'army' and return to Paris, the army had almost ceased to exist. More serious even than the loss of men was the loss of 500 cannon, 10,000 wagons and 200,000 muskets and sabres.

Defeat in Russia was followed by the massing of a new coalition against him, a popular coalition which was supported not only by 'sovereigns' but by 'people of all ranks'. Castlereagh, who, like Tsar Alexander, realized the changed nature of the struggle, was far more effective at the Foreign Office than he had been as minister of war and played a big part in the successful formation of a new alliance. He encouraged the Russians and the Prussians, who had signed a treaty of alliance in February 1813, to come to a genuine and deeper understanding. In March 1813 the Prussians declared war on Napoleon, and although they were defeated at Lützen and Bautzen, Napoleon was driven to sign an armistice with them on 4 June which gave them time to recover. Castlereagh signed the Treaty of Reichenbach with them and the Russians in the same month, binding them not to make a separate peace. Meanwhile, Austria, which under its shrewd Chancellor, Metternich, had offered mediation, went over the 'allies' on 24 June. For the first time since Napoleon's rise to power, France was confronted by the four great powers simultaneously. If only they could keep together, they were bound to win.

It was not easy for Castlereagh to bind them together in one single confederacy pledged to resist 'the unbounded and faithless ambition of an individual', for behind the will to defeat Napoleon there were conflicting aims and purposes. In October 1813 at Leipzig Napoleon was decisively defeated in the Battle of the Nations, but the allies were reluctant to follow up the victory by invading France. Mutual mistrust was coupled with fear of a French national resistance similar to that of 1793 or to the Spanish resistance to France in 1808. It was to counter further Austrian peace proposals (the Frankfurt proposals), centred on the principle of giving France its 'natural frontiers', that Castlereagh was sent out to allied headquarters in January 1814. After difficult negotiations, he finally persuaded the allies on 1 March 1814 to agree on 'certain fixed principles of common interest' and to sign the Treaty of Chaumont, which bound them yet again to make no separate peace and to continue the war, if necessary, for another twenty years. The objectives of victory, it was agreed, included 'an enlarged and independent Holland, a confederated Germany, an independent Switzerland, a free Spain under a Bourbon dynasty, and the restitution of the Italian States'. To maintain such a settlement the great powers agreed to remain in alliance for twenty years after the war: to cement their understanding with hard cash, Castlereagh promised that Britain should contribute twice as much towards what was hoped would be the final allied effort as any other of the powers.

Less than a month after Chaumont, the allies led by Tsar Alexander, entered Paris on 31 March 1814. On 4 April Napoleon abdicated in favour of his son, but it was too late. The rump of the French Senate, organized by Talleyrand, voted for the recal of the Bourbons, Louis XVIII returned, and Napoleon was exiled to Elba.

As events turned out, this was not quite the end of the story. At the end of February 1815 Napoleon escaped from his island exile and on 20 March re-entered Paris 'without firing a shot'. The representatives of the allied powers were meeting in Vienna to try with difficulty to work out a lasting 'peace settlement'. At once they declared Napoleon an outlaw, 'the disturber of the peace of the world', and pledged themselves to destroy him. This time, there was to be no prolonged struggle, and the decisive victory, as was fitting, belonged to Wellington, who had been present as British delegate at Vienna when the startling news was received. Abandoning the ballrooms and lobbies of the Austrian capital, he hurried to Belgium, the key continental outwork of the British security system and the original bone of contention in 1793. Along with Blücher, the Prussian general, who commanded 120,000 men at Liège, Wellington with 100,000 men (whom he sweepingly and characteristically dismissed as an 'infamous army') set out to defend the Belgian frontier against Napoleon's rapidly massed forces. His strategic plans were ill thought out and he did not foresee what line of approach Napoleon would adopt, but although in his own simple words, 'Bonaparte has humbugged me', he emerged victorious. At Waterloo on 18 June about 72,000 Frenchmen faced Wellington's 67,000 men, of whom less than a third were British. 'I tell you', Napoleon remarked on the eve of battle, 'that Wellington is a bad general, that the English are bad troops, and it will be a picnic.' Whatever the deficiencies of Wellington's strategy, this was a completely false assessment. From the early morning to the evening of the battle the British centre stood firm in the mud, and beat off successive French attacks. Finally, the arrival of Prussian detachments under Blücher permitted Wellington to counter-attack with his cavalry and to rout the main part of the French army. 'The finger of providence was upon me', was Wellington's comment, although he admitted that the battle was 'the nearest run thing you ever saw in your life'. Four days after Waterloo Napoleon abdicated yet again and soon afterwards surrendered to the captain of a British ship, H.M.S. *Bellerophon*, which was cruising off the French coast. 'The most powerful, the most constant and the most generous of my enemies', as he now described the British, packed him off to the remote island of St. Helena, where he lived unhappily until his death in 1821.

4. THE SINEWS OF WAR

How had it been possible for Britain to wage almost continuous war from 1793 to 1815 and eventually to emerge victorious? The answer clearly did not lie in inspired political leadership, in co-ordinated grand strategy, or, despite the size of the army (350,000) during the last stages of the war—the period of what Cobbett called 'the gorget and the sash'—in the strength of British land forces.[1] Looking at the struggle as a whole, the two main decisive material factors were naval and economic. It was above all else the seas, the source both of Britain's wealth and greatness, which saved the country and ensured ultimate victory.

Organized sea-power, symbolized in the fleet, 'the defence which reason and nature so clearly point out to us',[2] was employed in a less dramatic and spectacular way after Nelson's triumph at Trafalgar, but the frequent inaction of the fleet was itself a sign of mastery. Collingwood maintained the defence of the Mediterranean through seven years of continuous French military expansion, while British vessels overseas won victories in places as far apart as Martinique, St. Domingo and Senegal. Britain's naval supremacy was based neither on superior naval equipment—the industrial revolution had not yet affected naval construction or methods—or even on the superior discipline and morale of the ordinary sailors. The means of naval recruitment—by the press gang, or through bargains with magistrates to attach vagabonds and prisoners to the service or even by employing foreigners—did nothing to guarantee a reliable force. It was rather the plentiful supply and qualitative superiority of British officers and the organization of the naval command which differentiated the two opposing fleets. Until his death at sea in 1810 Collingwood stood out in particular, in Creevey's phrase, 'the prime and sole minister of England, acting upon the sea, corresponding himself with all surrounding states, and ordering everything upon his own responsibility'.[3]

While the navy was keeping the ocean lanes open, patrolling the coasts of the colonies and providing convoy cover for merchant-men, the merchant service as a whole, through all the vicissitudes of

---

[1] Many critics of military organization during the war complained that Britain was 'the only country in Europe that has not a regular, fixed, well-known rule by which to arm ourselves for offence and defence in time of war'. For a fiery criticism see C. W. Pasley, *An Essay on the Military Policy and Institutions of the British Empire* (1810).

[2] *Political Register*, 1 April 1815.

[3] Quoted Mackesy, *op. cit.*, p. 396.

economic warfare, was laying the foundations of an overwhelming
peace-time supremacy. Although the French and their allies captured
on an average 524 merchant ships a year between 1795 and 1810,
this loss, even in the worst years, amounted to only 3 per cent of the
total British tonnage. As the war went on the pay of merchant
sailors soared, but marine insurance rates significantly fell, from as
much as 25 per cent in the 1790s to as little as 6 per cent in 1810.
British overseas trade continued to expand in sharp contrast to the
languishing of French trade; there was a tremendous rise in exports
from 1812 to 1815, and as a portent of things to come, a newly
built steamship arrived in London from Glasgow in 1815 after a
voyage of 1,500 miles.

The continued resilience of British overseas trade depended, of
course, not only on shipping space—this does not seem to have been
a limiting factor—but on the productive powers of a newly developing industrial society. While Napoleon failed to develop French
industry under the blanket of protection which the war and the
inevitable abrogation of the Eden Treaty provided, British industry,
immune from competition, continued to expand. Different sectors
of it were affected in different ways, but at least down to the forma-
lization of Napoleon's Continental System (1806–10) and the
promulgation of Britain's retaliatory Orders in Council (from 1807)
most industries showed continued growth.

Progress in cotton and woollen textiles from 1793 to 1807 was
interrupted only by the financial crises of 1797, 1799 and 1803, and,
as one cotton spinner put it, whenever the industry 'received a blow,
the rebound was quite wonderful'.[1] The invention of the cotton gin
in the United States in 1793, the year when war broke out, led to
an enormous increase in American exports of raw cotton (from
about ½ million pounds in 1793 to over 20 million pounds in
1801): plentiful supplies and still expanding markets created such
a favourable business situation that in the summer of 1802 there
were about twenty factories in construction in or near Manchester.
Although there was a break in prosperity in 1803 and pessimists
claimed that 'dullness of trade' would continue until 'Bonaparte was
settled', it was a sign of British textile supremacy that Bonaparte's
soldiers were wearing British greatcoats when they defeated the
Russians in 1807. In the West Riding of Yorkshire, Benjamin Gott
of Leeds was manufacturing clothing and blankets for the armies

---

[1] Quoted by E. Baines, *History of the Cotton Manufacture* (1835) pp. 358–9.

of England, Russia, Prussia and Sweden, and even older centres of the woollen industry, like Norwich, enjoyed a war-time boom.

Britain's second great industry, the iron trade, directly associated with war requirements, was relatively prosperous throughout the whole period from the outbreak of war until the Peace of Amiens in 1802, and even after peace had been signed, 'the impetus derived from recent developments was sufficient to carry iron production across the gulf'.[1] The demand for ordnance was the main cause of growth, and the great supply establishments at Woolwich and Enfield, backed up by the distant Carron works in Scotland, were enterprises the scale of which Napoleon could not match. Nor could he make use of the new British techniques which were increasingly superior to those of the continent. But there were other reasons for growth besides the demands of government—limitation on iron supplies from Sweden and the Baltic, for example, and the still multiplying commercial uses of iron by machine-makers and manufacturers of domestic equipment. There was such a rapid increase in demand that at the turn of the century ironmasters were complaining of a shortage in coal supply, and iron works were greatly increasing the scale of their operations. By 1806 the three largest iron works in the kingdom were located in the newly booming area of South Wales.

The third great industry, for it could now be described in such a way, was agriculture, and the war guaranteed that the 1790s were a golden age of agriculture for the new large-scale farmers and the smaller men alike. The enclosure movement continued at a rapid pace and new ploughland was opened up; there was a marked increase in capital investment in farms; transport improvements widened the range of markets; the Board of Agriculture, set up by Pitt in 1793, spread propaganda relating to new methods and techniques. Although the prices of agricultural products fell from 1801 to 1804, they remained high for a decade after 1804, and a renewal of large-scale agricultural 'improvements' dissipated fears and grievances which had been expressed in the first four years of the new century. Landlords benefited from high rents and tenant farmers from war-time prices, and the output of tillage crops in 1815 was 50 per cent greater than it had been twenty years before.

While agriculturalists continued to do well during the last ten years of the war, industrialists faced far more complicated problems between 1806 and 1811 than they had faced in the previous period of

[1] T. S. Ashton, *Iron and Steel in the Industrial Revolution* (1951 edn.), p. 146.

hostilities. The series of Orders in Council (twenty-four in all) introduced by Grenville and the Ministry of all the Talents and continued far more extensively by Portland's government, were blamed for businessmen's problems far more than the Berlin decrees or Napoleon's Continental System. Taken together, the Orders declared France and her allies in a state of blockade, banned trade between French ports and other enemy ports and between enemy colonies and their mother countries, and allowed neutrals to trade with France and her allies only if they were selling British goods or if their vessels first touched at an English port, declared, unloaded and reloaded their cargoes, and paid a duty. In other words, that residue of foreign trade which had not already been disturbed or strangled by Napoleon was strictly controlled by the British government. 'The enemy had declared that Britain should have no trade. The reply was that the enemy—and the word was used in its widest sense—should have no trade except through Britain.'[1] Licences were issued to individual merchants to contravene the Orders in Council, but they were as unpopular with most business-men as the system itself.[2]

Already suspicious of government interference and prone to blame Westminster rather than Paris for business difficulties, British manufacturers and merchants attacked the Orders-in-Council from the start. They had no conception of the need for 'economic warfare' and were alarmed by its immediate results both in Europe and America. They were even more alarmed—particularly those manufacturers who depended on the American market—when the neutral United States passed the Embargo Act of 1807 and followed it up two years later by the Non-Intercourse Act, which closed American harbours to both British and French vessels.

Alarm was tempered at first by continued experience of pros-perity. French industry was in no position to meet all the continental demands made upon it nor could Napoleon devise an efficient administrative system to prevent the smuggling of British goods into Europe, not only through Portugal, but through places as far away as Salonika, Venice and Trieste. Despite Napoleon's efforts to make the commercial war 'the central point in the entire internal and external policy of France',[3] there was a lusty boom in many parts of

[1] A. F. Fremantle, *England in the Nineteenth Century, 1806–1810* (1930), pp. 226–7.
[2] There is need for a good monograph on the Orders in Council. For business opposition, see *P.P.* (1812). *Reports of Committees.*
[3] See E. F. Heckscher, *The Continental System* (1922), p. 88.

Britain in 1808 and 1809. Losses in trade with the United States were made up by gains in Spain and Portugal, after the beginning of the Peninsular War, and in Brazil and Latin America. This latter trade had a highly speculative tinge—in a famous phrase of the economist J. R. McCulloch, 'some speculators actually went so far as to send out *skates* to Rio Janeiro'—but when the speculative element is discounted, 'more Manchester goods were sent out in the course of a few weeks than had been consumed in the twenty years preceding'.

Such good times could not last, and Britain faced a serious economic—and political—crisis in 1810 and 1811. The speculative boom collapsed, prices fell sharply, the number of bankruptcies increased and in the manufacturing districts there was large-scale unemployment. At the same time, there was first a loosening and then a tightening of Napoleon's blockade. To add to social tension there were bad harvests in 1809 and 1811 and the expectation of one in 1810. In all the great industrial centres, manufacturers and merchants clamoured for a total abolition of the 'disastrous and stupid' Orders in Council. Fifty thousand inhabitants of Manchester had pressed for revocation even in the relatively good year 1808: in 1810 and 1811 the pressure increased, and the war as a whole became unpopular. In Birmingham, where it was estimated that almost half the total volume of the city's output was produced for the American market, there were 9,000 people in receipt of poor relief in the summer of 1811 and 'every manufacturer is overloaded with stock'.[1] A young banker, Thomas Attwood, was given the task of presenting the city's case against the Orders, backed by a united front of businessmen and artisans. 'Never in any former instance, or upon any other subject, were the genuine feelings of by far the greater majority of the inhabitants of the town so strongly excited, or so unequivocally expressed.'[2] Urban demonstrations in many other British cities—supported and at times organized by the ambitious young Whig politician Henry Brougham, counsel for the Liverpool merchants in 1808—provided a sharp reminder to Perceval's government that business opinion could no longer be overlooked. Early in 1812 Brougham succeeded in securing a committee of the House of Commons to inquire into the state of trade: it sat for six weeks and examined over 100 witnesses from thirty manufacturing towns. In their fight against the Orders, the merchants and manufacturers

[1] *Minutes of Evidence against the Orders in Council* (1812) pp. 30–1.
[2] *Aris's Gazette*, 9 April 1812.

had moved one stage further on the road to self-expression. Behind them was the movement of the 1780s: in front of them were the outspoken and often radical movements of the post-war years.

The difficulties of the years 1810 and 1811 were better exploited by Brougham than by Bonaparte. When British harvests were disastrous and food prices had risen so high that thousands faced starvation, Napoleon was unable to resist the pressure of French grain growers who after a run of good harvests were anxious to export their surpluses to starving Britain. Making a serious miscalculation in 1810, based on a fundamental misunderstanding of the political situation, Napoleon came to the conclusion that if he could force Britain to export gold to buy wheat, disastrous inflation would cripple Britain's will to resist. There was inflation in wartime Britain as we shall see, but it was relatively mild, and Napoleon, with his eyes fixed on Britain's adverse trade position, forgot Britain's increase in national income and output. It would have been far better for him in 1810 to have tried—he might not have succeeded—to starve Britain out or at least to add to the social tension in the British manufacturing districts. Instead, he let the critical moment pass.

In 1812 the new government of Lord Liverpool abandoned the Orders in Council, and, to make the freeing of trade complete, Napoleon abandoned the Continental System too. The epitaph on Napoleon's policy was a memorandum of December 1812. 'Undoubtedly', he informed his minister of commerce, 'it is necessary to harm our foes, but above all we must live.' In England the epitaph on the Orders in Council was publicly recited. Fifty thousand people cheered Attwood and his fellow delegates on their return to Birmingham from London after the government had made what Castlereagh regarded as an unprecedented concession to middle-class pressure; a few months later, in Tory Liverpool during a spirited election where both sides were compelled 'to resort to speechmaking and demonstrations', Brougham got near to winning the seat from Canning. The cheering and excitement at the change in government policy could not prevent a war with the United States (June 1812–December 1814), partly although not entirely inspired by American trade and shipping grievances.[1] From a

---

[1] The most active anti-British influences in the United States were to be found in the west, and they were more concerned with Canada than with shipping. See J. W. Pratt, *Expansionists of 1812* (1925).

military and naval point of view, little that happened during the war deserves to be remembered (although Toronto was burned and Washington attacked): from an economic point of view, the war encouraged both British free traders and American protectionists.

The revival of British trade and exports between 1812 and 1815 could not quite blot out the memory of business grievances and dissatisfaction during the previous period. Just as Pitt's war against the Revolution had begun in face of the hostility of a substantial number of rich businessmen, so the war against Napoleon ended with at least some businessmen conscious only of the business opportunities it had wasted and the burdens which it had entailed.

To assess the nature and extent of the burdens, it is necessary to take into account two basic points. First, the long wars with France were not total wars. As Dr. G. M. Trevelyan has written, 'the war was in the newspapers, but it scarcely entered the lives of the enjoying classes'.[1] Jane Austen, for example, had two brothers at sea during the wars, but she kept warfare almost entirely out of her novels. From an economic as well as a military point of view, war never became 'the great industry, directing, distorting, and dominating the whole of the nation's economic life'.[2] Whereas statisticians during the Second World War reckoned that three civilian workers were needed to keep one fighting man in the field, during the Napoleonic Wars it was estimated that one civilian worker could maintain two fighting men.[3]

Second, whatever the privations of war—and they were many—continued economic growth, including the growth of capital equipment, relieved the strain. What a well-known statistician, Patrick Colquhoun, called 'new Property . . . annually created by the Labour of the People'[4] permitted an increase in employment and a rise in productivity. 'Many, who from deficient activity or mediocrity of parts, would, in a state of peace, have necessarily remained unemployed, were brought by the war into situations attended with income.'[5] Contemporaries seldom attempted to deny this. Arthur Young, with characteristic exaggeration, claimed that as a result of the catastrophe of 1789 'Britain became the emporium of the world, and such a scene of wealth and prosperity filled every eye in this

[1] *Illustrated English Social History* (1952), vol. IV, p. 4.
[2] W. K. Hancock and M. M. Gowing, *British War Economy* (1949), p. 13.
[3] *Ibid*, p. 14: See also J. Lowe, *The Present State of England* (1822).
[4] *A Treatise on the Wealth, Power and Resources of the British Empire* (1814).
[5] Lowe, *op. cit.*, p. 30.

happy country, as the sun before had never shone upon.'[1] More discriminating observers admitted that 'the mass of the people did not suffer as severely as would seem probable. The country was not overrun by a hostile force; industry and commercial activity were not checked, but rather increased, and, although taxation was high, the produce of land, and of every article of manufacture being paid for in proportion, the war except to fixed incomes, made but a trifling difference.'[2] It was Colquhoun's conclusion that 'war, accounted in former days a season of embarrassment and poverty, assumed in the present age the appearance of a perido of prosperity.'

Granted the basic reliability of these general assessments, what was the nature of the 'burpens', and which economic interests and social groups bore them?

In the first place, there was the burden of rising prices not only on people with fixed incomes but on the poorest and weakest sections of the community. Dear food meant high rents for landlords and large profits for tenant farmers: it also meant starvation for the poor, not only the congested poor of the new towns but the village labourers themselves. Wages did not keep pace with prices. Dear timber, bricks, and glass meant inferior housing for those who could not afford to respond to the opportunities of a free economy. The rising rate of interest on government stock limited all forms of 'social investment'.

The two main periods of price rise were from 1793 to 1801, when government policy was markedly inflationary, and from 1811 to 1814, when many prices reached a nineteenth-century peak. Although poor consumers had only restricted ways of expressing their discontent in such situations—rioting was the most natural way —more sophisticated observers blamed the Bank of England; a Select Committee of the House of Commons was appointed in 1810 to enquire into the causes of the high price of bullion. Its diagnosis —over-issue of notes by the Bank—and its main recommendations —that cash payments by the Bank of England, which Pitt had suspended in 1797, should be resumed—were not acceptable to those who placed the needs of the war above the dictates of 'sound finance', and a further sharp rise in prices followed. In fact, the Bank was by no means entirely responsible for the price rise. Inflationary budgets, bad harvests, exchange depreciation and

---

[1] *Inquiry into the Value of Money in England* (1812), p. 77.
[2] W. A. Mackinnon, *op. cit.*, p. 134.

commercial speculation, particularly when taken together, explain much which at the time was blamed on the Bank. Wherever the cause lay—and it was in the heart of the 'free economy' itself—the consequences were felt by that section of the community least able to do anything about them.

In the second place, there was the burden of mounting taxation. To meet the exceptional demands of war-time expenditure, a government can rely on three expedients—to borrow money, to create money through the government's bank, and to raise additional taxes. Between 1793 and 1815 taxation covered nearly a half of total British government expenditure: the corresponding figure for the First World War was far lower, and it was not until the Second World War, when administrative as well as economic conditions were very different, that it was exceeded. During the first few years of the French Wars, however, Pitt did not rely on taxation but on borrowing. The size of the loans raised increased from £11 million in 1794 to over £32 million in 1797, and it is not surprising that in the latter year there was a serious financial crisis. Unbalanced budgets, foreign remittances in loans and subsidies, abnormal imports of grain, the re-establishment of a metallic currency in Paris and finally, after paper credit experiments, a run on the English country banks, led to a drain of gold from Britain and a serious fall in reserves which led Pitt first to suspend cash payments by the Bank of England and second, to attempt substantially to increase taxation. What he called 'the necessity of raising a large proportion of the supplies within the year' launched him on the course of war finance by taxation, which came to be regarded by the Victorians as the great tradition of British economic policy. At first, he tried to increase the amount raised from indirect taxation, but in 1799 he introduced the income tax, a direct tax which his opponents branded as 'inquisitorial' and 'iniquitous'. It was not until 1806, when the administration of the tax had been perfected, that it began to produce substantial results, but between April 1806 and April 1816, the year when it was abolished, it produced £172 million for the exchequer. After it was levied at a stable rate of two shillings in the pound, the rise in the total amount collected reflects the economic development of the country. Different sorts of taxpayers were treated differently. Fund-holders and office and pension-holders had their incomes taxed at source: industrialists found it easier to evade their obligations. It is significant that even in East Lancashire, the most highly developed industrial area in the country, Schedule A of the tax—that on rent and real property—produced between two and three times as much as Schedule D—the tax on profits from trade and commerce, manufactures, professional earnings and salaries.[1]

The amount raised from income tax never amounted to more than one-sixth of a year's supplies including loans, or one-third of total taxation revenue, and customs and excise duties remained more lucrative means of raising money, quadrupling in yield between 1790 and 1815. These duties, along with the assessed taxes, fell on all sections of the community, but they hit the poor (who were exempt from income tax) far harder than they hit the consumers of luxuries. It was the 'middle and industrious classes of society', however, who complained most. 'Why rejoice in the midst of rivers of blood' one of their spokesmen asked bitterly in 1809, 'while the burden of taxation presses so heavily on the middle classes of society, so as to leave the best part of the community little to hope and everything to fear?'[2] Such complaints helped to forge middle-class consciousness, and to push into general use the concept of a 'middle class'.[3] The poorer sections of the community were politically paralysed and had fewer opportunities of ventilating their far more serious tax grievances.

In the third place, despite the large share of war costs paid for out of taxes, the national debt continued to grow. It rose from £228 million in 1793 to £876 million in 1815, and at the same time the annual interest charge increased from less than £10 million to over £30 million, a figure larger than the whole government outlay in 1792. Although from 1806 onwards the annual amount raised in taxation was sufficient to cover the cost of the war and the pre-war interest on the debt, it could never meet the heavy interest charges on the debt incurred during the first period of the struggle. In 1815 interest on the national debt accounted for more than half the total government expenditure, and taxpayers had to continue to pay for the war long after it had ended. It is not surprising that fund-holders began to be regarded as 'spongers' and 'parasites'. Their hold on

---

[1] See A. Hope Jones, *Income Tax in the Napoleonic Wars* (1939).

[2] *Monthly Repository* (1809).

[3] There was a significant association of Protestant nonconformist sentiment and economic grievance in the emergence of specifically 'middle-class' sentiment. The dissenters were conscious that they occupied 'precisely that middle station in society which is most affected by the stagnation of trade and the increase of taxation'. J. Bennett, *History of the Dissenters 1818–38* (1839), p. 240. The term 'middle class' was first popularized in dissenting periodicals.

the country was the nation's most important 'permanent' burden, and it was a burden carried by the poor rather than the rich, for income tax itself (including direct taxation on fund-holders) was abolished—against the wishes of the government—in 1816. The rising national income of the whole community permitted the enormous burden of new debt to be met, but that section of the community least able to bear it—'the lower orders of society' or 'the working classes', as they were increasingly beginning to be called—was expected to contribute most.

Just as the war effort was sustained with no apparatus of government control or any suggestion of a philosophy of 'fair shares for all', so the transition to peace was made with no attempt to lift the burdens of the broad masses of society. They were, indeed, increased. Although during the war 'combinations' of workers by no means completely disappeared,[1] skilled craftsmen sometimes gained wage increases, and hand-loom weavers were given renewed livelihood in some places because of the difficulty and expense of installing sufficient new machines, once the war ended cyclical and technological unemployment added to labour's problems. War and peace were seen as part of the same unfolding pattern of distress and despair.

So far, the chief bearers both of the temporary and permanent 'burden' seem to have been the poor. There was, however, in the fourth place, a real economic cost of the war, which it is impossible to measure precisely. The war meant many foregone as well as realized opportunities; probably the cotton industry, for all its prosperity, would have developed at a faster rate without the war. War-time international trade in textiles, for example, would have developed more smoothly had it not been for difficulties in securing supplies, dislocation of traffic arrangements, and delays in deliveries and receipts. Conditions would have been easier too for the pottery industry, which Wedgwood and his fellow-manufacturers had helped to create. Furthermore, the war entailed much uneven and unequal industrial development. There was heavy over-expansion in the iron industry, for instance, which led to inevitable post-war contraction and unemployment. In agriculture, both heavy war-

---

[1] They existed both in the Midlands and the North, and in 1808 and 1810 a general spinners' union in Lancashire organized unsuccessful strikes for 'equalization' of spinners' wages at Manchester rates. In 1802-6 there was joint action by weavers in Gloucestershire, Somerset and Wiltshire, and the movement was in touch with Yorkshire.

time capital investment, embarked upon in a period of high prices, and the opening up of large amounts of marginal land for cultivation carried with them inevitable post-war difficulties. Heavy debt charges had to be met in a period of falling prices, when much marginal land ceased to be profitable to cultivate. There are still vestiges of abandoned farms of the Napoleonic Wars, situated high on moorland ridges, far away from modern farming areas. Finally, the differential cost of the war—the total of war-time government expenditure minus the estimated total of government expenditure assuming that there had been no war—was £1,573 million, implying an annual average almost as large as the total differential cost of the whole of the Crimean War. Much of this cost was economically 'unproductive'. Bonaparte was beaten, but who could tell what would have been the shape of British economy and society if the war effort had not been deemed necessary?

5. IDEAS AND MORALE

Neither the economic sinews of war nor the military and naval effort were regarded by large numbers of Englishmen as the clue to victory. 'It is to the cultivation of the moral qualities', wrote the liberal *Morning Chronicle* in 1815, 'that England is indebted for her power and influence. From the want of them France may be mischievous, but she will never be great.'[1] The wars against France reinforced the movements for the reformation of manners and the enforcement of a stricter morality; in many ways, indeed, they widened the 'moral gap' between Britain and the Continent as much as they widened the economic gap. The longer the struggle went on, the more ideas—particularly abstract ideas—were regarded as dangerous on this side of the Channel; only moral standards, supported by 'vital religion', were guarantees of social order, national greatness, and individual salvation. They were held to be necessary foundation both of morale and of victory.

During the first years of the struggle, the opponents of the Revolution made much of its atheism and infidelity. 'Most fortunately for the interest of religion and morality or of their prudential substitutes at least', wrote Coleridge long after the wars were ended, 'the name of Jacobin was everywhere associated with that of Atheist or Infidel.'[2] The implications for Britain were clear. 'Those

[1] 2 February 1815.
[2] *Aids to Reflection* (1825).

who are hostile to the British Constitution, are almost always equally hostile to the Christian revelation.'[1] In face of the catastrophic terrors of the French Revolution, however, it was necessary to emphasize the 'vital' rather than the 'rational' aspects of the Christian revelation; the Evangelicals were thus placed in a better position to preach a relevant message for generations at war than less 'enthusiastic' Churchmen. Their cry that Britain's distemper 'should be considered rather as a moral than a political malady'[2] permitted them—indeed, compelled them—to appeal to all sections of society.

The Evangelicals remained a minority within the Church of England and were bitterly attacked by both clerical and lay enemies of 'fanaticism', but they were able to accomplish much of long-term significance in the war-time atmosphere. With the assistance of Wesleyan Methodists, who numbered 213,000 in 1815, and various older dissenting groups, they successfully encouraged the 'vigorous principle of enlarged and active charity',[3] particularly during years of economic and social strain like 1811 and 1812. They attacked abuses of ecclesiastical organization, like clerical absenteeism (Jane Austen turned to this question in *Mansfield Park*, 1814). They refused to whitewash political scandals; Wilberforce, for example, voted in the House of Commons in 1805 for the trial of Lord Melville (a blow which hit Pitt hard)[4] and four years later for an enquiry into the conduct of the Duke of York. In that year Perceval, who sympathized with Evangelicalism, ceased to call parliament on Mondays so that members should not have to travel on the Sabbath. The independent action of Evangelical members of parliament had made them into a recognized 'party of the Saints', a small but influential circle in the group politics of the period from 1801–1812. Their notions of morality were well brought out (to the point of caricature) in a well-known sketch of a 'spiritual barometer', prepared in 1800. The highest point of the barometer was 'glory' and the lowest point 'death and perdition'; in between came the theatre, 'frequent parties of pleasure, much wine, spirits, etc.', luxurious entertainments, levity in conversation and fashions. At

---

[1] B. Porteus, *A Charge delivered to the Clergy of the Diocese of London* (1799), p. 15.

[2] W. Wilberforce, *A Practical View of the Prevailing Religious System of Professed Christians* (1797), p. 415.

[3] *Ibid.*, p. 337.

[4] 'What a comfort', was Hannah More's comment on Melville's successor, 'to have a cabinet minister who *prays* for the success of his measures'. Quoted M. Jaeger, *op. cit.*, p. 50.

the half-way point of the barometer were indifference, 'family worship only on Sunday evenings', private prayers frequently omitted, 'family religion wholly declined'.[1] To provide a suitable spiritual atmosphere in which the barometer could function, they fostered voluntary associations, such as the Church Missionary Society, founded in 1799, and the British and Foreign Bible Society, set up in 1804 and managed jointly by Evangelicals and dissenters. While the threat of invasion hung over England, Bibles, which they considered the best antidote to it, were distributed in thousands.[2] Eight years later in another critical year, they emphasized the power of the Bible during moments of internal danger. 'If the security of the state depends upon the loyalty and morals of its people, by what other means [than Bible reading] can you contribute so essentially to the preservation of order, to the authority of the law, and the stability of government?'[3] But the Bible was the key to the salvation of other nations as well as of Britain. No group stressed international action, and particularly Christian action within the Empire, more vigorously than the Evangelicals and their friends.[4] Not only could they claim a large share in the successful abolition of the slave trade in 1807, but they founded bodies like the African Association (1806) to watch the African coast, set up a negro colony in Sierra Leone which was not based on slavery (1784), and persuaded Parliament, in face of opposition both from the East India Company and other Christian bodies, to appoint a bishop and three archdeacons for India (1813). They even secured the insertion into the new East India Charter (1813) of a clause investing the Board of Control in London with authority to overrule decisions of the Company refusing licences to missionaries. Their dream was a Christian India, bound to Britain more by the ties of 'vital religion' than by economics.

The efforts of the Evangelicals and their allies, supported by other influences, undoubtedly led to a genuine improvement in morals and manners in Britain during the French wars. Nearly all contemporary observers agreed about the change, whether they

---

[1] *Evangelical Magazine*, December 1800. Quoted M. J. Quinlan, *Victorian Prelude* (1941), p. 115.
[2] Two and half million copies of the Bible were issued by the British and Foreign Bible Society between 1804 and 1819.
[3] *Christian Observer*, July 1812.
[4] The older nonconformist sects were also interesting themselves more and more in missionary action. The Baptist Missionary Society was set up in 1793 and the London Missionary Society(a Congregationalist organization) two years later.

approved of it or not. At the base of society (so it seemed) people 'became wiser, better, more frugal, more honest, more respectable, more virtuous, than they ever were before'[1]; at the peak of society, although wickedness continued to flourish, 'the wicked seemed more wicked, and the good, better'.[2] The romantic movement with its heroes and its villains heightened the contrast, but moral earnestness rather than poetic imagination made the contrast possible. Although the first generation of post-war Britons was still a cruel and violent generation by modern standards, many habits which had been taken for granted in the past were now regarded as 'frivolous' or out of place. In such circumstances the Evangelicals were torn between the need to focus attention on continued wickedness and the justifiable desire to point to moral progress. It was characteristic of their attitudes that Wilberforce, who thought that Napoleon's escape from Elba had been a manifestation of Divine displeasure, a sign that moral reformation in Britain had not been pushed far enough, went on a few years later to remark that he saw 'in every part of this country new proofs presenting themselves of the diffusion of religion'.

Because the Evangelicals were a minority, the methods they pursued to secure their objectives were in some ways as significant as the objectives themselves. Just as the Methodists, for all their habitual loyalty to the state, bequeathed to working-class radicals useful forms of effective organization—'class meetings' and 'class leaders', for example—so the Evangelicals, whose deepest hopes were centred not on this world but on the next, bequeathed to middle-class liberals a whole apparatus of efficient organization. Their use of magazines and tracts, their willingness to hold public meetings, their appeal to opinion and their foundation of voluntary societies pointed forward to the highly organized political movements of the middle classes later in the nineteenth century. Thus, the organization of the new morality, if not the new moral outlook itself, was a pointer to change rather than a permanent guarantee of stability. Perhaps those conservative members of the Church of England who branded the Evangelicals as 'spiritual Jacobins' were nearer the truth than they knew.

Most of the real Jacobins in Britain, however, had little sympathy with 'vital' religion. Paine and Hannah More were clearly ranged

---

[1] Francis Place Papers, B.M., Add. MSS. 27,828, f. 61.
[2] Hannah More, quoted by M. Jaeger, *op. cit.*, p. 74.

against each other in the 1790s; during the last stages of the war, Cobbett, who was regarded as a 'Jacobin' by most of his enemies, including the government, attacked 'canting Methodists' and Bible societies just as violently as fund-holders and rotten boroughs. Hazlitt, who admired Napoleon as much as he revered the French Revolution, and Bentham, who evolved a new philosophy of reform, joined in lamenting the 'torrent of fanaticism'. To understand the approach of these men to the problems of war-time society, it is necessary to turn from morals to ideas, for although resistance to the Revolution made ideas dangerous and forced them either underground or into expensive editions (like Godwin's *Political Justice*) it could never suppress them.

By 1798, as we have seen, the first phase in the 'intellectual' history of the French Revolution and its impact on Britain was over. The British 'Jacobins' had been tried; some of them had been acquitted, thanks to eloquent defenders, like Erskine, and independent jurymen. Others had recanted, and attempted either to find new political philosophies or to abandon politics altogether. At a Westminster dinner in 1800 Fox was toasting not the liberty of the press but its memory. The government had demonstrated as firmly as it could that it was unwilling to tolerate 'subversive' attacks on the British Constitution. As Lord Braxfield had put it at one of the Scottish trials, 'two things must be attended to which require no proof. First, that the British Constitution is the best that ever was since the creation of the world, and it is not possible to make it better'.[1]

Braxfield might not have read Burke, but as a result of Burke's influence, the defence of the Constitution had been given a new twist. Burke revered the Constitution not for its reason but for its *mystique*. Instead of talking about clocks, Burke talked about trees. He questioned all geometrical and mathematical arguments (which were to him as irrelevant in politics as they were in gardening) and employed analogies and metaphors based on Nature to defend 'a Constitution, whose sole authority is, that it has existed time out of mind'. There was a necessary place in politics for prejudice just as there was in religion, and the aristocratic prejudice was an essential ingredient of a good society. Rights and freedom were grounded in history not in 'political science', and even those 'rules of prudence' which were laid down so clearly in England in 1689 were 'founded upon the known march of the ordinary Providence of God'.

[1] P. Mackenzie, *Life of Thomas Muir* (1831), p. 108.

The arguments used by Burke and his opponents in the early 1790s long survived the war. Burke's plea that history should never be taken lightly, and that radicalism lacked reverence, strongly influenced later generations of thinkers, including one of the seminal thinkers of the nineteenth century, Coleridge the ex-revolutionary, and one of the outstanding 'romantic novelists', Sir Walter Scott. Coleridge did not adopt but rather adapted Burke's views, and evolved a unified Conservative philosophy which allowed for progress as well as tradition[1]; Scott in the Waverley novels (the first of which was published in 1814) personalized many of Burke's ideas and reached a reading public which cared little for political pamphlets. The views of Burke's opponents also reappeared time and time again in different guises. Godwin's complaint that Burke 'reversed the genuine propensities of man' and taught his countrymen to 'seek the public welfare, not in alteration and improvement, but in a timid reverence for the decision of our ancestors',[2] was never quite forgotten, although many of his other views became distinctly unpopular. Paine's stress on natural rights and his contempt for Burke's *mystique*, particularly Burke's suggestion that mankind is 'a herd of beings that must be governed by fraud, effigy and show',[3] continued to move discontented reformers. Above all, a comment by Godwin's wife, Mary Wollstonecraft, that behind all Burke's 'plausible arguments and witty illustrations', the defence of property and 'contempt for the poor' were always conspicuous was to have widespread repercussions in the future. Neither Pitt nor Wilberforce could kill such viewpoints any more than they could finally stamp out the apparently dying embers of popular radicalism. In 1801, when radical ideas were very much in the background, Major Cartwright met Wilberforce, with whom he was on friendly terms, in Westminster. 'Among other friendly expressions, he (Wilberforce) said he hoped we should meet in a better world: I answered that *I hoped we should first mend the world we were in.*'[4] The French Revolution and Malthusian economics might blast Godwin's dream of the perfectibility of man and make

---

[1] Another ex-revolutionary, Southey, was so disturbed by the course of events in 1809 that he wrote: 'Almost the only wish I ever give utterance to is that the next hundred years were over.'

[2] *An Enquiry Concerning the Principles of Political Justice and its Influence on General Virtue and Happiness* (1793), Book III, ch. VII.

[3] *The Rights of Man*, p. 24. Cf. Godwin, Book V, ch. XV, 'Of Political Imposture.'

[4] F. D. Cartwright (ed), *Life and Correspondence of Major Cartwright* (1826), vol. I, p. 300.

simple hopes become complicated,[1] but they could not undermine legitimate hopes of political and social improvement.

Some of these hopes were reinforced by the war-time conversion of Jeremy Bentham to radical reform, for if Coleridge was the first seminal mind of the nineteenth century, Bentham was the second. From 1807 to 1810 Bentham, under the powerful influence of his friend and neighbour James Mill, came to believe that political reform was the precondition of all other reform, including reform of the law. Refusing to build politics on a foundation of 'natural rights'—in this he contrasted sharply with Paine and the French revolutionaries—Bentham was as insistent as any revolutionary on the folly of accepting institutions merely because they were old or respected. He was 'the great questioner of things established',[2] including the British Constitution itself. In the name of 'the greatest happiness of the greatest number', of 'utility' (which for Burke had been a conservative concept), he pleaded for a review of all existing morals and legislation. Once converted to democracy, he demanded in his *Parliamentary Reform Catechism*, first written in 1809 but not published until 1817, equal electoral districts, annual parliaments, household franchise and reform of electoral procedure, on the grounds neither of history nor of 'natural rights' but of interest. As things stood, England was being governed by a minority in the partial interests of a minority; only the 'democratical, which is the universal interest', could secure the greatest happiness. 'Talk of *balance*: never will it do: leave that to Mother Goose and Mother Blackstone.'[3] Reform needed to be advocated in conformity to the 'science of government'. Appeals to antiquity on the lines of Cartwright and the eighteenth-century radicals were neither necessary nor sensible, and all political claims were to be advanced on their intrinsic merit and utility.

Bentham's philosophy rested on eighteenth-century foundations, but it was of the greatest practical use in the nineteenth century, when it began to influence consciously or unconsciously whole groups of politicians and administrators. Godwin's hope of

---

[1] Godwin had argued that 'the road to the improvement of mankind, is in the utmost degree simple' (Book V, ch. XXV). Paine said the same of the duty of Man, which 'is not a wilderness of turnpike gates, through which he is to pass by tickets from one to the other. It is plain and simple.' (*Op. cit.*, p. 51.)

[2] J. S. Mill, *Dissertations and Discussions*, vol. II. (1859), p. 332. It was John Stuart Mill in brilliant essays on Coleridge and Bentham who first described them as 'seminal minds' of the century.

[3] *Works*, vol. III, p. 450.

abolishing government, on the grounds that men's interests are naturally identical, was replaced by Bentham's 'commonsense' policy of reforming government, on the grounds that men's interests must be artificially identified. Bentham's philosophy was one-sided and it contained within itself contradictions and unresolved alternatives. In its most effective form, however, it gave an impetus to all ideas of practical 'improvement'—in law, politics and administration. It might do nothing, as Coleridge and later writers suggested, 'for the spiritual interests of a society', but it permitted Britain gradually to carry out 'silent revolutions' which produced just as far-reaching and abiding consequences as the turbulent revolution of 1789.

The development of Bentham's democratic ideas belongs to the last stages of the Napoleonic wars and marks a significant departure from old-style radicalism. Corresponding to this intellectual development, but by no means completely identified with it, was a second phase in popular political agitation, which began in 1806. Reform ideas, old and new, were increasingly canvassed between 1806 and 1812. The new phase gathered speed relatively quickly after the previous period of indifference. In 1805, when fear of foreign invasion had not yet evaporated, Sir Francis Burdett, an ardent and colourful political reformer, met the aged but still self-confident Horne Tooke, whose career, like that of Major Cartwright, links eighteenth and nineteenth centuries. 'Your political principles', Burdett remarked, 'at present are as much out of fashion as your clothes.' 'I know it', replied Tooke, 'but the fashion must one day return or the nation be undone.'[1] It was Burdett more than any other single person who revived the fashion; the centres of his activities were London and Middlesex, for long the main theatres of fashion in English politics. In 1806, backed by William Cobbett, the former Tory who finally broke with his old patron Windham, and Francis Place, the ubiquitous radical tailor who skilfully sewed together the threads of London reformist politics, he began to enliven the metropolis. Although at the general election of 1806 Burdett was defeated in Middlesex, Cartwright at Boston, Cobbett at Honiton,

[1] J. H. Tooke, *Diversions of Purley*, vol. II (1805), p. 15. Cf. one of Cartwright's comments in 1797. When Tooke wrote to him that the cause of reform was 'dead and buried', Cartwright scribbled in the margin: 'But J.C. is a believer in the resurrection.' Stalwart opponents of men like Burdett complained as early as the elections of 1802, when Burdett stood as a candidate for Middlesex, that the struggle at the election had been 'not between the supporters and opponents of the existing administration, but between Government and Jacobinism'. See J. Bowles, *Thoughts on the late General Election* (1802): *A Letter to the Freeholders of Middlesex* by An Attentive Observer (1804).

and their approved candidate at Westminster, they had successfully raised the radical flag against both Whigs and 'Tories', accusing them both of narrow factionalism, economic corruption and subservience to vested interests.

Experience of the Ministry of All the Talents led the 'radicals' to believe that all 'parties' were mere 'ins' and 'outs', alike in their dependence on 'corruption'. After the fall of the ministry Burdett triumphed at a new Westminster election, largely as a result of the energetic efficiency of a Westminster Committee which set a new standard of popular electioneering. The growing influence of Cobbett in the country and the presence of Burdett in the House of Commons was a sign that future politics would be monopolized neither by the followers of Pitt or Fox: indeed, most of the Whigs, already divided on so much else, hated the 'inflammatory' and 'irresponsible' propaganda of Burdett and his friends more than they distrusted the tactics and strategy of their parliamentary opponents. Whitbread continued to lend his support to parliamentary and administrative reform, but Grey and the Grenvilles were cautious and aloof even on those occasions, like 1809, when the demand for reform seemed to be stirring again among 'the most respectable part of the elective body of the United Kingdom—the yeomanry, the house-keepers, and the middle ranks of society'.[1] A motion proposed by Burdett in June 1809, advocating a plan of parliamentary reform, secured only fifteen supporters in the House of Commons: it seemed to justify an earlier remark of Burdett that the House of Commons 'is the only spot in the world where the people of England are spoken of with contempt'.[2] There was a more forcible justification in store in 1810 when Burdett was committed to the Tower for denouncing in Cobbett's *Political Register* a decision of the House of Commons to imprison for contempt a London radical, Gale Jones. Burdett's committal was the signal for London mob action, reminiscent of 1780, and for a flood of provincial petitions demanding 'an immediate and radical reform'. Bentham, who took full account of Burdett's weaknesses of character, nonetheless recognized the importance of his work: in addition Bentham was influencing Francis Place and being influenced in turn by Cartwright. Progressive Whigs

---

[1] *Morning Chronicle*, 17 April 1809. Many of the Whigs had lost all interest in attacking 'placemen', and believed that they were better placed in Parliament than anywhere else. See B. Kemp, *op. cit.*, pp. 107–8. At the same time they were uninterested in more radical schemes for the extension of parliamentary representation.

[2] Quoted M. Roberts, *op. cit.*, p. 239.

also were producing plans of moderate reform, like that of Thomas Brand, which while they stopped short before Cartwright's 'political reformation', went far enough to appeal to one school of reformers. At last, to try to rally the scattered forces, a new reform society was set up in 1811, including among its members Burdett and Cobbett, Henry Hunt, a new leader, and Christopher Wyvill, an old one, and such prominent personalities as Coke of Holkham. A year later, as a further sign of union, the Hampden Club was formed to bring together leading reformers. To ensure 'respectability', its members had to be men of substance paying a subscription of two guineas and drawing an annual income of at least £300 a year from land. Although the Club had strictly limited purposes, it made it possible for Whigs like Cartwright to keep in touch with the 'politicians'; founded in a year of 'distress' and disturbance,[1] the Club pointed the way to the Whig-radical politics of the post-war world. Its relative failure to mobilize opinion showed the continued weakness of 'ideas' as a moving force in agitation.

'Distress'—to use the word most favoured by contemporaries— was the most effective catalyst of discontent. During those wartime years when bad harvests and high food prices coincided with business depression and urban unemployment, morale tended to fall and ideas to spread. The threat to business prosperity in the government's Orders-in-Council policy made businessmen more receptive to ideas of reform—including abolition of the income-tax, a demand which the reform societies of 1811 exploited to the full —and less willing to take the activities of government for granted. Those businessmen who were also Dissenters—and Dissent, as we have seen, was particularly strong in the industrial North—had an added grievance in 1811 when Sidmouth, not then in office, attempted to control more closely nonconformist preaching activities; vigorous provincial opposition by men of 'grave deportment and puritanical aspect'[2] led to the abandonment of the measure,[3] and a year later a 'New Toleration Act' repealed seventeenth-century restrictions on

---

[1] Cartwright toured the provinces, and later helped to encourage the founding of many less exclusive provincial Hampden Clubs. When friends criticized his political journeys he replied, 'English gentlemen are perpetually travelling. . . . Some go to see lakes and mountains. Were it not allowable to travel for seeing the actual conditions of a starving people?' (*Life*, Vol. I, p. 45).

[2] Lord Holland, *Further Memoirs of the Whig Party* (ed. Lord Stavordale, 1905), p. 101.

[3] The Wesleyans, who led the agitation, thereby aligning themselves for the first time with the older Nonconformists, stressed the influence of Nonconformists in 'raising the standard of public morals, and in promoting loyalty in the middle ranks, as well as subordination and industry in the lower orders of society'.

certain nonconformist activities. In 1813 toleration was granted to Unitarians.

The new business prosperity of the last three years of the war lowered the middle-class political temperature again, but the new working classes, more helpless victims of 'distress', were less easily contented. In bad years earlier in the course of the war, like 1795 and 1800–1, they had been driven to riot and disturbance; in 1811 the 'Luddites', named after a legendary leader, Ned Ludd, set about machine breaking and 'disturbing the peace' in industrial areas. Their motive was not simply ill-considered hostility to machinery as such (this certainly played its part) but a desire to resist wage reductions and to demonstrate workers' solidarity *vis-à-vis* their employers. There was widespread unrest. In Nottingham it was claimed that local disturbances had 'no parallel in history since the troubled days of Charles the First'. In Lancashire and Yorkshire there was evidence of quasi-military discipline, oath-taking and the use of numbers instead of names. In certain places, the 'Luddites' raised the slogans of parliamentary reform, although their activities were far removed from those of the respectable and substantial members of the Hampden Club and hostile to the political radicalism of their most politically conscious employers.[1] The government, representative of order if not of opinion, was bound to take the 'Luddites' seriously and employed an army against them as large as that which Wellington was leading in the Peninsular War. Frame-breaking was made a capital offence, and a new Watch and Ward Act was passed (1812) to try to tighten local security arrangements. Although popular unrest subsided in 1814, it burst out again during the next few years and darkened the first years of peace.

The continuity of working-class discontent suggests that changes in the industrial structure of the country and fluctuations in the means of livelihood were more important than the war itself in stirring both hand and machine workers. Such workers might have little sympathy with the French or with Bonaparte, but there was a limit to their passivity. They might be drawn into popular religious movements like the Primitive Methodist Connexion, the most successful of all Methodist offshoots, which was established in the Potteries in 1812, but some of them at least could not avoid

---

[1] *Leeds Mercury*, 23 November 1811. This important liberal provincial newspaper, an organ of manufacturing opinion, accused the rioters of attributing their 'distress' to low wages and better machinery instead of to 'the long continuance of a heart-sickening war, without visible object, and apparently without end'.

'politics'. When a Methodist minister in Halifax refused in 1812 to bury a workman who had been shot while trying to break into a local mill, the workmen of the neighbourhood treated their dead comrade as a martyr and so threatened the minister that 'his friends judged it hazardous for him to proceed to his country appointments alone'.[1] Memories of incidents of this kind were not easily forgotten and in the disillusionment of the post-war period they continued to inflame the discontented. Not only was Waterloo soon followed by Peterloo (1819),[2] but the reminiscences of wartime distress often overshadowed the tales of the Glorious First of June or of Trafalgar.

That they did not completely blot out the victories of the war was due to two elements in English society, the first of which—the new morality—has already been discussed. The second was an older element—loyalty. To Coleridge the feeling of allegiance or loyalty was as essential a condition of permanent political society as 'restraining discipline', and Britain had demonstrated the strength of loyalty both to Church and King during the long wars; to Scott and to many of his contemporaries, the clue to action was that suggested by the Major in *Old Mortality*, 'I am no politician and I do not understand nice distinctions. My sword is the King's, and when he commands, I draw it in his cause.' Perhaps the final point to consider in an assessment of British morale is the extraordinary popularity of George III even during the last years of his life when he was blind and incurably insane. In a remote village at East Witton in Yorkshire, there is a church built in 1809 with an inscription, which reads: 'In the year of Our Lord 1809 when the People of the United Empire grateful for the Security and Happiness enjoyed under the Mild and Just Government of their Virtuous and Pious Monarch returned Solemn and Publick Thanks to Almighty God that by the Protection of Divine Providence His Majesty King George the Third had been preserved to enter the fiftieth year of his Reign.' Much was to happen, not least of all to the monarchy, between the fiftieth year of George III's reign and the fiftieth year of Queen Victoria's, but the 'virtuous and pious monarch', supreme head of the Church, reviled by the Whigs and revered by many of the rest, could command much more than swords.

[1] See R. B. Wearmouth, *Methodism and the Working-Class Movements of England, 1800–1850* (1937), p. 63.
[2] See below, pp. 209–11.

4

THE POLITICS OF TRANSITION

1. King, Ministers, and Parliament

Georges III did not die until 1820, although for long he had lost all contact with the world of reality. In the meantime the Prince Regent, with little obvious virtue or piety, continued to accept the 'safe government' of Lord Liverpool which had been formed as a second best in 1812.

Increasingly that government, which lasted until Liverpool was struck down by paralysis in 1827, came to rely on its own strength rather than on royal favour or differences of opinion and outlook among its opponents. In its early days it had scarcely been expected to survive its infancy; before many years had passed it had succeeded in consolidating the forces of order and authority while its opponents still remained weak and ineffectual. Although its parliamentary supporters were only loosely attached to each other and were frequently difficult to control, the government eventually attracted to itself most of the conflicting groups which had struggled against each other in the previous decade. Canning, after disbanding his 'party' in 1814, joined the administration as President of the India Board two years later and eventually became foreign secretary after the suicide of Castlereagh in 1822; Wellesley, who had quarrelled so bitterly with Liverpool in 1812, made his peace and became Lord-Lieutenant of Ireland nine years later; Wellington, the hero of Waterloo, joined the cabinet in 1818. The aristocratic Grenvilles finally cut themselves adrift from the Whigs in 1817 and, after toying with the idea of becoming a 'third party', gave their full support to the government on the basis of a patronage compact in 1821. Liverpool succeeded, indeed, in uniting the old Pittite forces which had coalesced in the first struggle against the French Revolution, and in addition to bringing together well-established figures with a past behind them, men like Sidmouth, Wellington, Castlereagh, and Canning, he encouraged bright young men with a future, like

Palmerston, Peel, and Huskisson. Behind the régime, through all its changes, there still lingered the memory of Pitt himself, 'that illustrious Statesman, whose name will ever be dear to England— that Pilot who sat at the Helm, and with a firm and collected mind weathered the Storm, when the raging elements threatened to over-turn at once all those monuments of national greatness raised by the accumulated wisdom of ages.'[1] And associated with Pitt was a 'system' of government, 'the only system which . . . can preserve in equilibrium the balance of our unrivalled Constitution, which can preserve it from all encroachments of monarchical ascendancy, of aristocratic pride, of popular delusion'.[2] By 1827 there were too many disputes about personality and policy to permit the perpetua-tion of this balance, but that the 'system' lasted so long was a tribute to Liverpool.

The prime minister possessed exactly the right blend of qualities to act as a mediator and a reconciler both of men and ideas. His father, Charles Jenkinson, who had risen through the patronage politics of the eighteenth century, groomed his son for high office, but it was character rather than family influence or outstanding political ability which took Liverpool to the top. Contemporaries stressed his 'pure and unquestioned integrity', and men who dis-agreed about everything else were united in respecting his honesty, fairness, and kindness. Modern historians have recently begun to pay adequate tribute to his mediatory rôle in the field of policies and ideas. 'He was representative of his age in a way that few statesmen have been, for he reflected both its prejudices and its enlightenment in exact proportions. . . . He seems, at one moment, to be looking back to the eighteenth century, at another to have set his face towards the prosperous commercial world of the high nineteenth century.'[3] But he was in no way conscious of being a Janus-like figure, for he did not detect the possible inconsistencies in his own outlook, or probe the basic philosophical antagonisms of many of the members of his administration.

The respectability of the prime minister and his tolerance of opposing points of view contrasted sharply with the notorious profligacy of the Prince Regent and his increasingly hysterical prejudices. The poet, Leigh Hunt, described him as 'a libertine

---

[1] These phrases were employed at a metropolitan meeting of Pitt Clubs in 1826.
[2] J. A. Atkinson, *Memoir of the Rev. Canon Slade* (1892), p. 92.
[3] W. R. Brock, *Lord Liverpool and Liberal Toryism* (1941), p. 34.

over head and ears in debt and disgrace . . . without a single claim on the gratitude of his country or the respect of posterity', and the Duke of Wellington remarked not only of George IV but of his brothers (including the unsavoury Duke of Cumberland) that they were the 'damn'dest millstone about the neck of any Government that can be imagined'. The whole royal family, indeed, was held in public contempt and lampooned each week in popular newspapers and periodicals.

There is little doubt also that between 1812 and 1830, when George IV died unmourned and unlamented, there was a waning of royal power as well as of royal popularity. In 1812 it was generally assumed that if the Regent had so chosen, he could have replaced Perceval and later Liverpool by Grey and Grenville or Lord Moira and the 'King's friends'; by 1830 it was clear that royal freedom of choice had been severely limited with respect to both men and measures. Although George liked 'to talk grandly to make people imagine that his prime minister was a sort of maître d'hotel which he might dismiss any moment that it happened to suit him',[1] his ministers knew better. They were bullied, cajoled, irked, frustrated, obstructed, and sometimes made conscious of their insecurity of tenure, but at critical moments it was they and not he who won. His favours, whims and confidences were still more important than those of most later monarchs, but they were not as decisive as those of most of his predecessors had been.

George's deficiencies of character—his lack of responsibility and pertinacity were more serious disqualifications in politics than his debauchery—and his unpopularity in the country were not the sole causes of the waning influence of personal monarchy. In tidying up the administrative and fiscal system, Pitt had severely limited the whole flow of Crown influence. Liverpool followed the same course, and disgruntled believers in the eighteenth-century 'system' of government complained that the influence of 'what they call corruption is, for practical purposes, too small rather than too great'. In 1822 Charles Arbuthnot, joint secretary to the Treasury (thereby patronage secretary) and husband of one of the most amusing political diarists of the century, warned that if the 'just and necessary influence of the crown' were further reduced, 'it will be quite impossible for any set of men to conduct the government of this country'.[2]

[1] *Journal of Mrs. Arbuthnot* (1950), vol. I, p. 79.
[2] Quoted A. S. Foord, *loc. cit.*

Arbuthnot was right in pointing to the implication of diminishing influence for the government rather than for the King, for there is no evidence that George IV was as worried about the subject as Liverpool, or later on, as Wellington. It was they and not the King who had to handle a House of Commons where the ministerial group of members was seldom large enough to guarantee safe divisions or to provide strong leadership in controversial debate. Liverpool, at a half way stage in the history of constitutional practices as of so much else, could depend neither on an efficient patronage system nor a disciplined party machine. Nor were his ministers assisted by a sufficiently large and skilful civil service to free themselves from the burden of administrative detail and to take their places as 'political' leaders in the House.

In such circumstances there was still scope for independent action on the part of individual members of Parliament, either singly or in 'interests', and for continued royal influence if not for ultimate control. Both forms of action pressed hard on government, at least sporadically. There was no guarantee that the government would get its way in the Commons even on major matters of policy. In 1816, for example, by 238 votes to 201 the Commons threw out the income tax which both Vansittart, the chancellor of the exchequer, and Liverpool himself regarded as essential to fiscal stability; the majority included many habitual supporters of the administration. In 1821 and 1822 a formidable cross bench coalition of supporters of the 'landed interest', led by Charles Western, the Whig member for Essex, struggled hard to change the outlines of economic policy.[1] Throughout the whole period individual members of Parliament could bargain for and obtain select committees to investigate important social and economic questions of the day, whatever the members of the government felt about them. It is not surprising that Liverpool was frequently driven to complain both to his friends and to George IV, as he did in May 1819 (when George was still Regent), of the difficulties of 'recovering that weight and influence which ought to belong to every government' and which was threatened by 'the evil temper and disposition which has been so apparent in some of the late proceedings of the House of Commons'. If he did not complain in turn to the Commons

---

[1] 'The country gentlemen treat the government exceedingly ill', wrote Wellington in 1822. 'What I complain of is their acting in concert, and as a party independent of, and without consultation with the government.' Quoted W. R. Brock, *op cit.*, p. 130.

about the difficulties of remaining on good terms with George, he certainly complained frequently enough in private. In June 1821, for example, Mrs. Arbuthnot reported that after Lord Liverpool had received a box from the King at Carlton House, he had thrown it on the ground, 'torn the letter, abused the King and declared he would resign'.[1] In the same year, the King refused him an audience, while seeing three of his colleagues. Such royal whims proved as irksome to Liverpool's successors as to himself. Even Wellington, for all his loyalty to the throne and his early position as a 'special friend' of the King, complained later that George 'was the worst man he fell in with in his whole life, the most selfish, the most false, the most ill-natured, the most entirely without redeeming quality'.[2]

In this situation, one possible way of regulating relations between prime minister and Parliament and prime minister and King was to work through recognized intermediaries. Liverpool did not find the use of such channels easy. He made little effort to call parliamentary party meetings or to have them managed efficiently when they were called: he placed little political reliance on either Arbuthnot or William Holmes, Treasurer of the Ordnance and Tory 'whip'; all he demanded from his supporters in Parliament was 'a generally favourable disposition'. 'I shall never attempt to interfere,' he added, 'with the individual member's right to vote as he may think consistent with his duty upon any particular question.'[3] As far as contact with royal intermediaries was concerned, Liverpool was rightly suspicious. He disliked Sir William Knighton, who became private secretary to the King in 1822, and refused him the rank of privy councillor when the King asked for it. Knighton told Arbuthnot on one occasion that 'Lord Liverpool and I ought for our mutual interests to be like *man and wife*'.[4] Certainly Liverpool, who might not have shared Mrs. Arbuthnot's comprehensive opinion that Knighton was 'the greatest rogue in England', did not see their constitutional relationship in such intimate terms.

---

[1] *Journal of Mrs. Arbuthnot*, vol. I, p. 100.

[2] *Ibid.*, vol. II, p. 266.

[3] Quoted W. R. Brock, *op. cit.*, p. 101. Requests for support to members of Parliament by the leader of the House were still not made in the name of cabinet or party in 1815. 'It is painful for me', Castlereagh wrote to Peel in May 1815, 'to feel myself obliged by a sense of duty to the Prince Regent's Service to represent to the Official Friends of the Government . . . the indispensable necessity under the present circumstances of the session, of giving their constant Attendance throughout the Evening.' (Peel Papers, B.M., Add. MSS. 40,307, ff. 111–123.)

[4] *Journal of Mrs. Arbuthnot*, vol. I, p. 269. Mrs. Arbuthnot also remarked that Knighton loathed Liverpool, *ibid.*, p. 262.

To complete this outline picture of Lord Liverpool's position as prime minister, it is necessary briefly to examine his relations with his cabinet colleagues, with the parliamentary 'opposition', and with what, for want of a better term, was still called 'the People'.

Liverpool was never an autocratic chairman of the cabinet or a vigilant watchdog over the different departments of the administration. Politically experienced as he was—he had held each of three secretaryships of state and had been connected with the India Board —he made little attempt to guide the work of men as different as Sidmouth and Canning, Castlereagh and Wellington. He looked back to Pitt, but he did not try to imitate him. George IV complained, indeed, in 1823, that 'the misfortune of this government is that it is a government of departments'.[1] It was fortunate that the departments were for the most part in capable hands, but in making the complaint George IV did less than justice to Liverpool's own rôle in welding together an effective group, to his skilful negotiation within what was in effect an 'inner cabinet' of key men, to his unobtrusive employment of checks and balances in the larger body, and to his far from unintelligent general scrutiny of financial and economic policy. Although the King was still able on occasion to use his authority to keep particular individuals both inside the cabinet (for example, Sidmouth from 1821 to 1824) and outside it (Canning in 1821), and even to object to its size, he could not break growing cabinet responsibility for policy. In 1821, when Liverpool was pressing for Canning to be included in the cabinet, against the wishes of many of his colleagues as well as the King, there was a moment, according to Hobhouse, when other members of the cabinet agreed 'to carry on the Government without Lord Liverpool, if he should determine to resign for the sake of Canning'.[2] Yet two years later Liverpool wrote to Arbuthnot on the occasion of another contemplated resignation: 'There is no reason why any of my colleagues should follow me, but I think the King will find himself very much mistaken if he supposes that if he dismissed me because it was *his royal will and pleasure* . . . that Canning, Peel, or anyone of my colleagues would remain behind.'[3] When in 1824 Wellington established a confidential relationship with the King and

---

[1] *The Letters of King George IV* (ed. A. Aspinall, 1938), vol. III, pp. 38–9.
[2] *The Hobhouse Diary* (ed. A. Aspinall, 1947), p. 65.
[3] *The Correspondence of Charles Arbuthnot* (ed. A. Aspinall, 1941), p. 58.

a small 'Cottage Coterie' tried to sway foreign policy, it was the Duke and not Liverpool who was deserted in the cabinet, because his colleagues feared that they 'should be supposed to be giving support to the King's favourite'. Thus, while conflicts about personalities and policies threatened to destroy the cohesion of the cabinet in the 1820s, there were other forces pulling it together, not least of all Liverpool's personal hold. In 1826 Peel put the matter very clearly. 'I should feel it dishonourable to allow one Member of the Government, and that Member the head of it, to make himself a sacrifice—and if he retired . . . yet I could not but consider that his retirement under the circumstances, would be a dissolution of the government.'[1] Pitt had never been able to claim loyalty quite as strong as this.

Certainly the parliamentary 'opposition' could not. It was still unsure of its aims and duties, of its place in the Constitution. The Regent's decision in 1812 to abandon not only the Whigs but also the Carlton House 'party' led by Lord Moira (who was safely removed from the English domestic scene when he became Governor of Bengal in 1813) helped to break the traditional hope of opposition—the coming to power of a new occupant of the throne. At the same time, those advanced Whigs like Henry Brougham who wanted to enliven opposition by making spirited appeals to 'the People' outside Parliament—even outside the limited electorate—met with solid resistance from more traditional Whigs who had little interest in waging an uninterrupted political struggle with government. Brougham was just as important in stirring up opposition to the income tax in 1815 and 1816 as he had been in leading the fight against the Orders in Council a few years earlier, and he looked to the public concern for 'retrenchment' as 'the richest mine in the world', but the successful agitation in the immediate post war period was not the prelude to the emergence of a rejuvenated popular Opposition well rooted in the constituencies. Social struggles between 1816 and 1820 in both London and the provinces divided the Whigs and the 'People', broke up the tenuous political understanding between Grey and Grenville, and encouraged some traditionalist Whigs to retire from routine politics altogether rather than face complicated and persistent moral and political choices. Brougham was looked on with grave suspicion, and neither of the post-war Whig leaders in the House of Commons, George

[1] Peel Papers, B.M., Add. MSS. 40,306, f. 184.

Ponsonby (until 1817) or George Tierney, his successor, was able enough to challenge the government effectively.

In 1820, however, what seemed a heaven-sent opportunity was offered to the Opposition. When George IV came to the throne, the question of his broken marriage with the eccentric and flamboyant Princess Caroline of Brunswick assumed central importance, for was Caroline, whom he hated, to be recognized as Queen? This particular royal problem had a long history. George and Caroline had married in 1795, ten years after George had secretly—and illegally—married Mrs. Fitzherbert, a Roman Catholic widow, and from the start the official marriage was a fiasco. George went on his own licentious way, and Caroline too—coarse and exhibitionist—was sufficiently indiscreet to be accused in 1805 of having an illegitimate child. Although cleared by what was called at the time 'the delicate investigation', Caroline felt herself wronged, and succeeded in winning many supporters in Britain, some of them in influential positions. Brougham became her staunchest backer, looking to her in much the same way that Whigs had looked to the Prince of Wales and unscrupulously advocating in 1813 that it was important 'to take her along' as 'a Constitutional means of making head against a revenue of 105 millions, an army of half a million and 800 millions of debt'.[1] He kept in close touch with her after she had left the country in 1814—by this time a favourite with the crowds as well as the politicians—and while the Regent was trying in vain to persuade Lord Liverpool to secure him a divorce and free him from 'the cruellest as well as the most unjust predicament that even the lowest individual, much more a prince, ever was placed in'. A commission was appointed to enquire into the Princess's dubious conduct in Italy, and in 1819 drew up a report producing considerable circumstantial evidence against her. This was the background to the events of 1820. On the death of George III, Caroline returned to England, determined to vindicate her rights as Queen. She was wildly cheered in the streets and welcomed, a little tentatively, by the Whigs, who saw the rich possibilities of 'renewing the old and natural alliance' between themselves and 'the People'. So unpopular was the new King that this alliance seemed likely completely to discredit him. When he asked that Caroline's name should be omitted from the Anglican liturgy, there were many who felt with one of

[1] *The Creevey Papers*, (1903), p. 179.

her advisers that she still had a place in the Prayer Book at least in
the prayer for 'all that are desolate and oppressed'.

This awkward and unsavoury situation forced Liverpool's government in the summer of 1820 (at the expense of losing Canning) to
take proceedings against Caroline, who was accused of adultery and
scandalous behaviour. Her conduct while abroad in Italy justified
the framing of such charges, while her willingness to forsake
advisers like Brougham for radical extremists like Alderman Wood
of London, contemptuously dismissed by Brougham as 'a citizen
and a fishmonger' (George called him 'that beast Wood'), shocked
responsible opinion. The crowds were still with her, however, and
Brougham, who acted as her attorney, skilfully maintained popular
excitement at fever pitch. When Liverpool introduced a Bill of
Pains and Penalties in the House of Lords to deprive Caroline of
her title, prerogatives, rights and privileges, there were spicy press
reports about the unreliability of government witnesses, a rush of
petitions from the provinces, and a vigorous attack on the government both inside and outside Westminster, during which no means
of ridicule and contempt were spared. 'For fifteen days', wrote a
contemporary historian, 'the whole people was obscene.' At last
the Bill of Pains had to be withdrawn before it even reached the
House of Commons, and Liverpool, who had never wished to be
drawn into this vulgar struggle, was compelled to yield to the
pressure of opinion. Ministers' windows were broken and the whole
city of London was illuminated as part of the popular rejoicings.

George IV never really recovered from the humiliation of these
events, but Liverpool did. Queen Caroline was soon forgotten by
most politicians and faded from the public gaze. She died in 1821.
The government, which had seemed on the point of breaking up,
found a new lease of life. Recovery took time, however. In December 1820 Huskisson told Canning that the ministers would 'break
down or be broken down before Easter', even when allowance had
been made for the blunders of their opponents. Certainly at this
time the King was dissatisfied with Liverpool and anxious to find a
new prime minister. Even when reluctantly he came to see how
difficult it was to get rid of Liverpool, he resolutely refused to allow
him to bring Canning back into the government. Such pique could
not last. By the end of 1821 the King was asking Liverpool for
advice 'as my friend', and the prime minister had strengthened his
government by settling with the Grenvillites, making Peel home

secretary, and Wellesley Lord Lieutenant of Ireland. A few weeks after the suicide of Castlereagh in August 1822, the King had to accept Canning in his place, although he coated the bitter pill with the sugar of royal 'grace and favour'. Further cabinet changes, engineered by Liverpool, prepared the way for the 'liberal toryism' of the last few years of his administration.

The return of Canning and the gradual change in the mood of Liverpool's ministry reflected in some measure the new importance of 'opinion' in national life. Politicians like Canning or, on the Whig side, Brougham, depended on their political skill in addressing meetings and mobilizing support, not on backstairs influence or connexion[1]; their actions inside and outside Westminster—and the actions of Liverpool and the old guard of ministers too—were increasingly scrutinized by the press and discussed by a bigger 'political publick' than had existed in the past. From the date of the reconstruction of the ministry, which was completed in 1823, an attempt was made to appeal to 'opinion', to keep the actions of government in line with the spirit of the times.

This was a significant change. The reaction of ministers to most manifestations of opinion before 1820, particularly the 'opinions' of the press, was hostile. Privacy was preferred to publicity, the secrecy of the drawing room to the bright lights of the stage. *The Times*—from 1814 onwards printed by steam-driven machinery —might argue that newspapers 'constitute one of the great springs of a society so highly civilized and so completely organized as that of Great Britain',[2] but most traditionalists thought them a nuisance at best and a serious political danger at worst. Increased stamp duties were introduced in 1815, and further action was taken to control the press in 1819. It was hardly surprising in such circumstances that the opposition had a far better press than the government, and as a result the feeling grew that there would have to be a closer harmony between government and 'opinion' if the balance of the Constitution were to be maintained.

Robert Peel, the new home secretary in the reformed adminis-

---

[1] George IV objected in 1823 to 'the passion which seems to exist for speech making out of time and out of proper place. What would Mr. Pitt have said, if in his days, Ministers and others belonging to the government had indulged in such inconvenient practices?' (*Letters of George IV*, pp. 38–9).

[2] 8 June 1815. Cf. the opening sentences of *The Periodical Press of Great Britain and Ireland* (1824). 'The Periodical Press of Great Britain . . . is the most powerful moral machine in the world, and exercises a greater influence over the manners and opinions of civilized society than the united eloquence of the bar, the senate and the pulpit.'

tration, described public opinion in 1820 as a 'great compound of folly, weakness, prejudice, wrong feeling, right feeling, obstinacy and newspaper paragraphs'.[1] It was fortunate for Liverpool that even before 1820 there was little solidity in this hotch-potch of diverse ingredients. Wrong feeling was balanced by right feeling, folly by obstinacy, the clamour of the press by the unconcealed indignation of the influential and at times frightened opponents of noisy publicity and free comment. The excesses of radicalism—the word 'radical' was one of the newly popular words of the post-war period—and the challenge to order, coupled with distrust of the inexperience and 'irresponsibility' of the Whigs, ensured a solid foundation for public support of the government in stormy years like 1819. After the reconversion of the ministry Liverpool looked for new and more 'enlightened' support among 'the great commercial interests of the country', even though the switch in appeal meant incurring the suspicions of some of his hitherto most fervent followers. Increasingly the second of the two new political labels of the period —'liberal'—was applied to members of his own ministry.

The break in the early 1820s can be exaggerated. In the background of both periods of Liverpool's administration were the mounting pressures of a complex society, where social differences were greater, economic forces more variegated, and political issues more persistent than they had ever been before. Liverpool, unlike many of his eighteenth-century predecessors, could not rely on the provision of sound administration alone. Popular or unpopular, he had to decide and to act; even to resist was itself a form of action. The responses of his government to the two basic problems of the new complex society—the articulation of 'issues' (some of them involving legislation and all of them setting new terms of reference in politics) and the challenge to order—revealed the difficulties in steering government through strange new seas.

2. 'CASH, CORN, AND CATHOLICS'

The three main issues which the government had to try to settle after the end of the war were summed up later in the century by one of Peel's first biographers under the catchy heading—'Cash, Corn and Catholics'.[2] They were not the only issues, but they were

---

[1] J. W. Croker, *Correspondence and Diaries* (1884), vol. I, p. 184.
[2] W. Cooke Taylor, *The Life and Times of Sir Robert Peel*, vol. I, (1846–51), p. 1.

all central, they were all raised before 1815, and they all continued to capture the attention of the country for more than half a century.

Of the three, the Catholic question had most complicated the course of politics before 1815. It was a question which involved a whole range of important problems—the royal prerogative, the nature of civil rights, the place of religion in the constitution of the state, and the government of Ireland. On all these problems there was room both for debate and deadlock. Governments fell or were built up around conflicting attitudes to these crucial issues. Pitt had resigned as prime minister in 1801 because the King considered Catholic emancipation an 'improper question'. The Ministry of all the Talents had been replaced in 1807 because it also moved towards a solution of which the King did not approve. Sidmouth, Perceval, and Liverpool had risen to power because they were prepared to support the King on this issue; but so sharply did even natural conservatives disagree about the right answers to the leading questions that from 1812 to 1827 Catholic emancipation was made an 'open question' in the cabinet, and totally different views were expressed about it by different ministers. To complicate matters still further, different views were expressed about it by the same people at different times, as they were also in the case of corn and currency. The life of Peel, for example, whose political career was bound up with the settlements of all these big issues, involved many shifts of position, and in retrospect could be justly regarded as an epitome 'of the progress of public opinion in England'.

Although Catholic emancipation did not come to the forefront of national politics until 1800, behind the conflicts of that year was the centuries-old controversy concerning relations between England and Ireland. During the 1780s, as we have seen, Pitt tried in vain to improve economic relations between the two countries; during the 1790s, in a new situation, coloured by the excitement of the French Revolution, he attempted to quieten growing political, economic and religious turmoil in Ireland by conciliating Irish Catholics (in an important Relief Act, forced through the Protestant Irish Parliament in 1793). The climax of his policy was the preparation of an Act of Union between the two countries designed to join together 'a pigmy with a giant in strength, commerce and freedom for mutual support'. There was little doubt that unless there were some bold solution to Anglo-Irish problems, England would suffer as much as Ireland. Indeed, armed rebellion in Ireland in 1798, the product of despair rather than of propaganda, led one contemporary to remark that 'Ireland in its present state will pull down England. She is a ship on fire and must be either cast off or extinguished.'

Although a bold answer to the Irish question was needed—it could never be a solution—three years before the rebellion broke out it was clear that any real attempt at a comprehensive answer would lead to major crises in English politics. In 1795, when for a few months (after Pitt's coalition with the Portland Whigs) the liberal-minded Earl Fitzwilliam was in power in Dublin, George III with his usual stubbornness showed beyond all doubt that he would never countenance full Catholic emancipation. Fitzwilliam was abruptly recalled, and the King set out on paper a point of view which he retained for the rest of his life in his periods of both clarity and insanity—that in both countries there should be only one Church Establishment, to which 'those holding any civil establishment must be conformists'; that although the claim of religion was sometimes discounted by 'persons of rank', 'the bulk of the nation has not been spoiled by foreign travel and manners, and still feels the blessing of having a fixed principle from whence the source of every tie to society and government must trace its origin'; and that, quite apart from any considerations of national feeling, his Coronation oath bound him 'not to Assent to the Repeal of the Act of Supremacy or the Test Act in favour of Roman Catholics'.[1]

The rebellion and its aftermath compelled Pitt to take a different line from the King, but even without the pressure of such circumstances his own temperament and ideas would have made him unhappy about the existing government of Ireland. In 1800 he bribed the Irish Protestant Parliament into supporting an Act of Union—it had resisted the measure a year earlier—and tried to follow it up, as many of his supporters had promised, by introducing a Catholic emancipation bill. Catholics—and Dissenters—should be admitted both to Parliament and to office on taking an amended oath of allegiance; their priests should receive state assistance; and the title system should be revised. Such a measure, Pitt told the King, 'would be attended with no danger to the Established Church or to the Protestant interest in Great Britain or Ireland. . . . Now the Union has taken place . . . it could never give any such weight in office or in Parliament, either to Catholics or Dissenters, as could give them any new means (if they were so disposed) of attacking the

[1] Quoted D. G. Barnes, *George III and William Pitt* (1939), pp. 343–4; 348–9.

Establishment'. In any case, 'those principles, formerly held by Catholics, which made them considered as politically dangerous, have been for a course of time gradually declining, and among the higher orders particularly, have ceased to prevail.'[1]

Pitt's logic did not satisfy George III's scruples, and he made little effort to use the great measure of political power he possessed to try to win over or overbear the King. With the King on the verge of another mental breakdown, Pitt did not wish to coerce him: in any case, he attached great weight to the King's wishes in determining his own 'public duty'. He resigned informally on 3 February, formally on 14 March, 1801 (on completely amicable terms with the King), and helped Addington to form a new ministry.[2] Between the beginning of February and the middle of March, George III had a recurrence of insanity, and rather than add to his anxieties or support a temporary regency, Pitt promised not to revive the question of Catholic emancipation during the King's lifetime, and furthermore to resist any attempts on the part of other statesmen to reopen the subject. Although the King temporarily recovered, both Pitt and his contemporaries knew that to try even to discuss Catholic emancipation with the King after 1801 would be likely to lead to a further bout of insanity.

At the same time, they also knew—at least the more enlightened of them—that it was a tragedy that any possible answer to the Irish question would provoke the use of a royal veto. Pitt might be prepared to tolerate this state of affairs, and men like Addington might share and indeed buttress the King's prejudices, but the more liberal of the opposition Whigs felt disgruntled and thwarted. During the Ministry of all the Talents, Fox moved with great caution, but a subsequent Whig attempt to open the highest commands in the army and navy to Catholics (and Dissenters) provoked the unyielding opposition both of the King and of Sidmouth and his group within the cabinet. Even after the attempt had been dropped, the King insisted on a 'positive assurance' that the issue would never be raised again. The refusal of Grenville and his colleagues to withhold, 'under the various circumstances which may arise, those Councils which may eventually appear to them indispensably necessary for the peace and tranquillity of Ireland' led to the downfall of the coalition government. From 1807 to 1812,

---

[1] Quoted *Ibid.*, pp. 372–3.
[2] See above, p. 143.

in opposition, the Whigs more and more became 'the party favouring the Catholics', although they failed to understand the complexities of the Irish political and religious situation, were divided about tactics, and, as in the question of parliamentary reform, showed little sympathy for independent popular movements. Their defence of 'liberal' principles was not a means to popularity in England. At the general election of 1807, they had to contend with the full force of the 'No Popery' cry of their opponents and the rallying of support to the old cause of Church and King; the conservative churchman and later prime minister, Spencer Perceval, was careful to point out to his constituents at Northampton that 'though it is a peculiarly sacred duty in His Majesty to defend the established religion of his kingdom from all approach of danger, yet it must, I am persuaded, be felt by you to be the common duty and interest of us all.'[1] An alliance of popular feeling and royal intransigence seemed likely to block the cause of emancipation for years to come, particularly when there was so much apathy among the non-committed. 'I care no more for a Catholic than I care for a Chinese', a backbench M.P. remarked. He had previously stated that he had 'no great faith in Catholic emancipation. I think that there is a radical and rooted antipathy between England and Ireland'.[2]

The accession of the Prince Regent marked no substantial change in the attitude of royalty to emancipation, for despite his friendship with Moira and the Whigs George soon disappointed all Catholic expectations. The only change came after the formation of Liverpool's ministry when Catholic emancipation became an open question and ministers were given full freedom as individuals to vote as they wished on what was perhaps the most controversial question of the day. This concession to tolerance did not mean much in practice. Closed minds continued to deal with the newly opened question, and there was little sign of an imminent change of policy. The 'Friends of the Church'—the Established Church—seemed as secure as they ever had been: their leaders, Sidmouth and Eldon, knew that however strong 'liberal' pressure proved to be, they still had powerful reserves of popular anti-papal ill-feeling to fall back upon.

It took more than ten years for a change of mood to become apparent in the House of Commons, but in the meantime the Whigs

---

[1] Quoted S. Walpole, *The Life of Spencer Perceval* (1874) vol. I, p. 247.
[2] Quoted M. Roberts, *op. cit.*, p. 94.

and emancipationist supporters of the government like Canning and Grenville never faltered in their belief in the need for emancipation. The change of mood was registered in the increasingly narrow parliamentary majorities on the many emancipation motions which were proposed by Irish members or radicals. In particular, younger men were in favour of emancipation (Peel was the great exception) and the *Morning Chronicle* could remark that the opposition to Catholic claims would be defeated one day 'not by the march of improvement, but by the march of death'.[1] Although Liverpool himself never voted for Catholic emancipation and made his last big speech on the subject in opposition to an emancipation motion proposed by Sir Francis Burdett in 1825, he left little doubt that he did not believe that emancipation could be put off indefinitely. While George IV talked of his Coronation Oath just as firmly as his father had done, Liverpool was anxious to avoid any suggestion that he would follow Pitt's line of surrender in 1801. 'He is aware,' he informed the King in 1821, when an emancipation bill was being debated in the Commons, 'that there is an increasing spirit in favour of the Roman Catholics, and he is therefore most anxious for the sake of the King's own quiet that His Majesty should not be prevailed upon to commit himself in any way upon the subject.'[2] On party grounds alone, Liverpool was anxious not to lose the goodwill of the emancipationist members of his own cabinet, who were the mainstay of its other policies. To an increasing extent 'liberality' on the Catholic question was correlated with general interest in improvement and reform, and Liverpool himself was coming to see that the state of national affairs, considered as a whole, demanded a persistent re-examination of traditional principles.

Emancipation bills were passed in the Commons in 1821 (Plunket's bill) and 1825 (Burdett's bill) but rejected in the Lords. The same fate met other bills which stopped short of emancipation but further lifted Catholic disabilities (e.g. Nugent's bill of 1823 which Liverpool supported). After Burdett's bill had gone through the Commons, Liverpool felt that he ought to resign. 'You would not wish me . . . to close a long political life with disgrace,' he wrote to a colleague. 'This must inevitably be the case if I now appear to be clinging to office when my opinions have been over-

[1] Quoted by E. Halévy, *The Liberal Awakening, 1815–1830* (1949 edn.), p. 263.
[2] Quoted *Letters of George IV*, vol. II, p. 424.

ruled in the House of Commons. . . . Such being the state of things, the *crisis* cannot be averted for many months. . . . Whenever the *crisis* *does* come, the Protestants must go to the *wall*.'[1]

Although there was a slight accession of 'Protestant' strength at the general election of 1826, the Protestants duly went to the wall in 1829 when emancipation was carried not by the Whigs but by the Duke of Wellington and Peel in face of violent ultra-Protestant opposition from many of their own followers. The details of the crisis must be recounted later,[2] for it was of critical importance in the story of the break-up of the 'Pittite' coalition which had governed Britain with only short breaks from 1794 and of the sequence of events which brought the Whigs back to power in 1830. Two elements in the background of the crises must be clarified at this point, however, for they are relevant to an understanding of the place of 'issues' in the period of Liverpool's ascendancy. First, the movement for Catholic emancipation was given a new twist in 1823 when Daniel O'Connell, an Irish Catholic barrister, usually known as 'the Liberator', founded the Catholic Association in Ireland not only to press for emancipation but for repeal of the Act of Union. O'Connell, who was able in 1824 to levy a 'Catholic rent' of one shilling a year on the members of his association, won considerable support from the Irish peasantry and built up his organization into a most effective pressure group. The suppression of his Association in 1825 did not mark the end of its mission, for the Order of Liberation took its place, and O'Connell was determined to go on challenging English authority at every point. The work of O'Connell made it impossible for English governments to remain open-minded—or neutral—on the emancipation question: an issue, which had been persistently shelved, now acquired new urgency. Second, quite apart from O'Connell's personal contribution, events in Ireland were moving towards a climax. In 1828 and 1829 destruction of life and property was reported from many areas, secret societies were flourishing, and civil war seemed imminent. To the British government the claims of order were more insistent than the pressures of organized opinion, and a long-discussed controversial issue became, as Liverpool had foreseen, a matter of practical government.

The Catholic issue was not the only issue in English politics

---

[1] Hist. MSS. Comm., *The Bathurst Papers*, p. 583.
[2] See below, pp. 230–3.

which governments were eventually compelled to face. Two other issues—'cash and corn'—emerged from the complexities of English society itself, and governments could not escape them even in the decade before 1825. As issues they were intimately inter-connected. 'It is absurd to talk of [the] price [of corn] without referring to money; and it is impossible to alter the quantity of money without affecting prices.'[1] There were many technical points 'intricate and foreign to the taste of country gentlemen'[2] (as they have been to most historians), yet the debate about corn and currency was not only about intricacies but fundamental questions, such as the place of agriculture in society, the relationship between consumers and producers, the composition of Parliament, the competing claims of landlords and industrialists, and the proper rôle of government. These subjects captured the attention of all 'interests', of Whigs, Tories, and Radicals alike.

It was the corn law of 1815 and the return to 'sound money' in 1819 which set the terms of the post-war controversy, and it was not until the 1840s that the Bank Charter Act of 1844 and the repeal of the corn laws of 1846 (both measures carried by Sir Robert Peel) brought to a near-conclusion debates which stretched back into the heart of the Napoleonic Wars. The debates were always conducted at different levels. There was a highly technical discussion between 'political economists', a noisy and emotional conflict between economic interests, a zig-zag argument among politicians, many of whom changed their minds, and eventually a war of highly-organized political associations, employing new resources of propaganda and the old language of crusades.

The corn law of 1815 prohibited the entry of foreign corn into Britain until the home price reached 80s. a quarter, with 67s. as the corresponding figure for colonial wheat. This government measure, which was bitterly attacked at the time as 'most obnoxious and ill-advised', was the product of a landed parliament, which from 1813 onwards had been investigating and reporting on conditions in the corn trade. From 1813 to 1815 the fortunes of the landed interest, particularly the farmers, suffered first as a result of an immense crop (followed by a drastic fall in prices) in 1813, and second from a harvest of poor quality in 1814 and renewed imports of foreign corn. Irish landlords were the first to protest, and Sir Henry Parnell,

---

[1] Sir James Graham, *Corn and Currency* (1826), p. 21.
[2] *Ibid.*, p. 22.

an Irish landlord, was the chairman of the Commons Committee
of 1813, which in the first instance was framed to deal with Ireland
alone and in its first report produced exclusively Irish evidence.[1]
Complaints that Parnell was interested only in an 'Irish job' were
drowned in the English landlords' grievances of 1814 and 1815.
English agricultural spokesmen too demanded post-war protection
'to give farmers confidence', to maintain a stable British output, to
obviate dependence on foreign countries, and to offset the burden
of enormous taxes borne by the landowners. Such arguments
appealed to a majority of members of Parliament far more than the
counter-arguments which were presented in scores of petitions
from the provinces and backed by the violence of the London mob.[2]
With angry crowds pacing the streets outside, Parliament carried a
measure which affronted not only the London mob but some of the
most powerful commercial and industrial interests in the country.
Manchester millowners protested that the bill would raise the price
of labour and handicap manufacturers in their conquest of foreign
markets. Westminster petitioners maintained that it was 'wiser to
import [corn] from countries where it can be grown at a low price
. . . than to diminish the national capital and increase the price of
bread in attempting to force it from barren spots at home by an
enormously expensive method of cultivation'. The recalcitrant
minority of twenty-one in the House of Lords, who insisted on their
right to enter a written protest in the House of Lords *Journal*,
remarked tersely: 'Monopoly is the parent of scarcity, of dearness
and of uncertainty. . . . To confine the consumer of corn to the
produce of his own country, is to refuse to ourselves the benefit of
that provision which Providence itself has made for equalizing to
man the variations of season and climate.' Most political economists
(with the important exception of Malthus) followed David Ricardo
in demanding complete free trade in corn as beneficial not only to
the country as a whole but to every interest except that of the landlords. The selfishness of the landlords, they argued, should not be

---

[1] For the story of the background of 1815, see D. G. Barnes, *A History of the English
Corn Laws* (1930), ch. VIII. There is room for more detailed research on the relation of
the Irish granary to English agriculture and politics in the late eighteenth and early
nineteenth centuries.

[2] The mob ran riot, and after blocking streets and breaking windows, attacked the
house of Frederick Robinson, later Viscount Goderich and first Earl of Ripon, at that
time vice-president of the Board of Trade and sponsor of the bill in the Commons.
Three soldiers and a butler in Robinson's household fired on the crowd, killing several
people, including a woman.

allowed to check the progress of the wealth and population of the country. Radicals did not fail to draw the lesson that 'any hope of success in restricting the importation of corn must arise from the people not being fairly represented—from the want of Parliamentary Reform.'[1]

This range of arguments, most of which were to be repeated time and time again during the period from 1815 to 1846, shows how significant the corn law question was from the start in the history of public opinion. Different interests and classes took up different stances. The landlords, who had done so well during the war, welcomed the corn law which they believed would help to maintain their high war-time rents. They claimed to speak also on behalf of tenant farmers and small freeholders, and even of agricultural labourers, although there were conflicts of interest between landowners and tenants and between farmers and landless labourers. Manufacturers disliked the bill, but they could scarcely use the argument that it would keep wages too high if they wished to gain the support on this issue of skilled artisans and unskilled workers. Thus, English society in 1815 was too complex in its structure to permit an easy and straightforward antagonism between town and country; other antagonisms cut across the old dividing line.

William Cobbett was one of the few writers in 1815 to predict that the new corn law would not produce the economic results the landlords hoped to achieve, but would only exacerbate social conflicts. Within one year, his prediction seemed justified—in spite of the corn law, the price of wheat fell from 71s. 6d. in March 1815 to 52s. 10d. in January 1816—and within seven years the prophecy had undoubtedly come true. The law was rigid and inflexible, but the ports opened and closed as the price level fluctuated. There was no steady price for the home farmer. After a brief taste of increased incomes again, by 1820 and 1821 both landlords and farmers were raising the cry of 'distress' louder than ever before, and a Select Committee of the House of Commons was set up to consider the scores of petitions which had poured in from the rural areas. A second Select Committee was set up in 1822, when the report of the first had proved unacceptable to many members of Parliament.

The members of the landed interest, in so far as the different elements within it were united between 1815 and 1822, did not agree among themselves about remedies. Some 'agriculturasses',

[1] See C. R. Fay, *The Corn Laws and Social England* (1932), pp. 42-3.

as Cobbett called them, pleaded for *more* protection, thereby provoking a new counter-attack by manufacturers, foreign traders and town labourers; others demanded a drastic reduction in taxation, rigid public economy and a forcible reduction of the interest on the national debt; a more numerous group attacked the currency policy of the government, which they claimed had cancelled out all the useful effects of the act of 1815.[1]

At this point in the movement of protest, the corn and currency questions clearly overlapped—indeed, for a time, they became one and the same question. In 1819 the House of Commons agreed that the Bank of England should resume cash payments, which had been suspended by Pitt in 1797. This return to gold, which was decided upon after long and at times tense debate, led to an immediate improvement in Britain's foreign exchange position, and gold began to flow into the coffers of the Bank of England. But the domestic effects of the return to gold were far more controversial. Prices, which had already fallen sharply from their war-time peak of 1814, fell sharply again between 1819 and 1821, much more sharply than Ricardo, the main advocate of the immediate return to gold, had anticipated. The circulation of notes under £5 in value was reduced from £7,400,000 in February 1819 to £900,000 in August 1822. There were vigorous complaints not only from agriculturalists like Sir John Sinclair that the interests of the City of London had triumphed over the interests of the soil, but also from iron-masters and some other industrialists that full employment had been sacrificed to 'sound money'. According to Thomas Attwood, the Birmingham banker and ironmaster, 'Peel's Act' had created 'more misery, more poverty, more discord, more of everything that was calamitous to the nation, except death, than Attila caused in the Roman Empire.'[2] Yet one group of industrialists strongly backed Peel. The leaders of the cotton industry, who looked to greatly increased international trade, strongly favoured a gold standard. 'We want a regulating medium', the treasurer of the Manchester Chamber of Commerce remarked in 1821, 'and there is nothing like

[1] Lord Byron in his *Age of Bronze* (1823) described the collapse of the 'landed interest'. Napoleon's 'vices', he said, 'destroyed but realms, and still maintained your prices':

> 'But corn, like every mortal thing, must fall,
>   Kings—conquerors—and markets most of all'.

[2] B.R.L. *Report of the Proceedings of the* (Birmingham) *Town's Meeting*, 13 December 1830. Thomas's Tory brother, Matthias, agreed that the act was 'one of the most impolitic and mischievous measures that was ever adopted in this country.'

gold for that purpose.'[1] There was thus an alliance in 1819 between the City, the orthodox political economists, and the cotton interest, which was to gain in strength during the next thirty years, and to help reshape the whole of British commercial policy.

From our twentieth-century vantage point it seems indisputable that the most violent contemporary critics of Peel's act in 1819 were exaggerating their case, that the fall in prices after 1815 was not a purely British phenomenon and was influenced by many non-monetary factors, including the rise in industrial productivity and the fall in costs. What is equally indisputable, however, is that these opponents were something more than crude inflationists asking for unlimited paper money and that they had a genuine case which still demands attention. Their criticism of the gold standard was often well reasoned. The terms on which the return to gold was made can still be challenged; it is undeniable that the lack of uniformity in the price fall made it injurious to particular interests; above all, a heavy burden was imposed on debtors, those who had contracted obligations during the wars. One of the most important groups of debtors was the farming group. They had acquired their debts in a period of high prices and booming demand; they now had to pay heavy interest charges during a period of falling prices and at times competitive trade. The technical details of currency manipulation were thus of great importance to corn growers however little they understood them. And it was easy for critics to forget the details and attack political economists, with their 'false speculation' and 'abominable theories', and 'change-alley people' who seemed to be in charge of high policy. 'Faith! they are now become *everything*. Baring assists at the Congress of Sovereigns, and Ricardo regulates things at home.'[2]

Although the government was loath between 1815 and 1822 to accept its full responsibilities for legislation to deal with these controversial issues—preferring to rely upon open parliamentary debates rather than on the imposition of official policies and upon the reports of select committees rather than on background departmental investigation—it could not indefinitely shirk the responsi-

---

[1] *Wheeler's Manchester Chronicle*, 25 August 1821.

[2] See *Political Register*, 4 September 1819. The critics of the 1819 Act were divided. Sir Thomas Lethbridge, a spokesman of the landed interest in Parliament, what Cobbett contemptuously called 'the Collective Wisdom', disliked the return to gold; Cobbett, who hated 'rag money' and supported the gold standard, objected to the terms on which the return had been made. He asked for a simultaneous reduction of the national debt, fiscal reforms and what he called 'an equitable adjustment.'

bility of taking action and, if need be, of defending it. There were complaints in 1819 that the government was trying to trap the opposition in Parliament to advocate measures which it wished to put into effect but for which it was reluctant to accept full responsibility, but by the middle '20s ministers had to be prepared to frame and advocate economic policy much more resolutely than their predecessors such as Vansittart had done. They were frequently divided about it, for corn and currency remained bitterly controversial questions, yet men like Robinson, the chancellor of the exchequer after 1823, and above all Huskisson, who became president of the Board of Trade and a member of the cabinet in the same year, were clear about the need for official action and exceptionally lucid in their exposition of 'abstract topics' in the House of Commons. They were indeed the political personalities who provided a link between the Age of Pitt and the Age of Gladstone. Huskisson, who had been vice-chairman of the Bullion Committee of 1810 and a member of the Peel Committee of 1819, was already an economic expert. In 1821 as draughtsman of the report of the Select Committee on Agricultural Distress he succeeded in converting the final document from a discontented protest of corn growers into a stalwart defence of the national return to gold. Placed in power, he contrived, with the help of new-style civil servants like James Deacon Hume to raise the Board of Trade 'to a consequence before unknown' and in better times than the immediate post-war period to frame a comprehensive economic policy. He swept aside trade barriers between Britain and Ireland, abolished cumbrous customs duties, reduced protective duties to more moderate proportions, cancelled bounties, and permitted the free export of gold. Believing at the same time in the need for freer trade and in the desirability of maintaining imperial links and imperial protection, he broke the fetters of the 'old colonial system', removed those provisions of the restrictive Navigation Acts which turned colonies into satellite appendages of the mother country, and boldly reformed the intricate network of shipping regulations and discriminations. As part of this policy of encouraging freedom and initiative, he wished to reform the corn law of 1815. He was in a better position to demand change now that he was no longer handicapped by the difficulty of answering the landlord's *tu quoque* argument—why free our trade while manufacturers and traders are heavily protected? The splits of opinion on the corn question within the government after 1826 played a big part—though not as big a part as the splits on the Catholic question—in breaking up the coalition which still looked back to Huskisson's greatest political hero, Pitt.

Before examining in more detail the 'liberalization' of Liverpool's government in the 1820s and the background of the splits which followed his resignation, it is necessary to examine the response the government made to the social disorder which followed the return to peace. If the issues of economic policy drew the government into controversies with the landed interest and the business classes, the issue of public order drew them into struggles with the industrial working classes. The new complex society had an ambitious and restless middle, but it also had a turbulent and discontented base. Between 1815 and 1820, in particular, the turbulence and discontent seemed to threaten the whole fabric of society—the economic order as well as the Constitution.

3. THE CHALLENGE TO ORDER

The return to peace had meant no immediate improvement in the condition of the working classes. Rapid demobilization, a cessation of government orders, a fall in urban employment and a heavier burden of indirect taxation than before hit the workers harder than any other section of the community.

In 1816 and early 1817 there was gloom in the countryside and distress in almost all industrial areas. At Birmingham 'nearly a fifth part of the population were receiving weekly relief'; in the iron-producing area of the Black Country there was the 'silence of unmingled desolation' inside many of the great ironworks and the cries of angry men outside; in Lancashire weavers were complaining that 'now, when the waste of war is over, our sufferings are become more general and deeper than ever'; at Newcastle-on-Tyne the colliers were rioting in the same grim mood as the farm labourers of Ely and the townsfolk of Bridport. All over the country, as one Lancashire radical, Samuel Bamford, put it, 'whilst the laurels were yet cool on the brows of our victorious soldiers . . . the elements of convulsion were at work amongst the masses of our labouring population.'[1]

[1] *Passages in the Life of a Radical* (1844 edn.), vol. I, p. 6.

Although there was a marked improvement in the economic climate in the summer and autumn of 1817, continuing through 1818, 1819 was one of the most troubled years of the nineteenth century. It was then that working-class 'distress' took the clearest political form it had ever taken, and there was a consequent fierce struggle between the forces of 'movement' and the defenders of order. Not surprisingly, some historians have chosen these tense years between Waterloo and Peterloo as the nearest point Britain ever reached to social revolution.

There was, in fact, little real sign that Britain was going the way of France twenty-five years earlier, although many frightened contemporaries thought so. While there was a highly distinctive mood of anger, alarm and strain, in many ways the general pattern of working-class agitation between 1815 and 1820 was typical of the whole pattern of subsequent agitation, at least until the rise of organized trade unions and political parties. The place of London in the strategy of agitation was changing. Although its Common Council was in the vanguard of reform in 1816, as in the eighteenth century, and carried an address to the Prince Regent designed 'to represent our national sufferings and grievances, and . . . to suggest the measures . . . indispensably necessary for the safety, the quiet and the prosperity of the Realm',[1] the provinces supplied most of the energy behind the new campaigns. The main spur to political activity was unemployment; in times of full or relatively full employment, such as 1818, there was a marked decline in political pressure and a keener concentration on industrial action—strikes for higher wages, battles not with 'government' or 'authority' but with the employers.

The provincial pattern varied from place to place. In Birmingham, for example, where small masters worked in close contact with skilled artisans, where there was easy social mobility, and where workshops employed little labour-saving machinery to 'throw workers out of their jobs', class antagonism was far less sharp than in Manchester. There, many workshops were already large and increasingly impersonal, the biggest cotton lords were separated from their workmen by social barriers which looked at times as if they might become barricades, and the development of machinery pushed handloom weavers to the brink of despair. In Manchester, even the demand for the extension of the suffrage was associated

[1] *The Times*, 10 December 1816.

with the claim that it would give additional 'power to every man to protect his own labour from being devoured by others' and later with securing 'the labourer the fruits of his own labour . . . and every British subject a full participation in all the privileges and advantages of British citizens'.[1] Against this social and economic background there was a political contrast between the two cities. In Birmingham an alliance gradually took shape between employers and employed—it went back to the united agitation against the Orders in Council in 1812 and made use of 'currency' arguments— more money in circulation would mean more effective demand, more employment, more social peace; in Manchester, competing agitations gathered momentum in bad times, while open hostility concerning factory conditions, wages, hours of work and the cost of living was usually the keynote of good times. In both cities reformers placed great emphasis on 'the need for union'—the most significant political slogan of the times—but in Manchester 'union' was increasingly thought of exclusively in terms of the joint economic action of the working classes, and in the 'good year' 1818, attempts were made to form a 'Union of all Trades' in industrial Lancashire. Even before that, millowners were complaining that 'the Classes of Persons . . . that have been most formidable to their Employers, by their Combinations, are the Calico Printers and Cotton Spinners, who labouring in large numbers in . . . Factories . . . have for many years past been almost every year in some place or other in a State of Combination against their respective employers.'[2]

It was the Manchester (and Lancashire) rather than the Birmingham (or London) pattern of discontent which created most fear between 1817 and 1820. In the 'bad year' 1816–17, the Manchester working classes organized a march on London, the so-called march of the Blanketeers: although 'the mob was unarmed and conducted themselves quietly', local magistrates, assisted by cavalry, were careful to see that most of them got no further than Stockport. In the 'good year' 1818, there were fierce strikes both of spinners and weavers. This time, the Manchester magistrates, no longer concerned with a threat to the Constitution and by no means well-disposed themselves to the dissenting millowners, were sympathetic to the weavers' demands, but the employers were adamant. Their

---

[1] *Wheeler's Manchester Chronicle*, 28 October 1826.
[2] P.R.O. H.O./42/149; 5 March 1816.

failure to make any concessions, particularly to respond to the demand for a legal minimum wage, turned the disgruntled workers back to politics again, and in 1819, the worst of all years, the weavers led the radical campaign, which culminated in August at the Massacre of Peterloo. The shift in tactics is well illustrated in a letter written by a Manchester reformer to the *Manchester Mercury* on the eve of Peterloo. 'As to the present distress, *you* and those of your kidney say that it's all owing to bad markets, want of trade with foreigners and such like. . . . The root of the evil in my judgement, lies deeper by a long way. . . . We are unsound in the vitals—there's the seat of mischief—the Constitution's become rotten to the core. . . . Corruption's at the very helm of the State . . . and what's the remedy, then? Why *reform*—a radical complete Constitutional *Reform*.'[1] The events that followed have, in retrospect only, a grim inevitability about them. When on 16 August thousands of workers from Manchester and the surrounding cotton districts gathered peacefully in St. Peter's Field to listen to Orator Hunt[2]—their injunctions were 'cleanliness, sobriety, order and peace', and among their slogans was 'No Corn Laws'—the magistrates, scared of an uprising, employed the local yeomanry to arrest him. When the forces of the yeomanry proved inadequate, they called in regular cavalry to disperse the crowds. A savage struggle followed in which eleven people were killed and over 400 wounded. Within a few days the damning term 'Peterloo' had been coined.

During the summer of 1819 there were many other mass meetings and political demonstrations in different parts of England—on 12 July, for example, an enormous crowd had gathered in Birmingham to elect Sir Charles Wolseley, a radical of extreme views but good family, 'Legislatorial Attorney and Representative' of the city —but it was 'Peterloo' which roused national political excitement to fever pitch. There was an immediate national outcry among both radicals and Whigs. Two days after Peterloo, Cartwright, who had been present at the big Birmingham meeting, was writing that 'the *crisis* in my judgement, is very favourable for affecting a union, with the *radicals* of the better sort among the Whigs, and I am meditating

---

[1] *Manchester Mercury*, 10 August 1819. Quoted by D. Read, 'The Social and Economic Background to Peterloo', in *Transactions of the Lancashire and Cheshire Antiquarian Society*, vol. LXIV (1954).

[2] An earlier meeting, planned for 9 August, to elect Orator Hunt as popular representative for Lancashire, had to be cancelled when the Manchester magistrates and the government declared this purpose illegal.

on means to promote it.'[1] The Common Council of London protested to the Regent; the Whig Lieutenant of the West Riding, Lord Fitzwilliam, was dismissed from his post for criticizing the action of the authorities. The government added to the tension by congratulating the magistrates for 'their prompt, decisive, and efficient measures for the preservation of the public peace'. Both journalists and poets[2] made sure that the memory of Peterloo would never fade: it remained vividly alive for generations to come, and inspired hundreds of new reformers.

But the 'crisis' did not lead to the civil war and revolution which many 'respectable citizens' feared, even though in 1820, as we have seen, the Queen Caroline case drew Whigs and radicals closer together and threatened the existence of Liverpool's government. The main reason for the relief of tension was the fact that economic conditions improved again, and as Cobbett said, 'I defy you to agitate a fellow with a full stomach.'[3] At the beginning of 1820 the *Manchester Mercury* pointed out that prices were rising and merchants were predicting a new period of prosperity. Before the end of 1821 the *Morning Chronicle* could smugly report that 'Peace, Cheerfulness and Industry, with their estimable train of advantages' had returned to the 'extensive towns of Manchester, Salford and their widespread neighbourhood'.[4] The years between 1821 and 1825 justified promise and prediction. In Birmingham and the Black Country, as in Lancashire, conditions improved, unemployment fell as iron prices rose, and discontents melted away. The culminating point was reached in the years 1824–25, which some economic historians have considered as the first truly modern cyclical boom in British economic history. Certainly at that time there was a stock market boom as well as a peak of industrial activity, and a wave of speculation as well as a burst of real investment. While the market value of Mexican and South American shares soared and the daring turned to South America as a new Eldorado, the volume of domestic building broke all previous records. During the whole of the first fifty years of the nineteenth century, the figure for brick production

[1] *Life and Correspondence of Major Cartwright*, vol. II, p. 137.
[2] Shelley wrote not only his well-known *Masque of Anarchy* with its famous lines 'I met Murder on the way—He had a mask like Castlereagh' and 'Ye are many—they are few', but also a sonnet *England in 1819* which referred to 'rulers who neither see, nor feel, nor know'.
[3] See *Birmingham Journal*, 12 November 1836.
[4] *Morning Chronicle*, 27 October 1821. See A. Redford, *Manchester Merchants and Foreign Trade, 1794–1858* (1934), ch. VI. The neighbouring towns were of great political importance, as they contained the most disgruntled workers.

in 1825 was surpassed only in 1846 and 1847. 'On all sides', the *Annual Register* claimed in 1825, 'new buildings were in the process of erection.' The King's speech for that year proclaimed that there had never been a period in the history of the country when 'all the great interests of society were at the same time in so thriving a condition'.

The fortunes of reform movements between 1820 and 1825 conform to the pattern which had taken definite shape in the years 1815 to 1820. In no part of the country was the popular political momentum of the years 1819 and 1820 maintained. Energy was diverted first to religion—there were Methodist revivals in Lancashire and Cumberland, and in 1823 there were two thousand conversions in Cornwall in a fortnight[1]—and then to trade unionism. What were still illegal combinations of labour multiplied in numbers, struggled for wage increases to meet rising food prices and frequently won impressive victories in strikes or 'turn-outs' as they were usually called. It was the growth of such combinations, and the erroneous assumption by political economists that if only combinations were made legal they would diminish both in numbers and strength, that in 1824 led Parliament—itself misled by a Select Committee controlled not by the government but by the philosophic radical, Joseph Hume, and Francis Place—to repeal the Combination Act of 1800.[2] As a result, in the prosperous conditions of late-1824, trade unions sprang into existence on all sides, and in such diverse industries as textiles, dyeing, mining, and shoemaking there were strikes. The disappointed Hume complained bitterly of the immoderate and imprudent actions of organized workers which were 'estranging their best friends, and gradually raising the community against them', but the unions continued to grow. In 1825 —a year of very high food prices—Parliament passed a new Combination Act which permitted the existence of trade unions but strictly limited their ability to strike. By the time that it came into effect, the boom had broken, and at the end of 1825 there were signs of the popular return to politics which was to reach its climax in the prolonged agitation for a Reform Bill.

The reactions of the 'authorities' to urban and working class discontent between 1815 and 1825 were more complex than has sometimes been suggested. The main representatives of order were the local magistrates, many of whom, like the Manchester magis-

---

[1] A. Stevens, *History of Methodism* (1860–5), vol. III, pp. 225–6.
[2] See above, p. 136.

trates, belonged to the squirearchy or the Anglican clergy and had little sympathy with the new millowners. Their chief anxiety was that there would be an assault on property from below and that the local means of defence would prove inadequate. Lacking the assistance of organized police forces, they frequently swore-in special constables or appealed to the home secretary for the assistance of troops. Some of them apparently believed in Francis Place's metaphor, that cutting down and trampling down the people was no different from cutting and trampling furze bushes on a common; others, however, maintained that it was a Christian duty to maintain the Constitution and to punish forcibly all those who tried to subvert it. Finally there were some who showed sympathy and understanding. In a memorial sent to Sidmouth only a few weeks before Peterloo the magistrates of Salford Hundred emphasized 'the deep distresses of the manufacturing classes of this extensive population' and added, 'when the people are oppressed with hunger we do not wonder of their giving ear to any doctrine which they are told will redress their grievance.'[1]

There was a regular network of correspondence between the Home Office and the magistrates, and both authorities made use not only of formal rhetoric and argument but of spies and agents employed to probe and sometimes even to stir up the political underground.

The attitude of Liverpool's government at the centre was not dictatorial. It was conditioned by fear of an insurrection which it might not easily be able to master. The limited number of troops at its disposal made the Home Office more cautious than the local magistrates and usually anxious to calm them. Liverpool and his ministers no doubt preferred charity (soup kitchens and good works) and subsidizing church building—£1 million was spent for this latter purpose by Liverpool's government in 1818 and a further £500,000 in 1824—to creating an efficient police force or repressing by force all signs of unrest. But they felt that it was their duty to support unpaid local magistrates, even when the magistrates were nervous and precipitate. It was not Sidmouth but Canning who remarked after Peterloo that 'to let down the magistrates would be to invite their resignation, and to lose all gratuitous service in the counties liable to disturbance for ever.'[2]

---

[1] Quoted F. A. Bruton, 'The Story of Peterloo' in *Bulletin of John Rylands Library*, October 1919.
[2] Quoted W. R. Brock, *op. cit.*, p. 112.

By curbing civil liberties whenever sedition seemed likely to
spread, the government claimed—quite inadequately—that it was
merely supporting the magistracy. In 1817 the Habeas Corpus Act
was suspended and three other restrictive measures were passed,
including a tightening up of the control of public meetings. After
Peterloo the army was increased by 10,000 men and the 'Six Acts'—
'gag acts'—were passed. Drilling and military exercises were
prohibited, magistrates were empowered to search for and seize
arms, the right to hold public meetings was further limited, and the
freedom of the press was severely restricted. In passing these
dangerous measures, the government believed that 'the alarm in the
country is now considerable and we ought to take advantage
of it'.

Undoubtedly the government had a considerable measure of
support among the 'respectable' and privileged groups both in
town and country. Just as in the early years of the French Revolution
'loyal' opinion had crystallized and expressed itself in bodies like
the Association for Preserving Liberty and Property against Republicans and Levellers, so in 1817, and even more so in 1819, there were
Whigs as well as Tories, manufacturers as well as squires, who feared
the 'excesses' of popular movements and the 'irresponsibility' of
their chosen leaders. 'Is there one among them with whom you would
trust yourself in the dark?' Grey asked in 1819. 'Look at them, at
their characters, at their conduct. What is there more base, and more
detestable, more at variance with all tact and decency, as well as all
morality, truth and honour? A cause so supported cannot be a good
cause.'[1]

If such were the views of Grey, it is not surprising that members
of local Pitt Clubs, still battling against 'atheistical philosophy,
jacobinism and diabolism', demanded strong action on the part of
both government and magistrates. They refused to hold the government responsible for distress and they saw the political crisis
in terms not of high food prices, unemployment and misery but of a
'deluded people', driven astray by malicious and treacherous agitators; an inflammatory press, seizing on every grievance; underground conspiracies, bound together by secret oaths, intimidation
and crime; and woolly-minded supporters in high places, bewitched
by the March of Mind and the advance of 'liberal' principles.

Between 1820 and 1825, this coherent but reactionary version of

[1] Quoted *ibid.*, pp. 117–18.

contemporary events and opinions was challenged by critics of many kinds; between 1825 and 1830 it broke down and later on, in the quiet middle years of the century, the good Liberal-Conservative Walter Bagehot found it difficult to believe that there ever could have been Six Acts at all. It is necessary, however, for the sake of full understanding to try to reconstruct the bits and pieces of the 'Tory case'.

The phrase 'the deluded people' reflected a patronizing paternalism which was out of date in some of the most advanced factory areas and in the areas where the hand-loom weavers faced hunger and despair. At its best it was tinged with genuine Anglican religion and dependent on a traditional hierarchical view of society.

The attack on 'seditious leaders' was bound up with aristocratic and squirearchical conceptions of political authority; local family power as well as central government seemed to be challenged by demagogic 'politicians' touring the country, taking up issues which they did not fully understand, and stirring the rabble to violent action.

Distrust of the press followed logically and was never difficult to justify. In Liverpool's view the press was 'the real source of the evil—but one more subject to embarrassment as a source of legislation, than any of the other evils of the day'.[1] When all newspapers were viewed with suspicion, it was not surprising that working-class newspapers were considered especially dangerous. In particular, radical papers like Cobbett's *Weekly Political Register* and Wooler's *Black Dwarf* (1817–24) were condemned for trying to turn simple people into dupes 'of the basest and most profligate of men'. Before the 'gagging acts' were passed Cobbett fled to America in 1817—he returned with the bones of Tom Paine two years later—and there were such incidents as a Shropshire magistrate ordering two men to be 'well flogged at the whipping post' (under the Vagrancy Act) for distributing copies of Cobbett's *Register*.[2]

The 'Tory' emphasis on 'underground conspiracies' seemed well placed when in 1820 Thistlewood, leader of a group of London extremists, was arrested for organizing a gang to murder the cabinet. The Cato Street conspiracy, as it was called, had all the ingredients of a fictional conspiracy for chilling law-abiding citizens.

[1] Quoted *ibid.*, p. 117.
[2] Quoted A. Aspinall, *Politics and the Press*, p. 46. The magistrate remarked that since his action 'I have heard of no others being circulated in this neighbourhood'.

Finally the scornful condemnation of the friends of disorder in high places permitted supporters of the government to indulge in many favourite occupations—baiting the Whigs, bullying the 'sentimental', and satirizing the 'march of intellect'. The most eloquent of 'Tories', like Southey, saw 'the steam engine and the spinning engines, the mail coach and the free publication of the debates in parliament' as part of one enormous modern complex. 'Hence follow in natural and necessary consequences increased activity, enterprise, wealth and power; but on the other hand, greediness of gain, looseness of principle, wretchedness, disaffection, and political insecurity.'[1] Not all supporters of the government— who included many owners of new steam engines and converts to a liberal commercial system—looked so deeply into the consequences and contradictions of 'improvement'. There were many indeed who, while prepared to put down disorder forcefully, anticipated Macaulay in believing that 'it is not by the intermeddling of Mr. Southey's idol, the omniscient and omnipotent state, but by the prudence and energy of the people, that England has hitherto been carried forward in civilization; and it is to the same prudence and the same energy that we now look with comfort and good hope.'[2]

4. THE MARCH OF INTELLECT

Liverpool realized the need for change himself. His replacement of Sidmouth by Peel as home secretary in 1822, the change from Castlereagh to Canning at the Foreign Office, the substitution of Robinson for Vansittart, and the entry of Huskisson into the cabinet, ushered in a period of 'liberal' rule. None of these changes, taken separately, marked a sharp break. When Peel became home secretary he found the pattern of reform in criminal law already set; a committee of 1819, the result of the work of Romilly, Sir James Mackintosh and Sir Thomas Fowell Buxton, had laid the foundations for a major revision of criminal law, and Henry Hobhouse was already under-secretary of state. When Canning replaced Castlereagh, he did not have to formulate a completely new foreign policy: Castlereagh had already been moving unhappily in a direction which Canning followed with enthusiasm. At the Board of Trade, Wallace, the energetic vice-president, had carried out useful work before

---

[1] For Southey's views on 'improvement', see *Sir Thomas More: or Colloquies on the Progress and Prospects of Society* (1829).

[2] *Edinburgh Review*, January 1830. Macaulay's powerful but often unconvincing reply to Southey is one of the most forthright statements of the belief in 'improvement'.

Huskisson went there and recognized the need for 'a full and complete revision of our commercial system'. He was annoyed indeed in 1823 at the promotion of Huskisson over his head. The bright new look of the Liverpool government was not an illusion, but neither was it the first move in a political conjuring act. It was because the times were changing that the government changed. Not only was the country at last in a genuine 'state of peace', but the presence of new elements in society—mercantile and industrial—was increasingly recognized.

Peel's reforms at the Home Office demonstrate clearly the new approach to problems of government. In the early nineteenth century, for all the pressure of humanitarians, like Romilly, and penal reformers, like Bentham, attempts at relaxing the severity of criminal law were stubbornly opposed by the government, and statutes creating new capital offences were still being enacted. In 1812 for instance, it had been made a capital offence to destroy lace frames and machinery. Only slowly did reforming opinion take shape, petitions against the existing criminal law begin to be presented in Parliament, and Parliament itself show genuine initiative. The real turning point came not in 1822 when Peel went to the Home Office, but in 1819 when Sir James Mackintosh's motion for the appointment of a 'Committee of Inquiry' into the criminal laws was carried against the government by a majority of nineteen. The *Report* of the committee constituted an invaluable review of the state of crime in the country, of the punishments awarded in the courts, and of constructive plans of reform; and Peel, on taking up office, soon made known his intention of considering 'the whole question of criminal law'. The Whig *Edinburgh Review* neatly but not without bias summed up the story. 'Common sense requires an obvious improvement: an Opposition member brings it forward, and is overpowered by sarcasms, invectives and majorities. But public opinion decides at once in its favour, and gradually diminishes the majority, in each succeeding year, till the scale is turned, and independent men of all parties became anxious to see the alteration effected. Suddenly the minister proposes the reprobate project as a government measure, and converts, while he laughs at, his former adherents.'[1] Discounting the bias, it is certainly true to say that Peel was proud of reforms which most of his predecessors would have resisted to the utmost. He introduced consolidated legislation to

[1] Vol. XL, March 1824.

cover three-quarters of all criminal offences on the statute books, abolished capital punishment for a very large number of crimes, revised the scale of lesser punishments, improved legal procedure and conditions of imprisonment, and in 1829 created a new (and highly controversial) Metropolitan Police Force. Powerfully assisted by Henry Hobhouse, Peel approached the task of reform not as a doctrinaire—Bentham still thought him 'weak and feeble'[1] —but as a sound administrator, sensitive to the claims of humanity. 'Tory as I am,' he declared in 1827, 'I have the satisfaction of knowing that there is not a single law connected with my name, which has not had for its object some mitigation of the severity of criminal law, some prevention of abuse in the exercise of it, or some security for its impartial administration.' It was before and not after the great Reform Bill of 1832 that Peel first saw the work of a 'Tory' as the implementation of 'judicious reforms' and the refusal to defend abuses merely because they were old.

Peel and Canning were never on intimate terms with each other— to Arbuthnot, Peel 'appeared to have the worst opinion' of Canning and said that 'he was a sort of person he should be very sorry to have a *tête à tête* with'[2]—but as foreign secretary, Canning made an even greater appeal to 'liberals' than Peel did. After Liverpool had manœuvred him back into the government, Canning came to dominate the ministry, directing his remarkable oratorical gifts to the exposition of foreign policy. It was in relation to Europe, indeed, rather than to England that the word 'liberal' was first employed. Canning's defence of European and South American liberalism against the pressures of organized authority, which George IV described as 'wise and comprehensive principles by which the peace and general interest of Europe were bound together',[3] alienated not only Princess Lieven, the brilliant wife of the Russian Ambassador, and Metternich, but also those English Tories who acquired the name 'Ultras' in the course of the 1820s. Canning was essentially a nationalist, refusing to take into consideration 'the wishes of any other sovereign, the feelings of any other Government, or the interests of any other people, except in so far as those wishes, those

---

[1] He admitted that Peel 'has given a slight impulse to law improvement in a right direction.' Quoted by L. Radzinowicz, *A History of English Criminal Law*, vol. I (1948), p. 574.

[2] *Journal of Mrs. Arbuthnot*, vol. I, p. 271.

[3] Quoted A. G. Stapleton, *George Canning and His Times* (1958), p. 411. For details of his foreign policy, see below pp. 346–50.

feelings and those interests may, or might, concur with the just interests of England',[1] but his nationalism had powerful international repercussions. His support of Spanish and Portuguese 'constitutionalism', his scorn for the principle of 'legitimacy', and his vigorous welcome to the new independent Spanish American states all entailed battles inside the cabinet and rebuffs and indignant comments outside it. His eloquence seemed 'elaborate and artificial' to confirmed Whigs, but much opposition was disarmed, and just before Liverpool was struck down by paralysis in February 1827, Brougham paid tribute to 'those sound, enlightened, liberal, and truly English principles—principles worthy of our best times and of our most distinguished statesman—which now govern this country in her foreign policy.'

Canning's foreign policy—particularly his recognition of the independence of the Spanish American states—was well adapted to the economic requirements of Britain's export interests, but he himself paid relatively little attention to the large-scale changes in commercial and economic policy, 'the study of which was perhaps the least suited to his taste'. In this field of action, Liverpool, Robinson and Huskisson were in the foreground, with Adam Smith and David Ricardo further back. Adam Smith was frequently quoted; the economist Ricardo, who made himself very unpopular with the country gentlemen, won the praise of a traditionalist like Lord Grenville. 'Radical as he was I consider Ricardo's death', Grenville remarked, 'as a great loss both to the country and to Government'.[2] The willingness of government to respond easily and naturally to new economic ideas was well brought out before the transformation of Liverpool's government by the prime minister himself. In 1820 on the eve of receiving a deputation of London merchants in favour of free trade—'free imports without retaliation and no duties except for revenue'—Liverpool told Thomas Tooke, the famous statistician and Baltic merchant who drafted it, that 'there was not a principle, not a sentiment in which he did not entirely and most cordially concur'.[3] Indeed before and after 1815 Liverpool made many

---

[1] Just after coming into power, he wrote to a friend—'for *Europe* I shall be desirous *now* and *then* to read *England.*' Quoted *ibid.*, p. 364.

[2] Quoted W. R. Brock, *op. cit.*, p. 188. The *Morning Chronicle*, 21 May 1824, describes how among the select audiences gathered to hear the first Ricardo memorial lectures were Huskisson, Canning, Peel and Liverpool.

[3] T. W. Tooke and Newmarch, *History of Prices*, vol. VI, (1857), p. 340. Tooke maintained that at this time, 'the simple truth is that the Government . . . were far more sincere and resolute free traders than the merchants of London.' *Loc. cit.*, p. 342.

characteristic free trade utterances of his own, which demonstrated the influence of political economy on his mind. As early as 1812 he noted, 'it has been well said in a foreign country, when it was asked what should be done to make commerce prosper, the answer was *laissez-faire*, and it was undoubtedly true that the less commerce and manufactures were meddled with the more they were likely to prosper.' In 1820 he added: 'If the people of the world are poor, no legislative interposition can make them do that which they would do if they were rich.'

The new economic policy of Robinson and Huskisson was a logical application in practice of economic aphorisms of this kind. It met with opposition from agriculturalists, protectionist manufacturers, and diehard opponents of all innovations, political and economic.

Although Huskisson had supported the corn law of 1815 and had maintained that 'to ensure a continuance of cheapness and sufficiency, we must ensure to our own growers that protection against foreign import which has produced these blessings',[1] his economic programme was suspect to farmers in the mid-'twenties. During his election campaign at Liverpool in 1826 he was reported as saying, 'the whole question is settled, and the trade in corn is to be free, and corn is hereafter to be admitted upon a duty to the great benefit of the shipowners and the trading part of the community in general.'[2] Wellington protested to Lord Liverpool against this alleged statement, which Huskisson denied having made, and there were many signs of internal cabinet difficulties on this question which came to a head after Liverpool's resignation. The country gentlemen were 'dreadfully alarmed' at both Huskisson's 'theories' and his 'threats', and although Liverpool, while he was active, did his best to talk the language of 'arrangement between the great interests' of British society, there were many Tories who felt that Huskisson was prepared to sacrifice the landed interest to the rest.

Old-fashioned industrialists were also alarmed. One of the most important of the protectionist manufacturing interests was the silk industry, many of the representatives of which protested against the abolition of the prohibition on the import of manufactured silk in 1824 and the introduction of a 30 per cent duty instead. Unlike the cotton manufacturers, the silk masters believed that the prosperity

[1] Quoted W. R. Brock, *op. cit.*, p. 219.
[2] *Ibid.*, p. 223.

of their luxury trade depended on strong protection, and put up a hard but unavailing resistance to the government's proposals.

The diehard opponents of all innovations, political and economic, disliked intensely the economic policies Liverpool and Huskisson were advocating. 'Liberality', wrote the Ultra lawyer Redesdale, 'is the word of the day . . . it is seriously threatening the British Empire with the overthrow of all its ancient institutions by which it has been nourished.'[1] Huskisson, remarked a provincial Tory paper, 'was a Jacobin in 1793, and all his life has been connected with, is indeed the leader of the politico-economic party which has done more mischief to the nation than any party ever entrusted with power.'[2] So long as economic conditions remained good, as they were until the autumn of 1825, there was limited scope for such complaints. When the great boom of 1825 collapsed, however, many people blamed Huskisson's 'theories' for the distress which followed. Bank failures, stock exchange collapse, and business bankruptcies in the autumn and winter of 1825 introduced a new phase in English politics. Everywhere people showed a 'disposition to attach blame to the Government for the privations they are experiencing'.[3] The government became the villain of the piece as it was becoming in France, and this anthropomorphic conception of crisis, as it has been called,[4] did much to make popular reform politics active again. Liverpool's optimistic view that 'any attempt to interfere by the authority of Government would only aggravate the evil instead of remedying it'[5] was bound to provoke frustration and anger. In London, Manchester, Birmingham, and the agricultural areas of the country there were all the by now familiar fruits of 'distress' from machine breaking to the revival of radical political societies. Even commentators who pointed out that the extent of distress was frequently exaggerated were bound to take account of the problems it raised. 'There is something in the frequent recurrence and long continuation of these distresses', one commentator wrote, 'which staggers one, and almost makes one doubt whether our plan of society is a safe or happy one for the most of the people. Their condition is generally better, but it is surely much more precarious

---

[1] *Lord Colchester, His Diary and Correspondence* (1861), vol. III, p. 300.
[2] *Birmingham Argus*, March 1830.
[3] P.R.O. H.O./52/11, 21 October 1830.
[4] See E. Labrousse, 'Comment naissent les Révolutions?' in *Actes du Congrès Historique du Centenaire de la Révolution de 1848* (1948), pp. 1–20.
[5] Quoted W. R. Brock, *op. cit.*, p. 204.

than in countries much worse governed, and that enters deeply into
the estimate of human happiness.'[1]

This interesting comment acquires greater significance when it is
placed in the context of the general literature of 'happiness' and
'improvement' in the complex society of the 1820s. Liverpool,
Canning, Robinson and Huskisson, for all their 'liberalism', were
not the most vocal exponents of theories of improvement or
philosophies of happiness. By the time that Distress quickened the
pace of English popular politics, 'the schoolmaster', in a famous
phrase of Henry Brougham, 'had been abroad in the land'. Extensive though the reforms of the Liverpool government had been,
they had not satisfied extreme reformers or dampened the enthusiasm
of the militant minority for parliamentary reform. Although the
question of parliamentary reform was not discussed at all in the
House of Commons in 1824 and 1825, in almost every important
town and city in the kingdom by that year there was a small group
of people who believed in 'the diffusion of the principles of rational
and constitutional freedom',[2] in 'enlightened and liberal principles',
and in the 'march of intellect'. Most of these groups were middle-
class in character and included a majority of dissenters, and they
were beginning to be familiar with the sort of arguments which the
friends of Jeremy Bentham advocated in the new national periodical
the *Westminster Review* founded in January 1824 to challenge the
well-established Whig *Edinburgh*, founded in 1802, and the Tory
Quarterly, founded in 1809. There was a link between Unitarianism
and Utilitarianism, and it was a Unitarian, W. J. Fox, who remarked
in the first number of the *Westminster* that the public was everywhere
coming into its own, even in literature, where 'flattering dedications'
were 'defunct' and 'all our great poets write for the people'. In
relation to politics, the young John Stuart Mill, still under the
influence of a rigorous Benthamite education, drove home the lesson.
'The most effectual mode of doing good to mankind by reading is
to correct . . . errors; to refute opinions which are generated only by
partial interests . . . ; and to attach honour to actions solely in
proportion to their tendency to increase the sum of happiness,
lessen the sum of misery.'[3]

[1] R. P. Smith to E. J. Littleton, 23 October 1826. Quoted C. R. Fay, *Huskisson and his Age* (1951), p. 153.

[2] *Birmingham Inspector*, 4 January 1817, one of a whole series of similar local periodicals.

[3] *Westminster Review*, February 1824. The *Edinburgh Review*, attacked by Mill, itself

Benthamite ideas spread, often in crude form, not only among the middle classes in the provincial cities (particularly through local newspapers) but among undergraduates and working men, particularly working men in London. 'My essays are the text books of the young men of the Union of Cambridge', James Mill wrote in 1825.[1] In the same year, the Benthamites founded University College, London, open to members of all religions or none, to provide a less expensive and more utilitarian education for the sons of the industrial and commercial middle-classes than that provided in Oxford and Cambridge, while Brougham published his celebrated *Practical Observations upon the Education of the People*, which sold 50,000 copies in a few weeks and quickly went through twenty editions. It advocated 'the gospel of the alphabet', more cheap books and more popular instruction. The Mechanics' Institute movement, which had its origins in early nineteenth-century Scotland, began work in London in 1823, and under the influence of Brougham, 'the most able and eloquent friend of the Mechanics now living',[2] soon took root in the provinces. Finally, the Society for the Diffusion of Useful Knowledge, founded in 1827, started its noisy and often inefficient work of educating the new artisan class. Economic change had already prepared the way: in 1826 it was remarked of 'lean, unwashed artisans' in Birmingham that they discussed 'the maxims of Government and the conduct of their rulers quite as rationally as some of the theorists in higher places' and of 'the industrious class' in general that 'it is snatched from routine' and 'withdrawn from ignorance—the principles and applications of the useful sciences are unfolded to it'.[3]

The 'liberal' members of Liverpool's government were relatively uninterested in or even hostile to this movement of thought and feeling in the country, although Huskisson was elected the first president of the Liverpool School of Arts and he and Peel were subscribers—along with Sir Walter Scott—to the Edinburgh School of Arts in 1825. Canning criticized Brougham's views on the need for the spread of popular education and aligned himself with Tory critics of what Dr. Folliott in Peacock's *Crotchet Castle* called 'the

maintained that 'the sacred thirst for science is becoming epidemic, and we look forward to the day when the laws of matter and mind shall be known to all men'. (August 1825).

[1] Quoted E. Barker (ed.) *Mill's Essay on Government* (1937), p. x.
[2] *Mechanics' Magazine*, preface to vol. 3 (1824).
[3] Quoted in the *Mechanics' Magazine*, 3 June 1826.

reading rabble'. Peacock's brilliant satire on what he called the 'Steam Intellect' Society has done more to preserve the memory of the S.D.U.K. than its educational achievements. 'I am out of all patience with this march of mind', Dr. Folliott exclaimed at breakfast one fine May morning: 'Here has my house been nearly burned down, by my cook taking it into her head to study hydrostatics.'[1] Dr. Folliott was far from being alone in his complaints. Scores of pamphlets were written warning of the danger of education 'exalting' the poor 'above their humble and laborious duties'; Coleridge prayed, 'from a popular philosophy and a philosophic populace, good sense deliver us'[2]; Cobbett thundered against 'Scotch feelosophy' and education by too many books; Lord Eldon is claimed to have believed that the march of mind would one day or the other direct 'a hundred thousand tall fellows with clubs and pikes against Whitehall'.[3] *The St. James's Chronicle* said of Mechanics' Institutes; 'A scheme more completely adapted for the destruction of this Empire could not have been invented by the author of evil himself.'[4]

It was in vain that the Mechanics' Institutes pleaded that they were outside politics or that a 'greater degree of knowledge' would strengthen 'the firmness of the bond which unites all orders of society'. The 'march of intellect' was unpopular with all those people in society who believed that education was socially dangerous. The unpopularity was enhanced by two further prejudices— the first, a prejudice against industrialism itself, which the Steam Intellect Society and similar organizations treated as a matter of pride; the second, a prejudice against the new doctrines of political economy, which seemed to be bound up with all enterprises of this kind. Whenever defenders of the Mechanics' Institutes used arguments like 'it is to our manufactures that we owe our national superiority. It is by our manufactures that we must maintain it',[5] they alienated not only Ultras who preferred 'the Wisdom of Ancestors' to the 'torch of Intellect',[6] but moderate men in the

[1] *Crotchet Castle* (1831), ch. II. It is a serious mistake to confuse Peacock's own views and sympathies with those of the eminently quotable Dr. Folliott.
[2] *The Statesman's Manual* (1816), p. 47.
[3] Place Papers, B.M., Add. MSS. 35,148/6–6b.
[4] *Ibid.*, 27,824, f. 80.
[5] *Stockport Advertiser*, 16 September 1825.
[6] J. S. Mill in *The Spirit of the Age*, a series of articles for the *Examiner* in 1831 (reprinted and ed. by F. A. Hayek, 1942), described how the two slogans were 'bandied from mouth to mouth' and turned into 'sarcastic jibes of hatred and insult'.

government, who were still pledged to Liverpool's view that 'the landed interest ought to have the predominant weight. The landed interest is in fact the stamina of the country.'[1] Wherever the praises of political economy were sung, they jarred many listeners. Political economy, as represented either by the Political Economy Club, founded in 1821, or in the popular tracts of Harriet Martineau, was thought of not as a neutral science of wants and resources, but as a partisan apologia for a new economic system. Huskisson and Robinson were suspect as part of the same political economists' circle. The general indictment against the whole 'march of intellect' —columns and flanks—was well stated in the preface to the *Gentleman's Magazine* in 1832; 'Philosophical or speculative theorists, and political economists have been so long experimentalizing and administering empirical nostrums to the naturally robust constitution of John Bull, that he is rapidly sinking from his once vigorous condition to weakness and decrepitude.'

The year 1832 marked, of course, the triumph of reform, and between the crash of 1825 and the bill of 1832 there was a renewal of interest in the question. That this was so was due more to the prevalence of distress than to the march of intellect, more to divisions in the ranks of the government than to accession of strength to the Whigs. Between 1827 and 1830, English politics were in a state of flux and the differences of opinion and outlook, which Liverpool had bridged, became open points of contention. Some strange new alignments developed in the process.

5. POLITICS IN FLUX

At ten o'clock on 17 February 1827, Liverpool was found lying paralysed on the floor of his breakfast room; during the following month, it became clear that he would never resume office. Before his death in 1828 political differences were coming to a head and 'the air was thick with rumours of impending change'. The Catholic question could no longer be kept an 'open' question, and Liverpool foresaw imminent 'crisis'; the corn law question had produced sharp divisions inside the cabinet, and although Liverpool was prepared to stake his reputation on a new corn law prepared by Huskisson, many of his colleagues were inflexibly opposed to it; the personality and foreign policy of Canning inspired continued

---

[1] Quoted W. R. Brock, *op. cit.*, p. 36. The view was held much more strongly still by writers like Coleridge.

distaste and distrust among Tories like Wellington and the Ultras, whose main complaint against Liverpool was 'the tyrannical influence acquired over him by Mr. Canning'.[1]

Nonetheless, it was Canning who was chosen by the King as the new prime minister in the spring of 1827. Possible alternative choices—Peel, greatly junior to Canning both in age and experience, and Wellington, who had almost disqualified himself by accepting the position of commander-in-chief on the death of the Duke of York—were not so much directly rejected by the King as shelved during the course of a month of what Professor Aspinall has described as 'masterly inactivity'.[2] As in 1812, George IV tried to evade his constitutional responsibility of choosing a prime minister; once it had become abundantly clear during the dilatory negotiations that a solidly 'Protestant' government could not be formed, the choice of Canning became inevitable. The King had been won over between 1825 and 1827 to a liking for him instead of an aversion, and the opposition of the great families of the country to a 'charlatan *parvenu*' only strengthened the King's belief that he was fighting the pretensions of the great aristocratic cliques which had tried to monopolize office during his father's reign. To the 'public' and the press, however, the choice of Canning was not so much a new incident in a sequence of old battles as a victory for opinion; it was generally said, in London at least, that the choice was the most popular with the people that had ever been known.

Such popularity did little to make Canning's political tasks at Westminster easier. Seven cabinet ministers who had served under Liverpool, including Wellington and Peel, refused to serve under Canning[3]; many backbencher Tories were bitterly opposed to him. Only Canning's energy and resourcefulness won him through. Having failed to persuade the 'Ultra' Tories to reconsider their position he turned to the Whigs. Grey, who viewed Canning with contempt and declared that the son of an actress was *de facto* disqualified for the position of prime minister, stood aloof and hostile. But Lord Lansdowne, the representative of a different Whig tradition, the Duke of Devonshire, Tierney, William Lamb (later Lord Melbourne), and Stanley all accepted office. Brougham was friendly, believing that the era of the Ultras was at last over, and

---

[1] *Journal of Mrs. Arbuthnot*, vol. II, p. 81.
[2] *The Formation of Canning's Ministry* (Camden Society, 1937).
[3] Wellington also resigned his post as commander-in-chief.

Lord John Russell, already a staunch advocate of parliamentary reform as he was to be for the rest of his long political life, offered outside support. The accession and support of such 'Whigs', along with the continued presence in the government of 'liberals' like Huskisson, Robinson and Palmerston, seemed to have shifted the whole basis of English politics. Mrs. Arbuthnot might report that Canning's new government was known as the provisional government or less formally as 'the warming pans', but in fact Canning had built up a strong team in almost impossible circumstances. The price was unbridled opposition from his old colleagues. 'Party spirit seems as if it would now run most furiously high in both Houses. In the Lords they are becoming like the House of Commons in violence'.[1]

The violence was demonstrated in the course of the debates on Huskisson's corn bill, which Liverpool had accepted. Rejecting the idea of total repeal or of a fixed duty, Huskisson proposed a sliding scale of duties, pivoted on a normal point of 60s. a quarter. The agriculturalists considered that the sliding scale offered inadequate protection, and although the bill passed the Commons, the Duke of Wellington, after a misunderstanding with Huskisson, carried a protectionist amendment in the House of Lords. As a result of the passing and later the repassing of Wellington's amendment, the government did not proceed with the measure. 'The long promised free trade in Corn', a radical newspaper commented bitterly, 'has been knocked on the head by the hero of Waterloo—and the people in consequence must, in the future, square their appetites to the superficies of British soil—or failing this, remove to climes where nature's gifts are not exclusively confined to the enjoyment of the wealthy, but are freely diffused among all classes.'[2] Canning himself saw the dangers of such criticism: from his 'liberal-tory' standpoint he considered that the Lords were inviting a struggle between 'property' and 'population'.[3]

Such warnings were not to come from Canning's lips for long. In July 1827 Lord John Russell had written: 'If Canning lasts, the Ministry will last.'[4] He did not last, and on 8 August died in the house at Chiswick where Fox had died twenty years before. His death in no sense eliminated the conflicts and divisions within the

---

[1] *Journal of Mrs. Arbuthnot*, vol. II, p. 115.
[2] Quoted D. G. Barnes, *A History of the English Corn Laws* (1930), p. 197.
[3] Quoted A. G. Stapleton, *op. cit.*, p. 350.
[4] *Early Correspondence of Lord John Russell* (1913), vol. I, p. 249.

old Pittite ranks, and it made it much more difficult to maintain the understanding between Canningites and Whigs. The new prime minister, Robinson, who had been created Lord Goderich at the time of the formation of Canning's ministry, was weak and ineffective when placed in a position of leadership. The King strongly objected to the strengthening of the Whig element in the administration, but Goderich could find no new support from other quarters. After months of wrangling, ineffective bargaining, and tears, Goderich, sick and jaded, resigned in January 1828. In the course of his short prime ministership he had never met Parliament. It was with genuine relief that Mrs. Arbuthnot wrote on 10 January, 'at last this most disreputable Government has come to an end'.

Her hero Wellington came back into power with Peel as his henchman in the Commons, but it soon became abundantly clear that he could not restore order to English politics. Remaining in office for more than two years, he moved in the middle of a world where politics became increasingly complicated and economic 'distress' more prevalent and widespread. The Duke was not a good prime minister, for he could never understand that political colleagues were not military subordinates and that policy was a matter of opinion as well as authority. He had other weaknesses too. A stinging epigram about him ran that he had a 'social contempt for his intellectual equals, and an intellectual contempt for his social equals'.[1] The contempt was mingled with tactlessness and occasional impetuosity, a by-product of his remarkable and transparent honesty. Such a combination of attributes—some of them the exact opposite of Liverpool's—was well contrived to ensure the final collapse of the Pittite 'coalition', to shatter into bits and pieces the groups which were already at loggerheads in 1828.

Wellington's first quarrel was with the Canningites and their moderate supporters. By including them in his ministry, he alienated the Ultras (and Mrs. Arbuthnot). By treating their carefully thought-out opinions as signs of mutiny, he made them angry and unsure of themselves. Huskisson was in any case a sensitive and awkward leader of the group and although he reached a compromise with Wellington on the old question of the corn law—carrying a bill similar to that of 1827 with some protectionist modifications—he broke with the prime minister on a minor issue of parliamentary reform. Two boroughs—Penryn in Cornwall and East Retford in

---

[1] Quoted C. R. M. F. Cruttwell, *Wellington* (1936), p. 101.

Nottinghamshire—were found guilty of serious corruption. Huskisson and his friends, going further along the road to parliamentary reform than Canning had ever done, favoured the transfer of their franchises to the large unrepresented cities of Manchester and Birmingham. There was a near-precedent in 1821, when the franchise of the delinquent borough of Grampound had been transferred to Yorkshire, but counties—even partly industrial counties—were not quite the same as enormous new industrial cities, and in 1821 further representation of Yorkshire had been deliberately preferred to new representation of Leeds. The traditionalist members of the government in 1828 favoured the absorption of Penryn and East Retford in their local hundreds, and were strongly opposed to enfranchising new cities through a 'back-door' measure. Although a compromise was patched up between the Canningites and the orthodox Tories—the franchise of Penryn was to be transferred to Manchester and the borough of East Retford was to be absorbed in its hundred—the House of Lords would not support the enfranchisement of Manchester. Huskisson and his friends now felt themselves free to turn down the East Retford proposals. They voted against the government, and Huskisson, without much careful thought, offered to resign. Wellington immediately accepted the resignation in May 1828 and would not allow the reluctant and embarrassed Huskisson to change his mind. As a result, the Canningites—already disliking Wellington's foreign and commercial policy—resigned *en bloc*. The fact that they had broken with the Duke ostensibly on a matter of political as distinct from economic reform or foreign policy showed the direction in which the new parliamentary winds were blowing. 'They all went and because they considered themselves a separate party and bound to act together, right or wrong, it was intended to be what Mr. Wilmot calls a *general strike*.'[1]

The new Wellington cabinet was solidly Tory, and Wellington and his friends could now for a brief moment believe that they had purged the government of all its 'theoretical' and subversive elements. There were three soldiers in the cabinet, and Palmerston, who left the War Office behind him after nineteen years of continuous service, sarcastically likened the minds of the new ministers

[1] *Journal of Mrs. Arbuthnot*, vol. II, p. 195. Wilmot Horton (Mrs. Arbuthnot forgot that he had added the Horton to his name in 1823) was a minor politician and undersecretary for war 1821–8.

to cartridge paper. Yet the discipline of the new 'military ministry' soon left something to be desired, largely because of the nature of the orders Wellington gave. In the course of 1828, influenced by the opinions of a 'Protestant' Lord Lieutenant in Ireland, who doubted whether he could safely depend on a partly Catholic army and police, he came to the conclusion that he had no alternative but to carry the one measure the Ultras really detested, the emancipation of the Catholics. In courageously carrying emancipation almost as a military operation, he provoked his second quarrel, a much more bitter quarrel than his earlier estrangement with the Canningites, and lost the support of those who had previously been his warmest friends. As a result of the complicated cross-voting which followed the passing of Catholic emancipation in 1829—the Ultras were a much less disciplined and coherent group than the Canningites—the Whigs were eventually able in 1830 to return to power. When they went on to introduce a large-scale measure of parliamentary reform in 1831, they could even claim that they were not the first to dabble with the ancient Constitution. The first assault had been made by Wellington himself, the man who claimed to be the most stalwart defender of the old order. It was in 1829 not in 1831 or 1832 that a provincial paper, specially edged for the occasion in black, exclaimed —'Died, full of good works, deeply lamented by every HONEST BRITON, MR. CONSTITUTION. His decease took place on the 13th of April in the year of our Lord 1829, at the House of the *Incurables*.'[1]

It is necessary to sketch some of the details of how Wellington came to introduce Catholic emancipation and the most important consequences of his decision. In a sense, the way for him was prepared by a decision which was not his own and which related to Protestant dissenters in England, not discontented Catholics in Ireland. In February 1828, Lord John Russell, backed by a powerful Nonconformist pressure group, the United Committee (of Congregationalists, Baptists and Unitarians), introduced a bill for the repeal of the Test and Corporation Acts in so far as they excluded Protestant Dissenters from office. At first Wellington and Peel opposed it, then they tried to compromise. The bill was eventually carried with very minor additions. Eldon regarded it 'as bad, as mischievous, and as revolutionary as the most captious Dissenter would wish it to be'[2]; Russell, reading the writing on the wall,

---

[1] *Birmingham Argus*, 1 May 1829.
[2] H. Twiss, *The Public and Private Life of Lord Chancellor Eldon* (2nd edn., 1844), vol. III, p. 45.

made a much shrewder comment. 'It is really a gratifying thing to force the enemy to give up his first line, that none but Churchmen are worthy to serve the State, and I think we shall soon make him give up the second, that none but Protestants are. Peel is a very pretty hand at hauling down his colours.'[1]

There was little time for reflection on the significance of the repeal of the Test and Corporation Acts before Sir Francis Burdett on 8 May 1828 brought forward the same motion on Catholic relief which had been rejected by a majority of 4 in 1827. This time it was carried by 6 votes, although the Lords went on to throw it out by 181 votes to 137. Wellington opposed the proposal, but he did not try to refute the principle of emancipation itself: instead, he talked of waiting for quieter times, a favourite Tory manœuvre throughout the rest of the nineteenth century. The argument ran that when times were noisy it was always wiser to wait for a period of tranquillity; when times were quiet, it was a sign of lack of public interest in change and everyone was happy and contented with things as they were. It was, in fact, noisy times which made Wellington and Peel yield in 1828 and 1829, just as noisy times eventually made them yield on the corn laws in 1846. Both of them preferred 'hauling down colours' to a collapse of governmental authority.

When in May 1828 Wellington reconstituted his cabinet after the withdrawal of the Canningites, he placed Vesey Fitzgerald, Irish member of Parliament for County Clare, at the Board of Trade. This necessitated a by-election, but since Fitzgerald was an emancipationist there seemed every likelihood that he would be safely returned again. Instead Daniel O'Connell saw the possibilities of the situation and himself stood as a Catholic candidate, receiving a clear majority of the votes. The result of the Clare election drove Wellington and (more reluctantly) Peel to concede Catholic emancipation. They realized that another general election would produce a flood of Catholic members, and that a change in the law was necessary to preserve legality and order in Ireland. When they announced their conversion in February 1829, the outcry of their own 'Ultra' supporters was unrestrained. Brunswick Clubs thundered against the threats to the constitution of Church and State; over 500 anti-Catholic petitions were organized, and Peel, who felt bound to resign his seat at Oxford and ask his constituents for a vote

[1] *Early Correspondence*, vol. I, p. 272.

of confidence, was beaten in an exciting by-election, during which his opponents taunted him with the couplet

> Oh! Member for Oxford! you shuffle and wheel!
> You have altered your name from R. Peel to Repeal.[1]

Wellington himself was goaded into fighting a duel with Lord Winchilsea, one of his most violent opponents in the House of Lords.

Wellington's standing and his approach to emancipation made it possible for him to carry the measure more easily than any other political personality could have done, and both Parliament and King gave way under his influence. George IV tried tears and kisses, threats to retire to Hanover and even dismissal of his ministers, but Wellington made it abundantly clear to him that there was no alternative to Wellington; finally in great pain he wrote to Wellington on 4 March that 'as I find the country would be left without an administration, I have decided to yield my opinion to *that* which is considered by the Cabinet to be for the immediate interest of the Country.'[2] It was an important moment not only in the history of the Catholic question but in the history of monarchy. The bill went ahead and in April Parliament finally decided to admit Catholics to its benches and to all offices except those of Lord Lieutenant General and of Lord Chancellor in both England and Ireland, and Lord Keeper and High Commissioner of the General Assembly of the Church of Scotland. As an anti-democratic safeguard, the Irish freehold qualification for voting was raised from 40s. to £10.

One hundred and forty two people, including many English county members, voted against Catholic emancipation, and from April 1829 to November 1830 they were an angry and confused group. Some of them, a small number, were even prepared to demand parliamentary reform, preferring the 'People' to Parliament and maintaining that a wider suffrage would have ensured a majority in the House of Commons against emancipation. In June 1828, for instance, the Marquis of Blandford introduced a series of propositions in the House of Commons, declaring that the system of borough representation was venal and corrupt. Others, a larger group, were prepared to vote against Wellington even if it meant (quite irrationally) allying themselves with the Whigs. Perhaps only a little less irrationally

---

[1] *Birmingham Argus*, January 1829.
[2] See R. Fulford, *George IV* (2nd edn., 1949), p. 222.

Wellington received a large measure of support, not only from Whigs but from radicals—and philosophic radicals at that. On the occasion of his duel with Winchilsea, Bentham sent him a letter of remonstrance, 'more solicitous for the life of the leader of the Absolutists than he is',[1] while independent Whigs urged the Duke to go on to introduce parliamentary reform and 'satisfy nine-tenths of the reformers with a moderate and reasonable change'.[2] Never had the opinions expressed been so contrary and the political situation in greater flux. 'Party', remarked Lord Holland in February 1830, 'seems to be no more.'

The situation still remained extremely fluid in 1830 although there were some signs that 'the gratitude the old Opposition has felt for the carrying of the Catholic Bill' was 'fast wearing out'.[3] Distress was producing louder demands not only for parliamentary reform but for remedial economic measures—greater economy, repeal of the corn laws, or, more vociferously at this time, demands for currency reform.

In the middle of this confused period two events occurred which in retrospect seemed to have changed the political balance—the death of George IV on 26 June and the bloodless July Revolution in France which led to the overthrow of the Bourbons. The immediate significance of the second of these two events in English history has probably been overrated,[4] but the first had three practical consequences—the necessity for a new general election; the accession of a King, William IV, who was felt, however slender the evidence, to be 'a King of England and not the King of a faction'[5]; and the end of the long-standing royal veto on Grey. The election, which followed the formal dissolution of Parliament on 24 July did not greatly clarify the long-term prospects of Wellington's government —there were both government and opposition gains in the small number of contested seats—but it certainly did not improve them in the short run. After the new Parliament had met, radicals of various persuasions pointed increasingly to the example of France. 'The success of the Mobs and either the unwillingness or inability

---

[1] *Dispatches*, vol. V, pp. 546–7.
[2] *A Letter to the Duke of Wellington on the expediency of making Parliamentary Reform a Cabinet Measure* (1830).
[3] Sir Robert Heron, *Notes* (1851), June 1830.
[4] See N. Gash, 'English Reform and French Revolution in the General Election of 1830' in *Essays Presented to Sir Lewis Namier* (1956), pp. 265–6.
[5] B.R.L., Birmingham Political Union: Speeches at a Dinner to celebrate the French Revolution.

of the soldiers to cope with them in Paris and Brussels', wrote Peel in October 1830, 'is producing its natural effect in the Manufacturing districts, calling into action the almost forgotten Radicals of 1817 and 1819, and provoking a discussion upon the probable results of insurrectionary movements in this country.' [1]

Against this background Wellington showed no signs of political mastery. He had failed in the course of 1830 to capitalize on the goodwill of the Whigs. The possibilities of his reaching an understanding with the small band of Canningites were dashed when Huskisson, a victim as well as a protagonist of 'improvement', was killed by a railway train drawn by Stephenson's *Rocket*, at the opening of the Liverpool and Manchester Railway in September. The Ultras were still restive and although some of them were now giving him support again, a large number were hostile or unreliable. At last on 2 November the Duke with one speech changed the political situation far more than the death of George IV or the French Revolution had done; in reply to a moderate and well-reasoned speech by Grey, Wellington carelessly and provocatively replied that he did not believe that the state of the representation could be improved, or that any constitutional innovator could do better than copy that which already existed. The Constitution, he added, had the support of the country, and so long as he held any 'station' in the government, he would always feel it his duty to resist reform proposals.

Whigs and radicals alike were stirred into resolute opposition by Wellington's unpropitious speech, the Canningites were angered, and even many moderate supporters of the government were upset. Only a group of Ultras fully shared these sentiments, and certainly Wellington's unoriginal statement of the old Tory case did little to rally them all to his side. When on 15 November Sir Henry Parnell, an Irish Whig—the original sponsor of the corn law of 1815 although he had changed his opinions about it and had become a resolute financial reformer—proposed that a Select Committee be appointed to investigate the Civil List accounts, the government was defeated by 233 votes to 204. Governments had survived hostile votes in the past, but on this occasion, confronted with a majority which included Whigs, Canningites, independent men and Ultras, Wellington resigned. He was perhaps glad to be free for a time of the cares of office and certainly Peel was relieved not to have

[1] Quoted by N. Gash, *loc. cit.*

to face the continued complications of a difficult parliamentary situation in which the government was left with smaller and smaller room in which to manœuvre. Wellington believed that the Whigs would find it difficult to resolve the differences between 'conservatives' and 'demagogues', while the commentator Greville was convinced that 'it is a hundred to one that whatever they do, they will not go far enough to satisfy the country'.[1]

Grey, who was invited by William IV to form a ministry, was dependent on the support of other groups in the House of Commons, and his ministry was a coalition under Whig leadership of those groups, including the Canningites, which had combined to defeat Wellington. It was this ministry, which was far from being a coherent 'party' ministry—the Whigs themselves were divided—that re-awakened English politics.

[1] *Greville Memoirs*, 17 November 1830.

5

REFORM

1. THE WHIGS AND REFORM

THE return of the Whigs to power meant that some sort of reform bill was inevitable; it was not certain, however, what exact form their bill would take. In the debate in the House of Lords, which provoked Wellington to his spirited but tactless defence of the unreformed legislature, Grey was candid enough to acknowledge that he had not prepared a specific plan of reform. The demand for reform had appeared for many years on Whig party banners side by side with 'retrenchment', 'civil and religious liberty', and 'the abolition of colonial slavery', but it had been talked about in general terms for so long that practical difficulties had been slurred over or left to be handled by particular politicians, of whom Henry Brougham and Lord John Russell were by far the most important. Russell had declared himself in favour of disfranchising rotten boroughs in 1819, and in 1820 had introduced the first of his measures for disfranchising particularly notorious constituencies. The second of these, for disfranchising Grampound, successfully passed the House of Lords in 1821. At that time Grey believed that there was no reasonable hope of carrying a comprehensive Reform Bill in his lifetime, and it was not until 1830 that he found both challenge and opportunity. Grey was a natural conservative, a *grand seigneur*, and he approached reform from this standpoint. He set out to show in his own words 'that in these days of democracy and Jacobinism it is possible to find real capacity in the high aristocracy'.[1] His new ministry was composed almost entirely of members of the aristocracy and to a large extent of peers; there

---

[1] Quoted H. W. C. Davis, *The Age of Grey and Peel* (1929), p. 228. Grey also believed that to resist 'the spirit of the age' was 'certain destruction . . . even Russia was unable to resist a handful of rebels' (*ibid.*, p. 227).

were only three commoners in a cabinet of thirteen.[1] Six or seven relatives of Grey himself were members of the administration. There were certainly far more people in this government who distrusted Henry Brougham than admired him, and it was only with difficulty that Brougham took his place in the government as Lord Chancellor.

The composition of the new government brings out clearly the importance of the intricate network of aristocratic 'connexions' among 'the friends of liberty and order, the old constitutional Whigs of England'. The leading Whigs were born not made; only a few outstanding individuals, of whom Macaulay, the greatest of Whig historians, was the chief, ever penetrated the inner citadels of Whiggery after starting as complete 'outsiders'. The citadels were the town and country houses of the great magnates —estates like Woburn, the home of the Duke of Bedford, 'a kingdom in miniature', or that 'splendid shrine' of London Whiggery, Holland House. It was in such houses, in Brooks's Club, and in the pages of the *Edinburgh Review*, that the theories and ideals of Charles James Fox were kept alive to nourish a new generation. The most popular Whig personality was Lord Althorp, leader of the House of Commons. Although he 'never gave birth to an original idea in his life, nor did he ever utter an eloquent expression', he had great resources of character and made his colleagues feel 'safe and right' so long as he was in a position of authority. 'He is the tortoise', said Melbourne, 'on whose back the world reposes'.[2] His Whiggery was beyond question and like most of the greater Whig magnates he had his heart in the land not at Westminster. 'He came out of the fields and woods and to the fields and woods he returned.'[3]

Attached to the Whig connexions in 1830, rather than fully integrated in one compact group, were the various 'interests' which had depended on Whig support for generations—a large part of the ' money interest ' in the City of London; a sizeable share of the 'manufacturing interest' of the industrial provinces, associated with men like John Marshall, the rich Leeds flaxmaster, or Edward Baines, the editor of the *Leeds Mercury* ; the main forces of old Dissent, represented in Parliament from 1784–1830 by William

[1] If Lord Palmerston, an Irish peer who sat in the House of Commons, is counted as a 'commoner' there were four.
[2] Quoted Lord David Cecil, *Lord M* (1954), p. 78.
[3] E. Myers, *Lord Althorp* (1890), p. 240.

Smith, who was also chairman of one of the most important dissenting institutions, the Dissenting Deputies, from 1805 to 1832. He
and John Wilks, founder and secretary of the Protestant Society
(set up in 1811), hoped to mobilize Whig members of Parliament in
the cause of 'civil and religious liberty'. These 'interests' were all
concerned with ideas and principles as well as with the achievement
of immediate practical objectives; there were other groups, too,
for whom ideas counted for everything. These were the 'opinion
groups' struggling for social and political changes, and they were
prepared to work through the Whigs (while criticizing them unceasingly) because they could not work at all through no-change
administrations such as Wellington had talked of in his last speech.
Many of the Utilitarians, for example, recognized the need for joint
action with the Whigs in the cause of 'improvement', and pressed
for extensive and searching reforms. They knew the strength of
vis inertiae outside Parliament and the timidity of short-sighted
politicians inside it. While objecting to Whig half-measures, they
realized the need to co-operate against those public men who
dreaded not only great changes but small ones, and would not act at
all because they did not know when and where 'innovation once
begun, though it be but a trifle' would end.[1] Bentham himself
stated the case for limited co-operation very clearly in the dark
days of 1818—'the Tories are the people's avowed enemies . . .
On no occasion under the ever-increasing weight of the yoke of
oppression and misrule, from any hand other than that of the parliamentary Whigs can the people receive any [*sic*] the slightest chance
(talk not of relief) for the retardation of increase'.[2] Bentham showed
more sympathy towards the Whigs than towards popular Radicals
such as Cobbett and Hunt, whose struggles he watched 'with much
the same eye as the visitors of Mr. Carpenter—the optician—contemplate the rabid animals devouring one another in a drop of
water.'[3]

The Whigs, exclusive and aristocratic though they were in their
attitude to government, were ready to accept political innovations.
Indeed, they believed that unless the privileged sections of the
community were prepared to adapt and to 'improve', waves of dangerous and uncontrollable innovation would completely drown

[1] *Westminster Review*, April 1824.
[2] *Plan of Parliamentary Reform*, p. cccxxvii.
[3] Quoted A. Bain, *James Mill* (1882), p. 333.

the existing social order. While their opponents in 1830 believed that a considerable measure of parliamentary reform would lead to national catastrophe, the Whigs maintained that only a considerable measure could prevent a catastrophe. Pointing to the 'universal feeling' that reform was necessary at that time, Grey told the King that 'not to do enough to satisfy public expectation'—he was careful to add as a true Whig, 'I mean the satisfaction of the rational public'—'would be worse than to do nothing'.[1] Two days later, he was more explicit. 'Any measure . . . to be useful must be effectual. Anything that was not so would only leave a feeling of discontent, which would press for further concessions . . . I am myself convinced that public opinion is so strongly directed to this question, and so general, that it cannot be resisted without the greatest danger of leaving the Government in a situation in which it would be deprived of all authority and strength.'[2]

Whigs and Tories were agreed during the crucial debates of 1830–32 that democracy was an unpalatable and dangerous form of government, that 'a stake in the country' was an essential title to political power, that landed property had a special part to play in guaranteeing the stability of the social order and the authority of the Constitution, that the 'wild'—as distinct from the 'rational'—part of the public should not be left undisturbed to exercise pressure on governmental policy. The Whigs, however, were responsive to some of the movements of change and responsible in relation to the rest. There were some Whigs too who went much further than Grey in their willingness to innovate, just as Whitbread had been prepared to go much further twenty years before. Lord Durham, for example, the son-in-law of Grey and Lord Privy Seal in the new government, was a man who declared publicly that he watched 'with regret every hour which passes over the existence of acknowledged but unreformed abuse'[3]; Brougham, in some ways perhaps less radical at heart than Durham, proclaimed eloquently but somewhat unrealistically: 'We don't now live in the days of Barons, thank God—we live in the days of Leeds, of Bradford, of Halifax and of Huddersfield. We live in the days when men are industrious and desire to be free.'[4]

---

[1] *The Correspondence of the Late Earl Grey with H.M. King William IV* (ed. Henry, Earl Grey, 1867), vol. I, p. 52.
[2] *Ibid.*, pp. 65–6.
[3] C. New, *Lord Durham* (1929), p. 254.
[4] *Leeds Intelligencer*, 29 July 1830.

The framing of a Reform Bill by the new government was left to a small committee of four, which included neither Brougham nor Grey himself. They were instructed by Grey to draft a plan of reform 'of such a scope and description as to satisfy all reasonable demands, and remove at once, and for ever, all rational grounds for complaint from the minds of the intelligent and independent portion of the community.'[1] Lord Durham, Lord John Russell, J. W. Ponsonby[2] and Sir James Graham, the last of whom was Grey's surprise choice, spent the late autumn and winter of 1830–31 discussing the outlines of the new measure. Their main problems were those of deciding which places should lose and which secure members of Parliament, and what voting qualification would enfranchise the 'middle classes' without creating thoroughly 'popular' constituencies. Their solution of these problems was kept secret until 1 March 1831, when Russell, who was not a member of the cabinet, introduced the Reform Bill to the House of Commons.

As Russell outlined the government's proposals to 'deal mildly but firmly with the rotten Boroughmongers' and to purify the electoral system, it soon became clear to the crowded House that the Bill went much further than had been anticipated. Russell took his stand between 'the two hostile parties' of diehards and Radicals, 'neither agreeing with the bigotry of those who would reject all Reform, nor with the fanaticism of those who contend that only one plan of Reform would be wholesome or satisfactory': he talked of amending abuses and averting convulsion, of restoring public confidence in the 'construction and constitution of the House of Commons', and of converting the House from 'an assembly of representatives of small classes and particular interests' into 'a body of men who represent the people, who spring from the people, who have sympathy with the people, and who can fairly call upon the people to support their burdens in the future struggles and difficulties of the country'.

In detail, Russell proposed completely to disfranchise small boroughs of less than 2,000 inhabitants, most of which were under the influence of a particular local patron, and some of which, like Old Sarum, were green mounds or heaps of stone. He went on to propose the semi-disfranchisement of a second group of small

---

[1] *Correspondence of Earl Grey and William IV*, vol. I, appendix A, p. 461.
[2] Ponsonby was called to the House of Lords as Viscount Duncannon in 1834.

boroughs with a population of under 4,000, allowing each borough one instead of two members. Of the 168 vacancies thus created, 42 were to be filled by new borough seats, including eight new London seats and seats for Manchester, Leeds, and Birmingham; 55 were to be devoted to the provision of additional members for counties, to augment what had traditionally been regarded as the most 'independent' element in the representative system; and nine new places were to be given to Scotland, Ireland and Wales. The remaining vacancies were not to be filled at all, so that the new House of Commons was to be significantly smaller than the old. As far as the conditions of voting were concerned, the 40s. freehold vote was to be retained in the counties, but in the boroughs the vote was everywhere to be offered to the £10 householder, the man who occupied— either as owner or tenant of one landlord—buildings of an annual value of £10.[1] The 'real property' and 'the real respectability' of the new centres of population would thus be given political weight, and the national electorate would be enlarged by 'about half a million persons, and these all connected with the property of the country, having a valuable stake amongst us, and deeply interested in our institutions'.

Although there was little that could be called revolutionary in Russell's proposals and he used the word 'property' as frequently as his opponents, the first Tory speaker in the debate, Sir Robert Inglis, stated unequivocally that the bill amounted to a revolution, 'a revolution that will overturn all the natural influence of rank and property'. This theme was taken up by most later Tory speakers and was not dropped until after a Reform Act was carried in 1832. The Tory opposition stressed five points. First, the bill by suppressing the small boroughs and standardizing the borough franchise was an uncompensated confiscation of private property and of corporate and customary rights, an exercise in 'robbery and pillage'. Second, the new 'experimental system' of representation was as full of anomalies and absurdities as the old historic system [2] and could not be thought of as a permanent settlement. Third, influence would inevitably pass from the landed to the industrial areas of the

---

[1] The £10 household franchise was hedged round by conditions—e.g. occupation for at least twelve months before qualification and payment of poor-rates. It was also augmented by other franchises. See below, p. 263. For the 40s. freehold, see above, p. 101.
[2] It was the Tory Croker who drew attention in March 1831 to facts which Radicals were to 'expose' for the next two decades—that some small boroughs retained two members while far bigger places were 'to be put off with *one*'. (*The Croker Papers*, vol. II (1884), p. 110.)

country, to the places with the biggest population and to 'the active, pushing, intelligent people' [1] (this was not flattery), who would soon outmatch the country squires. Fourth, as Wellington later put it, the new representative system would make it impossible for the King's government to be carried on because there would be inadequate patronage to back up a strong executive, and the House of Commons would be placed too much at the mercy of 'public opinion'. The King would in consequence be circumscribed in his choice of ministers, while genuine talent could not be nurtured in 'pocket boroughs'. Fifth, this particular measure of parliamentary reform would merely be the prelude to further parliamentary reform and eventually the destruction of all existing institutions, beginning with the House of Lords, but going on to include the Church, the Monarchy and private property itself. In Croker's grim words to Sir Walter Scott, there would eventually be no King, no Lords, no inequalities in the social system; 'all will be levelled to the plane of the petty shopkeepers and small farmers; this, perhaps not without bloodshed, but certainly by confiscations and persecutions.' [2] Many of these prophecies based on fear were expressed in wild language and were extravagant in their content, but Peel, who kept as aloof as he could do in the course of the protracted Reform Bill debates, stated the essence of them simply and without rhetoric. 'When you have once established the overpowering influence of the people over this House . . . what other authority in the State can—nay what other authority in the State ought to—control its will, or reject its decisions?'

Long-term Tory prophecies, whether founded on reason or fear, were countered by Whig defence of ordered change and by cogent assessments of the necessities of the immediate situation. The extension of the franchise was moderate and limited. Property would still be represented, but commercial and industrial as well as landed property would be 'hitched' to the Constitution 'in the love and support of the institutions and government of the country'. The increase in county representation would limit the power of the new forces of industrialism and allow the soil to retain its influence; the influence of the aristocracy would be upheld in a more purified form.

---

[1] A phrase of Alexander Baring, himself no orthodox country squire.

[2] *The Croker Papers*, vol. II, 113. Cf. W. Playfair, *Inevitable Consequences of a Reform in Parliament* (1792). 'Between the present imperfect, though successful mode of representing the people' and universal suffrage (one man, one vote) 'I see no medium, no point to stop at.'

The choice of new constituencies was not determined simply by a population formula but by the desire to have a fair representation in Parliament of the interests of 'manufacturing capital and skill'. The composition of the new House of Commons would thus facilitate a more careful attention to the problems of a changing society. Most important of all, *not* to introduce a carefully-thought out plan of reform would be to open the door to an uncontrollable popular demand for reform, which would be certain to destroy the constitution both of government and society.

Most if not all of these arguments were expressed in the early debates on the Reform Bill in March 1831. They were challenged by radicals, some of whom regretted not only the failure of the Whigs to introduce the ballot (it had appeared along with a proposal to reduce the duration of Parliament to five years in the first draft of the Committee of Four) but continued to plead for shorter Parliaments, a closer check by constituents on their members, and a wider suffrage than that offered by Russell.[1] In fact, the Whigs went as far as they possibly could have done in the light of their traditions and outlook, and they were accused by their aristocratic enemies— and Peel—of losing their dignity, betraying their order, and threatening the safety of the nation. Although Grey began by being remarkably optimistic about the chances of the bill passing, it soon became clear that the Whigs were not sure of a majority in the Commons and that they were faced with almost certain defeat in the Lords. When the second reading of the bill passed the Commons on 22 March by a majority of one vote (302 votes to 301, the largest recorded division of the unreformed House of Commons) it soon ran into difficulties at the committee stage, a Tory motion objecting to the reduction in the total number of members of Parliament for England and Wales being carried against the government by eight votes. After tense scenes in both Houses and a difficult interview between the Whig ministers and the King, William IV consented to a dissolution. The question of reform was now to be put directly—almost in the fashion of a referendum—to the unreformed electorate. Whereas the general election of 1830 had been, like most elections before it, concerned with many issues or with none, the election of 1831 was

---

[1] Orator Hunt, who recalled the memories of Peterloo in his Westminster speech, claimed that he had not heard a single new argument in the course of the debate. 'All that has been said in this House has been said twenty years ago by the weavers of Lancashire.'

an election fought entirely around the question of reform. There had never been such a single burning question of the hour.

The appeal to the electorate to choose was in many ways as significant as the content of the subject on which they were called upon to express an opinion. Liverpool had maintained firmly that public opinion, while it ought to have weight in the determination of policies, ought not to have so great a weight as to prevent the House of Commons from exercising its deliberative functions. The *Quarterly Review* argued on the eve of the introduction of the bill in 1831 that 'as the object of rational legislation is not to gratify the people's prejudices, but to take care of their interests, that system of government must be wanting in a most essential point, which is incapable of *protecting the people from themselves*', and Peel took the same orthodox line in the early debates of 1831, preferring the 'reason and calm judgement of this House' to 'some intrinsic and higher authority—the feelings and wishes of the people'. He was actually speaking in the House when Parliament was prorogued, and he warned his hearers that if the bill passed 'we shall have one of the worst despotisms that ever existed . . . a parliament of mob demagogues—not of wise and prudent men'. Wellington echoed the same view, objecting to the choice of 'delegates' for a particular purpose rather than the conventional 'deliberation upon matters of common concern'. The decision of the Whigs to press for dissolution in March 1831 pushed the whole reform question back to 'the people'; it was to be pushed back to them again in October 1831. To assess the response of 'public opinion' and the different ways in which it was organized, it is necessary to turn away from Westminster to the constituencies, and to examine the geography of discontent on the eve of and during the elections of April 1831. The cry of 'the bill, the whole bill and nothing but the bill' rang from one end of the country to the other. As a result, the Whigs got the mandate they demanded, and the bill, amended in various ways, could go further through another and even more exciting phase.

2. The Geography of Discontent

Enthusiasm for reform in the country as a whole was bound up not only with a theory of the franchise or an assertion of abstract principles but with the demand for other, sometimes even more radical, measures which had little chance of passing under an unreformed Parliament. 'It must be recollected', wrote a Newcastle radical, 'that a Reform in Parliament is only a MEANS to an end . . . the ENDS which that House of Commons is to accomplish are yet to be obtained.' [1] Because of the differences in social structure, economic organization and political tradition in different parts of the country, the 'ends' envisaged varied—in Birmingham, Attwood and his friends pressed for currency reform; in Manchester, stress was laid on the corn laws; in old closed corporations or cathedral towns like Exeter, emphasis was placed on the need for breaking down exclusive vested interests—but everywhere the answer to the most pertinent question, 'what did we want the Reform Bill FOR ?' was 'that it might do us some good; that it might better our situation'. This, argued William Cobbett, whose *Political Register* was in the vanguard of the popular reform movement, 'was what the people wanted the Reform Bill for, and not for the gratification of any abstract or metaphysical whim'. [2]

The popular radical approach to reform, well articulated by 1831, was a compound of three elements—a protest against 'distress', a theory of rights, and the dream, or rather series of often inconsistent dreams of 'a different system after the Reform Bill is disposed of'. [3] The sense of distress, whether exaggerated or not, was as crucial as both theory and dreams. 'It was often said', Thomas Attwood maintained, 'that it was the Duke's declaration against Reform which drove him from office, but with this opinion he differed. It was at least the distress of the country which primarily led to the agitation of Reform, and had it not been for that, his Grace's declaration, however abrupt and unjustified, would have had no consequences. Distress was the cause—Reform the effect.' [4]

Although the strength of the popular radical appeal in the provinces was considerable, when Russell introduced the Whig bill there were two problems which could seldom be evaded in most places—first, the division between popular radicals and more conservative reformers, and, second, difficult relations between the Whig oligarchy and popular associations which had been set up to press for reform.

The approach to reform of economically powerful and socially established urban mercantile and manufacturing groups was sub-

[1] N.R.L. *Outline of a Plan for a Northern Political Union* (1831).
[2] *Political Register*, 22 June 1833.
[3] B.R.L. *Report of the Proceedings of the Birmingham Political Union*, 17 May 1830.
[4] B.R.L., *Report of the Proceedings*, 30 July 1832.

stantially different from that of popular radicals. With considerable
initial reluctance these groups had come round increasingly to the
viewpoint that they needed direct representation in Parliament to
safeguard their interests. Hitherto they had feared the effects on the
smooth conduct of business of local political turmoil at election
times, and had usually been content to rely on county members or
representatives for neighbouring constituencies to protect their
urban interests in Parliament. In the eighteenth century Burke had
pointed out the lack of interest in parliamentary reform in places like
Birmingham, and the first generation of industrialists, like Matthew
Boulton, had certainly been unwilling to embroil themselves in
election politics. With the growth of trade, however, and the increasing complexity of economic issues, the demand for separate
representation of acknowledged seats of wealth, industry and
commercial enterprise, gained in intensity. As a local Wolverhampton businessman put it: 'Fifty years ago we were not in that
need of Representatives, which we are at present, as we then manufactured nearly exclusively for home consumption, and the commercial and manufacturing districts were then identified with each
other; where one flourished, both flourished. But the face of affairs
is now changed—we now manufacture for the whole world, and if
we have not members to promote and extend our commerce, the
era of our commercial greatness is at an end.'[1] The same argument
was used in Birmingham, Leeds, and Bradford; it was employed by
Lord John Russell in 1820 and again in 1831; it influenced many
moderate Tories, including the 'Waverer' group who in the later
history of the Reform Bill struggle attempted to prevent final
deadlock. The argument was neither democratic nor popular: the
Manchester Guardian, dismissed by its radical opponents as 'the foul
prostitute and dirty parasite of the worst section of the millowners',[2]
firmly maintained that the problem of reform was to 'prevent those
voters who belong to the class in society which is most accessible
to bribes from over-laying and rendering of no avail the independent
suffrages of people in a superior station'.[3]

Because of class cleavages in Manchester, which went back before
Peterloo, the extremism of much working-class opinion, and the
caution of many of the 'respectable' middle classes, Manchester could

---

[1] B.R.L., *Reports of the Principal Staffordshire Reform Meetings*, 14 May 1832.
[2] Quoted by C. Driver, *Tory Radical* (1946), p. 321.
[3] 8 December 1827.

not take the lead in the provincial struggle for the Reform Bill. Nor could the new industrial cities and towns of the West Riding, where economic and technical changes in the woollen and worsted industries were more recent than those in cotton and where there was bitter antagonism between new factory masters and operatives. There was perhaps no section of the Northern middle classes more enthusiastic in the cause of reform than the Yorkshire manufacturers roused by Edward Baines and the *Leeds Mercury*. They had chosen Henry Brougham as their candidate for the West Riding in 1830 and they went on to choose Macaulay as candidate for Leeds in the first 'reformed election' of 1832, but their very enthusiasm stirred working-class opposition to 'Whig' parliamentary reform and encouraged the operatives to press for a shortening of the working day and the end of 'child slavery' in the mills. It was in September 1830 that a discontented land agent, Richard Oastler, wrote his famous letter to the *Leeds Mercury* drawing attention to the plight of the Bradford factory children, and in April 1831, when Grey was appealing to the country and Baines was rallying the millowners, Oastler went on to publish his *Manifesto to the Working Classes of the West Riding*, which made no mention of parliamentary reform at all, but urged workers to demand from all candidates at the election a straight pledge in favour of a ten-hour working day.

Birmingham and the Midlands, along with Newcastle in the North-East, were the areas of leadership in the battle for parliamentary reform, just because it was possible there to 'harmonize and unite' the various 'materials of discontent'.[1] In December 1829 Thomas Attwood set up in Birmingham a 'Political Union of the Lower and Middle Classes of the People' to press for parliamentary reform. With the model of the Catholic Association very much in mind, Attwood was an opportunist in tactics, proclaiming himself a 'Tory' in the early months of the Union and offering support to the Marquis of Blandford in his Ultra reform proposals. After the Whigs had introduced their Reform Bill he came round to their support, joining hands with all those who believed that 'the present is the most eventful political crisis in the country'. Although Attwood placed currency reform first in his own programme, he did not insist on all members of the union being currency reformers; the object of the union, as proclaimed at its first big meeting on 17 May 1830, was to 'collect and organize the moral power of the country

B.R.L., *Report of the Proceedings of the Birmingham Political Union*, 17 May 1830.

for the restoration of the people's rights, to conciliate the passions, the prejudices, and the interests of all, and to bring all to unite in one common bond of union together.'[1] With this purpose in view, Attwood soon secured the support of Burdett and Cobbett, of Joseph Parkes, the Utilitarian, and of William Pare, the Owenite. It was never easy to maintain a completely united front, but in May 1831, when Grey appealed to the country, the Birmingham Union was not only strong locally but had set the pattern for the emergence of similar 'political unions' in other parts of the country. By July 1830 there were more than ten of them; by December, they had been founded in places as far apart as Glasgow, Manchester, Liverpool, Sheffield, Newcastle, and Coventry; by March 1831, when Grey was pressing for a dissolution, the King warned him of the dangers of national 'convulsion from the Land's End to John o' Groats.' 'Miners, manufacturers, colliers, labourers,' he went on, 'all who have recently formed unions for the furtherance of illegal purposes, would assemble on every point in support of a *popular* question, with the declared object of carrying the measure by intimidation. It would be in vain to hope to be able to resist their course, or to check disturbances of every kind, amounting possibly to open rebellion.'[2]

This prognostication would have been sharply challenged by the leaders of the Birmingham Political Union, to whom most of the other unions looked for guidance, since the Union claimed that it was a pillar of peace and a means of canalizing discontent in an orderly fashion. Later in the year when alarmed opponents of the unions were to claim that 'England is now actually governed by the Political Unions: the Parliament of Birmingham issues edicts',[3] John Stuart Mill paid tribute to the 'half-dozen leaders at Birmingham, who . . . act under the most intense consciousness of moral responsibility'.[4] This view was not, however, shared by the Whigs, and relations between the Whigs and the new associations posed serious problems in both the summer and autumn of 1831 and the spring of 1832.

At heart, Grey was as suspicious of the organized unions as was the King. At a later phase in the struggle, he tried deliberately to curb their activities and authority, but in March 1831 he found it

[1] B.R.L., *Report of the Proceedings of the Birmingham Political Union*, 17 May 1830.
[2] 21 March 1831, *Correspondence of William IV and Earl Grey*, vol. I, pp. 179–180.
[3] Quoted in *The Bristol Riots* by a Citizen (1832), p. 26.
[4] *Letters of John Stuart Mill* (1910), vol. I, p. 7.

necessary to point out to the King first that 'we did not cause the excitement about Reform. We found it in full vigour when we came into office' and second 'that the excitement which now exists is directed to what, I think, is a safe and legitimate object. In the event of a dissolution, it would act in support of the King and Government.' He went on to warn the King that 'if a contrary direction is given to it, you will probably see associations all over the country; and when once they have felt their power, the history of the Catholic question will show the consequences that may be expected.'[1] Lord Durham added that if the King refused a dissolution, 'feelings of disappointment, of almost reckless despair' would sweep the country. In other words, for all the Whig fear of commotion, it was the existence of the political unions and of the radical forces they represented which were their strongest arguments in persuading the King to dissolve Parliament. And at the elections which followed, it was the vigour of provincial reforming opinion which permitted Grey to go ahead with a secure parliamentary majority.

The basically conservative nature of the Whig approach to problems of discontent had been made clear before the elections of 1831 in the policy pursued by Lord Melbourne at the Home Office. Agricultural 'distress' in 1829 and 1830 had led to what has been described as the 'village labourer's revolt'. When Melbourne took office, 'the respect for property, which for generations had been an almost unbroken rural tradition, seemed to be suddenly melting away. Incendiary fires lit up the darkness of the hungry night throughout thirteen of the Southern Counties.'[2] The destruction of threshing machines, the burning of hayricks and cornstacks, the protest against tithes, the demand for living wages, and anger against the operation of poor laws were all elements in a spontaneous movement, which quickly spread from Kent to Dorset. One of Melbourne's first acts as home secretary was to issue a circular to the magistracy, asking them to act with promptitude, vigour and decision. He went on to repress the outbreaks ruthlessly and without mercy. Special commissions were sent to try the rioters in December 1830, and as a result of the trials nine labourers were hanged, 457 transported, and nearly as many imprisoned for varying terms. These domestic measures destroyed a revolt, which for a time seemed likely to add a Continental element to the English story of

---

[1] 22 March 1831. *Correspondence of William IV and Earl Grey*, vol. I, p. 186.
[2] W. M. Torrens, *Memoirs of Viscount Melbourne* (1890 edn.), p. 224.

political movement. 'There has long been a sullen discontent among
the peasantry of England,' Henry Hetherington, the editor of the
Poor Man's Guardian, exclaimed at the height of the crisis, 'may the
Aristocracy take warning in time.'[1] Melbourne took warning, but
acted in the opposite way from that which Hetherington demanded.
He refused to consider positive measures to relieve distress and
made it clear that for all their willingness to introduce a Reform
Bill the Whigs were determined to maintain the constitution of civil
society and the rights of property. The whole duty of government,
Melbourne believed, was to prevent crime and to preserve contracts.
He went on to prosecute journalists friendly to the rioters, including
Cobbett, who had argued that 'amongst the tradesmen, even of the
metropolis, *ninety-nine out of a hundred* are on the side of the labourers.
It is not that they *approve of the destruction of property* ; but they think
that these means, desperate and wicked as they are *in their nature*,
will tend to produce THAT GREAT CHANGE which all, who do not
live on the taxes, are wishing for.'[2]

Cobbett was triumphantly acquitted, and the first instalment of
GREAT CHANGE came as a result of Whig action and continued
urban pressure, but Melbourne's actions had sharpened the antipathy between popular radicals and members of the government.
The 'insincere and dirty' Whigs were never popular in the Political
Unions and were hated by many of the factory operatives of the
North. There was thus a latent sense of conflict and disillusionment
even in the first months of the reform agitation before the Whigs
were swept back into power by the small unreformed electorate.
The conflict and disillusionment were to burst out at a later date;
for the moment, however, during the elections themselves there was
an irresistible wave of excitement for reform. Wherever there was a
large and popular constituency, the reformer was in almost every
case returned. At Liverpool, for example, General Gascoyne, who
had proposed the motion which led to the defeat of the government,
was defeated after having diligently represented the city for more
than thirty years.[3] Four reformers were returned for London, and
of the eighty-two county members, almost all were pledged to the
bill. 'The county members', Greville pointed out in the middle of
the results, 'are tumbling about like ninepins.' 'Never, perhaps,'

<hr>

[1] P.R.O., H.O./40/25.
[2] *Weekly Political Register*, 4 December 1830.
[3] Gascoyne is said to have promoted 200 local bills at the instigation of his constituents.

wrote another contemporary when all the results were announced, 'had any election worked so complete a transformation.'[1]

3. THE TRIUMPH OF REFORM

The political effects of the election became clear from 24 June onwards. It was then that Russell introduced a new Reform Bill, showing only minor modifications from the first. This time, the bill passed its second reading with a large majority of 136 votes (367 votes to 231). It lagged in committee, for delay was the only tactical instrument left to the opposition. Finally, on 22 September it was carried by 345 votes to 236 and was sent on to the House of Lords. The Tories had contested the fate of each condemned borough, and one important new amendment was passed at the instigation of the Marquis of Chandos, who later became the second Duke of Buckingham. Chandos proposed that county votes should be given not only to 40*s*. freeholders but to tenant farmers who occupied on their own account land at a rent of not less than £50 a year. Although Althorp opposed the measure on the part of the government, and another landlord, Lord Milton, complained that the amendment would place electoral power 'not in the hands of individuals but of an oligarchy composed of the members of the Bench of Quarter Sessions', it was carried by 232 votes to 148. The so-called Chandos clause was certainly designed to reinforce the landlord interest, for many of the tenants-at-will who were now given the vote were dependent on their landlords.[2] It is significant that many Whigs supported this expression of natural 'influence', while many Radicals approved of it simply because it implied an extension of the total electorate. A subsequent proposal of Orator Hunt to give the vote to every urban householder, whatever the amount of his rent, found Hunt in a minority of one.

Only one new argument was advanced by the Tories in the course of these debates. Croker, who had already directed attention to the multitude of anomalies in the new system, pointed out that as a result of the Whig proposals Britain north of the Trent would gain 110 members at the expense of the southern and agricultural part of the country. The coalfield would gain what the cornfield lost. Peel adopted the same view. Son of a calico printer though he was,

---

[1] W. N. Molesworth, *The History of the Reform Bill of 1832* (1865), p. 198.
[2] Other extensions of the county franchise gave votes to £10 copyholders and £10 leaseholders of not less than 60 years.

he argued that at all times 'it is necessary to protect the agricultural interest from the augmenting influence of the manufacturing districts'. Russell, a landed proprietor and member of the great Bedford family, was left to reply that ministers had been realistic and had merely recognized the importance of 'those vast depôts of manufacturing wealth, which during the last thirty years have constantly been increasing'.

Once the Reform Bill had passed the Commons, the urgent question then arose—'What will the Lords do with it?' The question had constitutional, political and social implications, and many popular orators warned the peers that they would be abolished along with the rotten boroughs if they defied the public will. The Birmingham Political Union decided to call upon all its members to refuse to pay taxes if the Lords refused to pass the bill. Despite such warnings and the arrival of wagon-loads of reform petitions from various parts of the country, the Lords rejected the bill on 8 October by 199 votes to 158.

This gesture of defiance provoked an immediate and prolonged outburst of opposition in the country. London itself was the centre of organized and spontaneous demonstrations, and a new political body, the National Political Union, was founded by Francis Place and his friends (including one old reformer of the 1790s, Thelwall) with some support from London skilled artisans. It would have nothing to do with the extreme radical demand for universal suffrage and annual parliaments, and there was soon a working-class breakaway from it, but it rallied London in support of the government in the constitutional crisis. Place was at the centre of the web of London radical politics at this time and he turned the Union into a reasonably efficient instrument, speaking in the name of 'all reformers, of the masses—of the millions'. Meanwhile in Birmingham monster meetings of the Political Union, with as many as 150,000 people estimated to be present, were urging all reformers to unite peacefully but unflinchingly to resist the activities of a 'faction' of the aristocracy. A celebrated—and much criticized— letter from Lord John Russell to Attwood seemed to give official blessing to this entreaty. 'It is impossible', Russell wrote, 'that the whisper of a faction should prevail against the voice of a nation.'[1]

---

[1] Quoted along with a letter from Althorp to Attwood by C. M. Wakefield, *Life of Thomas Attwood* (1885), p. 179. For a defence of the Lords see *Blackwood's Magazine*, vol. XXX (1831), p. 304 ff.

Where the organized power of the unions was weak, in cathedral towns, for instance, and in parts of London, there were many violent incidents in October and November 1831. The highly unpopular boroughmonger, the Duke of Newcastle, who had asked in 1830 why he should not do as he liked with his own property, was assaulted and his home attacked by a London mob; the windows of the Duke of Wellington's house were broken; the Duke of Cumberland was dragged from his horse on his way back from the House of Lords and rescued with difficulty by the police. The Archbishop of Canterbury and other bishops who had voted against the bill were insulted, jeered at, and hooted. There was rioting and arson at Nottingham and Derby, Worcester and Bath, and finally on 29 October the city centre at Bristol was sacked by an angry mob in the worst riots of the year. The words 'liberty' and 'slavery' which had frequently been on the lips of the Bristol slavery abolitionists were taken up by the crowds, and the weakness of both mayor and military left the mob free to do much as it wished.

The leaders of the Birmingham Political Union claimed that disastrous sequences of events in places like Bristol would have been avoided if there had been a well-organized local Political Union, but Grey and some of his colleagues (if not Russell) were very suspicious of the influence of the unions at this time. The prime minister agreed with the King that the establishment of unions was 'far more mischievous and dangerous than any proceedings of a more avowed and violent character, palpably illegal and treasonable', particularly if they tried to set themselves up on a permanent footing. He maintained, however, that they could not be dissolved until the Reform Bill had passed. Restating the Whig assumption on which the whole Reform Bill had been based, he concluded that once the question of reform was settled, 'all the sound part of the community would not only be separated from, but placed in direct opposition to associations whose permanent existence every reasonable man must feel to be incompatible with the safety of the country. Under such circumstances these Unions could not long continue to exist, and all the real influence and power of society would be united with that of the government in putting them down.'[1] When in November the Birmingham Political Union attempted to reshape its structure and arrange its members in local 'sections' with a paramilitary organization, 'a gradation of ranks and authority', the

[1] *Correspondence of William IV and Earl Grey*, vol. I, p. 410.

government issued a proclamation declaring that such an organization was unconstitutional and illegal. In consequence, Attwood and his friends chose to yield gracefully to the official decree.

The situation in the autumn and winter of 1831–32 remained confused quite apart from the rioting and the organization of Unions. In October 1831, cholera, the harbinger of political excitement all over Europe, made its way to England, spreading alarm and adding to excitement. To some it was a sign of divine displeasure, to others of faulty human organization.[1] In the meantime, there were widespread rumours of dissension within the government between reformers and anti-reformers, and in the country signs (disputed then and since) of a decline in the vigour of local enthusiasm for the bill. Three by-elections were won by the Tories in Dorset, Pembrokeshire, and Liverpool while, just as significant, working-class elements in many places were showing noticeably diminished interest in a bill which gave them no direct benefits. In many places, indeed, they were setting up small but militant associations of their own to demand a genuinely radical bill. The National Union of the Working Classes, founded in April 1831 by a group of London working men influenced by the teachings of Robert Owen and led by William Lovett, a compositor, Henry Hetherington, the journalist, and John Cleave, a former follower of Cobbett, was pressing both at public meetings and in the columns of the *Poor Man's Guardian* for universal suffrage and 'obtaining the just rights of the labouring part of society'.[2] At the Blackfriars Rotunda, the headquarters of this group, there were regular and unrestrained complaints against the government. From the North of England, Orator Hunt was reporting working-class indifference or opposition to the bill, and a little later a Manchester radical operative, referring to votes for the mill-owners and not sparing his language, was pronouncing the Reform Bill 'the most illiberal, the most tyrannical, the most hellish measure that ever could or can be proposed'.[3] There were several such straws in the wind suggesting to discontented Tories that there might soon be 'an enforced natural union between

---

[1] When the government proposed a National Fast Day, the National Union of the Working Classes called it a National Farce Day (*Poor Man's Guardian*, 24 March 1832). In the House of Commons on 20 March, Spencer Perceval, the Tory relative of the dead prime minister, in a remarkable outburst claimed that cholera had been 'hanging over the country as a curse from the first day on which the Bill was introduced, and a curse it hath been upon the country from that time to this'.

[2] *Poor Man's Guardian*, 27 August 1831.

[3] *Ibid.*, 11 April 1832.

aristocracy and disfranchised population—against a vulgar privileged "Pedlary" '; the new £10 voters.[1]

Before the suggestions could amount to anything substantial, Russell introduced a third Reform Bill on 12 December 1831. It changed the test for borough disfranchisement and introduced several changes in the list of condemned constituencies, saving some which had hitherto been doomed to the loss of one member; it abandoned earlier and never popular proposals to reduce the total size of the House of Commons and distributed the seats, which hitherto were to have been suppressed, among a mixture of old and new boroughs; it simplified the conditions relating to the £10 suffrage; and it allowed freemen in boroughs, if resident, to retain their votes. The second reading of the new bill was carried by a majority of 162 votes (324 votes to 162) in December 1831. To all stalwart reformers the question now was, as one writer put it, not 'what will the Lords do?' but 'what will be done with the Lords?'[2]

There were, indeed, only three possible answers to the question. The first was for the government to surrender to the Political Unions and the mob; this answer it could never accept. The second was to reach a compromise about the nature of the Reform Bill itself and to meet some of the objections of the moderate Tories who were prepared to have a measure of reform but not the 'Bill, the whole Bill, and nothing but the Bill'; the government had, indeed, already made deliberate concessions in the third bill which went a considerable way to meeting the criticisms of the so-called Tory 'Waverers' or 'Trimmers', a group associated with Lord Wharncliffe and Lord Harrowby. It could go no further without alienating opinion outside Parliament. The third was for Grey to make the House of Lords yield either by getting the King to create sufficient new peers to carry the bill, or by threatening that there would be such a creation unless the Lords ceased their resistance.

While the Commons was debating the third bill in committee, Grey was wrestling with the difficult constitutional problem of the creation of additional peers. He was not happy himself about the consequences of creating peers on a large scale even if the King was willing to create them. 'I wish to God', he wrote in January, 'that it could be avoided! I sometimes think we should have done better

[1] *The Croker Papers*, vol. II, p. 115.
[2] W. N. Molesworth, *op. cit.*, p. 306.

to resign on our defeat in the House of Lords.' When Althorp
pointed out that if the bill were lost again because no peers had been
created, 'every one of us will be utterly and entirely ruined in
character', Grey continued to waver, pronouncing the creation of
peers 'a measure of extreme violence' and 'a certain evil, dangerous
as a precedent'. In trying to cajole and soothe the King, he was also
trying to cajole and soothe himself. After the King had made a
somewhat vague promise in January 1832 to create what peers were
required, although only if the need for them was 'certain', Grey
was pressed by some of his colleagues, including Althorp as well as
Durham and Brougham, to have them created at once. He resisted,
sharing the King's fears and knowing that a large number of
his colleagues in the Cabinet, including the ex-Canningites Palmerston and Melbourne, felt as he did. His cautious approach proved
justified when the unaugmented House of Lords passed the second
reading of the bill—'Waverer' votes were crucial—by a majority
of 9 (184 votes to 175) on 13 April.[1]

Even now, the crisis was not over. It had to go through one final
and exciting phase before the Whig triumph was complete. In
committee, a motion proposed by the Tory, Lord Lyndhurst, that
against Grey's express wishes consideration of the disfranchising
clauses of the bill should be postponed until after the enfranchising
clauses had been debated, was carried by 151 votes to 116 on 7 May.
Grey with the backing of an almost unanimous cabinet decided to
ask the King either to create at least fifty peers or to accept the
resignation of his ministers. The King, who had been listening to
other counsellors than his cabinet—his wife was generally blamed—
had become increasingly alarmed at the 'convulsion' of public
opinion and the protests against hereditary authority, and accepted
the government's resignation. To underline the seriousness of the
new constitutional crisis, the House of Commons went on to pass
a resolution imploring 'His Majesty to call to his councils such
persons only as will carry into effect, unimpaired in all its essential
provisions, that bill for the Reform of the representation of the
people which has recently passed this House.'

For several days there was grave political and constitutional
deadlock. The Political Unions, which had been relatively quiet
earlier in the year, held mass demonstrations to 'speak a tyrant
faction's doom'. In Birmingham, where there had never been any

[1] The Commons had carried the third reading by 355 to 239 on 23 March.

important rift between middle-class and working-class reformers throughout the struggle, Attwood and his friends pledged themselves on the day of Lord Lyndhurst's motion to seek a more radical reform if the government's bill was modified or shelved. As the situation worsened the Union recruited many new members and dedicated itself to fighting the battle of reform through to final victory. In the words of its hymn,

> We raise the watchword, Liberty!
> We will, we will, we will be free.

In Manchester, where social divisions had hitherto handicapped joint action, a mass meeting was arranged to protest against the actions of the House of Lords. Above all, in London, which was now at the heart of the political struggle, a campaign was planned to try to make it impossible for a Tory government to take office. Old London institutions, like the Livery, appealed to the Commons to vote no supplies to a Tory government, and the Court of Common Council set up an emergency committee to meet from day to day. Francis Place, assisted by radicals of all hues, placarded the streets with the slogan, 'to stop the Duke go for gold'. His idea of a run on the banks was coupled with a scheme to organize a collective refusal to pay taxes. More ominously still, the leaders of the Rotunda joined hands with Place and there was talk of barricades and pikes, whilst Daniel O'Connell reminded a cheering audience at Westminster that 'Charles I had been beheaded for listening to the advice of a foreign wife'.

Meanwhile, the anti-reformers tried in vain to form a Tory government willing to carry an attenuated reform bill of its own. Peel, troubled by haunting memories of Catholic emancipation, and rightly afraid of seeking to introduce a measure which would make a mockery of his earlier resistance to all projects of extensive reform, refused to take office. Wellington, conscious only of his 'duty' to his sovereign and of the danger of creating additional peers, did his best to find a team of ministers willing to act, but the political task was too much for him, quite apart from the problems created by the pressure of outside opinion. On 14 May, Wellington's spokesman in the House of Commons, Alexander Baring, was compelled to announce that the commission given to the Duke to form a ministry was 'entirely at an end'.

The King, who had by now lost all his popularity in the country, was left with no alternative but to ask for Grey again. Impotently angry at the way events had worked out, he kept Grey and Brougham standing when they went for their interview, but he was obliged to give them the vital note granting them permission to have enough new peers created to secure the passing of the Reform Bill. The King's secretary, Sir Herbert Taylor, who had played an important part behind the scenes throughout the whole story of the bill, followed up this granting of royal permission by sending a circular note to the bishops, the moderates, and the most active leaders of the Tory opposition in the House of Lords reminding them that it would not be necessary to create new peers at all if the Tory peers dropped their opposition. Although a handful of peers continued to protest strongly against the bill and accused Grey of acting in an 'unconstitutional' manner, the bill went through its committee stage in six days, and was read for a third time on 4 June, 106 peers voting for it and only 22 against. It received the royal assent on 7 June.

Two interesting speeches were made in the last stages of the Commons debate. First, Peel, who opposed the bill to the last, warned that when in the future the question of the corn laws was raised by the government, 'the precedent formed by the present occasion will be appealed to, and if they should be placed in similar circumstances of difficulty and excitement, the danger to the public tranquillity will be made a plea for overturning the independence of the House of Lords.' The old shadows of 1829 traversed his mind, and he could not foresee the distant shadows of 1846 when he was to repeal the corn laws and Wellington to immobilize the House of Lords. Second, Russell made a declaration which soon became famous, stating that the ministers regarded 1832 as a 'final' measure. Neither Peel nor Russell proved very far-sighted in 1832 in gazing into the future. An extreme radical writer put the matter more concisely in October 1832. 'The promoters of the Reform Bill projected it, not with a view to subvert, or even remodel our aristocratic institutions, but to consolidate them by a reinforcement of sub-aristocracy from the middle classes. . . . The only difference between the Whigs and the Tories is this—the Whigs would give the shadow to preserve the substance; the Tories would not give the shadow, because stupid as they are, the millions will not stop at shadows but proceed onwards to realities.'[1]

[1] *Poor Man's Guardian*, 25 October 1832.

Some historians have made much of the 'correctness' of Tory prophecies in 1831 and 1832, and have gone so far as to claim that on the 'high historic and philosophical plane, the tory case against reform was irrefutable'.[1] Such an assessment is highly debatable. Quite apart from the fanciful fears of the new shape of politics, many of which were not realized in the near future and some of which have never been realized, the Tories were themselves in a sense responsible for the dimensions of change in the Reform Bill of 1832. The gravity of the political situation in 1831 and 1832 arose from 'the fault of those who had delayed Reform so long that it was necessary to do in one bill and at one time what ought to have been done long before in twenty bills, spread over more than a century'.[2] It is unprofitable in history to pursue such 'moral' judgements too far and dangerous to try to dole out 'high historic and philosophical' praise and blame. The Whigs themselves were always prone to do it, weaving together a tapestry of 'Whig interpretation', and recently they have been criticized far more sharply than the Tories by modern historians. In fact, however, without the specific Whig contribution to the 'settlement' of this question in 1832, the course of nineteenth-century English history might have been very different. By making it possible for an unreformed House of Commons to reform itself, the Whigs were successful under the leadership of a highly traditionalist peer in relieving the danger of revolution and in attaching to the Constitution 'the middle classes who form the real and efficient mass of public opinion, and without whom the power of the gentry is nothing'.[3] It is impossible to say what would have been the fate of traditional British institutions if the political system had not been adapted in 1832 to fit the needs of some of the most active members of a new economy and a new society. Only in such circumstances might all the fears of the Tories have been realized. Certainly the Whigs in 1832 did a good deal to prevent the extreme radical vision of the future from becoming a reality: they made sure—to use their own language—that the 'age of improvement' would not be suddenly transformed into an age of 'disruption'.

More important than Tory fears in the years which immediately followed the passing of the Reform Bill were the hopes reformers placed in it. Some of them had regarded the bill as the birth year of a

[1] N. Gash, *Politics in the Age of Peel* (1953), p. 9.
[2] W. N. Molesworth, *op. cit.*, p. 334.
[3] *Correspondence of William IV and Grey*, vol. I, p. 376.

new era, and although radicals like Cobbett emphasized that 'the Reform Bill can no more rectify our ills than it can have caused them',[1] many people thought of the new measure as 'the great bill for giving everybody everything' or for 'making everybody equal'.[2] The news of the passing of the bill was greeted throughout the country by banquets, illuminations and the ringing of church bells. In Birmingham, to which, according to Durham, the 'country owed Reform . . . and its salvation from revolution',[3] the painter, R. B. Haydon, drew several sketches of the 'brave men' of the Political Union; in addition, plans were made for the construction of an enormous 'Clarence Vase', inscribed with the names of all those peers and members of the House of Commons who voted for the bill. In tiny Liskeard in Cornwall—the closed Corporation and freemen of which had hitherto returned two members to Parliament —a cannon captured during the Napoleonic Wars was moved by an excited crowd a little after midnight on 6 June, 1832 from its 'imprisonment' on a hillside into the middle of the community. The name 'Grey' was painted on it 'in recognition of the noble Earl so named, whose Administration had given the Elective franchise to tens of thousands of the People'. With symbolic gestures of this kind as well as with speeches the Reform Bill was welcomed, and it is important in assessing the significance of the measure to recall John Bright's phrase that if the bill was not a good bill (by that he meant a genuinely radical bill) it was a great bill when it passed. It was the manner of its passing rather than its content or its immediate consequences which made men look back proudly to the struggles of the past and look forward hopefully to an 'age of reform'. Ebenezer Elliott, the Sheffield mechanic and poet, looked back to the pioneers of the 1790s who had been imprisoned or transported for their beliefs:

> O could the wise, the brave, the just
> Who suffer'd—died—to break our chains;
> Could Muir, could Palmer, from the dust,
> Could murder'd Gerrald hear our strains . . .

Others looked forward to the continued pressure of opinion on the citadels of government and even to a new social order, which would permit further change.

---

[1] B.R.L., *Report of the Proceedings of the Birmingham Political Union*, 7 May 1832.
[2] Samuel Warren, *Ten Thousand a Year* (1841).
[3] Quoted J. K. Buckley, *Joseph Parkes of Birmingham* (1926), p. 109.

4. THE NEW ELECTORAL SYSTEM

Among those people who did not look forward with eagerness to the new age of reform was William Wordsworth, who remarked that if the bill passed he would retire to a 'safe and conservative government like Austria'. He had no reason to be so despondent. Conservatism was not crushed in 1832, and the reformed electoral system was a blend of old and new; the House of Lords not only survived but revived, and even the House of Commons elected at the first general election under the new system turned out, as the diarist Greville admitted, 'to be very much like every other parliament'.

The agricultural South continued to be over-represented, both in terms of population and interests, at the expense of the North and even more of London. Ten southern counties with a quarter of the population of England had a third of the total representation; urban Middlesex, however, with a greater population than industrial Lancashire, was significantly under-represented and returned 14 members as against Lancashire's 26. At the same time there were big changes. Cornwall's representation was reduced from 44 to 13. Fifty-six English boroughs, all but 15 of which were in the South, lost their representation entirely; Weymouth had its representation reduced from four to two, and 30 other boroughs, of which 21 were in the South, lost one of their two seats. Twenty-two new boroughs were created—five of them metropolitan, 14 of them growing industrial towns in the North and Midlands—with the privilege of returning two members, and 20 secured the right of returning one member. Although there still remained five tiny boroughs with an electorate of less than 200 (Reigate had 152) and 115 members still sat for boroughs with an electorate of less than 500, the substitution of names like Huddersfield and Rochdale, Bradford and Stoke-on-Trent for Tregoney, Wendover, Appleby and Old Sarum was a belated recognition of the necessary political consequences of the industrial revolution. Some of the big new London constituencies like Tower Hamlets and Finsbury had over 7,000 voters on the roll.

Conditions in large boroughs of this kind were necessarily different from those in the pocket boroughs or near-pocket boroughs which still remained or were in some cases created by the act. For all the new uniformity of the borough franchise, there was still place for great variety in the new system. Whereas in pocket boroughs like Calne, represented in 1831 by Macaulay and on the eve of the second Reform Bill in 1867 by Robert Lowe, the arch-enemy of further reform, nominees of great families continued to be returned, in the big boroughs there were often incessant demands by organized constituents for policy programmes and 'pledges' from their members. They were not always given. Certainly in Birmingham Attwood, triumphantly returned at the election of 1832, was strong enough to resist them, claiming that they were sought for only by a 'rag tag and bob-tail'[1]; even in London itself where Francis Place and the National Political Union advised constituents that 'the conduct, private as well as public, of every candidate should be scrutinized . . . and pledges should be given by him to the electors in the most solemn manner',[2] there were difficulties about the practice. The issues it raised demonstrated the new range of 'democratic' political problems in 'large towns and populous districts'.

While borough seats were thus redistributed in 1832, 65 seats made available as a result of the disfranchisement of the rotten boroughs were handed over to the counties, significantly increasing total county representation.[3] If a strict population test had been applied, however, county voters would still have been seriously under-represented in relation to the rest. The 345,000 English county voters controlled 114 seats; the 275,000 borough voters 327 seats. The 1832 act was not based on such a mathematical formula; it continued to perpetuate a representative system based on 'interests' rather than on the mere counting of heads, and since the social system of the agricultural counties still depended not on numbers but on the deference shown to great families, it is unrealistic to talk of county under-representation in 1832. A majority of counties plus small boroughs still proclaimed the dominance of the landed interest, which the Chandos clause set out further to protect. Nor did the influence of landed families, big or small, stop short at the boundaries of the borough constituencies. The Boundary Commissioners, who were given the task of fixing borough boundaries after the act had passed, sometimes added adjacent rural parishes to small boroughs, thereby assisting the process implied in the Act of transferring local influence from borough proprietors and small closed oligarchies to

---

[1] B.R.L., *Proceedings of the Birmingham Political Council*, 3 July 1832.
[2] Place Papers, B.M., Add. MSS. 27,796, f. 144.
[3] A third member was given to seven counties, while twenty-six counties previously returning only two members were divided into two divisions, each with two members. Yorkshire, with its densely populated industrial West Riding, was given six members instead of four.

neighbouring landlords and gentry. Many of the constituencies classed as boroughs (Banbury or Peterborough for instance) included what were in fact 'veiled rural districts', and the main test of difference between them and segments of the counties was neither economic life nor social structure but the electoral qualification.[1]

In the boroughs, although the universal qualification was the £10 household test hedged round by residential (twelve-month) and other qualifications, the occupation, as owner or tenant of one landlord, of buildings of an annual value of £10 meant very different things in different parts of the country. Russell himself admitted that the proportion of £10 houses varied in the towns from one-sixth to one-half, although the national average was one-third or one-quarter: the percentage of £10 houses in Reading was twice that in Wigan. In Leeds, the working classes were almost completely debarred from the franchise since they lived in houses of £5 to £8 in value: in Manchester, where rents were higher, more working-class voters were added to the register. In London, rents were so high that the £10 clause enfranchised most genuine householders. These differences were defended by Althorp as making for continued diversity in the electoral system, and they bring out clearly the lack of mathematical logic in the act. Reform was not considered as a gateway to equality, despite the popular tales that the act 'made every man as good as everybody else'. The £10 test was simply a rough property test designed to keep out a large part of the population from the franchise and to satisfy the rest; in old 'popular boroughs' such as Preston with the tightening of residential qualifications many of the artisans lost their votes immediately and others were swamped by the new £10 voters.

The £10 householder was soon to acquire the status of an ideal citizen in the eyes of those who wished to stop short at the settlement of 1832. In fact, not only did the status of the £10 householder vary in different parts of the country, but the boundary line of £10 simply marked, of course, the lowest limit of the new franchise. In 1832 two-thirds of the new voters were estimated to have houses of more than £15 in value. From the start there was no homogeneous social class associated with the £10 householder electorate, and the choice of a financial criterion provided a shifting basis for the electorate of the future. Quite apart from the growth of income of

[1] For this point and many other important points on the new electoral system, see N. Gash, *op. cit.*, chs. III, IV and V. I have drawn heavily on the facts and statistics set out in Professor Gash's masterly analysis.

particular social groups as a result of the growth of national wealth, changes in the value of money complicated the mathematics of the suffrage, and during the middle years of the century, as a result both of rising standards of living and rising prices, many people had become £10 householders who fell outside the calculations of 1832. For this reason alone it is difficult to see how there could have been any ultimate 'finality' about the 'system' of 1832.

In the counties, the vote continued to be retained by 40*s.* freeholders with the addition of £10 copyholders, leaseholders[1] and tenants-at-will paying rent of not less than £50. At the same time, freeholders in boroughs could vote in the county where the borough was situated if they did not occupy their freehold or if its value was between 40*s.* and £10. Such freeholds included river rights and canal shares, market tolls and titles to property as well as land, and permitted Birmingham and Leeds 'freeholders' to exercise power in Warwickshire and the West Riding. The influence of such freeholders, generally speaking, was far smaller than that of landlords and gentry, but it was resented by those who shared the Duke of Wellington's fear of the creation of a 'formidable active party against the aristocratic influence'.[2] As the Duke recognized, there were independent elements in the countryside—blacksmiths, carpenters, masons and, above all, dissenters—who were willing to provide focal points of opposition and might possibly unite with 'freeholders' from the towns. The attack on 'deference' and indirectly on 'influence' usually came from such quarters. But Wellington was right in qualifying his fears with the consolation that 'the gentry have as many followers and influence as many voters at elections as ever they did'. Certainly most social forces in the countryside made for gradual rather than revolutionary change, and 'influence' remained an essential ingredient in the new 'system', particularly when there was no ballot to permit secret voting. Lord Stanley could argue in 1841, for example, that 'it was known that when a man attempted to estimate the probable result of a county election in England it was ascertained by calculating the number of the great landed proprietors in the county and weighing the number of occupiers under them.'[3]

[1] Ten pound leaseholders of not less than sixty years and £50 leaseholders of not less than twenty years.
[2] *The Croker Papers*, vol. II, p. 206.
[3] Quoted *Leeds Mercury*, 8 July 1841. See the important article by G. Kitson Clark, 'The Electorate and the Repeal of the Corn Laws' in the *T.R.H.S.* (1951).

The effect of the new system of representation was to increase the total electorate by about 50 per cent, one Englishman in five now having the privilege of the vote (in Scotland, the figure was one in eight and in Ireland one in twenty). No one had the vote, however, unless he had first registered and paid a registration fee. Such provisions gave a great incentive to political organizations to encourage registration. In May 1835 the Tories set up a small standing committee at the Carlton Club in London to supervise registration arrangements and to collect information on the state of party strength in the constituencies; two years later Peel advised his supporters to 'register, register, register'. In 1835 the moderate radical Reform Association, founded the previous year by Lord Durham, set up a registration office in London and established branches in the country. 'We must organize our association in London', wrote its skilled organizer, Joseph Parkes, to Durham, 'to work the Reform Bills—to point out to the country the facility and effect of organization, prearrangement and funds by small annual subscriptions for registration especially.'[1] A few years later, the Anti-Corn Law League was to turn registration activity into a powerful business concern, adding its supporters to the rolls, having the names of its political opponents removed whenever possible, and exhorting its followers to invest money in property which would convey a 40*s*. freehold vote for a county division.[2]

If registration pointed the way forward to new techniques of party organization, the abuses of the old electoral system were by no means finally disposed of in 1832. Some pocket boroughs survived, where family influence remained stronger than party feeling; in 1858, indeed, Trollope in *Dr. Thorne* described towns in his far from completely fictional Barsetshire which returned members to Parliament, 'in spite of Reform Bills, past, present and coming, in accordance with the dictates of some neighbouring magnate'. In his maiden speech in the House of Commons in 1837 Disraeli declared that since the 1832 act 'the stain of boroughmongering had only assumed a deeper and darker hue, and that intimidation was more highly organized than even under the old system'. It was still possible to buy a seat, and there were many corrupt boroughs, like Stafford, where 1832 did little to purify politics. Of the 1,000 voters at the 1832 election there, it was calculated that 850 had been

---

[1] Quoted J. K. Buckley, *op. cit.*, p. 137.
[2] See below, pp. 312 ff.

bought. Many elections in less notorious places were corrupt and violent, and in some of the new industrial constituencies, like Huddersfield, election results were as dependent on local influence as results in the old rural areas. In London itself, the member of Parliament for Marylebone told the House of Commons in 1852, 'scarcely a tradesman in Regent Street or Bond Street' was not subject to the intimidation of 'men of high character, or rather of high station', who gave orders how to vote. The 1841 Parliament was known as the 'Bribery Parliament', and more than ten years later in 1852 the barrister-novelist, Samuel Warren, argued that 'bribery is seen perhaps in fuller action at the moment than ever before, as is testified on all hands by those competent to form an opinion on the subject'.[1]

It is difficult to determine to what extent corruption was the instrument candidates chose to 'influence' the electorate and to what extent it sprang from the 'wickedness' of the electors themselves. There was no legal limit on the amount which could be spent by candidates at elections; and free rides, free drink and free food were expected by voters almost everywhere. At black spots like Sudbury, which was so steeped in corruption that it was completely disfranchised in 1844, the party spirit which prevailed was not affected by the political situation but by a 'contest of the parties amongst themselves as to which shall make most money at elections'.[2] 'Principle', wrote the *Morning Chronicle*, 'is unknown among the electors, the far greater proportion of whom are free burgesses of the lowest order, and require feasting and treating and other weighty considerations to bring them to the poll.'[3] Even when financial corruption was restricted, there was often violence. At Hertford there were fights between hired gangs of gipsies and bargees, and abduction of hostile voters by 'bullies' at Lewes and by 'lambs' at Nottingham. Although there were brave radical candidates who stood up manfully for the cause of 'purity' at election times, they sometimes upset and dispirited fellow-radicals by their 'naïve enthusiasm' for a 'pure' election, and in some radical strongholds, like Leicester, it was the radicals themselves who were responsible for most of the 'fun'. They rounded up late voters and

---

[1] *Manual of Election Law* (1852).
[2] Quoted N. Gash, *op. cit.*, p. 160.
[3] 7 January 1835. This account may well have been written by Charles Dickens, and certainly Sudbury was one of the places very much in his mind when he wrote his famous description of the Eatanswill election in *The Pickwick Papers* (1837).

gave them a comfortable night's lodging and a free breakfast, and in some cases provided them with free clothing. So-called 'runners' or messengers, some of them reputed to be so lame that they could scarcely walk, received payments averaging 17*s*. 6*d*. a head in the days following the poll.[1] At Devizes it was said that one of the candidates, Dr. Bowring, had to pay the voters three times as much as was normal because he did not believe in the Holy Trinity.

Only after important changes had modified public manners and institutional morals, and a succession of Acts of Parliament had restricted bribery, did this state of affairs materially improve. Until it improved, we must draw a sharp contrast between the high-sounding principles of the Whigs in framing the act of 1832 and the imperfect means which were available to politicians and the public when they set about 'working' it. Although they continued to talk the language of 'reform', political reformers could often do little to transform the intricate patterns of influence and tradition. Although they and their Conservative opponents were bound to pay increasing attention to the language and techniques of 'party', there could be nothing like a complete party government. Indeed the development of a full party system was held in check by traditional social forces far more effectively than the development of the factory system had been. Provincial interests were not dependent on party; party was dependent on them. The social system depended on 'influence'; the political system continued to register that 'influence' in all the multifarious forms it took—not only the influence of landlords over their tenants, but of masters over servants, employers over workmen, clergy over their congregations, and even customers over shopkeepers. While there were revolts against 'influence', some of them successful, it would have been impossible for organized national 'parties' to impose their will or their programme on the country as a whole, even had they been strong enough centrally to try to do so.

As it was, not all constituencies were contested, for the restricted franchise, the expense of elections, the balance of local interests, the number of double-member constituencies, and the slow development of national party machines still made for compromise when possible. The first election of 1832 was sharply contested by any previous standards. The fifty contests in English and Welsh counties

---

[1] See A. Temple Paterson, 'Electoral Corruption in Early Victorian Leicester', in *History* (1946).

and the 144 in English and Welsh boroughs were considerably more than double the number of contests at the general election of 1818, for example, and four times as many as at the general election of 1790,[1] but later elections in 1837, 1841 and 1847 were quiet, only just over two-fifths of the constituencies being contested in the last of these years. The return of Peel to power in 1841, one of the most important political turning points in early Victorian England and a sign that the Whigs had not secured a monopoly of parliamentary power by their actions in 1832, was achieved not by a dramatic national political contest in every constituency, but by a general process of Whig political erosion between 1832 and 1841. Divisions among his opponents, the exploitation of new tactics of parliamentary and electoral management, and four general elections in nine years made the reversal possible, not a national swing of the political pendulum. And Peel himself regarded his victory not so much as the victory of a party as a challenge to himself and his administration to prove their loyalty and efficiency in the Queen's service.

5. REFORM BY INSTALMENTS

From 1832 to 1841 the Whigs were in office with a diminishing degree of parliamentary and outside support. The election of December 1832 produced an enormous majority for them. 'There exists no *party* but that of the Government', Greville wrote in February 1833; 'the Irish act in a body under O'Connell to the number of about forty; the Radicals are scattered up and down without a leader, numerous, restless, turbulent, and bold . . . the Tories without a head, frightened, angry, and sulky; Peel without a Party, prudent, cautious, and dextrous, playing a deep waiting game of scrutiny and observation.'[2]

Some of the Whigs no doubt over-rated the extent to which they had destroyed the political power of their Tory opponents and saw the politics of the future in terms of a contest between themselves 'representing monarchy, aristocracy, wealth and order on the one hand, and a small, but fierce and active body of republicans and anarchists on the other'.[3] In this they were soon to prove completely mistaken. While they were pursuing further useful reforms—

---

[1] H. Jephson, *op. cit.*, vol. II, p. 150.
[2] L. Strachey and R. Fulford (ed.), *The Greville Memoirs* (1938), vol. II, p. 361.
[3] J. A. Roebuck, *History of the Whig Ministry of 1830* (1852), vol. II, p. 417.

the continued amendment of the criminal law, the rationalization of legal procedures, the municipal reform act, the final abolition of slavery (1833 and 1838), the termination of the last monopoly of the East India Company (the China Trade) and the preparation of a new Poor Law—their majority was dwindling away. Three problems were responsible for their unanticipated difficulties—Ireland, the split between Whigs and radicals, and the death or the retreat from politics of some of the most influential Whig leaders.

The Whig ministers disagreed about how to deal with Ireland which remained the scene of great violence and disorder and, under the continued leadership of O'Connell, was beginning to press hard for total repeal of the Act of Union. The disagreements were marked even before the Reform Bill passed. Russell and Durham favoured concessions to Ireland, including an adjustment of Church property, but Stanley, the Chief Secretary for Ireland, was strongly opposed to such projects and was prepared to use coercion to maintain law and order. By mid-1832, behind the façade of truce, dissension was so marked that O'Connell announced his intention to impeach Stanley in the reformed Parliament on grounds of his gross misconduct of Irish affairs. These conflicts pointed the way to the difficulties of 1833 and 1834. The first Whig measures relating to Ireland were, however, measures of reform. Ten out of twenty-two Protestant bishoprics were suppressed and the Church Cess, an Easter tax, was abolished. Assistance was given to Irish educational projects, and a Board composed of both Catholics and Protestants was set up in Dublin. None of these measures won any large body of support in Ireland, and they were followed in February 1833 by the introduction of a Coercion Bill (a measure for one year only). Among its other provisions it empowered the Lord-Lieutenant to prohibit and disperse public meetings. At once there were bitter divisions in the Whig Cabinet and before the bill finally passed in April, Durham had left the government in anger and Stanley had moved from the Irish secretaryship to the Colonial Office. When the question of the renewal of the bill came up later in the year, Althorp made it clear that he also strongly opposed the restrictions on public meetings. He was thereby drawn into conflict with Grey, who followed the same line of argument as Stanley and threatened to resign unless the whole bill were passed. By May 1834 the Whigs were completely at loggerheads with each other, and when Russell impetuously but resolutely declared in the Commons that he would like to see part of the wealth of the Protestant Church of Ireland devoted to other purposes in the name of 'justice to Ireland', Stanley, Graham, Goderich, and Richmond immediately resigned from the government. As Stanley put it in a much quoted note to Graham: 'John Russell has upset the coach'[1]: it was a metaphor which the political cartoonists of the day seized on with avidity. A few months later Grey resigned when he discovered that some of his colleagues were still attempting to conspire with Wellesley, Lord-Lieutenant of Ireland, and O'Connell to qualify the policy of coercion. Tired of politics and anxious to get back to his estates, Althorp retired with his prime minister, but was persuaded to stay on as chancellor of the exchequer and leader of the House of Commons until his father's death the following November. The new leader of the government was Lord Melbourne, under whose genial and leisurely chairmanship the Whigs were to wither away.

Attempting to evolve an Irish policy not only broke up the Whig cabinet but exacerbated Whig relations with English radicals. O'Connell had established powerful links with English middle-class radicalism in the course of the reform struggle, and in 1833 and 1834 he tightened the links both in Parliament and outside. In May 1833, for example, there was an enormous demonstration of the Birmingham Political Union 'for the purpose of petitioning His Majesty to dismiss his ministers'. Before a crowd estimated at 200,000, O'Connell spoke words which rang as effectively in Birmingham as in Irish ears. 'Twelve months ago', he said, 'the people gave the ministers the raw material of liberty to work up into a beautiful web of freedom in the land; but like unskilful or idle citizens they were breaking the web to pieces.' A Birmingham radical manufacturer, G. F. Muntz, was more blunt. The Whigs, he said, were 'always professing to support the interests of the people, but always acting in opposition to their professions.'[2]

In Parliament antagonism between Whigs and radicals flared up almost as soon as the reformed Parliament met, but when the radicals contested the re-election of the Speaker the government had an overwhelming majority of 241 to 31. Soon afterwards, when O'Connell proposed that the formal Address to the Crown should be referred to a committee of the whole House, because the King's speech had contained unnecessarily bitter references to Ireland, his

---

[1] C. S. Parker: *Life and Letters of Sir James Graham* (1907), vol. I, p. 187.
[2] B.R.L., *Report of the Proceedings*, 20 May 1833.

proposal was defeated by 428 votes to 40. These heavy defeats showed the numerical limitations of a radical group, which included many of the 'new men' of 1832—Attwood, John Arthur Roebuck, a close friend of John Stuart Mill, George Grote, a classical scholar and active Benthamite, and John Fielden, a Lancashire manufacturer—as well as old parliamentary Radicals like Joseph Hume and the great national radical figure, William Cobbett. But the fact that most of the radicals cut a worse figure in Parliament than outside it did not take the sting out of radicalism. It rather made the parliamentary radicals, divided about much else, into unrepentant advocates of further parliamentary reform and supporters of continued 'movement' in politics. They were critical questioners of all established institutions, objecting in particular to the retention of sinecures, the presence of '300 titled paupers' on the Pension List, and the assessed taxes on windows, houses and paper. Supported by an influential stamped and 'unstamped' press, many of them were talking of the need not only for propaganda but for comprehensive national education. Their biggest votes, however, were mustered on questions of further political reform. Grote gathered 106 supporters against the government's 211 when he introduced a resolution in favour of the ballot, and 164 votes were collected against the government's 213 on a further motion in favour of triennial parliaments.

The radical desire to keep politics alive contrasted sharply with the disinclination of the Whig ministers to spend all their time debating political questions. Some of the Whigs were prepared on occasion to make political speeches outside Parliament—Brougham, for instance, made a 'speechifying tour' of Scotland in 1834 which his enemies described as a 'vagrant, grotesque apocalypse', and even Grey made a well-reported speech in Edinburgh. Some of them even claimed, as Brougham did, that they 'rejoiced, delighted and gloried, in office and out of office, in every opportunity of meeting the people to render an account to them of this stewardship'. For the most part, however, the responsibilities of public trust were usually weighed against the claims of family and local stewardship. During the Reform Bill crisis Althorp had always opened letters from his bailiff before he opened the rest of his post; when the new crises of 1833 and 1834 disturbed the unity of the cabinet, he rejoiced in the opportunity of returning to 'the fields and woods'. Melbourne became prime minister in 1834 only after considerable hesitation. 'I think it's a damned bore', he said; 'I am in many minds what to do.'[1]

It was not surprising that in November 1834, when Althorp quitted the Commons altogether on succeeding his father as Earl Spencer, Melbourne found it difficult to maintain an effective Whig cabinet in office. He told William IV of his difficulties in a long and confidential interview at the Pavilion in Brighton, and the King, who had lost all confidence in the government and strongly disliked Melbourne's proposal to promote Lord John Russell, used the occasion to get rid of his ministers altogether. Relations between William and his government had been strained by differences of opinion on Ireland and by the King's dislike of radicalism and of 'itinerant speechifying, particularly by individuals holding high office', but he could not have dismissed his ministers in November 1834 unless Melbourne had acted weakly and given him a more than adequate opportunity. Less than two years after the triumphant elections of December 1832, Whig ineptitude had produced a situation in which the King could once more ask the Duke of Wellington to form a ministry. The Duke accepted without hesitation, although he declared that he would serve only until Peel, who was travelling in Italy, returned to London.

The constitutional implications of the change of ministers in November 1834 were argued at considerable length in 1834 and 1835. The first comment of *The Times* was that 'the Queen has done it all'. It was well known how the Queen had regretted the change of ministry in 1830 and how hostile she was to reform, but it certainly did not need the Queen to prod the King into action in 1834. His dislike of both Brougham and Russell was strong, and he was quick to seize Melbourne's half-proffered resignation and turn it into a near-dismissal. Many of Melbourne's supporters were ready to join with the Radicals in branding the King's action as 'unconstitutional', but Peel, who hurried back to London to head the new ministry, accepted full responsibility. 'I am responsible for the assumption of the duty I have undertaken,' he stated categorically 'and, if you please, I am by my acceptance of office responsible for the removal of the late government.' In taking formal responsibility from the King, Peel was clear that the King had dismissed his ministers. A memorandum of February 1835 in the Peel Papers declares in unequivocal language that 'the last Change of Adminis-

[1] Quoted Lord David Cecil, *op. cit.*, p. 11.

tration was his [the King's] own immediate and exclusive Act. He removed Ministers, whom he considered no longer capable of carrying on the Business of the Country with advantage, and He called to his councils others whom he considered deserving of his Confidence.'[1]

Some historians have maintained that the King's actions in 1834 controverted the Reform Bill of 1832. Although it is difficult to see how, his wishes were ultimately ineffective because of the bill. Wellington and Peel failed to win a majority at the general election of December 1834, and although they continued in office until April 1835 they were unable to secure adequate support in the House of Commons, and had to resign. In the meantime, Peel in a well-known election address to his constituents, usually known as the Tamworth Manifesto, accepted the Reform Bill of 1832 as a 'final and irrevocable settlement of a great constitutional question' and pledged himself and his colleagues to review institutions and to redress abuses and grievances 'without infringing on established rights'. His manifesto was recognized at the time as an important constitutional innovation. 'In former times', wrote the Tory *Quarterly Review*, 'such a proceeding would have been thought derogatory and impugned as unconstitutional, and would have been both; but the new circumstances in which the Reform Bill has placed the Crown, by making its choice of Ministers immediately and absolutely dependent on the choice of the several constituencies . . . have rendered such a course not merely expedient but necessary.'[2]

Peel reduced the Whig majority, won the support of *The Times* and tried to introduce useful pieces of reforming legislation, but his efforts failed in face of stormy Whig-radical opposition. While Grey warned the Whigs to oppose the radicals as strongly as the Tories, and Stanley and his friends proclaimed the existence of a 'third party', separate from both Whigs and Tories, the main body of the Whigs and radicals joined hands with the Irish to drive Peel from office. O'Connell reached an understanding with Russell in February 1835 in the so-called Lichfield House Compact, whereby the Whigs were assured of Irish votes in the Commons; and after the government's resignation, the King had no alternative but to recall Melbourne, who formed a new ministry which lasted amid increasing difficulties until 1841.

[1] Peel Papers, B.M., Add. MSS. 40,303, f. 10. The King used the weakness of the Whigs in the House of Lords as an argument.
[2] *Quarterly Review*, vol. LIII, April 1835.

From the start the new ministry, which left out Brougham and Durham, was weak and lacked effective leadership. Melbourne was 'the companion rather than the guide of his ministers', out of place in an age of rapid change. His temperamental conviction of *dolce far niente* was far removed from the philanthropic Toryism of those who wished to restore the old order, if need be by legislation, and from the aggressive *laissez-faire* philosophy of those who wished government to reorganize the legal and institutional framework of the country to permit the maximum individual freedom for merchants and manufacturers. He cared little for 'improvement' and disliked the new middle classes—'all affectation and conceit and pretence and concealment'. After Queen Victoria came to the throne in 1837 he found a new and absorbing personal interest in life, but by then the political and economic difficulties of his ministry had begun to multiply.

Neither Melbourne's personality nor Whig difficulties, however, could bring the policy of reform by instalments to a standstill. Not only were there Whig leaders like Lord John Russell who believed in 'popular' and 'improving' legislation, but a relatively small and enthusiastic group of reformers were continuing to demand changes in the name of the greatest happiness of the greatest number. Jeremy Bentham died in 1832, but his influence lingered long after his death through disciples like Edwin Chadwick and Dr. Southwood Smith. Indeed, the Benthamite period in English history was only beginning in 1832.

Although contradictory deductions could be drawn from Bentham's 'science' of legislation and administration, the main influence of his teaching after 1832 was to quicken the demand for comprehensible and uniform law and for efficient government. While middle-class manufacturers and merchants were starting to organize themselves to secure freer trade and less government interference, Benthamites of the stamp of Chadwick were pressing for a concerted attack on 'sinister interests' and stating the case for the public interest with increasing force. During the 1840s there were to be many signs of conflict between the view of the political economists that 'each [man] in steadily pursuing his own aggrandizement is following that precise line of conduct which is most for the public advantage'[1] and the view of the Utilitarian theorists that increasing government intervention was necessary to reconcile and

[1] Quoted E. Halévy, *The Growth of Philosophical Radicalism* (1928), pp. 500–501.

harmonize diverging interests. During the earlier decade of the 1830s, however, political economists and administrative reformers marched side by side in a campaign against the inconsistencies and wastes of traditional government. They were denounced by the defenders of the 'old Constitution of Church and State', yet the policy of 'improvement' which they advocated could never have been carried out in many of its details without the acquiescence of Peel and the 'responsible' Conservatives, and the growing recognition in informed circles that the legacy of the past included not only Burke's venerable and ancient trees of the forest but also much dead wood.

In introducing reforms, the Whigs were assisted by thorough initial investigation and survey. Indeed, the method of arriving at the decision to legislate was itself a sign of the times. In the period after 1815 the task of investigation and recommendation of new lines of policy had been left largely to Select Committees of the House of Commons, and the number of such committees increased sharply. During the 1830s much greater use was made of Royal Commissions, which included not only members of Parliament but 'experts' in political economy and administration; opinion outside the House of Commons was tapped and put to public use.[1] By 1849 more than 100 Royal Commissions had been set up, and almost every major piece of social legislation introduced between 1832 and 1867 was preceded by this type of investigation. The *Royal Commission for inquiring into the Administration and Practical Operation of the Poor Laws* set up by Earl Grey in February 1832 was the prototype, and the way was being prepared for an age of Blue Books, the reports of the Commissions, which not only kept members of Parliament informed but were read by large numbers of people in the country, sometimes even as 'best sellers'. There was thus a direct link between the use of 'experts' in the 1830s and the development of a new climate of opinion later in the century.

Among the Whig reforms, which included important real property legislation and the abolition of archaic legal institutions, two big measures stood out—the Municipal Corporations Act of 1835 and the New Poor Law of 1834. The first of these measures was fittingly described by Joseph Parkes, one of its chief architects, as the

---

[1] For the origins and development of Royal Commissions, see H. D. Clokie and J. W. Robinson, *Royal Commissions of Inquiry* (1937). The authors describe the reports of many commissions of enquiry before 1832, including the Commission on the Common Law (1829).

'postscript to the Reform Bills'; the second set the framework for social policy for the rest of the century.

In July 1833 a Commission was appointed to enquire into the existing state of municipal government in England, Wales and Ireland, and Joseph Parkes was appointed its secretary. Its chairman, John Blackstone, Parkes succinctly described as 'an excellent Rad, Ballot, etc.'[1]; its twenty-two Commissioners set about discovering conditions in the old corporations—when they began, they did not even have a list of such corporations to assist them—and in April 1835, after examining all 'the chartered hogsties', as *The Times* called them, they produced a powerful and lucid though biased report, followed by an appendix in five large volumes. On the basis of this report, the Whigs introduced a comprehensive measure of local government reform dissolving over 200 old corporations and setting up in their place 179 municipal boroughs to be governed by elected councils. Local constitutional peculiarities were swept away and the municipal franchise was granted to all ratepayers. The councils were no longer to be permitted to use their property for the benefit of their members or for the special advantage of individuals; they had to transfer all income to a 'borough fund' and to allot any surpluses to the 'public benefit of the inhabitants and the improvement of the borough'. Accounts had to be properly audited.

It is not surprising that the radical Parkes hailed the measure as 'a smasher—a grand point to get Household Suffrage and a thorough purge of the existing Corporations. . . . We clear the roost from top to bottom—Town Clerks and all—abolish all old names except Mayor and Town Clerk—give a simple Town Council.'[2] More surprisingly, Peel did not oppose the bill, although Parkes believed that he would be bound to take up 'his proper anti-reform position' and other writers declared that the old corporations 'were dear to him as the apple of his eye'. Peel was learning the lesson of the times more quickly than Melbourne; 'he saw that no Ministry could hold together for any length of time which resisted [borough] reform'.[3]

---

[1] Quoted J. K. Buckley, *op. cit.*, p. 118.
[2] Quoted *ibid.*, p. 122.
[3] J. Grant, *Random Recollections of the House of Commons* (1836), p. 118. Lord Lyndhurst and the Tory peers in the House of Lords amended the bill out of all recognition— 'Damn Peel! What is Peel to me?' Lyndhurst is said to have asked; but Wellington imposed a firm discipline, many of the amendments were withdrawn, and the bill passed. Checks and balances were introduced by the Lords, however, including the creation of borough 'aldermen', which were designed to limit 'democracy'.

The 1835 act was a natural complement of the 1832 act in that the demand for reform of the closed corporations had figured prominently among the objectives of the local reformers of 1830–2, particularly in those towns where oligarchic corporate organization was regarded as more corrupt and cramping than even the un-reformed House of Commons. When a Select Committee of the reformed House of Commons reported in June 1833 that 'corporations, as now constituted, are not adapted to the present state of society', Thomas Latimer, the vigorous editor of the *Western Times* in Exeter, who was sometimes known as 'the Cobbett of the West', was moved to take pride in the fact that 'the principles with which we commenced our labours, and the opinions on corporations we have expressed from the first (whiggish, radical and revolutionary though they were denounced as being . . .) are now the avowed principles and opinions, not merely of the public at large, but even of those who are generally the last to be enlightened on these subjects—we mean the government itself.'[1] The passing of the act of 1835, which did not apply to London, was hailed in most of the reformed boroughs as a move towards real self-government, and the work of defining the borough boundaries, dividing them into wards and drawing up lists of qualified voters was carried out so rapidly that the first municipal elections were held within three months of the act becoming law.

For all the sense of triumph in 1835 it is important not to consider the new act as the instrument of an enthusiastic 'civic gospel'. The functions of the newly elected councils were few, and contemporaries saw the triumph in terms of an extension of the principle of representation rather than as a means to comprehensive municipal action. Cheap government was a radical cry in the towns as well as at Westminster, and the 'shopocracy', which came to play an important part in local government, was hardly a socially progressive force. The drive to secure local acts of Parliament to permit improvement through collective action was limited not only by financial considerations but by the narrow civic sense of many of the new councillors, and there were no means of adequate central control to safeguard standards of local government or to widen the scope of administrative initiative. Much of the work of civic improvement was still left to Improvement Commissioners, whose tasks were not immediately taken over by the new town councils, and as late as

[1] Quoted R. S. Lambert, *The Cobbett of the West* (1939), p. 65.

1848 there were thirty towns where the local councils had no powers of draining, cleansing and paving, and sixty-two towns where there was no local authority of any kind carrying out such duties. It was with justice that Chadwick later complained in a famous phrase that 'such is the absence of civic economy in some of our towns that their condition in respect to cleanliness is almost as bad as that of an encamped horde, or an undisciplined soldiery'.[1]

As the towns grew, they outpaced both existing technical knowledge and communal responsibility, and the new representative framework of 1835 by itself could do little to ensure improvement. Furthermore, it was only after 1835 that many large new centres of population like Manchester and Birmingham were incorporated. The act of 1835 did not automatically incorporate such thriving new cities. They had to apply for charters, and the subsequent local battle for incorporation centred more on questions of privilege and representation than of good government. In Manchester, which was incorporated in 1838, 'the low, blackguard leaders of the Radicals', very different from 'philosophic radicals' like Parkes, joined with the Tories in opposing incorporation, and it was left to the 'shopocracy' to carry the day; in Birmingham, which was incorporated in the same year, public-spirited reformers like R. K. Douglas, the editor of the *Birmingham Journal*, maintained that 'local institutions alone guaranteed and fostered a conviction among the people that government was a matter which every man ought to take an interest in',[2] but it was not until more than thirty years later that the civic gospel captured Birmingham and men of the calibre of Joseph Chamberlain set about transforming the incompetently managed city and suburbs.

The second large-scale reform measure of the Whigs, the Poor Law of 1834, had more important immediate repercussions than the Municipal Reform Act of 1835. The Royal Commission which prepared the way for it was appointed before the Reform Bill had become law. It reported in 1834 and the conclusions it reached laid the foundations for the famous act of that year which Chadwick, secretary to the Commission, described as 'the first great piece of legislation based upon scientific or economical principles'.[3] The claim was misleading in that the commissioners (who included the

---

[1] *The Sanitary Condition of the Labouring Classes* (1842), p. 44.
[2] Quoted C. Gill and A. Briggs, *History of Birmingham* (1952), vol. I, p. 221.
[3] Quoted S. E. Finer, *The Life and Times of Sir Edwin Chadwick* (1952), p. 69.

outstanding political economist, Nassau Senior) made no attempt to analyse the causes and nature of poverty, but it was fair and accurate in relation to the new administrative machinery created by the act. The framework of the new Poor Law discarded independent parish control of relief and introduced nearly all the administrative devices which were to be used later in the century in making English local government efficient—central supervision by a Board of Commissioners, central inspection, central audit, a professional service controlled by locally elected bodies, and the carving out of 600 new and manageable *ad hoc* administrative areas, the so-called Poor Law Unions. In providing these essential devices as part of a Benthamite experiment in efficient government, the act of 1834 was far more logically designed than the Municipal Reform Act of 1835. Both parish vestries and local justices of the peace lost their poor law powers, and the new elected Boards of Guardians were in turn 'guarded' by the Central Board which laid down a minimum standard of performance. There was sharp criticism of these proposals from defenders of the old local system of parish rule, but Chadwick, who had no fears of centralization, dismissed as 'cant' the description of parish rule as self-government and 'the glory of Englishmen'.[1]

The background of the new Act was the mounting pressure of poor rates, which after a period of falling prices were still almost as large in 1832 (£7 million) as they had been in the grim post-war year, 1817. Some parishes were much harder hit than others. One Buckinghamshire village reported in 1832, for example, that its expenditure on poor relief was eight times more than it had been in 1795 and more than the whole rental of the parish had been in that year. The debate on the best way not only of financing but of handling the poor had been continuous since the eighteenth century and had already produced several distinctive and irreconcilable statements of points of view. Cobbett and Hunt criticized the old Poor Law because it did not give paupers enough, and talked of the 'rights' of the poor; Owen and Attwood demanded constructive employment of the poor; Malthus argued that the Poor Laws should be dispensed with altogether since they encouraged the growth of an under-fed population; many people, untouched by any single coherent philosophy, attacked the Speenhamland allowances policy because it was expensive and 'pauperizing' in its consequences.[2]

---

[1] Quoted S. E. Finer, *ibid.*, p. 78.
[2] See above, p. 59.

The Poor Law Commission saw its task as organizing 'a measure of social police' which would encourage the development of a free market for labour, but it did not want to go as far as Malthus and abolish the Poor Laws altogether. It believed that in certain circumstances 'relief may be afforded safely and even beneficially', but it was careful to specify what those conditions were.

Broadly speaking the two guiding principles of the commission which were enshrined in the act of 1834, were the workhouse test and 'less eligibility'. First, an able-bodied man seeking poor relief had to seek it in a workhouse, or not at all. Outdoor relief along with the allowance system was to be abolished. There would thus be an incentive, it was argued, for paupers to find their place in a free and more mobile labour market. Second, relief inside the workhouse was to be made as uncongenial as possible by irksome regulations, the absence of social amenities, the provision of poor food, and the imposition of strict discipline. 'Every penny bestowed that tends to render the condition of the pauper more eligible than that of the independent labourer', the commissioners declared, 'is a bounty on indolence and vice.' As soon as 'the condition of the pauper is made less eligible than that of the independent labourer, then new life, new energy is infused into the constitution of the pauper; he is aroused like one from sleep, his relation with all his neighbours, high and low, is changed; he surveys his former employers with new eyes, he begs for a job, he will not take a denial—he discovers that everyone wants something to be done'. In other words the abolition of outdoor relief and the threat of the workhouse were magic wands to abolish poverty and unemployment.

These two simple principles, which for all their beautiful language nonetheless, as Thomas Carlyle sarcastically remarked, emboided a 'simple secret known to all ratcatchers', were the theoretical foundations on which the administrative structure of the new Poor Law was built. They were delusively simple even in relation to the society of their day. They were designed to deal with agricultural rather than industrial pauperism, with the England south of the Trent where the allowances system had been freely applied by the justices, rather than with the industrial England north of the Trent, where there was already a considerable amount of involuntary unemployment, particularly in bad years. When an attempt was made to apply the new Poor Law to the north of England in 1837 there was an immediate outcry among the factory workers who already 'enjoyed' a free labour market, and it proved impossible to abolish outdoor relief. In the South, where the act was ruthlessly applied, the allowances system was slowly crushed out, but only with strain and suffering. As the years went by, the principle of less eligibility was gradually whittled down and modified. To place under the same stringent discipline the young, the sick, the aged, and the able-bodied—neither Chadwick himself nor the Commissioners had wanted different 'classes' to be concentrated in 'mixed' workhouses—proved as much of a strain to the administrator as a burden of grievance to the poor, and by the second half of the nineteenth century the new Poor Law became almost as subject to local variation as the old Poor Law of the eighteenth century. Only the stigma of the workhouse remained.

The introduction of the new Poor Law in 1834 was approved by Peel as much as by Melbourne, but it aroused bitter opposition from old-fashioned Tories as well as popular Radicals. It was carried in the Lords only because the government commanded more proxy votes than its opponents. The gap between popular and philosophical radicalism was no wider than the gap between Eldonite Toryism and the new conservatism of Peel. To John Walter, the proprietor of *The Times*, the new Poor Law was 'a plan which might draw the country yet further from its ancient habits and ultimately change the character of Englishmen'.[1] To Richard Oastler, the Tory-Radical in the West Riding, the act was a denial of Englishmen's traditional rights. Oastler had already inspired the factory operatives to develop an organized agitation for factory reform and had bitterly opposed a Whig Factory Act of 1833, which while restricting children's working days and introducing a factory inspectorate, fell far short of the operatives' demand for a ten-hour working day. The new Poor Law, he exclaimed, separated husbands from wives in the workhouse, and was as 'unconstitutional' as it was immoral. Senior and Chadwick were 'the Empson and Dudley' of Somerset House, the headquarters of the new Commission.

The opposition to this thoroughly Benthamite reform demonstrated the difficulties of finding agreed solutions to the pressing problems of the 1830s. There was a marked divergence between those who considered the new Poor Law as evidence of 'improved' legislation and those who regarded it as a cruel and inhuman tamper-

[1] Quoted R. L. Hill, *Toryism and the People* (1929), p. 98.

ing with established rights and institutions, or more generally
between those who saw utilitarian tests of governmental efficiency as
safeguards of progress and those who considered them to be corro-
sive and ultimately socially destructive. The divergence was a main
theme of English history between 1834 and 1837; from 1837 to 1846
it remained prominent in a dramatic period of political cleavage.
There was no shortage during these years of working-class rebels
and of eloquent intellectual prophets who claimed that the political
structure created by the Reform Bill of 1832 and the reform by
instalments which followed it totally ignored the basic problems of
society. These were the testing years of the new industrial system as
well as of the new Constitution. Before England could cross the
threshold into the Victorian age of balance it first had to go through
the ordeal of prolonged social and economic crisis, and the crisis
necessarily involved major political reorientations. That the reorientations were made without violent revolution was the result
of a combination of circumstances and personalities. For all their
weaknesses the Whigs had shown between 1830 and 1835 that
large-scale changes could be made without bloodshed. The lesson
was not lost on their Conservative opponents, particularly on Sir
Robert Peel. Out of the conflicts he and not the Whigs or the
Benthamites emerged as the dominating figure, leading the country,
as *The Times* put it in his obituary notice in 1850, 'from the confusions
and darkness that hung round the beginning of the century to the
comparatively quiet haven in which we are now embayed'.[1]

There was one other crisis in the 1830s which was not social and
economic, but religious. The early reforming zeal of the Whigs,
their alliance with the Dissenters in the cause of religious freedom,
their dislike of the attitude of a majority of the bishops in the
House of Lords during the Reform Bill debates, and their tampering
with the Irish Church made many staunch supporters of the Church
of England fear that a reformed Parliament would end by reforming
not only the State but the Church. The sense of danger was communicated in Whig speeches. If the Lords opposed the Whig
government on any vital matter, Macaulay wrote in 1833, 'he would
not give sixpence for a coronet or a penny for a mitre'. It is not
surprising that there was indignation and alarm. A young Oxford
don, John Henry Newman, travelling in the Mediterranean in the
winter of 1832 and the spring of 1833, was not alone among church-

[1] 4 July 1850.

men in having 'fierce thoughts against the Liberals'. He refused to rest his eyes on the tricolour flying on a French ship at Algiers, and out of the encircling gloom he wrote his famous hymn *Lead Kindly Light*. The light was to lead Christians in many directions before the 1830s were over, and in the meantime the rousing cry of the 'Church in danger' stirred up much heat. A few militant Dissenters fanned the flames with such violent and provocative language that it seemed at times as if England was about to be drawn into a 'Continental' battle between clericalism and anti-clericalism. Such fears were exaggerated, however, for Whig enthusiasm to achieve all-out Church reform did not survive the general election of 1837, and the Dissenters were never completely united and certainly were far from being completely anti-clerical. They were not in themselves 'a political party or capable of becoming such',[1] and for the most part their language was more restrained than that of their Anglican opponents, some of whom were anxious to 'institute a crusade against the triple alliance of infidelity, liberalism and papistry'.[2]

Newman and the leaders of what soon became known as the Oxford Movement were anxious to distinguish their position both from that of Tory critics of all reform proposals[3] and from that of the 'Church party', 'a party more numerous by far than [the] three theological ones' (the Liberal, the Evangelical and the Tractarian), a 'party of order', 'created by the legal position of the Church, profiting by its riches and by the institutions of its creed.'[4] Nurtured in Oxford, the Tractarians sought an older and a more abiding authority than an Erastian Established Church. Keble's famous sermon in 1833 on 'National Apostasy', and his fervent protest against the proposal to secularize a portion of the revenues of the Irish bishoprics, talked not of temporal abuses but of Parliament's 'direct disavowal of the sovereignty of God'. It was the spiritual force unleashed by Keble, Newman, and Edward Pusey rather than the strength of their urgent protest against the parliamentary reform of the Church of England which ensured their survival. Their *Tracts for the Times*, the

[1] *Eclectic Review*, January 1839. This was the monthly organ of the Congregationalists, launched in 1805.
[2] *Church of England Quarterly Review*, January 1837. This was the first issue of this periodical.
[3] The Tractarians had no common political outlook. John Keble was a natural conservative, but Hurrell Froude was disgusted by some of the Tory attacks on the Reform Bill. See R. H. Froude, *Remains* (ed. J. H. Newman and J. Keble, 1838–9), vol. I, p. 250.
[4] *Kingsley* v. *Newman* (1913 edn.), pp. xxv–xxvi.

first number of which appeared in 1833, was concerned not so much with the fleeting facts of the present as with the eternal 'authority' of the Church. It was only in the middle years of the century that questions of vestments, ritual, and liturgy became dominant in the Anglo-Catholic movement, at least in popular controversy. By then Newman had left the Church of England for the Church of Rome (1845), the Tractarians who remained within their own communion had helped—at the cost of great controversy—to revivify its intellectual and spiritual life, and the power had gone out of the 'alliance' between the Whigs and the Nonconformists. Lord John Russell, indeed, was prepared to play on every form of prejudice, including No-Popery, within the Church of England. His Ecclesiastical Titles Bill of 1851 banning the use of Roman Catholic titles in England was rightly described by the Quaker, John Bright, as 'little, paltry and miserable—a mere sham to bolster up Church ascendancy'. In 1835 the members of the noisy Protestant Association, celebrating the tercentenary of the introduction of the Protestant Bible, did their best to harass the Melbourne Ministry; in 1851 Russell used the same kind of people to thunder against his opponents.

The main Whig measures of the 1830s were far from paltry or little, although they did not go as far as Nonconformists wished. They included the commutation of tithes (1836), the Marriage Act of the same year which allowed Dissenters to be married in their own chapels, the legalization of civil marriage with local registration of births, weddings and deaths, and, most important of all, the setting up of a permanent Ecclesiastical Commission in 1836 to redraw the boundaries and redistribute the income of dioceses. The House of Lords opposed much of this legislation, qualifying, for instance, the Marriage Act so that Nonconformists had to have their marriages announced before the Poor Law Guardians. The Ecclesiastical Commission, however, was strongly supported by Peel, who as a stalwart Churchman was responsible in his short ministry for appointing a committee of enquiry into Church revenues which he hoped would strengthen rather than weaken the position of the Establishment. The practical reforms which the Commission made possible—the ban on the holding of plural benefices over two miles apart, the augmentation of stipend of many poor parish priests, and the diminution of enormous episcopal incomes—were as important to the survival of the Church of England as an institution in a new age as any of the movements of reform from within her own ranks.

Indeed for all the opposition of the Tractarians, it was the Whigs who by their reforms allowed new spiritual forces the means of expressing themselves, and it was some of the fiercest critics of those reforms who were least interested in the 'spiritual renovation' of the Church.

The hopes of the militant Dissenters in the mid-'30s that Church rates would be abolished and the 'disgraceful connection between church and state' dissolved were dashed long before the general election of 1837, when the Whigs made it finally clear that they intended to carry their ecclesiastical reforms no further. Their last proposal—to abolish Church rates and to raise an equivalent amount of revenue, £250,000 annually, from the better management of Church lands and from additional pew rents—was carried by only 273 votes to 250 and was killed in the House of Lords. By 1840 they were modifying the constitution of the Ecclesiastical Commission so that all bishops became *ex officio* commissioners. From the late 1830s onwards the Whigs left the dissenting cause to the Dissenters themselves and to the radicals. In the early 1840s the militant Dissenters were to glory in 'the dissidence of dissent', and to inspire organizations like the Religious Freedom Society, founded under Radical presidency in 1838, and the Anti-State Church Association, founded in 1844. Although such political preoccupations were not to the taste of many of the more quiet Dissenters, they acted as a leaven in almost every political agitation, particularly in the provinces. Unless the excitement and frustration of the period between the abolition of Nonconformist disabilities in 1828 and the end of the Whig policy of reform by instalments is recaptured, it is impossible to understand the energy and emotional fervour of Dissent in the years of cleavage which followed 1837.

6

SOCIAL CLEAVAGE

1. REFORM AND THE WORKING CLASSES

NEITHER the Dissenters nor the Tractarians (nor for that matter
the Whigs) understood the new working-class aspirations of
the 1830s and '40s. No real concessions had been made to
'democracy' in 1832, and Grey and his colleagues did little to suggest that action would be taken in the future to deal with the problems of 'distress'. Opposition to Whig measures and belief that the
Reform Bill was 'a mere *trick* to strengthen . . . the tottering
exclusiveness of our "blessed constitution" '[1] antedated the passing
of the bill, although general disillusionment was slower to take
shape. In the *Poor Man's Guardian*, published unstamped in defiance
of the newspaper tax, Henry Hetherington and his friends of the
National Union of the Working Classes thundered against what
they called a 'delusive, time serving, specious and partial measure';
criticizing the transfer of votes to a 'small and particular portion of
the community', the petty masters and the 'middle men',[2] they
pleaded in the name of the 'useful classes' for universal suffrage,
vote by ballot, annual parliaments, and the removal of all property
qualifications. Behind these political demands was a mass of accumulating social and economic grievances. Economic conditions in
1833 and 1834 were relatively favourable—good harvests coincided
with full employment—but it was made unmistakably clear that if
the plight of the 'suffering millions' became more serious, then
large-scale independent working-class political action would
follow.

While times remained good, however, it was difficult, as a witness
before a Select Committee put it in 1833, to get the working classes
'to talk of politics'. 'Do you think the working classes of Stafford-

---

[1] *Poor Man's Guardian*, 24 September 1831.
[2] *Ibid.*, 30 July 1831.

shire ever show political discontent so long as they are doing well in their particular trade?' he was asked. 'Not at all' was the reply.[1] In deviating from this pattern the more sophisticated London workers and some of the skilled artisans in the big cities were exceptional. They looked forward rather than backward, pitching their hopes not in a golden age in the past but in the future. Enjoying higher wages than other labour groups and frequently engaging in educational activities, they prided themselves on being 'the intelligent and influential portion of the working classes'. They were prepared to take part in a whole series of working-class organizations with different names and even different purposes. Thus William Lovett, a cabinet maker by trade and later one of the Chartist leaders, was a member in turn of the first London Co-operative Trading Association (1828), the British Association for Promoting Co-operative Knowledge, the Metropolitan Political Union, the National Union of the Working Classes, the movement for the unstamped press, and the London Working Men's Association.

The difference in experience and outlook of different sections of the labouring population makes it difficult to employ the term 'working classes' with any degree of precision. Local differences were so marked, occupations were in many cases so rigidly demarcated, factory operatives were in so different a situation from hand-loom weavers or domestic nailmakers, self-educated artisans were separated by so wide a gap from rough casual labourers that, as a well-known economist put it as late as 1846, 'in order to represent with perfect fidelity the state of the labouring population it would be necessary to describe each class separately'.[2] Several attempts were made between 1830 and 1836, however, to establish working-class unity. The success of the 'middle classes' between 1830 and 1832 inevitably stimulated working-class reactions and heightened a sense of separate interest. 'We are the people', declared William Benbow, one of the first advocates of a national strike, 'the Grand National Holiday', 'our business is with the people and to transact it we must take it into our own hands.'[3]

Various theories were current which set out to provide a rational basis for the distinctive action of the working classes. The first was the theory of Robert Owen. Although for most of his life Owen

[1] Quoted W. W. Rostow, *British Economy of the Nineteenth Century* (1948), p. 120.
[2] W. T. Thornton, *Over-population and its Remedy* (1846), p. 10.
[3] Quoted G. D. H. Cole and A. W. Filson, *British Working Class Movements* (1951),

did not analyse social questions in strict class terms, he emphasized that labour is the source of all value, distinguished forcibly between 'bees' and 'drones', and pleaded for co-operation instead of competition as the basis of the industrial system. Owen had begun his career as a Manchester manufacturer in 1790 and ten years later had moved to New Lanark, where his mills and community institutions soon became showplaces for visitors from all over the world. He attributed his business success not to his own efforts but to the social forces of the age, particularly the exploitation of the new 'scientific power', and he argued in general terms that social environment determined individual character and not the reverse. His *New View of Society* (1813) proclaimed this theory to the world, and between 1813 and 1819 he tried to persuade his aristocratic contemporaries to plan productive relief for the poor and to seek for a better social order. His failure to win the full support of the aristocracy and of the government led him to devote his energies to building model communities, social microcosms where drastic changes could take place without outside interference, but when in 1828 his famous community at New Harmony in the United States collapsed he returned to England to make a definite appeal to the 'labouring class'. By this time Owenism had already attracted many disciples in England, among them William Lovett and his fellow members of the British Association for Promoting Co-operative Knowledge. They believed both in his theory of society and in the growth of co-operative production and retail stores, and looked to Owen as a leader because he had convinced them that 'working-men sustained the whole superstructure of society'[1] without fully sharing in its benefits. As early as 1821 a Co-operative and Economical Society had been launched in London, with its own magazine the *Economist*, and six years later the most successful of early co-operative societies was founded at Brighton by Dr. William King, a Cambridge graduate and the real pioneer of the co-operative store.

During the Reform Bill struggle Owenites and Co-operators continued to preach their doctrines to small but enthusiastic audiences and held national congresses at Manchester and Birmingham. In the period of business prosperity between 1832 and 1834, they poured their energies into the creation of a national 'trade union movement'. Owen, who was autocratic rather than democratic in temperament, an ideologist not a politician, suddenly found himself

[1] *Poor Man's Guardian*, 31 December 1830.

at the head of a huge working-class movement, the Grand National Consolidated Trades Union, founded in February 1834, which had as its objective the unity of the working classes in a decisive but peaceful struggle to inaugurate the Owenite millennium.

Three writers strongly influenced by Owen—John Gray, William Thompson, and Thomas Hodgskin—developed a whole system of socialist economics before the G.N.C.T.U. was launched. Gray's *Lecture on Human Happiness* (1825), Thompson's *Labour Rewarded* (1827), and Hodgskin's *Labour Defended* (1825) all began their analyses with a statement of the labour theory of value and an assertion that capital was simply stored-up labour. They went on to demand that labour should receive the full product of its efforts. They had read widely—in Godwin, Bentham and Ricardo as well as in Owen—and they made it their main purpose to direct attention to 'misery in the midst of all the means of happiness'. In the new industrial society, wrote Thompson, 'hostile camps of the employers and labourers are everywhere formed'[1]; 'to relieve distress', Hodgskin declared in 1832, 'only one of two things can possibly be done; either the quantity of wealth must be augmented, or it must be better and differently distributed. . . . As . . . political changes have not effected, and cannot effect the expected benefits, men will necessarily turn away from political alterations as unproductive of good, and inquire into the sources of evil, and the means of drying them up.'[2] It is scarcely surprising that radical social analysis of this kind alarmed conservatives far more than radical political propaganda, and liberal reformers of the 'Steam Intellect Society', who believed in 'improvement', joined their conservative opponents in emphasizing that such socialist doctrines, 'harmless as abstract propositions' would end in 'maddening passion, drunken frenzy, unappeasable tumult, fire and blood'.[3] The danger of working-class 'contamination' seemed real, for the doctrines were circulating in an industrial context among the Lancashire trade unions of the 1820s. John Doherty, the Owenite leader of the Grand General Union of all the Operative Spinners in the United Kingdom and later of the National Association for the Protection of Labour (1830), talked repeatedly on public platforms of labour's rights and pleaded unremittingly for trade-union unity in his news-

[1] Quoted by R. K. P. Pankhurst, *William Thompson* (1954), p. 57.
[2] Quoted by E. Halévy, *Thomas Hodgskin* (1956 English edition), p. 127
[3] Quoted Pankhurst, *op. cit.*, p. 201.

paper *The Voice of the People*. In 1833 Doherty joined hands with
Oastler in the battle for the ten-hour working day and on his death
was described by Lord Ashley as 'one of the most faithful to a cause
that ever existed'.[1]

The G.N.C.T.U. was merely one, albeit the biggest, example of a
number of large national unions created between 1831 and 1834,
concerned not simply 'to obtain some paltry rise or prevent some
paltry reduction in wages' but to establish 'for the productive
classes a complete dominion over the fruits of their own industry'.
In the words of the working-class journalist and later Chartist
leader Bronterre O'Brien, 'an entire change in society—a change
amounting to the complete subversion of the existing "order of the
world" is contemplated by the working classes. They aspire to be
at the top instead of at the bottom of society—or rather that there
should be no bottom or top at all.'[2]

An Operative Builders' Union was founded in Manchester in
1832 as a federation of existing builders' unions; its highest authority
was a Grand Lodge or Builders' Parliament, meeting twice a year.
The union attempted to recruit all builders to its ranks and to
create a 'Builders' Guild' to eliminate contractors and start co-
operative building schemes as a prelude to the taking over of the
whole industry. Curiously enough in its manifesto it quoted Sir
Robert Peel on the necessity of taking 'our own affairs into our
own hands'; the first number of its journal the *Pioneer* (7 September
1833) talked more ambitiously of putting 'poverty and the fear of it
for ever out of society'. While the builders were setting out to
secure 'the whole moral regeneration of society', cotton spinners in
Lancashire and Scotland, clothiers in Yorkshire, and potters in
Staffordshire were also recruiting hundreds of new members and
there was talk of a 'universal compact' to bind trade unionists of
every kind together.[3]

The attempt to persuade all workers to join the big unions
produced inevitable conflict with the manufacturers. Owen himself
had stressed the need for peaceful collaboration, but some of his
strongest supporters, including James Morrison, the editor of the
Pioneer, talked in terms of the class struggle and demanded workers'
control. In any case, it was difficult to keep trade-union action in

---

[1] Quoted G. D. H. Cole, *Attempts at General Union* (1953), p. 153.
[2] *Poor Man's Guardian*, 19 October 1833.
[3] *Pioneer*, 26 October 1833.

the localities on the same high plane as that on which Owen himself moved, and there were increasingly tough local struggles in the last few months of 1833 between combinations of workmen and counter-combinations of employers. The most important of them was at Derby where in November 1833 the masters and manufacturers of the town passed a resolution refusing to employ any member of a recently formed trades union. Notices were served and a thousand men were soon idle. The Derby workers were militant, and the national unions were in no mood to allow any kind of local capitulation. Circulars were sent to operatives in all parts of the country, donations collected, and a committee appointed to direct a plan of campaign. The Derby 'turn-out' was thought of as a trial of strength which the unionists would have to win if they were to achieve their ultimate purposes.

It was the difficulties of the Derby trade unionists which provided the immediate stimulus for the setting up of the G.N.C.T.U. in February 1834. A few months earlier in October 1833 an Owenite conference had been called to form a 'Grand National Moral Union of the Productive Classes of the United Kingdom' with Co-operative as well as trade-union support. The G.N.C.T.U. by contrast was entirely a trade-union body. Central control of the new organization was to be entrusted to a Grand Council meeting twice a year and to a full-time Executive Council of paid members. Below this level there was to be a vertical organization of each trade from branch to Grand Lodge and a horizontal organization of federated trades, all trades being linked both in the districts and in the centre. Members were to pay a shilling levy, co-operative workshops were to be set up, and each district was to have its own educational, recreational, and social security system. The trade-unionist periodicals did not hesitate to compare favourably this elaborate structure with that of Parliament. 'There are two Parliaments in London at present sitting', the *Crisis* observed in 1834, 'and we have no hesitation in saying that the Trades Parliament is by far the most important, and will in the course of a year or two be the more influential.'[1]

The comprehensive scope of the new organization was a testimony to the far-reaching and 'utopian' dreams of 1832 to 1834. In practice, however, the G.N.C.T.U. was dogged with insurmountable difficulties for the whole of its short life. The four major trade unions—those of the builders, the potters, the spinners and the clothiers—

[1] *Crisis*, 22 February 1834.

did not join and retained their separate identity. The new factory workers as a whole were aloof, preferring the fight for a shorter working day. Finally, there were many instances of trade particularism within the G.N.C.T.U., above all in London, and of deviations and secessions. For all the high-sounding phrases of its constitution, the G.N.C.T.U. remained a snowball movement and never became a routine institution. For all its emphasis on the millennium, it became a prisoner in a web of local and national emergencies. Called into being as a result of the costly dispute at Derby, it soon faced equally serious difficulties in London and the West Country. Failure at Derby and the defeat of a tailors' strike in London divided its leadership and split the movement. By August 1834 it had almost completely collapsed, Morrison was ousted by Owen, and Owen turned back again with relief from the comprehensive problems of a mass organization to the safer confines of a co-operative sect.

Unionism of every kind suffered a series of setbacks in 1834 and 1835. Financial and organizational weaknesses, the recruitment in good times of large numbers of merely nominal members, and the immeasurably greater strength of employers made the setbacks inevitable, but for all the inevitability there was a sense of bitterness and disillusionment. As fast as the workers became organized they put forward wage demands to their employers: the employers retaliated by declaring open war on the unions. Throughout 1834 there were strikes and turn-outs in nearly all parts of the country and growing union activity even in the agricultural areas.

One of the provincial unions of this period has passed into all the history books—the Friendly Society of Agricultural Labourers at Tolpuddle in Dorset, founded in October 1833 several months before the G.N.C.T.U. It had its own grand committee of management, its grand lodge and its entrance fee of one shilling, and its object, stated in restrained language, was to secure for all its members, by fair means, a just remuneration for their labour. Despite its profession of peace, the local magistrates arrested its leader, George Loveless, a labourer and Methodist preacher, and five other people, and after an unfair trial for administering unlawful oaths to unionists transported them to Australia. The Whig government, with Lord Melbourne primarily responsible, was an active partner in the repression. The Dorsetshire martyrs are rightly regarded as among the founders of English trade unionism and the twentieth-century

T.U.C. looks back to them with reverence and pride. Even in relation to the immediate circumstances of 1834, the sequence of events at Tolpuddle was of considerable importance, for a Dorchester Committee was set up in London, on the initiative of the G.N.C.T.U., with William Lovett at its head. It organized protest meetings and the collection of petitions in all parts of the country, and served as the most important link between the trade unionism of 1832–4 and the political Chartism which followed it. While employers in many parts of the country were forcing their workers to abandon the unions on penalty of immediate dismissal and the government was employing spies and encouraging legal action to suppress the unions, there was a fairly general move back to political action. In June 1834, for example, the striking Leeds clothiers 'succumbed to a vital law of necessity, returned to work and dissolved the old Unions',[1] and the *Poor Man's Guardian* drew the moral that nothing less than universal suffrage was necessary to break the workers' chains.

Before there could be a full return to militant working-class politics, there had to be a turn in the economic situation. Already in 1836 Thomas Attwood in Birmingham was pinning his hope of a new burst of political action on a bad harvest and a million unemployed, but the time was not yet ripe. Between the failure of the G.N.C.T.U. and the early months of 1837 working-class political activity was confined to small groups, of which by far the most important was the London Working Men's Association, founded in June 1836 by Hetherington and Lovett. It was pledged to independent working-class action and included in its manifesto the key sentence, 'if they whose interests are so identified [the working classes] do not investigate the causes of the evils that oppress them, how can they expect others to do it for them?'[2] The L.W.M.A. was the child of London reform politics and the parent of the famous National Charter of 1838. It is essential to examine the national appeal of the Charter in the light of what went before as well as what came afterwards. It provided a new symbol of unity, the new centre of a gathering snowball of local grievances and aspirations, but it is a document which must be related directly to the chronology of distress and the intricate interplay of protest

[1] *Pioneer*, 21 June 1834.
[2] For the background of the L.W.M.A. the best source is Lovett himself, *The Life and Struggle of William Lovett in His Pursuit of Bread, Knowledge and Freedom* (1876).

movements and organizations in the months which preceded its drafting. In 1837 and 1838 that interplay depended above all else on large-scale economic and social crisis which alarmed 'responsible opinion' as much as it stirred the working classes.

2. CRISIS

One of the main Owenite journals in the great burst of trade union expansion was called the *Crisis*; the choice of name was a tribute to the sense of challenge in the air and to the vigour of the belief that industrial society was universally doomed unless it was reshaped on a co-operative instead of a competitive basis. The English social and economic crisis of 1837 and 1838 was serious enough in its practical implications without the need of apocalyptic Owenism to give it extra colour. Although it was the economic implications of the crisis which had the most significant political consequences—the formation of two great extra-parliamentary pressure groups, the Chartists and the Anti-Corn Law League—it was the social implications which fascinated a generation of prophets of catastrophe and captured the attention of the more critical members of society. Whig platitudes seemed totally inadequate at a time when 'the condition of England' became the leading question of the day. Indeed to Thomas Carlyle, the most eloquent prophet of the age, both the heavy arguments of the political economists and the whole of Parliament itself with its 'deep-rutted routines' and its crude panaceas were equally inadequate. 'Such a Platitude of a World', he wrote in *Past and Present* (1843), 'in which all horses could be well fed and innumerable working men could die starved; were it not better to end it, to have done with it?' The economic crisis of 1837, like the further crisis of 1842,[1] involved more than the statistics of industry and trade; it touched the mainsprings of human emotion and imagination. The discontents were far more profound than anxieties about figures in businessmen's ledgers or the best way for a working-class family to make ends meet; they determined the way of thinking of a whole generation. Men as different as Engels, the friend of Karl Marx, and Thomas Arnold, the headmaster of Rugby, were conscious above all else of a divided society, of Disraeli's 'two nations between whom there is no inter-course and no sympathy'. They spoke of a 'cash nexus' taking the

---

[1] The two crises were related. See R. C. O. Matthews, *A Study in Trade Cycle History Economic Fluctuations in Great Britain, 1833–42* (1954).

place of an older and richer pattern of social relationships, of a sense of imminent collapse, of a worse catastrophe than the French Revolution. Distress after 1815 had quickened the pace of English politics; in the late 1830s and early 1840s it dominated the whole mood of the nation.

Some account of the detailed economic record of the years 1836 to 1850 is a necessary prelude to any understanding both of politics and of literature. Between 1832 and 1836 the Whigs had been favoured not only by plentiful employment but by a run of good harvests. The price of wheat fell from 63*s*. a quarter when the Reform Bill was passed to only 36*s*. at the end of 1835. The year 1836 marked a turning point. Not only did the run of good harvests come to an end, but there were signs of a financial crisis (beginning with strains in the United States) which broke the trade boom. In 1837 there was a serious recession, during which merchants were obliged to sell for moderate prices goods which they had bought when prices were exceptionally high. By April of that year Liverpool merchants were complaining in a petition to Parliament that 'the distress of the mercantile interest is intense beyond example and that it is rapidly extending to all ranks and conditions of the community . . . the prudent with the imprudent . . . spinners and labourers with the manufacturers themselves', while from Birmingham the cry came that 'unless remedial measures be immediately applied a large portion of our population will shortly be thrown out of employment . . . with alarming consequences to all classes of the community'.

By the summer there were 50,000 workers either unemployed or on short time in Manchester.[1] Although there were some signs of a qualified revival in 1838 and 1839, there continued to be considerable unemployment in particular areas, including Lancashire and the Midlands, and serious political unrest. A somewhat better year followed in 1840, but in 1841 the recession moved into depression again and there was no gloomier year in the whole nineteenth century than 1842. Prolonged business difficulties and four years of harvest dearth made England unhappy and afraid, a country of conflict and despair. Bread was dear, and flesh and blood were cheap. Movements of protest and revolt swept the country.

The period from 1843 to 1850 was one of revival broken by a further financial crisis in 1847 and considerable unemployment in

[1] *Manchester Times*, 17 June 1837.

the textile industries in 1847 and 1848. The boom of the mid '40s was based largely on the rapid expansion of railways, although an improvement in export trade in 1842 and 1843 did something to establish it. Between 1839 and 1843 no new railway lines were opened to supplement the railways constructed between 1825, the opening of George Stephenson's Stockton and Darlington, and the peak year of 1836; by contrast, between 1844 and 1847 (inclusive) 442 railway acts were passed by Parliament and more than 2,000 miles of track were opened. The railway construction boom, with its emphasis on amalgamation and consolidation, overshadowed all other economic developments of the period and not only provided an enormous volume of direct employment but stimulated the demand for the products of other industries, particularly iron, coal and engineering. By 1845 there was much talk of a 'railway mania', far bigger than the canal mania of the 1790s, but inevitably involving wild speculation as well as substantial genuine investment, and in October 1845 the railway bubble was pricked. A crisis in the railway share market was followed by the reappearance of unemployment in Lancashire and the Midlands and a rise in the expenditure on poor relief. More serious financial and economic difficulties ensued in 1847 and 1848, when the need for large grain imports to meet bad harvests led to a loss of gold, credit stringency, and some business failures. While the price of corn rose to 100s. a quarter, a shortage of raw cotton led to short-time working in the Lancashire mills. Old tensions reappeared and social conflicts became once more acute. By 1847 and 1848, however, the government was no longer the passive spectator of the economic scene that it had been ten years earlier. Peel, who became prime minister in 1841 and stayed until 1846, had replaced Whig platitudes with deliberate economic and administrative decisions, culminating in the redeal of the corn laws in 1846; the sting had been removed from middle-class politics, and the way was prepared for another economic revival as soon as food prices fell and the immediate crisis in business confidence had been overcome. Quite apart from governmental policy, the inherent vitality of an expanding economy was sufficient to carry the country safely through political storms which made Europe the centre of a series of revolutions in 1848. In particular, railway construction itself, which some contemporaries blamed for the new crisis, was a stabilizing factor counterbalancing weaknesses in other sectors of the economy and making possible a widening of markets and a lowering of transport costs. By 1850 the weight of crisis had been lifted and the *Annual Register* could comment without undue optimism that 'the domestic affairs of the British nation presented a tranquil and, with partial exceptions, a cheering aspect'.

This brief account of the crests and troughs of the period 1836–50 provides a background for the politics of social cleavage. Three points about the background are of special importance.

First, there was plenty of scope in the changing economic circumstances of the period for different sections of society to assert grievances and to press for remedies. In times of bad trade, particularly from 1838 to 1842, merchants and manufacturers were driven to demand changes in national economic policy. The fact that they had gained the vote in 1832 made their actions more effective. The composition of Parliament did not mirror their strength in the new economy, but they were at least in a position to put pressure upon it. The Anti-Corn Law League became their chosen instrument. In times of hunger and unemployment, which went with bad harvests and bad trade, the labouring section of the population also had every inducement to make political demands, although for them a reform of Parliament seemed a necessary priority. Working-class political organizations, many of which were drawn together in the Chartist movement, were almost bound to diverge from movements backed by businessmen and merchants, for there was an immediate if not an insuperable clash of interests which was reflected within the factory and the new industrial town. Interests were translated into class terminology. The 'middle classes' saw their struggle as a battle against the 'aristocracy', the 'working classes' as a battle for their own rights. Finally, farmers too had their grievances, which were by no means fully expressed by the big landlords, many of whom received incomes from urban development, coal mines, railways or industry as well as from land[1]; the farmers found it difficult to make their voices heard above the clamour of contesting interests and they were on the defensive between 1841 and 1846. All the contending interests and classes in society in the 1840s liked to argue that they were acting in the 'national interest', but their claims were challenged in both the strident utterances of prophets like Carlyle and the cautious administrative decisions reached by Sir Robert Peel.

---

[1] See D. Spring, 'The English Landed Estate in the Age of Coal and Iron' in *J. Ec. Hist.* (1951).

Second, it is difficult to generalize about conditions in different parts of the country and over quite narrowly separate periods of time. The railways were helping to make one single England in the 1840s; it was not already there. There was a vivid contrast not only between the big city, the small town and the countryside—Lancelot Smith in Charles Kingsley's novel *Yeast* found the conversation of town labourers 'like the speech of savages'—but within different areas of the big city and different parts of the national countryside. In *Mary Barton* (1848) Mrs. Gaskell turned from middle-class Manchester to the 'recesses' of the city, emphasizing what Carlyle called 'the infinite abysses' of local social life in an industrial setting: in her novel *North and South* (1855) and in her *Life of Charlotte Brontë* (1857) she assumed that the ways of the North and even its language would be quite unfamiliar to her readers south of the Trent. Charlotte Brontë herself well summarized the appeal of locality in a passage in *Shirley* (1849) where she described a working-class disturbance: 'A yell followed this demonstration—a rioter's yell—a North of England—a Yorkshire—a West Riding—a West Riding-clothing-district-of-Yorkshire rioter's yell.' Literature is much more revealing than economic data for the understanding of the attitudes of contemporaries to the social gulfs of the 1840s. These gulfs were beginning to fascinate novelists in a decade when Society novels were giving way to novels about society, and books about fashion, particularly the old silver-fork novels of the 1830s, were becoming increasingly unfashionable.[1] Nearly all percipient writers of the 1840s not only concentrated on the problem of the relationship between rich and poor but seized on the coming of the railway as a great historical divide not only in their own but in the nation's life. The greatest of early Victorian novelists, Charles Dickens, is typical in both these preoccupations. He looked to the power of benevolence (or the Christian spirit) to draw the different sectors of society together, and particularly in *Dombey and Son* (1841) he brilliantly noted many of the most important social effects of the coming of the railway.

The economic effects of the railway revolution were obvious enough—they permitted the cheaper movement of goods, particularly heavy and perishable goods, and they widened local markets. Socially, as Dickens saw, railways not only enabled the new

---

[1] See K. Tillotson, *Novels of the Eighteen-Forties* (1954); W. O. Aydelotte, 'The England of Monk and Mill as Reflected in Fiction' in *J. Ec. Hist.*, Supplement, 1948.

passengers to travel faster—at as much as fifty miles an hour instead of twelve—but to rub shoulders with people they had never met before and even to catch glimpses of the 'other world' on the side of the railway track. There is little doubt that railways, unlike the motor-car in the twentieth century, had a basic democratic tendency or at least that they levelled social distinctions without eliminating the thickest lines of division. George Hudson, the railway king, who caught a glimpse of the full possibilities of a railway system, was a lion of London society before his dubious financial methods led to his ruin. Of one railway, the Birmingham to Rugby, Thomas Arnold wrote, 'I rejoice to see it and think that feudality is gone for ever. It is so great a blessing to think that any one evil is really extinct.'[1] In the long run, through the growth of a daily post, a national newspaper system, cheaper travel, and national commodity markets, railways helped to unify England in a way that hitherto had not been possible.

The rapid rate of economic change in the 1840s, of which the railways were both a symbol and a cause, was assessed in radically different ways by different writers, even by those who agreed on much else. The comfortable view, expressed by political economists and by statisticians like J. R. Porter, was that material progress was itself the basic form of progress, the lasting improvement, and all else was superstructure. Many of the writers who emphasized that fair distribution counted as much as large-scale production, would have agreed with this basic value judgement or at least have been tolerant about it. 'It's this steam, you see, that has made the difference; it drives on every wheel double pace, and the wheel of fortune along with 'em.'[2] There were other people, however, who were less satisfied and contrasted the present very unfavourably with the past, often not in a mood of nostalgia but of genuine social criticism. Dickens did not feel the pull of the past, but many novelists, poets and artists did. While Carlyle was returning in *Past and Present* to the world of the Abbot Sampson in the twelfth century, discovering there a genuinely creative attitude both to work and to wealth, and trying to depict the nineteenth-century present in historical terms, the Gothic revival in architecture was beginning to modify considered judgements on taste. Augustus Pugin was as interested in the spiritual implications of the Gothic revival as he was in the

[1] A. P. Stanley, *The Life and Correspondence of Thomas Arnold* (1877), vol. II, p. 388.
[2] G. Eliot, *The Mill on the Floss* (1860), Book VI, ch. V.

design of buildings, but so popular did the break from Georgian styles become that by 1847 *Punch* could fear that 'we shall be treated by posterity as people who live in the Middle Ages, for everything around us partakes of the mediæval character'. There was an element of escape in some of the manifestations of the desire to look back—certainly there was in the fanciful mock mediæval tournament in Eglinton Castle in 1839, in the chivalrous capers of George Smythe, Lord John Manners and the 'feudal circle' of 'Young England', and in the dream of a monastic revival [1]—but there was also an element of deep discontent with a new society which seemed to be always growing and always to be going astray. That element was to be reinforced in mid-Victorian England by John Ruskin who paid his first visit to Venice in 1841. For him and his disciples the Middle Ages, which had served as a source of thrills and romance for Coleridge and the terror novelists of the early century and as a noble pageant for Sir Walter Scott, became a store-house of lessons for the reshaping of Victorian economic life. [2] The orthodox political economist's view of 'improvement' was 'corrected' by relating the new industrial age of steam and railways to great ages of creative effort in the past.

After plumbing the social depths of the 1840s, to go back to the apologists of the new economic order like Andrew Ure and W. Cooke Taylor[3] or even to the bare economic chronicle is like returning to a world of platitude. Nonetheless, it was the economic crisis of 1837–42 which provoked much of the heart-searching, as did the further crisis of 1847 which was followed by the wave of revolutions on the Continent. During the political crisis of the Reform Bill the *Athenaeum* had remarked that 'no one talks of literature in these stormy and changeful times . . . no attention is paid to anything but speculations on reform and change of rulers.'[4] The economic crises were different; they raised fundamental questions such as the position of the individual in the new society, the relationship

---

[1] See C. Whibley, *Lord John Manners and His Friends* (1925). 'Young England' was strongly influenced by Kenelm Digby's *Broad Stone of Honour or the True Sense and Practice of Chivalry* (1829). For Disraeli's association with 'Young England', see W. F. Monypenny and G. E. Buckle, *The Life of Benjamin Disraeli* (1929 edn.), vol. I, part I, ch. 6. The *Communist Manifesto* (1848) called Young England 'half lamentation, half lampoon' but added that, 'at times by its witty and incisive criticism' it struck 'the bourgeoisie to the very heart's core'.

[2] See below, pp. 473 ff.

[3] Andrew Ure's *Philosophy of Manufactures* (1835) was an eloquent statement of the manufacturers' point of view: W. Cooke Taylor, *Tour in the Manufacturing Districts of Lancashire* (1842) painted a favourable picture of Lancashire conditions.

[4] 12 May 1832.

between different social groups and the fate of the nation. Yet for all their searching the social critics discovered no adequate remedies and missed many features in English society which accounted for the fact that England, like Russia but unlike most European countries, did not have a revolution in 1848; they ignored or underestimated the practical reforms of the 1840s, the appeasement of the middle classes, the achievement of Peel, the pull of deference in the countryside, the influence of religion. They failed also to examine with sufficient care 'the other nation', the existence of which they were the first to realize. They misinterpreted its activities and its prospects both in 1837 and ten years later. Engels, the young visitor from Germany, foresaw an imminent revolution. 'It is too late for a peaceful solution,' he exclaimed in 1844; 'soon a slight impulse will suffice to set the avalanche in motion.'[1] Carlyle as late as 1850 was still echoing some of the same fears.

In fact, the 'other nation' was itself broken up, as we have seen, into many kinds of sub-nations. The economic, educational and temperamental gulf between skilled and unskilled workers was wide enough for John Stuart Mill to consider it the equivalent of a class divide. Even without full recognition of their political rights, the skilled working classes could hope for material gains under the new economic system and for a minimum freedom to organize and agitate. They were not likely to be revolutionary for long, unless they were incessantly provoked. The village labourers, increasingly distinct in outlook from the town labourers and far less easy to organize, were either content to defer to their betters or had been cowed by local magistrates and the government during a decade of repression. The worst-off section of the working-class population, the hand-loom weavers, were a slowly declining force, and while they gave a note of urgent anger to Chartism they could not properly sustain it in good times. Their plight was a tragic one and political economists could give them no helpful advice but to 'flee their trade' and beware sending their children into it 'as they would the commission of crimes'.[2] If in periods of falling prices—the normal

[1] *The Condition of the Working Class in England in 1844* (1892 edition), p. 298. 'Prophecy', he remarked (p. 297), 'is nowhere so easy as in England, where all the component elements of society are clearly defined and sharply separated.'
[2] See the *Report of the Commission on Hand-loom Weavers* (1841). It was a classical statement of classical political economy, characteristically different in tone from a S.C.R. of the House of Commons on the same subject in 1835. The difference illustrates the contrast between the two techniques of investigation. The first enquiry was dominated by humanitarians, the second by political economists. See G. J. Stigler, *Five Lectures on Economic Problems* (1949), ch. 3.

situation between 1815 and 1846—the hand-loom weavers tried to increase their output, then the prices of their products fell further and their incomes did not rise. If they mobilized their children's labour, their children suffered with them. But when the rôle of the hand-loom weavers and of other displaced labour groups like the framework knitters is fully examined, it becomes clear that they were not the cohorts of revolution but the tragic victims of the rise of the machine. Only a relatively small number of doctrinaires like George Julian Harney, and a mass of immigrant Irish labourers, who poured into England in large numbers in the 1840s—it was estimated in 1835 that one-fifth of the population of Manchester was Irish [1]—were potential revolutionaries. The doctrinaires had considerable influence in certain cities, Newcastle for example,[2] but they were never able to dominate the national politics of the day. Of the Irish it may be said that either they were absorbed into the new economic system as 'navvies' and casual labourers or they were tossed here and there continuing to harbour their national grievances. So long as O'Connell lived and was regarded as the 'Liberator'—he died in 1847—most politically-minded Irishmen stood aloof from Chartism, but in 1847 and 1848 they were so prominent in the movement that *The Times* could call the Chartism of 1848 'a ramification of the Irish conspiracy'.[3] That conspiracy could be countered on its own ground.

If the English working classes were not as revolutionary in the late 1830s and 1840s as many frightened contemporaries thought or as many militant Chartists hoped, this does not mean to say that they were not often hungry. The debate on the effect of the industrial revolution on living standards goes on, and there is plenty of evidence, some of it conflicting, to suggest that some workers were 'better off' economically in the 1840s than they had been twenty years before. The consumption per head of some commodities was increasing, the real wages of particular groups of workers had increased, and some of the expressions of grievance were the result of better opportunities for self-expression and organization in the concentrated centres of population than had hitherto been the case. But there is general evidence too on the other side. The Leeds

---

[1] J. H. Clapham, *An Economic History of Modern Britain* (1939), vol. I, p. 61.
[2] Tyneside miners and wireworkers carried banners at meetings in 1838–9 bearing such slogans as 'Liberty! or I shall make my arrows drunk with blood, and my sword shall devour flesh', *Northern Liberator*, 28 December 1838.
[3] 10 April 1848.

labour economist John Francis Bray wrote in 1839 that 'the millions are a doomed class . . . their constitution is unimprovable and their wrongs irremediable',[1] while the classical economist John Stuart Mill argued as late as 1848 that it was doubtful whether any of the inventions yet produced had 'lightened the day's toil of any human being'. 'They have increased the comforts of the middle classes', he went on, 'but they have not yet begun to effect those great changes in human destiny, which it is in their nature and in their futurity to accomplish.'[2]

The third point to stress about the economic background of the period from 1838 to 1850 was that the working classes, whether 'better off' or not, enjoyed nothing that could be called social security. Their well-being fluctuated from year to year as the result of pressures that they could not control. Not only did the cost of living bob up and down but so too did the chances of employment. When the workers were fully employed they might on occasion enjoy 'a rough and rude plenty'[3]; when they were unemployed they were subject to the bleak provisions of the new Poor Law of 1834.

Independent working-class action to meet these social contingencies took various forms. Friendly societies played an important part in providing material help and support just as they had done in the late eighteenth century; they grew rapidly in the 1830s and 1840s, and two of them—the Manchester Unity of Oddfellows and the Foresters—were so large that they were viewed with suspicion by those who scented danger when working-men from different parts of the country were gathered together in national federal bodies. In 1842 Sir James Graham, Peel's Home Secretary, appointed a registrar of Friendly Societies and laid down that all such societies should be enrolled.

Alongside the Friendly Societies trade unions continued to operate, although they were smaller and less ambitious than the enormous Owenite societies of the previous period. Highly skilled craftsmen, associated in bodies like the Journeymen Steam Engine and Machine Makers' Society, had organizations which in some ways pointed forward to the new model unions of the mid-nineteenth century, while in the grim year 1842, a year of strikes and riots in the textile industries, the miners created a new Miners'

[1] *Labour's Wrongs and Labour's Remedies* (1839), p. 67.
[2] *The Principles of Political Economy* (1915 edn.), p. 751.
[3] Quoted from an Oldham working-man's letter of 1845 in a Historical Association pamphlet by W. H. Chaloner, *The Hungry Forties* (1957), p. 8.

Association with headquarters at Wakefield in Yorkshire. The potters, tailors, cobblers and flint glassmakers, too, were active in the early 1840s, and in 1845 a new National Association of United Trades for the Protection of Labour was set up.

These trade-union efforts were not the most important manifestation of working-class action in the period from 1836–50, for they could only influence a relatively small section of the working classes and they lacked the skilled leadership and centralization of funds which were provided in mid-Victorian England. The third form of independent working-class action was co-operation. The best-known example of this response to the economic and social environment was the Rochdale Equitable Pioneers' Society founded in 1844. Although it was not the first of such bodies, it was certainly the most influential; the Rochdale co-operative store for the sale of clothing and provisions was merely one branch of its organization —the need for co-operative production was emphasized as much as co-operative distribution—and the Pioneers also directed attention to bad housing, intemperance, and the importance of democratic control in a voluntary movement. 'Benefit', 'security' and 'welfare' were three of their watchwords.

The fourth form of independent working-class action was Chartism, the attempt to secure the six points—universal manhood suffrage, annual parliaments, voting by ballot, equal electoral districts, no property qualifications for members of Parliament, and payment of members. Behind this political formula there was not only the weight of the radical tradition but what the *Morning Chronicle* called 'the cry of millions suffering under a diseased condition of society'. The Charter was accepted in August 1838 by a variety of working-men's groups which agreed to merge their agitations in one common struggle. From that time onwards the history of Chartism was inextricably bound up with the national crisis. 'Required, as we are universally, to support and obey the laws', the Chartists exclaimed, 'nature and reason entitle us to demand that in the making of the laws, the universal voice shall be implicitly listened to'. The 'universal voice' was soon louder than that of Carlyle.

3. THE CHARTISTS

The basic document, the Charter, was drawn up by the London Working Men's Association in consultation with Francis Place and a number of radical M.P.s, including J. A. Roebuck and Joseph Hume. In 1836 the L.W.M.A. had published a scathing document, laced with statistics, *The Rotten House of Commons, being an Exposition of the Present State of the Franchise.* 'Is the Landholder, whose interests lead him to keep his rents by unjust and exclusive laws a fit representative for working men?' it asked in the style of middle-class radicalism. The second question marked a break not only with the aristocracy but with the merchants and millowners. Was the 'capitalist' (it used the name) any more suited to the task? His 'executive monopoly of wood, iron and steam enables him to cause the destitution of thousands [and he has] an interest in forcing labour down to the *minimum* reward.' The demand for a popular House of Commons was stated in down-to-earth language. 'The House of Commons is the People's House, and *there* our opinions should be stated, *there* our rights ought to be advocated, *there* we ought to be represented or we are SERFS.' Most Chartists, unlike the leaders of the G.N.C.T.U., were firm believers in a parliamentary ideal, but they had no use for its present sponsors. They looked neither to Whigs nor Tories, and after the General Election of 1837 when there were serious radical defeats—J. A. Roebuck, for instance, was beaten at Bath—they depended little on parliamentary radicalism either. They built up an extra-parliamentary organization which, since it was bound by its composition and nature to propose measures which a half-reformed House of Commons could never accept, became more important as an example of mutual working-class self-help than as a lever of legislative change.

Historians of Chartism must concern themselves more with its inner politics and with its place in English society than with the very limited way in which it fitted into the practical politics of the day. From the start there was no realism in the claim of a London Chartist at a meeting in February 1837 at the Crown and Anchor Tavern that 'in 1832 the working classes by their moral and physical organization beat the Tories for the sake of the Whigs—by the same means they can in 1837 beat both Whigs and Tories for the sake of themselves'.[1] Such a claim, however legitimate the aspiration behind it, was quite unpractical, and the Chartists were doomed to failure even before the final form of their Charter was drafted. Much of their energy was devoted to the discussion not of ends but of means, but even had they agreed (which they did not) about means,

---

[1] Quoted in the *Lovett Scrapbook*, vol. I, B.R.L.

they could never have forced their conception of Parliament on the country. Only in years of economic crisis when 'the knife and fork question' dominated politics had they any real opportunity of winning sufficient working-class support to intimidate if not to convince the government. When economic conditions improved after 1842 they inevitably lost ground. They came into prominence again in 1848, but by that time the forces of order had been consolidated and the middle classes had been appeased.

Although the L.W.M.A. sent out missionaries to set up local working-men's organizations and produced the final draft of the Charter in May 1838, initiative soon passed to other working-class movements in the provinces. The Birmingham Political Union had been formally revived nearly a year earlier and had pressed hard for household suffrage, triennial parliaments, the ballot, payment of members, and the abolition of the property qualification. In December 1837 it demanded unity in the name of 'the People'. 'Before the majesty of their united will', it declared boldly, 'Whigs and Tories, and all dark and deceitful things will flee away as the shadows disappear before the rising sun.'[1] After sending out missionaries to Scotland and Wales as well as England it was quickly drawn into the network of working-class politics, linking up with the L.W.M.A. and in August 1838 accepting the Charter as the basis of its own propaganda. Its petition, drawn up by the editor of the *Birmingham Journal*, became as familiar to early Chartist crowds as the Charter itself. 'Heaven has dealt graciously by the people, but the foolishness of our rulers has made the goodness of God of none effect.'

At the enormous Birmingham meeting of 6 August 1838, when the Charter was accepted as the programme of a united national movement, the voices of the L.W.M.A. and the B.P.U. were augmented by a new voice, that of Feargus O'Connor. It was a powerful Irish voice, designed to appeal to large crowds of overworked, uneducated and hungry people, and it soon became—or so O'Connor and his supporters believed—the voice of Chartism itself. Before the Birmingham meeting O'Connor had already established himself in the troubled North of England, where the agitation for factory reform and against the new Poor Law of 1834 had stirred working-men to the point of rebellion. Oastler in the West Riding and J. R. Stephens, a Methodist preacher in Lancashire, had already

[1] Place Papers, B.M., Add. MSS. 27,819, f. 153.

drawn revolutionary distinctions between the law of Malthus and the law of God, and had demanded 'sturdy resistance' from the Northern operatives. O'Connor, who had quarrelled bitterly with the L.W.M.A. in 1837, led the angry crowds of 'fustian jackets and unshorn chins' from an attack on the 'twin bastilles' of the factory and workhouse to a fight for the Charter. He had little sympathy with the tactics of men like Lovett and Attwood. His newspaper, the *Northern Star*, first published in November 1837, gave full details of the local struggles and the forms of central leadership for which the more militant local Chartists craved. Before 1838 was out, the *Northern Star* was selling 50,000 copies a week, and O'Connor had won active support in the strongholds of many other working-class leaders. He had gained a foothold in London in the earlier 1830s and had quarrelled with Lovett about working-class politics long before the Charter was published: in 1838 he succeeded in gaining a foothold in Birmingham and the Midlands also, particularly among the heavy-industry workers of the Black Country. He was even beginning to be known in the small towns of the West Country where there were decaying pockets of industry. It was a feature of Chartism that it flourished in such soil as well as in big new industrial cities like Manchester. Only in the remote country-side and in towns like St. Helens, where there was a considerable variety of occupations and a fair degree of prosperity, did it find growth difficult. Wherever it grew, the appeal of O'Connor grew with it.

The main purpose of the nation-wide Chartist meetings in the summer and autumn of 1838 was to elect representatives to a Chartist convention to prepare a petition to Parliament stating the Chartist case. In February 1839 the convention met in London. It proudly called itself the People's Parliament and was convened the day before Parliament itself gathered; some of its members even put the letters M.C. after their names. The members of the Convention had plenty of time on their hands, for their petition was not ready until May. The more they talked, the more the differences between their backgrounds and attitudes became apparent. They were united on the Charter itself but on little else, and as soon as they started to debate what they would do if the petition were rejected by the House of Commons, they quarrelled bitterly. Some of them wanted the convention to deepen its roots in the country and to become a kind of anti-Parliament: others wanted 'ulterior measures' to intimidate the real Parliament—a 'national holiday' or 'sacred month', withdrawal of money from banks, or the use of physical force. The tone of some of the extreme speeches is well illustrated in a sentence of Dr. Fletcher, the delegate from Bury in Lancashire—'he would not recommend the use of daggers against a Rural Police, but he would recommend every man to have a loaded bludgeon as nearly like that of the policeman's as possible'[1]; Harney, who wore the red cap of liberty to show that he was a revolutionary Chartist, put the matter more tersely, 'before the end of the year, the people shall have universal suffrage or death'. Such speeches alienated the more moderate members of the convention, beginning with J. P. Cobbett, the lawyer son of the great radical, who left on the first day. He was soon followed by the Birmingham middle-class delegates, led by Attwood. By the time that the convention decided to move from London to Birmingham on 13 May it had already lost many of its members, and a series of questions it put to its local supporters about the right tactics to pursue in the future were bound to provoke further disagreement. Its decision that 'peace, law and order shall continue to be the motto of this convention' was immediately qualified with the proviso 'so long as our oppressors shall act in the same spirit'.

In July 1839 the House of Commons rejected by 235 votes to 46 a motion by Thomas Attwood that it should go into committee to consider the Chartist petition. Attwood talked more of the currency question than of universal suffrage; Disraeli took the opportunity to affirm that however much he disapproved of the Charter he sympathized with the Chartists; Russell called the Chartists a 'fraction of the working classes'. The debate showed how little the Chartists could expect from the House of Commons, as did all later parliamentary debates on Chartism. The numbers at the convention subsequently became even smaller and the language more violent, and after riots in July some of the Chartist leaders, including Lovett himself, were arrested at Birmingham and sent to gaol; others were arrested later in the summer. After long and acrimonious debates the rump of the convention which had returned to London was dissolved in September 1839.

The arrest of well-known Chartist personalities and the failure of the convention threw back on local leaders the burden of maintaining Chartist vitality. A confused period followed in which some leaders

---

[1] Quoted M. Hovell, *The Chartist Movement* (1925), p. 128.

opposed the use of force, others supported it in argument, and a few supported it in practice. On the dark and stormy night of 3 November 1839, John Frost, a draper, ex-mayor, ex-magistrate and member of the convention, led a few thousand Welsh colliers in an armed march on Newport, a monster demonstration against the arrest of Henry Vincent, a popular Chartist leader in Wales and the West. The demonstration failed, and with it any possibility of bigger attempts to concert physical force measures. Frost and the other leaders were sentenced to death, and although as a result of a series of meetings and demonstrations throughout the country the sentences were commuted to transportation for life, much of the power had gone out of Chartism. By the end of June 1840 at least 500 Chartist leaders were in gaol. In the North of England General Sir Charles Napier, who was appointed to the command of the Northern District of the army in February 1839, was skilful enough to 'calm things down' as well as to maintain order. His sympathies were genuinely with the Chartists, and they were more effective in practice than the noisy sympathies of men like Disraeli. 'Would that I had gone to Australia and thus been saved this work, produced by Tory injustice and Whig imbecility', he wrote in his *Journal* in April 1839; 'the doctrine of slowly reforming when men are starving is of all things the most silly: famishing men cannot wait.'[1]

It was, above all else, the continued existence of hunger which kept Chartism alive. Out of the tribulations of 1839–40 a genuine effort was made to create a more effective Chartist organization. Before this date there had been no national Chartist organization at all, and most local organizations had been weak. Some of the Scots Chartists led the way in 1839 in pressing for a system of strong and 'enlightened' organization which would secure payment of members' dues and spread the gospel of reform as the means to 'good government and pure and virtuous institutions'. Their example was copied in Newcastle and in London, and in July 1840 a Manchester conference, dominated by the followers of Feargus O'Connor, founded the National Charter Association. Although the Corresponding Societies Act of 1799 was still in operation, and it was illegal to form societies with branches, the N.C.A. went far to centralize leadership, to provide machinery for collecting regular subscriptions (1*d.* per week), and to mobilize support in the smallest

[1] Sir W. Napier, *The Life and Opinions of General Napier* (1857), vol. II, p. 22.

units of the association—wards and 'classes' of ten. The new
association made considerable progress, but its local organization
was often weak and careless, and it was never supported by Lovett
or most of O'Connor's fiercest critics. On leaving gaol in 1841
Lovett turned to educational reform and set up a society for the
'political and social improvement of the people'; he was more
violently criticized by O'Connor than ever before. So too was
Bronterre O'Brien, the first theorist of Chartism, who finally broke
with O'Connor in 1842. The N.C.A. became O'Connor's organization, and after its leader had spent a few months in prison in 1841,
it was the N.C.A. which drafted a new petition to Parliament to
reconsider the Charter. This time the Chartist case was rejected by
287 votes to 59, Roebuck seizing the opportunity to attack O'Connor
as a 'malignant and cowardly demagogue'. The most eloquent
speech was that of Macaulay who affirmed that universal suffrage
would be 'fatal to the purposes for which government exists' and
was 'utterly incompatible with the existence of civilization. In
every constituent body throughout the empire capital and accumulated property' will be 'placed absolutely at the foot of labour'.

   From the date of the defeat of the second petition in 1842 Chartism
lost much of its vitality. Even before the business revival began, the
appeal of Chartism was being undermined not only by personal and
sectional differences but by the growing power of the Anti-Corn
Law League and the revival of trade unionism. O'Connor himself
became increasingly interested not in the six points of the Charter
but in a scheme for settling families on the land as permanent
smallholders. He glibly emphasized his 'faith in progress, in the
perfectibility of every human mind',[1] but he saw resettlement on
the land as a means to greater agricultural production and to greater
individual 'self-reliance'. There was no suggestion of common
ownership in his proposals, which were first mooted in 1841 and
took formal shape in the setting up of a Chartist Co-operative Land
Society in 1845. From 1845 to 1847 the Land Plan dominated
Chartism. That it ultimately failed, crashing in 1848, was no indication that it lacked an appeal in the early and mid-1840s. There
were considerable numbers of working-men who looked back to
the land and dreamed of independence instead of 'enslavement and
degradation'; they were as confused as O'Connor about the sort of
economy and society they wanted, but their confusion merely drew

[1] *The Labourer*, vol. I (1847), p. 73.

them nearer to him. When he compared the effect of machinery on working-men's lives with the effects of the coming of the railway on horses, he was talking not to Chartist theoreticians like O'Brien or Chartist educators like Lovett but to unhappy and frustrated people. He certainly did not stop to ask himself, as O'Brien did, whether a revived and probably conservative peasantry would take the slightest interest in the political programmes he and his fellow Chartists were advocating. To his left-wing critics he declared boldly, 'my plan has no more to do with Socialism than it has with the comet'.[1]

The economic crisis of 1847 and 1848 turned Chartism back to the six points and gave it a final lease of life. As news was received of revolutions in Italy and France in the early spring of 1848, the Chartists began to organize a third petition (this time with five points, the ballot being dropped). A new convention was called to London—it included only five men who had been present at the first convention of 1839—and after persistent bickering decided that if the new petition were rejected it would summon a National Assembly. O'Brien opposed these tactics on practical grounds and complained that O'Connor had 'discredited all the efficient advocates of Chartism'. He was out of tune with most of the delegates, however, and full-scale plans went ahead for a mass demonstration on Kennington Common and the presentation of the new petition on 10 April.

The so-called 'fiasco of Kennington Common' did not bring Chartism to an end, but it demonstrated clearly why from the start the movement had been doomed to failure. Before the mass demonstration took place, the home secretary, the Duke of Wellington, and a large number of special constables (including Prince Louis Napoleon, soon to be Napoleon III), took formidable precautions to protect property and preserve law and order in the metropolis. The Chartist decision to go ahead with their plans even though the home secretary announced that a procession from the Common to Westminster would be illegal, was more a piece of *bravado* than of courage or sound judgement. The London Chartists were in fact badly organized,[2] and as Harney remarked later 'every hour the strength of our adversary, and our own weakness became more

---

[1] *Northern Star*, 15 April 1843.
[2] London had never really been an effective Chartist centre, and at the Convention of 1839 delegates had been shocked by public apathy.

and more apparent'.[1] When the great day came there was a smaller Chartist crowd on the Common than had been anticipated, and O'Connor immediately capitulated when the Superintendent of Metropolitan Police told him to abandon the idea of carrying the petition *en masse* from South London to Westminster. Heavy rain brought the speeches to an end, and the crowd dispersed. The petition was subsequently shown to include large numbers of forged signatures—what petition of the period would not?—and Parliament was able to dismiss Chartism for a third time with no great difficulty. The provincial flames took longer to quench, and after the national Assembly had been called in May there were serious Chartist disturbances in the north of England, particularly where there was a powerful Irish element in the population.

Perhaps the most important point that the whole story of Chartism demonstrated was not the weakness of the English working classes in the society of the 1840s but the strength of the middle classes. On the eve of the demonstration 'the shopkeeping and other middle classes' in London had complained of the 'apathy and inaction of the government' and pressed for a display of strength,[2] and in an interesting letter written after the Kennington Common incident by Lady Palmerston to Mrs. Huskisson, one sentence about 'our revolution' stands out. 'I am sure that it is very fortunate that the whole thing has occurred as it has shown the good spirit of our middle classes.'[3] There would never have been such an abundance of 'good spirit' had it not been for the energetic performance and achievements of the great middle-class organization which, like Chartism, grew out of the economic depression—the Anti-Corn Law League. The contrast between the two movements is not only a contrast between the melodramatic and irresolute domination of O'Connor and the effective and at times brilliant leadership of Cobden: it is a contrast between two segments of a divided society.

4. THE ANTI-CORN LAW LEAGUE

The Anti-Corn Law League was the second great extra-parliamentary pressure group which emerged from the economic crisis of 1838–9 and the radical impasse in the House of Commons. On 14 March 1839, Melbourne declared 'before God' that to leave the

---

[1] *Northern Star*, 2 February 1850.

[2] C. E. Trevelyan to Russell, 4 April 1848. P.R.O. 30/22/7. (I owe this reference to Mr. F. C. Mather.)

[3] Quoted C. R. Fay, *Huskisson and His Age* (1951), pp. 137–8.

whole agricultural interest without protection was 'the wildest and maddest scheme that has ever entered into the imagination of man to conceive'; six days later, a great meeting of delegates from different anti-corn law associations, which had been established in various parts of the country, decided to found a national organization to be called the Anti-Corn Law League. Its object was simple and direct—the total repeal of the corn laws.

Until the depression, interest in the question of the corn laws, which had been strong after Waterloo and in the 1820s, greatly diminished. There were operative anti-corn law societies like the Mechanics' Anti-Bread Tax Society at Sheffield, but 'no person above the rank of a small tradesman' bothered to pay much attention to the cause in the early 1830s : in 1836 an Anti-Corn Law Association was set up in London, but it lacked unity of purpose and effective leadership. Anti-corn law literature preceded anti-corn law organization. In 1827 Colonel Thomas Perronet Thompson produced his famous *Catechism on the Corn Laws* with its brilliant sequence of questions and answers: in 1830 Ebenezer Elliott, 'the Bard of Free Trade', wrote his *Corn Law Rhymes* with their accent on the pathos and tragedy of hunger and the social contrasts between a handful of 'wicked monopolists' and the starving thousands:

> Ye coop us up and tax our bread
> And wonder why we pine,
> But ye are fat and round and red
> And filled with tax bought wine.

Even Elliott admitted, however, that before the pathos and tragedy of the social situation could be generally appreciated and the proper conclusions drawn, businessmen had to feel the pressure of falling profit margins and economic failure. 'Wisehead, at last', he remarked, 'was born of Empty-Pocket in a respectable neighbourhood; and from that moment Monopoly began to tremble.'[1] Richard Cobden, the leader of the national agitation, was less rhetorical but equally frank. 'I am afraid', he said, 'that most of us entered upon the struggle with the belief that we had some distinct class interest in the question.'[2] Pride in the triumphs of industry and an acute sense of the urgency of its current problems gave momentum to the repeal agitation from the start.

[1] *More Prose and Verse* (1850), vol. I, p. vi.
[2] Quoted by J. Morley, *The Life of Richard Cobden* (1881), vol. I, p. 95.

The struggle began very modestly in Manchester in September 1838, when seven men, including the old Manchester radical Archibald Prentice, meeting behind a dingy red curtain in a room above the hotel stables, set up the Anti-Corn Law Association. Very quickly, however, the new association mobilized influential support among Manchester liberals and businessmen, won over the Chamber of Commerce and began corresponding with other associations in different parts of the country. A lecturer was appointed as a missionary of free trade, and Joseph Parkes, with all his wide experience of political organization, was selected as agent in London. George Wilson, the talented chairman, who had served his political apprenticeship in the movement for the incorporation of Manchester, and Richard Cobden, a Manchester manufacturer with a Sussex farming background, who rightly became known as 'the impersonation of the free trade principle', were shrewd tacticians in refusing to merge the demand for total and immediate corn law repeal in a wide programme of radical reform. They saw the advantages of a single formula which everyone could understand and they accurately assessed the particular appeal of that formula in the new industrial areas of England.

Although the formula had very practical implications for harassed middle-class manufacturers, it had moral undertones as well and could be made to appeal to a broad coalition of interests. Richard Cobden, in particular, soon came to the conclusion that free trade in corn would settle four outstanding problems at the same time. First, it would guarantee the prosperity of the manufacturer by affording him outlets for his products. Second, it would relieve 'the condition of England question' by cheapening the price of food and ensuring more regular employment. Third, it would make English agriculture more efficient by stimulating demand for its products in urban and industrial areas. Fourth, it would introduce through mutually advantageous international trade a new era of international fellowship and peace. The only barrier to these four beneficent solutions was the ignorant self-interest of the landlords, 'the bread-taxing oligarchy, unprincipled, unfeeling, rapacious and plundering'.[1]

The presentation of the case of the repealers in these terms turned a political movement into a moral crusade. Not only was class interest 'widened into a consciousness of a commanding national

---

[1] J. Almack, *Character, Motives and Proceedings of the Anti-Corn Law Leaguers* (1843).

interest', but that interest was conceived in humanitarian and religious as well as economic terms. The very language of men like Cobden and even more later on of John Bright was dominated by Biblical metaphors and images. Texts sprang to their lips as easily as statistics,[1] and they hoped that Manchester would become identified to all eyes with their cause, 'just as Jerusalem was the centre of our faith'.

The Anti-Corn Law League was not a democratic body. Control was vested in a council of large subscribers, each subscription of £50 carrying with it one vote. Cobden was its master tactician and in 1841 he made his famous alliance with John Bright, the Quaker industrialist of Rochdale, whereby they both pledged themselves not to rest until the corn laws were repealed. The accession of Bright to the movement brought to its service not only a great orator, who was scathingly effective both in social denunciation and in homely moralizing, but one of the key figures in the unfolding story of nineteenth-century English Liberalism. His enemies accused him of extremism, of impetuosity, and of pitting class against class; his friends and supporters began to regard him as a prophet, relating shifting practical politics to the eternal truths of the moral law.

The League was never the pure-hearted and utterly unselfish crusade which Bright claimed it to be. Whatever may be said of its objective, its arguments were often inconsistent and contradictory[2] and its means were sometimes controversial and even dubious. Its speakers drew different deductions, for instance, in their analysis of the likely effects of repeal on wages—some claiming that it would reduce money wages and thereby make British industry more competitive, others arguing that through increased employment it would raise them. Cobden himself on one occasion prophesied that there would be no catastrophic fall in wheat prices after repeal; more frequently he maintained that the consumer was paying a large and unnecessary tax on a staple commodity. The methods of the League were as mixed as its arguments. They included not only the peaceful pursuit of missionary propaganda but the same sort of pressure on the electorate as the older political parties were prepared to employ. In particular, the utmost importance was attached to registration, and great efforts were made both to create new votes for free traders

---

[1] For instance, 'Behold, I have heard that there is corn in Egypt; get you down thither, and buy for us from them, that we may live and not die.'

[2] See *The Speech of Mr. George Game Day at Huntingdon, 17 June 1843* (1844), for an extremely effective contemporary analysis of League arguments.

and to remove hostile Conservatives from the register. The League created an extremely effective organization, which has rightly been claimed as an important milestone in the development of English political institutions. Conservative critics attacked it as the 'foulest and most dangerous combination of modern times', and *The Times* condemned Cobden and Bright as 'authors of incendiary clap trap', but such denunciation was as exaggerated as the high moral claims of many of the League's sponsors. In fact, the Anti-Corn Law League was a successful experiment in the formation and management of *national* public opinion, and with its large funds, its efficient centralized office organization, and its consistency of purpose, it challenged existing ideas not only of political machinery but of the scope of politics itself. It showed a marked advance on earlier local forms of political organization, like the Birmingham Political Union, and an enormous advance when compared with bodies like the General Chamber of Manufacturers which had tried for the first time to mobilize business interests in the 1780s.[1] In its style it owed much to the movement for the abolition of slavery[2]; in its structure it pointed forward to later organizations like the National Reform Union and the Reform League of the 1860s.[3]

It was in 1841 when the decision was taken to start contesting elections that the League began to loom large in national life, and at the general election of that year a number of Leaguers were elected to Parliament, including Cobden himself at Stockport. The parliamentary foothold, which the Chartists lacked, was invaluable to the cause. 'You speak with a loud voice', Cobden came to realize, 'when you are talking on the floor of the House; and if you have anything to say that hits hard, it is a very long whip and reaches all over the kingdom.'[4] In March 1845 the whip was cracked near at hand. After listening to a long factual speech by Cobden, Peel crumpled up his notes and said to his colleague, Sidney Herbert, who was sitting next to him, '*You* must answer this for *I* cannot'.[5]

Peel had already gone far to liberalize trade in his budget of 1842 and had reformed the corn law of 1828 in the same year, but the League was not satisfied by what it regarded merely as concessions.

---

[1] See above, pp. 116–17.
[2] Cobden admitted this, and related both earlier movements and his own to the 'Wesleyan model' which he felt they had intentionally or unintentionally copied. See Morley, *op. cit.*, vol. I, p. 126.
[3] See below, pp. 496–7.
[4] Morley, *op. cit.*, vol. I, p. 211.
[5] *Ibid.*, p. 213.

In the grim summer of 1842 there were violent denunciations of Parliament by inflammatory League speakers, and working-class riots and strikes in the north of England for which not only the Chartists but some of the members of the League were held to be in part responsible. Some Leaguers prodded their workpeople into striking, and others who were local magistrates neglected their duties in order to allow the movement to get under way. When they saw that working-class leaders were men more interested in 'a fair day's wages for a fair day's work' than in immediate repeal they changed sides and helped to suppress the revolt.[1]

The aftermath of this episode was a tense scene between Peel and Cobden in the House in 1843. Cobden declared that he held Peel personally responsible for the dangerous situation in the country and the overwrought Peel, whose secretary had just been assassinated by a madman, retaliated by claiming that Cobden was actively encouraging a mood of violence and disturbance, even threatening him with assassination. When times improved and the corn laws were repealed, Peel was generous in paying special tribute to Cobden, who had advocated repeal 'with untiring energy', 'from pure and disinterested motives'.

Between 1841 and 1846 the success of the League fluctuated with the state of the harvests and the economic conditions of the masses of the population. In 1841 and 1842, when harvests were bad and unemployment widespread, there were remarkable advances both in propaganda technique and organization. More characteristic than the flirtation with violence was the appeal to 'the politics which flow from pity, the politics of the gospel'.[2] A great conference of ministers of religion at Manchester in August 1841—Wesleyan Methodists were conspicuously few—led to a diffusion of repeal ideas from scores of pulpits. The organizer of the conference was George Thompson, a leading figure in the abolitionist cause, and considerable emotional energy was generated in the attempt to prove the corn laws 'anti-scriptural and anti-religious, opposed to the law of God'. Nor were the simpler techniques of organization forgotten by the League. The new Penny Post, introduced in 1840, was employed to collect funds and to distribute tons of tracts—as

[1] See G. Kitson Clark, 'Hunger and Politics in 1842' in *J.M.H.* (1953), for a full and sensitive analysis of the context and significance of the disturbances. 'The evidence', he concludes, 'does not point to a real danger to the state, but . . . to a very serious fissure in the community.' The leadership of the league was itself divided.
[2] *Report of the Conference of Ministers of All Denominations on the Corn Laws* (1841).

many as three and a half tons of tracts were delivered from Manchester in a week. From December 1842 onwards the *Anti-Corn
Law Circular* was published weekly instead of fortnightly, often with
tracts stitched into its pages, and subsidies were paid to the London
Sun. The new magazine the *Economist*, which first appeared in 1843,
received the full support of the League. In addition, there were more
characteristically 'Victorian' propaganda devices, many of which in
Cobden's phrases marked off the League as 'a middle-class set of
agitators'. 'We have obtained the co-operation of the ladies', he went
on; 'we have resorted to tea parties.'[1] Anti-Corn Law League
bazaars were held, where customers could buy free trade hand-
kerchiefs, anti-corn law breadplates and teapots and anti-monopoly
pin cushions.[2] In January 1843 a Free Trade Hall built in six weeks
and capable of holding seven to eight thousand people was opened
in Manchester on the site of the Peterloo massacre. It was to be used
exclusively by the League.[3] By that time a centralized £50,000 fund
had been established to guarantee the success of the organization.
It was followed by a £100,000 fund in 1844, when businessmen were
more prosperous than two years before. Cobden and Bright were
very efficient money-raisers and there was no lack of wealthy
provincial donors, like Thomas Thomasson of Bolton, who was
often the first man to put down his name in collection lists, never
for sums of less than £1,000. To try to tap the support—financial
and otherwise—of London, the League moved its office to the
capital early in 1843, and went on to organize 136 meetings there
during that year, some of them in Drury Lane theatre. The move
had great psychological importance and helped to win over the
London press which had previously been able to sneer at the League
as a provincial product. 'A new power had arisen in the state', wrote
The Times, 'and maids and matrons flock to theatres as though it were
but a new translation from the French. . . . We acknowledge that
we dislike gregarious collections of Cant and Cotton men. But we
cannot doubt that whatever is the end of this agitation, it will expire
only to bequeath its violence and its turbulence to some successor.'[4]

In 1843 the limbs of the organization were stretched into the

---

[1] Quoted Morley, *op. cit.*, vol. I, p. 249.
[2] The great Manchester bazaar of 1842 was described as having more of 'the
character of a great art Exposition than of a mere bazaar'. It pointed the way forward
to the Great Exhibition of 1851.
[3] The imposing Free Trade Hall in 'the Lombard-Venetian style of architecture',
which was badly bombed in December 1940, was opened in 1856.
[4] 18 November 1843.

countryside as well as the metropolis and the towns. Up to this point, the League had mainly emphasized the evil effects of the corn laws on operatives and industrialists, shopkeepers and merchants. It now turned its attention to the tenant farmers and the village labourers in the countryside. Cobden and his colleagues stressed that protection was no substitute for improved farming, the only sound foundation of a healthy agriculture, that the corn laws disorganized corn trade and prices, that the interest of tenant farmers diverged sharply from those of their landlords, particularly in such matters as leases and game laws, that village labourers were among the most oppressed sections of the population, and that farmers' prosperity depended on industrial demand. League propaganda in the country had a real though limited appeal. Most farmers were unconvinced and some supported protectionist counter-organizations, such as the Essex Agricultural Protection Society which began to follow the example of its opponents in making appeals to public opinion.[1] A loosely-knit central co-ordinating body, the Anti-League, as it has been called, mobilized much protectionist support, but it found the task of sustaining a prolonged agitation far more difficult than the League. It was not easy to agitate in a social environment where the 'noise made by lecturing and talking' at an Anti-League meeting might drive the local landed gentry to fear that one of their own speakers 'would raise up a revolution'.[2] Outside that rural environment, though the Anti-League made some efforts to win the support of the working men, it had little real chance of appealing successfully to the Chartists.

Relations between the Anti-Corn Law League itself and the Chartists were often equally difficult in the industrial areas, although by 1843 the League was by far the stronger of the two pressure groups, and at a famous Northampton debate in August 1844 Cobden won a great success over Feargus O'Connor, who had to end by agreeing with Cobden that the corn laws were a great evil. Matters had not always been so simple. Many Chartists considered the League in its early days as an interloper, and the demand for free trade as a means to lower wages and a red herring to divert workers from the central battle for parliamentary reform. League meetings were noisily interrupted or broken up, and 'fustian confronted broadcloth, the dignity of nature against the distinction of wealth'.[3]

[1] For farmers' attitudes, see A. Somerville, *Whistler at the Plough* (1852).
[2] See G. L. Mosse, 'The Anti-League' in *Ec. Hist. Rev.* (1947).
[3] *Northern Star*, 3 July 1841.

The basis of opposition between the two bodies was essentially class antagonism. There was little in common between the *Northern Star* with its attacks on the 'millocrats' and the *Circular* with its skilful homilies and its carefully weighed statistics. Whatever the ideas of the Chartists concerning free trade—some were convinced protectionists, others repealers—they were agreed in treating the Leaguers with suspicion as members of a different section of society. At the general election of 1841 many of them supported the Tory candidates. When in 1840 in Sunderland the free traders called on the Chartists to aid their agitation, the two local Chartist leaders, both moderate repealers, replied: 'What is our present relation to you as a section of the middle class? It is one of violent opposition. You are the holders of power, participation in which you refuse us; for demanding which you persecute us with a malignity paralleled only by the ruffian Tories. We are therefore surprised that you should ask us to co-operate with you.'[1]

One serious attempt was made in 1841 and 1842 to bridge such class cleavages, the Complete Suffrage Union. It was preceded by an abortive attempt at Leeds in the autumn of 1840. Significantly enough the centre of the new agitation was Birmingham, normally a stronghold of social peace, and the sponsor was a Quaker, Joseph Sturge, a corn miller and formerly a leader of the local anti-slavery movement. Sturge and his friends set out in November 1841 to build a popular organization based on both repeal and an extension of the suffrage. A wider suffrage, they believed, would not only extend political justice in the same way that abolition of the corn laws would extend economic justice; it was necessary also in order to push legislation like the repeal of the corn laws through a half-reformed Parliament.

At the peak of its popularity the Complete Suffrage Union claimed between fifty and sixty branches in different towns and cities, and won the support of the new magazine the *Nonconformist*, edited by Edward Miall, who published an important series of articles in the autumn of 1841 on the 'reconciliation of the middle and labouring classes'. Officially the League stood aloof from the new movement; in fact, its leading members disagreed about the correct way to deal with the political arguments Sturge put forward. Some of them, like Bright, gave considerable support to Sturge, and in April 1842 attended the Birmingham conference of the Union, which was also

[1] *Northern Liberator*, 23 May 1840.

attended by Lovett, O'Brien, Vincent and many of the Chartist leaders. Cobden was lukewarm in public and hostile in private—he did not want to divert energy from the battle for repeal—and his fears seemed justified when the conference carried the six points of the Charter and divided only on the policy of retaining the name 'Charter' in the new plan of campaign. A further conference in December 1842 split on this second issue and revealed the depth of class divisions. It was attended by O'Connor and many of his followers, and all the Chartists present, including moderates like Lovett, stood by the name which had now become a symbol of everything in which they believed. The conference broke up when Sturge and his friends, completely outvoted, left the hall. That the class feeling was not confined to one side is clearly demonstrated in a remark by Sturge's biographer; 'Mr Sturge's friends felt thankful that this result left him at liberty honourably to withdraw from much uncongenial fellowship.'[1]

The failure of the Complete Suffrage Union and the weakness of the Chartists in the years after 1842 left the Anti-Corn Law League almost a monopolist in the pressure-group politics of the years 1842–6. In the decisive years 1845 and 1846, when the corn law question was forced to the attention of Peel and was dividing his party, the Chartists were silent. How far Peel was converted to repeal by the League is a different and difficult question. For long, protectionists had been suspicious of him and repealers had considered him as the great hope. As early as 1842, for instance, Ebenezer Elliott wrote that 'Peel, I have long thought, understands our position, and will do his best to prevent the coming catastrophe, but he wants moral courage.'[2] Between 1842 and 1845 Peel's 'understanding' grew. He became convinced that the corn laws were not necessary for the prosperity of British agriculture and that if it could be shown that they were causing suffering they would have to be repealed. In May 1845, before the failure of the Irish potato crop provided an opportunity for change, Cobden was convinced that Peel was only waiting for a suitable occasion to abolish the corn laws. The conversion of the prime minister to free trade, however, certainly did not imply an acceptance of the full Cobdenite doctrine. He was more interested in practical questions than in ideologies. Faced with a difficult situation—famine and unrest in Ireland—he decided that the

[1] Quoted by H. Richard, *Memoirs of Joseph Sturge* (1864), p. 318.
[2] G. S. Phillips, *Memoirs of Ebenezer Elliott* (1852), pp. 103–4.

moment had come to act, and Cobden himself admitted that 'the League would not have carried the repeal of the corn laws when they did had it not been for the Irish famine and the circumstances that we had a Minister who thought more of the lives of the people than his own continuance in power'.[1]

The background of Peel's decision must be re-examined in the light of his policy as prime minister between 1841 and 1846. It must be remembered in a more general context, however, that by 1845 the forces opposed to repeal had been broken up and sharply reduced. For all the League's attack on the landlords as the villains of society, many of the big landlords, particularly those with urban and industrial properties, like Earl Fitzwilliam, had little interest in continued protection. The most active group which demanded protection was made up of tenant farmers, whose agitation on the eve of repeal was in line with a whole series of agitations in which they had taken part after the end of the war in 1815. Many of the tenant farmers felt that they were betrayed in 1846 as they had been by the Currency Act in 1819, and on both occasions it was Peel who had been responsible. Their angry feelings were demonstrated by the fact that in the parliamentary division list of 1846 107 county members voted against repeal and only 25 in favour. But the 'country party' was a minority both in the electorate and in the economy, and its political power had declined between 1815 and the 1840s. Behind the scenes, the administration—particularly the administration of the Board of Trade—had long depended on convinced free traders, men like Deacon Hume and J. R. McGregor, who took free trade arguments for granted in their evidence before the one-sided Select Committee on Import Duties in 1840. At the front of the political stage, the Whigs changed their minds in 1845 and 1846. In the middle of the potato crisis in 1845 Lord John Russell, the Whig leader, in his famous Edinburgh letter, announced his abandonment of Whig belief in a fixed duty on corn and his conversion to full free trade. In the divisions of the next year only nine Whigs voted against repeal, five of whom were county members. Such a notable degree of loyalty and support suggest that the attitude of the Whigs in 1846 was very similar to that they had displayed in 1832: they recognized that aristocracy had to make concessions if it wished to retain its social and political force. Between 1846 and 1852 the Tory protectionists in turn had to make their peace with the new fiscal

---

[1] G. J. Holyoake, *Sixty Years of an Agitator's Life* (1892), vol. II, p. 229.

system. Mid-Victorian England did not dismantle the landed aristocracy, as Bright had desired, but it accepted almost without question the necessity of free trade. As a prize essayist of the League, Henry Dunckley, proudly affirmed in 1854, 'it would be just as reasonable to accept the Ptolemaic system as the true philosophy of the heavens, or the physics of the schoolmen as a true exposition of the laws of nature, as to admit the theories of Protection in questions relating to industry and commerce'.[1]

Economic historians have recently reduced the economic arguments in favour of repeal in the 1840s to something like their true proportions. The most important protection of British agriculture before and after 1846 was not the existence of the corn laws but the geographical protection afforded by the difficulties of importing large quantities of foreign corn from great distances and tapping new sources of supply outside the area of European production. The claim of the League that the abolition of the corn laws would open up an enormous range of foreign markets was exaggerated and only sketchily supported by statistical enquiry: the chances of British manufacturers being successful in overseas markets depended on other factors besides the corn laws. The prosperity of mid-Victorian England did not rest entirely or even mainly on the decisions arrived at in 1846, but on a variety of economic circumstances many of which had little to do with either the positive or the negative actions of government.

When exaggerated statements of economic cause and effect are discounted, the main significance of the battle against the corn laws stands out as being social and political. The League mobilized middle-class opinion and secured some working-class backing in its struggle against 'the lords and great proprietors of the soil'. During the course of that struggle the British aristocracy as a whole was criticized more sharply than it had ever been criticized before—on economic, social, political and moral grounds. Whereas in 1830–2 only that section of the aristocracy which resisted all reform was bitterly attacked, in the years before 1846 some of the leaders of the League spared no landlord, not even the landlord who was in favour of repeal. They felt that 'their pride as an order' as well as their interests were at stake. Far-sighted commentators—including Peel himself—had prophesied in 1832 that the effect of the Reform Bill would be to destroy the social system which the corn laws

[1] *Op. cit.*, p. 97.

attempted to bolster. The League did its best to make the prophecy
come true.

But 1846 was not a complete middle-class triumph. The aristocracy yielded, the working classes were never completely convinced,
and the prime minister responsible for the surrender did not
conceive of his own actions in terms of middle-class strategy. Peel
was as sensitive as his Tory opponents, but more realistically so, to
the bogey of a 'dull succession of enormous manufacturing towns,
connected by railways, intersecting abandoned tracts which it was
no longer profitable to cultivate'. In his speech announcing the
repeal proposals he continued to claim, as he had always done, that
'the land is subject to particular burdens' and that equivalent
compensation in some form or other was necessary to replace the
unconditional loss of duty. Repeal had been necessary in the
national interest, and not in the interests of town versus country or
businessmen versus aristocrats. This was a fundamental thesis which
Peel proclaimed in the summer of 1846 when he urged that the object
of the repeal had been 'to terminate a conflict, which according to
our belief, would soon place in hostile collision great and powerful
classes in this country'. Unless that conflict were terminated, the
aristocracy would never be 'popular' again, the 'middle classes'
would be drawn away from their industry, and the 'working classes'
would be alienated.

Such a thesis contrasted boldly with the only thesis which
Cobden and the leaders of the League considered logical and in
keeping with the 'spirit of the age'. Perhaps the most interesting
exchange of political letters in the nineteenth century was that
between Cobden and Peel three days before Peel was defeated by a
hostile coalition of political opponents after repeal had been passed.
In a letter, which Cobden described as 'exclusively for our own eyes',
Peel was told flatteringly that he represented 'the IDEA of the age
and it has no other representative among statesmen'. He was asked
to appeal to the nation on the hustings cry of 'Peel and Free Trade',
and was guaranteed the support of 'every important constituency'
in the country. 'Now I anticipate what is passing in your mind',
Cobden went on. 'Do you shrink from the post of governing
through the *bona fide* representatives of the middle class? Look at
the facts, and can the country otherwise be ruled at all? There must
be an end of the juggle of parties, the mere representatives of
traditions, and some man must of necessity rule the state through

its governing class. The Reform Bill decreed it; the passing of the Corn Bill has realized it.' In his reply Peel completely by-passed the middle-class Marxist arguments used by Cobden, and talked not in terms of social classes and political necessities but, instead, of personal inclinations and public duty. 'I must be insane', he said in his most revealing sentence, 'if I could have been induced by anything but a sense of public duty to undertake what I have undertaken in this session.'[1] To understand the nature of Peel's reply—why he rejected the logic of the League—it is necessary to turn in more detail to the successes and dilemmas of his great creative ministry from 1841–46, a ministry which because of what it accomplished split his party.

5. PEEL AND HIS ACHIEVEMENT

Between 1832 and 1841, when he came back into office with a large majority, Peel steered the Conservative party through many difficult seas. At the election of 1841 the party was a far stronger and more efficient vessel than it had been either during the Reform Bill debates or in the short-lived Peel-Wellington ministry of 1834–5.

Peel himself was not directly responsible for the main work of party building. He was not interested in the details of routine management, but he exercised great influence on his parliamentary party and determined the general direction in which it moved. While F. R. Bonham, who had been chosen as Tory election manager in 1832, reorganized the party from his desk in the Carlton Club—his work was brilliantly but unreasonably caricatured by Disraeli in his account of Mr. Tadpole in *Coningsby*[2]—Peel succeeded both in reuniting his supporters in the House of Commons and in appealing to an increasing body of respectable opinion outside Westminster. Bonham and his assistants helped to mobilize provincial Conservative feeling, encouraged the creation of a network of local Conservative associations and clubs, and supervised registration arrangements; Peel provided what was equally indispensable, leadership and direction.

Three features of his direction of the fortunes of the party were of special importance. First, he avoided what he considered 'factious' opposition and claimed that it was necessary to support the Whig government whenever its members espoused Conservative

---

[1] The letters are printed in Morley, *op. cit.*, Vol. I, ch. xvii.
[2] It was denied at the time that Tadpole *was* Bonham.

principles, 'as I apprehend they must do if they mean to maintain the cause of authority and order'.[1] As a believer in strong government Peel had no desire to weaken the executive. He detested 'anti-governmental principles' for their own sake and preferred the claims of public authority to those of political doctrine. 'We adopt the principles which used to be said to prevail in an administration,' he told 300 of his followers in 1838; 'we not only adopt the principles of a government. We perform many of its functions.'[2] Second, as a corollary of this emphasis, he refused to flirt with radicals or to support those members of his own party like Oastler who wished to outbid the Whigs and to re-state the Tory case in radical terms. Third, also as a necessary corollary, he expected his followers to show the same restraint and responsibility which he showed. He was well aware, as a parliamentary commentator put it in 1836, that the very existence of the Conservative party was 'bound up in him'. The same writer described Peel's followers as 'clay in the hands of the potter', but he went on to point to a possible flaw in the arrangement. Peel, he claimed, 'felt that he could with impunity conceal from them the course he intends to pursue on any given question', knowing that 'however much they may disapprove of that course, they will soon be compelled, by the necessity of the case, to feign, if they do not feel, a disposition to acquiesce in it.'[3] This was to be a fatal flaw. The time was to come when Peel, pre-eminently a man of his own counsels, was to turn his back on the Speaker and his face towards his party, as was his wont, and not receive the expected cheers. When that time came—on the corn law question in 1845 and 1846—his sensitivity to charges of 'treachery' would make the crisis more acute.

This shrewd character sketch is fully corroborated by the evidence of other commentators. Lord Ashley, who never got on with Peel, once described him as 'an iceberg with a slight thaw on the surface'.[4] Daniel O'Connell compared his smile to the gleam on the silver plate of a coffin lid. Newman maintained that it was 'pitiable that such a man should not have understood that a body without a soul has no life, and a political party without an idea no unity'.[5] The young Disraeli, who was in a strong position as a

---

[1] Quoted G. Kitson Clark, *Peel and the Conservative Party* (1929), pp. 83–4.
[2] Quoted W. Cooke Taylor, *Life and Times of Sir Robert Peel* (1846–51), vol. II, p. 57.
[3] J. Grant, *Random Reflections on the House of Commons* (1836), pp. 105–122.
[4] E. Hodder, *The Life and Work of the Seventh Earl of Shaftesbury* (1887), p. 183.
[5] Quoted by R. L. Hill, *Toryism and the People* (1929), p. 68.

brilliant and resourceful coming politician to exploit the deficiencies of an experienced statesman, seized on all these points of weakness in 1845 and 1846. He attacked Peel's sense of responsibility, confounding it with a love of office, criticized his willingness to listen to experts, calling it a burglary of other men's intellects, dismissed his moderation as the absence of principles, and thought of his 'practical mind' as a mind completely untouched by the power of imagination. Above all, at the height of the crisis he played on Peel's 'treachery'. Like the Turkish Lord High Admiral, Peel, he said, had steered the fleet into the enemy's port.

Such comments and criticisms would not have been so telling had Peel been the leader of a party with a reasonably common set of interests and an agreed philosophy. Many of the country gentlemen who supported Peel from 1832 to 1846 did not share his views either on society or on political economy. Some of them joined with Oastler and the Tory-radicals of the North in questioning the philosophy of 'improvement' and in violently attacking the 'Demon called *Liberalism* who is now stalking through the land . . . assuming first one name and then another; March of Intellect, Political Economy, Free Trade, Liberal Principles, etc., but always destroying the peace of the cottage and the happiness of the palace.'[1] Some of them, like the leaders of the new Operative Conservative societies in the industrial towns and cities, were willing to try to protect labour as well as corn, believing that 'the natural protectors of the labouring poor are the owners of the soil'.[2] Some of them still resented the new currency system and the extension of it in the 1840s, while others were deeply concerned about the new fiscal programme to which Peel was increasingly committed. In face of Peel's careful advocacy of 'practical reforms' they were often inarticulate, preferring loyalty to argument, but they were more loyal to their own way of life than to their parliamentary leader. The roots of their loyalty stretched deep into local life and touched religion as well as politics. In Liverpool they called themselves 'Real True Blues and Loyal Jacks'; in Cornwall, they produced a member of Parliament, Sir Richard Vyvyan, eighth baronet of Trelowarren, who was among the first to protest against what he regarded as Peel's attempt to 'convert a body of high-minded noblemen and gentlemen into a regiment of partisans'.[3] Both the

---

[1] Quoted by C. Driver, *Tory Radical, The Life of Richard Oastler* (1946), p. 295.
[2] See R. Oastler, *Letters to the Duke of Wellington* (1835), pp. 35–41.
[3] Quoted by R. L. Hill, *op. cit.*, p. 65.

parliamentary discipline and the programme of 1841–6 chafed them, and Sir James Graham, Peel's chief lieutenant at the Home Office, remarked early in 1845 before the final crisis broke that 'the country gentlemen cannot be more ready to give us the death-blow than we are to receive it. If they will rush on to their own destruction, they must have their way'.[1] After the split Peel himself admitted that he was 'much more surprised that the union was so long maintained than that it was ultimately severed'.[2]

Peel did not conceive it to be his duty between 1832 and 1846 to seek his programme from the members of his party. Indeed, between 1835 and 1841 he looked more to the weakness and divisions of his opponents than to platform manifestos as a guarantee of a Conservative return to power. The prelude to his electoral success in 1841 was not the vigorous presentation of a 'Tory' or 'Conservative' case about the corn laws or any other leading subject but the evident incapacity of the Whigs to manage the affairs of the country properly. He would have come to power without an election in 1839 if there had not been a dispute with the young Queen about the politics of the ladies of the bedchamber, but the Whigs were not in a position to profit from their renewed lease of life. The weaknesses of Melbourne's administration were brilliantly satirized by W. M. Praed, the Tory poet,

> To promise, pause, prepare, postpone,
> And end by letting things alone:
> In short to earn the people's pay
> By doing nothing every day.

Praed died in 1839, but after 1839 the weaknesses became even more apparent. In particular the finances of the country were in a hopeless state, and Peel drew an unusually lively picture of Sir Francis Baring, the Whig Chancellor of the Exchequer, 'seated on an empty chest, by a pool of bottomless deficiencies, fishing for a Budget'. Four successive Whig budgets had shown a deficit and the government had been persistently defeated in the lobbies on several issues, including the Budget, when Peel carried by one vote a no-confidence resolution in June 1841. Parliament was dissolved, and at the subsequent general election the Whigs, whose calculations of their chances were completely inaccurate, were heavily defeated.

[1] C. S. Parker, *Sir Robert Peel* (1891–9), vol. III, p. 172.
[2] *Ibid.*, vol. II, 347. Cf. the prophecy of the *Edinburgh Review* in 1840 (vol. LXXI, p. 313): 'His ostracism may be distant but to us it seems certain.'

At the election of 1837 the Conservatives had been in a minority of 24; at the election of 1841 they had a majority of 78. In 1841 the Crown, as Melbourne put it, 'for the first time' had 'an Opposition returned smack against it'.[1]

The election of 1841 was not fought on the single issue of the corn laws, although Russell had brought the Whig ministry to a close by suggesting a programme of freer trade and a fixed duty on corn in place of the sliding scale of 1828, and the Anti-Corn Law League was active in mobilizing local opinion. Many of Peel's supporters in the constituencies advanced extreme protectionist views, but Peel himself stated that the details of trade policy should not be settled at the hustings but left to the 'dispassionate consideration' of Parliament. The election of 1841 was no more a direct election about the corn laws than the election of 1830 had been a direct election about parliamentary reform, and on both occasions the pressure of distress counted for as much as abstract theories. In the contested constituencies the situation was often confused. The Chartists and some of the radicals showed that they preferred the Tories to the Whigs for reasons which Peel did not accept. At a Nottingham by-election in April 1842, for instance, the Tory candidate, John Walter, was enthusiastically supported by a group of radicals on the ground that he had opposed the New Poor Law of 1834, and in many constituencies where the poor law was detested 'the vital issue was the condition not of trade, but of the people'.[2] Feargus O'Connor advised Chartists to support the Tory candidates, and there were hectic and colourful scenes in many constituencies where the largely voteless Chartists were determined to show that they were none the less a local political force to be reckoned with. To complete the mixture of motives and alignments, there were undoubtedly many people in 1841 who looked to Peel personally as the most effective prime minister the country could find at a moment of acute national difficulty. 'The elections are wonderful', wrote Croker, 'and the curiosity is, that all turns on the name of Sir Robert Peel.'[3] For once Greville agreed with him. With Tory successes at Liverpool, Hull, Leeds, Bradford, Nottingham,

[1] *Letters of Queen Victoria* (1907), vol. I, p. 276. In 1835 too the electorate had show unmistakably that it did not want Wellington and Peel.

[2] B. Kemp, 'The General Election of 1841' in *History* (1952). See above, p. 281. One of Walter's opponents was Joseph Sturge, and the support given by some Chartists to Walter was a blow to the whole philosophy of the Complete Suffrage Union. O'Connor himself won Nottingham in 1847.

[3] Parker, *Peel*, vol. II, p. 475.

Bristol and the City of London, it seemed clear that 'there was a general feeling of satisfaction and security (in the country) by the substitution of a real working government for the last batch'.[1]

'A real working government' was, in fact, the main consequence of the election of 1841. It was between 1841 and 1846 that all Peel's finest qualities were revealed, for although the range of administrative activity was much more restricted than it is in the middle of the twentieth century, the problems to be tackled almost all demanded freshness of approach, thoroughness of grasp and the capacity to take decisions. Peel impressed his personality and outlook on his well-balanced cabinet with exceptional force. Though he stressed the importance of departmental investigation and activity, he himself strictly supervised the business of each branch of government. Ashley, who did not approve of Peel's policies on 'social and moral questions', dismissed the administration on one occasion as 'a Cabinet of Peel's dolls',[2] but later in the century Lord Rosebery described Peel as 'the model of all prime ministers' and paid tribute to the way in which 'he was conversant with all departmental questions, and formed and enforced opinion on them'.[3] Much more than a co-ordinator, Peel was the personal genius of his administration, but the strain of his office told on him severely, particularly during the political battles of his last two years in power. In 1845, for instance, he wrote that he defied 'the Minister of this country to read all that he ought to read, including the whole foreign correspondence; to keep up constant communication with the Queen *and the Prince*; to see all whom he ought to see; to superintend the grant of honours and the disposal of civil and ecclesiastical patronage[4]; to write with his own hand to every person of note who chooses to write to him; to be prepared for every debate, including the most trumpery concern; to do all these indispensable things, and also to sit in the House of Commons eight hours a day for 118 days.'[5] It is not surprising that in the light of this assessment of his duties as prime minister—a conception of the office in complete contrast to that of his predecessor Melbourne—Peel became a hero of the Victorian gospel of work. The limitations of a Ten Hours Bill he

---

[1] C. C. Greville, *Journal of the Reign of Queen Victoria* (1887), vol. II, p. 52.
[2] Hodder, *op. cit.*, p. 319.
[3] *Miscellanies* (1921), vol. I, p. 197.
[4] Peel stressed in his letter to Cobden in 1846 (see above, pp. 324–5) that 'the odious power which patronage confers' was one of the heaviest of his responsibilities.
[5] Parker, *Peel*, vol. III, p. 219.

never applied to himself, and the scores of statues erected after his death in the industrial towns of the North revealed him to the nation as an ideal type of the age.

Peel's administrative pre-eminence, as much as his industry and sense of responsibility, inspired the band of Peelites who remained true to their leader to the end of their lives. '*He* is my leader still though invisible', the Duke of Newcastle wrote to Lady Peel more than a year after Peel's death, 'I never take a step in public life without reflecting, how *he* would have thought of it.'[1] The young William Ewart Gladstone, who was made vice-president of the Board of Trade in 1841 and president in 1843, owed an enormous amount to Peel and was in the strict line of succession from him. In a new setting and intermingled with contrasting elements, the Peelite strain was to give a particular colour to later English Liberalism just as it had influenced the whole course of earlier nineteenth-century Toryism. Peel was never a party politician in the modern sense of the word and it was consistent with the whole of his career that in 1846 he did not hesitate to put the claims of duty to his conscience, to his sovereign and to posterity before the claims of his party. His ministry nonetheless was a political as well as an administrative bridge in nineteenth-century English history.

So diverse and many-sided is the world of politics that Peel's vigour and industry failed to fascinate those who wanted politics in the 1840s to be perpetually fierce and exciting. It had always been so in Peel's lifetime. Men had contrasted him unfavourably with Canning in the early 1820s. The force of Canning's oratory had thrilled them to admiration and hatred; Peel they associated with subjects which often appeared barren and uninviting, like the reform of the criminal law. For all the cataclysmic backcloth, there were many subjects of this sort in the 1840s and Peel had to appear far more frequently as a teacher than as a prophet. The duel between Peel and Disraeli in 1845 and 1846 provided one more scene of a recurring drama in politics—the experienced administrator, forced to be didactic, and the brilliant rebel, forced to combat experience with imagination. In a sense, English Conservatives in every generation have to choose (if the talent is available) between a Disraeli and a Peel. There is no doubt that between 1841 and 1846 the talents of Peel were more urgently necessary, that however much Disraeli disliked slogans based on 'Ancient Institutions and Modern

[1] Quoted *ibid.*, p. 559.

Improvements',[1] a policy designed to reconcile rather than to revert was necessary. Disraeli himself had no positive policy and did little in Parliament to justify his pre-occupation as a novelist with the 'condition of England question'.[2] The difficulty was that Peel had to be didactic not only in handling Disraeli, who after all was young enough and able enough to learn even when he did not admit it, but the heterogeneous rank-and-file of his party. What worried him increasingly was how to make his own unindustrious followers continue to support the executive when it seemed to threaten their interest. 'How can those who spend their time in hunting and shooting and eating and drinking', he complained to his wife in the middle of the final corn law crisis, 'know what were the motives of those who are responsible for the public security, who have access to the best information, and have no other object under Heaven but to provide against danger, and consult the general interests of all classes?'[3]

Before the political crash came, the achievements of Peel and his ministers were threefold—to restore and reform the national finances, to introduce legislation to deal with pressing social and economic questions of the day, and to tighten up and make more efficient the work of administration. The three achievements are best considered in reverse order, for the first of them was inextricably bound up with the fall of protection and led relentlessly to the split of 1846. It was, however, the most striking of the achievements, for there were serious weaknesses in Peel's handling of social questions, and both he and his colleagues held that a return to economic prosperity would, through better conditions of living, relieve social distress far more effectively than legislation. In the long run they were right, but in the short run they found themselves bitterly opposed by political opponents on all sides. As for the improvements in administration, they depended more on Peel's general direction and the choice of able departmental heads than on drastic modifications of administrative machinery.

Two examples of the change in mood within the administration have been examined in detail by historians. At the Home Office, Sir James Graham, Peel's 'second self', knew more about business

---

[1] Mr. Tadpole in Disraeli's novel *Coningsby* preferred the word 'ameliorations' to 'improvements' on the grounds that 'nobody knows what it means'.

[2] He did not, for instance, support an 1842 motion in favour of outdoor relief to the poor, which mustered only twenty-two radical votes; he attacked the education grant of 1839; he took no part in the Mines Act debates; and he voted against the Public Health Act of 1848.

[3] *Private Letters* (ed. G. Peel), p. 273.

than 'the rest of all the government put together'[1]; his experience in
the Whig government of 1830–4 had given him knowledge and
opportunity, and he had been personally responsible at the
Admiralty for the abolition in 1832 of the old system of control
through three overlapping Boards and the setting up of a centralized
Board of the Admiralty responsible to Parliament. He had won the
praise of economy-minded radicals like Hume, and admirers of
his achievement asked for the 'same system of consolidation' in
the Army. By 1841 Graham along with Stanley had moved across
to the Tory ranks, and so close were his opinions to those of Peel
that *Punch* once commented that they 'were two persons with
only one intellect'.[2] Graham shared—and to some extent exaggerated—Peel's weaknesses as well as his virtues. He was cold,
meticulous, and essentially a public servant, out of sympathy with
popular movements of every kind; he believed, moreover, in the
rigid supremacy of the laws of political economy. 'The lot of
eating, drinking, working and dying must ever be the sum of
human life among the masses of a large portion of the human
family.'[3] At the Home Office, while he considered every social and
political problem of the day with careful attention and never tried
to evade the necessity of taking action, his bleak attitude towards
people was always bound to alienate those who believed either in
Tory-radical panaceas or in the Chartist formula.

To the presidency of the Board of Trade Peel appointed Lord
Ripon, formerly Lord Goderich,[4] but Gladstone, vice-president and
responsible departmental head in the House of Commons, took
over the duties of the presidency in 1843. Although Gladstone was
disappointed at first by his new assignment, he quickly realized that
'governing packages' was a most important task in the new economy.
He was assisted by capable officials, superior in calibre to most of
those in other governmental departments. To established figures
like J. R. MacGregor and J. R. Porter, the statistician, he added
Thomas Farrer who later rose to be permanent secretary (and
president of the Cobden Club) and Stafford Northcote, who later
became leader of the Conservative party in the House of Commons.
It was with the assistance of this well-administered Board of Trade
that the fiscal revolution of the ministry was carried out.

---

[1] This was Gladstone's comment. Quoted Morley, *op. cit.*, vol. I, p. 248.
[2] *Punch*, vol. I (1841), p. 54.
[3] *Hansard*, 3rd series, vol. C, 773–781.
[4] See above, p. 228.

Administration without legislation in the 1840s was impossible. The 'strong government' which Peel regarded as necessary could not follow the eighteenth-century practice of dispensing with ideas and clearly defined objectives. Much of the legislation of the ministry was necessarily contentious, for it touched powerful interests—corn and sugar were prominent in defence, cotton in attack—and compelled the government to concern itself directly with occupational and professional groups like factory owners, doctors, teachers and engineers. There was thus inevitable delay in passing legislation and in carrying it out. Furthermore, the success of legislation depended not only on departmental initiative, parliamentary debate, and general goodwill outside, but on Royal Commissions, which examined conditions in all parts of the country, and on an effective inspectorate which supervised the response of interested parties to their new legal responsibilities. The detailed examination of differences in local statistics (local death rates, for example) and standards of achievement was itself a spur to comprehensive national action; so too was the vigilance and pressure of local inspectors, professional men close to practical problems at a new level of national administration.

The most important link between administration and social legislation was still the Poor Law of 1834, and Peel and his colleagues decided without hesitation to extend it for another five years. The scope of poor law policy was wide enough to touch many other social questions, and the effective national control of public health was in a sense a by-product of it. Already before 1841 the poor law framework had been adopted for the registration of births, marriages and deaths (1836), and in 1842, Chadwick's masterpiece, the famous report on the *Sanitary Condition of the Labouring Classes*, made its appearance. It was followed a year later by the appointment of a Royal Commission on the Health of Towns, which published its conclusions in 1845. National public health reform did not come until 1848, but it was in the period from 1841 to 1846 that sanitary evils were exposed, recommendations made, and opinion mobilized. A Health of Towns Association, founded in 1839, did its best to popularize the view that 'the heaviest municipal tax is the fever tax', and although it lacked the tactical skill and concentration of purpose of the Anti-Corn Law League, it had some success with its propaganda. The delay in getting a public health act on the statute book was a measure of the administrative difficulties, the strength of 'sinister interests', and the underlying *vis inertiae* of large sections of the public, and it finally needed fear of a cholera outbreak as well as the revelation of existing horrors to speed up legislation.

By the Whig Act of 1848 a General Board of Health was set up consisting of three members. Chadwick was to be one of them. The local machinery of public health was left to Town Councils where they existed, and where they did not to entirely new authorities, Local Boards of Health. The act created many difficulties and in 1854 the General Board of Health was dissolved: none the less, the passing of the first piece of national health legislation was a sign that the 'Sanitary Idea' had established itself as a leading idea of the age, just as the constitution of the new health authority reflected the influence of the Poor Law of 1834 on the structure of administration.

Outside the framework of the Poor Law important social measures still depended on the initiative of philanthropists and 'experts', and Graham at the Home Office never went as far as the most important of the religious philanthropists, Lord Ashley, desired. Ashley, heading a strong pressure group outside Parliament, was offered only a Household, not a cabinet, post in 1841. He believed in the unremitting exposure of social evils, and was driven by a fierce Evangelical energy which never left his conscience quiet or allowed him to stay still. Graham was troubled by no such promptings. He regarded large-scale governmental interference with the labour market as the 'commencement of a "Jack Cade" system of legislation', and consequently the two big social measures of the period —the Coal Mines Act of 1842 and the Factory Act of 1844—both fell short of Ashley's aspirations and far short of the aspirations of the organized working-class movement in the North.

The Mines Act, which was introduced by Ashley on the basis of the influential illustrated report of the Commission on the Employment of Children in Mines, was nominally supported by Graham, but the government qualified its provisions and did little to secure its passing. The act was none the less useful in that it forbade the employment underground of women and of boys under 10, and provided an inspectorate (of whom the chief was a remarkable social investigator and public servant with a long and varied career before him, H. S. Tremenheere)[1] to enforce it. The Factory Act fixed a

[1] See an illuminating article about him by R. K. Webb, 'A Whig Inspector', in *J.M.H.* (1955). Tremenheere had interesting experiences behind him too. In 1830, while reading for the bar, he attended Rotunda meetings in London, and spread anti-Radical propaganda amid the 'garlic & onions & a wilderness of sweets'. See above, p. 254.

6½-hour maximum working day for children under 13 and a maximum of 12 hours for women. During the course of the debates Ashley pleaded forcibly for a Ten Hours Bill which would afford 'a slight relaxation of toil, a time to live, and a time to die; a time for those comforts that sweeten life, and a time for those duties that adorn it', and despite Graham's opposition carried a ten-hour amendment by nine votes. By using party pressure the government turned the tables on Ashley at a later stage (by seven votes), and after refusing to compromise on eleven hours carried the final version of their bill by a large majority. The Factory Act, like the Mines Act, was a substantial step forward, the logical outcome of the administrative experience of the previous decade, but it was a grudging step in the name not of justice but of charity. It was not until 1847 that the Ten Hours Bill was passed with majorities of 108 and 63 on the second and third readings, after support had been given it both by Whigs and Protectionists. Macaulay spoke for the first when he argued that he could never believe that 'what makes a population stronger and healthier and wiser and better can ultimately make it poorer': the Protectionists, who had supported Ashley less firmly than the Whigs in 1844, were converted to support of the Ten Hours Bill in sufficiently large numbers to ensure the passing of the measure.[1]

The development of public education was just as difficult to achieve as the control of exploitation in the labour market. Long before the 1840s, Whitbread in 1806, Brougham in 1820, and Roebuck in 1833 had brought forward bills for creating a rate-aided system of education. The 'march of intellect', they believed, needed a nationally enforced discipline, and the State would have to supplement the work of the two main voluntary educational societies—the British and Foreign School Society (founded in 1807) which included both Churchmen and Nonconformists, and the National Society (founded in 1811) which was exclusively Church of England. In 1833 the Whig government, encouraged by Brougham, made a grant of £20,000 'for the purpose of education' to be shared between the two societies, and in 1839 the grant was increased to £30,000. At the same time a special committee of the Privy Council was set up to administer the grant, and inspectors were appointed to examine the work of the schools.

[1] For a brief study of the relevant voting statistics in 1844 and 1847 see W. O. Aydelotte, 'The House of Commons in the 1840s', in *History* (1954).

The main obstacle to the further development of an educational system was the religious zeal of the sponsors of the voluntary societies, and the first project of the new committee—a 'Normal College' for the training of teachers—could not be realized because of the clash between Anglican demands for complete control and Nonconformist emphasis on religious liberty. However, the secretary of the new committee, Dr. James Kay, later known as Kay-Shuttleworth, was an energetic believer in the 'claims of the civil power to control the education of the country'. His career provided yet another link between poor law and education, not unlike the link between poor law and public health, for, after beginning his professional life as a physician and helping to fight the cholera in 1832, he had served as an Assistant Poor Law Commissioner under the 1834 act. He was a firm believer in the principles of 1834 and made his first educational experiments in pauper schools. Less stubborn than Chadwick and more willing to compromise, he was able to accomplish much behind the scenes and in 1846 to lay down regulations which marked the first stage in the creation of a teaching profession. He was fairly described by W. E. Forster, the sponsor of the first Education Act of 1870, as 'a man to whom probably more than any other we owe national education in England'.

Both he and Graham failed, however, in the biggest single legislative reform relating to education between 1841 and 1846, and religion was the cause of their failure. In the Factory Act of 1833 it was laid down that children working in factories must attend school two hours a day; in 1843 Graham proposed to reduce the hours of work of children in such a way that they would either have the morning or the afternoon free to attend compulsory grant-aided trust schools. The trustees of each school were to include the parish clergyman, two churchwardens, and four other persons, including two millowners to be nominated by the local magistrates in special session; the schoolmasters were to be churchmen, although special provision was to be made for the instruction of children of dissenters by ministers of their own persuasion. Although Graham, encouraged by Brougham, made a forceful plea for factory education, the religious implications of his proposals roused a storm of protest among Dissenters, the Wesleyans joining with the older Nonconformists to force the government first to modify and then to jettison its proposals. Extreme Churchmen

were almost as hostile as the Dissenters, and Graham only succeeded
in adding to his personal unpopularity. The cause of education was
seriously held back by what Peel called the 'sorry and lamentable
triumph' of the Dissenters, and a renewed bout of voluntary activity
was no substitute for what would have been an extremely important
national reform. The moral of the story, however, was that there
can be no large-scale social reforms unless there is a reasonable
measure of agreement about values and priorities. The economic
and technical arguments for education were less powerful in the
1840s than the arguments for scriptural literacy, and Kay-Shuttleworth was in a tiny minority in refusing to believe that the best
condition of the working classes was one of 'unenterprising contentment, uninstructed reverence, and unrepining submission'.

Cheap bread was to prove even more contentious than cheap
education, but other economic reforms were carried by the government without stirring up violent controversy. They were designed
to regulate the legal and institutional framework of business without
controlling or supervising it. In 1842 district bankruptcy courts
were set up—a central court had been created eleven years before—
and soon afterwards imprisonment for debts of less than £20 was
abolished. In 1846 a uniform system of district county courts,
'agreeable to the constitution and genius of the nation', was set up
all over the country. The speedier and more effective administration
of justice was a chief aim of Graham as well as of shopkeepers,
tradesmen and merchants. Although there was little violent opposition, there were complaints from some of Graham's own colleagues
that there 'was a growing tendency to withdraw the administration
of business, judicial, financial or administrative, from the hands of
the upper classes of society and to rest it on paid officers of the
Crown'. The complaints were accentuated, indeed, by the fear that
if the new machinery were ever perfected, the landlords would
'degenerate into an idle and useless class of society'.[1]

Two important measures in 1844 were designed to give greater
order to banking and to company finance. The Bank Charter Act of
1844, like so much other legislation between 1841 and 1846, was
the product of decades of controversy between experts and of
repeated parliamentary enquiries into the stability of banking. It
was designed, as Peel put it, to secure 'by gradual means the establishment of a safe system of currency' and in drafting it Peel drew

[1] C. S. Parker, *The Life and Letters of Sir James Graham* (1907), vol. I, pp. 333-5.

on the advice of the Bank of England and the writings of the 'Currency School' (with Samuel Jones Loyd, later Lord Overstone, as its main spokesman) which had argued in favour of pinning the amount of money in circulation to gold, and developing automatic devices to ensure the stability of the currency. In approaching complicated currency questions, Peel showed many of the same qualities of mind that he displayed in relation to the corn laws. He was not doctrinaire, and yet he helped to lay the foundations of orthodoxy. The main features of the act, which followed an earlier Whig act of 1833, were four—the concentration of note issue in the Bank of England; the division of the structure of the Bank of England between two watertight departments, one dealing with issue, the other with banking; the limitation of notes issued by the Bank to a fixed sum (£14 million), any further issues to be backed by gold bullion; and the weekly publication of accounts. Peel's Act of 1844 not only prepared the way for the Victorian supremacy of the Bank of England: it provided a link with the rest of his economic policy. His belief that within the new system financial adjustments would be automatic—the level of prices and employment being adjusted by inflows and outflows of gold and consequently by movements in interest rates and the volume of credit—appealed to those powerful economic interests in the country, of which cotton was the most important, which depended on a sound currency and an active international trade. The Act was passed with little debate, and Peel's promise that it would prevent 'reckless speculation' and ensure the 'legitimate reward of industry' rang true. The financial crisis of 1847 sharpened criticism of the Bank of England once more, as did further crises in 1857 and 1866, when the Act had to be suspended, but the structure built in 1844 survived until the wars of the twentieth century. Although effective central bank management and techniques took years to evolve, the Victorians could look back to Peel as the architect of a confident economic order.

The rationale of the Companies Act of 1844 was somewhat similar to that of the Bank Charter Act. It did not attempt to foster a policy of business expansion or to encourage economic growth through the provision of limited liability; it rather set out to tidy and to systematize, to check 'reckless speculation', and to ensure 'the ligitimate reward of industry'. A parliamentary committee had reported in 1844 that 'for years the world had been at the mercy of anyone who chose to publish an advertisement, call himself a company, and receive money for assurances and annuities'.[1] There was no control over the directors of incorporated companies, accounts were irregularly kept, and there was inadequate publicity. The 1844 Act laid down that all companies had to be registered, and that they had to publish their prospectuses and balance sheets. Although most English business was not organized in incorporated companies in 1844, the reforms were rightly regarded as guarantees of business 'improvement'.

The 1844 Companies Act did not apply to those companies which had been specially sanctioned by Parliament. It thus left out the railways, the main form of joint stock business enterprise in the 1840s. Although railways drew directly on the savings of thousands of small local investors, encouraged the emergence of great tycoons, of whom George Hudson was outstanding, and relied upon very dubious methods of finance, the attempt by government to regulate them effectively in the public interest was doomed to failure. The main reason was that the railway interest was always strong enough in the House of Commons to defeat any proposals which were regarded as dangerously restrictive.[2] When Gladstone proposed in 1844 (following the advice of a Select Committee) that all new railway Bills should include clauses giving the State the right of revising fares and charges and the option of purchasing railways outright after twenty years, the boldest clauses in his bill were whittled down and ultimately the option was never realized.

A study of Gladstone's approach to company and railway legislation leads naturally into the further study of the greatest and most publicized of the achievements of Peel's ministry—the restoration and reform of the national finances and the creation of a new fiscal system.

Peel's first task on taking office was to remedy the disastrous financial situation. The deficit for the current year was estimated at well over £2 million, and Peel did not believe that it could be disposed of by 'Whig expedients'. His own comprehensive solution

---

[1] *Report of the Select Committee on Joint Stock Companies* (1844).

[2] A few members of the House followed Colonel Sibthorp in declaring themselves 'conscientiously opposed to the introduction of the railways', but the majority were shareholders and at least one-seventh were railway directors. Colonel Sibthorp also 'conscientiously opposed' Catholic emancipation, the Reform Bill of 1832, free trade, the Public Health Act of 1848, and the Great Exhibition of 1851. He claimed the credit for the Chandos clause of the 1832 Reform Act, which he wished to introduce before Chandos proposed it (see above, p. 251).

included two major changes, both of which he had previously opposed—the restoration of the income tax and the general reduction of protective duties. The first of these measures was designed not only to make good the immediate deficit, but to enable the second objective to be achieved, thereby 'compensating the country for its present sacrifices'. The reduction of protective duties, Peel held, would assist industry, expand trade, and improve the lot of the 'labouring classes of society'.

The first big tariff reductions were made in the bold but experimental budget of 1842 introduced by Peel himself. Out of 1,200 articles then subject to the tariff 750 were reduced. By 1844 the government deficit had been turned into a substantial surplus, and the income tax, set at 7*d.* in the £, had been more or less accepted by the public. Peel went on in 1845 to strike off another 430 articles from the tariff list and to reduce the duties on many other commodities. The import duty on raw cotton and the excise duty on glass were abolished in this second great reform, as were all the remaining taxes on exports. The duties on timber and sugar, which touched colonial interests, were further lowered, and the tariff system as a whole took the broad shape which it was to retain into the twentieth century.

This chain of fiscal reforms increasingly alarmed those members of Peel's own party who believed that the climax of his policy would be the repeal of the corn laws. In March 1845 before the corn law crisis itself, Graham complained that he and Peel were 'scouted as traitors' although 'we have laboured hard, and not in vain, to restore the prosperity of the country, and to give increased security to the aristocracy by improving the conditions and diminishing the discontent of the great masses of the people.'[1] There was no reason, however, for Graham to sound so surprised. The *Manchester Guardian* was describing one of Peel's speeches in Parliament as the speech of a 'special pleader for the Anti-Corn Law League'.[2]

Peel was in further difficulties with his own supporters in April 1845 when he proposed a government grant of £30,000 to assist in the rebuilding of the Catholic College at Maynooth in Ireland. Although he won the support of many of the Whigs, of whom Macaulay was the most vocal, nearly half his own supporters voted

---

[1] Croker, *Correspondence and Diaries,* vol. III, p. 31.
[2] 4 June 1845.

against him, and 'Protestant' opinion was mobilized in the country with even more vigour and organizing skill than in the 1820s.[1]

> How wonderful is Peel! [*Punch* declared]
> He changeth with the Time,
> Turning and twisting like an eel
> Ascending through the slime.

Of the members of his own party who voted against him, 108 were to vote against him on the bigger issue of corn-law repeal in 1846.[2] The split on Maynooth was indeed a preview of the split to come.

It was Ireland which precipitated not only the 'religious' split but the economic division. The bad harvest of 1845 and the threat to the Irish potato crop impelled Peel in November to try to persuade his cabinet to suspend the corn duties immediately by Order in Council and to summon parliament to reform the existing laws. He failed to hold his ministry together, and for a brief moment in December handed over 'the poisoned chalice' of government to Russell, who in his *Edinburgh Letter* had openly abandoned the Whig policy of a fixed duty in favour of total repeal. Russell failed to form a government, and before the end of the month Peel returned to power with a reconstructed cabinet, which did not include Lord Stanley, the most determined of the Tory Protectionists. The way was prepared for the impassioned and dramatic debates on the corn laws which split his party and determined the shape—or shapelessness—of English politics for generations to come.

Peel made five great speeches on the corn question before the laws were repealed by a majority of 98 in May 1846, with 231 Conservative backbenchers voting against him and only 112 on his side. When Peel said that he looked to posterity to justify him, Disraeli pointed out that posterity was a limited assembly 'not much more numerous than the planets', and that in the last resort free politics were more dangerous than free trade. 'Maintain the line of demarcation between parties', Disraeli exclaimed, 'for it is only by maintaining the independence of parties that you can maintain the integrity of public men, and the power and influence of Parlia-

---

[1] A central Anti-Maynooth Committee demanded 'a mighty effort' to secure a 'majority in the House of Commons based on Protestant Principles'. See A. S. Thelwall, *Proceedings of the Anti-Maynooth Conference* (1845).

[2] 'Young England' was split on Maynooth, however, which provided 'the occasion' if not the cause of its dissolution. Manners voted for the grant, Smythe took a middle line, and Disraeli opposed. This vote was the only occasion on which Bright and Cobden voted in different lobbies, Cobden for, Bright against.

ment itself.' One of Peel's admirers, Sidney Herbert, presented exactly the opposite thesis when he remarked that 'it has been said that party is part of our constitution. I think it is contrary to the whole spirit of our constitution'. Peel in the moment of drama still stood by the essentials of conduct he had always followed, and his old and loyal colleague Wellington piloted repeal through the House of Lords so successfully that in its last stages it was passed by show of hands without a division. It was characteristic of the prime minister that he refused to dissolve Parliament and appeal to the country on the issue of free trade, because he felt that such an appeal would influence public opinion just when 'repose' was needed[1]; and when, just as the Corn Act received the royal assent (June 1846), he was defeated on a different issue, an Irish coercion bill, and had to give way to Russell and the Whigs, he pleaded for the same 'conservative opposition' which he had advocated after 1832.

Between 1846 and 1850 Peel's national stature was almost un-challenged in the country. He had split the party which had been built up laboriously between 1832 and 1846, but he had retained the loyalty of the officers, while losing the support of many of the troops. Among the faithful were the most able administrators and best-known figures in his ministry—men like Graham, Gladstone, Dalhousie, Sidney Herbert, Cardwell and Aberdeen. 'To be a Peelite', Rosebery has maintained, 'was a distinction in itself; it denoted statesmanship, industry, conscience.' The strain of public duty without public office weakened and divided the Peelites, but Peel himself towered above considerations of party, in many matters the confidant of the Whig government, in others the mediator between contending groups. On his sudden death in July 1850, a few days after being thrown from his horse on Con-stitution Hill, the Queen and many of his fellow-countrymen felt that they had lost England's greatest statesman. Large numbers of workingmen sent in their pennies to help pay for statues in his memory. There was no more revealing witness to the magnitude of his achievement; and disillusioned Chartists, who had always experienced difficulty in collecting pennies for the movement, were the first to direct attention to the contrast.

[1] See above, p. 325.

7

BRITAIN AND THE WORLD OVERSEAS

1. FROM SETTLEMENT TO REVOLUTION

THE contrast between violent upheavals in Europe in 1848 and relative peace and order at home gave comfort and confidence not only to the English aristocracy but to the middle classes. 'Whilst almost every throne on the Continent was emptied or shaken by revolution', a writer in the *Annual Register* for 1848 observed, 'England stood firm, and even appeared to derive increased stability from the events which convulsed foreign kingdoms.'[1]

Such observations, which continued to be made throughout the whole of the mid-Victorian period, derived both from basic complacency and from pride and prejudice. English institutions were deemed superior to the institutions of other countries, and there seemed to be little reason for Englishmen to have too much to do with foreigners except as teachers and customers. At the edges of Englishmen's attitudes to the outside world there was usually the sense, well expressed by Mr. Podsnap, that other countries were a 'mistake', or the reflection of the young man in Tennyson's *The Princess*,

> God bless the narrow seas!
> I wish they were a whole Atlantic broad.

At school, it was claimed in a little textbook which sold thousands of copies that every child might say

> I thank the goodness and the grace
> Which on my birth have smiled,
> And made me in these Christian days
> A happy English child.[2]

---

[1] See the *Manchester Guardian*, 12 April 1848, which linked economic prosperity with political order and claimed that 'our Constitution is not a mere name, but a living and authoritative guarantee for social order and individual rights'.

[2] *Near Home or the Countries of Europe Described* (1855), p. 4. French instability was

It is impossible, however, to dismiss Englishmen's place in the early nineteenth-century world in the language of self-satisfaction or isolationism. There was usually a debate in England about foreign policy and not a single line of agreed action. While political economy and liberal principles provided guides to foreign policy for many Englishmen, others were strongly influenced by romanticism, particularly in exciting periods, like the Greek War of Independence in the 1820s: the revolutions of 1848 themselves were welcomed by those Chartists and radicals who believed that they had 'shaken European tyranny to its deepest foundations',[1] and after they had been crushed, an angry correspondent wrote to the *Social Reformer* complaining that England had done nothing to go to the rescue of the oppressed. 'Her armies may broil in India or parade at home— her navies may rot in harbour or meddle with barbarians—but civilized people may fall unaided.'[2]

The post-1815 debate on foreign policy began with the peace settlement itself, the settlement which was challenged in 1848. If in 1815 there was little popular discussion about foreign affairs outside parliamentary circles and the London world of affairs, there was a vigorous debate in Parliament itself. Brougham and the more militant Whigs strongly criticized Castlereagh's surrender to European 'reaction', not knowing that Castlereagh in private was referring to the Holy Alliance (September 1815) between the absolute monarchs of Russia, Prussia and Austria as 'a piece of sublime mysticism and nonsense'. A small group of Whigs voted against the peace treaties, objecting to such provisions as the return of the Bourbon monarchy in Spain, while the radical *Black Dwarf* attacked Castlereagh personally for 'intriguing away his country's interests' and adopting 'the accursed principles of legitimacy'.[3] In the period of domestic repression between 1815 and 1820 they detected a sinister association between the government and the foreign autocracies.

In fact, during these years Castlereagh refused to identify Britain too closely with the policies of the European powers, although at

summarily dismissed in this fascinating guide. 'Sometimes they have a king, and sometimes they send him away and will have none' (p. 10). One of the main virtues of England was that it was a country with 'many Bibles' where 'the people may learn about God . . . and that heavenly place where saints and angels dwell'.
[1] J. Barker, *The Reformers' Almanac* (1848), p. 165.
[2] *Social Reformer*, 25 August 1849.
[3] 2 April 1817; 10 December 1817.

the same time he did his best to maintain the system of diplomacy by conference which had been agreed upon by the great powers of Vienna. He resisted Russian attempts to convert the congress system into a means of imposing a programme of concerted anti-revolutionary intervention, and before he committed suicide in 1822, Britain had begun to part company with the other great powers on the question of intervention to maintain autocratic government in Spain, Portugal and Sicily. It was not that Castlereagh felt any sympathy with liberal movements or with protests against autocracy; he was afraid of general commitments. The Austrian ambassador in London once said that he was 'like a great lover of music who is at church; he wishes to applaud but he dare not'.[1] By 1820, however, Castlereagh was not only afraid to applaud but less willing to listen to music. He was saying firmly of his continental colleagues, 'if they will be theorists we must act in separation'.[2] He did not live long enough to attend the Congress of Verona in 1822, at which Britain broke with her war-time allies and the congress system was doomed, but had he lived it is likely that he would have followed the same course.

His successor, Canning, helped to make foreign policy exciting and interesting to people who had taken little interest in it before, and used the issues it raised to achieve popularity in home affairs.[3] He exploited the existing differences between Britain and her war-time allies, turning them from a matter of concern into a matter of pride, and at the same time transforming the presentation of the case for non-intervention from a negative into a positive one. He was assisted in his boldness by the fact that, unlike Castlereagh, he had taken no direct part in the peace settlement. Very quickly he was regarded by most European statesmen and rulers as a dangerous radical, an assessment which reinforced his popularity at home, at least outside the cabinet. Although he was fundamentally as anxious as Castlereagh to maintain peace and as unwilling to convert the breach with the autocratic powers into a scheme for the 'liberal regeneration' of Europe, he went far to satisfy both English and foreign liberal aspirations. The opposition he faced inside Liverpool's cabinet and the bitterness of the attack on him by the Duke of

---

[1] Quoted C. K. Webster, *The Foreign Policy of Castlereagh* (1931), p. 326.

[2] For his 1820 State Paper, see H. W. Temperley and L. M. Penson, *Foundations of British Foreign Policy* (1938), pp. 47 ff. The authors rightly describe this document as 'the most famous State Paper in British history'.

[3] See above, p. 218.

Wellington for 'upsetting all our foreign policy'[1] are a measure of the rôle he chose to play.

On the two crucial issues of Spain and Greece Canning won the sympathies both of political economists and of romanticists. Through the Duke of Wellington, Britain's representative at Verona, he refused to approve of the great powers giving a blessing to the entry into Spain of French troops, sent there to back the Bourbon king and to suppress the Spanish liberals. He asked Parliament to increase the size of the navy from 20,000 to 25,000 men and announced that Britain would in no circumstances permit the permanent military occupation of Spain, the violation of Portuguese territory, or the appropriation of any part of the Spanish American colonies. This last declaration in particular met with the full approval of the trade and business interests which looked to South America as to a new Eldorado. While Canning could not stop the French from entering Spain in 1823—that would have meant a war which he had no desire to wage—he was able to tell the French ambassador 'be yours the glory of a victory followed by disaster and ruin, be ours the inglorious traffic of industry and an ever-increasing prosperity'.[2] He was able too after a long struggle in the cabinet formally to recognize the republics of Mexico, Buenos Aires and Colombia in 1825. In the most famous of all his phrases: 'I resolved that if France had Spain it should not be Spain with the Indies; I called a New World into existence to redress the balance of the old.' The recognition in the same year of the independence of Brazil—as a monarchical empire—crowned Canning's South American policy.

The Greek situation, directly raising the problem of Britains' relations with Russia, was far more difficult to manœuvre and provoked more serious cleavages in English opinion. It was one episode in the complicated politics of the Near Eastern question, a question in which Russia and Austria had an even more immediate interest than Britain had. Before the outbreak of the French Revolution, Pitt had expressed (in face of Fox's opposition) Britain's interest in the integrity of the vast and sprawling Ottoman Empire and his opposition to Russian aggrandisement[3]; the same attitude can be noted during Canning's spell at the Foreign Office from

[1] *The Journal of Mrs. Arbuthnot*, vol. I, p. 203. Cf. later a comment in October 1823: 'There are some people who like to fish in troubled waters & Mr. C. is one of them. . . . A year ago, we were on terms of friendship with every Court in Europe. Now we are bickering & sparring with them all.' (*Ibid.*, p. 269.)
[2] Quoted E. Halévy, *The Liberal Awakening* (1949 edn.), p. 175.
[3] See above, p. 128.

1807–9 when an Anglo-Turkish treaty of friendship was signed. The Peace Treaties of 1815 excluded all references to Turkey and Turkish possessions, but, as Castlereagh saw, it was impossible to leave the Near East out of the international picture. Russia had made substantial gains from the Turks during the Napoleonic Wars and her pretensions inside the Ottoman Empire were considerable. By the Treaty of Kutchuk Kainardji in 1774 she had secured certain ill-defined rights of interference on behalf of the Christian subjects of the Sultan—and there was an obvious danger of international crisis if open revolt broke out in any of the Turkish provinces.

When the Greeks, inspired by a mixture of motives, rebelled against the Turks in March 1821 and went on to proclaim a constitution for independent Greece in January 1822, they immediately posed difficult questions for the great powers. Was the revolt against Turkish authority analogous to the revolts of Liberals in the West against the forces of order and legitimacy? Was Greece another Spain? Or were the rebels to be treated as Christian subjects of an infidel power in need of encouragement? With the support of Castlereagh, Metternich successfully persuaded the Tsar to allow the Turks freedom to suppress the Greek revolt as they wished. Although the Tsar found it difficult to maintain his respect for constituted authority throughout the ensuing struggle, by the summer of 1827 the Sultan's troops, organized by his powerful and efficient vassal Mehemet Ali, Pasha of Egypt, and led by Mehemet's son Ibrahim, had won back from the rebels almost the whole of the Greek mainland.

The Greeks secured the sympathy and support of liberals, nationalists, and romantics all over Europe. In England there was tremendous enthusiasm, and volunteers, among whom Lord Byron was outstanding, hurried to fight in the Greek cause. Conditions in Greece itself did not correspond to the Western liberal image. There were fierce divisions between different groups of rebels, little real contact between 'freedom-loving intellectuals' and fanatical peasants of the Morea, and at all times and in all places a confused muddle of glory and plunder. None the less it was the image and not the reality which mattered in England and Europe, and it was the image as well as the relevant bundle of British interests which Canning had to take into account. Once again political economy and romanticism converged.

Canning's first action in relation to Greece—the recognition of the Greeks as belligerents in March 1823—was due as much to economic pre-occupations as to philhellene pressure. He refused to go beyond recognition or to join in a European conference to 'settle' the issue, for, in line with the policy which he had inherited from Pitt, he feared Russian interference and was anxious not to alienate the Turkish government. He was not interested in a war either for 'Aristides or St. Paul'. Acknowledging, however, in 1826 that Ibrahim Pasha was repressing the Greeks in such a brutal manner that the Russians under their new Tsar Nicholas I (who came to the throne in December 1825) might intervene alone, he set out to reach a realistic agreement with Russia. Wellington was sent to St. Petersburg, and in April 1826 a protocol was signed by which Britain and Russia agreed that they should jointly mediate, that Greece should become a self-governing Turkish dependency, that neither of the signatories should seek any gains from Turkey, and that other powers should be invited to sign and to take part in mediation. In July 1827 France signed the Treaty of London re-affirming these objectives, and the new allies pledged themselves to interfere to settle the Greek question unless the Turks accepted an armistice within fourteen days. Austria still stood aloof, advocating the same policy of non-intervention which Metternich had laid down in 1821.

To try to achieve this 'settlement' the three allies sent a fleet to the Eastern Mediterranean. When the Turks refused an armistice, there soon followed a brisk naval battle at Navarino (20 October) during which the Turkish and Egyptian fleets were destroyed, but no concerted attempt was made to direct the allied fleets from Navarino to Constantinople and to drive the Sultan into acceptance of the armistice terms. Canning's policy, for all its apparent success in balancing interests, failed to move the Turks, while at the same time it dealt such a decisive blow to Turkey that only Russia seemed to be the gainer. It is not surprising that the news of Navarino alarmed that section of English opinion which was anxious above all else to safeguard the position of Turkey, and that the King's speech in January 1828 deeply lamented the 'conflict . . . with the naval force of an ancient ally'.

By the time of Navarino, however, Canning was dead. In the last period of his life he had boldly intervened in Portugal (December 1826) 'to defend and preserve the independence of an Ally', and in support of the young Queen Maria had sent both ships and troops to Lisbon. Wellington had threatened resignation then; it was he and not Canning who had to deal with the aftermath of Navarino, and he could not prevent the outbreak of war between Russia and Turkey in 1828. By the Treaty of Adrianople (September 1829) the defeated Turks were compelled to pay an indemnity, and to surrender to Russia the Danube delta and the fortresses dominating the road south into Asia Minor. A Russian garrison remained for five years in the Danubian principalities, and after French troops had expelled Ibrahim's army from the Morea, Greece became completely independent in February 1830.

Wellington's foreign policy between 1828 and 1830 was in sharp contrast to that of Canning. He was willing to play a subordinate rôle in Europe and to cut British commitments. He withdrew British troops from Portugal and thus allowed Dom Miguel, Queen Maria's uncle and the representative of autocracy, to restore despotism; he reduced Canning's estimate of budget expenditure by £500,000; he watched almost helplessly while Charles X's authoritarian, unpopular and ambitious French government tried to establish closer relations with the power which he considered increasingly menacing, Russia. The Canningites could legitimately claim that 'Great Britain has abdicated the "umpire's throne" and has converted herself into an "adversary of constitutional freedom"'.[1]

When Wellington's government was defeated in November 1830, Lord Palmerston at the age of 46 became foreign secretary in Grey's government. He remained there from 1830 to 1841—with the exception of the few months of Peel's minority ministry in 1834-5—took over again from 1846-51, and as home secretary (1852-5) and prime minister (1855-8 and 1858-65) never abandoned his preoccupation with foreign policy until his death in 1865. It is thus impossible to understand the development of nineteenth-century British foreign policy without carefully surveying his attitudes and decisions. In time, indeed, he became the personification of England both at home and abroad. He certainly regarded himself as the consistent defender of British interests, and with experience he deliberately chose, as Canning had done, to advertise those interests and to make Englishmen conscious of them. Behind the scenes he was an indefatigable worker, a master of the techniques

[1] *An Authentic Account of Mr. Canning's Policy* (1830), p. 49.

of diplomacy, able to talk to diplomats as easily in French as in English, supremely competent in drafting despatches and unravelling complicated issues, never the prisoner of a diplomatic 'system'. In the middle of the stage, he was a brilliant showman, conscious of the need for publicity, particularly through the rising national (and nationalistic) press, enjoying the thrill of great occasions, knowing how to appeal to the rising middle-classes and even to working-men too. So well did he learn how to handle shopkeepers, merchants and manufacturers that he was once described as 'the finest meteorological instrument in England, who indicated with the greatest fidelity the temperature of the middle classes'.[1] An easy-going, pleasure-loving aristocrat at heart, he eventually became established as a 'universal favourite', 'Lord Evergreen'. His only consistent opponents were Cobden and Bright—the men of the Manchester School—and they would have been opposed to the architect of any active national foreign policy whether he had possessed Palmerston's personal characteristics or not.

Between 1830 and 1841 Palmerston had to deal with a changing Europe, in which the settlement of 1815 was increasingly criticized and disturbed by European liberals and nationalists. Before he came into office the bloodless French Revolution of July 1830 had overthrown Charles X and pushed into power Louis Philippe, the 'citizen king'. Palmerston welcomed the change with enthusiasm, as he always welcomed the emergence of constitutional régimes overseas. In 1832 he told the House of Commons that 'the independence of constitutional States . . . never can be a matter of indifference to the British Parliament, or, I should hope, to the British public. Constitutional States I consider to be the natural Allies of this country.' He was to show later on in Belgium, the Iberian Peninsula, Switzerland, and Italy how much weight he attached to constitutional government. 'It is impossible without a constitution', he wrote to the British Ambassador in Vienna in 1841, 'fully to develop the natural resources of a country and to ensure for the nation security for life, liberty and property. I hold that there is no instance in past or present times under a despotic government where these objects have been attained.'[2] He went much further than Canning in actively assisting the cause of European liberalism and in claiming the right to protect it against autocratic pressure,

[1] Quoted by Webster, *The Foreign Policy of Palmerston* (1951), vol. II, p. 793.
[2] *Ibid.*, p. 787.

and, when the revolution of 1848 broke out, all his sympathies were with the moderate opponents of the old and decaying social and political order.

Nonetheless, the main cornerstone of Palmerston's policy was national interest, and he found it necessary to emphasize that 'we have no eternal allies and no permanent enemies. Our interests are eternal, and those interests it is our duty to follow.'[1] He wanted Britain to be 'the champion of justice and right', but he wanted her to interpret that task as she herself chose.

The Belgian revolt of August 1830 touched a traditionally sensitive area of British interests, the same area which had prompted Pitt to act in 1793. Recognizing the justice of the Belgian case, Palmerston worked patiently and skilfully to check French ambitions in Belgium, to avert a war, and to secure a permanent settlement. He employed diplomacy by conference to secure his objectives, thereby in a sense looking back to Castlereagh rather than to Canning. After the Conference of London (1831) had agreed to establish a new independent Belgian state with great power guarantees of its neutrality and integrity, there still remained innumerable practical difficulties, particularly the refusal of the Dutch to accept the settlement, and it was not until sanctions had been applied against Holland that peace was assured. The Tories talked in vain of the dangers of a 'Dutch war', and although the final treaty about Belgium was not signed until 1839, 'the glorious name of Palmerston' had become associated for all time with the making of a new state. He had been fortunate during the first stages of the Belgian question in that the Tsar was preoccupied with Poland, Metternich was busy in Italy, and Prussia lacked effective political leadership, but his personal success was none the less real.

In 1839 also in the Near East Palmerston was on the way to achieving his second great success. The situation there had remained complicated after the Treaty of Adrianople as a result of the continued internal weakness of the Ottoman Empire and the active ambitions of Russia. In the first instance, Palmerston suffered a diplomatic defeat. In 1832 a quarrel between the Sultan and Mehemet Ali—who had deservedly been congratulated by Bentham for his internal reforms—led to war between vassal and master, and the Egyptian armies occupied Syria and opened the way to Constantinople. Appeals by the Sultan to Britain for help were turned

---

[1] *Hansard*, 3rd series, vol. XCVII, p. 122

down—the British fleet was over-committed elsewhere—and as a last resort Turkey turned to Russia. By intervening alone, the Russians were able at Unkiar Skelessi in July 1833 to secure an extremely favourable eight-year treaty of mutual defensive alliance and assistance with the Turks. To Palmerston the most objectionable part of the treaty was the agreement of the two powers to consult confidentially on all their respective interests. This, he said, made the Russian ambassador the chief cabinet minister of the Sultan. Palmerston's first reaction was to try to stop the ratification; his more mature policy was to give the British ambassador discretionary power to summon the British fleet at the request of the Sultan. He regarded this as a defensive policy to be employed only after Russia became the aggressor, believing, as many of his fellow countrymen believed, that Russia was 'pursuing a system of universal aggression on all sides, partly from the personal character of the Emperor, partly from the permanent system of the government'[1], and became increasingly concerned not only about the integrity of Turkey but its capacity to reform itself from within.

Palmerston's concern was put to the test in 1839 when Mehemet Ali and the Sultan went to war for a second time. This time it was the Sultan who took the initiative—against British advice—but the sequence of military events was the same. Once again Ibrahim's armies advanced from Syria; once again they threatened Constantinople. To make matters worse for the Turks, the Sultan died before the news of Ibrahim's victories reached him and was succeeded by a rather bewildered boy of 17, while the Turkish fleet deserted to the enemy. It looked as if the Ottoman Empire was to be delivered not to the Russians but to Mehemet Ali. In this serious emergency the ambassadors of the five great powers in Constantinople agreed—on Metternich's initiative—to present a collective note to the Sultan (27 July 1839) asking him not to engage in direct negotiations with Mehemet Ali. Agreement between the powers stopped at this point, and it was against this background of crisis and divergence that Palmerston, employing all the diplomatic weapons in his armoury and having to handle a divided cabinet in London—on one occasion he threatened to resign—achieved a great personal triumph and an important public settlement.

---

[1] Quoted L. Ashley, *Life of Lord Palmerston* (1879), vol. I, p. 296. Wellington withdrew the discretionary order in his brief tenure of the foreign secretaryship in 1835, and Palmerston inserted limitations after 1836.

Broadly speaking Palmerston's aim throughout the tangled negotiations was to maintain an independent Turkey as strong as possible and to check the power of Mehemet Ali, whom he dismissed as 'an ignorant barbarian'. Aware of the nature of the basic divergences between the powers, he was anxious to maintain peace and to keep London the effective centre of the diplomatic web. In the course of negotiations, a deep rift between Britain and France became apparent. The official French view was that Mehemet Ali could not and should not be forced to leave Syria; in many French circles he was regarded as 'un nouvel Alexandre', as the possible founder of a new Francophil Arab empire in the Middle East. Palmerston feared that Mehemet was or would be a French 'puppet'; that his ambitions, if unchecked, would lead to his controlling both the main routes to the east; that France and Russia might come to a mutual understanding about him. To check these 'dangers', Palmerston himself drew into closer relations with Russia, and in 1840 forced the weak and reluctant Whig cabinet to allow him to abandon France and to sign a quadruple agreement with Russia, Austria and Prussia (15 July) imposing terms on Mehemet Ali and promising to help the Sultan to enforce them. The decade-old understanding between Britain and France which had made Thiers, the new French prime minister, exclaim in March 1840 that Britain 'is our natural ally and in the East our necessary ally' was broken, and the way was prepared for the bombardment of Beirut and the defeat of Ibrahim Pasha by combined British, Austrian and Turkish forces. After the fall of Acre, news of which reached the Western capitals towards the end of November, it was clear that Mehemet Ali's power to create an Arab empire in the Middle East had been completely broken.[1] In July 1841 the four powers declared that their common interests had been served, and, along with France (at last brought back into the 'concert') and Turkey, they signed the Convention of the Straits which affirmed the 'unanimous determination' of the Sultan and the five signatories 'to conform to the ancient rule of the Ottoman Empire, by which the passage of the Straits must always be closed to foreign warships, so long as the Porte is at peace'. For all the reference to 'ancient rule', the great powers were in fact signing the first large-scale international agreement on this zone of contention and conflict.

[1] Wellesley in an unsolicited testimonial to Palmerston called his achievement 'the ablest act both of diplomatic and military policy that ever within my memory has proceeded from the British Cabinet'. Quoted Webster, *op. cit.*, vol. II, p. 732.

Palmerston's success lay in both the manner of his achievement and in the ends he secured. He had proved the value of unflinching determination and consistency of purpose in face of both domestic and foreign opponents. He had broken Mehemet Ali, ensured the preservation of Turkey, induced Russia to renounce her exclusive privileges in Constantinople, and organized a concert of Europe to achieve his ends. It is important, however, in estimating the extent of his triumph to look at it in its full perspective. In the long run, Turkey was too decayed to be preserved, and any suggestions of dramatic reform—like one which the Turks conveniently produced out of the hat in November 1839—were conjuring tricks, not genuine promises of regeneration. Furthermore, Russia's decision to renounce her privileges at Constantinople was a voluntary act of the Russians themselves, meeting Russian needs and inspired by Russian motives. A full study of Russian diplomacy is as relevant to understanding Russo-British relations as a study of Palmerston's diplomacy. There was still scope for serious disagreement between the Russian and British governments in the following period, and there were no reasons for believing that the initial situation of 1839, when the Tsar was preoccupied with family affairs and annoyed at the Turkish distraction, would repeat itself. Finally, Palmerston alienated many genuine supporters of Anglo-French friendship in Paris. To some extent the alienation was inevitable, because of divergences of outlook and tortuous French diplomacy, but Palmerston's extravagant language and bouts of truculence made the gulf wider than it need have been.

The Whig cabinet fell in September 1841 two months after the Straits Convention had been signed, and the new foreign secretary, Lord Aberdeen, who had held the same position for a short period before 1830, made it his main task to restore good relations between Britain and France. To understand the problems he had to face it is necessary to look back to Palmerston's policy towards France before the Near Eastern crisis of 1839–40.

The original bases of the Anglo-French 'alliance' which Thiers complained was being destroyed between 1839 and 1841 were the 'constitutionalism' of the French government after the Revolution of 1830, and Palmerston's distrust of Metternich's policies in Germany and Spain. Sir Frederick Lamb, Britain's ambassador in Vienna, had remarked succinctly in 1832 that 'the principle of movement and that of repose are at war openly or underhand throughout Europe and people are much more liberal or the reverse than they are Frenchmen, or Germans or Italians'.[1] Palmerston's policy was pursued against this background, particularly after September 1833 when the Russians and Austrians in three agreements, loosely called the Treaty of Münchengrätz, bound themselves to the support of monarchical solidarity and conservative principles and, at Metternich's instigation, agreed to maintain the *status quo* in Turkey so that they could concentrate on resisting 'revolution' in the West. They guaranteed each other's Polish possessions and promised mutual assistance in case of rebellion. Münchengrätz was in a very real sense the Holy Alliance in miniature, stripped of its 'sublime mysticism and nonsense'. The aims it expressed were diametrically opposed to those of English and French liberals and radicals, who were attached to the cause of Polish independence, anxious to unite the forces of European liberalism, and interested in the Near Eastern question only in so far as it might drive a wedge between the two great autocratic powers, Russia and Austria.[2]

Palmerston was no radical, but he joined with the French in April 1834 in a Quadruple Alliance of the 'constitutional states' of the West—Britain, France, Spain and Portugal—and conceived of it as 'a powerful counterpoise' to the three absolutist monarchies of Eastern Europe. He even hoped that 'all the smaller planets of Europe will have a natural tendency to gravitate towards our system'. There was an element of suspicion in his calculations however—the fear that France would act by herself as she had done in 1823. The terms of the alliance bound the Regents of Spain and Portugal with French and British help to compel Carlos and Miguel, the leaders of the forces of autocracy in their respective countries, to leave their own soil. The Portuguese problem was quickly settled when Miguel left Portugal and in 1836 Queen Maria married a Coburg husband; in Spain, where it was less easy for the British navy to interfere, cruel war continued between Carlists and 'constitutionalists' (backed by a contingent of British troops) until 1839. Relations between Britain and France became seriously strained over the complex Spanish question—there were differences even

[1] Quoted Webster, *op. cit.*, vol. I, p. 177.
[2] In the context of the Near Eastern question, however, Münchengrätz took the sting out of Unkiar Skelessi. Austrian interests in the Near East were not at this time significantly different from those of Britain, and the agreement between Russia and Austria to preserve the existing sovereignty of the Ottoman Empire against subversion either by a regency or by a complete change of dynasty (Mehemet Ali) was a check on Russian policy.

when the Quadruple Alliance was signed—and if Palmerston was occasionally too frank and impatient, Louis Philippe as early as 1835 was flirting with Metternich to disturb the West-East pattern of 1834. Palmerston certainly recognized the necessity of an understanding with Britain's nearest neighbour: 'It is of great importance', he told one of his envoys in 1836, 'not only to be well with the French government, but to appear to all Europe to be so. England alone cannot carry her points on the Continent; she must have allies as instruments to work with.'[1]

Between 1841 and 1846 the high-minded Aberdeen in London and Guizot in Paris, for all their mutual desire to revive the '*entente cordiale*', found themselves unable to avoid difficult and contentious issues. There were disputes about the methods used to put down the African slave trade, involving the right to search ships, about the control of Tahiti, and nearer home about the governments of Greece and Spain. More alarmingly, behind the European differences was the ambitious and increasingly dangerous private policy of Louis Philippe. Tired of ostracism, Louis Philippe longed for full recognition as a partner of the powerful sovereigns of the East. The main centre of trouble was once again Madrid, a city of limitless international intrigues, and the main issue was the Spanish marriage question—who should wed the young Queen Isabella and her sister. Isabella's position had been safely established after the final defeat of the Carlists in 1839, and Louis Philippe's strongest wish was to place an Orleanist prince—or at least a Bourbon prince—on the Spanish throne. Aberdeen, who for all his high-mindedness was weak at heart and completely lacking in Palmerston's diplomatic skill, followed what Palmerston described as diplomacy by 'sliding scale', even giving general assurances to Guizot that he would not support a Coburg candidate. Palmerston was quite realistic when he challenged Aberdeen and stated openly in the House of Commons in August 1844, that 'influence abroad is to be maintained only by the operation of one or the other of two principles—hope and fear. . . . Powerful countries should be taught to fear that they will be resisted by England in any unjust acts either towards ourselves or towards those who are bound in ties of amity with us.'[2]

---

[1] Quoted Webster, *op. cit.*, vol. I, p. 414. He also recognized the danger of France (with its Mediterranean navy) becoming closely associated with Russia. 'It must not be forgotten', he remarked, 'that the one great danger to Europe is the possibility of a combination between France and Russia.'

[2] *Hansard*, 3rd series, vol. LXXV, p. 1870.

The open failure of the *entente* came after Peel's defeat and Palmerston's return as foreign secretary, at the age of 62, in 1846. Making no reference to previous conversations between Aberdeen and Guizot, Palmerston wrote a memorandum taking the exclusion of an Orleanist candidate to the Spanish throne for granted: he went on a month later to lay down that he did not think that the French had any right to exclude a Coburg prince. Louis Philippe this time acted with resolution. At the end of August 1846 he announced the betrothal of his son to Queen Isabella's sister and of Queen Isabella to her cousin, Don Francis, who was generally reputed to be impotent. The Anglo-French *entente* was at an end, and the autocratic monarchies were consequently given a free hand to repress the increasingly discontented liberal and national elements in Eastern Europe. In November 1846 Russia, Austria and Prussia destroyed what little was left of Polish independence, and between 1846 and 1848 Louis Philippe and his erstwhile Liberal ministers tried to come to terms with the other Europe, the Europe of Metternich. This time the diplomatic problem centred on Switzerland, where Guizot and Metternich together encouraged Catholic separatist elements in their attempt to break away from the Swiss federation, and Palmerston was left alone to save Swiss unity and independence. To confirm his position as the one remaining defender of liberal principles and the unflinching opponent of Metternich, he sent Lord Minto on a mission of enquiry to Italy in 1847. 'Italy', Palmerston told Russell in July 1846, 'is the weak part of Europe, and the next war that breaks out in Europe will probably arise out of Italian affairs.'[1] Wherever Minto went, including the papal states, he advocated the merits of 'a system of progressive improvement'.

The leaders of the other Europe, who now included Louis Philippe, were exchanging views early in 1848 as to the best means of checking British policy, but before they could get far, they were all toppled from their eminence. Louis Philippe went first—in Palmerston's phrase, one of 'the cunning who outwit themselves'.[2] Metternich, who had long foreseen the catastrophe, followed: 'Happy would it have been', Palmerston commented, 'if this had happened some years ago.'[3] Revolutions were soon in progress in

---

[1] Quoted H. C. F. Bell, *Lord Palmerston* (1936), vol. I, p. 412.
[2] Ashley, *op. cit.*, vol. II, p. 56.
[3] *Ibid.*, p. 57.

France, Austria, Prussia, Hungary and Italy. Only Russia with its lumbering social system and Britain with its highly-developed economy and its constitutional government, remained unscathed. Both had outlets for discontent—the one in the wastes of Siberia, the other in new lands overseas—but both were necessarily drawn into the complicated politics of a restless Europe. Before examining Palmerston's approach to the problems of 1848–9 it is useful to go back behind the chronicle of the years from the settlement of 1815 to the outbreak of the revolutions to examine the machinery of British policy and to uncover the main determinants of British power.

2. NATIONAL INTEREST AND NATIONAL POWER

Between 1815 and 1848 the effective control of foreign policy lay in the hands of only six foreign secretaries—Castlereagh, Canning, Dudley, Aberdeen, Wellington and Palmerston. During the same period there were eight prime ministers and twelve home secretaries. The task of foreign secretary was as onerous as it was responsible. Much of the routine work of a growing department as well as the conduct of high policy fell on the shoulders of the foreign secretary himself. In 1815, at the end of the wars, thirty-three people were employed in the Foreign Office; in the 1830s, after Canning had spent much time modernizing procedure and rules of business, Palmerston was still depending on a staff of thirty-nine and writing himself the drafts of any despatches of great importance.[1] 'When I see the assistance Metternich has', wrote Lamb from Vienna, 'my only wonder is how our English Secretary of State can get through his business at all.'[2] While the scope of foreign policy was extending yearly—as expressed, for instance in the number of Foreign Office despatches—and while the volume of information released to Parliament and the press was also rising in an unprecedented manner, the official machinery for managing foreign relations was inadequate and archaic. Almost everything depended on the personality of the foreign secretary himself.

The great exception, of course, was the dependence of the foreign secretary on information gathered from ambassadors who,

---

[1] In 1858 an additional assistant under-secretary was added, and during the 1860s in addition to the chief clerk and three other clerks dealing with audit, estimates and accounts, there were eight senior clerks, each with an assistant, in charge of eight divisions, into which the countries of the world were divided.

[2] Quoted Webster, *op. cit.*, vol. I, pp. 56–7.

because of difficulties in speedy communication, operated almost independently, particularly at moments of crisis. Travel times were long by late nineteenth-century standards—in the suden political crisis of 1834 which led to the recall of Wellington andPeel, it took Peel, travelling 'at the utmost speed', twelve days to get back from Rome to London [1]—and news as well as people moved slowly. It was not until 1850 that a submarine cable was laid under the English Channel,[2] until 1866 that the Atlantic cable was effectively in use, and until 1871 that the Viceroy of India couldsend a telegraph message from Simla to Washington by way of an evening party in London. The diplomatic (and military) geography of the world was thus quite different in the first half of the nineteenth century from the diplomatic geography of the twentieth century. Not the least point of difference was that there was no Suez Canal until 1869, after the end of the period described in this book.

It is difficult to generalize about the calibre of British ambassadors. Although there were career diplomats at the newer courts of the Hague, Brussels, Stockholm, and across the Atlantic in Washington (a *chargé d'affaires* was left to handle a difficult question of mediation in Washington in 1835–6) the diplomatic prizes went to political or personal nominees. When Palmerston took over in 1830 he found Tory diplomats in control, for instance, at Berlin, St. Petersburg and Madrid (Lord Sidmouth's nephew: 'his very name', said Palmerston, 'was against him'). Before long he had placed in four of the key diplomatic posts—Paris, Vienna, Madrid, and Constantinople—men with whom he was on good terms and with whom he could communicate freely and intimately. They by no means always agreed with him, however, and there was much scope in this period for individuals to stamp their personalities on the offices they held. George Canning's cousin, Stratford Canning, first Viscount Stratford de Redcliffe, stands out in this respect. He became a précis writer in the Foreign Office in 1807, served very briefly in Copenhagen as his first post, and as early as 1808 made his first acquaintance with Constantinople and the Levant. In 1812 he negotiated the treaty of Bucharest between Russia and Turkey; in 1824 he was handling the problem of Alaska; in 1825 he was back in Constantinople, directly concerned with the problem of the Greek revolt, and finally from 1842 to 1858 he was ambassador

---

[1] The journey took fifty-nine hours in the late 1860s.
[2] The Irish cable was not laid until 1853.

in Constantinople, the dominating figure in the local diplomatic corps.

In their daily operations the ambassadors, great or small, lacked a highly trained, expert staff to assist them. Like the foreign secretary in London they had to depend for the most part on men whose qualifications were always open to doubt. In addition they were either hindered or helped by a flood of attachés, well-connected young men who treated the diplomatic service as a finishing school.[1] The social prestige of diplomacy counted for more than any material benefits received, for foreign embassies felt the distant hand of the Treasury cutting expenditure as much as did the foreign secretary himself in London. While Palmerston was compelled to reduce the efficiency of the courier service (already far slower than the private banking service of the Rothschilds), the pressure was felt abroad in different ways—an attempt was made in Paris for example to sell the embassy building which Wellington had bought cheaply in 1814, and at Constantinople there was no decent residence at all.

The increasingly rich but socially divided Britain of the period from 1815 to 1848 was prepared to spend only a tiny fraction of its resources on diplomacy, and even that fraction was resented. The pressure of the Treasury sprang simply from the demand for 'retrenchment' which country gentlemen and urban radicals shared. In the *Extraordinary Black Book*, a radical catalogue of 'incomes, privileges, and power', the section devoted to ambassadors and diplomatic missions began with the sentence: 'There is no branch of our multifarious civil services which requires to be more keenly investigated, and more unsparingly curtailed than our foreign embassies.' The condemnation was bound up, as was Bright's indictment in the middle of the century, with an attack on the aristocracy. If men of a 'high order of talents, but of private station in society were to be selected for foreign missions', it went on, 'the national business would be incomparably better done, and the extravagance of the diplomatic service might be corrected without a murmur.'[2]

Similar arguments were used in relation to the far bigger sums of

---

[1] For changes in the attaché system and the attempt of the Foreign Office to subject it to closer control, see S. T. Bindoff, 'The Unreformed Diplomatic Service, 1812–60' in *T.R.H.S.* (1935). By 1860, out of seventy-eight attachéships, thirty-four were paid. Bright could then describe the well-connected but paid employees of the Foreign Office as the recipients of aristocratic outdoor relief.

[2] 1831 edn., p. 183.

money devoted to foreign loans, raised privately, and to defence expenditure, although some selected loans—like a notoriously ill-managed 'Liberal' loan to Greece in 1825—won radical support and were sponsored by men like Hume and Bowring. The radicals, indeed, were inconsistent in the 1820s and 1830s in pressing for more vigorous support for Liberal movements overseas and at the same time refusing the necessary means to make such a policy effective. It was only Cobden and Bright at a later date who showed any consistency in their approach to this question, logically relating their view of Britain's 'interests' to their estimate of financial and moral commitments.

Military expenditure was, of course, a main target of radical criticism, bound up as it was with traditional dislike of a standing army, with growing resentment at the association of the army with the system of social privilege, and with disapproval of the unequal taxation system. The last point is particularly pertinent, for although Britain in 1830 was spending only about one-sixth of its national income on government, interest on the national debt, a debt largely built up in time of war, accounted for more than half the total public expenditure, and the cost of the army and navy for more than half the rest. The fiscal system in operation was regressive,[1] and it was not until Peel reintroduced the income tax in 1842 and set about reducing indirect taxation that those with higher incomes were taxed according to their capacity to pay. The burden of taxes on the poor seemed directly related, as the Whig wit Sydney Smith put it, to 'the inevitable consequences of John Bull being too fond of glory'.[2] In 1851 G. R. Porter, the statistician, calculated that during the first half of the nineteenth century the national defences had cost the country more than £1,200 millions, $52\frac{1}{2}$ per cent of which had been expended in fourteen years of war, and the remaining $47\frac{1}{2}$ per cent in thirty-five years of peace.[3] In 1846, the year that the corn laws were repealed and with the peaceful-minded Aberdeen as foreign secretary, over 28 per cent of total government spending was devoted directly to the army and navy.

[1] The share of total revenue borne by the customs was higher after 1815 than before 1793 and continued to rise until Peel's reforms. Specific duties levied at a fixed sum on each pound of merchandise were relatively higher too as a result of the post-war price fall.

[2] For Smith's brilliant description of John Bull being taxed from the cradle to the grave, 'at bed or board, couchant or levant', see S. Buxton, *Finance and Politics* (1888), vol. II, pp. 19–20.

[3] *Progress of the Nation* (1851 edn.), p. 506.

Although the navy was the main support of Britain's post-war foreign policy, the necessary element of power behind the diplomatic moves of both Canning and of Palmerston, it was not until Peel's ministry of 1841–6 that annual expenditure on the navy (except in 1844) exceeded annual expenditure on the army. There was always room for debate on the size of both estimates and the way in which they were allotted, and radicals like Joseph Hume, who was dismissed by Palmerston in 1822 as a 'dull and blockheaded fellow', established their parliamentary reputation by incessant probing and criticism. On one occasion in 1835 Hume spoke more than forty times in one night.

To understand the relationship between official policy and the views of the opposition it is necessary to turn not only to statistics but to the concept of 'national interest' which successive foreign secretaries tried to safeguard. The most vital cluster of British interests centred on Britain's position as a maritime and commercial nation, and it is not surprising that there was little domestic criticism of those sections of the Vienna settlement which strengthened Britain's command of world ocean routes. By the terms of the first Treaty of Paris (1814) Britain received the Cape of Good Hope, Heligoland, Malta, Ceylon, Mauritius and islands in the West Indies. These places were not acquired for their colonial wealth—Europe's richest overseas colony, the Dutch East Indies, was handed back to Holland—but for their strategic importance and their harbour and supply facilities. In the subsequent bargaining at Vienna Britain went on to secure from the other great powers agreements for opening certain rivers to navigation and (less effectively) for abolishing the slave trade.

The strength of this second preoccupation illustrates the way in which maritime power expressed itself in vigorous leadership on broader issues than narrow 'national interest'. Wilberforce insisted to Castlereagh that 'it would be shocking to restore to Europe the blessings of peace' and at the same moment to create 'traffic in the persons of our fellow-creatures',[1] and Castlereagh did his best to meet Wilberforce's entreaties. For the whole period from 1815 to 1850 successive British foreign secretaries were directly concerned with enforcing the implementation of abolitionist promises made by foreign powers and with securing the enforcement of abolition where no agreements had been made. The struggle was a difficult

[1] Quoted by R. Coupland, *The British Anti-Slavery Movement* (1933), pp. 154–5.

one—the number of slaves transported across the Atlantic actually increase in the late 1830s—and involved elaborate systems of naval patrol. Palmerston, who used the navy to such useful effect in supporting the cause of Liberalism in Portugal and Greece, was the most eloquent defenerd of an energetic assault on all foreign slave ventures. 'Is it not the duty of every government and of every nation, on whom Providence has bestowed the means of putting an end to this crime', he asked Parliament in 1844, 'to employ those means to the greatest possible extent?' Bright criticized Palmerston's 'benevolent crotchet for patrolling the coasts of Africa and Brazil' and maintained that the commercial system was being put out of gear by 'our meddling with this slave question', but Palmerston's action received very great public approval.[1]

The ideological implications of Britain's maritime and commercial power served then to focus attention on an extended obligation. There were in addition certain practical deductions which could be and were derived from the facts of British sea power. It was in Britain's interest to protect trade, wherever protection was feasible. The business background of Canning's South American policy accounted for much of the support it received, and the British recognition of Buenos Aires, Mexico and Colombia took the form cf signing commercial treaties with them.[2] In weighing the merits of Palmerston's policy in the Near East in 1839 and 1840 it is relevant to note the increase of British trade in the Levant between 1830 and 1839, the growing importance of the corn trade, the difficulties implicit in Mehemet Ali's policy of maintaining monopolies in cotton and coffee, and the importance—before the opening of the Suez Canal—of the land route to India.[3] It was in 1839 too that an outrage committed on a British crew near Aden led to the occupation of the town and its hinterland, which were later to become an essential link in British means of communication with India and the Far East. In the Far East itself there was a similar but more spectacular series of moves in the same year and after a brief war between Britain and China the Treaty of Nanking (1842) ceded Hong Kong to Britain and opened up five treaty ports, including Shanghai, to foreign trade. The war with China was known as the Opium War—for British traders objected to the Chinese prohibition

---

[1] *Ibid.*, pp. 177 ff.

[2] See W. W. Kaufmann, *British Policy and the Independence of Latin America* (1951).

[3] For some of the problems involved, see V. J. Puryear, *International Economics and Diplomacy in the Near East* (1935).

of foreign opium supplies—but opium was merely a pretext. What was at stake was the willingness of the Chinese to admit foreigners and foreign imports to their soil. On this occasion the core of British interest was associated not with ideology, as in the case of the anti-slavery movement, but with the simple desire to develop trade and to maintain prestige. Palmerston was just as eloquent, however, in talking of British leadership—'we stood at the head of moral, social, and political civilization', he declared—as he had been when denouncing the slave trade.

What was Britain's cluster of interests in Europe, where Palmerston had to cope with allies and rivals, and where, like other foreign secretaries, he believed in the paramount importance of peace as 'our ultimate object'? Essentially British interests derived from Britain's geographical position—an island off the coast of Europe and not a full part of it, an island moreover with a population less than that of any other great power except Prussia. It was usually in moments of crisis, like 1793, that statements of immediate British interests in Europe were made clearly and concisely. At the beginning of his Foreign Office career, however, Palmerston made it abundantly clear that he recognized the importance to Britain of a neutral and independent Belgium free of French influence or indeed of the influence of any other great power or combination of powers. While being clear-sighted enough not to accept the King of Holland's arguments for the continued existence of a Dutch-Belgian buffer state, he acknowledged that it was necessary to permit Belgium to be prosperous without destroying the economic position of Holland. At the opposite end of Europe, he quickly came to the conclusion after taking office—it was not his opinion before he took over—that Britain's interests depended on the maintenance of Turkish integrity and independence. It was a momentous decision which involved great risks, but it is difficult to dispute the view that quite apart from the merits of the British desire to keep the Russians out of Constantinople, Europe as a whole was not ready in the 1830s or 1840s to wrestle with the ponderous problems of Turkish disintegration. In the Iberian peninsula too Britain had strategic and commercial interests, centred not only on Gibraltar but on the River Tagus in Portugal; Canning had been particularly sensitive to the problems of this area,[1] and Palmerston followed the same lines of action.

[1] See above, p. 347.

As far as the land mass of Europe between the Channel and the Straits was concerned, British foreign secretaries from 1815 to 1848 continued to talk of the 'balance of power' as an operative maxim. Castlereagh, like Metternich and the war-time allies, had believed in stopping France from becoming gigantic in order that she might be great; France was not only treated generously in 1815, but allied occupation was terminated two years ahead of schedule and in 1818 the reparations bill was written down to about one-fifth of the original figure. Castlereagh argued that as a result of the peace settlement 'calculations of prudence' had become simpler in the post-war world; the number of geographical units had been reduced and 'there remain but few Pieces on the board to complicate the Game of Publick Safety'.[1] Canning in his turn emphasized the need for 'respect for the faith of treaties—respect for the independence of nations—respect for that established line and policy known by the name of "the balance of power in Europe" '[2], while Palmerston claimed the right to resist any attempts to derange 'the existing Balance of Power', and 'to alter the relative strength of States'.[3] His major fear was another Tilsit—an alliance between France and Russia, and he recognized the importance of a stable Austrian Empire in Central Europe, a 'central bulwark' in any system of balance.

For all such talk—and it was almost continuous—the phrase 'balance of power' begged many questions. How far was it automatic? How far did it depend on a European concert? Did it imply 'dictating affairs of nations most remotely situated and apparently unconnected with ourselves'? Castlereagh, who believed in the virtues of organized concert while he was far from blind to its disadvantages, came to understand the impossibility of uniting Europe in a scheme of general intervention against 'moral contagion' and 'military revolt'. This did not prevent his critics, among whom was the young Russell, from attacking his policy as a deviation from the old system of balance, necessitating a shift in the rôle of Britain from the holder of the balance to one single voice in an 'Amphictyonic Council'.[4] Canning emphasized that the attempt to main-

[1] Quoted Temperley and Penson, *op. cit.*, p. 59.
[2] R. Therry, (ed.) *The Speeches of Canning* (1828), vol. V, p. 4.
[3] Quoted Temperley and Penson, *op. cit.*, p. 136.
[4] *A Letter to the Right Honourable Lord Holland on Foreign Politics* (1819). Castlereagh on one occasion at least spoke of 'the counsels of the great powers' being unified in such a manner that they created 'the efficiency, almost the simplicity of a single state'. Quoted Halévy, *op. cit.*, p. 131.

tain a balance was part of 'our duty to ourselves' rather than of our duty to others. In a Europe where the balance was changing Palmerston never relaxed in his efforts to defeat the aims and aspirations of that particular country or group of countries which he regarded as the most dangerous element in any given international situation. In the early 1830s he focused his attention on the Eastern powers and on Metternich's leadership of 'the other Europe': in 1839–40 he vigilantly concentrated on France. The most cogent of his opponents in both these situations was Richard Cobden, then a little-known public figure. His criticisms were far more thorough than those of Russell, for he challenged the whole conception of a balance of power. He did not object to Russian control of Constantinople and to Austrian domination in Europe, and he joined with Bright in denouncing Palmerston's attempt to enforce the abolition of slavery. He considered the balance of power a deceptive slogan designed to lure Britain into dangerous entanglements all over the world, and demanded a cheap foreign policy based on the 'commonsense' of disarmament and free trade in place of the expensive display of glory and gunpowder.[1]

Cobden's criticism was lit up by an intense internationalism, grounded in belief in a free-trade Utopia. It was in starkest form, however, as a cogent and even a corroding analysis, that it challenged the way in which Palmerston and his supporters viewed the relationship between British interests and British power. Cobden wanted to deflate British foreign policy; Palmerston, accused by a section of the more romantic radicals of not supporting liberal causes with sufficient fervour, wanted Britain to 'count for something in the transactions of the world'. He wanted London to be at the centre of the diplomacy of his age. 'It is not fitting,' he held, 'that a country occupying such a proud position as England . . . should lock herself up in a simple regard to her own internal affairs, and should be a passive and mute spectator of everything that is going on around.' As soon as the issues of foreign policy were stated in such terms something much more than concern for a European balance of power was involved. British 'opinions' counted as well as British 'interests', a set of beliefs about government and society—both instinctive and deliberate—as well as a catalogue of obligations and entanglements. Palmerston's belief that a large measure of initiative

---

[1] See in particular his pamphlets *England, Ireland and America* (1835) and *Russia* (1836).

and leadership should be supplied by a powerful Britain, and that 'England is strong enough to brave consequences'[1] contrasted sharply with Cobden's belief that Britain's foreign policy should merely be a modest by-product of her economic supremacy. What Cobden did not see was that behind Palmerston's language of leadership was a genuine sense of the limits of effective action and a knowledge of the practical arts of diplomacy, and that he was always anxious to avoid a general war or to over-commit limited British forces. Palmerston found it increasingly difficult during the last stages of his life to maintain his influence in a Europe where organized German military power was becoming a key factor. It was at the mid-point of his mature career—the revolutions of 1848 and their aftermath—that both the strength and weakness of his approach to international questions was displayed, and in 1850 and during the Crimean War, before the new Europe took shape, that the English debate on his policies was most heated and far-ranging.

3. 1848 AND AFTER

The revolutions of 1848 were heralded by liberals and nationalists all over Europe as a decisive break with the world of the past, and the springtime of a new age. For a time, as in 1789, Paris seemed to be at the centre of a new continental 'movement' which would carry new nations and new classes to victories far more sweeping and decisive than any that Palmerston had ever dreamed of. In Baden, Württemberg, Saxony, and Bavaria there were noisy demonstrations by enthusiastic crowds; in the capital of Prussia, Frederick William IV, after hesitating between appeals to his soldiers and to his subjects, promised his 'dear Berliners' constitutional government; in Austria the Emperor retired to Innsbruck while a National Assembly in Vienna played with plans for a new liberal order; in Italy, Milan and Venice drove out Austrian troops from their territories, and Charles Albert of Sardinia offered them support, promising in a memorable phrase that 'Italy will do it herself' and achieve unity and independence; in Hungary Kossuth and the nobility were driven further and further along the road to revolution. The Hungarian poet, Petöfi, admirer both of Burns and Byron, a few years earlier had prophesied the universal mood of 1848:

[1] Quoted Ashley, *op. cit.*, vol. I, p. 146.

I dream of days of bloodshed
In which an old world dies,
And see from smoking ruins
A phoenix world arise.

To Palmerston 1848 meant above all an 'avalanche of despatches' and a welter of new preoccupations; his main interest was to prevent revolution from turning into international war. Secondary interests were associated with the continued maintenance in a changing Europe of a balance of power. Despite his refusal to recognize the 'system' of Metternich, Palmerston shared few of the dreams of Petöfi or the European intellectuals who gave the revolutions their dynamism. He preferred the language of 'improvement' to the more general talk of 'movement' and believed that 'large republics seem to be essentially and inherently aggressive'.[1] He saw himself as a mediator and a pacifier, although as always he played his part in a flamboyant rather than a subdued style.

His policy towards the revolution in France, which seemed to be the key to European politics everywhere else, was well summarized in a letter to the British ambassador in Paris before the month of February was through. 'We desire friendship and extended commercial intercourse with France, and peace between France and the rest of Europe. We will engage to prevent the rest of Europe from meddling with France . . . the French rulers must engage to prevent France from assailing any part of the rest of Europe. Upon such a basis our relations with France may be placed on a footing more friendly than they have been or were likely to be with Louis Philippe and Guizot.'[2] Basically this trust was justified. The French revolutionaries were not disposed to place their country at the head of a new revolutionary crusade. The poet Lamartine, propelled into power by jets of his own rhetoric, shocked some timid English Tories by his 'Manifesto of the Fourth of March' announcing the repudiation of the settlement of 1815, but he publicly emphasized that the French revolution was not an attempt to create disorder in Europe and privately wrote to Wellington telling him to read the declarations of the Provisional Government in their 'real sense' and not at their face value. Palmerston, therefore, was not confronted in 1848 with a dangerous neighbour threatening European peace, and by 1849, when the various European revolutions had collapsed

[1] Quoted *ibid.*, vol. II, p. 73.
[2] *Ibid.*, p. 71.

or been suppressed, France had lost in authority and leadership.
It was against this background that Palmerston welcomed the rise
to power inside France of Louis Napoleon, first as President in
1848 and then three years later after a *coup d'état* as Emperor. The
English foreign secretary looked behind Napoleon's admitted
ambition to the services he had performed in checking 'the deplorable state of society' in France. In making such a conservative
assessment Palmerston went further than English opinion both in
the Whig cabinet and in the streets, and alienated both English
nationalists and supporters of the exiled Guizot.

It was during the pre-Napoleonic period, when France was still
ruled by a provisional government, that Palmerston tried to check
independent French action in Italy and to make his own contribution to an Italian settlement. His policy in Italy in 1848 was a logical
continuation of the policy of the Minto mission. He sympathized
with the cause of Italian constitutionalists and tried to encourage
them as much as possible, and when Charles Albert went to the
support of the anti-Austrian rebels in Milan and Venice he recognized that whether his actions were justified or not, 'he could not
help doing so'. The failure of Palmerston's subsequent policy shows
the weakness of good intentions. For all his sympathy with Italian
liberals, Palmerston based his actions not on a belief in Italian
emancipation and unity but on two general propositions—first that
the French should not act in Italy alone, and second that Austria
would be a stronger country and thus a more stable element in the
European balance if her Italian possessions were abandoned. The
Alps, he maintained, were Austria's natural boundary and her best
defence, and there was no necessary clash between Italian romanticism and Austrian realism. The maintenance of Austria was 'an
object of genuine interest to all Europe and to no country more
than England'. Unfortunately for Palmerston the Austrians did not
see the logic of this appraisal, and the Queen, along with a section
of the Whig cabinet, did not accept the practical implications which
derived from it. Palmerston was thus unable to make any substantial contribution to the solution of the Italian question. If there
was no 'war of principles' in Italy in 1848–9, with France and Austria
as the contending champions, this was the result of muddled French
policy rather than of English mediation; the most that could be said
for Palmerston was that when France did intervene alone in spring
1849 (in Rome) it was not as a liberator but as a guardian of order,

an equivocal rôle which embarrassed Louis Napoleon as much as it angered the Italian nationalists. The very temporary 'solution' of the Italian question in 1849—the restoration of the *status quo* of 1815—was determined neither by Britain nor by France but by the military weakness of the Italians and their inability to defeat their Austrian masters. Prince Schwarzenberg who took over in Vienna after the defeat of the Austrian liberals was a believer in force and saw the opportunities of separating England and France from each other. When Palmerston protested against the ruthless way in which Radetzky repressed the remnants of Italian resistance, Schwarzenberg replied in language which permittedof no easy answer: 'Lord Palmerston regards himself too much as the arbiter of Europe. For our part we are not disposed to accord him the rôle of Providence. We never impose our advice on him in relation to Ireland; let him spare himself the trouble of advising us on the subject of Lombardy.'[1]

The voice of Schwarzenberg was one of the new voices of reaction and repression which were growing louder in the Europe of 1849. In Italy the limitations of Palmerston's policy were shown; in Germany, where he never displayed quite the same sympathy for unification or liberal constitutionalism, the limitations were equally apparent and in the long run more serious. Palmerston was in no position in 1848 to show initiative and to teach lessons to German politicians, and on one specific issue—that of Schleswig Holstein— he opposed German claims and prepared the way for many difficulties in the future. He wished these two duchies to remain Danish and thereby to keep Denmark big enough and strong enough to preserve the Baltic balance of power. But he could no more maintain the *status quo* in Schleswig Holstein than he could secure change in Italy. After the estates of the two duchies broke with Denmark in 1848 and appealed to the German Confederation for support, Prussian troops marched in and expelled the Danes. Palmerston, exaggerating the interest of Russia and Sweden in maintaining Danish power, was soon lost in the intricacies of fruitless mediation —with no allies abroad and with little public interest in the question at home. An armistice agreement in August 1848 between Frederick William IV and the King of Denmark owed little to him, but it helped to undermine the cause of the German liberals at Frankfurt without permanently settling what soon became one of the trickiest

[1] Quoted A. J. P. Taylor, *The Italian Problem in European Diplomacy* (1934), p. 191.

problems in European diplomacy. The Schleswig Holstein question was on the margin of history in 1848, but the subsequent collapse of the liberals and nationalists in Frankfurt was to dictate the shape of international politics for more than a century. Henceforth the realization of German unity was to depend not on talk but on deeds, not on freedom but on discipline, not on thinkers but on soldiers, not on ideas but on power. Both the nature of the German question and the means taken to handle it made it inevitable that the influence of Britain in Europe would necessarily diminish after 1848. Schwarzenberg had challenged Palmerston's implicit assumption that London should be the centre of ideas and advice: a school of new German 'realists' deflected Palmerston's policy far more effectively than Cobden.

The drive for and ultimate realization of German unity exposed the inadequacies of an active British foreign policy. It was not at once, however, that the balance of power which Palmerston appreciated and understood was shattered. From 1848 to 1865, the year of his death, a combination of circumstances diverted attention from the facts of the future: the circumstances included Britain's continued and increasing economic power, the further stages in the struggles for Italian unification, delay in Prussian reorganization, the dreams of Napoleon III, and above all the Crimean War.

The link between many of these issues was Austria, the lumbering multi-national state which had interests in three of Europe's danger areas—Italy, Germany and the Balkans. In contemptuously rejecting Palmerston's interpretation of Austrian interests in Italy, Schwarzenberg was not disinteresting himself in any way in Germany. Indeed he did not wish to limit Hapsburg commitments in any way. When in May 1849 Prussia offered assistance to the Austrians to help suppress the Hungarian revolution on condition that Austria should recognize Prussia's supremacy in the new Germany, the offer was turned down. Instead Schwarzenberg accepted the unconditional assistance of Tsar Nicholas I, who feared that successful revolution in Hungary might reopen the whole of the dangerous Polish question. At this critical date in the history of counter-revolution all things connected. French intervention in Rome saved Nicholas from the fear of revolutionary intervention elsewhere, and he recognized the French Republic on the same day that he announced his intervention in Hungary. Further east, he signed an alliance with Turkey providing for a joint occupation of the Danubian princi-

palities of Moldavia and Wallachia which the Russians had entered
as a counter-revolutionary measure in July 1848.

It was at this point in the counter-revolution that the determinants of Palmerston's policy can be most clearly separated out. He
welcomed the restoration of the 'central bulwark' of Austrian power
and even the intervention of Russia, adding that he hoped it would
be finished off as quickly as possible. The sympathy and kindness
he had hitherto shown to representatives of the Hungarian revolution had always stopped short at positive intervention or war. He
disliked Kossuth's deposition of the Hapsburgs and his design for a
Danubian federation, and while he knew that Kossuth was popular
among English radicals and that public feeling ran strong in favour
of the Poles, he had promised the Tsar in April 1848 'never to do
anything underhand or ungentlemanlike on those matters'.[1] When
Nicholas acted a year later, therefore, he made no attempt to protest.
Later in 1849 he refused to give any support to Prussia when it
was clear that all hopes of German unity under Prussian leadership
were being thwarted by the Austrians. Although he remarked on
one occasion that Germany under Prussia 'would be the best solution
and a solid barrier between the great Powers of the Continent',[2]
he disapproved of Frederick William's behaviour and strongly supported the Danes when hostilities were revived in Schleswig Holstein in March 1849. When Prussia and Austria signed an agreement
at Olmütz in November 1850 it marked a complete Prussian surrender; a further alliance between them in May 1851 included a
Prussian guarantee of Austria's territory in Italy.

Although Palmerston accepted the principle of intervention
against the revolution in Hungary, he characteristically opposed the
way in which that intervention was carried out. He wrote to the
British ambassador in Vienna comparing Austrian 'atrocities' with
those of negroes in Africa and Haiti and describing their troops as
'the greatest brutes that ever called themselves by the undeserved
name of civilized men'[3]; when Nicholas I, who had also disapproved of Austrian savagery, went on to demand from Turkey
the extradition of four Polish generals who had fled there after the
rising, and the Austrians asked for the return of 4,000 Hungarian
refugees, Palmerston supported the Turks in their refusal to let the

[1] Quoted Ashley, *op. cit.*, vol. II, p. 79.
[2] Quoted A. J. P. Taylor, *The Struggle for Mastery in Europe* (1954), p. 37.
[3] Ashley, *op. cit.*, vol. II, p. 105.

men go. British and French fleets moved to the Near East—a British squadron actually entered the Dardanelles—and although Palmerston refused to sign a formal treaty with the Turks, he believed that once again, in partnership with France, he had upheld the freedom of the Ottoman Empire. The Near Eastern crisis of 1849 was of short duration. It showed, however, that Palmerston was convinced that in the Near East Britain had a genuine 'interest' at stake, that Britain and France, the allies of the not far distant Crimean War, could already move in concert, that sea-power made all the difference to the effectiveness of British foreign policy, and that the preoccupation of the forces of European order with the task of internal pacification still left Britain with a rôle to play. It showed too, however, that Palmerston had made many enemies in England during the course of the last two years. Quite apart from extreme radicals who accused him of betraying the liberal cause, there were 'Broadbrims' in the cabinet who opposed British intervention in the Near East. Just as ominous, the Queen was increasingly resentful both of Palmerston's methods and his policies. Throughout the difficult months of 1848 she had expressed strong support of the Austrian case in Italy and a complete lack of confidence in the foreign secretary's ability to protect national honour and to preserve peace. She even pleaded with Lord John Russell, the prime minister, to appoint a new foreign secretary who would eschew 'intemperate language' and restore good relations with old friends. Russell refused, giving as a reason his desire to avoid 'internal trouble' and his fear of 'making Palmerston an enemy by displacing him', but the Queen persistently returned to the attack.

An ideal opportunity for a full public review of Palmerston's foreign policy was presented not long after the successful British action at Constantinople. On his way back from the Dardanelles Admiral Parker called in at Athens to try to enforce the dubious claims for compensation of a Portuguese Jew, 'Don Pacifico', who by the accident of birth in Gibraltar claimed British citizenship. When the British minister failed to get satisfaction from the Greeks, Greek ships were seized and a general blockade was proclaimed. There were protests from Russia and France, the Russians accusing Britain of 'abusing the advantages afforded by her immense maritime superiority', but the Greeks had to make an abject surrender after a secret session of their two Chambers.

The 'Don Pacifico' case rallied all Palmerston's enemies in

England. Prince Albert and the Queen were infuriated with his 'mode of doing business', *The Times* dwelt on the 'tissue of caprices, machinations, petty, contentious and everlasting disputes',[1] and Peelites like Aberdeen contrasted the state of affairs in 1846 when Britain was 'honoured, loved and respected by every state in Europe' with the anger and opposition of all overseas countries in 1850. They were so anxious to point out Palmerston's weaknesses that they forgot how much had happened in Europe between 1846 and 1850.

In June 1850 a motion of confidence in Palmerston's foreign policy proposed by the radical Roebuck was carried by 310 votes to 264 after a notable debate which ranged far and wide over the whole of Palmerston's policy. In a remarkable speech, which his opponent, Gladstone, called 'a gigantic intellectual and physical effort', Palmerston discussed the Greek incident—legitimately underlining the faults and failings of the Greek government and declaring boldly that all British subjects like Romans of old could rely on 'the watchful eye and the strong arm of England'—and defended the main sequence of his actions in 1830s and 1840s. Turning to the revolutions of recent years, he branded as revolutionaries not only the wild men of Europe but the blind men, those who 'dammed up the current of human improvement until the irresistible pressure of accumulated discontent breaks down the opposing barriers'. Standing as a reconciler of freedom and law, Palmerston won much moderate support. He was opposed by a dazzling galaxy of leaders— by Gladstone, who saw in his policy merely 'a rash desire, a habitual desire, of interference'; by Peel, who a few days before his death warned against converting diplomacy from 'a costly engine for maintaining peace' into an agency of 'angry correspondence' and conflict; by Cobden, who urged non-intervention in the domestic affairs of other nations and rated 'the maintenance of peace, the spread of commerce, and the diffusion of education' above all the 'labours of Cabinets and Foreign Offices'; and by Disraeli who made a rash and tasteless speech, which exposed his ignorance of the main facts of recent international relations. Essentially the debate was about the rights of British intervention overseas rather than the correct way of interfering, and on that ground Palmerston secured a great personal success.

At the end of 1851, however, he was pushed from office. Con-

[1] 22 June 1850.

tinued disputes with Prince Albert and the Queen made his position difficult, and Russell retained him at the Foreign Office only because he knew that his weak government would fall without him. There was a quarrel between them about the right of Palmerston to meet the exiled Kossuth in London and matters finally came to a head when in December Palmerston expressed approval of Louis Napoleon's *coup d'état* to the French ambassador before consulting the Queen or the cabinet. Russell who, like the Queen, was tired of the unrepentant foreign minister, replaced him by Lord Granville, a close friend of the Prince Consort. In a formal note to Russell the Queen claimed that Palmerston had not only committed 'faults in form and method' but had embarked upon 'a personal arbitrary perversion' of the basic principles of policy. She asked for the shape of British foreign policy in the future to be more specifically defined and an account given of 'how the general principles are to be practically adapted to our peculiar relations with each Continental State'. In his reply Lord Granville showed just how difficult it was to do what the Queen—and doubtless every subsequent student of nineteenth-century diplomatic history—wanted. He talked vaguely of the encouragement of 'moral, intellectual and physical progress among all other nations'; he stressed the importance of the security of foreign trade; he demanded a better diplomatic service; and he pleaded nobly that 'this country should in her relations with other States do by others as they would be done by'. But he finally had to admit that 'with regard to occurrences likely to have international consequences, no general rule can uniformly be applied'.[1] In the meantime, while these platitudes were being pennep, the fall of Palmerston had been greeted throughout Europe as a triumph for the counter-revolution, and in Vienna Schwarzenberg gave a ball in honour of the news.

4. THE CRIMEAN WAR

The year when Palmerston fell from power—1851—was the year of peace and the Crystal Palace. A gigantic olive tree planted inside the palace was regarded as a symbol of international concord, just as the rows of machinery at the Exhibition were seen as tokens of economic community through trade and manufacture. Yet there was a hollow note about most of this propaganda. The peace of 1851 depended not on the triumphs of free trade but on the victory

[1] Printed in Temperley and Penson, *op. cit.*, pp. 183–6.

of the forces of counter-revolution in Europe, and there was something fragile and precarious about even the pacific record of the English people itself. Within three years the London olive tree had become as anachronistic as the 'trees of liberty' planted in 1848 in the streets of Paris, and Tennyson in his poem *Maud* (1855) was welcoming enthusiastically the coming of the Crimean War:

> For the peace, that I deem'd no peace, is over and done,
> And now by the side of the Black and the Baltic deep,
> . . . flames
> The blood-red blossom of war with a heart of fire.

The Crimean War was a popular war which appealed to all sections of the community. 'The nation is still in its essentials the same as it was forty years ago', wrote *The Times*, 'sound to the core, true to itself, animated by a spirit . . . which has neither been contaminated by unexampled prosperity nor degraded into a mere power of calculating profit and loss by the sordid doctrines of a shallow and ungenerous utilitarianism.'[1] In other words, Patriotism had not been buried with Protection either in 1846 or in 1851. Unfortunately, as *The Times* itself was soon to emphasize, Patriotism was not enough. The Crimean War brought with it tragic disillusionments rather than spectacular victories. Against its stormy background Palmerston for the first time became prime minister and ended the war as the 'man of the hour'. The irony was that had he been at the Foreign Office the war might have been prevented. There is no better vindication of his policy than the contrast between his firm grasp of essentials and the good-natured ineptitude of Lord Aberdeen who as prime minister of a Whig-Peelite coalition ministry, which lasted from 1852 to 1855, allowed the country to drift into war.

The immediate origins of the Crimean War sprang out of a local squabble between Roman Catholic and Greek Orthodox monks for the control of the Holy Places in Jerusalem. Napoleon III, seeking for prestige, maintained the ancient French patronage of the Catholic Church; Nicholas I stood by his claims to exercise authority not only over the Jerusalem monks but over the whole ten million Orthodox Christians in the Turkish Empire. Afraid of French pressure not at Jerusalem but at Constantinople, and concerned to stem what he still regarded as the 'cause of revolution', Nicholas tried to win English support by reviving talk of an agreed and

---

[1] 9 November 1854.

mutually advantageous partition of the Ottoman Empire. 'When *we* are agreed,' he told the British Ambassador, 'I am quite without anxiety as to the rest of Europe. It is immaterial what others may think or do.' Feeling that the British government under Aberdeen would not closely associate itself with the French, and considering himself sure of Austrian backing, Nicholas sent Prince Menshikov to Constantinople in February 1853 to re-establish Russian prestige. On the Tsar's orders Menshikov put forward the largest possible Russian claims, which were to be followed up, if need be, by a display of force. At this point the Turks, advised but not unduly influenced by the British ambassador Lord Stratford de Redcliffe, gave way on the Holy Places question, but held out against Russia's comprehensive demands over protection of Christian subjects which even Aberdeen thought 'unreasonable' and Palmerston provocative. In consequence a British fleet was ordered to Besika Bay outside the Dardanelles in June 1853, and was joined by a French fleet a few days later.

Russian anger at the Turkish rejection of the Menshikov proposals induced them to cross the River Pruth and to march into the Danubian provinces of Turkey in June 1853. Palmerston, who was home secretary in Aberdeen's coalition government, proposed resolute action and the sending of the British fleet through the Straits. He was over-ruled by the cabinet, however, and steps were taken instead to hammer out in Vienna a diplomatic compromise in the names of Austria and Prussia as well as of England and France. By this time, although the Russians would accept mediation the Turks were unwilling, and on October 1853 they declared war on Russia. They were still far from sure of British support. Aberdeen was loath to prop up the Turkish Empire, and his foreign secretary, Lord Clarendon, wrote with annoyance, 'the beastly Turks have actually declared war'. Many responsible sections of British opinion backed Aberdeen. 'We see not how any man who gives the smallest thought to the consequences and chances of lighting up the flames of war', a provincial newspaper put it, 'can urge upon us such a mad and murderous enterprise.'[1]

The advocates of war were held back until at the end of November 1853 the tense international situation became critical. When the Russian fleet attacked and destroyed an inferior Turkish squadron at Sinope on the Black Sea, the power balance was shattered.

---

[1] *Sheffield and Rotherham Independent*, 23 July 1853.

'Sinope', wrote *The Times*, 'dispels the hopes we have been led to entertain of pacification. . . . We have thought it our duty to uphold and defend the cause of peace as long as peace was compatible with the honour and dignity of our country . . . but now war has begun in earnest.'[1] Though the 40,000 readers of *The Times* were a strategic group in the population, the government still hesitated, and it was not until January 1854 that the pressure of opinion and the fear of independent French action drove the divided cabinet (Palmerston had actually resigned in December 1853, nominally on a different issue, but had consented to rejoin the ministry) to send the British fleet into the Black Sea with instructions to confine the Russian navy to its base in Sebastopol.

Officially war between France, Britain, and Russia did not begin until the end of March 1854. In the intervening period it became clear that Russia could not rely on the support of the two conservative countries of Eastern Europe, Prussia and Austria. The apparently all-powerful decision-maker of 1849 was now in complete isolation. It had certainly not been Nicholas's intention to provoke a major war with Britain and France, but critics of British policy, like Cobden and Bright, offered no satisfactory alternative policy to that followed by the British government. In condemning the war-like language of Palmerston and thundering against the mischievous delusion of 'balance of power', they failed to make clear the weaknesses of Russian policy or to attribute a fair share of blame to the vacillations of Aberdeen. It is significant that Gladstone and the Peelites, who were the last people to advocate an adventurous foreign policy, came to recognize the necessity for a war to vindicate 'the claims of public law against the ambitions of an aggressor'.

The Crimean War, however, cannot be understood from a perusal of the motives of members of the British government. Throughout Britain there was a powerful current of popular Russophobia. Earlier in the century, several English writers had argued that the Russian objective was to capture Constantinople, and that once Constantinople was captured, the conquest of India and universal dominion lay within Russia's 'easy grasp'. They familiarized important sections of the reading public with the view that only enslaved peoples anxious for their own liberation could

---

[1] 13 December 1853. By that time the *Sheffield and Rotherham Independent* too was claiming that 'mere talking to the Tsar will do nothing . . . the time appears to be at hand when we must act so as to dissipate the evil designs and efforts of Russia' (17 December 1853).

drive the semi-barbarous Russian despots back into the steppes of
Asia.[1] Nothing fundamentally new was said or written by Russo-
phobes in 1854 and 1855 which had not been said by 1830, but in
the post-1848 world the critics of Russia stirred not limited sections
of the reading public but large crowds of people. Ex-Chartists, like
Harney, warmed to a struggle against the universal enemy of the
popular cause; Davi Urquhart,d the most militant of all Russo-
phobes, set up 'working men's foreign affairs committees' to study
Russian 'crimes' as well as to condemn them; the cities, particularly
Sheffield and Newcastle, rallied giant demonstrations; and the press,
growing yearly in influence, stimulated eager excitement. The very
representative radical and co-operator G. J. Holyoake talked of
'an unknown and unsuspected instinct of race'[2] stirring in his blood,
and confessed an undiscriminating patriotism while the war was in
progress. When what he felt was a premature peace was signed, he
refused to illuminate his office in Fleet Street, preferring to display
a large placard bearing Elizabeth Barrett Browning's verses on the
continued plight of Poland, Italy, and Hungary.

The excitement of British opinion meant that all the war-time
actions of the British government (and the conduct of Prince Albert
and the Queen) would be scrutinized by 'the people' just as anxiously
as the actions of the Russians themselves, and that there would be a
demand for the war to continue until a 'real victory' had been won.
Paradoxically, therefore, the ambitious Napoleon III, who tired of
the war first, ultimately became the hero of the minority peace party
in England, even of men like Cobden and Bright, while extreme
English radicals of a crusading temperament continued to press for
large-scale changes which would have altered the European balance
far more drastically than any European statesman wished to do.

Popular dreams in England of resolute action against the Russians
in Finland, of marches deep into the Ukraine, and of open declarations on behalf of Polish and Hungarian freedom were abruptly
broken during the course of the war, which was fought in the
distant Crimea, 'the eye tooth of the bear', and was punctuated by
persistent diplomacy. Failure to achieve quickly either ambitious
general hopes or strictly limited objectives such as the capture of

---

[1] See J. H. Gleason, *The Genesis of Russophobia in Great Britain* (1950).
[2] *Life and Letters* (1908), pp. 3–5. Holyoake made the illuminating admission that
'such was the insularity of birth and race that I for a long time mistrusted all people not
English. . . . Judging from myself, I regarded the coast towns of England as though
they were inhabited by alien races.'

Sebastopol, soon provoked radical sections of English opinion to protest more violently against the ineptitude of the government in London than the wickedness of the Russians. In the terrible Crimean winter of 1854-5 the Aberdeen government fell after trying in vain to resist a radical motion, introduced by Roebuck, to have a parliamentary committee set up to inquire into 'the condition of the army before Sebastopol'. When the voting figures were announced—305 to 148—they were greeted not with the usual cheers but with profound silence followed by derisive laughter. The government had been condemned, in the words of a contemporary, to 'the most ignominious end recorded of any Cabinet in modern times'.

The crisis did not end with the defeat of the Whig-Peelite coalition. Derby would not form a ministry: Russell could not form one and Palmerston was left to take over, 'l'homme inevitable'. To begin with he was the creature of the people rather than their master; his first night in the House of Commons was a failure, and doubts were expressed among extreme radicals whether the 'whiskered wonder of over seventy years' was likely to lift the war out of the quagmire into which it had been forced by 'the aristocratic system, a system of total incapacity'. As the war-time situation improved in the summer of 1855, however, Palmerston began to stand out again as 'a Triton among the minnows'. In September news of the capture of Sebastopol reached London, and the first military objective of the war, which had been expected to fall during the first few weeks of hostilities, was at last in allied hands.

It was neither deficiency of courage nor the great strength of Russia which was the obstacle to British success—the facts of Russian power which had loomed so large in men's minds in the counter-revolutionary aftermath of 1848 looked much less impressive in 1854. The reason for disillusionment was simple. Although the workshop of the world, Britain was not well equipped to buy military glory. The desire to save money had reduced the effective size of the army to about 65,000 men at home, 40,000 in the colonies, and 30,000 in India on the eve of the Crimean War. The Militia Act of 1852 had set up a small reserve, just in time, but the annual spell of three weeks' training was as inadequate as the pay, equipment and armament of all the troops. There were no reasons in 1854 for feeling confidence in high military leadership. Lord Hardinge, the Commander-in-Chief, was 69, Lord Raglan was 65, and the youngest Major-General, Lord Lucan, was 54. It is not surprising that *The Times* quoted Chatham's comment on the officers appointed to command in the American war: 'I do not know what effect these names have on the enemy, but I confess they make me tremble.'[1] Even more serious, as the war soon revealed, the army machine was creaking and inefficient; there was no adequate provision for food, supplies, transport, or the care of the sick and wounded; and there was a shortage of intelligent leaders in the field, aggravated by the system of purchase of army commissions and promotions by seniority. It was a series of blunders which was responsible for the greatest display of bravery during the fighting—the famous Charge of the Light Brigade on 18 October 1854. The only great new personality to emerge from the struggle was not a hero but a heroine. Florence Nightingale, animated by an over-riding sense of service, not only won the love and affection of thousands of sick and dying soldiers, but pressed reforms on a frequently hostile military administration and revealed to the public its responsibility for the lives of the men at the front. At the same time her powerful ally, W. H. Russell, one of the first newspaper war correspondents, exposed every blunder in the Crimea with such ruthlessness that his critics at home accused him of treason.

Criticism did not stop at the higher command; it soon became associated with an attack on the aristocracy as a whole and even on the 'unconstitutional' position of Prince Albert. While working-class journals like the *People's Paper* pleaded for a Soldiers' Charter, businessmen as well as political radicals began to ask impatiently whether it might not be possible to employ in the conduct of affairs not 'men of influence' but men of property. They looked longingly to 'the great railway administrators and contractors, the men who manage lines of packets, who own and direct successfully the operation of whole fleets of merchant ships', and argued that men 'conducting their own operations with unfailing regularity' were the right kind of people to end 'repeated official blundering.'[2] Victory, on which such high hopes were centred, thus seemed to depend not merely on replacing Aberdeen by Palmerston but on casting the searchlight over all the hidden corners of English society.

Roebuck's demand for a Select Committee should be seen against this background; in pressing for full publicity Roebuck was demanding an investigation not only of foreign affairs but of

---

[1] Quoted C. Woodham Smith, *The Reason Why* (1953), p. 136.
[2] *Sheffield and Rotherham Independent*, 3 March 1855.

domestic administrative and social arrangements. Although his Select Committee failed to produce dramatic revelations and by the time that it reported Palmerston had re-established his own leadership, it cannot be doubted, as the American Nathaniel Hawthorne remarked, that the war gave the country a vast impulse towards democracy'.

When Sebastopol fell there was great public demand for more triumphs, and the Queen herself in congratulating the British commander urged him to 'lose no time in following up the great victory and driving the Russians from the Crimea'.[1] Napoleon III, however, was anxious by this time for peace, and the new Russian Tsar, Alexander II (Nicholas I died in March 1855), accepted in January 1856 four points which had been drawn up in Vienna in concert with Austria in July 1854. They laid down that a European guarantee of the principalities of Moldavia and Wallachia should be substituted for a Russian protectorate; that there should be international control of Danube navigation; that Russia's claim to protect all Turkish Christians should be rejected, and that instead the five great powers together should provide a guarantee; and that the Straits convention of 1841 should be revised 'in the interests of the Balance of Power in Europe'. It was only the last of these points which was really a matter of contention in the last stages of the war, for the Russians withdrew from the principalities in August 1854 and even earlier were prepared to abandon their claims to protect all Turkish Christians. The real issue in the last months of the war, at least as far as the governments were concerned, was Russian naval power in the Black Sea. By the time that the contestants met in Paris in February 1856 and a month later signed the Peace of Paris which brought the Crimean war to an end, relations between Britain and France had been severely strained and Palmerston had realized that any continuation of the war to achieve 'additional security' would have meant fighting alone.[2] While Napoleon was fêted in Paris as 'Emperor of Europe' there were ominous signs of public disapproval of the French on this side of the Channel, and the heralds who proclaimed the peace in London were hissed at Temple Bar. In Sheffield the local inhabitants, who had enjoyed great prosperity during the war, were advised that there was no justification for 'spending our time in processions or our money in gaslights'.

[1] *Letters*, vol. III, p. 143.
[2] For some of the diplomatic problems of the war, see G. B. Henderson's stimulating *Crimean War Diplomacy and other Historical Essays* (1947).

The war had cost Britain over 22,000 lives and over £50 million.
Was the expenditure worthwhile? The small and extremely unpopular group of peace-at-any-price radicals who opposed it said no
—it had brought with it '10 per cent income tax and 0 per cent
benefit to mankind'. Whereas radicals of a different persuasion, like
Roebuck, Harney or Karl Marx, looked to liberation and the
salvation of Europe by force, Cobden and Bright replied tartly that
their opponents were confounding 'the blowing up of ships and the
slaughter of thousands with the cause of freedom'. To Cobden and
Bright the danger of Russian power was a 'phantom', the necessity
of upholding Turkey an 'absurdity', and all British intervention
abroad costly 'meddling'. When war broke out, treasure chests were
squandered and angels of death were far more conspicuous than
angels of glory. Such views were not calculated to appeal to the
crowds during the Crimean War, and Bright's effigy was burnt in
the streets of Manchester to the cry of 'send him to old Nicholas'.
Nonetheless, Bright's lonely eloquence left a powerful impression
on a somewhat awed House of Commons and even moved Stratford
de Redcliffe when he visited the 'crater of a volcano' that was once
Sebastopol to ask, 'if this is a sample of the effects of war, who
would not be willing to join his [Bright's] peace party?' The question has been put by most historians of the Crimea ever since and
there has been something like a consensus, until recently, that the
war was the most unnecessary in the history of modern Europe.

It would be a mistake, however, to take for granted what Cobden
and Bright said. They prejudged the war from the start and did not
understand the importance of its results. The Peace of Paris ensured
that the Danubian principalities could become independent of
Russia, and at the same time neutralized the Black Sea. Neither of
these achievements can be dismissed easily. The first of them made
possible the eventual emergence of an independent Roumania; the
second, accepted under protest by the defeated Russians and
abrogated in 1870, nonetheless checked Russia in her advance
towards Constantinople and gave the Turks a new opportunity to
set their house in order. That the opportunity was not taken was
less significant than the very real blow dealt to Russian influence in
Europe as a whole. In the aftermath of the revolutions of 1848
Russian power had reached its peak; it was never to be so strong
again until the twentieth century. It is reasonable to argue indeed
that the ultimate unification of Italy and Germany was made far

easier by the new power situation created as a result of the Crimean War.

If the Near Eastern question as a whole was not settled in 1856 any more than it had been in 1841, the reason was that it was a question which could not be 'settled' in any final sense except on the basis of a strong Turkey or a supreme Russia. There was no hope of a permanent balance. Turkish promises to reform continued to mean little in practice despite Palmerston's hopes, and as the century went by the hope of a strong Turkey receded. As the certainty of disintegration grew, a new element entered into international calculations—the desire of Balkan nationalities to shape their own destinies instead of having them determined by the great powers. The significance of this new element was lost on both Palmerston and Cobden in 1856, but was already touched on by Gladstone, the man who later in the century was to review the whole Near Eastern question in moral terms, taking nationalism into account. In 1856, however, Gladstone spoke still very vaguely for the future, while Palmerston spoke for the present when he claimed confidently that the war had freed Turkey from 'eternal dictation' and had raised a 'firm barrier against future aggressions'. There was basic truth in the claim. For all the horror and hysteria of the Crimean War it was not without results.

5. FACTS AND IDEALS OF EMPIRE

By the time that the balance of forces in Europe was changing to Britain's disadvantage, Britain had built up and in many cases consolidated very substantial interests and power outside Europe. There was continuity in this process. Although most Victorian statesmen as well as spokesmen of the Manchester School professed a distaste for 'Empire' and talked of colonies as a 'millstone round our necks',[1] they were rarely indifferent to the development of active British overseas interests. In some cases there was a continued growth of what has been called 'formal Empire', the Empire of the flag; more frequently there was an expansion of 'the informal Empire' of trade, investment, and influence.[2] The expansionist process always depended on an amalgam of economic, ideological,

---

[1] A phrase of Disraeli in 1852, quoted Monypenny and Buckle, *op. cit.*, vol. I, p. 1201.

[2] The distinction between 'formal' and 'informal' empire is made clearly by C. R. Fay in the *Cambridge History of the British Empire* (1940), vol. II, p. 39.

and political impulses—on pressures from the periphery as well as from the centre.

In both 'formal' and 'informal' empire the same basic relationships can be traced—the romance of exploration, the development of trade, the movement of British capital, the creation of new forms of economic dependence, the pushing forward of the frontiers, and the emergence of new markets. Whereas in some territories, however, there was a constitutional problem of 'dominion'—as there was in Canada or Australia—in others there was only a problem of economic 'entry' and of the maintenance of political guarantees for continuous economic control. In neither set of circumstances were the problems simple. Constitutional developments between 1815 and 1867 in Canada, Australia, New Zealand, and Cape Colony were necessarily at least as tangled as constitutional developments in Britain, although most of the moves made were, as in Britain, towards increasingly representative government; the politics of control were equally complex, involving not merely peaceful trade or gunboat diplomacy—to take the two extreme techniques employed—but realistic assessments of the economic value of the territory concerned, the strength and resilience of its social and political structure, the readiness of its rulers to collaborate with the British, and the extent to which other European countries were prepared to allow Britain a free hand.[1]

For the expansionist process to be successful, flexibility above all else was needed, and if in some degree this was automatically provided as a result of a mass of separated and unco-ordinated decisions taken by scattered people (traders, missionaries, officials) thinking and working in all parts of the world, the range and variety of those decisions itself created further problems of adjustment and organization. The Colonial Office in London—organized as a separate unit again in 1812[2]—was always only one of many factors in the politics of empire. It was limited in the scope of its operations not only by the jealousy and opposition of other departments at the centre and the intermittent and often ill-informed criticism of members of Parliament, but by the development of new forces on the remote frontiers of exploration and settlement. Only a secretary of state of the highest rank and reputation could have rescued it

---

[1] See the stimulating but highly controversial article by J. Gallagher and R. Robinson, 'The Imperialism of Free Trade' in *Ec. Hist. Rev.* (1953).

[2] Its first permanent under-secretary was appointed in 1825.

from being forced to deal slowly and cumbrously with its mass of world-wide preoccupations, and few men of the highest calibre served in that position. It was not until 1836, when Sir James Stephen became permanent under-secretary, that systematic office routines were established. Stephen has been described as 'the most honourable, sensitive and self-critical of men',[1] but his critics lampooned him as 'Mr. Over-Secretary' or 'Mr. Mother Country'.

There were four groups in England who were specially interested in problems of Empire—investors, foreign trading concerns, missionary societies, and a small section of the radicals. Their interests were not identical, and except in special circumstances they did not agree among themselves or with the British government. The investors cared little for formal colonies as such—they were as interested in opportunities in South America as in South-East Asia—while the government did not consider that it was one of its responsibilities to go to their assistance when loans were in default or economic enterprises jeopardized. The missionary societies, who often had strong links with the government— Stephen was a loyal member of the Church Missionary Society and a nephew of Wilberforce—were frequently at loggerheads with the trading companies. Indeed, there was often a battle in distant places between gin and Bibles. While Wilberforce's successor, Fowell Buxton, was building up the Aborigines Protection Society after 1836 to safeguard the interests of innocent 'natives', the trading companies were frequently engaged in skirmishes and local struggles which made a mockery of the concept of trusteeship.[2] The section of the radicals which was most interested in Empire was led by Edward Gibbon Wakefield, one of the few early nineteenth-century Englishmen to realize the advantages of 'systematic' as distinct from 'haphazard' colonization. At a time when the Manchester School was condemning all colonies as expensive luxuries which required aristocratic governors and garrisons of troops to maintain them, Wakefield was pleading for a planned colonial land policy, organized emigration, and social as well as economic development.[3] His views

---

[1] W. L. Burn, *The British West Indies* (1951), p. 125.

[2] See W. Howitt, *Colonisation and Christianity* (1836). There was often, however, an alliance between missionaries and traders. John Williams in his *Narrative of Missionary Enterprises* (1840) asked for support of missions because they promoted trade, and Livingstone told a Select Committee in 1865 that 'wherever I have seen a mission established, the mission promotes civilization and commerce'.

[3] *The Art of Colonisation* (1849). For contrasting theories of colonization see K. E. Knorr, *British Colonial Theories* 1944); C. A. Bodelsen, *Studies in Mid-Victorian Imperialism* (1924).

had only limited appeal, but they could occasionally fire sparks in unlikely places. 'The *transmarine possessions* of England are a mine as yet partially explored', wrote an anonymous pamphleteer in 1834, 'inexhaustible in its treasures, requiring only population, with a moderate amount of capital to become of immense importance and wealth to the mother country.'[1]

As the nineteenth century went by, 'population' moved abroad not only to colonies but, like capital, to places where the opportunities seemed brightest. As a result the whole picture of overseas development was transformed. It is impossible to understand the way in which Britain fitted into the Victorian world without giving a very important place to the movement of men. In 1815 less than two thousand persons left the British Isles: in 1830 the figure was over 55,000; by the late 1840s and early '50s more than a quarter of a million emigrants were leaving in single years.[2] Although the Mecca of the United States had by far the greatest drawing power, for a time the discovery of gold in Australia provided a powerful counter-attraction and influenced over 80,000 persons to leave England for Australasia in 1852 alone. 'Auri sacra fames', wrote Lord Ashley in his *Diary*, 'what no motive human or divine, could effect, springs into life at the display of a few pellets of gold in the hands of a wanderer. This may be God's chosen way to fulfil his commandment and "replenish the earth".'[3]

Taking the period from Waterloo to the late 1860s as a whole, emigration became an organized industry with agents, shipping rebates, and propaganda offices, and more than seven million people left the British Isles—very large numbers from Ireland after the famine—about half of whom went to the United States, one-and-a-half millions to Canada, and one million to Australia. Most of the emigrants owed little to government assistance and large numbers of them crossed the seas in the most difficult and dispiriting circumstances. They were drawn or driven by different motives, personal, economic, religious, and social, and though it is possible to relate the general rhythm of movement to economic forces on both sides of the Atlantic and in England and the Antipodes,[4] the fascinating

---

[1] *Hints to All Parties* (1834).

[2] Many of the emigrants returned. In examining nineteenth-century emigration statistics, it is important to distinguish between gross and net emigration.

[3] Hodder, *op. cit.*, p. 450.

[4] See *inter alia*, U. Jerome, *Migration and Business Cycles* (1926); W. A. Carrothers, *Emigration from the British Isles* (1929); B. Thomas, *Migration and Economic Growth* (1954); W. S. Shepperson, 'Industrial Emigration in Early Victorian Britain' in *J. Ec. H.* (1953).

adventure story is best seen in something more than economic perspectives.

Without the safety valve that emigration afforded, it is difficult to know what would have happened to English—and certainly to Irish—society in the 1840s and '50s. Just as important, without the broad canvas of the world development English nineteenth-century history would seem strangely parochial and restricted.[1] Quite apart from voyages of discovery and exploration—Livingstone to Africa, Burton to Brazil and Tanganyika, or Layard to Nineveh—which the Victorians might well have described as 'Neo-Elizabethan'[2]—there were many boldly conceived schemes of settlement. *Reynolds's Newspaper* might sound a gloomy warning to oppressed workers that miserable though they were in England, they would be 'ten thousand times more miserable when turned adrift in some colony at the end of the world',[3] but this was to misunderstand the nature both of the challenge and of the opportunity. As the land utopias of the Chartists and early radicals faded into the background in the late 1840s and '50s, the far more exciting appeal of foreign settlement took its place. It was an appeal which looked not back to the past, as did so many working-class dreams, but forward to a new future. Although many emigrants were disappointed—large numbers of them returned—far more made their terms with the Australian city or the mid-Western frontier. They could even sing in the process

> Brave men are we, and be it understood
> We left our country for our country's good,
> And none may doubt our emigration
> Was of great value to the British nation.

As a result of emigration Britain secured an emotional as well as an economic frontier in distant parts of the world, and it was not difficult later in the century to paint a popular picture of the Empire very different from that of the Manchester School. Britain

---

[1] 'Great Britain', wrote Roebuck in 1849 (*The Colonies of England*), 'may by means of her colonies, acquire a power and influence which her own narrow territory might not permit her to attain.' Roebuck was born in Madras and brought up in Canada.

[2] Both Kingsley and Froude sang the praises of the Elizabethan sailors, and in *Westward Ho* (1855) Kingsley wrote enthusiastically of 'brave young England longing to wing its way out of its island prison, to discover and to traffic, to colonize and to civilize, until no wind can sweep the earth which does not bear the echoes of an English voice.'

[3] 5 January 1850. For the attitude of the trade unions to emigration, see R. V. Clements, 'Trade Unions and Emigration, 1840–80', in *Population Studies* (1955).

became the 'old country', the homeland, and there was ample scope for the emergence of theories of 'imperialism' which stressed sentiment as well as economics.

In the early and middle years of the century four main features of imperial development need to be noted in addition to the emigration of people—the continued expansion of formal empire, the rise of constitutional government in the colonies, the growth of foreign investment, and the final break-up of the 'old colonial system' of economics.

However much critics talked of the disadvantages of colonies— one member of Parliament suggested in 1822 that it would be better if Canada was 'sunk under the ocean'; another (Cobden himself) claimed in 1857 that 'if France took the whole of Africa, I do not see what harm she would do us or anybody else save herself'— successive British statesmen usually refused on grounds of prestige alone to abandon any existing colony. When Melbourne sent Lord Durham on his historic mission to Canada in 1838 to prepare the way for a new Canadian constitution, he told him that 'the final separation of those colonies might possibly not be of material detriment to the interest of the Mother Country, but it is clear that it would be a serious blow to the honour of Great Britain'.[1] Eleven years later Russell maintained that 'the loss of any great portion of our Colonies would diminish our importance in the world, and the vultures would soon gather together to despoil us of the other parts of the Empire'.[2] Between 1815 and 1870 important acquisitions were made in India—in 1858, one year after the Mutiny, control of India finally passed from East India Company to the Crown; in Burma; in South-East Asia, where Stamford Raffles, with little encouragement from London, founded the great new city of Singapore in 1819[3]; in New Zealand; the Falkland Islands; and in Africa. There was a chain of colonial wars in all parts of the world—for instance, the Burmese Wars of 1824–6 and 1852, the Afghan War of 1839,[4] the

---

[1] Quoted A. J. Harrop, *The Amazing Career of Edward Gibbon Wakefield* (1928), p. 103.
[2] Quoted W. P. Morrell, *British Colonial Policy in the Age of Peel and Russell* (1930), p. 208.
[3] In 1824, however, a neglected Anglo-Dutch treaty of considerable long-term importance consolidated the British position in Singapore, secured Dutch recognition, and opened the way for British extension of trade in the China seas. It marked the abandonment of the immediate post-1815 policy of concentrating on India and not interfering with Dutch interests further east.
[4] 'The moral effect of what we have done in Afghanistan', wrote a British officer on the spot, 'is not confined to that country but extended to the many discontented spirits in India and to the neighbouring states.' Quoted by K. K. Datta, *A Survey of Recent*

Maori Wars of 1860–72, and the Kaffir Wars, seven of which had already taken place by 1848.[1] The discovery of diamonds in Griqualand West in 1867, the year of the second Reform Bill, was the prelude to a new and adventurous period in South African history.

The rise of constitutional government in the growing centres of white emigration was far advanced by 1867. The Canada Act of 1840, while it did not go as far as Durham had suggested in his famous *Report*, united the two provinces of Canada which had been separated in 1791, and set up a bicameral legislature, a nominated legislative council and an elected assembly. From the mid-40s onwards, control of Crown revenues, patronage, lands, and tariffs passed to the Canadian authorities, and in 1867 the British North America Act created a new, federal and almost completely self-governing Dominion of Canada. The measure passed through the House of Commons 'as if it were a private Bill uniting two or three English parishes'. In Australia as in Canada, it was made clear in the 1850s that Britain had no desire to impose forms of government 'not in their judgement suited to their (Australian) wants', and although the idea of federation was slow to establish itself in a country of enormous distances, small population, divided interests, and uneven economic development, political change was far more rapid and radical than in England. The first responsible ministry took office in New Zealand in 1856, while the framework of representative government was established in Cape Colony in 1849 even though some of the colonists showed a considerable reluctance to forsake their distant farmsteads for the legislative chamber. By 1867 Gladstone could argue persuasively that freedom and voluntaryism were the strongest imperial ties that could exist.[2]

While new constitutional relationships were being created with what were eventually to become the 'dominions' of the twentieth century, relations with the problem child of eighteenth-century empire, the United States, were 'normalized' in the period from

---

Studies in Modern Indian History (1957). Indian historians have recently shown great interest in the relationship between Russophobia and British foreign policy in India, in the switch from the eighteenth-century French threat to British rule in India to the nineteenth-century fear of Russia.

[1] The seventh Kaffir war of 1846 cost the British taxpayer £1,000,000.

[2] For a sensitive study of this approach, see P. Knaplund, *Gladstone and Britain's Imperial Policy* (1927). For general accounts of imperial change, see Knaplund, *The British Empire* (1941); A. P. Newton, *A Hundred Years of the British Empire* (1940); C. E. Carrington, *The British Overseas* (1950); D. G. Creighton, 'The Victorians and the Empire', in the *Canadian Historical Review* (1938).

1815–60. At the end of the American War of 1812[1] none of the points of dispute between the two countries was settled, but in 1818 an agreement was negotiated whereby both Britain and the United States ceased to maintain naval forces on the Great Lakes. The contentious boundary between Canada and the United States was regulated in the north-east in 1842 (the Webster-Ashburton treaty) and in the north-west in 1846 (the Oregon settlement).[2] Four years later—and five years after Texas had been fully incorporated in the United States (1845)—the Clayton-Bulwer treaty settled outstanding problems on the southern frontier.

The cessation of territorial disputes was not the most important element in the realization of a new kind of Anglo-American relationship. Economics counted for more than politics or diplomacy even in the period before the Oregon dispute, the most difficult of the disputes, was settled.[3] Between 1815 and 1860 nearly half American exports went to Britain, and about 40 per cent of American imports came from Britain. The interdependence of the two economies was apparent in the history of commercial fluctuations in the 1830s; twenty years later British capital was poured into the building of American railways. It was characteristic of Richard Cobden, who had a very clear vision of future American economic potentialities, that he invested the subscription raised by his admirers after the repeal of the corn laws in shares in the Illinois Central Railway.

The growth of foreign investment drew British resources not only into the United States and the 'formal Empire' but into all parts of the world. Between 1815 and 1880, it has been estimated, over £1,000 million in credit had been accumulated abroad, no more than one-sixth of it in the formal Empire.[4] In 1815 foreign capital invested in Britain may have equalled the amount of British capital invested overseas; by the end of the period covered in this book the world was being 'redeveloped' by British investors. The whole world was the province of the British exporter too, and in no single year of the

[1] See above, pp. 166–7.
[2] For a study of the Oregon dispute see F. Mark, 'British Party Politics and the Oregon Treaty' in the *American Historical Review* (1932), and 'British Government Propaganda and the Oregon Treaty', *ibid.* (1934).
[3] When in 1849 Sir Henry Bulmer was named minister in Washington, Lady Palmerston told him that she regretted he was being 'thrown away on the stupid Americans'. Quoted T. Lever (ed.), *The Letters of Lady Palmerston* (1957), p. 307.
[4] See A. H. Imlah, 'British Balance of Payments and Export of Capital, 1816–1913', in *Ec. Hist. Rev.* (1952) and 'Real Values in British Foreign Trade' in *J. Ec. H.* (1948); L. H. Jenks, *The Migration of British Capital to 1875* (1938).

nineteenth century did the Empire buy much more than one-third of Britain's exports.

It was the possibility of unlimited and universal financial and commercial development which, among other reasons, predisposed the Manchester School to place the claims of an international economy above those of an imperial economy. The task of dismantling 'the old colonial system' was begun in the eighteenth century, and although tariff reformers like Huskisson retained and extended imperial preference, after the repeal of the corn laws in 1846 preferential tariffs were swept away. The fiercest battles were about timber and sugar—not only were powerful interests at stake but the whole way of life of the West Indies, the ideological issue of freedom versus slavery, even the future of the British navy. The repeal of the Navigation Acts in 1849, and the abolition of the preference on sugar in 1854 and on timber in 1860, were important milestones in the history of Victorian England.[1] Writing in 1828 Nassau Senior had exclaimed that 'the question of free trade is, next to the Reformation, the most momentous that has ever been submitted to human decision. . . . Slowly and reluctantly, and as if parting from our dearest friend, we have begun to withdraw from the restrictive system'[2]; by 1858 the dearest friend was a departed ghost, and the new Reformation had passed from the phase of revolt into the phase of dogma.

[1] See R. L. Schuyler, *The Fall of the Old Colonial System* (1945).
[2] *Three Lectures on the Transmission of the Precious Metals* (1828).

8

THE BALANCE OF INTERESTS

1. THE CULT OF PROGRESS

SENIOR'S reference to the parallelism of economic and religious changes was characteristic of mid-Victorian England, even though it was made in 1828, and much of the mid-Victorian writing about progress employed similar analogies and images. Unlike the 1840s, the 1850s and 1860s were years of internal balance and widespread though not universal contentment. The 1851 Preface to G. R. Porter's *Progress of the Nation* caught the new mood. 'It must at all times be a matter of great interest and utility to ascertain the means by which any community has attained to eminence among nations. To inquire into the progress of circumstances which has given pre-eminence to one's own nation would almost seem to be a duty.'

The cult of progress was very generally accepted by the mid-Victorians, and the defence of it was put forward by different people at different levels and, taking the period from 1850 to 1867 as a whole, in different ways at different times.

The simplest defence was a statement of the obvious. Scientific and technical advance in England was visible, it could be measured in figures and summed up in 'facts'. 'In this world', said Mr. Gradgrind in Dickens's *Hard Times* (1854) 'we want nothing but Facts.' There certainly were plenty of them. The population of England and Wales had increased from less than 9 millions at the first census of 1801 to nearly 18 millions in 1851, and the standard of living, despite all Malthus's gloomy prophecies, was beyond all doubt beginning to rise in the middle years of the century. By 1871 the total population was over 22 millions. Agriculture itself was producing greater yields, and the middle years of the century have rightly been described as a 'golden age of high farming', but the most obvious reason for the rise in national well-being was the increase in the supply of power and the number of machines. By 1850 the output of coal had reached 56 million tons a year; pig iron output was over two million tons—half the total world output; there were 1,800 cotton factories, employing 328,000 workers and using steam engines with 71,000 total horsepower; and there were over 5,000 miles of railway.

The industrial progress which these facts witnessed was indisputable, and it continued to depend on that same inter-relationship of business initiative and technical invention which had made possible the industrial revolution of the eighteenth century. New technical advance stimulated further 'improvements', and between the age of Watt and Arkwright and the mid-Victorian epoch there had been many far-reaching discoveries. In the coal industry Humphrey Davy's safety lamp, invented in 1815, 'operated as a complete renovation to many of the collieries which were then in a state of exhaustion', although it was adopted in some mining areas only very slowly. At the same time more thorough and effective working at the coal-face, the sinking of deeper shafts (one pit at Apedale in North Staffordshire had workings 2,145 feet below the surface), and the gradual development of more efficient transport, haulage, winding, and ventilation facilities led to rises in output. In the iron industry, the stimulus of new markets encouraged greater production, although the age of steel was just around the corner. The railway companies were large-scale customers in the boom of the 1840s; during the 1850s and 1860s the ship-builders also were extremely active, the net tonnage of iron ships built rising from about 13,000 in 1850 to nearly 65,000 at the end of the decade and more than 250,000 in 1870.

Alongside these developments in transport, there were less spectacular but equally important advances in engineering without which the new industrial economy would have broken down. Quite rightly the mid-Victorians chose engineers as their folk heroes. Many of them were men of the humblest social origins—George Stephenson was the son of a collier; Joseph Whitworth began work as a simple mechanic; James Rendel, one of Telford's surveyors and later engineer in charge of the building of the Birkenhead docks and the Portland harbour, came from a farming background. The railways gave an enormous impetus to the progress of mechanical as well as civil engineering, as indeed did the whole of the technical improvements described above. The Institution of Civil Engineers, founded in 1828, had described the qualification of their professional members as 'the art of directing the great sources of power in Nature for the use and convenience of Man': the mechanical engineers sung the praises of precision, uniformity, and speed. Four men in an acknowledged line of succession—Joseph Bramah,[1] Henry Maudslay, James Nasmyth, and Joseph Whitworth—made it possible to manufacture interchangeable standard parts and to use machine tools which could adjust measurement to a thousandth part of an inch. In George III's reign the first steam engines had been tailor-made, turned out slowly by craftsmen: in the middle of Queen Victoria's reign steam engines and other machines alike were being turned out by standardized routines. The industrial changes of the eighteenth century had led to a ransacking of Nature; Whitworth and his successors introduced gentler and more deliberate methods of control. The skilled artisans who worked for them were the aristocracy of mid-Victorian labour, increasingly specialized and increasingly conscious of the contribution they were making to national prosperity.

Industrial developments, demanding considerable capital as well as enterprise, were making it increasingly difficult by 1850 for artisans, however intelligent, to become businessmen, and most workers were looking to a union 'code' to protect their interests rather than to ownership or to profits. The businessmen themselves had established their position in the community, and they included a large number of 'routinizers' as well as innovators, men who adopted the techniques of others and competed in markets which they had not themselves made. They were still, however, for the most part self-financing in their capital expenditures. Although big concerns like railways relied on shareholders for their capital—in December 1845 the London Stock Exchange was quoting 260 different kinds of railway shares—family businesses and partnerships continued to dominate the industrial scene not only in old industrial districts like Lancashire or the West Midlands but in new boom areas like the Cleveland district of Yorkshire. It was on the basis of partnerships and dynastic inter-marriage that Middlesbrough, for instance, grew from a village in 1850 to a large new town in 1870, and the Middlesbrough region came to account for one-third of the total output of pig iron. Limited liability was extended to all

---

[1] Bramah also 'improved' the water closet, and invented the Bramah lock and the publican's pull-over beer tap.

registered companies in 1856—the new company code, the frame-work of which had first been provided in 1844, was consolidated in 1862—but the adoption of public company forms was slow in the period covered in this book, scarcely touching the cotton industry at all. Businessmen took advantage of the new transport system and of the financial services provided by the growing joint stock banks before they turned to an organized national capital market. They continued to depend on bills of exchange for their short-term transactions, although the City of London through its foreign discount business was more closely associated with overseas than with domestic economic development.

Many of the most active businessmen were still radical in politics: some, however, gazed beyond the mill gates or the factory walls to estates in the country. For all the new wealth created by industry and the attack of the Anti-Corn Law League on redundant feudalism, it was land which still carried with it most prestige. While it was far from easy for a successful businessman to become a 'gentleman' in his own lifetime, he could have reasonable hopes that his children, educated in the new public schools and perhaps marrying sons or daughters of the gentry, would eventually become 'ladies and gentlemen'. He could spend his declining years, if he wished, in 'hunting up genealogies' and spreading his wings 'for sublime apotheosis among the county families'.[1]

It is just as important, however, not to exaggerate the frequency of this 'businessman's progress' as it is to ignore it. Much emphasis was placed by the mid-Victorian industrialists on 'the hard way': they tended, indeed, to standardize business virtues, cataloguing them conveniently as self-help, character, thrift, punctuality, and duty. They gave little place to 'luck' or even 'advantages' in their explanation of occupational success, and they regarded insolvency as a manifestation of personal weakness. The facts that Gradgrind talked about were as 'hard' as the title of Dickens's *Hard Times* itself. In the North of England, in particular, the new business values were at the heart of the new society, contrasting sharply, as Mrs. Gaskell showed in her novel *North and South* (1855), with the values of the country. The progress of industrialization had accentuated the differences between the industrial and non-industrial areas of the country. By 1850 96 per cent of the cotton operatives lived in what was in effect one single unbroken cotton area—Lancashire, Cheshire,

[1] *Fortnightly Review*, December 1868.

Derbyshire, and a small section of the West Riding; over 86 per cent of the spindles and 94 per cent of the power looms used in the worsted industry were in Yorkshire; the woollen industry, which had once been widely dispersed, had reached almost its twentieth-century degree of concentration, only 7,000 people being then employed, for example, in the old, rich woollen area of Wiltshire. To Mrs. Gaskell there were two modes of life in Britain each with its 'own trials and its own temptations. The dweller in towns must find it as difficult to be patient and calm, as the country-bred man must find it to be active and equal to unwonted emergencies.'

The triumphant facts of industrial progress were proclaimed for all the world to see in the Palace of Industry of 1851, the Great Exhibition, which set out 'to present a true test and a living picture of the point of development at which the whole of mankind has arrived . . . and a new starting point, from which all nations will be able to direct their further exertions'.

The Exhibition, with its 13,000 exhibitors and its six million visitors, not only brought the facts to life, but invested them with a new romance. The smoke was far away and the self-made Joseph Paxton's giant glass building, the Crystal Palace, successfully suggested both fairy tale and success story. 'Quite in keeping is the building with the age', wrote a contemporary, 'it is the aesthetic bloom of its practical character, and of the practical tendency of the English nation.'[1] But the Exhibition was designed to display the works of other nations besides the English—pottery from Sèvres as well as from Etruria, fine black lace from Barcelona as well as printed calicoes from Manchester. There was no more vigorous assertion of national confidence than the internationalism of 1851.

In one sense the internationalism was real enough. Free-trade Britain, 'the workshop of the world', depended on other countries for both markets and supplies. The cotton industry was looking increasingly and successfully to new markets in India and the East; in 1850, one-quarter of British pig iron was exported as against one-tenth thirty years before; almost 60 per cent of the ocean tonnage of the world was under British registry. As far as imports were concerned—and they were as necessary to the new economy as exports—the English cotton industry was the biggest single American customer, closely linked with the plantations of the United States South; the woollen and worsted industries looked to

[1] For a fuller study of the Exhibition, see my *Victorian People* (1954), ch. 2.

an ever growing extent to distant Australia. Taking the trade statistics as a whole, Britain was a net importing country throughout the whole nineteenth-century 'age of improvement', and there were very few years indeed when a favourable balance of trade was shown. The mid-Victorians did not worry about this, for the deficit was more than made up by incomes from shipping, insurance, other services, and foreign investment. Shipping was particularly important in the middle years of the century. The tonnage of ships entering and leaving British ports more than doubled between the mid-'40s and 1860 and rose by another 50 per cent in the subsequent decade. It is impossible to understand international economic interdependence in the nineteenth century without devoting considerable attention to the merchant navy. But the interdependence was shown in other ways too. Thomas Brassey, for instance, was building railways on the Continent and throughout the world. Among his achievements were the Canadian Grand Trunk, key lines in Australia, Argentina, and India,[1] and even a small but historically significant military railway in the Crimea during the years of war. Against this background of economic internationalism—undisturbed by governmental manipulation of currencies[2]—there was scope for the enterprising exporter. The market value of British exports increased by nearly 300 per cent in the twenty-five years after the beginning of Peel's fiscal reforms in 1842, and long after the Great Exhibition there were abundant signs of British industrial as well as commercial and financial leadership.

There were signs, however, that the leadership might not be permanent, although most contemporaries did not clearly discern them. By 1867 not all the hard facts of economics were on the credit side. In the steel industry, for instance, which was providing a new technical basis for industry, England was to be less successful than in the earlier age of iron. Henry Bessemer, who was goaded by the military needs of the Crimean War into discovering a new way of producing high-tensile steel in large quantities, developed the converter process, the details of which he announced to the British Association in 1856. Although he and John Brown, the Sheffield

---

[1] In the thirty years between 1845 and 1875, about £95 million was invested in Indian guaranteed railways, most of it between 1858 and 1865.

[2] It was a sign of governmental non-intervention in the network of credit facilities that a loan for Russia was floated on the London money market *during* the Crimean War. It was in the 'ordinary way of business', the foreign secretary noted, and ought not to be interfered with. See H. Maxwell, *The Life and Letters of the Fourth Earl of Clarendon* (1913), vol. III, p. 107.

manufacturer of armour plating for the new iron-clad ships, made enormous profits out of the new techniques, the Germans and Americans were eventually to forge ahead on the basis of further British inventions. Economic progress in England continued, and in the late '60s and '70s output figures broke all existing records, but in the age of steel British industrial superiority could no longer be taken for granted. The element of monopoly which lay concealed in the great rise of national income and welfare was to be drastically reduced. Even before the Great Exhibition the *Economist* had sounded a disconcerting warning (Cobden often did the same) that 'the superiority of the United States to England is ultimately as certain as the next eclipse'; by the early 1870s—even as early as the second World Exhibition in Paris in 1867—far-sighted observers were beginning to realize that 'ultimately' did not mean sometime in the very remote future.

By then there were other forces at work in English society which were qualifying earlier statements of the cult of material progress. There had always been a group of Christian critics of 'the wilderness of our manufacturing world', men who looked back to Coleridge and refused to put their trust either in the 'March of Mind' or 'the efficacy of Civilization'. In setting out to evaluate economic change they turned not to the rise in output, but to 'the fatal cycle . . . of speculation, prosperity, over-production, glut, distress'.[1] Their pessimism was reinforced in the 1870s and 1880s by new currents of thought. They were a minority, however, and in mid-Victorian England there were far more protagonists of intellectual as well as material progress. H. T. Buckle, for example, the son of a wealthy London shipowner, in his revealing *History of Civilization in England*, the first volume of which appeared in 1857, took 'the progress from barbarianism to civilization' for granted. He was anxious only to investigate its causes, and when he visited the Crystal Palace he meditated on 'the bright promise of reward to man's genius and continued triumph over the blind powers of nature'.[2] History was 'the living scroll of human progress', inscribed with 'every successive conquest of man's intellect'.[3]

Two years after Buckle's first volume appeared, a much greater work, *The Origin of Species* by Charles Darwin, grounded belief in

[1] For the views of this group, see D. Forbes, *The Liberal Anglican Idea of History* (1952), *passim*. For other critics of the Victorian order, see below, pp. 472 ff.
[2] See A. H. Huth, *The Life and Writings of H. T. Buckle* (1880), vol. I, p. 78.
[3] *Edinburgh Review*, October 1851.

progress not as Buckle—or Porter—had done in the hard statistical facts of the present or in 'the defeat of the protective spirit' but in a scientific record of origins and evolution. Darwin's treatise ended with the extremely optimistic conclusion that 'as natural selection works solely by and for the good of each being, all corporal and mental environments will tend to progress towards perfection'. There had been many intimations of such a statement of evolution in the writings of poets and scientists; indeed, they had probed far more deeply than the political economists into the inner meaning of the processes of change, had taken the world of nature as well as the world of men into the reckoning, and had concluded that in time there would emerge 'a nobler type of humanity, which shall complete the zoological circle on this planet, and realize some of the dreams of the purest spirits of the present race'.[1] Tennyson, in particular, as early as 1832, was thinking along these lines, and he ended his *In Memoriam* (1850) with a powerful pronouncement of trust in a better world and a loftier race.

Both *In Memoriam* and *Origin of Species* appealed to sensitive minds far removed in quality and subtlety from the rough, tough businessmen or the unimaginative Gradgrinds. 'The generally faltering voice with which Tennyson expresses the ardour of his own hope '[2] evoked a warm response in people who would have been unimpressed by a statistical catalogue, while Darwin's basic optimism was shared by men and women who disliked the often strident association of material progress and Protestant individualism which was so common in popular exposition and at the Exhibition of 1851.

There was danger in the air, however, when belief in progress raised awkward questions like 'progress whither?' It was left to a later generation to try to answer them and to contemplate the full implications of the questions themselves, just as it was left to a later generation to wrestle with difficult economic questions after Britain's predominance had begun to be challenged. As early as 1886, in *Locksley Hall Sixty Years After*, Tennyson himself was recognizing the possibility of regression

> Forward then, but still remember how the course of time will swerve,
> Crook and turn upon itself in many a backward-streaming curve.

The image pointed to a future when the curves of economists were

[1] R. Chambers, *Vestiges of the Natural History of Creation* (1844).
[2] R. H. Hutton, *Aspects of Religious and Scientific Thought* (1901), p. 408.

to be treated more seriously than the curves of metaphysicians. For
the mid-Victorian present, however, one of the most authoritative
voices was that of Herbert Spencer, significantly an engineer by
training, a believer in rigid non-interference on the part of the
State, and an evolutionist (of a kind) before Darwin. 'The ultimate
development of the ideal man is logically certain', Spencer wrote in
his *Social Statics* (1851), 'certain as any conclusion in which we place
the most implicit faith; for instance, that all men will die.'[1] This
supremely dogmatic assertion did not stand alone. By a curious
completion of the circle, when Spencer went on to remark that the
student of society learns 'to recognize only a struggling beneficence'
behind existing evils and above all else is 'struck with the inherent
sureness of things', he was not far removed from Gradgrind's
confidence in the first chapter of *Hard Times*.

2. SOCIAL HARMONIES

Mid-Victorian confidence was based not only on economic
strength but on social balance. Taking the years from the Great
Exhibition to the second Reform Bill of 1867 as a whole—and they
have a remarkable unity—almost all sections of the articulate
community were able to show substantial gains. Rising prices,
which followed the period of falling prices from 1815 to near the
turn of the century, induced optimism; dependent as they were on
the buoyancy of markets not only in England but overseas, where
new lands were being opened up each year, and backed as they were
by the new gold of Australia and California, they helped in themselves to relieve many social tensions. The fact that the incomes of
businessmen, landlords, farmers, and artisans all rose together was
even more important in determining national mood. Profit margins
were high; rents increased—on a selected sample they went up in
the twenty years after 1850 from an average level of 20*s*. 6*d*. to 24*s*.
an acre[2]; farm prices did not rise as much as other prices, but
English farmers, protected by geography, received greater incomes

---

[1] Quoted J. B. Bury, *The Idea of Progress* (1913), ch. XIX. Darwin in his *Autobiography* (printed as part of *The Life and Letters of Charles Darwin*, ed. F. Darwin, 1887,
expressed considered doubts about Spencer. 'His conclusions never convince me: and
over and over again I have said after reading one of his discussions, "Here would be
a fine subject for a half-a-dozen years' work".' Darwin was suspicious of all deductive
reasoning.

[2] R. J. Thompson, 'Enquiry into the Rent of Agricultural Land in England and
Wales' in the *J.R.S.S.* (1907).

than they had done since 1814; real wages of factory operatives rose by 17 per cent between 1850 and 1865, the number of hand-loom weavers and 'domestic' workers decreased, and employment opportunities multiplied; while some skilled sections of the labour aristocracy, with a growing income differential separating them from the unskilled, were able, at least in boom periods, to vie with the members of the professional classes, who were themselves increasing in numbers [1] and prestige in the twenty years after the Exhibition. 'I cannot afford lamb, salmon, young ducks, green peas, new potatoes and such like', one of Samuel Smiles's captains of industry remarks, 'until after my hands have been consuming these delicacies of the season for two or three weeks.' [2]

Such a comment was conditioned by an age of unprecedented prosperity although, as we shall see later on, the prosperity was always qualified.[3] To contemporaries, however, the qualifications came second—if they came at all—and the prosperity first. There were signs everywhere of an expanding economy and a dynamic society—new industrial buildings, new Town Halls, above all new and large Nonconformist chapels; rich men mixing with titled men on the boards of railway companies and even in city offices; steam ploughs, first used in 1857, in the cornfields; overloaded ships in the harbours, of which one—I. K. Brunel's 'Great Eastern'—was a giant steam vessel not surpassed in size until 1901. It was easy to forget the seldom-visited slums of the cities and the hovels of the countryside because so much had been accomplished and was being accomplished elsewhere. Many of those who did not forget believed nonetheless that, given time, the relative decline in poverty would be followed by the abolition of (as yet unmeasured) destitution, simply through a continuation of mid-nineteenth century economic growth and a further diffusion of the principles of thrift, self-help, and hard work; and radicals like Henry Fawcett, the blind Professor of Political Economy at Cambridge, looked forward soberly to a society of well-fed, well-educated English citizens, with skilled artisans and peasant proprietors at the base sharing the values of those in positions of leadership and depending for hard manual work and domestic service on negroes and Chinese.[4] This projection into the future of the most coherent middle-class radical logic of

---

[1] The number of commercial clerks, for instance, doubled between 1851 and 1871.
[2] *Thrift* (1875), ch. IV.
[3] See below, pp. 448 ff.
[4] *The Economic Position of the British Labourer* (1865).

the age was the counterpart of Malthusian pessimism in the early stages of the industrial revolution.

Fawcett and his friends were far from being self-satisfied; they were anxious not to stand still, but to reshape English society by allowing the laws of political economy to reign supreme. They believed that the social harmonies of the mid-nineteenth century owed nothing to government, and that any intervention on the part of the State would tilt the balance in a dangerous way; they thus opposed both strong government and all talk of new social systems ushered in by legislation. Their less logical and less radical contemporaries were content to accept the social balance as it was without worrying at all about the challenge of ideal systems. Practice was more important than theory, limited improvements than organic transformations. Prosperity was real, and there was no need for 'panaceas'. After all, as one pamphleteer put it in 1852, 'suppose all our parishioners were put on a level in the scale of society to-day, before this day twelve months there would be an aristocracy among them, "a nobility without heraldry" '.[1]

The main political figure of the period, Palmerston, well expressed the main tenets of mid-Victorian beliefs about society both implicitly in his home policy[2] and explicitly in his speech during the 'Don Pacifico' debate. 'We have shown the example', he said, 'of a nation, in which every class of society accepts with cheerfulness the lot which Providence has assigned to it; while at the same time every individual of each class is constantly striving to raise himself in the social scale—not by injustice and wrong, not by violence and illegality, but by preserving good conduct, and by the steady and energetic execution of the moral and intellectual faculties with which his creator has endowed him.' According to this analysis, which is all the more interesting in that it was advanced in a debate about foreign policy, it was possible to reconcile economic change and individual mobility with traditional social balance and stability. In the 1860s Walter Bagehot re-stated the theory in a more general context. Distinguishing between English society and foreign societies founded either on caste (as in India) or on equality (as in the United States) he extolled the merits of the English system of 'removable inequalities', a system in which many people were inferior to and worse off than others but in which each might hope *in theory* (an

---

[1] P. Peace, *An Address on the Improvement of the Condition of the Labouring Poor* (1852).
[2] See below, pp. 420 ff.

important rider which Palmerston did not add) to be on a level with the highest below the throne.[1] One of the advantages of this social system, it was maintained—and this was why it was relevant for Palmerston to discuss it in a debate on foreign policy—was that it provided through 'mild social discipline . . . a wise and temperate substitute for those harsh police laws and perpetual interference with the freedom of private action generally enforced throughout the Continent and nowhere more so than in the revolutionized countries'.[2] Another advantage was that it made the economy more efficient. John Stuart Mill claimed that the most important distinguishing feature of 'modern life' was the fact 'that human beings are no longer born to their place in life . . . but are free to employ their faculties . . . to achieve the lot which may appear to them most desirable'.[3]

The appeal of this social analysis to mid-Victorians was a testimony to the difference in mood and outlook from the years which preceded and the years which followed. In both the 1840s and the 1880s there was open talk of 'class' divisions; in the 1850s and early 1860s the social framework was accepted, except during the Crimean War and on the eve of the Reform Bill of 1867, and when discussion moved from individuals to society, there was more emphasis on 'interests' than on 'classes'. The 'railway interest' dominated the scene at the beginning of the period, and at the end of the period Bagehot claimed that if the 200 railway members of Parliament chose to combine on a point which the public did not care for, they would be absolute. The 'City interest' was referred to as much as it had been in the middle of the eighteenth century. Relatively small interests like the licensed victuallers, the attorneys, or even the ecclesiastical lawyers were often in a strategic position to check legislation. The new and influential trade union, the Amalgamated Society of Engineers, founded in 1851, did not claim that it was its duty to secure the objects of a 'class' but rather 'to exercise the same control over that in which we have a vested interest as the physician who holds his diploma or the author who is protected by his copyright'. Little place was left in this welter of interests for strong

[1] See his essay on 'Sterne and Thackeray' (1864), reprinted in *Literary Studies* (1879).
[2] J. Walsh, *The Practical Results of the Reform Act of 1832* (1860), pp. 26–7.
[3] *The Subjection of Women* (1869), ch. I. For a contemporary criticism of the theory on the grounds that not to rise in society had become a matter of shame, see J. Ruskin, *Pre-Raphaelitism* (1851). For a useful general discussion, see W. Houghton, *The Victorian Frame of Mind* (1957), especially ch. VIII.

government. Bagehot believed that 'the most dangerous of all
sinister interests is that of the executive Government, because it is
the most powerful', and most of his contemporaries agreed that
government jobbery was a more serious danger to the community
than the unchallenged claims of sectional groups. The prestige of
government was as limited as its powers. As Frederic Harrison noted
in the 1860s, it was an ominous fact 'how feeble the various forms
of authority are growing in this country. Ministers, Governments,
Parliaments, parties, all yield to a mere push, squeeze with a slight
pressure, collapse mysteriously without warning'.[1]

Nonetheless mid-Victorian society did not allow the most vigorous economic group—the new businessmen—to reign supreme. In a
prosperous society which stressed not only active individuality but
the interplay of interests and the irrationality of social collision,
businessmen could not shape the whole of society in their own
image. They were checked both by the old 'landed interest' and the
new 'working classes'.

The members of the 'landed inteiest' long after the fall of protection continued to exercise great social and political authority. The
government of the counties was still in their hands—it was an
unpaid service—while at Westminster they were still firmly en-
trenched.[2] 'So vast is their traditional power', wrote an intelligent
observer, Bernard Cracroft, in 1866, 'so deep and ancient are its
roots, so multiplied and ramified everywhere are its tendrils and
creepers that the danger is never lest they shall have too little but
always lest they should have too much power, and so, even in-
voluntarily, choke down the possibilities of life from below.' At
the core of the Parliament of 1865 there was a 'cousinhood' of
landed families, which included well over half the members. The
House of Commons remained very closely attached socially to the
House of Lords; 71 baronets, 11 elder sons of baronets, 19 younger
sons of baronets, and 8 grandsons of baronets were joined by 37
peers or elder sons of peers, 64 younger sons of peers, and 15
grandsons of peers. In addition there were 100 commoners sitting
in Parliament connected with the peerage by marriage or descent.
'The Parliamentary frame', Cracroft concluded, 'is kneaded together

[1] *Fortnightly Review*, April 1868.
[2] In 1851 the *Quarterly Review* was still maintaining that 'the Constitution looks to
property, and especially that most stable form of property, *land*, as affording the
soundest, and indeed, the only safe basis of representation and government' (vol.
LXXVIII, p. 579).

almost out of one class; it has the strength of a giant and the compactness of a dwarf. For in this respect one Parliament is very much like another.'[1]

Even the economic importance of the landed interest necessarily remained considerable in an age when large improvement outlays had to be made in the countryside—on drainage and farm buildings in particular—and neither industry nor the State was willing to subsidize farming on any large scale. 'There is no other body of men in the country who administer so large a capital on their own account', wrote the agricultural economist, Sir James Caird, of the great landlords just after the end of the period covered in this book.[2] On the basis of existing evidence it is impossible to generalize on a national or even regional basis either about landlords' incomes and expenditures or the attitudes they displayed towards their tenants. Many landlords, however, were regional benefactors; some at least were receiving a large income from mineral rights and urban development as well as agriculture; some were employing considerable full-time administrative staff with well-organized estate offices; and some were fully conscious of their obligation to their tenants. It was not until after 1875 that relations between landlords and tenants were modified by law[3]; there were heavy losses of capital in land and, to quote Lady Bracknell in Oscar Wilde's *The Importance of Being Earnest*, 'all that can be said about land' is that 'it gives one position, and prevents one from keeping it up.'

In the light of what came later the position of the landed interest in the middle years of the century was still extremely strong. The same may be said of it in the light of what had gone before. After the corn laws were repealed Cobden and Bright wished to go on to mobilize opinion against 'the landlord spirit which is dominant in political and social life', to turn to a full-blooded attack on the game laws, on copyholds, entails and 'the eleventh commandment, primogeniture',[4] and to achieve not only free trade in corn but 'free

---

[1] B. Cracroft, 'The Analysis of the House of Commons' in *Essays on Reform* (1867).
[2] J. Caird, *The Landed Interest and the Supply of Food* (1878), p. 58. See also for the position at the beginning of mid-Victorian England his *English Agriculture in 1850–51* (1852).
[3] A Landlord and Tenant Act of 1851 empowered tenants to remove fixtures they had erected during their tenancy, subject to the option of the landlord to buy them. Even before this, some land reformers in the 1840s had tried to increase the security of the tenant in other ways, but the view of the 1833 Select Committee on Agriculture that 'the legislature can do much evil, but little positive good by frequent interference with the agricultural industry' still prevailed.
[4] Morley, *Cobden*, vol. II, ch. 2.

trade in land'. The attempt failed for many reasons. The issue was
too technical to win widespread support. For a time bodies like the
National Freehold Land Society, founded in 1849 with the blessing
of Joseph Hume as well as of Cobden, gained many enthusiastic
adherents, but in the period of mid-Victorian prosperity the political
sting was taken out of the question. Cobden himself pointed to
two of the main reasons for the failure—the reluctance of farmers
to associate themselves with the agitation, and the 'snobbishness of
the moneyed classes in the grand seats of commerce and manufacture'.[1] He saw as clearly as Bagehot that initiative in country
places was checked by 'deference' and that the strength of the
aristocracy depended on 'strong prejudices' in its favour among
'all ranks and classes of the community'. He saw too, as clearly as
Disraeli, that many businessmen were anxious above all else to be
considered as 'gentlemen', that concern about status was ultimately
more decisive than concern about income, and that many a successful businessman 'has his eye already upon a neighbouring
park, avails himself of his political position to become a country
magistrate, meditates upon a baronetcy, and dreams of a coroneted
descendant'.[2] Cracroft might complain that in a dynamic age
'the landlord's creed, pure and simple, is the creed of calm and
long possession . . . it has the dignity of repose and the serenity of
the everlasting landscape', but long possession could be an object
of envy as well as of hate, and repose itself could be considered the
most desirable of objectives.

If business dominance was checked by both the landed interest
and the social aspirations of businessmen, it was checked too by
the groups of skilled artisans who banded themselves into trade
unions. Superficially the ideas of the new model trade unions,
which looked to the Amalgamated Society of Engineers as a guide,
were similar to those of the more enlightened middle classes. The
leaders of the highly respectable 'junta' in London,[3] which included
William Allan, the leader of the engineers, George Odger, and
Robert Applegarth, the secretary of the Amalgamated Society of

---

[1] *Ibid.*, p. 515.   [2] 'The Spirit of Whiggism' (1836), reprinted in W. Hutcheon
(ed.), *Whigs and Whiggism* (1914), p. 349.

[3] The Junta leaders had enemies within the trade union movement itself, particularly
George Potter, the leader of the builders' strike of 1859 and later the highly opportunist but often irresponsible editor of the *Beehive*. Potter used the pages of his working-
class journal—at its peak in 1865 it had 8,000 readers—to encourage provincial strikes
and to attack centralized office leadership in London. In fact, however, he had no
coherent social and political philosophy to offer as an alternative to that of the Junta,
and in many matters he was less radical than either Odger or Applegarth.

Carpenters and Joiners, disliked most strikes, Odger comparing them to wars which were only justified by absolute necessity; they believed in thrift, temperance and 'steady habits'; they de- manded high contributions and built up large insurance funds; and they talked incessantly of 'responsibility'. In fact, while men like Applegarth were prepared to mix with Liberals and support the cause of parliamentary reform, they were not prepared to abandon labour solidarity and to put all their trust in individual advancement. 'I would have a man do a fair day's work for a fair day's wage', Applegarth told a Royal Commission,[1] and he was never afraid of accusing 'political economy' of depriving men of bread. He did not attempt to minimize the beneficial value of strikes on certain occasions and he complained that 'employers by their overbearing and tyrannical conduct, compel workmen to combine for their mutual protection'.[2] He objected firmly to 'that system of individualism, which gives Arkwright, Brunel and Stephen- son "full scope for the exercise of their extraordinary skill" but leaves the thousands less skilful to scramble through a selfish world as best they can'.

The responsible tactics of the Junta leaders did much to disarm middle-class criticism of trade unionism. 'We cannot help but honour and admire the sentiments of fraternal sympathy', Thomas Brassey, the great contractor, wrote approvingly, 'which prompt working men to promote each other's advancement in life by mutual aid and support.'[3] There was always some suspicion, how- ever, and often a hostility, the hostility reaching its peak in 1866 and 1867. A series of 'union outrages' in Sheffield and the revelation of a frightening record of intimidation and violence on the part of a small local union were used to provoke opposition to trade unions as a whole. At the same time a judgement in the Court of Queen's Bench in the case of *Hornby* v. *Close* placed trade union funds at the mercy of defaulting officials, for the Court laid down that trade unions, being at common law unlawful societies in restraint of trade, were not entitled to the benefit of the Friendly Societies Act

---

[1] *Report of the Royal Commission to inquire into Trade Unions and other Associations* (1867), Q. 117.

[2] When asked (Q. 7372) whether he wished 'to divide all the wealth equally', he replied, 'no, I do not entertain such revolutionary notions'.

[3] *Work and Wages* (1872), p. 25. For diametrically opposed views, see J. Plummer, *The Rights of Labour* (1859) and P. H. Rathbone, 'The Moral of the Sheffield Trade Outrages' (*Report of the Congress of the Social Science Association* (1867)). 'Labour is only a commodity (like fish) . . . the laws of political economy, rightly understood, are as much the laws of Providence as the laws of gravitation.'

of 1855 which protected friendly society funds. The Junta leaders were anxious not only to distinguish themselves from the local Sheffield 'agitators' but to strengthen the legal position of the unions as a whole. They pressed for a Royal Commission, and persuaded a minority of three of the Commissioners to conclude that 'the riots of the rough population have but very little bearing on the claims of such societies as the Amalgamated Engineers or the Amalgamated Carpenters'. Both majority and minority, while disagreeing about means, wished to protect trade union funds.

The minority report, which provided the inspiration for the subsequent trade union legislation of the liberal government in 1871, acknowledged that the expansion of trade unions was 'not the spasmodic growth of a temporary movement, but the progress of a stable institution'. It went on to add that 'the degree of completeness' to which trade union organization had attained, and the scale on which its operations were conducted 'are quite equal to that of a first-rate mercantile enterprise'. No contemporary note of praise could have been more firmly sounded. Yet it was not, of course, a mercantile enterprise which Allan, Applegarth, and Odger had created, but a new force in the life of society and ultimately in the political life of the nation. If the aristocratic obstacle to business dominance diminished in the last quarter of the nineteenth century, the working-class challenge increased. Although the trade union leaders of the middle of the century spoke mainly in the name of the skilled labourers, they made the subsequent rise of unskilled labour far easier than it otherwise would have been.

There was one final element in the mid-Victorian social balance which must be taken into account. Apart from aristocrats and artisans, the new intelligentsia and the rising civil service both resisted the dominion of wealth and the supremacy of business.

The English intelligentsia was neither rootless nor rebellious; at its centre, it was stable and assured, with enough property to buy leisure and independence and with sufficient association with government to keep it in touch with the conduct of national affairs. It had its own sense of 'cousinhood', and was as distinguished by good manners as by the weight of ideas. The origins of this intelligentsia, as Noel Annan has shown,[1] lay in a group of Evangelical,

---

[1] *Studies in Social History* (ed. J. H. Plumb, 1955), VIII, 'The Intellectual Aristocracy'. See also his *Leslie Stephen* (1951). There were, of course, conflicts within the 'cousinhood' and significant age differences between 'fathers' and 'sons'.

Quaker, and philosophical radical household⌐
century, the Macaulays and Stephens looking ⌐
Sect, the Wedgwoods to the industrial revol⌐
of the intelligentsia were able through their
through the articles which they contribute⌐
Victorian reviews to influence opinion, and while tney ⌐
unmistakably to their own age they always had sufficient confidence
and prestige to be able to criticize it.

The civil servants, too, were in no sense the English equivalent
of a continental bureaucracy. Many of them like Matthew Arnold,
a school inspector, or Sir James Fitzjames Stephen, legal member
of the council in India, were intellectuals themselves. Most of them
had contacts with the public schools and with the universities; most
of them placed 'character' on the same level as 'ability' and shared
the view of Thomas Arnold, architect of the Victorian public school
system, that 'the great work of government' was 'the highest earthly
desire of the ripened mind.'[2] They were almost all 'gentlemen', and
even many reformers of the civil service wished them to continue so.

The idea of the 'gentleman' is the necessary link in any analysis
of mid-Victorian ways of thinking and behaving, for as Taine, the
percipient French commentator, noted, 'these three syllables . . .
summarize the history of English society'.[3] Gentlemen had their
code; they often accepted the theory of progress but they were
always suspicious of the 'religion of gold'. It was difficult to define
exactly what a 'gentleman' was, but as Anthony Trollope, the
novelist, said, 'any one would know what it meant'.[4]

The strength of the ideal of the gentleman was well displayed
even in the writings of Smiles, the 'philosopher of self-help'. All
'true' gentlemen 'look each other in the eye and grasp each other's
hands', wrote Smiles, 'they know each other instinctively. They
appreciate each other's merits.'[5] They would no more think of
using their power for unworthy aims than of allowing themselves
to forget strict self-control. Such a picture was based not on observation but on rooted belief in a moral code, on the world of *ought*,
not on the world of *is*. It was the appeal of this perfect picture,

[1] See above, p. 70.
[2] Quoted A. P. Stanley, *op. cit.*, vol. I, p. 172.
[3] *Notes on England* (1872 edn.), p. 174.
[4] *Autobiography* (1883), ch. III.
[5] For Smiles's trust in the 'gentleman' see *Self-Help* (1859), ch. XIII. 'It is a grand old
name, that of gentleman, and has been recognized as a rank and power in all stages of
society.'

...ever, which helped to make the Victorian social balance what
...was, something quite different from the social balance of any other
country in any other period of prolonged prosperity.

3. POLITICS AND GOVERNMENT

It was taken for granted by most of the leaders of opinion in
the 1850s and 1860s that to sit in Parliament should be the highest
object and ambition of every English gentleman and that 'to serve
one's country without pay is the grandest work that a man can do'.[1]
In his famous study of the English Constitution (1867) Bagehot
maintained that the 'best government' was that managed not by the
many but by the 'select few', men who had enjoyed 'a life of long
leisure, a long culture, varied experience, an existence by which the
judgement is incessantly exercised and by which it may be incessantly improved'. Although he himself admitted that the flesh-and-
blood (as distinct from the ideal) members of the House of Commons
included some of 'the finest brute votes in Europe', and rather less
moderate critics added to the cry 'let us be governed by gentlemen'
the all-important rider, 'by all means if they govern well',[2] there was
a growing consensus of responsible opinion in the late 1850s and
early '60s that the House of Commons really did constitute 'a
deliberate assembly of moderate and judicious men'. They chose
rulers, Bagehot asserted, 'as we like rulers to be chosen. If they did
not, in a speaking and writing age, we should know.'

Before examining the process by which, according to Bagehot,
the rulers were selected, it is best to start in the constituencies and
to describe how the members of Parliament themselves were
chosen. At this level of politics there was a paradox. If Westminster
was a palace, the constituency at election times was often a pigsty.
In many places the élite had to stoop to conquer. Bribery, intimidation, and treating were still commonplace. Electorates were often
small—at Marlborough, Wells, Thetford and Knaresborough, for
instance, they were less than 300 in 1865, and at Arundel and Calne
less than 200—and there were frequent petitions challenging
election results. Beverley, for example, which Trollope contested in
1868, presented petitions in 1837, 1857, 1860 and 1868. Conditions
were different in the large, so-called 'popular constituencies', of
which Tower Hamlets with its 29,000 voters was the biggest. The

[1] A. Trollope, *Autobiography*, ch. XVI.
[2] L. Stephen, 'Popular Constituencies', in *Essays on Reform* (1867), p. 88.

political if not the physical atmosphere was clearer, there were frequent platform demonstrations, many exciting debates about political issues, and dozens of political clubs and associations whose resolutions and activities were reported in the local press. Large-scale bribery was impossible and 'the little puffs which produce a tempest in a teapot were powerless in a great popular body'.[1] As the Newcastle radical Joseph Cowen put it, 'when people declaim against the noise and dirt of the busy centres of population, they should remember the liberty we enjoy as a consequence of the mental activity and enterprise which have been generated by the contact of mind with mind brought together in great cities.'[2] Even in such places, however, the number of electors considered as a fraction of the population was often small. Birmingham with a population of nearly 300,000 had less than 10,000 voters in 1865; Leeds with over 200,000 inhabitants had just over 7,000 voters; Cowen's Newcastle with over 100,000 inhabitants had less than 6,000 voters; and even more striking, Bradford with an only slightly smaller population than Newcastle had an electorate of only 3,770. It was possible in some large places, particularly in Birmingham, for non-electors' associations to press for the choice of particular candidates and to enliven the election campaign, but democracy, still thought of as a bogey-word by most political theorists, was strictly limited in practice. It was not until the Reform Act of 1867 widened the electorate, the Ballot Act of 1872 introduced secret voting, and the Corrupt Practices Act of 1883 turned the poacher into the gamekeeper[3] and made election agents the guardians of public morals at election times, that century-old malpractices were cleared away. An earlier act of 1854, which for the first time defined bribery and undue influence, penalized these offences, and required an audit of election expenses, did not produce all the good results expected of it. In the mid-Victorian years it was the agent who usually set the pace for the candidate, skilfully bargaining with local interests, engaging in 'war stratagems' with his rival manipulators on the day of the poll, and shepherding his candidate—often to the candidate's discomfort and annoyance—both into backstairs lobbies and in front of hustings crowds. It is not surprising that many mid-Victorian novelists considered the

---

[1] L. Stephen, 'Popular Constituencies', in *ibid.*, p. 111.
[2] E. R. Jones, (ed.) *The Life and Speeches of Joseph Cowen* (1885), p. 406.
[3] See H. G. Nicholas, *To the Hustings* (1956), p. xii.

description of an election a congenial literary theme; after all, as
Trollope put it, 'no other great European nation has anything like
it to offer to the ambition of its citizens; for in no other great country
in Europe, not even in those which are free, has the popular constitution obtained, as with us, true sovereignty and power of rule.
Here it is so; and when a man lays himself out to be a member of
parliament, he plays the highest game and for the highest stakes
which the country affords.'[1]

The central party organizations played only a small part in the
choosing of candidates, and in the manipulation of the electorate
local influence counted for more than national pressure. In county
constituencies influence still often expressed itself in local compromises and agreements, and to qualify the paradox implicit in the
contrast between pigsty and palace it is necessary to remember that
a large number of such constituencies were usually uncontested[2]
and that there were strong social barriers to the success of candidates
who were not 'gentlemen'. Large numbers of M.P.s were deputy
lieutenants, prominent figures in the local yeomanry, and owners
of land in their constituencies. Lord George Henry Cavendish,
brother of the Duke of Devonshire, represented North Derbyshire
from 1834 through the whole period covered in this book, while
in 1865 Northumberland was represented by a Percy, a Ridley, a
Beaumont, and a Liddell. Preston returned a Stanley, Cumberland
a Howard, a Lowther, and a Wyndham, and Tamworth was served
by two Peels, one of whom it is true was educated not at Harrow
but at Manchester Grammar School. Even many of the large popular
constituencies preferred 'gentlemen', sometimes as radical candidates,
to 'politicians' or to outstanding local personalities. Lord Amberley,
for instance, contested Leeds in 1865, and won Nottingham,
Feargus O'Connor's old seat, as a radical in 1866. Although the anti-
aristocratic cry was sometimes raised—by Trollope's fellow-novelist
Thackeray, for example, at Oxford in 1857 when he promised to
fight not only 'to enlarge the constituencies but to popularize the
government of this country'[3]—it was generally unsuccessful.
Deference was a strong social force, and it seemed certain that 'so

---

[1] *Doctor Thorne* (1858).
[2] More than 180 English members of Parliament in 1865 had been returned un-
opposed.
[3] See J. Grego, *A History of Parliamentary Elections and Electioneering* (1886), pp.
398–402. 'We want a working man and neither a lord nor a bishop', a Leeds crowd
shouted in 1868 when Amberley's name was suggested again for the radical candidature.

long as the aristocracy is willing to provide us with legislators . . . the demand will equal the supply'.[1]

In fact, the main task of the members of Parliament during the mid-Victorian period was not yet legislation. For Bagehot the legislative aspect of the work of the Commons came third in normal times, subordinate in importance to the executive management of the State and the political education that parliamentary debates afforded to the whole nation. While the individual members of the House were loath to vote in such a way that they would be involved in the discomfort and expense of frequent dissolutions, the weak governments of this period, unsure of stable majorities, were anxious to avoid a mass of contentious legislation which might split the cabinet and threaten their precarious tenure of office. Active backbenchers were on the whole far more willing to criticize than to welcome legislative initiative, and in the course of their protracted discussions were quite uninterested in anticipating their twentieth-century successors and turning themselves—to quote a phrase of Professor Burn—into a kind of superior 'registration office'. They usually owed little to the central party, and they were prepared to devote as much 'outlay of brain' to the passage of a gas bill 'as might suffice to govern the Indian empire for six months'.[2] Their reluctance to legislate in the grand manner was determined not only by tactics but by their realistic assessment of the lack of interest in comprehensive change. They knew that 'a sense of satisfaction permeates the country because most of the country feels that it has got the precise thing that suits it', and instead of unsettling and innovating, they were content to 'let things take their way naturally, with a slight deflection hither or thither as things might require'.[3]

It was not only that sweeping statements of new general principles were viewed with suspicion: even old theories and principles were re-affirmed in far less firm language. In business 'rule of thumb' was thought more important than theory, and businessmen carried into the world outside the factory what Mill called 'the dogmatism of common sense'. The 'less eligibility' clauses of the Poor Law of 1834 were treated in many places more as high-sounding abstractions than as practical precepts, and there were almost as many variations

[1] L. Stephen, *loc. cit.*
[2] F. Harrison, *loc. cit.* For Professor Burn's comment, see his stimulating article, 'The Age of Equipoise: England (1848–1868)', in the *Nineteenth Century* (1949).
[3] A. Trollope, *The Prime Minister* (1876).

in the policies of local Boards of Guardians as there had been in
the administrative patchwork 'of the eighteenth-century poor law.
As far as parliamentary reform was concerned, the country was for
the most part quite uninterested. 'Lord John Grosvenor's Bill
against Sunday trading' (1855), wrote one political commentator,
'created five times more popular agitation and excitement than all
the reform measures united.'[1] Occasionally Bright's powerful
oratory could stir crowds in Manchester and Bradford—as in 1858
and 1859—but there was an underlying apathy which mocked
Bright's talk of 'a steady, ever-growing, irresistible tide of public
opinion'.

In the House of Commons itself the survival of parliamentary
reform as an issue during these years—official bills were introduced
in 1852, 1854, 1859 and 1860—is best explained in terms of a
delicately balanced political situation within Parliament itself rather
than in terms of sustained public pressure from outside. The reform
bills of ministers (the anti-reforming Palmerston introduced his in
1859) were less triumphant vindications of principle than useful
manœuvres to attract small marginal groups of members, and they
had the special advantage that they seemed highly unlikely to
succeed. Nothing could be lost by offering so-called 'fancy franchises' to East India proprietors, holders of Bank of England stock,
and even members of the Inns of Court and College of Physicians,
and something might be gained. Bright ridiculed these efforts, and
Russell, converted from belief in finality to support of further
reform, sharply criticized the 'subtle inventions of ingenious
theorists', but Bright, as we have seen, was unable to launch a
nation-wide movement, and in 1861 Russell temporarily abandoned
his hopes.

In these years of quiet, expediency was the 'only principle to
which allegiance is paid' and 'the old antithesis of principle and
expediency is absolutely forgotten.'[2] Only in the case of free trade,
which was accepted in 1852 by the old Protectionists of 1846 and
further implemented particularly in Gladstone's budgets of 1853
and 1861–6, was there any undeviating line of advance. In considering questions of tariff protection, *The Times* noted in 1858, 'we pass
out of the region of compromise and conjecture in which the
Politician is doomed to dwell, and get into the region of abstract

---

[1] Sir J. Walsh, *op. cit.*, p. 7.
[2] Lord Robert Cecil, 'Theories of Parliamentary Reform', in *Oxford Essays* (1858).

truth, which works out the conclusions deducible from its premises with something very nearly approaching to mathematical precision.'[1]

Some writers claimed, however, that the dominion of expediency had begun with Peel's acceptance of free trade in 1846 against the wishes of a substantial section of his own party. Since then, the argument went on, ministers had been unable to maintain properly demarcated lines of division between different parties. 'His Majesty's Ministers and His Majesty's Opposition, as our fathers knew them, two compact and always opposed bodies, are swept away.'[2] This historical analysis was misleading in that it exaggerated the tightness of party allegiance before 1846, but it seemed confirmed by the course of events after that year of party disintegration. Lord John Russell, Peel's irresolute Whig successor, restored weak government. His cabinet was divided and he was unable to press hard even for those measures which he believed necessary, like land reform in Ireland. By 1851 it had become abundantly clear both that his ministry could not hold together for long and that it would be difficult to replace it. His defeat on a radical motion in the February of that year was followed by several days of hectic excitement during which attempts were made to form a different ministry, but at the end of it all he had to come back with all his old colleagues, 'damaged, weak and unpopular'.

There was no hope of any immediate solution to the political problems of 1851, for the Whigs lacked cohesion and depended on radical and on Irish support, and there was inevitable tension unless they made concessions to the advocates of change. Whig prime ministers, strong or weak, always faced the dilemma of being at one and the same time leaders of a 'movement and agitation party' and the heads of governments. After Russell's quarrel with Palmerston in December 1851[3] the difficulties of maintaining an equilibrium increased, and Palmerston quickly had his 'tit for tat' for his dismissal when in February 1852 his vigorous opposition to the prime minister led to the downfall of the government by nine votes (135–126). From that time onwards almost every subsequent government until 1867 was openly weak in the House of Commons, and there were many examples of 'majorities collected God knows how and voting God knows why'. Although there was always a

---

[1] Quoted in an anonymous pamphlet *The Franchise. What shall we do with it?* (1858).
[2] *Ibid.*
[3] See above, pp. 375–6.

majority in the House of Commons of persons 'holding liberal opinions', they were never united as a party except for reasons of immediate political tactics.[1]

A second set of writers maintained that it was not Peel's betrayal of his party but his death in 1850 which took the backbone out of English politics. So long as he remained alive, they argued, he was a force to be reckoned with, even in opposition. He was frequently consulted by Russell on such varied matters as Ireland, the financial crisis of 1847, and the repeal of the navigation laws in 1849, and on at least one occasion the Whigs specially brought him up from Tamworth to speak in the House. There were many signs, however, that his 'Peelite' supporters, who numbered about ninety backbenchers after the election of 1847 but 'did not exercise any considerable degree of permanent influence as a body',[2] were beginning to be restive in the confused political situation. Some were turning to the Protectionists—in a debate initiated by Disraeli on agricultural distress in February 1850 more 'Peelites' voted with Disraeli than with Peel—while others were associating with the Whigs—twenty 'Peelites' voted with Palmerston against Peel in the 'Don Pacifico' debate.[3] The 'Peelite' leaders, men of considerable political and administrative experience, were tiring of 'the cold-baked meats of Praise and Self-approval' and were anxious to return to office. Peel's death in 1850 meant that key decisions about tactics had to be made by Gladstone, Graham, Herbert, and Newcastle; their personal characters and preferences rather than the pressure of a 'rank and file' or the goodwill of the Court, which they certainly possessed, were the main factors in the political equations of 1851 and 1852.

When Russell resigned in February 1851 there was much talk of a Whig-Peelite coalition without Palmerston, but it was not until December 1852 that a coalition was formed which had a Peelite leader, Aberdeen, a strong Peelite contingent in the cabinet, and Palmerston at the Home Office. Between February 1851 and December 1852 not only had Russell quarrelled with Palmerston but the 'tit for tat' had led to the formation in February 1852 of a short-lived Tory minority government led by Lord Derby and

---

[1] For a later statement of this view, see G. F. Lewis (ed.) *The Letters of Sir George Cornewall Lewis* (1870), p. 344.

[2] Morley, *Gladstone*, vol. I, p. 260.

[3] For the general position of the Peelites at this time see a useful article by C. H. Stuart, 'The Formation of the Coalition Cabinet of 1852', in *T.R.H.S.* (1954).

including Disraeli as chancellor of the exchequer. The position of the Tory group, Peel's old opponents in 1846, was as difficult in the mid-Victorian years as that of the Whigs—in many ways more so. Although many of the 'Peelites' had returned to the fold between 1846 and 1852, the name 'Conservative' had been adopted again in 1848, and Protection was abandoned as a party cry in 1852, the Tories were doomed to be a parliamentary minority in mid-Victorian England. Their government of 1852 was weak in names and ability, and their two later minority governments in 1858 and in 1866 exposed the inherent difficulties of their situation. Whether in government or in opposition, they were bound therefore to make their own particular contribution to the politics of expediency, and there was a large element of truth in the comment of the *Edinburgh Review* that the Derby government of 1852 was 'the first administration which reduced inconsistency to a system, and want of principles to a principle'.[1] The self-assured Derby had to rebuke the opportunist Disraeli on more than one occasion after 1852 for seeking a possible union with ultra-Whigs, like Lord Grey, the son of Grey of the Reform Bill, or with the Manchester School. Disraeli in turn resented Derby's reluctance to take office at moments of crisis—in 1855, for instance, during the bitter debates of the Crimean War—and there were times when the Conservative party seemed in serious danger of breaking up. That it did not disintegrate was of the utmost long-term political importance—as was the fact that it remained flexible and non-doctrinaire. It may be reasonably argued, indeed, that its flexibility and resilience, which disgruntled Tory critics continued to condemn as weakness and treachery, were more valuable long-term assets than either Whig intransigence or liberal principles. Derby and Disraeli between them—the one relying on social standing and representing a genuine aristocratic element in mid-nineteenth-century politics, the other depending on ambition and brains—guaranteed the future of the Conservative party.

It was on the occasion of the grouping together of the Whig-Peelite coalition of December 1852 that Disraeli made his famous and much-quoted remark that 'England does not love coalitions'. The coalition government certainly was more popular in the Commons than it was in the country, and even at the centre the arrangements made were dependent not on 'a coalition of party sentiment and feeling' but on a series of hard-driven bargains.

[1] Vol. CX (1859), p. 272.

'Everybody's principles', one Conservative declared, 'had united
with nobody's opinions.' While Derby's government had suffered
from a lack of outstanding personalities and administrative experience, Aberdeen's new government included 'five or six first-rate
men of equal or nearly equal pretensions, none of them likely to
acknowledge the superiority or defer to the opinions of any other,
and every one of these five or six considering himself abler and more
important than their Premier'.[1] The Ministry of All the Talents, as
it was soon called, included Russell at the Foreign Office,[2] Palmerston at the Home Office, Gladstone at the Exchequer, and Graham
at the Admiralty. It was a far from easy team for the 69-year-old
Peelite prime minister to hold together, and matters were made
worse for him by both the uncertain mood and alignments of backbenchers in the House of Commons and the emergencies he had
to face, the greatest of which was the Crimean War. After the
general election of 1852 Graham had written to Gladstone, 'it will
be an impossible Parliament. Parties will be found too nicely balanced
to render a new line of policy practicable without a first appeal to
the electors'.[3] Although no such appeal was made until 1857, the
1852 Parliament ran its course only because there was a perpetual
shifting of groups, a desperate hunt for places and a general dislike
of dissolution, and because in the middle of the war the ignominious
collapse of the coalition was followed by the setting up of a new
government led by Palmerston.

The Crimean War broke the mood of mid-Victorian politics and
focused attention on the need for sweeping changes in government
and administration,[4] yet its main result was not large-scale reform
but the perpetuation of Palmerston's ascendancy in English politics.
In almost every respect Palmerston was the perfect epitome of the
politically articulate England of his day, as much the representative
of the 'idea of the age' as Peel in very different circumstances had
been only ten years before. Averse to strong government and uninterested in organic reforms, he believed in gradual 'improvement'
and the continued prosecution of an active foreign policy. 'He was
a statesman for the moment. Whatever was not wanted now, whatever was not practicable now, he drove quite out of his mind.'[5]

---

[1] *The Greville Memoirs*, vol. VI, p. 384.
[2] He resigned in February 1853.
[3] Quoted Morley, *Gladstone*, vol. I, p. 428.
[4] See above, p. 382, below, pp. 433–5.
[5] A. Trollope, *Palmerston* (1882), p. 4.

Both his parliamentary strength and weaknesses were revealed in 1857 and 1858. When in 1857 a group of distinguished parliamentarians, including Russell, Gladstone, Disraeli, Graham, Cobden and Roebuck successfully banded together in the House of Commons to carry a vote of censure against the government's policy in China —Sir John Bowring, the ex-Utilitarian governor of Hong-Kong had ordered British military and naval forces to take action against the Chinese at Canton—Palmerston was able to brand them as an 'unprincipled combination' and to appeal over their heads to the electorate. When they complained of a 'penal dissolution', Palmerston taunted them with the remark that 'so far from looking upon renewed intercourse with their constituents as a punishment they ought to regard it as a triumph'. He knew well enough that he could paint a simple but compelling picture of innocent Englishmen and 'insolent barbarians' which would attract the support not only of ordinary electors but of organized commercial interests, such as the Manchester Commercial Association, and historically powerful bodies like the Court of Common Council in London. At the general election of 1857 the name of Palmerston was a 'convenient watchword' everywhere, and *The Times* in its first account of election results simply divided the successful candidates into Palmerstonians and anti-Palmerstonians: 'As we once had a Barebones Parliament,' the *Quarterly* added, 'so we are now to have a Palmerston Parliament.'[1]

The extent of Palmerston's victory entailed the almost complete annihilation of the Manchester School—Bright was defeated at Manchester and Cobden at Huddersfield—and demonstrated how much the cries of the 1840s had faded into the background. It also dealt a final blow to the 'Peelites', who for long had been a collection of leaders rather than a highly organized group. Their thin ranks had already been reduced by many further defections inside Parliament between 1852 and 1857 and at the election they lost important seats. Their final defeat and disappearance as an independent force was no cause for regret, and 1857 merely registered ten years of history. 'Individually', one acute contemporary writer put it, 'they are persons possessed of every claim to respect, but on public grounds few view with regret their extinction as a party. There was no standing room for them in the narrow line which separates the two sides of the House; they were at once a sign of the prevailing

[1] *Quarterly Review*, vol. CI (1857), p. 544.

disorganization and a cause of its continuation and extension. If they voted with the Minister, their adherence was deemed servile; if they voted against him, their opposition was thought factious. ... The constituencies, locally organized under the forms of political dualism abhor the *tertium quid*. ... Accordingly not a single person, we believe, has been returned to Parliament because he was a Peelite.'[1]

Despite the overwhelming victory of Palmerston in 1857, not even he could continue to hold a parliamentary majority together, and events in 1858 showed that the House of Commons was still intractable. Sheltering behind the Palmerstonian label were many Whigs and radicals whose support for him was strictly qualified in practice. Some were genuine reformers, unwilling to remain caught up for ever in the election propaganda of 'Bowringites' and 'pro-Chinese'; others, no doubt, agreed with the comments of the member for Great Yarmouth that it would have been better if the country had chosen a new Parliament upon some broader and more general basis than that of confidence in a particular minister upon a particular question.

The fall of Palmerston in 1858 was engineered not by critics of his conservatism but by opponents of his foreign policy. They asserted, not as they were wont to do, that it was too aggressive, but that for once in a while it had not been sufficiently firm. In January 1858 an English-made bomb was thrown at Napoleon III by an Italian conspirator, Orsini, whose plot also had been hatched on this side of the Channel. When the French protested against the lax security arrangements in England which had permitted a 'nest of assassins' to operate without check, Palmerston yielded with surprising readiness, and introduced a bill to amend the law of conspiracy by imposing a special penalty for conspiracy to murder. For once Palmerston's opponents found a popular cause to undermine his government. Russell, Graham, Bright, and Kinglake, the historian of the Crimea, who had a personal and public grudge against Napoleon, gathered enough support to beat Palmerston by nineteen votes. A minority Conservative government took office again, and there was talk that Palmerston had been finally eclipsed.

Like most prophecies concerning Palmerston, this one was wrong. He was back in office in 1859 for six years, this time with a more secure majority. To understand the emergence of the long

[1] *Ibid.*, p. 561.

ministry of 1859 to 1865, which was of crucial importance in re-shaping English politics, it is necessary to turn not only to the diffi-culties of the short-lived Conservative minority government but to the more general reaction against the politics of the preceding thirteen years.

To try to augment the strength of a Conservative minority govern-ment Derby turned in February 1858 both to Grey and to Gladstone and asked them to join his cabinet. In 1852 he had invited Palmer-ston, as he had done also during the abortive negotiations of 1855; Gladstone also had been approached in the second of these two years. Gladstone's refusal to serve in the Conservative government of 1858 was of considerable political importance, for he was still poised at this middle period of his life between his Conservative past and his Liberal future. While Derby was approaching him very gingerly, Bright was telling him with direct Quaker candour that if he joined a Conservative government he would be linking his fortunes with 'a constant minority . . . which is every day lessening in numbers and in power' and that if he remained 'on the other side' nothing could prevent him ultimately from becoming prime minister.[1] This was, indeed, to be the way ahead for Gladstone although he himself did not see it clearly in 1858. He was willing even, thinking more of Homer than of Derby, to accept a govern-mental mission to go to the Ionian Islands as Lord High Commis-sioner Extraordinary. It was not until 1859 that the real parting of the ways came for him, and even then the full significance of his choice became apparent only in retrospect. In the meantime, the Conservative government was forced in its few months of office to scramble for votes, to compromise on many issues, and to alienate some of its followers. When it introduced a controversial Reform Bill, there was restiveness and alarm among a section of country gentlemen who objected to 'voting black to be white or white to be black' at the bidding of Derby or Disraeli,[2] and in March 1859 the government was defeated by thirty-nine votes in a packed Commons on a motion of Lord John Russell. The debate had been as confused as the whole politics of the period. Some anti-reformers supported the government's bill, many reformers opposed it. In neither case did they strike any sparks in the country outside Westminster.

[1] Gladstone Papers, B.M. 44,112.
[2] See a letter from Henry Drummond to the Conservative Whip Sir William Joliffe in the *Disraeli Papers*, Joliffe XII, quoted W. D. Jones, *Lord Derby and Victorian Conservatism* (1956), p. 253.

After his defeat Derby asked the Queen to dissolve Parliament, and chose as two of his main election points the decline of the two-party system and the factious attitude of the opposition. In directing public attention to the awkwardness and inconveniences of the general parliamentary situation he was framing an indictment of thirteen years of English politics. Disraeli took the same line, going beyond denunciation of Russell—a restless and disruptive influence moving in an 'atmosphere of coalitions, combinations, *coups d'état* and cunning resolutions'—to a general criticism of the 'hocus pocus' of group as distinct from party politics. 'The real issue', he wrote to Derby, 'the broad, great issue is whether Parliamentary government is compatible with our existing institutions.'[1] Unfortunately in practice he had been as factious as anyone else, more than most, and it was difficult to reconcile his statements of constitutional principles with his political actions. He had pleaded forcibly and precociously in 1846 and on many later occasions for clearly defined party boundaries,[2] and was willing in 1859 to contemplate parliamentary reform if it would conclusively break the existing parliamentary deadlocks, but what he really wanted was personal power as leader of a stable majority in the House of Commons.

As a result of the general election of 1859 the Conservatives won thirty seats and a government was formed which lasted for six years. It was not, however, a Conservative government. Palmerston and not Derby led it, and Gladstone and not Disraeli was its outstanding political personality. A genuine line of division, instead of the spurious line chosen by the manipulators of parliamentary reform in 1858, helped to determine the composition of government and opposition. It was not on a domestic issue at all, but on the unification of Italy that the parties regrouped. In face of the agreement of Napoleon III and Cavour to launch a war of Italian liberation, the Conservative government tried to maintain an uneasy neutrality. It showed no sincere sympathy with the Italian cause and on occasion could not avoid appearing to treat Austria as an aggrieved victim of Cavour's ambition and French aggression. When the Italian war began in earnest in May 1859, Derby con-

---

[1] Quoted W. F. Monypenny and G. E. Buckle, *op. cit.*, p. 1612.

[2] See above, pp. 342–3. In 1848 he maintained 'that you can have no parliamentary government if you have no party government', and attributed weak government to 'the disorganization of party' (quoted *ibid.*, p. 924). See an important article by Gladstone expressing a somewhat similar point of view on 'The Declining Efficiency of Parliament', in the *Quarterly Review*, vol. IC (1856), pp. 521–70.

demned Austria's ultimatum but at the same time tried hard to restrain France and Sardinia. His policy, which was popular in the country, alienated some of the most powerful parliamentarians at Westminster, including Palmerston, Russell, and Gladstone, and helped to give a sense of unity to the opposition. Gladstone, who had first interested himself in Italian politics on a visit to Naples in 1851, had conversations with Cavour in March 1859 which converted him to the view that Austrian rule was as much to blame as Neapolitan backwardness for the problems of Italy. He later confessed that foreign politics had the chief place in his mind in 1859; Palmerston wished not only to pursue a more positive diplomacy but to revive the French alliance; Russell, as much of an 'old Italian master' as Palmerston himself, was willing as usual to do everything to defeat the government. Thus although the Conservatives had gained ground at the election, they were immediately confronted in the new Parliament by a formidable *bloc* of opponents, who were anxious to pursue a different policy. Gladstone voted for the government in a crucial no-confidence vote on 10 June, for a brief moment pushing foreign affairs to the back of his mind, but after the government had been defeated by thirteen votes in that division he was prepared to join the new government which Palmerston formed.

Once again Palmerston was the leader of an impressive-looking government which included his old enemy Russell at the Foreign Office and Gladstone at the Exchequer. The Queen had attempted to forestall Palmerston by sending for Granville, but the manœuvre failed and the new government not only lasted longer than any government since that of Liverpool but constituted a bridge leading from the group politics of the 1850s to the party politics of the late-Victorian England.

The coming into power of a government with reasonable security of tenure by no means brought to an end the group and interest politics of the mid-Victorian years—they were to be more tangled than ever in 1866 and 1867—but it did at least make for new alignments which pointed the way to the future rather than to the past. Until the critical debates on the eve of the second Reform Bill, which touched on the basic problems of society as well as of government, two factors continued to make for mild and unobtrusive government and compromise politics.

The first was the narrow gap between the opinions of members on one side of the House of Commons and the other. 'The spirit of the country', wrote Bagehot in *The English Constitution*, 'is quiet but reasonable, indisposed to sweeping innovations, and equally indisposed to keeping in the old Tory way, everything which is because it is. The moderate members of both parties represent this spirit very fairly. At a recent election a poor voter is reported to have said that both candidates were very nice gentlemen, but that for his part he could not see much difference between them; and this is the simple truth.' Palliser spoke much the same words in Trollope's *Phineas Redux* (1876)—'when some small measure of reform has thoroughly commended itself to the country so thoroughly that all men know that the country will have it—then the question arises whether its details shall be arranged by the party which calls itself Liberal or that which is termed Conservative. The men are so near to each other in all their convictions and theories of life that nothing is left to them but personal competition for the doing of the thing that has to be done.'

The second was the continued lack of general support for 'strong government' in the earlier nineteenth-century sense of the term. 'I was accustomed', the novelist George Eliot wrote of her father, 'to hear him utter the word "Government" in a tone that charged it with awe and made it part of any effective religion'[1]; her own generation cared little for such a *mystique*. Bagehot found it difficult to believe in 1858 that the famous Six Acts could ever have existed on the statute book, and Peterloo (and the French Revolution) were far more difficult for the mid-Victorians to understand than they are for people living in the twentieth century. With the diminishing danger to public order in the 1850s, there was a decline of fear. The important County and Borough Police Act was passed in 1856 providing central police grants to local authorities and setting up a police inspectorate, while the old British love of violence was being channelled harmlessly into reading about domestic crime or bloodshed overseas. With the growing wealth of the country and the consciousness that it owed little to government aid, there was a decline in respect. Individual members of Parliament still lived in a world of deference, but 'government' was usually treated with suspicion unless it was undoing old errors. In the no-confidence debate of 1859, Sidney Herbert said that he did not believe that a strong government in the old sense of the word was any longer

[1] Quoted W. L. Burn, *loc. cit.*

possible, 'nor do I think we want a strong government in the sense the country did formerly. Then society was weak, and a strong Government was necessary to repress and guide it. Now society is strong and dominates the government set over it.'

There was one feature of this 'strong society' which cannot be left out of an analysis of politics and government—public opinion, particularly as expressed in the increasingly influential press. It was, after all, the check imposed by 'a speaking and writing age' which Bagehot regarded as the ultimate check on the parliamentary choice of ministers. In previous periods of party fragmentation and weak executives, considerable power might have been exercised by the sovereign. Victoria's powers were limited, however,[1] as was her patronage, and 'public opinion', sharply opposed to both Queen and Prince Consort in the early stages of the Crimean War and unwilling throughout the period to welcome hidden exercise of the traditional royal prerogatives, was a growing force.

In 1850 F. Knight Hunt published his *Fourth Estate*, dedicated to the journalists of England and their 'constant readers'. It chose as its motto a phrase of Benjamin Constant, 'the press is the mistress of intelligence, and intelligence is the mistress of the world' and treated newspapers as 'a positive necessity of modern civilized existence'. The events of the 1850s and 1860s, particularly the Crimean War, enhanced the rôle of the press, gave journalists a greater independence and a more secure status than they had ever before enjoyed, and placed the growing reading public in a position where it could comment on decisions of high policy and criticize the daily actions of government. At the same time the abolition of the stamp duty on the anniversary of Magna Carta in 1855—the eagerly awaited objective of the Association for the Repeal of the Taxes on Knowledge—and the repeal of the paper duty in 1861 cheapened the price of newspapers and increased circulations. The number of readers of *The Times*, for instance, went up from about 40,000 in 1851 when it cost 5*d.* to 70,000 in 1861 when it cost 3*d.*, and the number of advertisements increased proportionately. The *Daily Telegraph*, which started as a small twopenny single sheet in June 1855, lowered its price and doubled its size three months later, and was the first penny daily deliberately seeking as many advertisements and as large a circulation as possible.

It was the rôle of the press as a critic rather than as a potential

[1] See below, p. 461.

manipulator of mass circulations which was most emphasized in the 1850s and 1860s both by supporters and opponents. While the reviews did much to 'teach the multitude of men what to think and what to say' in matters of taste as well as politics,[1] the newspapers with their 'audacity of censure' and 'exaggeration of flattery' contributed considerably to the weakness of government.[2] 'It is *The Times* which leads the Government and the House of Commons which follows'; one writer remarked, 'Ministers and Parliaments fear *The Times*, and *The Times* is not the least afraid of either.'[3]

The average daily circulation of *The Times* during the Crimean War was much greater than that of the other five principal London morning papers of the early 1850s put together—the *Morning Post* with which Palmerston was very closely associated; the *Morning Herald*, which had the *Standard* as its sister evening paper; the *Daily News*, which first appeared under Dickens's editorship in 1846; the *Morning Advertiser*, 'the journal par excellence of the public house'[4]; and the *Morning Chronicle*, which represented the views of the Peelites and was quietly swallowed up by the popular *Daily Telegraph* in 1862. A vigorous provincial press followed the same trends as the national press—the *Liverpool Daily Post* was founded in 1855, the *Manchester Guardian* became a penny paper in the same year and the *Birmingham Daily Post*, an offshoot of the older *Journal*, became a penny daily in 1857, but *The Times* still stood supreme. 'It leans upon no single class, it represents no exclusive party, it advocates no separate interest. It claims to embody and to express, and to a great extent it does embody and express the current opinion of all the intelligent and informed sections of the British community.'[5]

The new rôle of *The Times* in the confused political world of the 1850s is well illustrated by a small but significant episode in 1859. When Granville was entrusted by the Queen to form a government instead of Palmerston, he gave an account of the interview to Delane, the editor of *The Times*. Printed the following day, it greatly annoyed the Queen who naturally exclaimed: 'Whom am I to trust?'

---

[1] See a sermon of Newman in 1850, quoted Houghton, *op. cit.*, p. 104. The 1860s was a decade rich in reviews. The old quarterlies lost ground to monthly literary magazines and to reviews like the *Fortnightly Review* (1865).
[2] A remark of Croker, quoted A. Aspinall, *Politics and the Press* (1949), p. 4.
[3] Walsh, *op. cit.*, p. 112.
[4] Quoted E. E. Kellett, 'The Press' in *Early Victorian England* (1934), vol. II, p. 33. See also T. H. S. Escott, *Masters of English Journalism* (1911), esp. ch. VIII.
[5] Walsh, *op. cit.*, p. 98.

Granville, who had earned the title 'the polite' and had been a personal friend of the Queen and the Prince Consort since the time of the preparations for the Great Exhibition, denied that he had communicated anything to Delane and claimed that *The Times* report had been drawn up 'in a vulgar, inflated manner' from information received from leaky friends. In fact, he had written to Delane after seeing the Queen and the leakage was his own. Delane did not reveal this, and the truth only came out thirty years after his death. Later in the century Jowett was to include in his 'maxims for statesmen and others' the warning 'never tell'; it was Delane and not Granville who followed his maxim in 1859. To *The Times* 'even the secrets of the Palace were open'[1], and its reserve power was growing at the same time as its public appeal. In time it was to become part of the 'Establishment' itself.

4. RADICAL PRESSURES

Outside the circle of parliamentarians and readers of *The Times* there were certain radical groups at work in the 1850s which were eventually, for all their limited appeal, to influence the politics of the mid-'60s. They counted for little in good times, except during the Crimean War, but in 1857, a year of financial crash and diminished trade, when there was heavy unemployment in London and some of the provincial cities, they were strong enough to frighten conservative opinion. Wherever unemployed operatives demonstrated—in 1857 London workers set up a short-lived National Association of Unemployed Operatives—or trade unionists went out on strike—as did the engineers in 1852 and the builders in 1859–60—there was a sharp reminder that social conflicts were still unsolved. 'Education', a writer in the *Newcastle Weekly Chronicle* exclaimed in 1857, 'has as yet done little to remove the barriers of prejudice and ignorance which separate class from class in this country. The old fallacies still hold their ground; capital is still denounced as antagonistic to labour, and the possession of a "bit of land" still declared to be the infallible remedy for the ills the poor man is heir to.'[2]

Apart from Christian socialism, a highly imaginative and searching reaction of F. D. Maurice, J. M. Ludlow, Charles Kingsley and

---

[1] E. Cook, *Delane of The Times* (1915), p. 120.
[2] 23 January 1857. The *Weekly Chronicle* was purchased by Joseph Cowen in 1859.

E. V. Neale to the Kennington Common episode of 1848 and the spectacle of near-revolution, there were three main types of radicalism in the 1850s—the social radicalism of the inheritors of Chartism, the militant nationalistic radicalism of men like Roebuck, and the logical, consistent middle-class radicalism of Bright, Cobden and the Manchester School. It was almost impossible for these three radicalisms to coalesce. Ernest Jones, who kept the Chartist banner flying in the early 1850s, had no sympathy with Bright. His socialism, strongly influenced by Marx, ran counter to all Bright's views about the necessity of government non-intervention not only in economic matters but even in such 'moral' matters as the sale of intoxicants by licensed victuallers. Roebuck in his turn had little sympathy with either wing of what it was increasingly difficult to think of as one single movement. A militant supporter of the Crimean War, he quarrelled bitterly with Bright; a militant opponent of the trade unions, he sat on the Royal Commission of 1867 and opposed one by one the claims of men like Applegarth. By then, indeed, his radicalism was merging into Conservatism, as was the esoteric, conspiratorial radicalism of the wild and un-balanced Russophobe, David Urquhart. Bright and Cobden, who thought differently on many questions, were consistent in their Manchester School teachings, but some of their supporters found their discipline rather too strict. It was therefore only in the shocked eyes of the opponents of all kinds of 'social subversion' that all radicals looked alike, Bright, Roebuck and Jones, mischievous men who set class against class and did not understand what was good for them. Why indeed did they continue to exist? 'Civil and religious liberty are complete with us', wrote Lord Shaftesbury in genuine indignation, 'the people have not a wrong unredressed, nor the Radicals a right unattained, and yet their [the English radicals'] spirit is that of Mazzini, Ledru-Rollin and Kossuth.'[1]

Shaftesbury was right to choose foreign parallels, for it was foreign policy more than home policy which kept militant radicalism alive during the 1850s. Beginning with the revolutions of 1848 and Kossuth's visit in 1851 there was an almost continuous influence of exiles and outsiders on English politics, culminating in Garibaldi's visit in 1864. At the same time big foreign struggles, not only the Crimean War but the American Civil War and the Polish rising of 1863, broke the languor of English politics.

[1] Hodder, *op. cit.*, vol. II, p. 447.

The last Chartists were themselves strongly influenced by events on the Continent in 1848 and by the presence in London of considerable numbers of Polish and German exiles, among whom Karl Marx was outstanding. The Fraternal Democrats, formed in the autumn of 1845, made up a bridge movement between English and Continental radicalism, and Harney and Ernest Jones advocated a union of socialists and Chartists to prepare the English working classes for the 'achievement of their deliverance from the oppression of irresponsible capital'.[1] Jones interpreted the Six Points of the Charter in socialist terms, attempting after the disillusionment of 1848 and 1849 to build up a working-class party based on the Charter and something more—'Chartism under the red flag'.[2] A Convention in March 1851 marked the peak point of his agitation, for by the end of the year new divisions had appeared among the Chartists, Harney had broken with Jones, and there was a general mood of apathy in the increasingly prosperous industrial areas. Jones himself continued throughout the 1850s, however, to preach his socialist doctrines, particularly in the north of England. He was violently anti-Russian during the Crimean War, although in his magazine the *People's Paper* he pressed for 'justice to the English soldier' as well as an all-out struggle against Tsarist autocracy. In 1857 he unsuccessfully contested Nottingham on a radical land and manhood suffrage programme. Yet by 1857 he had become convinced despite all his previous opinions that a union between working classes and middle classes was necessary if reform was to be achieved, and was looking rather tentatively towards both Roebuck and Bright. In face of considerable opposition from his own supporters, who continued to maintain that 'the working classes must accomplish their freedom without the aid of any other class in society'[3] he drew nearer to middle-class radicalism after 1858 and was closely associated in the 1860s with the influential Reform League. When he ceased to publish his Chartist journals in 1860, the National Charter Association went out of existence.

The history of the middle-class radicalism with which he became entangled can be traced back to the so-called 'Little Charter' movement of 1848 and before that, of course, to the earlier radical agitations of the late eighteenth and early nineteenth centuries.

[1] *Northern Star*, 3 November 1849.
[2] *Red Republican*, 13 July 1850, quoted J. Saville, *Ernest Jones, Chartist* (1952), pp. 37–8, p. 41.
[3] *National Union*, May 1858. Quoted *ibid.*, p. 70.

After the corn laws had been repealed Bright was anxious to organize a movement to extend the suffrage, and in 1848 he joined with Joseph Hume and a group of parliamentary radicals to press for the Little Charter, household suffrage, triennial parliaments, and a more equal distribution of seats. Cobden was far less interested in the prospects of a new agitation along these lines than in freehold land schemes and financial reform—the reduction of government expenditure, heavier rates of tax on unearned than on earned incomes, and full publicity about fiscal policy—and he devoted most of his energies to supporting a network of provincial Financial Reform Associations, modelled on a successful organization founded in Liverpool in 1848. Bright persisted, however, in advocating organic political reform and drew Cobden into a society pledged to achieve both their objects—the Parliamentary and Financial Reform Association. The Association was not very successful. In demanding a further instalment of parliamentary reform it alienated the 'millocracy', the old supporters of the Anti-Corn Law League; in trying to conciliate 'the Manchester men' it irritated ardent working-class politicians. When it was eventually dissolved during the Crimean War, few lamented its passing. Its story had demonstrated the difficulties of bringing together unrelenting free traders like Bright and working-class leaders who cared little for the doctrines of orthodox political economy. It was not only the Chartists or ex-Chartists who objected to the refusal of Bright and his friends to consider labour as anything more than a commodity while being willing to treat labourers as responsible citizens. While Cobden was talking of the 'desperate spirit of monopoly and tyranny' in trade unionism and claiming that trade unionists might 'as well attempt to regulate the tides by force' as influence the rate of wages 'by coercion',[2] skilled trade unionists were accepting only such 'views of economical science' as their 'experience in the world and workshop' seemed to justify. It is not surprising that throughout the whole of the 1850s and 1860s the *Economist* argued persistently that 'the artisan classes' whether or not they had definite political opinions had 'strong class prejudices, strong class hopes'.[3]

The dissolution of the Parliamentary and Financial Reform

---

[1] Quoted J. A. Hobson, *Cobden, the International Man* (1919), p. 166.

[2] See above, p. 409; D. Chadwick, 'The Rate of Wages in Manchester and Salford, 1839–1859', in *J.R.S.S.*, vol. XXIII (1860); *T.N.A.P.S.S.* (1862), p. 801.

[3] 16 June 1860.

Association took place when the third division in radicalism, that
between the 'peace party' and the 'war party', had become an open
and dramatic cleavage. Cobden and Bright were not pacifists opposed
to war in all circumstances, but they considered that the Crimean
War was both a mistake and a crime. Their view that the Russian
menace was a myth and that the Turkish Empire was 'one of the
most immoral and filthy despotisms over one of the fairest portions
of the earth' was well defined by 1850, and while militant anti-
Russian radicals, by far the biggest group, were pressing Aberdeen
to go to war in 1854, Bright was giving his full support to a Quaker
mission, which included Joseph Sturge, to visit Russia to discuss
with the Tsar the possibility of maintaining peace. Once war broke
out, Cobden and Bright were as sharply criticized by many of their
old allies as they were by Palmerston. But even the militant radicals
were divided. One section led by Urquhart saw Palmerston as a
Russian-paid agent, and set up Working Men's Foreign Affairs
Committees in the provincial towns and cities to demand 'open
diplomacy' and a full exposure of an international Russian conspiracy; another section looked to Palmerston as a national leader,
while reserving the right to criticize the administrative and social
system on which he depended. The debates between the supporters
of Roebuck and the followers of Urquhart were just as heated and
noisy as the debates between the Manchester School and the rest,
and in Sheffield and Newcastle radical politics provided a range
of more clearly defined parties than existed at Westminster.

For all the radical divisions, the Crimean War undoubtedly gave
a great impetus to the re-emergence of radical attitudes. The
unemployment and high food prices of the grim Crimean winter led
not to demands for peace, as Cobden and Bright anticipated, but to
increasingly strident demands for a more energetic prosecution of
the war and the destruction of the 'aristocratical monopoly of
power and privilege'. Early in 1855 an Administrative Reform
Association was set up in London, 'brought into existence by the
exigency of the time'. Above all else, the new association which had
the backing of Roebuck, Dickens, and Samuel Morley, the rich
radical wire-puller of the age, sought full information about the
'real conduct' of public affairs, particularly in the Foreign Office, 'a
region of unknown powers and undefined responsibility'. 'There
must be an end put to every mystery of office', was the cry; 'how
the Administration of the country is carried on must be made plain

to the most ordinary capacity.'[1] Despite the differences between
Urquhart, Roebuck, and Bright, this was a cry which they could all
utter equally sincerely. Urquhart made his working-class followers
read Blue Books and ferret out facts on such obscure topics as the
statistics of Anglo-Turkish trade; Roebuck, in pressing for a
parliamentary select committee to investigate the management of
the war, had asked for what his opponents considered a kind of
inquisition 'unworthy of a free and generous people'; Bright was
one of the strongest critics of the Foreign Office establishment.

The campaign of the Administrative Reform Association, reaching its climax in mass meetings in Drury Lane theatre, was made
easier by the publication in 1855 of the famous *Report on the
Organization of the Civil Service*, prepared by Sir Charles Trevelyan
and Sir Stafford Northcote. 'Admission into the Civil Service', the
Report declared, 'is, indeed, eagerly sought for; but it is for the
unambitious and the indolent and incapable that it is chiefly desired.
Those whose abilities do not warrant an expectation that they will
succeed in the open professions . . . and those whom indolence of
temperament or physical infirmities unfit for active exertions, are
placed in the Civil Service, where they may obtain an honourable
livelihood with little labour and no risk.'[2] The full implications of
this Report were discussed not only at mass meetings of the
Administrative Reform Association and the State Reform Association, founded for those who could not afford to pay a guinea
subscription, but in Parliament, where there were revealing debates
on the need for army reform and open competitive examination for
the civil service. Reform resolutions proposed by Roebuck's friend,
Henry Layard, the excavator of Nineveh, were defeated by 359
votes to 46 after one of the most unorthodox backbenchers, Henry
Drummond, had taunted the administrative reformers with greater
inefficiency even than that of the government. 'See what a precious
mess they have made at Manchester', he declared. 'Filled as that
town was with Radicals and philosophers, they could not drain it.
And yet there was hardly a town in the kingdom which could be
more easily drained; for it stands upon two hills and any man of
ordinary common sense would at once have said, "Cut a ditch from
the top to the bottom and so drain it".'

Radical fervour burnt itself out in the last months of the war,

---

[1] Administrative Reform Association, *Official Papers*, No. 1, May 1855, p. 7.
[2] See below, pp. 442-5.

although there was violent criticism of the peace. Slowly between 1855 and 1858 there were signs of an attempt to achieve a Radical reunion. The change in the attitude of Ernest Jones has already been noted. In the meantime Bright too was driven to new action. At the general election of 1857 he lost his seat at Manchester, and almost immediately afterwards was adopted instead as member for Birmingham, 'the home of the most convinced, intelligent, and rational radicalism in England'. It was an important move, for in the 1860s as in the 1830s Birmingham provided through its social structure and local political tradition a basis for a 'thorough union' between working-class and middle-class radicals. In 1858 and 1859 Bright made Birmingham the key point in a new reform agitation which won the full support of Roebuck, and the limited support of Jones. There was a degree of radical unity and enthusiasm in these years which had been missing since 1846, and provincial reform associations, such as the Reformers' Union in the Midlands, the Lancashire Reformers' Union and the Northern Political Union in Newcastle sprang into life. Unfortunately for Bright and his fellow radical orators and organizers, the general public displayed relatively little interest, and hopes of large-scale reform had to be pitched in the future. Bright himself was optimistic and indomitable; even at the blackest hour after the election defeats of 1857, when Macaulay was comparing the defeat of the leaders of the Manchester School to the fall of the rebel angels, he wrote to Cobden what proved to be an extremely accurate forecast of the shape of things to come. 'Ten years hence those who live so long may see a complete change in the public mind on the questions on which the public mind has recently been so active and so much mistaken.'[1]

The change in mood and outlook between the late 50s and 1867 depended on four important new developments—the American Civil War, the conversion of Gladstone to belief in parliamentary reform, the death of Palmerston, and, perhaps most important of all in relation to the time sequence, a setback to economic prosperity in 1866 and 1867. It was only after these developments had taken place that radical pressure became fully effective.

5. ADAPTATION AND IMPROVEMENT

If there was little spectacular movement of the great radical tides between 1846 and 1860, except during the Crimean War, the

[1] See Morley, *Cobden*, vol. II, ch. VIII.

currents of 'improvement' continued to flow both in central and local government. Palmerstonians themselves accepted the necessity of 'progressive improvement' while emphasizing that 'it supposes no theory, rests on no pledge, makes no party, and is therefore the proper work of an unpledged legislature'[1]; Derby too was at pains to make it clear that Conservative ministries were not necessarily stationary and that in an age 'of constant progress . . . in politics, as in everything else, the same course must be pursued—constant progress, improving upon the old system, adapting our institutions to the altered purposes they are intended to serve, and by judicious changes meeting the demands of society'.[2]

At the national level 'improvement' took many forms, most of them continuations of tendencies already apparent in the more doctrinaire age of the 1830s and 1840s. Two royal commissions were at work on law reform in the 1840s, one dealing with the Common Law Courts, the other with Chancery, and although it was not until 1873 that the Supreme Court of Judicature Act tidied up the whole legal system and created a single series of courts, Common Law Procedure Acts were passed in 1852, 1854 and 1860, and Chancery Amendment Acts in 1852 and 1858. The criminal code was consolidated in the 1860s and a large number of obsolete laws began to be repealed. Transportation to Australia, which had been curtailed in 1841, was further reduced and the last convict ship sailed in 1867. At the same time there were improvements in the management of English prisons. In 1853 the Penal Servitude Act began the reorganization of long-term imprisonment, and a Youthful Offenders Act of a year later provided for sending young delinquents to reformatories and industrial schools. An act of 1869, following on an earlier act of 1842, virtually ended imprisonment for debt, the great evil which Dickens spent so much of his time attacking. Another Dickensian bogey, the patent laws, were modified although not basically altered by the Patent Law Amendment Act of 1852, which set up one Patent Office, reduced costs of registration, and revised procedures,[3] while after years of controversy and the full consideration of a select committee, the Divorce Act of 1857 provided for the first time a reasonably straightforward routine procedure for securing a divorce, much less expensive than that which existed before. 'It did away with the iniquity of a law which

---

[1] *The Times*, 31 March 1857.   [2] *Hansard*, 3rd series, CXLIX, p. 41.
[3] There was still room for improvement in the Patent Office. See V. G. Alexander, A Nineteenth Century Scandal', in *P.A.* (1950).

theoretically prevented divorce, but in reality conceded to the rich a right denied to the poor.'[1]

All these various reforms were in keeping with the spirit of the age. They were piecemeal, often unco-ordinated, and usually limited in scope. They did not destroy the old fabric but renovated it and cleaned its surface. They were almost without exception, genuine 'improvements', and they were frequently taken, along with limited liability, as testimony to the good sense and adaptability of an 'enlightened' epoch. The same could be said of university reform in 1854, when Gladstone, who had argued passionately in 1835 that Oxford should never be vexed by the 'interposition of Parliament', put reform of his university before the pressing problems of the Near Eastern question. Urban radicals wanted to go much further than he and to admit Dissenters to the university without any bar, to cheapen college education, and to reform the curriculum—but, backed by a small group of reformers inside the university, Gladstone reconciled the claims of the past with the needs of the present. 'The structure of this ancient university', he said, 'is so curious and complex, it has so much of history and tradition within itself, and such infinite variety and diversity attached to it, that it is impossible to deal with all its interests justly and considerately and at the same time do it in a few general and sweeping clauses.'[2] Many English institutions were of this kind and the fact that they survived both the industrial revolution and the clamour of critical middle-class opinion in the nineteenth century was a tribute to the cautious 'improvers' of mid-Victorian England. There was, after all, a large body of 'reasonable', 'liberal-conservative' opinion in the country which did not wish to sweep everything away. 'Well-regulated minds', to use the language of George Eliot, might still allow a place for 'the departed shades of vulgar errors', taking in 'a little Toryism by the sly', not prepared everywhere to see 'dear, old brown, crumbling picturesque inefficiency' give way to 'spick-and-span, new-varnished efficiency' with its 'endless diagrams, plans, elevations, and sections'.[3]

[1] A. V. Dicey, *Lectures on the Relation between Law and Public Opinion in England* (2nd edn. 1914), p. 347.

[2] See J. Morley, *Life of Gladstone*, Book IV, ch. 3.

[3] *Scenes of Clerical Life* (1858). John Morley paid tribute to J. S. Mill's *Dissertations and Discussions*, which came out in the same year as *Adam Bede* (1859) for teaching 'sympathy with the past, with the positive bases of the social fabric, and with the value of Permanence in States which forms the reputable side of all conservatisms'. (*Critical Miscellanies* (1888 edn.), vol. III, p. 131.

Turning from old institutions to new ones, from law courts and universities to mills and workshops, there were many parallel signs of 'improvement' in the approach to industrial relations. The Factory Act of 1847, amended in 1850 in order to close loopholes, had been concerned only with cotton textiles. In 1860 a new act provided for state intervention in bleaching and dyeing, and a year later lace factories also were controlled. The debates on these two bills revealed that many members who had been implacably opposed to factory legislation in the 1840s had changed their views. John Bright remained resolutely hostile to 'all legislative interference with the labour market', but Graham was typical of a whole group of members who admitted that they had been wrong in the 1840s and wanted to make amends for their earlier votes. On Shaftesbury's initiative a new commission was appointed in 1861 to investigate the employment of children in trades and manufactures. Its revealing reports, published at intervals between 1864 and 1867, laid the foundations for a new and comprehensive factory reform. Acts of 1864 and 1867 extended the definition of a factory to include 'any place in which persons work for hire' in the trades concerned; they directed attention not so much to the nature of the workplace as to the kind of employment. In addition they were concerned not only with hours of labour but with the risks and dangers of particular trades. Gladstone hailed the near unanimity with which these changes were accepted and the mitigation of suffering they achieved, while *The Times*, reversing many of its older attitudes, emphasized that 'to employ women and children unduly is simply to run into debt with Nature'.[1] The grimmest effects of free economic development were at last being regulated, however inadequately and pragmatically, and 'the economic counterpoise to the Industrial Revolution seemed to be on the very eve of fulfilment'.[2]

It is impossible to set the reforms of the 1850s and 1860s either in a completely Benthamite or a completely philanthropic humanitarian framework. Tidy divisions of the nineteenth century into ages of 'legislative quiescence', *laissez-faire* individualism, and modern collectivism [3] are rightly out of fashion among modern historians. In examining any single measure of mid-Victorian improvement it

[1] 4 March 1867.
[2] R. W. Cooke Taylor, *The Factory System* (1894), p. 96.
[3] See A. V. Dicey, *op. cit.* For a recent critical interpretation of Dicey's chronology see J. B. Brebner, 'Laissez-faire and State Intervention in Nineteenth-century Britain'. in *J.Ec.H., Supplement* (1948).

is difficult to separate and isolate the strands of motive and inspiration. John Stuart Mill used Benthamite premises to justify lines of action which his father would have detested; Shaftesbury was prepared to work with apparatus which had been constructed not by Tory-radicals but by utilitarian administrators; one of the most important reforms of the period, limited liability, was initiated neither by businessmen nor Benthamite defenders of freedom of contract but by a group of middle-class philanthropists most of whom accepted the title of 'Christian Socialists'.[1] Within political economy itself there were significant signs of a change of approach. Although its dogmatic adherents were still emphasizing that its tenets belonged to no single age or nation but were 'founded on the attitudes of the human mind', more flexible minds were turning to a 'science of observations, experience, fact and induction',[2] while among the general reading public the subject as a whole did 'not excite the same interest as formerly' nor was there 'the same confidence in it'.[3] Distinctions were fairly generally made between economic *laissez-faire* and social *laissez-faire*, and Samuel Smiles, who believed in most of the principles of liberal economics, was expressing a commonly held view when he attacked 'Nobody', a malevolent, invisible hand in the middle of the social world. 'Nobody adulterates our food. Nobody fills us with bad drink. Nobody supplies us with foul water. Nobody spreads fever in blind alleys and unswept lanes. Nobody leaves towns undrained. Nobody fills gaols, penitentiaries and convict stations. . . . Nobody has a theory too—a dreadful theory. It is embodied in two words—*Laissez faire*. . . . When people are poisoned by plaster of Paris mixed with flour, "let alone" is the remedy. . . . Let those who can, find out when they are cheated: *Caveat emptor*. When people live in foul dwellings, let them alone. Let wretchedness do its work.'[4]

For Smiles and most of those of his contemporaries who thought like him, the wisest way of tackling social evils was to combine the minimum of state interference with the maximum of voluntary co-operation. They were prepared to encourage the working-class co-operative movement, as were the Christian Socialists who played

---

[1] For an interesting recent account of the story, see J. Saville, 'Sleeping Partnership and Limited Liability, 1850–1856', in the *Ec. Hist. Rev.* (1956).

[2] W. Newmarch in *T.N.A.P.S.S.* (1871), p. 109. Newmarch himself, it is important to add, was a firm believer in less state interference. See T. W. Hutchison, *A Review of Economic Doctrines, 1870–1929* (1953), p. 4.

[3] W. Bagehot, *Economic Studies* (1880), p. 3.

[4] *Thrift*, p. 337.

an active part in it, and even to regard it as a kind of panacea. Smiles, Ludlow, Mill, and even Henry Fawcett were in agreement on this approach. They welcomed the growth of the working-class temperance, savings and insurance movements, the rise of new commercial insurance companies, with well-chosen names like the Prudential (1848), and the setting up of the Post Office Savings Bank which was founded in 1861. They extolled the independent working man who was no longer 'the sport of time and fate', who could 'look the world in the face' and 'dictate his own terms',[1] and failed to understand those poor people who were indifferent both to creature comfort and the spur of ambition. It was only rarely that a wise observer would admit that 'we know too little of the inward consciousness of the toiling and the suffering poor to be able to speak with any confidence of their own view of their own existence'.[2]

While recommending the principle of voluntary organization to others, the middle classes applied it very comprehensively themselves. In London and many of the large cities there were many poor relief societies operating side by side and sometimes in opposition to each other; 'the most fashionable amusement of the present age is philanthropy', a Liverpool journalist wrote in 1861,[3] and had he been more sensitive, he could have pointed to the way in which women—dissatisfied married women, maiden aunts, dedicated Christians—were particularly prominent in many of these bodies, in an age of sex inequality seeking fulfilment in the service of others. Octavia Hill in London was at the centre of a network of voluntary activities, believing all the time that 'personal and sympathetic intercourse with the poor' was more important than 'any organization'.

Perhaps the most important of all voluntary bodies in the 1860s was the National Association for the Promotion of Social Science, founded in 1857 with the aged Brougham as its first president and women prominent among its members. It concerned itself chiefly with discussion and propaganda on law reform, penal organization, education, local government and public health, although it dealt with many other questions too, and its published *Transactions* provide an invaluable source for the modern social historian.

---

[1] *Thrift*, p. 16.

[2] J. H. Thoms, *A Spiritual Faith* (1895). Quoted M. B. Simey, *Charitable Effort in Liverpool in the Nineteenth Century* (1951), p. 60.

[3] *Porcupine*, 1 June 1861. Quoted M. B. Simey, *op. cit.*, p. 56.

Among the other questions were workhouse 'visiting', women's employment, and 'the amicable adjustment of differences between employer and employed',[1] one of the thorniest of Victorian topics but one in which voluntary action was beginning to be important too. At a meeting in Leicester in September 1860 six employers and six operatives set up a board of arbitration for the hosiery industry: by the late 1860s there were many similar examples of voluntary local conciliation.[2] Eventually the Board of Trade itself was to recognize that voluntary agreement was more important than State action in setting the tone of industrial relations.

Public health more than any other single issue in mid-Victorian history could not be regulated by individual or group action, but needed the intervention of either local authorities or the State. The cause of 'sanitary reform' was actively supported by doctors, clergymen, novelists (George Eliot as well as Dickens and Kingsley) and politicians, but since it touched awkward problems of property rights, professional jealousies, and administrative 'centralization', there were difficulties in setting up adequate machinery. After the fall of the General Board of Health in 1854 and the relegation of Chadwick to private life, 'improvements' were cumulative rather than dramatic. By the Local Government Act of 1858 the administrative duties of the Board were transferred to the Home Office and its medical duties to the Privy Council. Doctors were registered in 1855, the first Nuisance Removal Act was passed in the same year, the first Food Adulteration Act was carried in 1860[3], and at the Privy Council Sir John Simon, Chadwick's successor, was a firm but tactful believer in 'sanitary science', the application of which he considered 'most nearly to embody the spirit and fulfil the intentions of practical Christianity'. Palmerston himself was a zealous advocate of sanitary improvement—his social record was more impressive than Disraeli's record before 1874—and his step-son, William Cowper, was an extremely active vice-president of the Council. Unfortunately politicians, administrators, and propagandists could accomplish little until there were new developments in

[1] Gladstone was in the chair at the special meeting in 1867 to discuss this topic. For a brief account of the Social Science Association, see an article with that title by B. Rodgers in the *Manchester School* (1952).
[2] See R. Kettle, *Strikes and Arbitration* (1866); H. C. Crompton, *Industrial Peace* (1887).
[3] Articles in the *Lancet* (1851–4), reproduced in newspapers, stimulated public interest. Later legislation, particularly an act of 1875, was needed to make control effective.

medical science and major changes in administrative structure. The latter were not secured until the Local Government Board was set up in 1871. Only in London was there any measure of real local government reform in the 1850s and '60s—the Metropolitan Board of Works was established in 1855—and everywhere else there was a chaos of areas and authorities. The mid-Victorians were never able or willing to devote sufficient sustained attention to the complicated questions of local government organization, and many other causes besides public health suffered as a result.

In the machinery of central government there were real 'improvements' between 1850 and 1867, although they were all in keeping with the spirit of the age rather than attempts to change it. The important civil service reforms, which have been described as 'the one great political invention in nineteenth-century England',[1] were designed not to democratize administration as some of the Crimean War reformers wished [2] but to cheapen it and to make it more efficient while preserving its traditional social framework. The prelude to reform was a series of departmental enquiries initiated in 1848 as a result of the pressure of a mixed band of supporters of economy in the House of Commons; successive governments continued them, and in March 1853 the chancellor of the exchequer, Gladstone, fresh from his study of university reform, instructed Sir Stafford Northcote and Sir Charles Trevelyan, who had been concerned with many of the earlier reports, to examine the question of civil service reform as a whole. They worked fast and without very close enquiry into conditions within the government departments, and their report was finished by September 1853 and published in March 1854. It appeared just in time to lend ammunition to the Administrative Reform Association, but the reforms actually carried out were far more limited in scope than those which Layard or Roebuck demanded.

Trevelyan and Northcote made three main recommendations—first, that the civil service be divided into two categories, a higher or 'intellectual grade' concerned with key decisions, and a lower or 'mechanical grade' engaged in routine copying; second, that in future both grades should be recruited by open competitive examination, the examinations to be conducted by an independent central board; and third, that promotion should be by merit and not by seniority.

[1] G. Wallas, *Human Nature in Politics* (1908), part II, ch. III.   [2] See above, p. 434.

The three proposals were warmly discussed not only by civil servants, many of whom resented the colourful denunciation of existing practices, but by politicians, university dons, political economists, and the public. The politicians included some who feared the effects of the loss of patronage on their prospects of political power. A memorandum by Trevelyan quoted in Morley's *Life of Gladstone* makes it clear that it could still be held realistically that 'a large number of borough members' were mainly dependent upon patronage for their seats,[1] and fifteen years later the patronage secretary was talking of 'the great advantage of the daily correspondence and communication with members of the party which the Treasury patronage gave me, to say nothing of the power which it placed in my hands'.[2] Other politicians were more worried by social anxieties. 'The more the civil service is recruited from the lower classes, the less will it be sought after by the higher, until at last the aristocracy will be altogether dissociated from the permanent civil service of the country.'[3] The Queen in turn expressed grave doubts about open competition, as did an influential section of the Whigs, and it was left to Gladstone, a few heads of colleges, and a cluster of professors to suggest that the new method would not entail a lowering of social standards in the service—a substitution of *parvenus* for 'gentlemen'—but would rather 'strengthen and multiply the ties between the higher classes and the possession of administrative power'. The civil service was to be thrown open not to the 'raw' middle classes but to the new educational *élite* of the public schools[4] and the universities. Whitehall was to be surrendered not to Manchester but to Oxford. Jobbery was to go, and education was to become the test, but social stratification was to remain.

Before Gladstone had time to act, Aberdeen's government had fallen, and his place was taken by George Cornewall Lewis, one of

---

[1] J. Morley, *Life of Gladstone*, Book IV, ch. IV. For the authorship of the memorandum and other more revealing documents of Trevelyan, see E. Hughes, 'Sir Charles Trevelyan and Civil Service Reform' in *E.H.R.* (1949). See also Professor Hughes's 'Civil Service Reform, 1853–5' in *History* (1942).

[2] This letter from G. G. Glyn is in the Gladstone papers and has been quoted by E. Hughes in a short article, 'Postscript to the Civil Service Reforms of 1855' in *P.A.* (1955). For Graham's powerful statement of the case in favour of patronage, see C. S. Parker, *The Life and Letters of Sir James Graham* (1907), vol. II, p. 210.

[3] Quoted Morley, *loc. cit.*

[4] Dr. Vaughan, the headmaster of Harrow, talked frankly of the new service providing an 'opening' for public school boys who, 'neither ignorant, nor dull, nor idle, nor dissipated', were condemned to 'years of inactivity' because they were unsuitable for the professions. Trevelyan himself said that the tendency of the measure was 'decidedly aristocratic'.

the critics of the proposals. The Order in Council of May 1855 regulating entry into the civil service was the product of his brain, and it was a characteristic Whig compromise. Civil service commissioners were appointed with the duty of ascertaining that entrants to the public service had the requisite qualifications, but the departments were left to nominate their own entrants. It was not until 1870 that open competition under Treasury control became the rule, with the Foreign Office still a significant exception. It may be argued that the reform of the civil service in 1855, like the reform of parliament in 1832, opened a door which could not be closed again, but in both cases the 'democrats' had no say in the initial decision.

The phrase 'Treasury control' is the key to the second great reform in central government in the 1850s and '60s, although more detailed research needs to be done on both the concept and the practice before historians can make neat and tidy generalizations.[1] What is clear is that alongside the growing stress on institutional morality in government there existed a strong sense of responsibility about the use and management of public money. In part this sense of responsibility derived from the accepted orthodoxies of mid-Victorian public finance, that individuals should be taxed no more than was absolutely necessary to cover certain essential national costs, and that government spending should be as small as possible; in part, however, it derived from strong personal convictions, ranging from a simple belief that 'honesty is the best policy' to a dedicated sense of the essential oneness of private and public duty.

In 1857 a Select Committee on Public Moneys, appointed in the previous year, recommended the systematic application of the appropriation audit (first applied to the navy in 1832) to all branches of public expenditure and the setting up of a committee of the House of Commons, nominated by the Speaker, to study the audited accounts annually. Four years later Gladstone set up the Public Accounts Committee of the House of Commons and, in 1866, by the Exchequer and Audit Act, further tightened up auditing procedure by creating the office of Comptroller and Auditor-General. The Comptroller was to be a most important public servant who, while appointed by the Chancellor, was to hold his office like a judge, independently of the executive. The suggestion that Gladstone at one time had thought of Cobden as the best

[1] For a brief, near-contemporary account, see H. D. Traill, *Central Government* (1892).

candidate for the post gives some idea of the importance he attached to it.[1] Although no Cobdens were appointed to the office, the annual reports of the Comptroller not only provided a useful basis for discussion in the Public Accounts Committee but permitted the Treasury (while having its own accounts scrutinized) to gain a far clearer idea of what each of the other government departments was doing. 'Treasury control' depended on such a disciplined procedure, and in its relations with other departments the Treasury changed after 1866 from a capricious despot into an enlightened tyrant. By the 1880s the permanent secretary to the Treasury considered that 'the theory of the control exercised by the Treasury was complete'.[2]

With the rise of Treasury control based on a disciplined system of central administration—the process was incomplete within the period covered in this book—the main tasks of adaptation and improvement had been accomplished. Before that date, however, the terms of politics were themselves changing and new forces were disturbing the balance described in this chapter. The National Association for the Promotion of Social Science disappeared in the 1880s before it had time to deal with all the items on its agenda; by then a new 'democracy' was challenging almost all the basic presuppositions of mid-Victorian policy and adding new and unforeseen tasks to the machinery of government.

Before examining the politics of the critical years of debate and conflict when England trembled on the brink of large-scale changes, it is wise to pause and to consider the kind of society which the mid-Victorians felt they were living in, the hopes and fears they expressed, and the differences of opinion which they were prepared to tolerate. It was not the least significant reason for the continued movement of the currents of adaptation and improvement described in the last part of this chapter that men of the calibre and influence of John Stuart Mill believed as an article of faith that 'it is only by the collision of adverse opinions that the remainder of the truth has any chance of being supplied'.[3] Faith in the existence of ultimate truths was the 'one intellectual certitude' in mid-Victorian England,[4] and it gave both unity and order to the mid-Victorian period.

[1] See F. Hirst, *Gladstone as Financier and Economist* (1931), p. 245.
[2] Quoted K. B. Smellie, *A Hundred Years of English Government* (1950 edn.), p. 165.
[3] *On Liberty* (1859), ch. II.
[4] Houghton, *op. cit.*, p. 14.

9

VICTORIANISM

1. 'THE VICTORIAN COMMONWEALTH'

THE adjective 'Victorian' was apparently coined exactly half way through the nineteenth century by an almost forgotten writer, Edwin Paxton Hood, who set out in his *The Age and its Architects* (1851) to relate the conditions of his own time to the whole 'development of the ages'. In a chapter called 'the Victorian Commonwealth' he began by describing it as 'the most wonderful picture on the face of the earth' and recorded as a 'fact' the observation 'perhaps on no other spot of ground has heaven ever grouped so bright a constellation of its best mercies'. He rounded off the comment with an appropriate biblical text, 'He hath not done so with any people'.[1] The 'fact' and its trimmings may properly be taken as evidence of enhanced national self-consciousness on the eve of the greatest period of Victorian prosperity.

In an England relatively undisturbed by violent class conflicts or political upheavals, there was room for the free exchange of ideas, the cultivation of enjoyment, the quest for personal fulfilment, even for personal rebellion. Though freedom was hampered by private reticence and social conformity, enjoyment was restricted by shibboleths, fulfilment was obstructed by convention, confidence was underscored by anxiety and doubt, and rebellion was confronted by stern orthodoxy and authority, the recognition of limits and barriers lent both edge and inner tension to much of the critical and creative writing of the period. Neither the edge nor the tension was universal, however. There was room also for humour, good nature, making allowances, and reaching compromises. There was above all—though some found it elusive—room for a sense of peace which was usually associated with familiar faces, scenes, and experiences.

---

[1] *The Age and its Architects* (1852 edn.), p. 73.

The domestic ties of the family itself were sung more loudly than at any other period of English history, and the large mid-Victorian family with so many children about the place that it was a necessary rule of reason that 'little children should be seen and not heard'[1] was hailed as 'the unit upon which a constitutional government has been raised which is the admiration and envy of mankind'.[2] There were as many treatises on 'domestic economy' in mid-Victorian England as on political economy,[3] all of them designed to foster 'happy families'. The phrase taken from a familiar hymn, 'sweet are the ties that bind',[4] was a key phrase in the 1850s and 1860s. The home was felt to be the centre of virtues and emotions which could not be found in completed form outside, and even in the ties of daily routine there seemed to be special harmony and peace. As Coventry Patmore, one of the most characteristic of Victorian poets, put it:

> Not in the crisis of events,
> Of compass'd hopes, or fears fulfill'd,
> Or acts of gravest consequence
> Are life's delight and depth reveal'd.
> The day of days was not the day . . .
> But, oh, the walk that afternoon
> We saw the water-flags in flower.[5]

It is perhaps nostalgia for this sense of inner peace against a background of an undisturbed landscape which has drawn the 'displaced persons' of the mid-twentieth century back to the Victorian Commonwealth to settle there 'like illegal immigrants for the rest of their lives'.[6] The prevailing feeling about Victorian England has changed completely since the revolt of Lytton Strachey and the intellectuals of the first quarter of the twentieth century, and in recent years elegant criticism has given way to exaggerated revival. In consequence, a fair appraisal of the Victorian Commonwealth demands a knowledge of historiography as well as of

[1] Some of the other necessary rules, e.g. 'A place for everything and everything in its place', and 'early rising', are well described in a book which ran through many editions, T. G. Hatchard, *Hints for the Improvement of Early Education and Nursery Discipline*. The sixteenth edition appeared in 1853.
[2] W. Cooke Taylor, in the *T.N.A.P.S.S.* (1874).
[3] Mrs. Beeton's *Book of Household Management* first appeared in 1861. It was one of a whole *genre*. See J. A. Banks, *Prosperity and Parenthood* (1954), Appendix I.
[4] Mill's phrase was 'the reciprocity of duty' (*The Subjection of Women*, ch. IV).
[5] *The Spirit's Epochs*, printed in *Florilegium Amantis* (ed. R. Garnett, 1879).
[6] B. Willey, *Nineteenth-century Studies* (1949), p. 52.

history. It is perhaps now beginning to be possible for the first time to see both anti-Victorian revolt and Victorian revival in perspective and to form an impression of the age itself and not of a distorted image of it. Two necessary qualifications for a fair appraisal are a sense of time and a sense of discrimination. The first enables the light and shade of successive Victorian generations to be recaptured, for there was never one single 'Victorian Commonwealth' beginning in 1837 and ending in 1901. The second enables a proper distinction to be made between Victorian achievements and Victorian failures. For all the achievements implicit in the dynamic economy and the free society, for all the wonder in 'the most wonderful picture on the face of the earth', many Victorians were lonely and isolated, and many others were 'stupid, vulgar, unhappy and unsuccessful'.[1] The loneliness adds to the melancholy beauty of much Victorian literature (Arnold's *Dover Beach* is a classic example); the vulgarity and stupidity still survive in many of the 'objects, the buildings, the pictures and the literature that have been left to us'. The deficiencies were there in the balanced England of the mid-Victorian years as much as in the England of the 1880s and '90s. G. M. Young, who considers 'the life of the university-bred classes' in the England of the 1860s to be 'the culminating achievement of European culture',[2] has also written that if you fall asleep tonight and wake up in 1860 your impression of Victorian England will depend on where you wake up.[3]

The most sensitive Victorians—and many of the least sensitive too—were as aware of the contrasts in the Victorian Commonwealth as historians writing in the twentieth century. E. P. Hood, for instance, devoted a large part of his book to the failings of his age. One Englishman in seven was a pauper; crime was 'well housed, well fed, educated and indulged' while poverty was 'crushed, trampled and left uncared for'; the rural 'Arcadias' were usually places of low wages, inferior diets, inadequate housing accommodation, and illiteracy, while the cities, symbols of progress and in themselves a 'great modern treatise on political economy', were scarred by dark areas still largely unvisited by the respectable members of society. 'Sparta', wrote Hood, 'had 300,000 slaves to 30,000 freemen; does not our situation in some sort resemble hers?

---

[1] H. House, *All in Due Time* (1955), p. 79.
[2] *Victorian England; Portrait of an Age* (1936), p. 99.
[3] *Last Essays* (1950), p. 214.

. . . Already we have a revolution, slumbering, but gathering power in all our cities, and still we pursue our way with intrepid stupidity, dreaming of Eden in the very midst of a reign of terror.'[1]

Hood's descriptions of the black spots of English city life were paralleled in many other studies of the 1850s and '60s. The most famous was Henry Mayhew's *London Labour and the London Poor*, the first volume of which appeared in book form in 1861. Two years before, George Godwin, the editor of *The Builder*, had published his *Town Swamps and Social Bridges*, and there was a considerable mid-Victorian literature of exposure of 'moral debasement and physical decay',[2] much of it 'making one-half of the people of London known to the other half'[3] or trying as Mayhew did to persuade those in 'high places' to 'bestir themselves to improve the conditions of a class of people whose misery, ignorance, and vice . . . is, to say the very least, a national disgrace'.

It is impossible to understand the Victorian Commonwealth without entering its underworld, part of which was inherited from the past, part of which was expanding yearly not only in London but in Liverpool, Birmingham, Manchester and all the large cities. And in the countryside, as Bagehot himself was at pains to stress, there were 'crowds of people scarcely more civilized than the majority of two thousand years ago'. 'Great communities', he concluded, 'are like great mountains—they have in them the primary, secondary and tertiary strata of human progress; the characteristics of the lower regions resemble the life of old times rather than the present life of higher regions.' As far as the implications of this social structure for politics were concerned, there were difficulties which even the Greeks did not have to face. They were not compelled to combine in their polity the labourers of Somerset and men like Mr. Grote, the philosophical radical. They 'had not to deal with a community in which primitive barbarism lay as a recognized basis to acquired civilization'. It was in italics that Bagehot printed his next two words, *'we have'*.[4]

'Victorianism'—the word was not coined by the Victorians—was neither a universally congenial nor a universally accepted moral and social concept in the Victorian Commonwealth. Its four main

---

[1] *Op. cit.*, p. 79.

[2] E.g. H. Gavin, *Sanitary Ramblings* (1861).

[3] J. Garwood, *The Million Peopled City* (1853); see also J. Hollingshead, *Ragged London in 1861* (1861).

[4] *The English Constitution*, ch. I.

elements—the gospel of work, 'seriousness' of character, respectability and self-help—were often proclaimed not because they were
conspicuous but because they were absent.

For all the Victorian emphasis on work not only as a means to
money, respectability and success, but as a supreme virtue, involving
both self-denial and creative accomplishment, there is much
evidence of scamped work, of absenteeism, above all of drudgery
in mid-Victorian England, particularly the drudgery of domestic
service on which many happy families depended. Carlyle from his
lofty eminence might pontificate that 'properly speaking all true
work is religion', and the Great Exhibition might render unqualified
homage to 'the working bees of the world's hive', but Smiles, the
most powerful advocate of the gospel, laid as much emphasis on the
existence of social sins as of social virtues, and rebels like John Ruskin
and William Morris left no doubt that their ideal of truly rich and
creative work was far removed from Victorian practice. Even taken
simply as a gospel, the Victorian belief in work often had an element
of escape in it, escape from nagging doubts and hidden despair.
Many breakdowns which were attributed to overwork were rather
due, as Lecky observed, to anxiety.[1]

'Seriousness' or 'earnestness' of character expressed itself in many
ways—in Carlyle's attack on 'Dilettantism', in Thomas Arnold's
ethos of the public school, in George Eliot's sense of public duty,
in the aristocratic Lord Granville's refusal to be 'a gentleman at
ease' and his willingness, as Lord Russell said, 'to postpone everything to public business'[2]—but there were many Victorian aristocrats who made no contribution to national life and many 'members
of the middle classes' who belonged to what Matthew Arnold called
the 'gay' and even 'rowdy' and not to the 'serious' section.

Respectability shone out as a virtue only when it was contrasted
with the lack of it; cleanliness, sobriety, forethought, and thrift
could never be taken for granted. 'Prodigality', Smiles wrote, 'is
much more natural to men than thrift [and] economy is not a natural
instinct but the growth of experience and example.'[3] The respectable
gained in their own estimation by shunning ways that others chose
to tread; and most of the propaganda to encourage thrift had an
element of cant about it. 'We have heard a man with a mass of

---

[1] *The Map of Life* (1899), p. 332. See the brilliant section on this subject in
Houghton, *op. cit.*, pp. 242 ff.
[2] Quoted A. L. Kennedy (ed.) *My Dear Duchess* (1956), p. 6.
[3] *Self-Help*, ch. I.

unpaid college debts of many years standing', a writer in the *Saturday Review* stated, 'urge the practice of thrift upon an assemblage of mechanics, everyone of whom had money in the savings' bank, with a fervour that astounded the few persons present who knew [his] . . . private position.'[1]

Self-help was not easily taught to a substantial majority of the total population, for most of them were in no position to practise it. Skilled artisans might turn with enthusiasm to Samuel Smiles—20,000 copies of *Self-Help* (1859) were sold within a year of its first appearance—as might ambitious youths from all sections of un-privileged society, but for large numbers of people the walls of necessity were too high and too thick. Hood was wise to distinguish between the needs of two classes—for the first, 'that all restrictions be removed in their seeking their own elevation', for the second that they should 'be lifted entirely from their present sphere, and surrounded by new circumstances and enlightened by new ideas'.[2]

Emphasis on all the four elements in 'Victorianism' reflected not smugness but the need contemporaries felt to discover a secure moral order which would enable them to harness the machine, to improve their standard of living and to coexist powerfully side by side in a country which had travelled far and fast since the 1780s.

There were many deviants from what we have come to call 'Victorianism'—Richard Monckton Milnes, for example, who in addition to encouraging mechanics' institutes and penny banks was an indefatigable collector of erotic literature and went to the Great Exhibition to admire 'lace shawls etc.',[3] or the Crimean War hero, the Earl of Cardigan, who had fought a duel in 1840, had been accused of adultery (and of spiriting away the chief witness against him) in 1843, and whose men in the Crimea wore 'tight cherry-coloured pants . . . as utterly unfit for war service as the garb of the female hussars in the ballet of Gustavus'.[4] There were, however, powerful forces which made for conformity and drove John Stuart Mill in his *Essay on Liberty* (1859) to complain that 'society has now fairly got the better of individuality'. Four of them were of special

---

[1] *Modern Characteristics, A Series of Short Essays from the Saturday Review* (1866), p.72. The *Saturday Review*, founded in 1855, was one of the most brilliant Victorian periodicals, a relentless critic of Victorian cant. 'Every good man', said the famous preacher Spurgeon, 'is born for the love of God and the hatred of the *Saturday Review*'.

[2] *Op. cit.*, pp. 97–8.

[3] See J. Pope-Hennessy, *Monckton-Milnes, The Years of Promise* (1950); *The Flight of Youth* (1951).

[4] *The Times*, 22 April 1854, quoted by C. Woodham Smith, *op. cit.*, p. 138.

importance—the reinforcement of the social and moral position of
the 'middle classes' as a result of continued economic growth; the
pressure of Evangelicalism on all sections of the new society; a
further reaction against the 'barbarism' of old customs and habits,
influenced partly by religion, partly by social change, partly by
what Bagehot called 'an extreme, perhaps an excessive, sensibility
towards human suffering'; and a growing sense of the 'seriousness'
of life not only in the world of work but even in the criticism of
that world. The Victorians were their own best critics, but in
almost all their criticisms they accepted premises which in retrospect
make them as 'Victorian' as the targets of their irony or their
indignation.

Before examining in more detail certain of these basic features of
'Victorianism' it is necessary to view the subject as a whole from
two quite different angles.

First, 'Victorianism' was not a completely new phenomenon. It
was rather the culmination of tendencies going back to the eighteenth century. The fifty years before Victoria came to the throne
have often been considered as a 'Victorian prelude' during which
changes in morals, manners, styles and tastes began to influence the
quality of life of the community. There was, of course, no single or
unbroken line of development. In Regency England, after the
Napoleonic Wars had ended, there was an ostentatious parade not
of the virtues but of the vices of Society; behind the stucco there
were cracks, but *bravura* was as much a feature of the age as squalor.
For all the arrogance of what Peacock called 'a steam-nurtured,
steam-borne, steam-killed and gas-enlightened race', there still
existed a luxury-living, gay and dissipated, vain and exuberant
minority. The romantic movement might eventually play itself out
in Victorian hymn-books[1] and even in the pulpit, but in the world
after the Napoleonic Wars it expressed itself in the life of Byron,
the teachings of Shelley, and the voluminous cravats and quilted
waistcoats of the Regency *beaux*. Nor did the spirit of Regency
England evaporate mysteriously in 1830, or even in 1837. There
were dandies in the early 1840s—even a few duels—and scandals in
the 1850s; old and new manners, old and new predilections overlapped in nineteenth-century society as much as in nineteenth-
century politics. If there was Victorianism before Victoria—Dr-
Bowdler published his 'bowdlerized' family editions of Shakespeare

---

[1] The first edition of *Hymns Ancient and Modern* appeared in 1861.

in 1818—there was a flavour of the Regency long after the Prince Regent had given way to the Prince Consort.

By the 1850s and 1860s, however, the code of honour was in eclipse and there was a marked tendency to distrust Regency clothes, Regency entertainments, Regency morals, and even Regency architecture. Journalists writing in 1850 on the significance of the death of Peel pointed out how he had outstripped his schoolmate Byron as the idol of the public; in the same year the Pavilion at Brighton was sold to the local Corporation, and admirers of the age's new architectural triumph, the Crystal Palace, dwelt not only on its exploitation of glass and iron but on the fact that its designer, Joseph Paxton, had become head gardener at Chatsworth at the age of 23 and since then, as engineer, railway director, and man of affairs had shown, as the Queen herself remarked, how the lowest were able to rise by their own merits to the highest grade of society. It only needed Martin Tupper, the author as early as 1838 of what is regarded as a supremely Victorian book of verse, *Proverbial Philosophy*—it had run through ten editions by 1850—to proclaim the transition from Victorian prelude to Victorian achievement.

> This double decade of the world's short span
> Is richer than two centuries of old;
> Richer in helps, advantages and pleasures,
> In all things richer—even down to gold.

Second, Victorianism from a different angle was 'the insular phase of a movement common to the whole of Western Europe and its offshoots beyond the seas'. Mr. Young has quoted a passage from Gogol which might have come straight from any mid-Victorian writer[1]; he might have referred also to examples of furniture from the Second Empire or to manuals of business success in the United States. What distinguished English Victorianism from foreign phenomena of a similar kind then and since was not only the peculiar characteristics of English liberalism—ranging from Mill's passionate belief in representative government and a free society to the non-explosive liberal-conservatism of Trollope and Bagehot— but the way in which that liberalism fitted into a shell of convention which itself was the product of centuries of puritan religion, voluntary effort, and the moulding of a complex social system which made for balance and not for domination. Above all else, what

[1] *Last Essays* (1950), p. 206.

distinguished England was a very special sort of monarchy and a Queen who gave her name both to her age and her Commonwealth. 'Victorianism' before Victoria there was, but she herself had no prototype and in many ways she could claim to represent the spirit of the age as faithfully as her devoted servant Peel and far more faithfully than her aged whipping-boy Lord Palmerston.

2. QUEEN, PRINCE, AND COURT

When Victoria came to the throne in 1837 at the age of 18 the monarchy was at a low ebb. There was little republican sentiment and much talk of 'altar, throne and cottage', but William IV's early popularity had withered away. Victoria's initial advantages were threefold—her youth, her sex, and her already clearly formed sense of duty. When George IV and William IV ascended the throne they had a past behind them; Victoria, whose succession to the throne had been far from certain, had only a future. Her sex, which might in different circumstances have been a handicap, enabled her to make a special appeal not only to the public but to her prime minister, Melbourne. He was fascinated by the 'girl-Queen' and she by him, and the first phase of their 'partnership' between 1837 and 1839 was stimulating and happy for both of them. Moreover, from the start the Queen displayed great strength of character and responsibility. She wrote in her journal on the day of her accession that she would do her utmost to fulfil her duty to her country, and despite her youth and lack of experience she immediately took it for granted that others would obey her. Her first triumph of character was over the experienced and worldly-wise Melbourne, whose occupations and habits she revolutionized. 'I have no doubt he is passionately fond of her as he might be of his daughter if he had one', Greville wrote, 'and the more because he is a man with capacity for loving without having anything in the world to love. It has become his province to educate, to instruct, and to form the most interesting mind and character in the world.'[1] He watched his language—usually 'interlarded with damns'—sat bolt upright rather than lounged in his chair, and greatly restricted the range of his anecdotes.

Victoria's childish resolves 'to be good' were in harmony with a new spirit in society, and Melbourne was responding to pressures which even at the time were applied not only by the Queen but by

[1] *The Greville Memoirs*, vol. IV, p. 93.

'respectable' opinion. He enjoyed the one form of pressure but hated the second. 'All the young people are growing mad about religion', he once lamented. As it was, he could scarcely protest when the etiquette of the Court was tightened up and the Queen revealed herself as a stern and self-determined moralist, on one occasion at least exposing herself to great unpopularity by wrongly 'suspecting the worst' of a member of her Court. Admission to the Court was made to depend on good character, and 'rakishness' which Melbourne thought 'refreshing' the Queen considered at best 'melancholy' and at worst 'bad'. Manners as well as morals changed. The relatively easy informality of 'drawing room' and 'levées', during which the King might talk frankly or even rudely to people he knew, gave way to far more restrained and dignified ceremonial. Victoria's own sense of dignity was prominently displayed in 1839 when after Melbourne's defeat in the House of Commons she quarrelled with Peel about the party affiliations of the Ladies of the Bedchamber and prevented him from forming a new government. 'The Queen maintains *all* her ladies', she wrote to Melbourne (her dignity had been the surface defence of her warm affection for her old prime minister) 'and thinks her Prime Minister will cut a sorry figure indeed if he resigns on this.'[1] Melbourne was back in office again for two more years and Peel, condemned simply because he did not share Melbourne's delightful qualities, was left with the cares of 'responsible opposition'.

The position was altered, however, as a result of the Queen's marriage in February 1840, and after the influence of her husband had established itself—almost at once—Melbourne was inevitably pushed more and more into the background. It had long been the ambition of King Leopold of the Belgians, the Queen's uncle and one of her earliest *confidants*, to marry his niece to her cousin, Prince Albert of Saxe Coburg Gotha, and there had been much gossip about the match from 1837 onwards. Fortunately for Victoria, the marriage which had been planned was also a marriage of love. Albert, in her own words, 'completely won my heart', and the wedding, celebrated quietly in St. James's Palace, with no signs of enthusiasm in the country, began the happiest period of her life. Her husband was still six months under the age of 21 in 1840 and he was a far from popular figure with the aristocracy, the crowds, or the House of Commons—by a majority of 104 votes the annuity

[1] *The Letters of Queen Victoria* (1907), vol. I, p. 206.

of £50,000 the government proposed to pay him was reduced to £30,000—but he was just as resolved as Victoria to take the task of government seriously and willing in so doing to sink 'his own *individual existence* in that of his wife'. Stiff and conservative, his first efforts were devoted to reinforcing the Queen's own desire to set an example of strict propriety at Court.

The difference between old ways and new was well brought out in an early clash of ideas with Melbourne about the nature of social morality. 'Character', Melbourne maintained, 'can be attended to when people are of no consequence, but it will not do when people are of high rank.'[1] Albert cared far less about rank than industry and integrity, and besides being willing to work long hours with a Germanic thoroughness that Smiles could not have excelled, he displayed all those 'Victorian' virtues of character which Melbourne regarded as unnecessary in a man of his station. His 'seriousness' of purpose is witnessed by the causes to which he gave his full support. His first public speech was at a meeting on behalf of the abolition of slavery; he was a vigorous advocate of scientific research and education, of official patronage of art, and of reformed universities; he took an active interest in the work of the Society for Improving the Condition of the Labouring Classes, founded in 1844, and when criticized by Lord John Russell for attending one of its meetings replied firmly that he conceived 'one has a *Duty* to perform towards the great mass of the working classes (and particularly at this moment) which will not allow one's yielding to the fear for some possible inconvenience'[2]; he helped to design and plan the building of a block of houses known as Prince Albert's 'model houses for families'; and last, but perhaps most important of all, he played such an important part in organizing the Great Exhibition of 1851 that if it had not been for his efforts, it is doubtful whether the Exhibition would have been held. In all these efforts Albert met with resistance and opposition, much of it centred in the country houses and the universities, places where old prejudices were strong and suspicions difficult to break down.

Albert had perforce to follow the dictates of self-help as much as Stephenson or Paxton, and on many doors which were open to them he had to knock loudly. Two years after the Queen had written in 1853 that the nation appreciated him and fully acknow-

[1] Quoted Lord David Cecil, *Lord M.*, p. 272.
[2] Quoted R. Fulford, *The Prince Consort* (1949), p. 144.

ledged what he had done 'daily and hourly for the country',[1] he
was being lampooned in the popular press and attacked in the clubs
more than ever before. If there was any truth in the Queen's claim
that he eventually succeeded in raising monarchy to 'the *highest*
pinnacle of respect' and rendering it 'popular beyond what it *ever*
was in this country',[2] it was entirely as a result of his own exertions
and courage. He had no deficiency of spirit. When times were
blackest for him on the eve of the Crimean War, he could still write
that he looked upon his troubles as 'a fiery ordeal that will serve to
purge away impurities'.[3]

Friendship with Peel was as important to Albert as friendship with
Melbourne had been to Victoria, and it helped in itself to set the
tone of mid-Victorian England. Between 1841 and 1846 the Queen
and her husband came to put their full trust in their great prime
minister and the causes for which he stood—sound administration,
strong government, and free trade. As early as 1843 the Queen
wrote to the King of the Belgians praising Peel as 'a great statesman,
a man who thinks but little of party and never of himself'[4]; after
Peel's death she wrote that Albert felt the loss '*dreadfully*'. He feels
'he has lost a second father'.[5]

There was something in common, indeed, between Peel and
Albert, not only in their dislike of the noisy clamour of party but
in their desire for practical improvement and their resentment of
unthinking aristocracies. During the Crimean War Albert complained of the 'hostility or bitterness towards me' not only of the
radicals but 'of the old High Tory or Protectionist Party on
account of my friendship with the late Sir Robert Peel and of my
success with the Exhibition',[6] and the bitterness certainly went
deep. If in the case of Peel the main taunt was one of betrayal of the
landed interest, in the case of Albert it was one of never having
belonged to it, of being un-English,[7] of working by slow deliberation, not by instinct, of paying attention to the wrong things in the
wrong way. In such a context of criticism even Albert's virtues

[1] Sir Theodore Martin, *Life of His Royal Highness the Prince Consort* (1875), vol. II,
p. 461.
[2] *Letters*, vol. III, p. 264.
[3] *Letters of the Prince Consort* (ed. K. Jagow) (1938), p. 206.
[4] *Letters*, vol. I, p. 578.
[5] *Ibid.*, vol. II, p. 305.
[6] K. Jagow, *op. cit.*, p. 204.
[7] 'Prince Albert was unloved', Greville maintained, 'because he possessed all the
virtues sometimes lacking in the Englishman.' Quoted Prince von Bülow, *Memoirs
1897–1903*), p. 336.

could appear as vices. He was ridiculed in *Punch* for trying to act
twenty different character parts; he was criticized in army messes
for his zealous interference; he was attacked in Cambridge University for trying to do too much as Chancellor, not too little. He had
won a hotly contested election for the Chancellorship in 1847, and
it is easy to guess the reaction of Cambridge dons to his earnest
desire to look at 'schemes of tuition' and examination papers on
subjects in which he was particularly interested. His collection of
information on every conceivable issue of public policy, his investigation of statistics, his preparation of memoranda, and his considerable European correspondence were all activities calculated to
alienate aristocratic holders of power. So too was his stern insistence
on the morality of the Court. There was an interesting incident in
1852 when the new prime minister, Lord Derby, submitted his list
of names for household appointments and Albert noted with horror
that 'the greater part were the Dandies and Roués of London and
the Turf'. The Prince cared little for aristocratic company or
aristocratic pursuits—in 1861, the year of his death, for instance, he
described Ascot as rendered 'much more tedious than usual by
incessant rain'—and he did not attempt to hide his preference for
the company of authors, scientists, social reformers, and pioneers of
education. 'Culture superseded blood, and South Kensington
became the hub of the universe.'[1] The result was that the Court
stood aloof from the rest of the London world, and had 'but
slender relations with the more amusing part of it'.[2]

Victoria did not share all Albert's enthusiasms or even understand
them. She cared little for the company of scientists, showed no
interest in royal patronage of art, and in only few of her letters
referred to literature. She delighted, however, in the Exhibition of
1851 and thrilled to the bravery of British troops in the Crimea. On
thirty occasions she visited the Crystal Palace, noting in her *Journal*
that she never remembered anything before that everyone was so
pleased with as the Exhibition; during the war she wrote that 'the
conduct of our *dear noble* Troops is *beyond praise*', said that she felt
as if 'they were *my own children*', and objected to those critics of the
military system who detracted from British victories by 'croaking'.
Just because she genuinely shared such English sentiments and was
not tempted, as Albert was, to seek for forms of intellectual expres-

[1] G. W. E. Russell, *Collections and Recollections*, part II (1909), p. 140.
[2] Bagehot, *The English Constitution*, ch. II.

sion, she was far more popular than he. She was not, of course, in any sense a democratic monarch responding to mass pressures or gaining publicity through the influence of mass communications, but she won loyalty and respect from the majority of the population, including the middle classes, many of whose qualities and limitations she shared. Perhaps the most vivid impression of her impact on English society can be gained from a perusal of newspaper reports of her visits to the provinces in the 1850s. In 1858 she visited both Birmingham and Leeds. Everywhere there were great crowds 'who behaved as well in the streets as could any assemblage of the aristocracy at a Queen's drawing room'. The local newspapers, while praising the interest of the Prince Consort in science and industry, reserved their loudest praise for a queen who 'is as it were partner with the great and multitudinous people who do gladly obey her, joins with them in legislation, shares with them in government, and makes them to a great extent their own rulers'. They extolled her combination of 'feminine grace and royal dignity' and her lofty eminence above all party faction, but above all they argued that 'what consummates the whole is, that she is a wife and a mother of so lofty a purity and discharging her duties so well that she forms the brightest exemplar to the matrons of England'.[1]

In the pages of Bagehot the same points are made in a sophisticated and acute analysis. The dignity of the monarchy, Bagehot believed, disguised from the unthinking masses of the population the working of the effective elements in government. 'The masses of England are not fit for an elective government; if they know how near they were to it, they would be surprised and almost tremble.' At the same time the claims of monarchy were bound up with religion and morality and thus with loyalty and virtue. Like the Yorkshire editor, Bagehot picked on the idea of 'family' as a means of bringing down 'the pride of sovereignty to the level of petty life'.[2] Not the least of the achievements of Victoria and Albert was to provide for the country a pattern of obviously happy domestic life which contrasted sharply with the pattern provided by all the Queen's recent predecessors. At her marriage ceremony the 'royal family' was a collection of aged and for the most part discredited minor personalities, better known for their defects than for their merits. By 1861, there were nine royal children, the eldest of whom, the Princess Royal, had already

---

[1] *Leeds Mercury*, 11 September 1858.
[2] *Op. cit.*, ch. II.

produced a grandchild for the Queen, the future Emperor William II of Germany. On more than one state occasion in the '40s and '50s the royal children accompanied the Queen. In 1849, for instance, on the occasion of her first visit to Ireland (she went there again in 1853 and 1861) she took her four children with her. 'They were objects of universal attention and admiration. 'Oh, Queen, dear', screamed a stout old lady, 'make one of them Prince Patrick, and all Ireland will die for you.'[1]

The death of the Prince Consort from typhoid fever in 1861 was a tragic blow to the Queen from which she never fully recovered. 'The loss of her husband', wrote Lady Lewis to her brother, Lord Clarendon, 'has changed her from a powerful sovereign (which she was with the knowledge and judgement of her husband to guide her opinions and strengthen her will) into a weak and desolate woman with the weight of duties she has not the moral and physical power to support.'[2] Conventional condolences meant nothing to her, and only those who could find the right words to demonstrate their understanding of the extent of her loss were likely to touch any chord in her heart. Strangely enough, it was Palmerston, with whom both she and the Prince had had so many differences and had fought such hectic battles, who found the correct phrase and wrote to her of the Prince as 'that perfect Being'.[3]

From 1861 to the end of the period covered in this book the Queen was in the deepest retirement, resolved irrevocably that Albert's 'wishes—his plans—about everything are to be my law'. Although she found some consolation in the affairs of her family and its network of associations with other European courts, and although she spent many peaceful days at Balmoral, her favourite home, she wore mourning, shrank from large crowds, and feared formal social gatherings. She hated the thought of appearing in public as a 'poor, brokenhearted widow' and declared that she 'would as soon clasp the hand of the poorest widow in the land if she had truly loved her husband and felt for me, as I would a Queen, or any other in high position'.[4] It was natural, though hard for her to bear, that the public could not appreciate the reason for her social abdication. In 1865 *Punch* printed a famous cartoon in

---

[1] Quoted M. G. Fawcett, *Life of Her Majesty Queen Victoria* (1895), p. 125.
[2] Quoted by O. F. Christie, *Th. Transition from Aristocracy* (1928), p. 235.
[3] Quoted Fulford, *op. cit.*, p. 275.
[4] *Letters*, second series (1926), vol. I, p. 267. She wrote a moving letter to Lincoln's widow in 1865.

which Paulina (Britannia) unveiled the covered statue and addressed Hermione (Victoria) with the words "Tis time! descend; be stone no more!'[1] Two years later the Queen was still lost in an unfinished winter's tale and Bagehot could dismiss her and the Prince of Wales in the tersest of phrases as 'a retired widow and an unemployed youth'.

In time the Queen's age and experience were to produce new waves of loyalty and admiration, but the comment of Bagehot is the epitaph on the mid-Victorian period. What would have happened had the Prince Consort lived is a speculative puzzle which has fascinated many specialists in historical 'ifs'. Disraeli believed that 'if he had outlived some of our old stagers he would have given us, while retaining all constitutional guarantees, the blessings of absolute government'.[2] It was a dubious estimate of future probabilities. For all Albert's belief (and that of Stockmar, his tutor) in strong government with a monarchy raised high above the noisy clamour of party and exercising unobtrusive but effective power, he was not able—nor was the Queen—to influence politics decisively even in the period of group politics from 1846 to 1859. For the most part the Queen and Albert were forced to 'maintain a position of neutrality towards the leaders of party on both sides',[3] discriminating against individuals, like Bright, but not against groups. When they were shaken out of their neutrality—by sympathy with the Peelites, for instance, in the early 1850s—they could act only within closely circumscribed limits,[4] while the royal disagreement with Palmerston about the methods and the objectives of British foreign policy left the Crown powerful but by no means supreme. There was no alternative to accepting Palmerston in the Crimean War crisis, and the attempt to make Granville prime minister in 1859 was a failure from the start. The Queen was even driven to the same conclusion as Disraeli and Gladstone in the 1850s, 'that out of the present state of confusion and discordance, a sound state of parties will be obtained and two parties, as of old, will again exist, without which it is impossible to have strong government'.[5] But the rise of

---

[1] September 1865.
[2] Moneypenny and Buckle, *op. cit.*, vol. II, p. 117.
[3] Martin, *op. cit.*, vol. I, p. 36. The Queen revised and checked passages of this kind in Martin's *Life*.
[4] Albert strongly disliked the power of the press, applying to it the motto 'Vox populi, vox Rindvieh' (blockheads), and maintaining that 'there is at all times something wrong with newspaper diplomacy and newspaper strategy'. See Jagow, *op. cit.*, p. 217.
[5] *Letters*, second series, vol. II, p. 464.

parties, particularly after the extension of the suffrage in 1867, was bound in the long run to limit royal power still further, and in the twentieth century 'strong government' could be provided only by organized party machines served by a neutral civil service and squeezing the monarchy out of politics altogether. Albert had believed that 'the exaltation of Royalty is possible only through the personal character of the sovereign. When a person enjoys complete confidence we desire for him more power and influence in the conduct of affairs',[1] but even this worthy Victorian maxim has lost most of its political relevance in an age when issues are discussed not only in courts and cabinets but in party meetings and when 'public relations' count for as much as private rectitude in determining popular reactions.

What was left after 1861 was a series of royal prejudices, which increased in intensity in the last thirty years of Victoria's reign, and the moral force of monarchy, whenever the Queen cared to emphasize it. That the force counted for much is well brought out in the comment of the great historian, W. H. Lecky, on 'the profound feeling of sorrow and admiration' which greeted the news of her death. 'It shows', he said, 'that the vulgar ideals, the false moral measurements, the feverish social ambitions, the love of the ostentatious and the factitious, and the disdain for simple habits, pleasures and characters so apparent in certain conspicuous sectors of society, have not yet blunted the moral sense or prevented the moral perceptions of the great masses.'[2] To appreciate the significance of the comment it is necessary to turn in greater detail to the morals, manners, tastes, and styles of the majority of the Queen's mid-Victorian subjects.

3. MORALS, MANNERS, TASTES, AND STYLES

While Queen Victoria shared many contemporary tastes and opinions, in one respect at least her conceptions of morality were somewhat different from those of a highly influential and articulate section of her subjects. She cared little for 'extreme views' in religion, and in teaching her children—surely the best test of religious outlook —she chose to dwell not on 'the supernatural features of the Christian religion, but rather upon the pure and comprehensive morality which it teaches as its essential and indestructible element'.[3]

---

[1] Martin, *op. cit.*, vol. II, p. 469.
[2] 'Queen Victoria as a Moral Force', in *Historical and Political Essays* (1908), p. 275.
[3] Fawcett, *op. cit.*, p. 131.

It is difficult to separate out ethical and theological problems in mid-Victorian England, but the Queen's views and those of Prince Albert were bound to appear vague both to the Tractarians whom the Queen disliked and held responsible for the religious disputes of her reign, and to the Evangelicals who believed in a divine plan of personal salvation through Grace.

The essentials of Evangelical morality, the dominant morality of the age, were well expressed in up-to-date language in a poem *The Upward Line*, which compared life's pilgrimage with a railway journey:

> The line to Heaven by us is made,
> With heavenly truth the rails are laid;
> From Earth to Heaven the line extends
> And in eternal life it ends.

'Repentance' was the station where the passengers embarked, 'God's word' was the First Engineer, God's love the Fire and His Grace the steam, and although there were many dark tunnels, all passengers on the 'glory ride' were sure that they would reach their ultimate destination. If, however,

> . . . neither truth, nor fire, nor steam
> Can make you willing to get in,
> Then sinners you will weep at last
> When Heaven is lost and time is past;
> The Heavenly trains are all gone by,
> The sinner must for ever die.[1]

The theme and the treatment were essentially Evangelical, but the sense of sin and the fear of death played almost as big a part in all formal Victorian religion; it certainly found a place in Tractarian sermons and writings. It should be remembered that Victorian England still had a high child mortality rate and that the experience of a large number of deaths within a family was a chastening and disturbing experience. Christians like Charles Kingsley, who believed in a vigorous 'muscular' religion, were numbed by bereavement; vague Christian sympathizers like Dickens wallowed in death-bed sentimentality.

In evaluating Evangelical or Tractarian statements of belief, the question immediately arises as to how far the conceptions of the influential and articulate were generally accepted by most people in

[1] Quoted C. B. Andrews, *The Railway Age* (1937), pp. 42–4.

the country. How many parents were anxious in teaching their children, as Prince Albert was, to 'root up the Covenant theory that man's nature is sinful'?[1] How many 'respectable citizens' behind a façade of Bible reading, family prayers, quiet Sundays and sober weekdays were grounding their morality in a deep sense of piety and personal faith? The great growth of Sunday newspapers in mid-Victorian England—the *News of the World* (1846) attracted a large working-class reading public by its sensationalism as well as its radical politics—suggests that piety was counterbalanced by vicarious pleasure even on a Sunday. The enormous number of prostitutes in London and the big cities—the Burlington Arcade was described by a writer in the *Saturday Review* as the 'Western counterpart of an Eastern slave market', and in 1857 the *Lancet* claimed that one house in every sixty in London was a brothel[2]—showed that not all the pleasure was vicarious. Pictures of mid-Victorian morality derived from the respectable novels in Mudie's Circulating Library or on sale at W. H. Smith's station bookstalls are notoriously unreliable. Indeed W. H. Smith, who by 1862 had built up a flourishing railway bookstall business, was nicknamed 'Old Morality' and 'the North Western Missionary'.[3] In such matters the respectable mid-Victorians often tried to hide the truth from themselves. It was regarded as a testimony to the readability of a great novelist like Dickens that 'in forty works or more you will not find a phrase which a mother need withhold from her grown daughter'.[4] Yet Dickens's morality owed nothing to Evangelicalism or Tractarianism. Much religion, he suggested, was a 'vent for bad humours and arrogance' and there was no authority for the Murdstones in the New Testament; David Copperfield's opinion that 'we can all do some good if we will' was far more appealing. Dickens's obituary notice in *Fraser's Magazine* (July 1870) rightly seized on the point that 'he spent no thought on religious doctrines or religious reforms but regarded the Sermon on the Mount as good teaching, had a regard for the village church and churchyard, and

---

[1] Quoted Fulford, *op. cit.*, p. 183.
[2] For a recent appraisal see C. Pearl, *The Girl with the Swansdown Seat* (1955). For a contemporary view, see Taine, *op. cit., passim*. He called prostitution 'a festering sore, the real sore on the body of English society' (1957 edn., p. 31). See also W. Logan, *The Great Social Evil* (1871).
[3] Sir H. Maxwell, *Life and Times of the Right Honourable William Henry Smith, M.P.*, (1893), vol. I, pp. 53 ff.
[4] F. Harrison, *Studies in Early Victorian Literature* (1895), p. 143. See also H. House, *The Dickens World* (2nd edn. 1942), *passim*.

quarrelled with nothing but intolerance.' The appeal of moral generalities was at least as great in mid-Victorian England as it is today.

It is certainly dangerous to assume that because there was a mass of religious pamphleteering in mid-Victorian England, there was a generally valid connection between strong religious convictions and everyday morality, just as it is dangerous to deduce from the ubiquitous preaching of the gospel of work the existence of an unremittingly industrious working-class population. Many Victorians were at pains to emphasize that theirs was an age when all religions were highly organized, but not on that account generally and profoundly believed in; an age of observance more than assurance. In evaluating outer forms of Victorian conduct it is necessary therefore to investigate not only the 'fundamental principles' of religion but the economic, social and legal sanctions which kept men 'good'. Just as the threat of the sack, the fear of the poor law, and the absence of unemployment benefit were more important than treatises and homilies in ensuring steady and disciplined work, so 'good behaviour' was conditioned not only by 'vital religion' or belief in the authority of the Church, but by the fear of the police and of eternal punishment and more generally by concern for social ostracism and stigmas.

The Religious Census of 1851 demonstrated what Christians had long feared, that a large proportion of the population of England were neither Church people nor of any other religion. Although the exact figures must be treated with great caution, it seems clear that at least one-half of the people who might have been expected to go to church or chapel in 1851 did not do so. Most of the non-attenders came from the working classes. and local clergy in the towns were almost unanimous in pointing to the difficulties of attracting 'mass' support. 'The Population consists chiefly of Colliers and Foundry Men', a Chesterfield clergyman wrote, 'whose habits are very unfavourable to moral and religious influences and to attendance upon public worship'; 'the population having been till recently all but destitute of church ordinances, has relapsed into a state of semi-heathenism', wrote a vicar in a new parish near Oldham.[1] The same story was told by many other

[1] These and later extracts from local sources have been taken from the *Ecclesiastical Returns* (H.O. 129, 1851). These have recently been studied along with the full statistics by K. Inglis in an unpublished Oxford doctoral thesis 'English Churches and the Working Classes'.

people before and after 1851. 'What is St. Paul's?' Henry Mayhew asked one of his London costermongers. 'A Church, sir, so I've heard. I never was in Church.'[1]

It was not enough to argue as some Anglicans did that shortage of Church accommodation was responsible for the failure to win over the 'labouring myriads', or to take the view of many proud and quarrelsome Dissenters that all was well with their own communions and that it was the Established Church which was at fault. There were fundamental reasons for anxiety. Many of them were social. Pew rents alienated many people who could not afford them. As the official 1851 *Report* put it, 'working men, it is contended, cannot enter our religious structures without having pressed upon their notice some memento of inferiority'.[2] Lack of good clothes was another deterrent. A rector in Worcestershire observed that 'many parents, well-disposed to attend Public Worship, absent themselves on account of their dress, and the same remark is applicable to their children'; more simply and eloquently, a Roman Catholic priest from Walsall wrote: 'There is a service on Sunday morning at 8.o for poor people who from want of proper clothes do not like to appear out of doors at a later period of the day—average attendance at this service 350.' Finally, there was a more profound social problem involved in non-attendance. Within the village or the small town, with its hierarchical society and its intensive social life, church-going was, at least as far as the 'respectable' were concerned, reasonably regular and unpremeditated. The large city with its social gulf between rich and poor posed many problems other than those of social order and public health.

For all the efforts of hard-working vicars and curates in smoky urban parishes, of Tractarian priests injecting colour into drab working-class districts, of Evangelical and Nonconformist city missioners deliberately cultivating rough and stony soil, and of the 318,000 Sunday School teachers (1851), there was much 'spiritual destitution' in mid-Victorian England, particularly among the poor. Ignorance and indifference were more widespread than 'secularism', although in London and the big cities there was a small but often influential group of sober-living working men who were animated 'with an inveterately hostile sentiment' towards religion.[3] Their

---

[1] *London Labour and the London Poor* (1851), vol. I, p. 21.
[2] *Census of Great Britain*, 1851. *Religious Worship in England and Wales* (1855), p. 90.
[3] H. Dunckley, *The Glory and Shame of Britain* (1849), p. 75.

morality was usually indistinguishable from that of Nonconformist lay preachers or regular chapel-goers, just as the morality of thoughtful agnostics and rationalists in higher places was indistinguishable from that of the accepted Christian guides and teachers of the day. Indeed many mid-Victorian Evangelicals were content to note the part their religion had played in improving English morals while admitting at the same time, however reluctantly, that by that 'we do not mean that great masses are converted to God but . . . that great numbers are under the indirect influence of the Christian religion'.[1]

The dominant morality of mid-Victorian England was very closely associated with the middle-class element in English society. Within that element Nonconformity remained more important than Anglican Evangelicalism, separated from it by a social as much as by a spiritual gulf. It was frequently a sign of social advancement for a Nonconformist businessman to abandon the chapel and turn to the Church. The Establishment conferred 'status', and in small market towns like Mark Rutherford's Bedford [2] or large cities like Mrs. Gaskell's Manchester, Nonconformists had to be content at best with wealth and comfort. Some of them were very frank about the association of religion and class and even gloried in it. 'Our mission', wrote the Congregationalist Binney, 'is neither to the very rich nor to the very poor but to that great middle section of the community.'[3] Such men often believed that the social influence of the middle classes would be sufficient in itself to ensure the diffusion of their moral ideas and to guarantee national moral standards. They saw themselves as the guardians of the Protestant conscience, of the authority of the Bible 'and the Bible only', and, divided though they were not only between sects but within sects, they were united in resisting Tractarianism on the one hand and latitudinarianism, the absence of clearly defined religious dogmas, on the other. The views they heard propounded in their chapels were not very different from the views expressed in the *Upward Line*—'the minister invariably began with the fall of man; propounded the scheme of redemption, and ended by depicting in the morning the blessedness of the saints, and in the evening the doom of the lost'.[4] In their daily

---

[1] *The Congregational Year Book* (1849), p. 76.

[2] For a fascinating picture of local Dissent, see all the books of Mark Rutherford (W. Hale White). *The Revolution in Tanner's Lane* (1881) describes religious life in Cowfold (Bedford). The only aristocratic street there was three-quarters occupied by church people.

[3] T. Binney, *Congregationalism and Modern Church Movements* (1882), p. 36.

[4] *The Autobiography of Mark Rutherford* (1881), pp. 6-7.

morality, they were often accused of narrow-mindedness and self-righteousness, but at their best they were vigorous and self-reliant. Their dislike of established ecclesiastical authority frequently moved alongside their dislike of State interference with the economic market, but there was a warmth and sincerity in their attachment to the so-called 'voluntary principle' in religion and their ideal of 'affectionate service'. Their main weaknesses were an inability to do justice to the opinions of individuals and groups with whom they disagreed, their tendency to run to cant and hypocrisy, their frequently cramped social life, and their emphasis on the moral side of life at the expense of the intellectual and cultural.[1] All these weaknesses were shared by large numbers of Victorians who were not Nonconformists: they were as much deficiencies of a social group as of a religious body.

The deficiencies of this group account in large measure for the weakness of Victorian tastes and the profusion of Victorian styles. 'Festus' Bailey, in his poem 'The Age' (1858), complained that

> What England as a nation wants is taste;
> The judgement that's in due proportion placed;
> We overdo, we underdo, we waste.

Narrowness of education, pride in possession, fascination with ingenuity, and a hankering after 'sublime display' led most of the mid-Victorians to prefer the ornate to the simple, the vast to the balanced. Their emphasis on 'morality' confused both the majority and the minority in their assessment both of old works of art and new creations. While Ruskin was trying to persuade his contemporaries that 'taste is the only morality', most Victorians looked not to the artist's integrity but to his private life, not to the 'deep significance' of taste, but to its externals. The way of life of the artist was thought to be especially conducive to 'immorality'—he lived in an atmosphere of 'periodical impecuniosity and much tobacco smoke'.[2] In consequence, if artists wanted approval they had to take care to emphasize the morality of their conduct. Some of them began their day's work with a prayer; most of them followed up the prayer with hard work 'in the sense of regular and unremitting industry rather than of self-torturing effort after the unattainable'.[3]

---

[1] Matthew Arnold, *Culture and Anarchy* (1869), *passim*.
[2] T. H. S. Escott, *England: Its People, Polity and Pursuits* (1887 edn.), p. 334.
[3] A. P. Oppé, 'Art', in *Early Victorian England*, vol. II, p. 130.

The 'unattainable' was not particularly prized by the middle classes, who were mainly interested either in old and established works of art, about which there could be no controversy, or in modern works based on obvious themes treated in a literal manner and calculated to evoke proper sentiment—the proper sentiment turning, of course, all too easily into lush sentimentality. Aristocratic patronage of art counted for far less than in previous periods of English history, and there was powerful opposition to the much canvassed idea, strongly supported by Prince Albert, that the State should step in as fairy godmother.

The middle classes not only could not buy 'taste': they frequently debased what taste remained. They liked anecdote in art, talked ponderously of the 'moral content' of a picture, preferred 'big pictures' to small ones, and allowed themselves the occasional luxury of intoxication with colour. The best-known Victorian pictures like Sir Edwin Landseer's *The Old Shepherd's Chief Mourner* (1843) with its anthropomorphic sheep dog or W. P. Frith's *Derby Day* (1858) with its crowded and detailed canvas, were the kind of paintings not only that the public wanted but that most lesser artists wanted to paint. At a distance, the pre-Raphaelite group of painters who set up a 'brotherhood' in the year of revolutions, 1848, and were soon the centre of a sharp controversy about both the subject-matter of art and the 'right' method of treatment, seem to fit into their age rather than to be in violent contrast to it. They attacked Frith's *Derby Day* not on aesthetic grounds but because of its subject, they were as preoccupied with precise realistic detail as their opponents, and most of them were fully accepted by the critics of the late '50s. Holman Hunt's *Light of the World* (1854) was a great public success, and Millais's *Bubbles* eventually became one of the most effective late Victorian advertisements.

Parallel developments can be traced in the story of architecture and design. In early Victorian England there had been a celebrated 'battle of the styles' between the 'Gothic' and the 'classical'.[1] Pugin's dedicated championship of Gothic was grounded in carefully considered principles; he related architecture both to religion and life, believed that there should be one style as there was one faith, and maintained that good buildings could be built only by good men. On his death in 1852—on the same day as the Duke of Wellington—Gothic had established itself (it was well represented

[1] See K. Clark, *Gothic Revival* (1950 edn.).

in the mediaeval court at the Great Exhibition), but in a world
where 'taste' depended more on businessmen than on ecclesio-
logists Gothic was only one style among many. Mid-Victorian
architects ransacked every age in the past and every country for
models and examples, and many new hybrid styles appeared.
Pugin had laid down austerely that 'there should be no features
about a building which are not necessary for convenience, construction and propriety' and that 'all ornament should consist of
enrichment in the essential construction of the building',[1] but the
mid-Victorians completely ignored this advice. They did nothing
either to implement the hopes of a small group of architects who
pleaded for a genuine 'contemporary style', which would make
intelligent use of nineteenth-century materials like iron and glass.[2]
They liked imposing public architecture with 'pretensions', wanted
it to demonstrate wealth, to abound in decoration, even in polychromatic effects, and to incorporate the elaborate symbolism of an
age of free trade and material progress.[3] In their domestic architecture they demanded solidity, permanence, elaboration, and rich
façades. Sir John Hartower's house in Kingsley's *Water Babies* (1863)
had been 'built at ninety different times and in nineteen different
styles'. It bore traces of the Parthenon, the Brighton Pavilion and
the Taj Mahal.

Inside the houses there was a similar bastardization of styles, a
love of rich and generous curves, a profusion of ornament, and a
lavish use of nineteenth-century materials such as papier-mâché and
silver plate.[4] The objects on display at the Great Exhibition revealed
many of the 'tastes' of the men of the 1850s, particularly their trust
in the relevance of the machine to the 'success' of 'art'. Objects were
especially prized which displayed mechanical ingenuity,[5] and there
was great public acclaim for 'steam machinery' which made it

---

[1] *True Principles of Pointed or Ecclesiastical Architecture* (1841).

[2] See, for instance, Vose Pickett, *A New System of Architecture, founded on the Forms of
Nature and developing the Properties of Metals* (1845).

[3] Leeds Town Hall (1853–8) is a good example. In a lively debate during the building
between the 'civic pride' party and the 'economists', the former insisted on a Tower
which was to be 'useless' but 'dignified and with pretensions'. The economic symbolism
of the Town Hall was as elaborate as the religious symbolism of Worcester College
Chapel (1864). It is interesting too to compare the elaborate, polychromatic Albert
Memorial (1863–72) with the early Gothic Martyrs' Memorial in Oxford (1841).

[4] Papier-mâché had long been made in Persia and was made in Birmingham in the
eighteenth century, but it was not until the mid-nineteenth century that it became
popular, particularly when combined with mother-of-pearl. The electro-plating process
was not discovered until 1836 and not commercialized until after 1840.

[5] N. Pevsner, *High Victorian Design* (1951), p. 33.

possible 'to produce involved tracery and deep undercutting' with far less labour than craftsmen of the past had found necessary.[1] 'Pleasing objects' could be turned out in great quantities to make their way not only into the villas of the middle classes but into the homes of the skilled artisans. Thus, there was 'progress' in art as well as in manners; whereas art in the past had previously gratified the tastes of the few, it now served the wants of the many.[2] Unfortunately, the fact that vast quantities of 'pleasing objects' and 'elegant trifles' were turned out in Birmingham or London was no guarantee of quality. There was always a danger of the 'swamping' of the good by the bad, and even established painters were afraid first of the fashionable daguerreotypes of the fifties and then of the camera. Landseer's brother told Frith in 1870 that science had at last produced 'a foe-to-graphic art'.[3]

Similar trends can be traced in the story of mid-Victorian music. The moral content of music was always stressed, and the charms of the artist and the virtuosity of his performance captured audiences more than the quality of the work performed.[4] Exaggerated importance was given also to the publication of cheap editions of oratorios and choral music—most of them either hackneyed or pretentious. Abroad England was regarded as an 'unmusical country', but one in which foreign musicians might make their fortunes[5]; the distinction was far more eloquent than a dozen volumes of Victorian musical appreciation.

Any evaluation of mid-Victorian tastes must necessarily depend on the taste of the commentator, and during the last twenty years the 'Victorian revival' has done much to rehabilitate many Victorian objects—from monuments and buildings to bric-à-brac. Indiscriminate praise has taken the place of indiscriminate blame, pilgrimages to Victorian sites are undertaken, and collectors have forced up the prices of many objects which earlier in the century were relegated to the dust heap or the lumber room. The Victorians would have appreciated our mid-century collectors, for they were great collectors themselves, and art was not so much integrated

---

[1] R. Hunt, *Handbook to the Great Exhibition* (1851), judged many of the exhibits in this way.

[2] W. Whewell, *Lectures on the Results of the Great Exhibition of 1851* (1852).

[3] W. P. Frith, *Autobiography* (1888), vol. I, p, 149.

[4] This was probably true too of the stage. For an interesting attempt to relate these manifestations of taste in different arts, see J. H. Buckley, *The Victorian Temper* (1951), esp. ch. VII.

[5] E. J. Dent, 'Music' in *Early Victorian England*, vol. II, p. 252.

in their society as superimposed on it. To take Victoriana out of museums and art galleries and put them in their proper place, it is necessary to understand the kind of society which wanted them and the far from unanimous views which were expressed about them at the time. In other words, it is necessary to turn in more detail to the mid-Victorian critics of Victorianism.

4. VICTORIAN CRITICS OF VICTORIANISM

Most of the critics were concerned with the rôle of money in the new society and the narrowness of outlook of the moneymakers. In the 1840s Carlyle had condemned the 'cash nexus' and had challenged 'mammon worship': in the 1860s, when the web of credit had stretched further and tighter, Dickens in *Our Mutual Friend* (1864–5) drew powerful sketches of the shams and inherent emptiness of the world of mid-Victorian finance. He had always been fascinated by the effect of money on character, and in a brilliant chapter on 'Podsnappery' (Book I, ch. II) looked behind the well-regulated and pre-eminently respectable routine of Mr. Podsnap's life to the shabby 'values' which sustained it. All the elements in Victorianism were sharply criticized in a few pages. Mr. Podsnap lacked taste. 'Hideous solidity was the characteristic of the Podsnap plate. Everything was made to look as heavy as it could, and to take up as much room as possible.' Mr. Podsnap had supreme confidence in his own moral integrity. 'He always knew exactly what Providence meant. Inferior and less respectable men might fall short of that mark, but Mr. Podsnap was always up to it.' Mr. Podsnap sheltered himself from those things in the world which he did not like. 'I don't want to know about it; I don't choose to discuss it; I don't admit it.' Mr. Podsnap believed in sheltering other respectable people too; he felt that there were certain subjects which ought not to be introduced 'among our wives and young persons'. The picture both of high finance and of spiritual poverty in *Our Mutual Friend* had a powerful influence on many discontented mid-Victorians, including William Morris who later in life published extracts from it in his socialist *Commonweal*. Dickens's novel, however, was in no sense socialistic, and very similar criticisms of traffic in shares, false pretences, and financial and social maladjustments can be found in the liberal-conservative Trollope's mordantly satirical masterpiece, *The Way We Live Now* (1875). Arthur Hugh

Clough, the poet, went further. In his revision of the *Decalogue*, he included the precepts

> Thou shalt not steal; an empty feat
> When it's so lucrative to cheat . . .
> Thou shalt not covet, but tradition
> Approves all forms of competition.

Disgust with the tissue of false values surrounding money-making was one of the forces leading the critics of Victorianism to sanctify the claims of hard and honest work. The chapter immediately following 'Podsnappery' in *Our Mutual Friend* is called 'The Sweat of an Honest Man's Brow'. Once again it was Carlyle who was the first great sage to draw the right lessons. 'Properly speaking, all true Work is Religion', he wrote in *Past and Present* (1843) and he went on to show how it meant 'communication with Nature' and revealed 'something of divineness' in even the humblest hand worker. Not even the cash nexus could completely ruin good work: 'Labour is ever an imprisoned God, writhing unconsciously or consciously to escape out of Mammonism.' These thunderous propositions, central to Carlyle's philosophy of life, were capable of becoming either platitudes—as they often were in the dullest pages of Samuel Smiles—or cornerstones of a new view of society as they were for Ruskin, Morris, and later still for the young Keir Hardie. John Ruskin in *The Stones of Venice* (1853) was the first to use them to support an unorthodox political economy which paid as much attention in its analysis to the man who worked as to the product he made. He attacked the division of labour on the grounds that it was not labour which was divided but men, and described 'the pestilential air' which surrounded contemporary social relationships. In his later writings, notably *The Political Economy of Art* (1857), *Unto this Last* (1862), and *Fors Clavigera* (1871–84), he united in one synthesis a theory of economics, an approach to art criticism, and a new prescription for national policy. 'The first duty of a state', he maintained, 'is to see that every child born therein shall be well housed, clothed, fed and educated, till it attains years of discretion.' He went on to admit that in order to achieve this 'the government must have an authority over the people of which we do not so much as dream.'[1] William Morris went further than

[1] E. T. Cook and A. D. O. Wedderburn, *The Works of John Ruskin* (1903–12), vol. II, p. 263.

Ruskin, and in 1883 became an active propagandist of socialism. In the period covered in this book, however, he was not taking an active part in politics but establishing his reputation as a poet and a craftsman in the decorative arts. His building of the Red House at Bexley Heath in Kent in 1859 was a deliberate reaction against the tastelessness of his age—'pedantic imitations of classical architecture . . . ridiculous travesties of Gothic buildings . . . and the utilitarian brick box with a slate lid'. He looked back to the Middle Ages, as both Carlyle and Ruskin had done, for an integration of taste, style, and social purpose, but he was no mere revivalist. His dream was of the future. 'Were the rows of square brown brick boxes which Keats and Shelley had to look on, or the stuccoed villa which enshrined Tennyson's genius, to be the perpetual concomitants of such masters of verbal beauty? . . . Was the intelligence of the age to be for ever so preposterously lop-sided?'[1] The building of the Red House and the foundation of his famous 'Firm' of decorators and craftsmen in 1861 were important incidents in the journey from mid- to late-Victorian England. Morris himself worked on everything the firm produced, designing, painting, dyeing, and weaving with his own hands. He tried to guide his customers towards a genuine appreciation of 'simplicity' and 'sincerity' in the creative arts. It was as a result of his experiences with the Firm that he came to the conclusion that 'a reform in art which is founded on individualism must perish with the individuals who have set it going'.[2]

Behind the social criticisms of Carlyle, Ruskin and Morris was a fundamental criticism of the competitive industrial society, founded on free enterprise and machine production, which had developed out of the older agricultural and mercantile society during the previous seventy or eighty years of English history: of the whole 'age of improvement' described in this book. Carlyle was never sure about remedies; he turned and twisted about, looking for 'captains of industry', 'heroes' and 'doers, not talkers', until many of his readers must have waited for the descent of that silence which he had always praised as 'the SILENCE of deep Eternities'. Ruskin was curiously whimsical, muddled, inconsistent, and indecisive for all his insight, and there is profound truth in a comment he made in a

---

[1] *The Collected Works of William Morris* (1910–15), vol. XXII, pp. 321–2.
[2] P. Henderson (ed.) *The Letters of William Morris to his Family and Friends* (1950), p. 187.

letter to his father in 1848: 'I seem born to conceive what I cannot execute, recommend what I cannot obtain, and mourn over what I cannot save.'[1] Morris found the answers to many of his most searching questions only after the social balance of mid-Victorian England had given way to a new period of cleavage and tension. None of the criticisms of Carlyle, Ruskin and Morris, however, can be overlooked. They make it impossible for posterity to take most of their fellow-Victorians at their face value.

There was a fourth critic who claimed that the effect of criticism depended not on prophetic fury but on 'the power of persuasion, of charm'.[2] Matthew Arnold was neat, orderly and ironical where Carlyle was rough, mysterious and metaphorical; he was liberal when both Ruskin and Morris were leaning towards socialism; he disliked abstruse argument and he liked to choose concrete examples. He was anxious 'to mediate not a view of the world, but a habit of mind', the open mind.[3] As surely as his fellow writers, however, Arnold criticized the lopsidedness of his age, and in a mass of miscellaneous writings[4] caught the manifold weaknesses—and sometimes the strength—of mid-Victorian England more effectively than any other writer in his generation.

His main aim was to teach his contemporaries the meaning of 'perfection', to carry into the heart of a society which seemed to care little for it an 'idea of the best', a feeling for the *quality* of life. Industrial civilization, he maintained, had encouraged a warping and stultifying 'faith in machinery' and a belief that greater material wealth was a 'precious end in itself'. The only counterpoise to such a faith in externals was a 'search after human perfection in an *internal* condition'. It was fortunate that there were 'in each class a certain number of natures with a curiosity about their best self, with a bent for seeing things as they are, for disentangling themselves from machinery ... for the pursuit, in a word, of perfection.' This minority, he argued, shared 'humanity' as their distinguishing

---

[1] Peter Quennell chooses this remark as a motto of his *John Ruskin, The Portrait of a Prophet* (1949).

[2] *The Works of Matthew Arnold* (1903–4), vol. XIII, p. 266.

[3] John Holloway, *The Victorian Sage* (1953), p. 207. Arnold called Ruskin 'provincial' and 'never much liked Carlyle', who in his view preached 'earnestness to a nation which had plenty of it by nature, but was less abundantly supplied with several other useful things'. (G. W. E. Russell (ed.) *Letters* (1901), vol. II, p. 222.)

[4] It is important not to take *Culture and Anarchy* in isolation from the rest of his work as so many literary critics have been prone to do. *Friendship's Garland* (1871), *Popular Education in France* (1861), and *Schools and Universities on the Continent* (1868) are of equal significance in assessing his social thought.

characteristic. The result was that, generally speaking, they had 'a rough time of it in their lives'. Both the economic and social system made it difficult for them to pursue 'the best'. The English aristocracy were 'Barbarians'. They had had their day, and in an age of rapid change showed a sterile 'inaccessibility to ideas'. They might still possess sweetness, but they had far too little light. The English working classes, 'the Populace', were still for the most part brutalized by the struggle for existence. They had a future, but in the Victorian present they were often raw and blind. One part was a 'rabble'; the other part looked up to the middle classes and sought to emulate them. The middle classes themselves, the Philistines, lacked both sweetness and light. They were the 'kernel of the nation', the pride of its propagandists, in a real sense 'preponderating in importance in late years', but they were narrow and prejudiced, handicapped by a 'defective type of religion', 'a stunted sense of beauty', and 'a low standard of manners'. Even worse, they were 'averse' to whatever might disturb them in the enjoyment of their 'vulgarity'. Arnold laid particular emphasis on the effects of their defective type of religion. As a whole, the middle class had 'entered the prison of Puritanism and had the key turned upon its spirit there for two hundred years'. The influence it had been able to exert on other classes in the community had been disastrously misused. 'Look at the life imaged in such a newspaper as the *Nonconformist* ; a life of jealousy of the Establishment, disputes, tea-meetings, openings of chapels, sermons, and then think of it as an ideal of human life . . . aspiring with all its organs after sweetness, light and perfection.'

It was easy to dismiss Arnold as a 'highbrow'—the word had not then been invented—and to regard him as a 'man who held a moral smelling-bottle at his nose, and exacted an impossible standard of life from a busy and strenuous people who had a living to get'.[1] It remains easy in retrospect to demonstrate how his own temperament, upbringing and circumstances shaped his view of 'perfection' both in literature [2] and in society and how he always looked at the problems of his country from the vantage point of his beloved Oxford, a university which 'by her ineffable charm keeps ever calling us nearer to the true goal of all of us, to the idea'. His view

---

[1] Sir Joshua Fitch, *Thomas and Matthew Arnold and Their Influence on English Education* (1899), p. 301.
[2] See J. S. Eells, *The Touchstones of Matthew Arnold* (1955).

of 'culture', however, was not a purely personal one. It was directly related both to the facts of difference between England and the Continent and to an already rich tradition of English critical thought. Arnold was right to direct attention to the neglected 'virtues' of French and German society, to plead for 'flexibility' and to query the rigid domestic presuppositions of much of English middle-class liberalism. 'Your middle-class man thinks it the highest pitch of development and civilization when his letters are carried twelve times a day from Islington to Camberwell . . . and if railway trains run to and from them every quarter of an hour. He thinks it is nothing that the trains only carry him from an illiberal, dismal life at Islington to an illiberal, dismal life at Camberwell; and the letters only tell him that such is the life there.'[1]

The critical view of 'perfection' he advocated was not his own individual discovery. It looked back to Coleridge, to the anti-utilitarian movement of the late eighteenth and the early nineteenth centuries, and to the growth of a society dependent on industrial change. Wordsworth had written at the very beginning of the century of the emergence of 'a multitude of causes, unknown to former times, (which) are now acting with a combined force to blunt the discriminating powers of the mind'[2]; Coleridge had distinguished between 'cultivation' (culture), which was difficult to nurture, and 'civilization', which just grew, and had gone on to describe the necessary rôle of a minority—the 'clerisy', he called it—in supervising the task of nurture; Newman, a subtle and appealing critic of his age, had talked of 'perfection' and of the difficulties of realizing it.[3] Even John Stuart Mill had criticized Bentham for not recognizing that 'man is a being capable of pursuing spiritual perfection as an end', and had looked to Wordsworth to discover 'the importance of poetry and art as instruments of human culture'.[4] Arnold carried the tradition of critical protest one stage further by providing a new terminology; at the same time, while accepting the fact that 'religion' at its best coincided with 'culture', he looked not to a religious group for the pursuit of 'sweetness and light', but

---

[1] *Friendship's Garland* (1871).

[2] Preface to the second edition of the *Lyrical Ballads* (1800).

[3] *The Idea of a University* (1852). Newman queried the whole philosophy of 'improvement', the doctrine that 'education, railroad travelling, ventilation, drainage and the acts of life, when fully carried out, serve to make a population moral and happy', *Apologia*, 'Note on Liberalism'.

[4] See his criticisms of Bentham in *Dissertations and Discussions*, vol. I, pp. 330–93: *Autobiography*, ch. VI.

rather to those people in every class of society who were endowed with an honest 'curiosity about their best selves'. He was no more happy about the actual state of religion in mid-nineteenth-century England than he was about the state of politics, but he saw how closely religion and culture were connected. 'At the present moment', he wrote rather later in his life, 'two things about the Christian religion must surely be true to anybody with eyes in his head. One is, that men cannot do without it; the other, that they cannot do with it as it is.'[1] It is essential to examine the whole of Arnold's cultural pedigree if his criticism of mid-Victorian England is to be put in its proper place.

Against this background and drawing upon his experiences as an inspector of schools (1851–86), Arnold pleaded above all else for a genuine national educational system which would go far towards guaranteeing the achievement of his main purpose. He disliked views of elementary education which concentrated on the commonplace and the practical; he attacked the 'commercial academies' of the middle classes on the grounds that they were designed simply to enable children to 'get on in the world'; he criticized equally strongly the limitations of the public schools, particularly those schools which were mainly concerned with turning out 'gentlemen'. He thus directed attention to the weaknesses of the two 'ideal types ' of Victorian character—the self-made man, Smiles's hero, and the 'gentleman', even the Christian gentleman whom his father had tried to produce in large numbers at Rugby School. He went on to query the over-confidence and negative attitude of Victorian 'advanced liberals', their dislike of all forms of state interference, and their indifference to the fate of the very poor.[2] 'You seem to think', Arnold told his fellow countrymen through the mouth of his Prussian 'stooge', Arminius, 'that you have only got to get on the back of your horse Freedom, or your horse Industry, and to ride away as hard as you can, to be sure of coming to the right destination.'

Arnold's uneasiness about where the two horses Freedom and Industry were carrying his country was matched by an equally

---

[1] *God and the Bible* (1875), Preface.
[2] The career of Mr. Bottles in *Friendship's Garland* illustrates all the weaknesses of an advanced liberal. Bottles, who had 'always gone straight as an arrow about Reform' and paid the expenses of a Church rates contest out of his own pocket, finally looked forward 'to marrying his deceased wife's sister'. This was a reference to an 'advanced reform' proposal which radicals brought before Parliament almost every year.

relentless uneasiness about where his own life was leading, and in neither of these manifestations of uncertainty was he exceptional or alone. Humphry House has rightly related ultimate Victorian questions concerning the immortality of the soul to immediate questions of 'self-culture' and individual fulfilment, and has quoted Tennyson's remark in 1872 that if he ceased to believe in any chance of another life, and of a great Personality somewhere in the Universe, 'he should not care a pin for anything'.[1] This was a dangerous prop for a superficially confident society to rely upon and 'in an age of material advance and scientific discovery, the will to know frequently overpowered the will to believe'.[2] The conflict between science and religion in particular underlined those mid-Victorian doubts which were as illuminating and eloquent as the noisiest or the most sophisticated criticism.

5. RELIGION AND SCIENCE

Although there were signs in the late eighteenth century that the pursuit of scientific enquiry and experiment upset those churchmen who were afraid of 'human presumption', deviation from Biblical orthodoxy, and intellectual 'Jacobinism', most early nineteenth-century scientists believed that there was a more confident link between science and morality than there was between morality and art. Some of them talked in familiar terms, as Paley had done, of Divine Design in the pattern of the Universe; others employed new theories of catastrophic geology to 'prove' the Flood [3] or, when these had been discounted, looked for manifestations of God's 'government' in the history of the natural world. 'Truth is always delightful to an uncorrupted mind', the Cambridge scientist, Professor Adam Sedgwick, wrote in 1845, 'and it is most delightful when it reaches us in the form of some great abstraction which links together the material and moral parts of nature.' [4] It was thought proper to extend the influence of science outside the laboratory and the study. The universities might prefer the classics, but in the popular education of mechanics and artisans in institutes and night

---

[1] Quoted H. House, *All in Due Time* (1955), p. 99.
[2] J. H. Buckley, *op. cit.*, p. 106.
[3] This was the view put forward by the most eminent English geologist, Professor William Buckland, in 1820. 'The grand fact of *an universal* deluge . . . is proved on grounds so decisive and incontrovertible, that had we never heard of such an event from scripture. . . . Geology of itself must have called in the assistance of some such catastrophe.' *Vindiciae Geologicae* (1820), pp. 23–4.
[4] *Edinburgh Review*, vol. LXXXII, p. 56.

schools, scientific as well as technical instruction was often included; an appreciation of Truth, it was believed, would make the workers not only better workers but better men. 'Science teaches us', Brougham wrote, 'to look on all earthly objects as insignificant and below our notice except the pursuit of knowledge and the cultivation of virtue—that is to say, the strict performance of our duty in every relation of society.' [1] The lessons drawn from science left many working men unmoved, but they had a special appeal for the middle classes who found in geology in particular a science which could account for their wealth—thick coal seams—and could enliven their leisure hours through the favourite Victorian pursuit of collecting fossils and shells. The British Association for the Advancement of Science was founded in 1831, largely as a result of the activities of geologists, with the twofold purpose of increasing public interest in useful knowledge and of inspiring scientific discovery.

Emphasis by scientists on the social and moral as well as the intellectual or utilitarian rôle of science was in many ways extremely unwise, for by the time of the revolutions of 1848 it had been demonstrated that 'science' might teach the wrong lessons as well as the right ones, and that there were bound to be difficulties in reconciling scientific conclusions with those of revealed religion. The enormous success of an avowedly popular book, Robert Chambers's *Vestiges of Creation* (1844),[2] alarmed orthodox scientists themselves. In his volume Chambers began with the solar system and ended with man; just as 'gravitation' was the 'one final comprehensive law' relating to inorganic life, so 'development' was the one great law relating to organic life. Organic forms had not been created in fixed groups at the beginning of the world, but had chronologically progressed, and 'man, considered zoologically, and without regard to the distinct character assigned to him by theology, simply takes his place as the type of all types of the animal kingdom'. Established scientists were the first to attack the *Vestiges*. Sedgwick believed, for example, that Chambers had 'annulled all distinction between physical and moral', and that the framework of natural theology which Chambers had retained was completely artificial.

---

[1] Quoted in G. C. Gillispie's extremely interesting and original study *Genesis and Geology* (1951), p. 195.

[2] It was published anonymously, went through four editions between 1844 and 1845 and eleven editions by 1860. One theory was that it had been written by Prince Albert. In fact, Chambers was a self-made man with a passion for popularizing all kinds of knowledge. He was a 'precursor' of Smiles as well as of the popular evolutionists.

Yet although scientists were able to point out scores of serious academic and scientific shortcomings in Chambers's work, they could not 'muzzle' a thesis which appealed both to poets like Tennyson and to secularist working men.[1]

Before Darwin gave a responsible scientist's answer in 1859 to the problem of the descent of man, the work of other responsible scientists was raising difficulties for those people who placed a simple trust in the infallibility of the Biblical record. Sir Charles Lyell, whose three-volume *Principles of Geology* (1830–3) destroyed the dramatic geological case for the Flood, had made it equally difficult to believe in the simple Biblical view that the world was created in 4004 B.C. His book created much popular interest but little scandal, for it was unimpeachably scholarly, and Lyell himself was extremely tactful and reserved, as conscious of his social as of his scientific rôle. He believed in man's absolute uniqueness and the immutability of other species, but had come to the conclusion that Mosaic chronology was 'an incubus on our science'.[2] This was a most important conclusion, for it not only altered the whole sense of time span, but left less and less of the record of the past to be explained in terms of supernatural intervention. In private circles in the '40s and '50s it was well known that most distinguished scientists, whatever their public utterances, agreed with Lyell that it was impossible to hold to a strictly literal interpretation of the Old Testament. Not only was the earth far older than the Bible suggested but, just as serious, the order of creation of the various living forms described in *Genesis* did not correspond with the order in which the creatures appeared in the rocks. At this point archaeology lent its aid to geology and natural history. In 1857 the first remains of Neanderthal man came to light, and the discovery of stone implements and other objects demonstrated conclusively that long before the time of Biblically-placed Adam there were beings on earth to whom the name of 'man' could not be denied.

Darwin's *Origin of Species* 'from the standpoint of the providentialist interpretation of nature . . . was a *coup de grâce* rather than an entering wedge'.[3] For years before 1859 the cautious, cultivated, retiring, and sickly Darwin was collecting facts about evolution—he wrote out a long and coherent statement of 231 pages in 1844 which included nearly every detail of the final theory—but he

---

[1] See above, p. 401.
[2] K. M. Lyell, *Life, Letters and Journals of Sir Charles Lyell* (1881), vol. I, p. 328.
[3] Gillispie, *op. cit.*, p. 220.

shrank from writing a book on a subject which he knew would cause great controversy. It was only when he read an article by A. R. Wallace in the *Annals of Natural History* in 1855 that he began to feel that it would be vexing 'if anyone were to publish my doctrines before me'[1]; the further revelation of the nature of Wallace's work and the pressure of his friends led him into producing *The Origin of Species*, one of the most important books of the nineteenth century,[2] a book based on the accumulation of a mass of detailed and carefully checked information.

It began with a brief but shattering introduction which stated simply that 'the view which most naturalists until recently entertained, and which I formerly entertained—that each species has been independently created—is erroneous'. Species were not immutable. Hereditary modification was possible under human control—the first part of the book was devoted to careful conclusions drawn from horse-breeding and pigeon fancying—and stood out as the main theme of natural history, the doctrine of Malthus applied to 'the whole animal and vegetable kingdoms'. During a relentless 'struggle for existence', 'natural selection' had determined the future of living creatures 'under the complex and sometimes varying conditions of life'. In the final paragraphs of peroration, with their stormy note of optimism,[3] Darwin claimed that there was 'grandeur' in his new view of life. 'Whilst this planet has gone cycling on according to the fixed laws of gravity', he concluded in a sentence reminiscent of Chambers, 'from so simple a beginning endless forms most beautiful and most wonderful have been, and are being, evolved'.

Darwin's sense of beauty did not impress a large number of his influential contemporaries. The most dangerous of his critics were not the Biblical fundamentalists—they had been shocked by so many scientific writings before 1859 that *The Origin of Species* was merely the latest and biggest blow—but those scientists who felt that Darwin had destroyed the much-treasured link between morality and science. The theory of spontaneous 'natural selection', they believed, substituted accident—or perhaps mechanism—for intelligent purpose in the world of nature. It was this aspect of Darwin's theory which T. H. Huxley, Darwin's great protagonist,

---

[1] Quoted W. Irvine, *Apes, Angels and Victorians* (1955), p. 80.
[2] A joint paper summarizing both his own and Wallace's views was read before the Linnean Society in July 1858 and published in that society's *Journal of Proceedings (Zoology)*, vol. III, August 1858.
[3] See above, p. 401.

claimed was new in 1859.[1] Darwin made little attempt to resolve the dilemma between chance and design; instead, he took the view that when he used the word 'spontaneous' he merely meant that he was ignorant of the causes of that which he so termed. His 'ignorance' on what after all was a key point in Victorian argument was as upsetting as his positive conclusions. It was his old Cambridge geology professor, Sedgwick, who had predicted a brilliant scientific future for him, who wrote that Darwin had revealed 'demoralized understanding' and had done his best to plunge humanity into 'a lower grade of degradation' than any yet recorded. Reverting to the argument he had advanced against Chambers, he maintained that 'there is a moral or metaphysical part of nature as well as a physical' and that a man who denied this was 'deep in the mire of fallacy'. In conclusion he objected to the manner of Darwin's conclusion, particularly the appeal to 'the rising generation'.[2]

Huxley, bold, brilliant, and pugnacious, did much to publicize Darwin's thesis and to defend it against more old-fashioned scientists. He spoke the new language of the 'rising generation', compared Darwin with Galileo and Newton, and warned his countrymen that 'the origin of species' was not the first, and would not be the last, of 'the great questions born in science, which will demand settlement from this generation. The general mind is seething strangely, and to those who watch the signs of the times, it seems plain that this nineteenth century will see revolutions of thought and practice as great as those which the sixteenth welcomed.'[3]

There was not the slightest doubt, Huxley later said, that if a general council of the Church scientific had been held in 1860 Darwin's views would have been condemned by an overwhelming majority. As it was, it was not the Church scientific but the Christian Church militant and non-militant which was quickest to give an opinion. Bishops, parish clergy, journalists, and laymen almost all condemned that part of Darwinism which they thought they understood, and only a few priests of the Church of England, notably Charles Kingsley,[4] showed any sympathy with the new

---

[1] See F. Darwin (ed.), *The Life and Letters of Charles Darwin* (3rd edn. 1887), vol. I, ch. V. In this chapter Professor Huxley describes the contemporary reactions to the *Origin of Species*.

[2] See Gillispie, *op. cit.*, p. 217; Irvine, *op. cit.*, p. 113.

[3] Quoted F. Darwin, *op. cit.*, vol. I, p. 283.

[4] 'Now they have got rid of an interfering God', Kingsley wrote to Darwin, a master-magician as I call it—they have to choose between the absolute empire of accident and a living, immanent, ever-working God.'

picture of evolution by natural selection. Darwin's main ecclesiastical antagonist was Bishop Wilberforce of Oxford who at a famous
meeting of the British Association at Oxford in 1860 asked Huxley
with studied politeness whether 'it was through his grandfather
or his grandmother that he claimed his descent from a monkey'.
The ecclesiastical case often rose to no higher a level than this,
but in reality the divided Church of England was shaken by the
impact of the new views in a way that a more authoritarian body
would not have been, and there was no single effective answer which
any Churchman could make at that time, with any hope of securing
general agreement. Throughout the 1860s and '70s Christianity as
'a system of ideas, aspirations and practices' was facing a far graver
challenge than the Church of England had faced as an ecclesiastical
institution in the 'Church in danger' days of the mid-1830s.

The challenge from science was not the only one, and there was
in fact an important intellectual link between the problems of the
1830s and those of the 1860s. Ever since the early Tractarians
began to examine the *origins* of ecclesiastical authority, many Anglicans were drawn into a study of history which might lead them out
of the Church of England either into the Roman communion or out
of Christianity altogether. The two Newman brothers—John Henry
and Francis—typified the choice. Pulled in the two opposing directions, the first passed from Protestantism to Roman Catholicism,
becoming a cardinal in 1879, while the second moved from Protestantism into a religious 'modernism' which stopped short at the
confused boundaries of agnosticism. 'It is as if', Basil Willey has
written in a most illuminating image, 'two rivers, taking their rise
in the same dividing range, should yet be so deflected by some
minute original irregularity of level, so that one pours its waters
into the Mediterranean, the other into the German ocean.'[1] Germany
was the great centre of Biblical criticism, but before German
influence helped to provide a scholarly foundation for a new
English view of the Bible as a historical document and of Jesus as a
historical figure, sensitive English intellectuals were already feeling
a sense of insecurity in the traditional Christianity of their fathers,
particularly Evangelical Christianity. 'Whether or not Anglicanism
leads to Rome', John Henry Newman was writing in 1840, 'so far is
clear as day that Protestantism leads to infidelity.'[2]

---

[1] B. Willey, *More Nineteenth-century Studies* (1956), p. 11.
[2] Quoted M. Ward, *Young Mr. Newman* (1952), p. 360.

George Eliot was an interesting representative of one team of travellers along Francis Newman's road. She began researching into the origins of Christianity in 1831 when she was living a quiet provincial life among English Calvinists and hovering in her own mind between the Evangelical and Tractarian arguments. One of the books she read was Charles Hennell's *An Inquiry Concerning the Origin of Christianity* (1838) which represented an English, rather than a German, tradition of rationalist enquiry. With Hennell and Charles Bray, a prosperous Coventry ribbon manufacturer, as her guides, she soon came to the conclusion that miraculous interventions do not occur in the course of nature, and on the basis of that conclusion she abandoned all her belief in the doctrines of Christianity and in the need for Church attendance. From 1844 to 1846 she was translating *Leben Jesu*, a German rationalist study by D. F. Strauss which talked of the 'Christ Myth' and treated Christianity entirely as a historical product.[1] It was thus through a study of human history and not through natural history that George Eliot and many of her contemporaries reached a position where they could no longer accept the Bible or the Church as sources of authority. Their position was clearly defined long before the publication of *The Origin of Species*.

There was another element in the English 'rationalist' protest. John Stuart Mill's *System of Logic* (1843) influenced intellectuals in the universities, and it in turn was influenced by Auguste Comte's new sociology. According to Comte and his English disciples, the Positivists, of whom the most able was Frederic Harrison,[2] society had a history of its own, an ordered course going through three stages of growth—the theological, the metaphysical, and the positive or scientific. In this last stage the Christian religion would give way to the religion of humanity, a genuine religion, demanding acts of worship, but completely free from the superstitions of the past. While Mill, influenced by Comte, pleaded for a clash and conflict of opinions out of which new truths, like new species, would emerge, Harrison and his friends pointed to the inevitable emergence of a moral system superior to that of Christianity. Not all the rebels

[1] For the details of George Eliot's early intellectual development and its relevance to her later career, see J. Bennett, *George Eliot* (1948).

[2] Harrison's college tutor, Richard Congreve, was the first Positivist preacher in England; he was a pupil of Dr. Arnold of Rugby. Harrison admitted that it was the Positivist view of history which was the first feature in its philosophy to appeal to him (*Memories and Thoughts* (1906), p. 15). Mill too was influenced by the 'connected view of the natural order of human progress' (*Autobiography* (1873), ch. V).

against traditional Christianity were so optimistic. Like the scientists, they could either view the process of human change with eager anticipation or they could contemplate it with alarm—and even with despair.

George Eliot, as an artist, and T. H. Huxley as a scientist, agreed with the Comtists that the abandonment of Christianity did not mean the abandonment of 'morality'. They believed instead that they had to be good for good's sake not God's, to cultivate broad human sympathies, and to find a moral 'aim' or 'object' in life. George Eliot held that 'in proportion as the thoughts of men and women are removed from the earth on which they live, are diverted from their own mutual relations and responsibilities of which they alone know anything to an invisible world which can only be apprehended by belief, they are led to neglect their duty to each other [and] to squander their strength in vain speculations'.[1] Huxley had no doubt that 'the ledger of the Almighty is strictly kept and every one of us has the balance of his operations paid over to him of every minute of his existence'.[2]

For those who did not abandon Christianity, though they often went through religious crises and experienced intense moments of 'honest doubt', three ways were open—complete indifference to the impact of science on older views of life and history, an attempt to adapt Christian argument to new challenges, and an obedience to the full authority of the Roman Catholic Church. The first choice was the most frequent, and there were enough disputes within the Church of England on matters of religious observance and discipline in the 1850s and '60s to keep conventional ecclesiastical energies active and passions alive. The world of *Barchester Towers* (1857) was far more satisfying to a large section of the clergy than the world of *The Origin of Species*. Those people who chose the second way were in an extremely difficult position, meeting with great hostility from both Evangelicals and Tractarians alike. When in 1860—the year of the foundation of the High Church English Church Union—seven talented members of the Church produced a volume of essays designed to cast off 'incrustations' from Christianity and to bring out the 'eternal import' of religion, they were attacked as 'Seven against Christ' by both Pusey and Shaftesbury.[3] Their essays were,

---

[1] Quoted Bennett, *op. cit.*, p. 25.
[2] L. Huxley (ed.), *Life and Letters of Thomas Henry Huxley* (1900), vol. I, pp. 219-20.
[3] *Essays and Reviews* (1860). The seven writers included Frederick Temple, Head-master of Rugby and later Archbishop of Canterbury, Mark Pattison, and Benjamin

in fact, reasonably mild and thoughtful attempts to 'reconcile intellectual persons to Christianity'.[1] Only one of the essayists referred to Darwin (very favourably), although there were frequent references to Biblical criticism, appeals to theologians to stop clinging to out-of-date theories of 'God's procedure towards man', and demands for further discussion by churchmen of contemporary intellectual issues. 'It is a stifling of the true Christian life', one of the most-criticized writers declared, 'both in the individual and in the Church, to require of many men a unanimity in speculative doctrine, which is unattainable, and a uniformity of historical belief, which can never exist.'[2]

For all the mildness of most of the seven writers, two of them were condemned officially by the Court of Arches and suspended from their offices for a year. All of them were rebuked by Bishop Wilberforce with as little subtlety as he had shown in his rebuke to Darwin. At the same time they were all sharply criticized by secularists and Positivists for not going far enough. It was Frederic Harrison and not Wilberforce who remarked that their views were 'incompatible with the religious belief of the mass of the Christian public, and the broad principles on which the Protestantism of Englishmen rests'.[3]

The third choice is best represented by John Henry Newman, although his methods of argument and the quality of his thinking were quite exceptional. In his *Apologia Pro Vita Sua* (1864), Newman described the Roman Catholic Church as a 'port after a rough sea' and added that from the time that he became a Catholic he never had one doubt. 'Ten thousand difficulties do not make one doubt.' Even before he became a Catholic, however, he had reacted strongly against attempts to relate the existence of God, as Paley did, to the Divine Design of the Universe and had come to the conclusion that the religious apologetics of the day discussed the wrong problems in the wrong way. He was neither surprised by Darwin's theory of evolution nor shocked by it, preferring to ground his faith

Jowett, later Master of Balliol College, Oxford. The *Quarterly Review* of January 1861, which included Bishop Wilberforce's attack on the book, went through five editions.
[1] E. A. Abbott and L. Campbell (ed.) *Life and Letters of Benjamin Jowett* (1897 edn.), vol. I, p. 345.
[2] H. B. Wilson, 'The National Council', *loc. cit.*
[3] *Westminster Review*, October 1860. Kingsley's anti-intellectual reaction was typical of those who did not want to think too much. 'Do not darken your mind with intellectual puzzles', he told his curate, '[they] may breed disbelief, but can never breed vital religion, or practical usefulness.' *Letters and Memories of His Life* (ed. F. Kingsley, 1877), vol. II, pp. 103–1.

not in 'mutilated and defective evidence' but in 'a right state of
heart'. His *Grammar of Assent* (1870) rejected all ideas of a 'balance
of arguments' to control and fix man's minds, and he was thus able
to by-pass not only the immediate problems of his age but the
technique of free discussion and enquiry which the leading spokesmen of his age considered the necessary means to increase understanding. Harrison believed that Newman's brother Francis much
surpassed him in 'mental versatility' and that 'the central ideas of
the Cardinal's philosophy are so wild and incongruous that we can
only account for them as intellectual "faults"(in the geological sense),
abysmal fractures produced by a truly "seismic" act of the will',[1] but
what Harrison craved for was what John Henry Newman considered basically unprofitable—the meeting of brain with brain,
Christians, atheists, Positivists and 'agnostics' (the word was coined
by Huxley in 1870) all together. It was a craving which has little
appeal in the mid-twentieth century, but it was satisfied for a time
by the remarkable Metaphysical Society, set up in London in 1869,
which really did bring many of the great men of the age together to
discuss the central philosophical problems of the day.

For Huxley—and he should have the last word as a scientist—it
was just as necessary as it was for the orthodox Anglican theologians
that one side should win the debate between science and religion.
He had no doubt which side it would be. After a struggle of 'unknown duration', which would have as its 'side issues vast political
and social troubles', 'free thought' would conquer and organize
itself 'into one coherent system, embracing human life and the world
as one harmonious whole'. It would need generations, however, to
complete the task, and 'those who further it most will be those who
teach men to rest in no lie, and to rest in no verbal delusions'. In
the middle of the vast political and social troubles which followed
the end of the period of mid-Victorian equilibrium, Huxley's prophecy already began to date. The conflict between science and
religion petered out, giving way to new debates about the nature
not of the Universe but of society. At the same time, the verbal
delusions persisted, the mid-Victorian quest for 'ultimate truths'
was followed by a period of flirtation with every form of historical
and moral relativism, and, above all, the sheer indifference to the
issues raised by both Huxley and Wilberforce increased.

[1] *Realities and Ideals* (1908), p. 393.

IO

THE LEAP IN THE DARK

1. PRELUDE TO CHANGE

To return from the world of religion and science to the world of politics is to return to another area of conflict and contention. Between 1859 and 1865, despite the continued presence and personal popularity of Palmerston as prime minister, it was impossible to suppress all the forces which were leading up to large-scale changes. Indeed by 1865 Palmerston was regarded by radicals of all shades as the great obstacle to reform, and they were making preparations for the change in political mood and opportunities which they believed would follow his death. Particularly in the large cities, 'inflammable masses' were easily stirred up by 'demagogues' (to use conservative terminology) or (in radical terminology) 'the tribunals of the people' were boldly challenging 'the absolute and unquestioned sway' of an unrepresentative parliament. There was a revealing episode when Palmerston himself visited Bradford in 1864. At a workingmen's meeting before he arrived, it was decided to receive him in stony silence and to present him with an address stigmatizing him as 'the greatest obstruction to every means of Reform'. Although it was impossible to apply these tactics rigidly, Palmerston was left in no doubt that there was a substantial body of local opinion which agreed with the tone of the address.[1] It was clearly a relief for him to leave Bradford a fortnight later and to go to his home constituency at Tiverton where he was sure of a friendly welcome and a display of affection and respect. After all, he could console himself, he was in his eightieth year, and in the year when he was born the town of Bradford scarcely existed.

It is significant that in his Bradford speech Palmerston dwelt on the triumph of free trade, and in this aspect of national policy his

[1] H. C. Bell, *op. cit.*, vol. II, pp. 391–2.

ministry from 1859 to 1865 did much to round off the work of the previous decades. Gladstone as chancellor of the exchequer was determined to complete the work of Peel and to bring to an end 'the controversy about Protection, so long the leading cause of agitation in the country and of political disorganization in this House', while Cobden was allowed as a private person to go to Paris and prepare an Anglo-French commercial treaty. They were both successful. Cobden's strenuous efforts culminated in 1860 with the signing of a ten-year reciprocal 'most-favoured nation' treaty, the model of many subsequent agreements. The French agreed to remove all prohibitions and to reduce at various dates duties on coal, coke, iron, steel, tools, machinery and most British manufactured products, first to a maximum of 30 per cent and later of 24 per cent. The British promised in return not only a reduction in the duties on French brandy and wines but 'a sweep, summary, entire, and absolute of what are known as manufactured goods from the face of the British tariff'. Gladstone, who hailed Cobden as the 'great apostle of free trade', incorporated the terms of the treaty in his budget of 1860, when he removed the duties on 371 articles (including paper), reduced the duty on many more, and looked forward to the abolition of income tax. Only 48 articles remained subject to duties, and in all cases the duties were for revenue and not for protection. In his further budgets from 1861 to 1866, Gladstone reduced the income tax from 10*d*. in the £ to 4*d*., sharply cut duties on sugar, cheese, and tobacco, and abolished the tax on hops. He took pains to emphasize the effect of taxation not only on enjoyment but on employment, and he was happy to note that the prosperity of England mounted every year. The total value of imports rose from £179 million in 1859 to £295 million in 1866, while the value of exports rose from £155 million to £238 million. Gladstone believed that his fiscal policy 'set free the general course of trade', and Cobden looked still further into the future and anticipated the abolition of customs houses altogether. 'I shall not live to see this great reform realized', he commented, 'but I have no more doubt of its realization than I have of the triumph of truth over error in any other question in which the moral and material interests of mankind are involved.'[1]

The fiscal achievement of Gladstone and Cobden can be properly understood only against the general political background of the

[1] Quoted F. Hirst, *op. cit.*, p. 197.

early 1860s. The old suspicion of Palmerston, which they both shared, remained alive. Gladstone was at loggerheads with his prime minister not only on the question of the paper duties—Palmerston disliked his anxiety to press the issue in 1861—but on matters of defence expenditure and foreign policy. In 1861, the year after the commercial treaty had been signed, there was a further French invasion scare, one which followed on naturally from a scare of 1859, and all the accompanying 'torrent of prejudice, passion and hatred' which inevitably went with such panics.[1] During the critical months there were times when Gladstone was near to leaving the government, and he was bombarded throughout with good radical advice not only from Cobden but Bright. It was Bright, indeed, who directed his attention to the rôle Gladstone could best play in the future. 'The men whose minds are full of the traditions of the last century', he wrote to him in 1861, 'your *chief* and your *foreign minister*, will still cling to the past, and will seek to model the present upon it', but 'the past is well nigh really past, and a new policy and a wiser and a higher morality are sighed for by the best of the people, and there is a prevalent feeling that *you* are destined to guide that wise policy and to teach that higher morality.'[2]

In these critical years Gladstone was as conscious as Bright that he was poised between two generations. Not only were Palmerston and Russell old men, but other old friends were disappearing from the national stage. Aberdeen died in the winter of 1860, Sidney Herbert in the summer of 1861, and Graham in the autumn of that year. The final death of Protection itself marked the end of an era, and with his usual propensity to seize on one big issue at a time and to devote himself to it with all the strength at his command, Gladstone was now ready for a new bout of political activity. His move on this occasion was to be decisive both in his own history and in that of the country. With old personal and political friends dead he turned to the 'people'; with free trade secured, he took up the cause of parliamentary reform.

In 1864, a year when he was once more wrangling with his prime minister about the cost of national defence, he made his first famous public statement on reform in the House of Commons during the

[1] Also the poetry, or at least the verse. While Tupper (along with Smiles) was extolling the Volunteers, Tennyson as Poet Laureate was giving the order 'Form, form, Riflemen, form'.

[2] Quoted W. E. Williams, *The Rise of Gladstone to the Leadership of the Liberal Party* (1934), pp. 47–8.

debate on a motion of a private member, Edward Baines, the Leeds liberal-radical, to reduce the franchise qualification in the boroughs from £10 to £6. 'Every man', Gladstone 'ventured' to say, 'who is not presumably incapacitated by some consideration of personal unfitness or political danger, is morally entitled to come within the pale of the constitution.' It was scarcely a revolutionary pronouncement—Disraeli had talked in 1859 of opening avenues to the mechanic 'whose virtue, prudence, intelligence and frugality entitle him to enter the privileged pale of the constituent body of the country'[1]—but it was greeted as a profound revelation of the state of Gladstone's mind. He received many messages of congratulation and support from local liberal associations and from individual reformers. 'A controversy which might have involved lingering evil', F. W. Newman told him, 'shall (now) be worked out with a minimum of exasperation between the orders.'[2] Although Gladstone qualified his declaration in the best Gladstonian manner and emphasized that he did not recede from the protest he had previously made against 'sudden, or violent, or excessive, or intoxicating change', he had gone on record as a defender of the *moral* right of responsible working men to the vote. It was always a political danger signal when Gladstone used the word 'moral' in such a context. His further argument that responsible workingmen possessed the qualities most needed for the proper exercise of the vote—'self-command, self-control, respect for order, patience under suffering, confidence in the law and respect for superiors'—could never be forgotten. Though Baines's bill was rejected by 274 votes to 56, an impetus was immediately given to radical agitation outside Westminster.

Palmerston strongly challenged Gladstone's statement and remarked that it was more like the sort of speech Bright usually made than a responsible utterance from the Treasury Bench. 'I entirely deny', he exclaimed, 'that every sane and not disqualified man has a moral right to a vote.' Furthermore, 'the function of a government is to calm, rather than to excite Agitation'.[3] The Queen for once was as grieved as Palmerston at the 'strange, independent act' of a cabinet minister, while many of Gladstone's Oxford University constituents were appalled. His ·inevitable defeat in

---

[1] *Speeches on Parliamentary Reform* (ed. M. Corry, 1867), p. 192. A similar phrase was used even earlier by Stanley in 1853.
[2] Gladstone Papers, B.M., Add. MSS. 44,403, f. 29.
[3] Quoted P. Guedalla, *Gladstone and Palmerston* (1928), p. 281.

Oxford at the next election in July 1865 finally removed all his social and intellectual inhibitions about taking up the reform question. 'Keep him in Oxford and he is partially muzzled; but send him elsewhere and he will run wild',[1] Palmerston told Shaftesbury a few days before the election took place. It was a good prophecy. When immediately after his Oxford defeat Gladstone set out to contest a county seat in industrial South Lancashire, he began his campaign in the Manchester Free Trade Hall by declaring that he came to the North 'unmuzzled'.[2] From that time onwards he 'used the masses to provide himself with the response which his nature craved, but which he had ceased to find in the social world in which he moved'.[3] As early as October 1864, indeed, he noted in his *Diary* after a provincial tour, 'so ended in peace an exhausting, flattering, I hope not intoxicating circuit. God knows I have not courted them. I hope I do not rest on them. I pray I may turn them to account for good. It is, however, impossible not to love the people from whom such manifestations come, as meet us in every quarter.'

There was an element of paradox in Gladstone's discovery of the 'crowds' in 1864, for though his declaration on reform coincided with a renewed growth of popular agitation in the country and he was hailed enthusiastically as the new leader of a 'Great Party of the People',[4] he did not adduce popular clamour as a reason for speaking as he did. Rather, he claimed that he deprecated working-class 'agitation' and preferred the 'individual improvement' of members of the working classes to organized class pressure. It is significant that one day before he made his pronouncement he had received a deputation from the Amalgamated Society of Engineers, asking him to modify the rules of the Post Office Savings Bank so that the Society could place its funds in the safe keeping of the government. It was evidence of 'responsibility' of this kind which most impressed Gladstone. A year earlier he had been pleased with the reply of another trade-union deputation to his question about the 'alleged indifference' and 'apparent inaction of the working classes as to suffrage'. 'Since the abolition of the corn laws', he was told, 'we tried to spend our evenings in the improvement of our minds.'[5]

[1] Hodder, *op. cit.*, vol. III, p. 188.
[2] The word 'muzzled' was in the news. Derby had just referred to the necessity of 'muzzling' Roman Catholics by the oath of abjuration. He is said thereby to have lost several Conservative seats in Ireland.
[3] P. Magnus, *Gladstone* (1954), p. 165.
[4] *Newcastle Daily Chronicle*, 13 May 1864.
[5] Morley, *Life of Gladstone*, vol. I, p. 759.

A powerful feeling that silent changes were taking place in the minds of members of the working classes, not unlike movements of the earth's crust—Gladstone used the simile in a speech of 1866— led him to broaden his own mind. He was influenced too by working-class 'character' as well as 'intellect', particularly the 'noble heroic conduct of the Lancashire cotton operatives during the cotton famine'.[1] When the American Civil War cut off the sup- plies of cotton to Lancashire in 1861–4—80 per cent of Lancashire's cotton came from the Southern states—there was inevitable un- employment and distress in Lancashire. The refusal of the cotton workers to despair, to riot and to condemn the American North, which was imposing a blockade, made Gladstone feel that it was 'a shame and a scandal that bodies of men such as these should be excluded from the parliamentary franchise'.[2]

The American Civil War was an important link not only in the sequence of events leading to Gladstone's conversion to belief in parliamentary reform but in the history of popular radicalism. The revival of interest in reform from the doldrums of 1860 owed much to two external forces—the American War and the visit of Garibaldi to England in 1864. The detailed story of their consequences is far from easy to disentangle, for as during the previous fifteen years, there were serious differences of opinion within the radical move- ment, particularly between London and the provinces and between those who were prepared to follow the lead of Bright and those who looked upon him and his friends with suspicion. Not all the radicals who cheered Garibaldi were prepared to join in moral crusades with Bright, and Bright himself was worried rather than pleased with the tumultuous reception given to the Italian hero of democracy. Despite the differences, however, it is true to say that the two events taken together quickened the demand for a new upsurge in English politics, and that as the tides rose Bright was inevitably pushed more and more into national prominence.

To Bright and a considerable section of the articulate working classes, the only real issue of the American Civil War was freedom versus slavery, and when the North won, Bright could proudly claim that 'the great triumph of the Republic is the event of our age

---

[1] Quoted Williams, *op. cit.*, p. 105.
[2] For an interesting cotton worker's diary of this period, see *The Diary of John Ward of Clitheroe, Weaver, 1860–64* (ed. R. Sharpe Prance, Transactions of the Historic Society of Lancashire and Cheshire, 1953).

and future ages will confess it'.[1] His view was not shared by many of those radicals who disliked the Manchester School. Roebuck was an outspoken parliamentary supporter of the South, while journals like the *Beehive* and *Reynolds* began by denouncing the Northern blockade which would cause 'millions in England to starve'.[2] As the war continued, however, Lincoln was added to the gallery of radical heroes, there was radical praise of 'Anglo-Saxon democracy', English aristocratic supporters of the South were denounced, and most of the hesitations of the first months of the struggle were forgotten. Gladstone had talked of a new Southern 'nation'[3] and even Cobden (disliking northern protectionism as well as southern slavery) had wavered, but Bright was successful from the start in relating the American struggle to the English domestic struggle, and in drawing out of it *moral* lessons. The English sympathizers with the North, who were very strong in intellectual circles, were greatly impressed by the evidence of English working-class support of a great cause. Richard Hutton, the editor of the *Spectator*, was driven to claim (rather idealistically and on dubious evidence) that 'the working classes have a livelier sympathy with the popular feelings and the lives of other nations than the classes now most influential in politics',[4] and Bright himself switched his arguments in favour of further extension of the suffrage from complaints against the burden of taxation and the weight of aristocratic mis-management to the moral challenge of a restless people. 'The class which has hitherto ruled in this country has failed miserably. It revels in power and wealth, whilst at its feet . . . lies the multitude that it has neglected. If a class has failed, let us try the nation!'[5]

The second external stimulus—the visit of Garibaldi in April 1864—was in some ways of as great importance to English radicalism as the Civil War. Garibaldi was identified with romantic democracy, and the Europe with which his name was associated was not tainted with the 'materialism' of the Manchester School. A meeting addressed by him in the Crystal Palace attracted 20,000

[1] See J. G. Randall, 'Lincoln and John Bright' in *Lincoln, the Liberal Statesman* (1947).
[2] *Reynolds's Weekly Newspaper*, 29 September 1861.
[3] Gladstone later confessed that he had made a 'mistake of incredible grossness' in ever thinking that the North would *not* win and in stating his opinion so brashly. In 1872 he settled by arbitration the long-standing official Anglo-American dispute of the war, the claims for damage done to Northern interests by the British-built ship, the *Alabama*.
[4] *Essays on Reform* (1867).
[5] G. B. Smith, *The Life and Speeches of John Bright* (1886), vol. IV, p. 510.

people, and when his visit was cut short and his provincial engage-
ments were curtailed—his 'indiscreet' statements had led to pressure
behind the scenes—the London Working Men's Garibaldi Committee organized a protest demonstration which was broken up by
the police. It was as a result of this incident that a new political
organization, the Reform League, was set up in February 1865 to
press for an extension of the suffrage and a programme of radical
reform. At its inaugural meeting Hartwell, an ex-Chartist, presided,
and alongside trade unionists like Applegarth, Odger and George
Howell, its bricklayer secretary, there were midde-class sympathizers, including the president, Edmond Beales, a barrister, and
Samuel Morley. Ernest Jones was made a vice-president. The new
League was not well organized but, as events were to prove, it was
in the right place at the right time, and its greatest strength lay in its
power to mobilize at least intermittently the not unimpressive forces
of metropolitan organized labour.

Before the Reform League was formed, the Reform Union had
been established in the North of England. It grew out of a series of
provincial organizations, the Leeds Working Men's Parliamentary
Reform Committee taking the initiative in calling a reform conference of middle-class and working-class reformers in November
1861. George Wilson, the veteran organizer of the Anti-Corn Law
League and delegate of the Lancashire Reformers' Union, was in
the chair, and there were signs of the old division between the 'working classes' and the middle classes which had been so important in
Northern politics at least since the 1830s. The same divergences
were demonstrated at an unproductive London conference a year
later, but in March 1864, the year of Gladstone's pronouncement,
a third conference[1] held at Manchester set up the Reform Union.
It was potentially a powerful body, because like the Anti-Corn Law
League before it, it could draw on considerable middle-class
support. There was, indeed, a curious parallelism between the way
radicalism was shaping in the early 1860s and the way it had shaped
in late 1830s. The Reform League was in some respects in direct
line with Chartism[2]; the Reform Union, by contrast, was organized
in the same building where the Anti-Corn Law League had planned

---

[1] There was no conference in 1863 because of the cotton famine.
[2] A smaller London organization, The London Working Men's Association, was
founded in February 1866 with a Chartist name as well as a Chartist programme. It
was responsible for pushing the leaders of the Reform League into active dependence
on London trade unionism.

its campaign, and the Manchester Free Trade Hall was the centre of its biggest demonstrations. There were tensions between the two new bodies as there had been persistent antagonism between the two earlier movements in the earlier period.[1] But the parallelism can be pushed too far. Among the few wealthy backers of the Reform League was Thomas Thomasson who gave £210 of the £2,520 collected in donations, and there was even a token payment from Bright's brother.[2] From the start Bright emphasized the need for 'a combined and friendly movement', and circumstances were far more propitious for attempts at concerted action than they had been in 1841 and 1842. This time, after all, the extension of the franchise to working men was beginning to look like a pre-eminently practical proposition, and great national political figures, of whom Gladstone was the most prominent, were beginning to throw their influence behind it.

Two additional changes were needed to ensure the success of the new reform agitation—the death of Palmerston and a break in economic prosperity. 'It is most humiliating', a member of the Reform League's executive remarked in September 1865, 'that the Reform question depends for its solution upon one man—Lord Palmerston.' The comment was fair and accurate—Palmerston's government had just won the general election of July 1865 and had increased its majority. Although a considerable number of the gains were secured by radicals—John Stuart Mill, for example, was elected for Westminster—it still seemed certain that 'Palmerston's life was a security against the introduction of a measure of reform'. His death in October 1865 before the new Parliament met prepared the way for a new period of open politics. 'The truce of parties is over', wrote Disraeli who welcomed the change as much as Gladstone, 'I foresee tempestuous times, and great vicissitudes in public life.'[3]

The tempests were to blow around the issue of parliamentary reform, which could no longer be ignored. Already most of the future protagonists had taken up their positions. Russell, Palmerston's aged successor, who was anxious to promote a measure before

[1] Although the League executive passed several resolutions in favour of co-operation with the Union, it also found it necessary on one occasion to forbid its members to take any part in the efforts of the Union to establish branches in London (Minutes, 10 May 1867).
[2] The Ledger of the League along with its Minutes is in the Howell Collection at the Bishopsgate Library. The Minutes are used in the following account.
[3] Monypenny and Buckle, *op. cit.*, vol. II, p. 158.

he died, had been carrying a reform bill with him in his pocket ever since 1854. Bright had helped to stir the country and was ready for a new bout of sustained agitation in which both Reform League and Reform Union would have a part to play. On the day after Palmerston died, Howell wrote to Bright that no time should be lost 'by the Liberal Party in arranging their tactics and organizing their forces', adding as an appealing postscript, 'think not this haste indelicate, the Tories are already at work'.[1] Gladstone, rising in popular estimation every month, had moved dramatically from the world of packages to the world of men. Robert Lowe, the Liberal critic of reform, had already delivered his first great speech against a reform bill in May 1865 on a second reform motion proposed by Edward Baines. He was as gloomy about the future as Russell, Gladstone and Bright were hopeful. 'If they [the great Liberal party]' he said, 'unite their fortunes with the fortunes of Democracy . . . they will not miss one of two things—if they fail . . . they will ruin their party, and if they succeed, they will ruin their country.'[2]

Lowe was one of a small group of supporters of the Palmerstonian government who profoundly distrusted the arguments used to support reform. He was not a Whig, although he had some Whig support, and while he was member of Parliament for one of the surviving small pocket boroughs, Calne, not even his worst enemies could claim that his opposition to reform was based merely on a desire to protect that which was his own or his patron's. There was less self-interest in Lowe than in Bright. He attacked reform not as a member of an aristocratic coterie defending an old order but as an intellectual—strongly influenced by Bentham—who wished to retain government by the educated against government by the masses. He believed that the half-reformed Constitution, the product of the Reform Bill of 1832, provided good government—the best legislative chamber in the world and the most 'respectable' electorate. 'The seven Houses of Commons that have sat since the Reform Bill, have performed exploits unrivalled, not only during the six centuries during which Parliament has existed but in the whole history of representative assemblies.' The burden of proof that change was needed rested squarely on the reformers. It was not

---

[1] Reform League *Letter Book*, vol. 7, p. 21.
[2] R. Lowe, *Speeches and Letters on Reform* (1867), pp. 61–2. All the quotations from Lowe are taken from this book unless otherwise stated.

enough to talk of the necessity or the inevitability of reform. 'The end being good government, in which of course I include stable government, before I give my assent to the admission of fresh classes, I must be satisfied that this admission will make the government better or more stable.'

Applying this test, Lowe came to three conclusions. First, any further measure of reform would transfer power to the ignorant. He greatly alienated working-class leaders by emphasizing this point with all the wit and power at his command, claiming in a particularly bitter phrase that if you wanted 'venality, ignorance, drunkenness and facility for being intimidated, or . . .impulsive, unreflecting and violent people' you found them not at the 'top' but at the 'bottom'. In a reformed Parliament such classes would have power. He refused to correspond with an angry member of the Reform League on the fairness of this judgment, telling him abruptly that 'with such a body . . . I have no courtesies to interchange'. All the evidence of 'improvement' which Gladstone used as the source material for his conversion to belief in an extension of the franchise Lowe dismissed as irrelevant, using an argument reminiscent of Smiles, that in the golden age of mid-Victorian prosperity most skilled artisans who were worthy of the vote could buy it by saving a fraction of their incomes and becoming respectable £10 householders. The number of borough voters in England and Wales had increased from about 282,000 in 1833 to over 514,000 in 1866,[1] although this was still only one in eighteen of the urban population. The way to elevate the working classes was not to bring down the franchise 'to the level of those persons who have no sense of decency or morality' but to keep it as a 'privilege of citizenship'. At this point in his argument, Lowe drew on his own experiences as well as on logic. He had spent eight years in Australia between 1842 and 1850, and he believed that universal suffrage as practised in Victoria and New South Wales led to the franchise being so despised that people hardly cared to pick it up from out of the gutter. When a shilling registration fee was introduced, the number of voters fell by a half. 'A franchise which in the estimation of those who have it is literally not worth a shilling, cannot be an elevation of the working classes.'

Second, Lowe argued that a large measure of parliamentary

[1] See J. Lambert, 'Parliamentary Franchises, Past and Present', in the *Nineteenth Century*, December 1889.

reform would destroy real leadership in Parliament. 'If you form your House solely with a view to numbers . . . you will destroy the element out of which your statesmen must be made. You will lower the position of the executive government, and render it difficult, if not impossible, to carry on that happy union between the two powers which now exist.' In other words, Lowe preferred the mid-Victorian balance, which excluded a working-class share in power, to an open democracy, and drew not only on Australian experience as a guide to wisdom but on political developments in America. He had been alarmed on a visit to the United States in 1856 to observe a passenger on a railway train asking his fellow-passengers in turn which man they thought should be President. This was not the right way to secure effective political leadership or to develop 'pure' government. 'You may have Democracy at any time', Lowe exclaimed. 'Night and day the gate is open that leads to that bare and level plain, where every ant's nest is a mountain and every thistle is a forest tree.'

Third, Reform would lead to the canvassing and carrying out of policies which would undermine national unity and prosperity. The working classes were interested in the vote not in itself but as a means to an end, and were already looking beyond political democracy to 'socialism'. Free trade, 'the most precious jewel in the world', would be in jeopardy if they were to acquire real power, and along with it the whole economic basis of 'improvement'. The machinery of the State might be used to assist strikes—Lowe was very conscious of the 'dangers' of trade-union rule—or even to lead the country to an ill-considered 'democratic' war. 'Once give working men the votes, and the machinery is ready to launch these votes in one compact mass upon the institutions and property in this country.'

Lowe thrilled the House of Commons in 1865 and 1866 with his great anti-reform speeches, which were interspersed with Latin tags and handy anecdotes, but he knew that his prospects of holding back reform by masterly oratory were strictly limited. Many of the members of the House of the Commons shared his opinions and prejudices—that is why they cheered—but, being convinced of the 'inevitability' of reform, they refused to lose public credit by opposing it. In the last resort, indeed, large numbers of Conservatives were as willing to woo 'Demos' as Russell and Gladstone were. It is not surprising that Lowe regretted the death of Palmerston

with an intensity that was shared by scarcely any other figure in
the House of Commons. 'It appears to me', he said in 1866,
'that we have more and more reason every day we live to regret
the loss of Lord Palmerston. The remaining members of his
government would seem, by way of a mortuary contribution, to
have buried in his grave all their prudence, statesmanship and
moderation.'

The government which succeeded that of Palmerston was headed
by Russell, in his seventy-fifth year, and Gladstone took over the
leadership of the House of Commons. There was no haste in gathering Parliament together. Although the political situation in Europe
was confused, the period of mid-Victorian tranquillity in England
did not end with a bang. The House of Commons elected in July
1865 did not meet until February 1866, and when at last it was
called together, it was more concerned with British policy in
Jamaica than with franchise reform. On 12 March, however,
Gladstone introduced a very mild reform bill, more moderate than
Russell's bill of 1860. The county franchise was to be extended to
include tenants paying an annual rent of £14 or more, and the
borough franchise qualification was to be lowered from £10 to £7.
The right of voting was also to be conferred on men who had had
a deposit of at least £50 in a savings bank for two years.

This gentle measure, which was strongly supported by Bright but
disliked by many radicals who felt it did not go far enough,
immediately ran into the sharp opposition of Lowe and a substantial section of the Conservatives. In discussions with the
Conservative, Adderley, before the details of the bill were
announced, Lowe promised the support of a sufficiently large group
of Liberals to defeat the government if it brought forward any
measure on the subject. 'What sort of a measure do you mean?'
Adderley asked. 'Any bill that lowers the borough franchise by one
sixpence', replied Lowe. In such an intransigent mood he prepared
for the beginnings of the great debate that was to push England
towards a new form of government. He soon gathered round him
more than thirty disgruntled Liberals whom Bright christened the
'Adullamites'—a sullen cabal cowering in the darkness of a small
cave. They were strong enough nonetheless to keep the government's majority down to five votes on the second reading of the
bill (318–313) after Gladstone had stated a few days earlier at a mass
meeting in Liverpool that 'we have passed the Rubicon, we have

broken the bridge, and burned the boats behind us'. It was a phrase
which necessarily appealed more to radicals in the country than to
'independent' members of the House of Commons, and the narrow
parliamentary margin was a warning that the bill would face severe
difficulties at the committee stage. Indeed after the vote 'the official
lives of the Ministers who introduced it were not worth a quarter's
salary'.[1]

In an attempt to meet the arguments of the Conservatives and of
Whigs like Lord Grosvenor who had refused to consider changes
in franchise qualifications without considering changes in the
distribution of seats,[2] Gladstone and Russell introduced a Redistribution Bill in May. Again it was extremely moderate in tone. Small
boroughs were not abolished altogether but 'grouped' together in
larger constituencies: Woodstock, Wokingham and Abingdon, for
instance, were to become one constituency with two members. It
was a timid proposal and it nearly led to the government's downfall.
The Liberal member for Wells, one of the boroughs to be grouped,
withdrew a motion against the principle of 'grouping' just in time,
for it would have been supported by the Conservatives if not by the
whole of the Adullamites. There was no withdrawal, however, of a
further Adullamite motion of Lord Dunkellin to substitute a
narrower suffrage in the towns for that proposed by the government, and when it was carried against the government by eleven
votes (315–304) Russell resigned.

The Queen pressed him to stay, for she was more concerned
about the situation in Europe than in England. On the day that
Lord Dunkellin gave notice of his motion (12 June) diplomatic
relations between Prussia and Austria were severed, and Prussian
troops entered Saxony and Hanover. While England was wrestling
with the problems of liberal reform, Bismarck was taking the
penultimate step in his drive to secure German unity and to establish
German leadership on the Continent. Russell insisted on resignation,[3]
however, and Derby and Disraeli once more returned to power,
again as a minority government. Before they had completed the
formation of their ministry, the Austrians had been overwhelmingly

---

[1] H. Paul, *op. cit.*, p. 33.

[2] Since 1831 this had been a standard device of enemies of reform who did not wish
to incur the odium of openly killing it.

[3] 'There are things which can and cannot be done', Gladstone stated bluntly, 'to
acquiesce in a further limitation of the enfranchisement . . . would cover us with shame
and *would not settle the question.*' (*Letters of Queen Victoria*, second series, vol. I, p. 336.)
Only extreme radicals wanted a dissolution so soon after the previous election.

defeated at the battle of Sadowa (3 July). It was characteristic of the mood of English politics that Derby hastened to tell Parliament that his government had no intention of 'interfering vexatiously, or to volunteer unasked advice' in Europe. Instead, it was concentrating on what to do next on the question of political reform. Only one thing seemed definite as far as reform was concerned—that it would be as impossible for Lowe to coalesce with Disraeli as vinegar with oil.[1] Soon after the new government had taken over, Lowe was writing to his brother: 'I hold Bright and his mob in such sovereign contempt that I require no external support to fortify me against their abuse. What I am afraid of is your friends *the Tories*, and above all, Dizzy, who I verily believe, is concocting a very sweeping Bill.'[2]

2. DISRAELI AND THE LEAP

It was Disraeli indeed who carried the new Reform Bill which, after years of intermittent agitation and sustained but detached debate, granted the vote to the working classes of the towns. He carried the bill not as a doctrinaire radical, standing firm on basic principles, but as a 'flexible' conservative, willing to go even further than Bright if he could thereby remain in office and enjoy the delight of outbidding his Liberal opponents. His readiness to abandon all his original proposals and safeguards was a measure of his desire to take the credit of settling the reform question and of 'terminating the monopoly of Liberalism'. He was even prepared to take the risk of breaking up his own party if he could so disorganize his opponents that he could win votes from their side as well as his own. The confused situation in the House of Commons helped him, indeed it laid the foundations of his strategy. The Conservatives were in a minority. If all the opposition groups had voted against them they would have been defeated by about seventy votes. Disraeli managed to communicate his infectious exhilaration and enthusiasm to enough of his own supporters to minimize the risk of a large-scale party split. They began to enjoy as much as he did the outwitting of their opponents, and only a small minority led by a Cecil—Lord Cranborne—complained that as a result of unparalleled 'political betrayal' the monarchical principle was dead, the aristocratic principle doomed, and the democratic principle triumphant.

[1] G. P. Gooch (ed.) *Later Correspondence of Lord John Russell* (1925), vol. II, p. 344.
[2] Quoted A. P. Martin, *Life and Letters of Viscount Sherbrooke* (1893), vol. II, p. 309.

When Derby and Disraeli returned to power, it was Derby who took the lead in proposing a Conservative reform bill, but by January 1867 Disraeli (who earlier had been all for delay) had come to the conclusion that the right procedure for his party to follow was not to set up a procrastinating royal commission on the subject, but to introduce general resolutions on reform at once and quickly to proceed to a reform bill. In making his new assessment he was as strongly influenced by reports from the provinces as by first-hand evidence of the activities of the campaign of the Reform League in the capital.

It was at this point in the story that the economic background in 1866 and 1867 began directly to influence politics. In May 1866 the great London financial house of Overend and Gurney had crashed and after a disastrous 'Black Friday' (11 May) on the Stock Exchange, there were ripples of economic disorder in all parts of the country. For three months the bank rate rose to 10 per cent and there was widespread unemployment. In July 1866 there were riots and disturbances in London, one of the worst-hit cities, the railings of Hyde Park were torn down (23 July), and Life Guards had to be summoned to the assistance of the police. Spencer Walpole, the historian home secretary, burst into tears when a deputation from the Reform League protested against the closing of Hyde Park to political demonstrations. Winter brought no relief. The harvest had been ruined by heavy rains and meat prices were high as the result of an epidemic of rinderpest which had begun in 1865.[1] To add to the distress, cholera, the regular harbinger of political excitement, made another of its dramatic reappearances, and Fenian disturbances not only in Ireland but in England and across the Atlantic created additional alarm. The deteriorating social and economic situation favoured a sharp spasm of political radicalism, and 'the people' were showing as clearly as they could that the reform issue could be trifled with no longer . The *Hornby* v. *Close* decision,[2] which threatened trade-union organization, drew many skilled artisans who had previously shown little interest in politics, into the reform movement, and a coalition of extra-parliamentary forces seemed to be massing both in the metropolis and the provinces. The more

---

[1] Government compensation to farmers hard hit by rinderpest was strongly attacked by the opponents of the 'landed interest'. Mill attacked the aristocracy, and Bright said he fancied the disease was 'much carried by foxhounds'.

[2] See above, pp. 409–10.

active public opinion became, the more tempted was Disraeli to resort to a policy of parliamentary opportunism.

It was neither external pressure nor unlimited opportunism, however, which lay at the root of his and Derby's desire to introduce a reform bill. The issue had been toyed with for so many years that there now seemed to be a perfect opportunity of getting it out of the way and taking the credit for a settlement. Although some Conservatives did not share this view and held instead, as their ancestors had done, that a large-scale reform bill would destroy the influence of rank, property, and education by increasing the force of numbers, they were a minority among the leaders of the party, stronger in the House of Lords than in the House of Commons and unable during the debates of 1867 to form an effective Conservative Cave of Adullam. They were capable of causing difficulties in the early stages of Derby and Disraeli's reform plans, but their power dwindled as the parliamentary struggle went on and the views of other Conservatives became more prominent. Urban Conservatives, like Samuel Robert Graves, the member for Liverpool, a wealthy merchant and ship-owner and former mayor of the city, saw Disraeli early in 1867 and told him 'only one opinion out of doors: settlement of the question'. Men like Graves were a growing group within the party: 'Without conspicuous oratorical power [they had] raised themselves to the front rank by moderation, honesty [and] skill in business . . . [and they were] brightening up the books of the party and making it look tidy and respectable.'[1] Other Conservatives favoured a settlement for different reasons—'easy-going men' because they 'wanted quiet times and a safe seat', 'indifferent men' because they 'were bored to exasperation by the prolonged controversy', 'earnest-minded men' because they saw in the continuance of the issue 'a bar to all useful legislation'.[2] The most imaginative of them, particularly the two leaders, were fascinated by the thought of bold reform for its own sake. Derby, before succeeding to the earldom, had helped to draft the Reform Bill of 1832; he had stood out in Parliament at that time as the 'Prince Rupert of debate'; he had displayed great sympathy for the poor of the London slums; during the Lancashire cotton famine he had shown great solicitude for the Lancashire artisans, and in 1864 he had rubbed shoulders

---

[1] Sir H. Maxwell, *op. cit.*, vol. I, pp. 310–11.
[2] See Lady Gwendolen Cecil, *Life of Robert Marquis of Salisbury* (1921), vol. I, p. 252, and ch. IX, *passim*.

with Garibaldi. As an unruffled aristocrat, he cared little for ten-pound householders as such, and in 1867 he could describe the promotion of household suffrage as the best 'of all possible hares to start'. Disraeli likewise claimed a long interest in reform, and directly related it to his belief in a natural alliance between aristocracy and people. A volume of his speeches, which he prepared in January 1867 was specially designed as propaganda to demonstrate the facts of Disraeli's career as a reformer. It was 'a complete and consistent record', the editor, Disraeli's secretary Montagu Corry, noted, and it would enable the country to see 'with what justness it has been asserted that the Tory party are disqualified from dealing with the most difficult of modern questions, that of reform'.[1]

The Queen's speech in February 1867 forecast measures which 'without unduly disturbing the balance of political power, shall freely extend the electoral franchise'; it was followed up six days later by the government's introduction of general resolutions on the need for reform. The resolutions were extremely general. They included, for instance, as a first clause, 'the number of electors for counties and boroughs in England and Wales ought to be increased' and as the ninth clause the delightfully vague suggestion that 'it is expedient that provision be made for the better prevention of bribery and corruption at elections'. The generality was in fact deliberate, for the resolutions were designed not to illuminate but to conceal. Pious platitudes were all that a divided cabinet could agree upon. 'I think resolutions are only safe as long as they are general', wrote Cranborne. Behind the scenes there was a wide difference of opinion between those Conservatives who wanted at most a 'small' reform bill and those who wanted a comprehensive 'great plan' as Disraeli was beginning to conceive it.

A majority of members of the House of Commons as a whole wanted something more substantial than vapid generalization, and under combined pressure from Gladstone and Bright on the one hand and Lowe on the other, the resolutions were eventually withdrawn. Lowe was irritated that Derby, who had joined the Adullamites in defeating the moderate Liberal measure of reform, was now prepared to introduce a reform bill of his own. Bright believed that the government was anxious 'to murder the cause and the question

---

[1] *Parliamentary Reform* (1867), p. 6. An edition of Gladstone's speeches, *Speeches* and *Addresses delivered at the General Election of 1865*, took a different line. It bore as its motto: 'He will shape his old course in a country new.'

by a course contrary to parliamentary usage and odious in the sight of all honest men'. If Lowe and Bright had had their way they would each have thrown out the resolutions for opposite reasons.

While the opposition to the resolutions was taking shape, there was a struggle within the cabinet between the 'small bill' group and the 'comprehensives' about the form of the government's legislation. On Saturday, 23 February, agreement was reached on a big bill, only to be broken when Cranborne and his two cabinet allies, Carnarvon and General Peel (Sir Robert Peel's brother) after spending a miserable arithmetical Sunday trying to work out the effects of the measure, decided that it went too far and threatened resignation. Very hastily after a ten-minute cabinet meeting on the Monday it was decided instead to revert to the small bill. This was only the beginning of the crisis, for it soon became abundantly clear that the House of Commons showed no interest in the small bill and treated the resolutions with contempt. Although Derby and Disraeli knew that Cranborne, Peel, and Carnarvon would resign, they had to go back again to the comprehensive bill, which was introduced in the House of Commons on 18 March. There were prophecies of the imminent downfall of the government, but in the exercise in the politics of manœuvre which was about to begin the government was strengthened rather than weakened by its loss of three men of rigid principle. At a party meeting Derby warned members that there would be a dissolution unless the bill was passed, and they rallied to his support. It was not long before Cranborne, like Lowe, was commenting rather wearily that he wished the House of Commons had carried Gladstone's safe and conservative Reform Bill of 1866.

The bill introduced on 18 March, while designed to establish the House on 'a broadly popular basis', was far from being an experiment in democracy. Like the small bill of February, it included checks and counterpoises and suggested no extensive redistribution of seats. The franchise in the boroughs was to be based on personal rating; all householders paying their own rates and possessing a residential qualification of two years were to be given votes. Lodgers and those ratepayers who compounded their rates with their weekly rents were not to be given votes.[1] The county franchise was to be based on a voting qualification of fifteen pounds' rental. In addition, special

---

[1] There was a provision whereby compounders could get their names on the rate book, but Disraeli did not believe that many compounders would use it.

franchises were to be introduced for special groups as in the bill of
1859. Graduation from a university, fifty pounds in government
funds, the Bank of England, or a Savings Bank, and membership of
learned professions were all to confer the right of voting, as was the
payment of one pound a year in direct taxes (not licences, thereby
excluding Bright's ratcatcher with two dogs). Dual votes were to be
conferred on those individuals who possessed special as well as
property qualifications.

Disraeli claimed that 237,000 urban ratepayers would get the vote
for the first time, 100,000 would be drawn in on the basis of the
'fancy franchises', and 171,000 electors would be created in the
counties. The direct taxation franchise would also give about
200,000 members of the 'middle classes' a second vote. The final
result of the passing of the bill, he suggested, would be a new social
balance within the electorate which would ensure a fair and stable
settlement. No single class would be preponderant; representation
would rest with the nation. One-quarter of the voting power would
belong to the aristocracy, one-quarter to the working classes, and
the remaining half to the middle classes. Parliament would not
become a mere representative assembly based on the brute force of
number; it would continue to mirror social interests and to
guarantee the continuation of good government.

The nature of the ultimate settlement was very different from
that envisaged by Derby and Disraeli in March 1867. In the course
of the debates between March and July, the bill was completely
transformed. A series of amendments was carried which not only
swept away the original safeguards but shifted the whole balance of
political power in Britain.

The reason for the transformation was the confused political
condition of the House of Commons—the general feeling that unless
a bill was passed the House would be branded as an 'utterly incapable and incompetent assembly',[1] the lack of monolithic party ties,
the absence of disciplined voting, and the suspicion of leadership
among the opposition Liberals. Gladstone, who began by wishing
to oppose the bill from the start, was not trusted by most members
of his own party, and the second reading of the bill was carried
without a division. 'I can hardly speak a word in the Commons',
Gladstone complained, 'especially if it in any manner opposes or
reflects on Disraeli with any confidence that some man will not rise

[1] H. Cox, *A History of the Reform Bills of 1866 and 1867* (1868), p. 132.

on the Liberal side to protest against it.' Although he went on to say that 'the best course is to avoid all acts of leadership which can be dispensed with', he could not resist suggesting that his party should follow him in committee in supporting an Instruction which would have made possible the restriction of the urban franchise. He wished to exclude those ratepayers who were paying less than £5 a year in rates, while at the same time enfranchising every householder above this line whether he paid his rates personally or compounded them through his landlord. In putting forward this compromise, Gladstone satisfied neither Adullamites nor radicals, with the exception of Bright who fully shared his distrust of 'the dregs of the working classes', the 'residuum', 'a small class which it would be much better for themselves if they were not enfranchised, because they have no independence at all'. Forty or fifty Liberal Members of Parliament, meeting in the tea room of the House of Commons, decided to oppose Gladstone. They included a sprinkling of Adullamites, a radical group led by Henry Fawcett, and several Russell Whigs 'who cannot bear Gladstone as their leader'. Their motives were very mixed. The Adullamites were afraid of 'a coming democracy and Trades Union tyranny'; the radicals wished 'to get the largest measure of reform whether it should come from the hands of the Government or from the Opposition'. Disagreed though they were in their principles, the members of the 'tea room group' were successful in checking Gladstone at this early stage in the story of the bill. This was the first real breach in the defences of an opposition which had to remain united if it had any chance of success.

Having failed to carry the party with him, Gladstone proceeded to act on his own. He gave notice of a series of amendments, the first of which he moved on 11 April. It proposed to admit the compound householder as well as the personal ratepayer to the franchise. Since it was known that Gladstone was proposing this amendment in conjunction with others which would exclude all ratepayers whose premises were rated below £5, he lost much Liberal support and actually gained the support of some Conservatives. The private preferences of members of Parliament were extremely difficult to sort out at this stage, for they were not only thinking about how they wanted to vote on the particular amendment before them but of the effects of the amendment on other votes in the future. Disraeli was in a strong position to exploit the division to the utmost. In a speech which he himself described as 'marvellous and memorable', he broke through the ranks of his enemies; 7 Conservatives voted with Gladstone, but 25 Adullamites, 12 radicals and 8 other members of the 'tea room group' voted with Disraeli, and nearly 20 other Liberals abstained. The government thus won its first crucial test by 310 votes to 289, and the House immediately adjourned for the Easter recess. There was talk in the lobbies that Disraeli was in such a powerful position that he 'would hold Gladstone down for twenty years'.[1]

It now seemed certain, as Disraeli put it, that reform could be carried 'in a canter'. 'There are no doubt breakers ahead', he wrote, 'but I feel great hope of our overcoming them, and of realizing the dream of my life, and re-establishing Toryism on a national foundation.'[2] After the recess, however, it was the radicals who took charge of the situation. They were fortified by nation-wide meetings urging the removals of all restrictions on household suffrage and the introduction of a franchise for lodgers, and in an atmosphere of mounting excitement they were able to carry amendment after amendment against the original proposals of the government. During the process of revision the Reform Bill took on an entirely new shape.

The first amendment, proposed by the radical member for Tower Hamlets, reduced the period of residential qualification for voters from two years to one. Disraeli opposed the amendment, but was beaten by eighty-one votes. The following night he announced that the government had decided to accept the change.

The second amendment, proposed by the radical member for Finsbury, W. T. M. Torrens, the biographer of Lord Melbourne and Sir James Graham, extended the borough franchise to lodgers who had occupied rooms for the whole of the preceding twelve months. The amendment was not put to the vote, for Disraeli at once accepted it. At this stage it became clear that he did not much care what amendments were passed so long as a bill of some kind was carried while a Conservative government was in power.

The third amendment was by far the most important. A Newark solicitor, G. Hodgkinson, proposed an amendment which abolished the distinction between compound householders and personal ratepayers. The technical issue of compounding had already been

---

[1] A. R. Ashwell, *Life of the Rt. Rev. Samuel Wilberforce* (1883), vol. III, p. 227.
[2] Quoted Monypenny and Buckle, *op. cit.*, vol. II, p. 262.

before the House on many occasions and was being talked about incessantly behind the scenes. Liberals disliked making the distinction between compounders and personal ratepayers into a test of fitness for political power, but they were so divided about what other test should take its place that Hodgkinson estimated that the majority against him would be about a hundred. He knew too that Conservatives would be unhappy about extending the electorate on the scale that his amendment entailed. There were nearly half a million compounders in England and Wales, comprising nearly 35 per cent of the total number of householders, although the percentage varied enormously from place to place. Brighton, for instance, had so many compounders that it would have had only fourteen new constituents if Disraeli's original proposals had been carried; Sheffield by contrast would have had almost complete household suffrage.[1] To the astonishment of Hodgkinson and particularly of Gladstone, Disraeli at once accepted the amendment, which was carried in a small House without a division. He had not made the relevant mathematical calculations—he consulted Lambert, the government's statistician after the debate—or taken the opinion of the cabinet, but he was anxious to 'extinguish Gladstone & Co.' and get rid of the most complicated reform issue once and for all while the going was easy. As it was, 'the compound householder ceased from a parliamentary point of view to exist, and a silence, only to be broken by the historian fell upon the burning question of lobby gossip'.[2] Lowe was left to ask indignantly what afterwards remained 'to save the Constitution from the hands of a multitude struggling with want and discontent'.

Hodgkinson became 'immortal', as Argyll put it, as a result of his success. His amendment virtually established complete and unlimited household suffrage as the foundation of the borough franchise in England and Wales. It only remained for Disraeli quietly and unostentatiously to drop the fancy franchises which provided a link with his earlier attempts at reform. Fawcett lamented the demise of the educational test, for he believed that education would make everyone a good liberal, but the property franchise and dual vote

[1] See H. Cox, *op. cit.*, ch. XII. Cox believed that the effect of differences in local compounding arrangements, based on whether or not parishes had accepted the Small Tenements Act of 1850, was quite capricious, and Disraeli's suggestion that there would be great variety in a franchise based on a personal rate-paying test was an after-thought.

[2] H. Paul, *op. cit.*, vol. III, p. 85.

went with few regrets. Various philosophical radical suggestions proposed by John Stuart Mill—including a proposal that electors should be allowed to vote for 'Members of Parliament in general' if they did not like their own candidates, and an amendment in favour of women's suffrage—were defeated without any difficulty. As it was, the bill in its new form went further than any bill which Bright had ever sought to introduce.

But there was more to come. The conditions of the franchise had been completely altered; so too were the clauses relating to the distribution of seats. In the past the Conservatives had always held firm on this question and had refused to increase the representation of the cities and large populous districts in the House of Commons. Notions of balance were cast on one side, however, in May and June 1867. An opposition member proposed a more drastic scheme of redistribution than the government had brought forward, and despite the opposition of Disraeli the amendment was carried by the large majority of 127 votes, 72 Conservatives voting against the government. The process of educating the Conservative party in the political facts of life—Disraeli's avowed purpose—had clearly gone a very long way. Although radical amendments to disfranchise all boroughs with a population of less than 5,000 were defeated—with Liberal help—and a new clause providing a third member for large cities was lost by eight votes, Disraeli made a backstairs compromise by offering third members to Liverpool, Manchester, Birmingham and Leeds. It was this 'unsavoury surrender' which bestirred General Peel to comment that the proceedings on the bill had taught him three things—that nothing had so little vitality as 'a vital point'; that nothing was so insecure as a 'security'; and that nothing was so 'elastic' as the conscience of a cabinet minister. Considering what Disraeli had said about General Peel's brother in 1846, it was an appropriate comment.

The bill as it finally emerged from the Commons in July was thus different at almost every point from the bill as it was first introduced.[1] It was far more 'democratic' than Disraeli, or indeed most of his opponents, had ever intended. Yet for Disraeli himself its passing was a parliamentary triumph of the highest order. A minority government had smashed the opposition and had carried its reform

---

[1] Of the sixty-one sections of the final Act, Cox complained that only four, including the title, were the work of the Conservative government. Eighteen had been taken direct from Gladstone's 1866 bill, and twenty-one of the rest were either omitted or altered. *Whig and Tory Administrations during the last Thirteen Years* (1868), pp. 51-2.

bill against all the expectations of its enemies; the greatest joy of the victory was the consciousness of an enemy outwitted and out-manoeuvred. 'It was not his bill (as it finally passed) but it had passed, and he, not his adversaries, sat on the Treasury Bench. "Sing, riding's a joy! For me, I ride".'[1]

In the House of Lords Derby steered the bill successfully in much the same way that Wellington had steered the repeal of the corn laws. There were many people including the Queen who hoped that amendments would be carried in the Lords to 'avert the dangers which many people apprehend from the great increase of democratic power',[2] and Lord Grey, the son of Grey of the Reform Bill, was among its many distinguished Whig critics. Derby made a powerful plea for unity, however, calling a meeting of Conservative peers at his London house where he told them not only that the bill was the most conservative measure that could be adopted and had the almost unanimous support of the House of Commons, but that his object throughout the whole of the session had been 'to act so as to place the Tory party permanently in power and not to place them in a position to be beaten as soon as they had served the purpose of the opposition'.[3] In other words, he wanted to break the deadlock of the previous twenty years. His views carried great weight and the bill went through the Lords with few important changes. The most conservative amendment was one proposed by Lord Cairns, a member of his own party. It proposed that in the new three-member city constituencies, the voter was to be given only two votes, thereby, it was hoped, aiding the minority party in securing one of the seats. In practice it had a different result from that which was intended, encouraging strong party organization in the big constituencies, particularly in Birmingham.[4]

In August 1867 the bill was read for the third time, and after Russell had recalled how Derby had once lost his seat to Orator Hunt,[5] the prime minister went on to make his well-known and frank appraisal of the measure. 'No doubt', he said, 'we are making a great experiment and "taking a leap in the dark", but I have the greatest confidence in the sound sense of my fellow-countrymen, and

---

[1] *Ibid.*
[2] *Letters, Second Series*, vol. I, pp. 434–5.
[3] See W. D. Jones, *op. cit.*, p. 317.
[4] See F. H. Herrick, 'The Origins of the National Liberal Federation', *J.M.H.* (1945).
[5] It was a fair tit for tat. In 1866 Disraeli had reminded Gladstone that Gladstone opposed the Reform Bill of 1832.

I entertain a strong hope that the extended franchise which we are now conferring upon them will be the means of placing the institutions of this country on a firmer basis, and that the passing of the measure will tend to increase the loyalty and contentment of a great portion of her Majesty's subjects.'

3. THE DARK: UNSOLVED QUESTIONS

Derby's frank admission that he had made an experiment and taken a leap in the dark is the terminal point of this book. The period from 1784 to 1867 ends therefore not with a full stop but with a question mark. What would the new England be like when the urban artisan had the vote and 'numbers' for the first time counted for more in the Constitution than property or intelligence? 'What an unknown world we are to enter', wrote Gathorne Hardy, one of Disraeli's main lieutenants in passing the bill, 'if the gentry will take their part they will be adopted as leaders. If we are left to demagogues, God help us!'[1]

The fact that we know what happened after 1867—that there was no sudden change in politics, that the 'age of improvement' did not suddenly end, that the working classes did not immediately come into their own, that the gentry still remained influential, that the middle classes continued to prosper, that there were a few more years of brilliant prosperity before new economic tendencies asserted themselves and social conflicts gained in intensity, should not divert our attention from the doubts and dilemmas of 1867 itself.[2] Contemporaries were sure that they stood at the beginning of a new era. In a telling simile Bagehot compared 'political country' to an American forest; 'You have only to cut down the old trees, and immediately new ones come up to replace them; the seeds were waiting in the ground, and they began to grow as soon as the withdrawal of the old ones brought in light and air.'[3] Bagehot was the intelligent voice of the middle years of the century; an older voice, that of Carlyle, gloomily recalled the worst years of the 1840s. He could see no hope for the future. 'Perhaps the sooner such a mass of hypocrisies, universal mismanagements, and brutal platitudes and infidelities comes to an end, if not in some improvement then in

---

[1] A. E. Gathorne Hardy (ed.), *Gathorne Hardy, A Memoir* (1910), vol. I, p. 212.
[2] For a quick early twentieth-century answer to the questions of 1867, see J. Bryce, *Studies in Contemporary Biography* (1911 ed.), pp. 306–10.
[3] Introduction to the second edition of *The English Constitution* (1872).

death and *finis*, may it not be the better?'[1] It was a grim question to close what in this book has been described as the age of improvement. How far was it representative?

England in 1867 was divided not so much between Liberals and Conservatives as between optimists and pessimists. Lowe, Shaftesbury, Cranborne and Carlyle from their very different standpoints feared the worst. The new Constitution would 'give mere numbers a power they ought not to have' and would destroy the traditional rôle of Parliament as a 'mirror of interests', expressing 'everything which gives weight and importance in the world without'. The extension of the suffrage would open the gates to dangerous forces which had previously been kept under control. The working classes would want to set up shop for themselves, and in seeking to create a 'poor man's paradise', they would not only turn to demogogues and wirepullers but would make good government impossible. The wide gift of the elective franchise would be a calamity to those who gained it as much as to those who had lost their exclusive power. The leap in the dark would be the first of a series of leaps, each more risky and frightening than the one before. 'The appetite for change can never be glutted', said Cranborne; neither Disraeli nor Gladstone, nor for that matter Bright, could appease it. 'When Mr. Bright is preaching moderation and caution, Mr. Beales (of the Reform League) will be just girding himself for the battle; and doubtless Mr. Beales already numbers among his lieutenants politicians who look upon him as absurdly behind the age. The Girondist always has a Jacobin behind him ready to trip him up.'[2] It was an old warning which recalled the panic of the 1790s, but there were new ones too. What could be worse than an English imitation not of French but of American democracy, with the tyranny of the majority, the manipulation of the caucus, and the rule of the least able? There could be no hope for the future when 'the old tree of English liberty which has been the slow growth of ages and the admiration of nations should be transformed into the brazen image of ignorance and intolerance which the worshippers of Trans-Atlantic equality wanted to set up'.[3] England did not even

---

[1] *Shooting Niagara* (1867). In his installation speech as Lord Rector of Edinburgh University a year earlier Carlyle had claimed that his country was 'all going to wind and tongue' and that it was in an 'epoch of anarchy—anarchy plus the constable'.

[2] Quoted Lady Gwendolen Cecil, *op. cit.*, vol. I, p. 283.

[3] Edward Horsman, a close colleague of Lowe, used this phrase in a debate in 1866. *Hansard.* 3rd series, CLXXXII, 98 f.

enjoy the two social conditions which made American political adjustment possible—a plentiful supply of land and the absence of powerful neighbours. In America land acted as a 'sedative' to political passion: in England it was an irritant.[1] In America there was no reason to fear the pressure of neighbouring despotisms; in Europe they were growing in political power and economic strength every year.[2]

An additional note of alarm was added to this formidable catalogue of anxieties by the fact that it was a Conservative and not a Liberal government which had made the leap in the dark. 'The Earl of Derby "hopes that all will turn out well"', a moderate Whig reformer, who supported the bill of 1866, remarked. 'Adventurous gamesters are always hoping for luck; that the right card will be dealt, the right number turn up on the dice, the right horse win. But hitherto it has not been considered good statesmanship to commit the destinies of our empire unreservedly to Fortune. We have been content to advance from precedent to precedent, to pass from the known to the unknown by slow and heedful steps. The policy of political "leaps" remained to be invented by a government which called itself Conservative.'[3] In other words, a period of sustained economic growth and of measured discussion of politics and society had ended in a desperate gamble.

The optimists chose very different grounds on which to base their faith in the future. Some of them believed that history was with them; as Gladstone put it to his opponents in 1866, 'the great social forces which move onward in their might and majesty . . . are marshalled on our side'. It was a vague but powerful conviction, and in some cases it was backed by strong feelings about the innate honesty and judgement of the working classes. Why fear the masses of the people? They were just as entitled to the vote as any other people. 'The real danger to England', Bryce declared, 'is not from the working class . . . but from the isolation of classes . . . and the alarming increase in the political, and still more in the social, power of wealth.'[4]

[1] This was not only Lowe's view but the argument of many pamphleteers. See, for example, *Reform* (London, 1867).

[2] The American example was held up by the Manchester School, and in one of his last speeches (at Rochdale) Cobden had urged that some rich man should 'endow a professor's chair at Oxford and Cambridge to instruct the undergraduates in American history'.

[3] H. Cox, *op. cit.*, pp. 278–9.

[4] 'The Historical Aspect of Democracy' in *Essays on Reform*, p. 277.

It is important to note that this new faith was as shot through by doubt as the old religious faith which was being challenged by the scientists. Richard Hutton, who believed that trade unions were models of class patriotism and that the spirit of working-class solidarity and service they inculcated would work wonders if it were turned to national account, none the less held at the same time that artisans were less thrifty than the middle classes, less disposed to be guided by those who were their superior in culture, less cautious in their political instincts, and less dominated by 'wholesome dread of a strong central power'.[1] The *Edinburgh Review* objected to the universal juxtaposition of the adjective 'intelligent' and the name 'artisan', and pleaded that if the working man was to be king, the public was at least entitled to ask that he should exercise his power like a constitutional monarch.[2] Many other supporters of reform were far less happy about the trade unions than Hutton was. They believed that they taught the working classes to know the secret of their own power and that they would not stop at the defence of the claims of skilled labour. Lowe was naturally even more apprehensive. As a rigidly orthodox political economist as well as an opponent of reform, he regarded trade unions as the cumbrous weapons of persons 'as ignorant of their own true interest as they are careless of the feelings and reckless of the interests of others'. John Stuart Mill too, for all his receptivity to the attractions of socialism,[3] was increasingly afraid of the tyranny of majorities, and, in particular, of a 'governing majority of manual labourers' limiting competition in the labour market, taxing or restricting machinery, and protecting the home producer against foreign industry. Even Bright feared rather than welcomed the enfranchisement of a dependent class, and was careful after 1867 not to identify his arguments with those of democracy. Disraeli was very careful to state in carrying his bill that democracy was a form of government with which he and his party had no sympathy.

For the most part the optimists found it easier to challenge the arguments of their opponents than to express a highly reasoned case

---

[1] *Ibid.*, R. H. Hutton, 'The Political Character of the Working Class'. He also believed that 'the artisans would never be well informed on small political questions and they will therefore look to large ones'.

[2] Vol. CXXVIII (1868), p. 490.

[3] He planned a book on socialism in 1869 fragments of which were subsequently pieced together by Helen Taylor in the *Fortnightly Review* (1879). Long before that, of course, he had been influenced by the St. Simonians and to a debatable extent by his wife. See H. O. Pappe, 'The Mills and Harriet Taylor', in *Political Science* (1956).

of their own. They disputed the view of Conservative theorists like Cairns that Parliament was a 'mirror of interests'. According to the young Dicey, who wrote an extremely stimulating essay in 1867 on 'the balance of classes', it was idle to hope to satisfy the demand for reform by praising 'a Parliament, the object of which is permanently to embody distinctions which Reformers desire to extinguish'. In particular, the optimists argued, 'to give to landowners and capitalists representation according to their influence is to perpetuate and, as it were, to stereotype that interest'.[1] They went on to challenge the view that the working classes as a whole would act as a solid *bloc* in the new politics of the post-1867 world. The working classes were themselves divided, as divided as the middle classes had been in 1832. They were not a homogeneous pressure group, and the one thing that would make them into such a group would be not the granting of reform but the withholding of it. In a world where reform was vetoed by the 'superior classes', working-class power would grow in the dark instead of in the sunlight. It might then become genuinely dangerous. Furthermore, as things were, large numbers of the working classes were in no sense levellers. They looked up to their betters as to 'a sort of divine Olympus, beautiful, sacred, above all things *intelligible*, just near enough to be perhaps not quite unattainable by their children, just far enough to lend enchantment to the view'. So long as social attitudes of this kind persisted, changes in the Constitution would not produce the disastrous consequences their opponents suggested. Finally, the critics of pessimism argued, the American (or Australian) parallel was quite misleading. In new countries all the units of society started on a dead level 'like drops of quicksilver on a mahogany table'. Democracy was not the consequence of constitutional or political arrangements, but the cause of them. To add to the difficulties of achieving good government in new countries, society remained in the melting pot. New immigrants, pouring into New York, swelled the population of the cities; further West, a moving frontier kept people unsettled and ill-organized. 'The conservative and organizing forces of local attachment, personal and family influence, do not yet act as they do here. For the same reason, the power of party organizations is disproportionately strong; there is nothing to withstand them.'[2]

---

[1] *Essays on Reform*, p. 77.
[2] Goldwin Smith, 'The Experiences of the American Commonwealth' in *Essays on Reform*. See also his *Reminiscences* (1910), p. 221.

It was the 'forces of attachment' in England which most made for optimism in 1867, particularly for the optimism of Derby and Disraeli. Both leaders professed 'the greatest confidence in the sound sense' of their fellow-countrymen. By that they meant something rather more than that they believed large numbers of working men would vote Conservative at election times. They were expressing much the same sort of confidence in the working classes that the Whigs had expressed in the middle classes in 1832. Artisans, like shopkeepers, could be hitched to the Constitution. They were not for the most part dangerous or revolutionary; they fitted into the social system rather than aimed at its destruction. Giving them the vote, the full badge of citizenship, would be 'the means of placing the institutions of the country on a firmer basis'.

If Gladstone's appeal to 'history' by no means satisfied the Liberals and was qualified even by radicals, Disraeli's appeal to 'good order' did not satisfy all the Conservatives. His critics concentrated, as Lowe had done, on the facts of the class struggle rather than on theories of interdependence, and condemned Disraeli's 'thimble-rigging'. 'In the social pyramid', wrote the *Quarterly Review*, 'the possession of the suffrage will unquestionably give to the poorer millions the power of plundering the wealthier thousands.' It was a groundless commonplace to say that 'the working classes had shown themselves worthy of confidence'. What sane man had ever taken the bars out of his windows and dismissed the police because of the general amiability of the neighbourhood?[1] These arguments were advanced with vigour after the defeat of the Conservatives at the first general election under the new Constitution in 1868 when, as John Stuart Mill put it, in reply to Mr. Disraeli's statement to the working classes that he had given them the franchise, they replied, 'thank you, Mr. Gladstone'. Though there were signs of Conservative wooing of the working classes in the big cities—in Birmingham, for instance, where while the Liberals were proclaiming that 'a man that is born a Tory hath but a short time to live and is full of humbug' and were printing the words 'no resurrection' at the bottom of mock funeral cards, the Conservatives were appealing deliberately to trade unionists [2]—

[1] Vol. CVIII (1860), p. 282.
[2] The Conservative candidate declared himself in favour of 'the fullest legal recognition' of trade unions, 'believing that if the law protects the Unions, the Unions will protect the law'. He also called the dwellings of the poor 'a disgrace to our civilization', and asked for legislation to 'improve the houses of the labouring classes and the

there were equally frequent signs of Conservative distrust of the policy proclaimed in the Reform Bill. 'This general election has been the Conservative Party's Sadowa', one Conservative put it, 'with this difference that we ourselves made the needle guns, and handed them over to our adversaries to destroy us with.' [1] 'The phantom of a Conservative democracy was a reality to many men of undoubted independence and vigour of mind', wrote the *Quarterly*, but 'the late elections and the vast revolution which these elections have sanctioned, have dispelled all delusion on that head.' [2] It was not until the elections went the other way in 1874 and Disraeli secured a majority that it was claimed without any reservation that 'the sincerity of the English people in their profession of attachment to their own institutions has been established beyond all question. The people are not shifting about for systems . . . they will not trifle with the institutions which have grown with their national life.' [3]

Disraeli cared less about the verdict of the reviews in 1867 than he did about his own intuitions. He compared the *Edinburgh* and the *Quarterly* to two first-class rival coaching inns which did a roaring trade until the railway came along; then, they found things altered. They did not understand the new age and instead of competing vigorously as they had before, they suddenly came together. 'The boots of the "Blue Boar" and the chambermaid of the "Red Lion" embrace, and are quite in accord in this—in denouncing the infamy of railroads.' It was not the least telling of the many railway metaphors which adorned mid-Victorian argument, and it was supplemented by a characteristic paean to Conservative improvement. 'In a progressive country change is constant; and the great question is, not whether you should resist change which is inevitable, but whether that change should be carried out in deference to the manners, the customs, the laws, the traditions of the people, or in deference to abstract principles and arbitrary and general doctrines.' [4]

workshops in which they toil'. He was exceptional, however. Many Conservative election pamphlets continued to slander the Catholics and to put religion in the centre of the picture. See *England in the Nineteenth Century* (1868); 'Irish Papists are bringing every power and every influence to bear against the Church and the Constitution of the United Kingdom.'

[1] W. Dasent, *Life of J. T. Delane* (1908), vol. II, p. 228.
[2] Vol. CXXVII (1869), p. 541.
[3] *Ibid.*, vol. CXXXVI (1874), p. 586.
[4] Monypenny and Buckle, *op. cit.*, vol. II, p. 291.

Such a defence of change necessarily implied that the constitutional reform of 1867 would be followed up by other reforms. Already Disraeli had his own agenda—social reform to knit the community even more closely together. If he was not specific at this time about what he wanted to do—he never had been—he certainly had the necessary background and imagination to work out a programme when the occasion arrived. The Liberals too had their agenda—new legislation to protect individual rights and to remove the remaining Nonconformist grievances, the demand for a national system of education (on the form of this they were and remained divided), and, above all, at least in Gladstone's mind, a settlement of the Irish question.[1] Disraeli's agenda was not placed on the cabinet table until 1874; Gladstone's was not only to inspire the legislation of the five years after 1868 but to influence the whole course of English politics until after the end of the century. He believed that all its main items were necessary corollaries of the extension of the suffrage, and in relation to one at least—education— Lowe joined with him in recognizing the urgent need for action. As Vice-President of the Council from 1859–64, Lowe had introduced a 'Revised Code' in education, based on payment by results in the schools and an attack on all educational 'luxuries'. He believed in an elementary educational system which would not 'raise children above their station and business in life, . . . but fit them for that business'. After 1867 he was convinced that for political as well as economic reasons elementary education was necessary. 'To compel our future masters to learn their letters' was a task which had become not merely desirable but essential.

What were 'our future masters' really like in 1867? In all the contemporary discussion about past, present and future which has been reported so far, the working classes were more talked about than talkers. What did they themselves say about the shape of things to come? They did not write sophisticated essays on reform or discuss the new world round a dinner table, but the better-off and more articulate sections had their own newspapers, their own clubs where ideas were exchanged and criticized, and their own agenda. They were zealous in their advocacy of trade-union claims and they wished above all else to see the legal position of the

[1] In March 1865 Gladstone had already conceded that the Irish Church Establishment was unsatisfactory and 'ministered to the wants of only one-eighth or one-ninth part of the community'.

trade unions changed to their advantage; some of them wanted
legislative action to shorten the working day and to extend the
factory acts; at least a minority of them looked to the total abolition
of pauperism and unemployment. Beales stated frankly that his aim
was 'that of promoting as much as possible the political power,
and by that power, the physical welfare of the people. Reform of
representation is only the means to our end, the end being the
material welfare of the great masses of the community'.[1] With such
a philosophy they were not frightened of American parallels or
concerned about the ultimate complexities of the American social
situation. 'Our American brethren', wrote the *Beehive*, 'have a more
correct knowledge of the duties belonging to them as men; a higher
estimate of the dignity and rights of labour; arising possibly from
the fact that they are treated as free men and citizens in their native
land, and not as serfs.' [2]

For all the power of this language, however, 'our future masters'
were by no means ready to take up a full political rôle in 1867. For
many years to come most of their leaders clamoured and agitated
as a pressure group within the English Liberal party rather than as
an independent force,[3] and many of the rank and file were like the
workers of the previous fifty years, indifferent to large-scale agitation
except in moments of distress or exceptional opportunity. They were
bound to admit too, that they were divided amongst themselves. In
a frank and lucid analysis Thomas Wright, the 'Journeyman Engineer', who won the praise of Matthew Arnold, spoke of a fixed
gulf between the artisan and the unskilled, of the contempt educated
working men often felt for the illiterate, of the lack of interest
superior artisans showed in 'levelling ideas' about the 'redistribution
of property'.[4]

Although Wright believed that education would make for
working-class unity and would permit labour to exploit its full

[1] *Morning Star*, 3 August 1868. Quoted F. E. Gillespie, *op. cit.*, p. 282.

[2] 13 January 1866.

[3] For a working-class programme, which specifically rejected the view that working-
class members of parliament should be 'class' representatives, see the *Beehive*, 16
November 1867. It listed the objectives of the working classes as political and social.
The former included the ballot and the return of working men to Parliament; the latter
included national, unsectarian education, legal protection for trade union funds, and
measures to improve housing and workshop conditions.

[4] *Our New Masters* (1873), *passim*. See also his *Some Habits and Customs of the Working
Classes* (1867). In its review of this book Dickens's *All the Year Round* (8 June 1867)
commented: 'Meanwhile, the working man remains a study—in some respects, too, a
problem—in great part a difficulty—in much a contradiction—but, on the whole, a
national hope and a national pride.'

political power, his admirer Arnold was already warning against the dangers of the future. 'Plenty of people will try to give the masses, as they call them', he said, 'an intellectual food prepared and adapted in the way they think proper.' [1] It was a more prescient warning to the 'new masters' at the end of one long chapter of the 'age of improvement' than most of the warnings about them. In new circumstances around the corner, the working classes were to win many triumphs, but they were no more able to create an England which they could completely control than the middle classes in 1832.

The exciting perspectives of 1867 made all things dramatic, every clause a landmark; in the middle of the twentieth century, the perspectives seem distorted, and the landmarks less prominent. Continuities count for more than contrasts. Not all the trees in the American forest were cut down. They still grow nearly a hundred years later, and though there is new light and air, much brushwood and old leaves still remain. In the meantime, the world outside England has changed more than England itself, and to catch a glimpse both of Victorian light and darkness concerning the problem of England's future place in the world, there is no better brief quotation than a note from Benjamin Jowett to Lady Amberley in 1866. 'I sometimes fear that with all our great wealth and commerce we are only an orange going to be sucked by France or America. . . . Do you ever think about your country? I do sometimes.' [2]

[1] *Culture and Anarchy*, ch. I.
[2] *The Amberley Papers* (1937), vol. I, p. 462. In April 1867 Disraeli remarked, 'Foreign affairs are very queer. I sometimes fear the worst is at hand.' (Quoted A. E. Gathorne Hardy, *op. cit.*, p. 207.) A writer in the *Annual Register* (1867) was even more contemplative: 'England . . . owes her great influence, not to military successes, but to her commanding position in the arena of industry and commerce. If she forgets this, she is lost . . . undoubtedly to the extent of having to give up the lead, and ceasing to be a first-rate power. The signs, for those who can read, are present, and can be plainly seen.'

As excellent bibliographies for this period are contained in several easily accessible works, the purpose of this note is simply to show the student the way to further study. Many of the lines to pursue have been summarily signposted in the footnotes; this note should be regarded as supplementary to footnote references and not complete in itself.

1. BIBLIOGRAPHIES AND GENERAL BOOKS

The *Oxford History* volume by J. Steven Watson on the period from 1760–1815 has not yet appeared, but E. L. Woodward, *The Age of Reform, 1815–70* (1938) is useful and has a good bibliography. The bibliography for the period after 1833 is brought up to date thoroughly and carefully (with excellent supplementary notes) by G. M. Young and W. D. Handcock in their collection of *English Historical Documents, 1833–1874*, vol. XII (I) (1956). For the beginning of the period, see J. Pargellis and D. J. Medley, *Bibliography of British History, The Eighteenth Century, 1714–89* (1951) and D. B. Horn and M. Ransome, *English Historical Documents*, vol. X, *1714–1783* (1957). All bibliographies can be kept up to date with the help of the *Annual Bulletin of Historical Literature* published by the Historical Association. E. Halévy, *A History of the English People in the Nineteenth Century*, vol. I, *England in 1815*; vol. II, *The Liberal Awakening*; vol. III, *The Triumph of Reform*; and, vol. IV, *Victorian Years*, is the best general history of the nineteenth century. G. M. Young, *Portrait of an Age* (1936) is the most subtle and illuminating interpretation. There are, as yet, no completely satisfactory general studies of the period between 1789 and 1815.

2. OTHER STUDIES

For recent surveys of the social and economic background of the late eighteenth century, see in particular T. S. Ashton, *The Industrial Revolution* (1948) and *An Economic History of England: The Eighteenth Century* (1955). For later economic history, see J. H.

Clapham, *An Economic History of Modern Britain*, vol. I, *The Early Railway Age, 1820–50* (1926); and, vol. II, *Free Trade and Steel, 1850–1886* (1932). W. W. Rostow, *British Economy of the Nineteenth Century* (1948) and A. D. Gayer, W. W. Rostow and A. Schwartz, *Growth and Fluctuations of the British Economy, 1780–1850* (1953) are also useful.

For an invaluable study of late eighteenth-century constitutional history, see R. Pares, *King George III and the Politicians* (1953). All students of constitutional problems owe a great debt to Sir Lewis Namier's *The Structure of Politics at the Accession of George III* (1930), and the volumes he is editing on *England in the Age of the American Revolution*. I. R. Christie's *The End of North's Ministry, 1780–2*, deals with the political and constitutional prelude to the period covered in this book. For a later period N. Gash, *Politics in the Age of Peel* (1953) is an admirable guide to the nineteenth-century electoral system. There are many lively ideas in K. B. Smellie, *A Hundred Years of English Government* (1950 edition) and B. Kemp, *King and Commons, 1660–1832* (1957). On foreign policy, there is need for a new synthesis, but the basic documents are to be found in H. W. V. Temperley and L. M. Penson, *Foundations of British Foreign Policy* (1938). There is a good bibliography with scintillating comments in A. J. P. Taylor, *The Struggle for Mastery in Europe, 1848–1914* (1954).

On intellectual, cultural, and social history, recent books of interest are R. J. White, *Waterloo to Peterloo* (1957) and F. W. Houghton, *The Victorian Frame of Mind* (1957). Both have brief but helpful bibliographies. See also *Ideas and Beliefs of the Victorians* (1949) and A. Briggs, *Victorian People* (1955). J. L. and B. Hammond, *The Age of the Chartists* (1930) remains a classic of historical writing, and their *The Town Labourer* (1917) and *The Village Labourer* (1912) are lively studies of social history.

On imperial history, in addition to the books cited in the footnotes, see V. T. Harlow, *The Founding of the Second British Empire, 1763–93* (1952). On Ireland two indispensable recent books are K. H. Connell, *The Population of Ireland, 1750–1845* (1950) and *The Great Famine, Studies in Irish History* (1957). See also J. A. Reynolds, *The Catholic Emancipation Crisis in Ireland, 1823–29* (1954). L J. Saunders, *Scottish Democracy, 1815–40* (1950) is an excellent study of basic changes in early nineteenth-century Scottish society, a period which has been somewhat neglected by Scottish historians.

GENERAL INDEX

ABBOT, CHARLES, first Baron Colchester, 113
Abercromby, Sir John, 143
Aberdeen, fourth Earl of (1784–1860), 343, 355, 357–8, 359, 362, 370, 377–9, 381, 382, 418
Abingdon, 502
Aborigines' Protection Society, 387
Adam, Robert and William, 38, 49
Adderley, Sir Charles, 501
Aden, 364
Administrative Reform Association, 433–4, 442
Adrianople, Treaty of (1829), 350
Adullamites, 501–2, 504, 506, 509, 510
Afghanistan, 390
African Association, 174
Agnostics, 488
'Agrarian Revolution', 41–3
Agriculture, 2, 11, 36–44, 50, 57–9, 163, 171–2, 203, 220, 249–50, 312–13, 314, 319, 323, 324, 394, 402, 403, 407–8, 418
Agriculture, Board of, 39–40, 163
Alabama, 495
Albert, Prince Consort (1819–61), 375, 376, 382, 429, 455–63, 464, 469, 480
Albert Memorial, 470
Alexander I, Tsar of Russia, 148, 158, 159
Alexander II, Tsar of Russia, 383
Alfred the Great, King of the West Saxons, 89
Allan, William, 408, 410
Althorp, Viscount, later third Earl Spencer (1782–1845), 39, 237, 256, 263, 270, 271, 272
Amalgamated Society of Carpenters and Joiners, 409, 410
Amalgamated Society of Engineers, 405, 408, 410, 493
Amberley, Lady, 523
Amberley, Viscount, 414
Amiens, Peace of (1802), 142, 144
Anti-Corn Law League, 265, 294, 297, 310, 312–25, 334, 397, 432, 496
Anti-Jacobin, 141
Anti-League, the, 319
Anti-Slavery movement, 81, 115–16, 150–1, 253, 269, 316, 357, 363–4, 365, 367
Anti-State Church Association, 285
Appleby, 104, 261
Applegarth, Robert, 408, 409, 410, 430, 496

Arbitration, Boards of, 441
Arbuthnot, Charles, 186, 188, 218
Arbuthnot, Mrs., 188, 227, 228, 229
Argyll, eighth Duke of, 511
Aristocracy, 10–11, 37–9, 92, 96–7, 99, 104, 215, 226, 236–7, 242, 251, 258, 259, 262–3, 268, 297, 323, 382, 404, 406–7, 415, 443, 450, 476, 503, 508
Arkwright, Sir Richard (1732–92), 21, 24, 38, 54, 63, 395, 409
Army, the British, 138–9, 142, 146–7, 150, 153–5, 158, 160, 161, 214, 362, 363, 381–2, 458
Arnold, Matthew (1822–88), 411, 448, 450, 475–9, 522–3
Arnold, Thomas (1795–1842), 294, 299, 411, 450, 485
Ascot, 458
Ashley, Lord, seventh Earl of Shaftesbury (1801–85), 326, 335–6, 388, 430, 438, 439, 486, 493, 515
Association for Preserving Liberty and Property against Republicans and Levellers, 134, 214
Association for the Repeal of Taxes on Knowledge, 427
Atkinson, Thomas, 78
Attwood, Thomas (1783–1856), 165–6, 204, 245, 247–8, 252, 254, 257, 262, 271, 279, 293, 307, 308
Austen, Jane (1775–1817), 10, 18, 48, 167, 173
Austerlitz, Battle of (1805), 148
Australia, 386, 388, 391, 399, 402, 436, 499, 500, 518,
Austria, 128, 135, 137, 139, 142, 148, 154, 159, 261, 347, 349, 352, 358, 359, 366, 367, 370, 372, 373, 378, 379, 383, 425–6, 502–3
Aylesbury 101

BACON, FRANCIS, 19
Badajoz, 158
Bagehot, Walter (1826–77), 89, 215, 404–6, 408, 412, 415, 426, 427, 449, 452, 454, 459, 461, 514
Bailey, 'Festus', 468
Baines, Edward, 51, 237, 247
Baines, Edward, his son, 492, 498
Bakewell, Robert, 35, 42
Balance of Power, 366–8, 372, 379, 380, 383
Ballot, 243, 271, 276, 286, 304, 413, 522
Ballot Act (1872), 413

526

General Index

INDEX TO FOOTNOTE REFERENCES